Customs and Beliefs of the |Xam Bushmen

Customs and Beliefs of the |Xam Bushmen

Edited by

JEREMY C. HOLLMANN

WITS UNIVERSITY PRESS

RINGING ROCKS PRESS

THE KHOISAN HERITAGE SERIES
Series Editor: David Lewis-Williams

Other titles in the Khoisan Heritage Series

Contested Images
Diversity in Southern African Rock Art Research
Edited by Thomas A Dowson & David Lewis-Williams

Voices from the Past
/Xam Bushmen and the Bleek and Lloyd Collection
Edited by Janette Deacon and Thomas A Dowson

Women Like Meat
The Folklore and Foraging Ideology of the Kalahari Ju/'Hoan
Megan Biesele

Rock Engravings of Southern Africa
Thomas A Dowson

Wits University Press
1 Jan Smuts Avenue
Johannesburg
South Africa
http://witspress.wits.ac.za

Ringing Rocks Press
P O Box 22656
Philadelphia, PA 19110-2656 USA
www.ringingrocks.org

ISBN 1-86814-399-6

Cover art: Pencil drawing by Daï!kwain / 171x213mm / May 1875
!gai or 'Padden; Toï aitye – Female Ostrich
Courtesy Iziko Museums of Cape Town

Book design and cover: Sue Sandrock Design, Johannesburg, South Africa
Printed and bound by: Creda Communications, Cape Town, South Africa

Customs and Beliefs
of the /Xam Bushmen

As given by
/A!kuŋta (Klaas Stoffel)
||Kabbo (Oud Jantje Tooren)
Diä!kwain (David Hoesar)
/Haŋ‡kass'o (Klein Jantje Tooren)
‡Kasiŋ (Klaas Katkop)

Recorded by
Wilhelm Bleek and Lucy Lloyd
between 1870 and 1880

Introduced, edited and annotated by
Jeremy C. Hollmann

Originally edited by Dorothea Bleek
and first published in nine parts in the journal Bantu Studies
between 1931 and 1936

Dedicated to
the /Xam teachers,
and to Wilhelm Bleek,
Lucy Lloyd, and
Dorothea Bleek

and
with my thanks to
David Lewis-Williams,
a brilliant thinker and an inspiring teacher

Contents

Acknowledgements

I thank Nancy L. Connor and Bradford P. Keeney of the Ringing Rocks Foundation for their sponsorship of this project, and Benjamin Smith, Director of the Rock Art Research Institute (RARI), University of the Witwatersrand, for giving me time to work on the book.

David Lewis-Williams nurtured my interest in the Bleek and Lloyd Collection (BLC) and initiated what we called the '*Bantu Studies* project' in the first place. Our teatime conversations often became informal BLC seminars – this book has benefited greatly from these sessions, as well as from David's grammatical expertise and critical attention. Janette Deacon shared her knowledge of the |Xam and |Xam-ka !aũ with me and made valuable comments on the manuscript; her work in relocating the places mentioned in the BLC ranks amongst the most important archaeological achievement in our country's history.

Nak and Alma Reichert, Jan Lötz, and Rina van Wyk spent hours with me in the field, showing me the places in |Xam-ka !aũ that appear in this book, as well as offering me their hospitality. I am most grateful to them all.

I thank Wendy Voorvelt for her beautiful map, which shows several of the BLC locations. I thank the Special Collections Information Services at the University of Cape Town, in which the BLC is housed, for permission to reproduce documents, photographs, maps and drawings, and Lesley Hart, Manager, for her thoughtful and patient guidance through the Collection. I am also grateful to Michele Pickover, Curator and Archivist of the William Cullen Library's Historical and Literary Papers Collection, University of the Witwatersrand, for her assistance in locating the *Bantu Studies* correspondence and permission to quote and reproduce portions. Personnel at Wits University's Central Records Office Archives also supplied me with information about *Bantu Studies*.

I am very grateful to my colleagues at RARI for their assistance with the project. Letitia Petersen worked through some of the notebooks with me. Elaine Macdonald identified the locust bird and acted as a sounding board for ideas. Bronwyn de Villiers helped to select and scan all the images used in this book. Willem Steyn made useful comments on the manuscript.

I thank Nina Mössmer for information about the locust bird, the blue cranes and the ant-eating chat.

I am also grateful to several experts for their help. Tom Güldemann of the Max Planck Institute in Leipzig, Germany places Dorothea Bleek's *Bushman Grammar* in the context of contemporary linguistic work on the |Xam language. Braam van Wyk, Professor of Plant Systematics at the Department of Botany, University of Pretoria, suggested the identity of the *ʃo-/õä* plant. I thank Elizabeth Retief, Principal Agricultural Scientist, and Mienkie Welman, Principal Scientist, both at the National

Botanical Institute, Pretoria, for their help in locating voucher specimens. I also thank Rob Toms, Researcher in Orthoptera and Ethno-biology at the Transvaal Museum (Northern Flagship Institution), for identifying the locusts in the narratives. Anthony Traill, Professor Emeritus and Honorary Research Fellow in the Department of Linguistics at the University of the Witwatersrand, assisted me to understand Wilhelm Bleek's ideas about language in terms of contemporary linguistic theory. I would also like to thank Veronica Klipp and Melanie Pequeux of Wits University Press for publishing the book.

Marthina Mössmer was the person upon whom I relied most for technical help and emotional support. She welcomed *Customs and Beliefs* into our home and has always (well, almost always) been ready to listen to and discuss anything about it. Thanks to her expertise, the preparation of the manuscript has been an almost stress-free process for me. Most importantly, however, it was Tina's companionship that made it possible for me to thoroughly enjoy the preparation of this book. Thank you, Tina! Finally I thank Martin and Anna for their patience, love and support while I was so busy.

Note from WIMSA

(Working Group for Indigenous Minorities in Southern Africa)

The San of today agree with one of the oldest of the |Xam teachers' aspirations that Bushman stories should become known by means of books (Bleek & Lloyd, 1911: x). Since the San of Botswana, Namibia and South Africa embarked on the WIMSA Oral Testimony Collection Project, they have valued the revival of the stories of an extinct group of their fellow San and of their language. To honour the memory of the |Xam, the San delegates at the WIMSA general assembly in 2000 decided to name the San Education and Culture Centre in the Yzerfontein area, 60 kilometres from Cape Town, !Khwa ttu, which means 'water pan' in the |Xam language. !Khwa ttu was chosen by the San to archive all materials such as cultural resource maps and historical and educational books resulting from the Oral Testimony Collection Project, which is conducted by the San for the San. On behalf of the San, WIMSA would like to thank Jeremy Hollmann for his efforts to make this unique collection *Customs and Beliefs of the /Xam Bushmen* available to the broader public and thereby also to the San.

Axel Thoma
WIMSA Co-ordinator
Windhoek

Foreword

Imagine being in gaol in a city hundreds of kilometres from your family and the stark rural landscape of your home. You try hard to remember every rock and every bush that is familiar to you. You are afraid to speak your own language. Your fellow prisoners and the warders do not understand your language and they call you stupid because you do not know what they say. Yet they are not stupid for misunderstanding you. One day, a strange man visits the prison and asks if you can teach him to speak as you do. He gets permission for you to live in the relative comfort of his home. Slowly you teach him and his sister-in-law how to use their tongues to make the click sounds in |Xam. You say the names of objects and actions to them over and over again until they get them right. They take a long time to write the words down, and then stumble over them again the next day. You wonder if they will ever learn. After a few months they can put a sentence or two together and they ask you to tell them stories. At first, you tell them simple things. They find it hard to grasp why you laugh when you do, and you hang back when you realise they don't know enough to comprehend the depth of the story. The metaphors so obvious to you are lost on them. Their god is not the same as yours and you fear they have only a superficial understanding of the significance of your customs. Gradually you realise that, even though they do not understand, this may be one of the last opportunities your people will have to record the knowledge that has taken thousands of generations to accumulate. Even if your pupils don't understand what you tell them, you press on to educate them a little more every day, knowing that you will not be able to convey everything. The string that binds you together may break at any time. As you well know, storytelling is only one way to learn. Speaking about bows and arrows will not teach them how to be hunters.

These could be the thoughts of ||Kabbo, the grandfather whose knowledge and patience were the cornerstone of the |Xam language and memories that were recorded in Cape Town in the nineteenth century. The extraordinary collection of |Xam (Bushman or San) customs, beliefs, folklore and personal histories, narrated between 1870 and 1879 by ||Kabbo, |A!kuŋta, |Haŋ‡kass'o, Diä!kwain, ≠Kasiŋ and !Kweiten ta ||ken, amongst others, to Wilhelm Bleek and Lucy Lloyd, is the only substantial record ever to have been written down verbatim in a Bushman language in South Africa. Although the |Xam language has not been used regularly for a century, the fact that these memories were recorded as they were spoken has enabled them to contribute to a revival of interest in the language, customs and beliefs of South Africa's first indigenous people. |Xam has become like South Africa's Latin and has taken its place in the country's coat of arms.

Extracts from the more than 10 000 manuscript pages of |Xam records, now in the Jagger Library at the University of Cape Town, have been published only sporadically, and at least a quarter of the original material remains in manuscript form only. The form of publication has ranged from full |Xam texts with English translation, to English summaries of the translation in both prose and poetry, and most recently, to Spanish translations from the English. In the early years the orthography of the |Xam was one of the stumbling blocks to full publication. In the preface to the first volume, entitled *Specimens of Bushman Folklore* and published in 1911, some 41 years after the first interviews took place, Lucy Lloyd noted that the typesetting at that time could only be done in Germany. It must have taken months for the corrected proofs to be sent back and forth by sea.

For the foresight in collating and publishing the originals of the facsimile reproductions in this book, however, we have to thank Dorothea Bleek (1873-1948), second youngest of the four daughters of Wilhelm Bleek and his wife Jemima, who was Lucy Lloyd's sister. The articles were published under the general title 'Customs and Beliefs of the |Xam Bushmen' in the journal *Bantu Studies* between 1931 and 1936, and as 'Bushman Grammar' in the *Zeitschrift für Eingeborenen-Sprachen* in 1928-29.

Dorothea Frances Bleek, known as Doris to her family, inherited the same spirit of dedication displayed by her father and aunt. She was only two years old when her father died in 1875 but she long remembered the times during her childhood when |Haŋ‡kass'o, Diä!kwain, his sister and her family lived at the Bleek home in Mowbray. When she was about ten years old, her mother took her and her three sisters to Berlin where they attended school and university. Amongst the subjects she studied while training to be a teacher was African Languages. Once she had qualified, she taught at a high school for girls in Cradock in the Eastern Cape from 1904-1907 and, while there, she and a fellow teacher, Helen Tongue, often went out into the countryside to find and make copies of rock paintings. When Helen Tongue's copies were published in 1908, Dorothea and her sister Edith wrote a foreword recounting their memories of the |Xam people they had known. Dorothea moved to Cape Town in 1908 to take over the responsibility of managing the |Xam records and to assist her aunt in preparing *Specimens of Bushman Folklore* (1911) for publication. She visited Prieska and Kenhardt in 1910 and 1911 to see if she could locate the descendants of any of the people her father and aunt had interviewed in Cape Town in the 1870s and 1880s. Although she met one elderly woman, |Ogan-an or Mikki Streep, who had been in Cape Town in 1884, she found no |Xam-speaking people who remembered any folklore, and few who could still speak |Xam.

Dorothea became a renowned scholar and ethnographer in her own right. She did pioneering fieldwork among the Naron in what is now Botswana and published the results in the 1920s, and she also visited the Kalahari, Angola and Tanzania to study Bushman and related languages. During this period, while Honorary Reader in Bushman Languages at the University of Cape Town, she worked sporadically on the |Xam records and, from 1928, when she was in her mid-fifties, began publishing the extracts reproduced here. The *Bushman Dictionary* that Wilhelm Bleek and Lucy Lloyd had begun, and that Dorothea Bleek almost completed, was published in 1956, eight years after her death.

For both Wilhelm and Dorothea Bleek, and for Lucy Lloyd and the |Xam, this endeavour was a labour of love. None of them received monetary rewards for learning the language of the other, nor for publishing what had been recorded. While Lucy Lloyd and Wilhelm and Dorothea Bleek may have achieved academic recognition, their purpose was not to enrich themselves, but to record the knowledge for generations to come. Each contributed to the integrity of the whole. In a tribute to Dorothea Bleek in the preface to *Cave Artists of South Africa* by A.J.H. Goodwin, published in 1953, Eric Rosenthal recalled attending a lecture Dorothea had given on rock art shortly after the end of World War II:

> Miss Bleek was not merely a great student of the Bushmen and their habits; she had lived among them and gained their confidence. And as I saw her stand in front of that audience of business men and journalists in modern Cape Town, I fell under the fascination of her bright, dark eyes and the charm of her personality. ... Dorothea Bleek did not want to talk about herself. What lay closest to her heart was the work begun by her father, continued by her aunt and left now for herself to bring to a conclusion. Nearly a century had gone by since this work was started, and it seemed as though its promise would at last be fulfilled.

Jeremy Hollmann, a Research Officer at the Rock Art Research Institute at the University of the Witwatersrand, has proved that the integrity of the work of the Bleeks and Lloyd is still intact. He has used twentieth-century knowledge of Bushman customs in the Kalahari, combined with Dorothea Bleek's *Bushman Dictionary* and the |Xam grammar, to throw new light on |Xam passages and English translations. His notes at the beginning of each part bring the texts alive again and give fresh insight into the beliefs and customs of the |Xam.

To promote the language, especially amongst the descendants of the |Xam, copies of this book will be placed in appropriate libraries and institutions where they will be available to all interested parties and to future generations.

Janette Deacon
Stellenbosch

Special terms and conventions

|Xam-ka !aũ

I use the phrase |Xam-ka !aũ throughout to refer to that part of the present-day Northern Cape Province commonly known as Bushmanland. |Xam-ka !aũ is the term that the |Xam teachers used for the area in which they lived (see the map of |Xam-ka !aũ; Lewis-Williams 2000: 9-11). The phrase means 'the |Xam's ground'.

***Sorcerors and sorceresses,* !gi:xa *and* !gi:tən**

Many of the |Xam teachings refer to the work of *!gi:tən* (sing. *!gi:xa*), a word which, literally translated, means 'full of *!gi:*'. The word *!gi:* is best translated as supernatural potency (Lewis-Williams 1981). ||Kabbo translated the word *!gi:xa* as 'toorman', Afrikaans for 'magician' (see Part VII, 'About the toorman'). Bleek and Lloyd adopted the terms 'sorceror' and 'sorceress'. In Part VI, Dorothea uses 'medicine man'. David Lewis-Williams (1981) uses 'shaman'. Since there are problems with all of these translations, I have decided to remain faithful to the Bleek and Lloyd translation of *!gi:xa* /*!gi:tən* as 'sorceror/ess', whilst rejecting the possible negative connotations associated with the English translation.

Reverso or rev. pages

When checking on the accuracy of their transcriptions with the |Xam teachers, Bleek and Lloyd made notes on the left-hand page of the notebook, opposite the page on which they had written down the narrative. The left-hand page is the reverso page – the back or reverse of the previous page. This convention means that, for example, page 4475 rev. is opposite page 4476.

Notebook references

The notebook reference has four components. For example, the reference L .V. 23: 2109 stands for the following:

- L = Lloyd, who transcribed the text; B = Wilhelm Bleek, who transcribed the text.
- V = Diä!kwain, the teacher. Bleek and Lloyd allocated each teacher a number using upper case Roman numerals; I = |A!kuŋta; II = ||Kabbo; IV = ǂKasiŋ; VI = !Kweitən ta || ken; VIII = |Haŋǂkass'o; IX = |Xaken-aŋ.
- 23 = the notebook number (in this case, Diä!kwain's twenty-third notebook).
- 2109 = the notebook page.

In the notes to each narrative I omit the first three components, that is, the transcriber's name, the teacher's name and the notebook number, for ease of reference, and I use only the four-digit notebook page number.

Pronunciation

Bleek, Lloyd and the |Xam teachers took great trouble to ensure that, as far as possible, the sounds of the |Xam words were accurately recorded. All of the |Xam words were therefore written down using phonetic script. In the great majority of cases, Bleek and Lloyd used the phonetic script adopted by the International Phonetic Association (IPA). I reproduce the signs most commonly used in the *Bantu Studies* texts.

Click sounds

Bushman languages are renowned for their click sounds, of which there are five in the |Xam language. I provide a guide to their pronunciation, based on Guenther (1999: 11):

| A dental click, produced by placing the tip of the tongue against the back of the upper incisors, creating a sound similar to our 'tsk, tsk' (used, for example, when chiding a child).

|| An alveolar lateral click, produced by placing the sides of the tongue against the sides of the upper row of teeth, creating a sound similar to what we might make when urging a horse on to greater speed.

ǂ A palatoalveolar click, produced with the tongue against the bony projection on the roof of the mouth (alveolus).

! A post (alveolar) click, produced by placing the front of the tongue behind the alveolus, creating a cork-popping sound.

ʘ A bilabial click, produced by pursing the lips and then releasing them to make a kissing sound. The labial click is found only in the Southern Bushman languages.

Other phonetic symbols

All symbols used are those of the International Phonetic Alphabet (IPA) and those in the *Bushman Dictionary* (Bleek 1956). Note that it is not always possible to provide sensible English illustrations for every instance; after all, |Xam is a language in its own right and quite different from English.

ə as in <u>a</u>lone

ŋ as in si<u>ng</u>

ʃ as in <u>sh</u>ip

x as in lo<u>ch</u>

§ a symbol that Dorothea Bleek adopted to stand for pressed vowel sounds because it was cheaper for the printers to use (Bleek 1956: Introduction)

ʔ glottal stop – a momentary closing of the throat (glottis), something like the way certain English dialects pronounce 'butter'

Vowels and Diacritical marks

These are used to indicate how to pronounce a vowel. A guide to pronouncing unaccented vowels is provided first. I thank linguist, Anthony Traill, for the following guide:

a as in Scots 'bad', 'grand', 'lad'

e as in 'bed', 'ten', 'set' (as long as you are not Australian or Cockney)

i as in 'see', 'he', 'we' (as long as you are not Australian or Cockney)

o as in 'paw, 'law' (as long as you are not Southern African)

u English does not have a cardinal 'u'; the nearest is the vowel in 'put' and 'look' in some dialects

: denotes length and is shown together with certain vowel symbols when the vowels are typically long

~ above a vowel indicates nasalisation

˘ above a vowel indicates an extra short sound

– above a vowel indicates a mid-tone

´ above a vowel indicates a high tone

.. above a vowel probably indicates that it is centralised, although (according to Professor Traill) centralised vowel sounds are not a ubiquitous feature of Khoisan languages, and Bleek and Lloyd may have used this sign to stand for another sound, although it is not clear what

ë sounds something like the vowel in 'sit' and 'with', particularly in South African English

ï the centralised 'i' sounds like 'children' (but not *tshooldren*, as in South African English)

Spelling and Orthography

There is considerable variation in the spelling of |Xam words in the Bleek and Lloyd manuscripts. In published narratives and in the *Bushman Dictionary,* these researchers attempted to establish a |Xam orthography. There are none the less many variant spellings of words and names, even within a single published volume. With the exception of people's names in the 'source' field that heads each narrative, and the spellings of words as they appear in omitted text and notes, I adopt Dorothea Bleek's *Bantu Studies* orthography, as well as the spellings given in her *Bushman Dictionary.*

The |Xam teachers

|A!kuŋta

As a young man of about 18 years old |A!kuŋta, also known as Klaas Stoffel, was the first of Bleek and Lloyd's |Xam teachers and spoke the Flat Bushman dialect. He arrived at the Bleek household in August 1870 and returned with ||Kabbo to the Strandberg in October 1873. Nothing is known of his subsequent life. He contributed two stories, 'The resurrection of the ostrich' (Bleek & Lloyd 1911), and 'The Lions and the Tortoise', published in *Customs and Beliefs*, as well as many examples of words and sentences, including an excerpt published by Dorothea Bleek in *Customs and Beliefs* called 'The Moon's speech'.

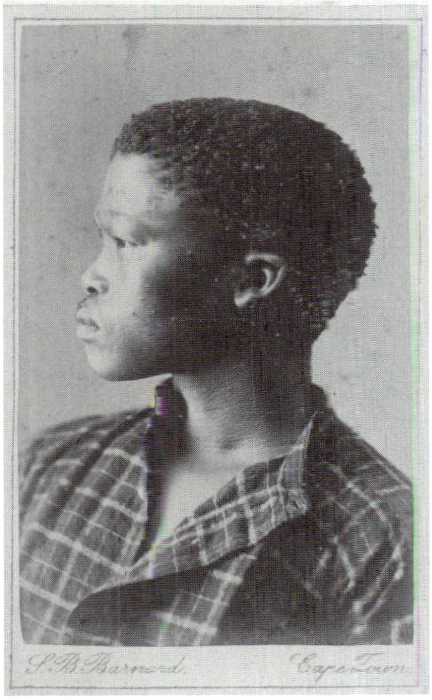

Courtesy South African Museum, SAL ALBX 19, INIL 15632 carte de visite of |A!kuŋta by S.B. Barnard, Cape Town, 1871

Diä!kwain

Courtesy UCT Libraries BLC 151 G1.8

Also known as David Hoesar (D.H. in the notebooks), Diä!kwain was about 29 years old when he began his work at the Bleek's house in late November 1873. He spoke the Grass Bushman dialect. Diä!kwain spent about four months with Bleek and Lloyd before leaving for his home near the Katkop Hills. He returned to Cape Town in 1874 and brought with him !Kweiten ta ||ken, his sister and Kasiŋ, his brother-in-law. His contribution to *Customs and Beliefs* is considerable and amounts to some 64 extracts chosen for publication by Dorothea Bleek.

Between 55 and 60 years old in 1871, when he began working with Bleek and Lloyd, ||Kabbo is considered the most knowledgeable of the teachers. He was apparently a *!gi:xa* or 'sorceror'. During his stay at the Bleek's home from 16 February 1871 to 15 October 1873 ||Kabbo dictated thousands of notebook pages in the dialect of the Flat Bushman people. He was also known as Oud Jantje Tooren (abbreviated to J.T. in the notebooks). He died on 25 January 1876 in |Xam-ka !aũ. Dorothea Bleek used 14 excerpts from his testimony in *Customs and Beliefs*.

||Kabbo

Courtesy UCT Libraries BLC151 G1.7, painting by W.H. Schroeder, ca. 1878

|Haŋ‡kass'o

Courtesy UCT Libraries BLC151 G1.2, painting by W. H. Schroeder, ca. 1878

|Haŋ‡kass'o was ||Kabbo's son-in-law and served two years in the Breakwater Prison with him. He returned to Cape Town some six years later and remained there for almost 2 years from January 1878 until December 1879. Although a lonely man who had very recently lost his wife and a child, |Haŋ‡kass'o was known for his lively narratives that incorporated songs and chants in the Flat Bushman dialect. His contribution to the *Customs and Beliefs* series, 65 extracts, is the largest of all the teachers. Nothing is known of |Haŋ‡kass'o since he left Cape Town in 1879.

ǂKasiŋ was also known as Klaas Katkop. He spoke the Grass Bushman dialect and was married to Diä!kwain's sister, !Kweiten ta ||ken. After his release from prison in Cape Town where he served time for culpable homicide, he spent about 4 months with the Bleek household before returning home in March 1874. He returned to Cape Town later that year with his wife and children and stayed for six months. He was about 42 years old at this time. ǂKasiŋ contributed one story, 'How an Old Woman asked a Chameleon for Rain' (see Part VIII), to the *Customs and Beliefs* series.

ǂKasiŋ

Courtesy South African Library

Pupil and scribe of the |Xam language

Dorothea Bleek

Courtesy UCT Libraries BLC 151

Dorothea Frances Bleek, daughter of the renowned linguist Wilhelm Bleek learned the |Xam language from her aunt, Lucy Lloyd, and devoted her life to editing and publishing the material dictated by the |Xam teachers. With her encyclopaedic knowledge of the Bleek and Lloyd Collection, Dorothea Bleek was able to select narratives by the main |Xam teachers who spoke directly about aspects of their culture which they felt were most important for people to know about.

Map of |Xam-ka !aũ – 1871

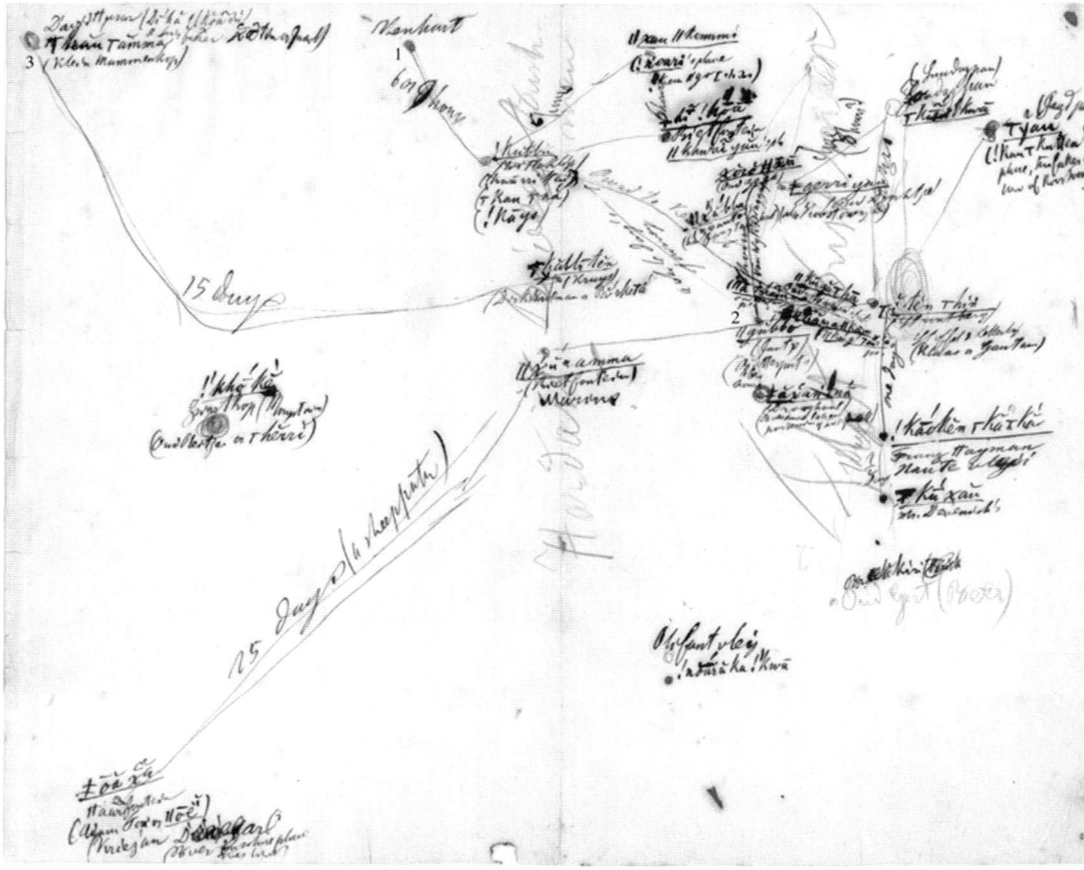

Courtesy UCT Libraries BC 151

Map of |Xam-ka !kaũ drawn up by Wilhelm Bleek in 1871 on ||Kabbo's direction showing the location of his home, the Bitterpits, relative to other places of importance.

Map of |Xam-ka !aũ – 1986

Adapted by Wendy Voorvelt, after Deacon (1986, 1988), Wilhelm Bleek and ||Kabbo (1871)

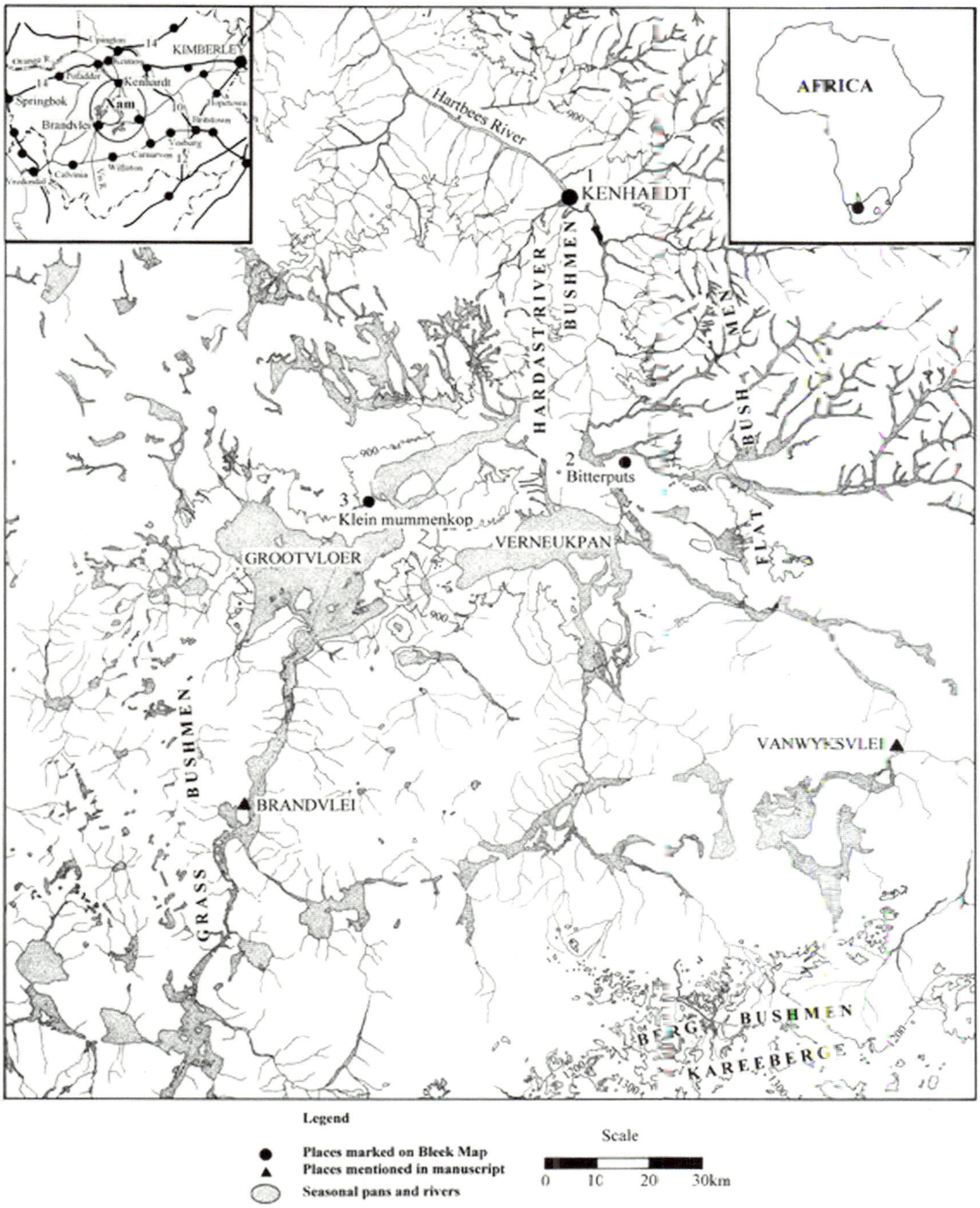

Map showing the regions occupied by different Bushman groups, as well as topographical features. Janette Deacon has re-located some of the places mentioned by ||Kabbo in the previous map.

Landmarks of |Xam-ka !aũ

The Bitterpits

One day on the train in Cape Town ||Kabbo sat next to a man who asked ||Kabbo where he came from.

'The black man … asked me: "Where dost thou come from?"

I said to the black man: "I come from this place."

The black man asked me: "What is its name?"

I said to the black man: "My place is the Bitterpits."' (Bleek & Lloyd 1911: 299)

Photo: Jeremy Hollmann

The |Xam teacher ||Kabbo owned the Bitterpits, a waterhole in |Xam-ka !aũ (see Deacon 1996b).

The pit has since been reinforced and covered. The name, Bitterpits, comes from the taste of the water, which is brackish and sulphurous.

The waterhole at the Bitterpits is concealed amongst the bushes to the left of the small dam.

Photo: Jeremy Hollmann

‘A boulder which is white. One stone, it is… Therefore people say a white boulder to it, for they feel it is white. It stands on the ground, stands on the dry river bed. It stood on the edge of the edge of the “lichte”.’

|Haŋ‡kasso, described this stone, which lies about three kilometres north of the Bitterpits (Deacon 1996b: 252). The stone is unique in its size (approximately one metre high and a metre and a half long) and remarkable for its colour.

Photo: Jeremy Hollmann

Photo: Jeremy Hollmann

Remains of a |Xam hut near the Bitterpits. The double row of stones in the picture is arranged in a semicircle. These stones were probably used to anchor bush screens and mats for the huts. The entrance to the hut is in the foreground. To the right of the entrance is an upper and lower grindstone. Charcoal from five hearths at this |Xam living site was radiocarbon dated and interpreted by Janette Deacon (1996b: 264-265) as dating from the early nineteenth century (1807 and 1818).

An upper and lower grindstone from a |Xam living site near the Bitterpits; a set of grindstones like this would probably have been used to grind grass seeds and other plant food, or to grind ochre, a stone that yields a reddish pigment used for decoration.

Photo: Jeremy Hollmann

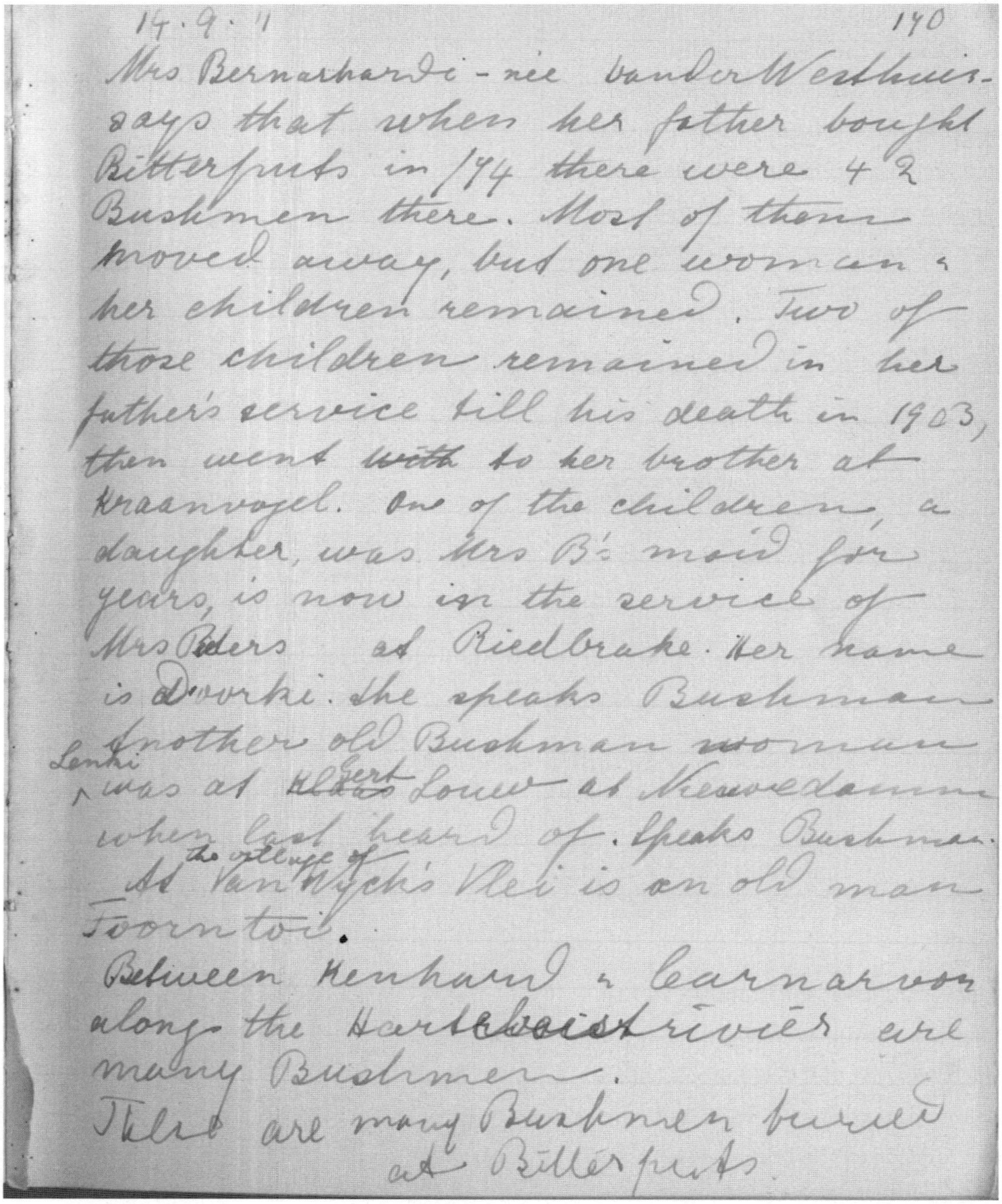

14.9.11 170

Mrs Bernarhardi - née van der Westhuis - says that when her father bought Bitterpits in '74 there were 42 Bushmen there. Most of them moved away, but one woman & her children remained. Two of those children remained in her father's service till his death in 1903, then went ~~with~~ to her brother at Kraanvogel. One of the children, a daughter, was Mrs B's maid for years, is now in the service of Mrs Peters at Riedbrake. Her name is Doorki. She speaks Bushman.

Another old Bushman woman Lenki was at ~~Klaas~~ Gert Louw at Nieuwedamm when last heard of. Speaks Bushman.

At the college of Van Wyk's Vlei is an old man Foorntoi.

Between Kenhardt & Carnarvon along the Hartebeest river are many Bushmen.

There are many Bushmen buried at Bitterpits.

Dorothea Bleek's notes dated 14 September 1911 record the fate of those who lived at the Bitterpits

Courtesy of UCT Libraries BLC 151 BZE 97/20 (8)

Dorothea Bleek's visit to Prieska

Many years after she had visited Prieska, a village in the |Xam heartland, Dorothea Bleek wrote that although the language and folklore seemed to be lost, 'Even at Prieska, the very old started the dance of former days after a feast of meat' (Bleek 1924: ix). These photographs may have been taken at the dance she mentions.

Courtesy of UCT Libraries BLC 151 BZE 97/20 (10)

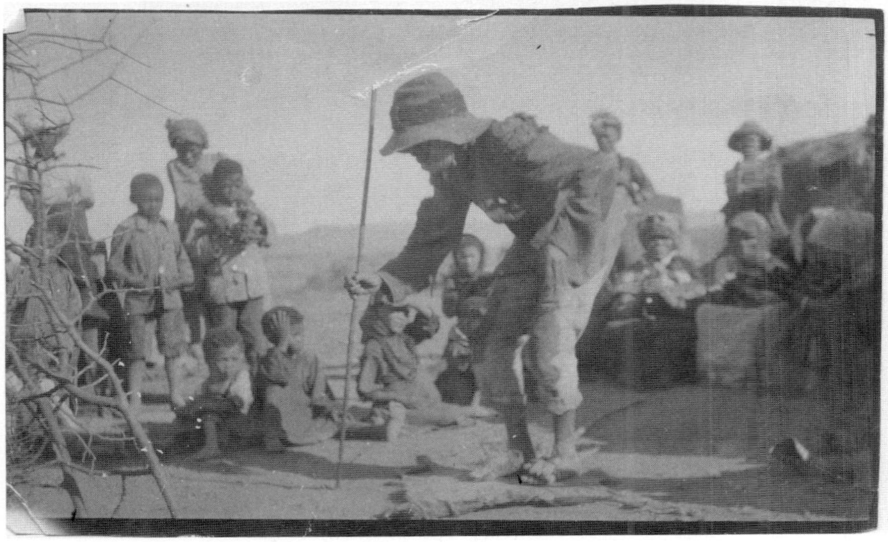

|Xam Bushman dancing, Prieska Location

Courtesy of UCT Libraries BLC 151 (no number)

|Xam Bushman dancing, Prieska Location

Courtesy of UCT Libraires BLC 151 (no number)

|Xam Bushman dancing, Prieska Location

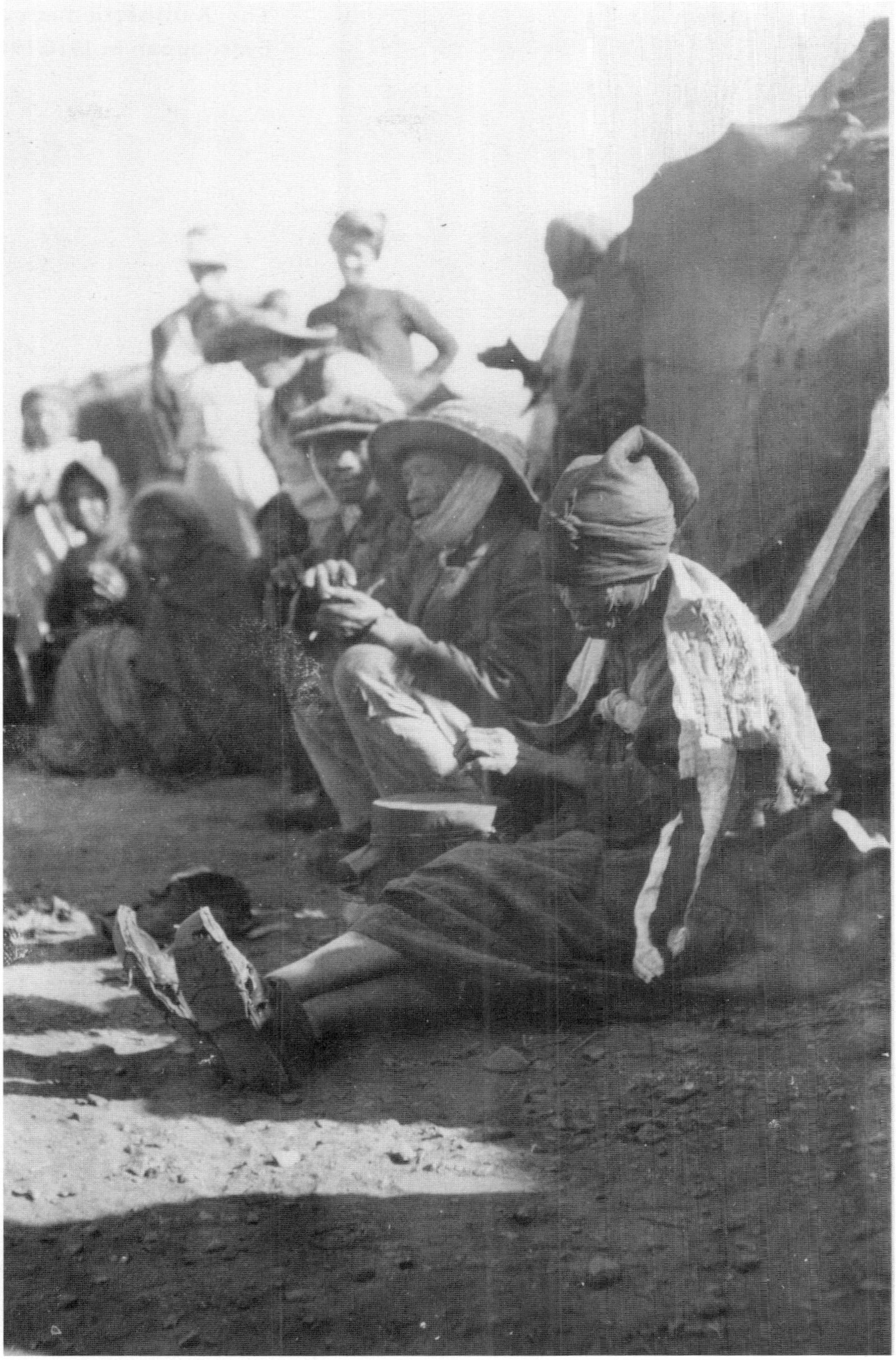

Courtesy of UCT Libraries BLC 151 BZE 97/20 (11)

|Xam dance at Prieska, with Kaiki playing the drum

The |Xam settlement at Eyerdoppan in 1910/1911

Courtesy of UCT Libraries BLC 151 BZE 97/20 (8)

Katren, Anna and granddaughter

Courtesy of UCT Libraries BLC 151 BZE 97/19 (34)

Bushman huts and screen, Eyerdoppan

Courtesy of UCT Libraries BLC 151 BZE 97/22 (38)

Bushman huts and screen, Eyerdoppan

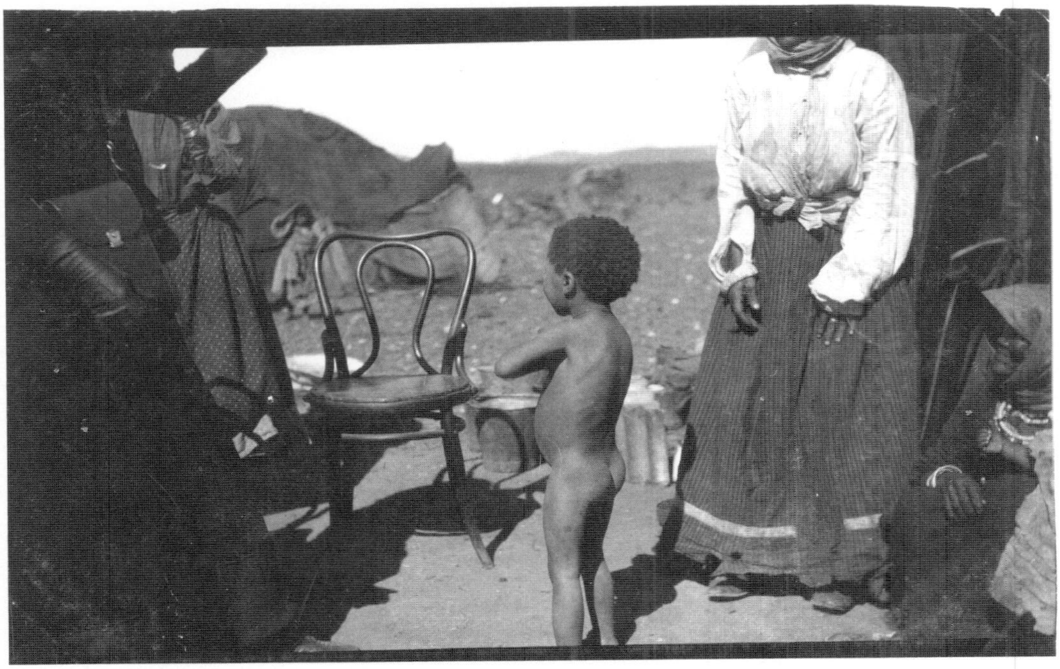

Courtesy of UCT Libraries BLC 151 BZE 97/20 (42)

|Xam child, Prieska

CUSTOMS AND BELIEFS OF THE |XAM BUSHMEN

EDITOR'S NOTES

The folklore published here was collected between 1870 and 1880 by the late Dr. Bleek and the late Miss L.C. Lloyd. It was taken down from the dictation of a number of /Xam Bushmen, that is members of the tribe living south of the Orange River. Some part of their collections was published in 1911 under the title Specimens of Bushmen Folklore, *Allen & Co., London; the translation of some further tales was published in 1923 under the title* The Mantis and His Friends, *Maskew Miller, Cape Town, but much remains unknown to the public. I wish to publish here in instalments the information concerning the beliefs and customs of these people. The text is given as dictated, using the orthography of the International Phonetic Association, excepting for the clicks, for which the ordinary symbols used in Bushman and Hottentot writings are employed. High and low tones are indicated by high and low dashes before the syllable. The translation is as literal as possible.*

Original note by Dorothea Bleek
Vol. 5 (1931), Part I: 179

Introduction

A popular story relates that, after many days spent visiting Inca ruins in Peru, a tourist asked the guide, 'But where are all the Inca today?' The local guide replied, pointing: 'There is one filling the tank of the tour bus' (Boonzaier et al 1996: 141). In the tourist's mind, the Inca were a people who belonged only in the past – the idea that Inca descendants still inhabited the country had not occurred to him.

A similar perception exists with respect to the |Xam and other Bushman[1] peoples in what is now South Africa. Because people no longer live on their ancestral lands, gathering *veldkos* and hunting, and because they have lost their languages and their ancestry is no longer 'pure', Bushman descendants have been invisible for a century or more. Today, however, South Africa's Bushman descendants have increasingly been making themselves heard in a variety of ways, political and cultural – it is no longer so easy to overlook their presence.

This book is intended as a contribution towards the reassertion of respect for and appreciation of Bushman cultures. The first part comprises a collection of narratives in which the voices of |Xam people – faithfully recorded by two remarkable scholars more than 100 years ago, and accompanied by a line-by-line English translation – speak of the beliefs, concepts and values that formed their world. The narratives, originally published more than 70 years ago in nine parts in the journal *Bantu Studies* (forerunner of the present *African Studies*), are an indispensable reference source for research in many disciplines. Unfortunately, however, the narratives are lost to people without access to the kind of library likely to hold copies of *Bantu Studies.*

Access to information about the |Xam language is similarly restricted. The second section of this book attempts to remedy this. It comprises a |Xam grammar, published by Dorothea Bleek in 1928 (Bleek 1928, 1929). When a language is recorded, but no longer spoken, its grammar is the key to its resurrection. With the grammar, the phonetic transcription of the |Xam and the translations to guide them, people can read the narratives in the original. But learning the language, its vocabulary and its grammar is not essential to using and enjoying this book – the customs and beliefs are still accessible to readers with no linguistic interest.

The Bleek and Lloyd Collection (BLC)

We have a group of extraordinary people to thank for the existence of the *Bantu Studies* narratives, which were selected from the 12 000 page Bleek and Lloyd Collection, now on the UNESCO Memory of the World Register. The actors and events associated with the BLC are well known (for example Vinnicombe 1976; Lewis-Williams 1981, 2000; Hewitt 1986; Deacon 1986, 1988, 1996a & b, 1997; Deacon & Dowson 1996; Skotnes 1996, 1999; James 2001), and I recommend readers to Janette Deacon (1996a & b) and David Lewis-Williams (2000) for the full story.

The year 1870 saw the first of the |Xam teachers, several of them prisoners of the colonial government, take up residence at the house of the linguist Dr Wilhelm Bleek in Mowbray, Cape Town. Everybody in the house must have known that the |Xam world as it was then – the customs and beliefs that regulated it, even the language – was threatened, and that the only way for it to survive the onslaught of social and economic change was to write it down.

The |Xam were the teachers, and Wilhelm Bleek and his sister-in-law, Lucy Lloyd, the pupils and scribes. They were just in time – when Dorothea Bleek, Wilhelm's daughter, visited the Great Karoo in 1910 and 1911 looking for her father's teachers, the stories were only vague memories, and the language all but forgotten (Bleek 1936; Traill 1996). Some of the poignant photographs taken on this expedition 92 years ago are reproduced in this book.

The *Bantu Studies* story

Although we are familiar with the Bleek and Lloyd Collection and the people who made it (Deacon & Dowson 1996; Lewis-Williams 2000), little has been published about the circumstances surrounding the publication of the *Bantu Studies* narratives.

When Lucy Lloyd (1834-1914), Wilhelm Bleek's co-worker and an accomplished linguist in her own right, published *Specimens of Bushman Folklore* in 1911, she dedicated it 'to all faithful workers' (Bleek & Lloyd 1911). Dorothea Bleek, born in 1873 to Wilhelm and Jemima, epitomised this ideal. She constantly sought out opportunities to publish and publicise the work that her father and aunt had collected.

The journal *Bantu Studies*, started in October 1921 by the Department of Bantu Studies at the University of the Witwatersrand, Johannesburg, was – as Clement Martyn Doke, renowned linguist and the journal's co-editor, wrote to Bleek – the 'most appropriate place' in which to publish the narratives.[2] It was dedicated to the study of the 'customs, life and languages of the Bantu peoples' (Doke 1927: 6). The first editor of *Bantu Studies*, John David Rheinhallt Jones, made it clear that, despite the journal's name, 'Khoisan material' was welcomed.[3]

Bleek wrote to Jones in 1931 advising him that she had sent him 'the batch of Bushman Folklore for *Bantu Studies* as promised', together with the added promise that 'If you can publish it soon, I shall be glad to follow it up with further installments'.[4] Jones and Bleek had evidently discussed the possibility of such a series and Bleek, in her characteristically efficient fashion, had selected and prepared the first of nine sections for publication in *Bantu Studies* as Part 1: Baboons (Bleek 1931).

The *Bantu Studies* material differs from the bulk of the BLC narratives. With her encyclopaedic knowledge, Dorothea Bleek was able to select narratives by the main |Xam teachers, ||Kabbo, Diä!kwain and |Haŋ‡kass'o, in which they spoke directly about aspects of their culture that they felt were most important for people to know about – the powers of certain special animals, the weather, rain and rain-making, and 'sorcery'.

Parts I to IV were published as 'Customs and Beliefs of the |Xam Bushmen'. The title was changed to 'Beliefs and Customs of the |Xam Bushmen' for Parts V to VIII. In Parts VII and VIII, as well as in 'Special speech', Bleek included the BLC notebook references for the narratives she used – these had previously been omitted.

In preparing the texts for publication, Bleek omitted any notes not directly related to the main point of the narrative, as well as certain instances of repetition. All these have now been restored. I remain true to various quirks in spelling, for example 'sorceror' rather than 'sorcerer', as used by Bleek and to the use of capitals or lower case within the text and notes as recorded by Bleek and Lloyd. In following Hewitt (1986) and Lewis-Williams (2000), I capitalise the initial consonant of all names of people – thus |Haŋ‡kass'o, not |haŋ‡kass'o.

Getting to grips with the narratives

Since the transcriptions are verbatim recordings 'written down from the lips of Bushmen', as Wilhelm Bleek put it (Bleek 1873:3), they preserve not only *what* was said but also *how* it was spoken. Thus, although the *Bantu Studies* narratives have been translated into English, their form and content still seem strange and difficult to fathom. The use of repetition in the narratives is a prime example. Repetition of words, phrases and ideas is used in oral cultures to develop the narrative and move it along (see 'Special speech'; Introduction). When the narrative is written down, however, the repetition tends to have the opposite effect – it slows down the narrative and makes it tedious and hard to follow. We must also remember that the |Xam teachers performed their narratives when writing was the only way to record speech – the technologies of sound recording and motion photography were yet to be invented. Consequently, there was no way of capturing the sounds of people speaking and singing in |Xam, as well as any accompanying gestures – these crucial elements are therefore missing from the narratives (Bleek & Bleek 1909; Guenther 1996; Lewis-Williams 2000).

In addition to these aspects of oral narratives, their subject matter is another challenge: the |Xam spoke about many ideas and concepts that require explanation for people who are unfamiliar with Bushman beliefs. I have tried to anticipate these and to clarify them by means of a short introduction for each of the nine parts published in *Bantu Studies*. Each introduction familiarises the reader with the ideas most relevant to that particular part by referring to other BLC narratives and to what other researchers have written about them. I have restored all of the text that Dorothea Bleek omitted, as well as all but a handful of the reverso notes, those omitted being mere technical points. I also clarify the meanings of words, comment on ideas, and suggest alternative translations.

The end of the |Xam?

In a frequently quoted comment, ||Kabbo – oldest of the |Xam teachers – is reported to have said that 'he much enjoyed the thought that the Bushman stories would become known by means of books' (Bleek & Lloyd 1911: x). He would no doubt be thrilled to see that the tide of obscurity has turned and that people are increasingly reading the BLC narratives for information and inspiration. My wish is that *Customs and Beliefs* should contribute to this trend.

Notes

1 There is currently a lack of consensus about the terms 'Bushman' and 'San'. Both have derogatory connotations and there seems to be no end in sight to the debate about which is most acceptable. I use the word 'Bushman' only as an adjective, referring to 'Bushman people' rather than 'Bushmen'. In doing so I mean to refer to a unique southern African culture, rather than to a means of describing a race of people.

2 AD843/RJ/Kb 32.2.3

3 AD843/RJ/Kb 32.2.3

AD843/RJ/Kb 32.2.3

PART I

BABOONS

From material collected by
Dr. W.H.I. BLEEK and Miss L.C. LLOYD between 1870 and 1880,
edited by D.F. Bleek

This number shows the Bushman's beliefs concerning baboons and his methods of dealing with them. The dividing line between mankind and the animal world is never very deep with the little hunters, it is therefore not surprising that they attribute to baboons many human characteristics. In doing so they give us insight into their own frame of mind, their respect for a girl's belongings, their belief in the sensations of the body foretelling danger, and in the body turning into clouds after death.

The next number will contain their beliefs and customs with regard to lions and other animals.

Dorothea Bleek's note to Part I
Vol. 5 (1931), Part 2: 179

By Harald Pager. Used with permission from the Rock Art Research Institute

'My grandfather … told me that baboons speak |Xam … that baboons are not like other things … they have their wives … they also resemble people.' Copy of Bushman paintings of humans and baboons from the Drakensberg/uKhahlamba.

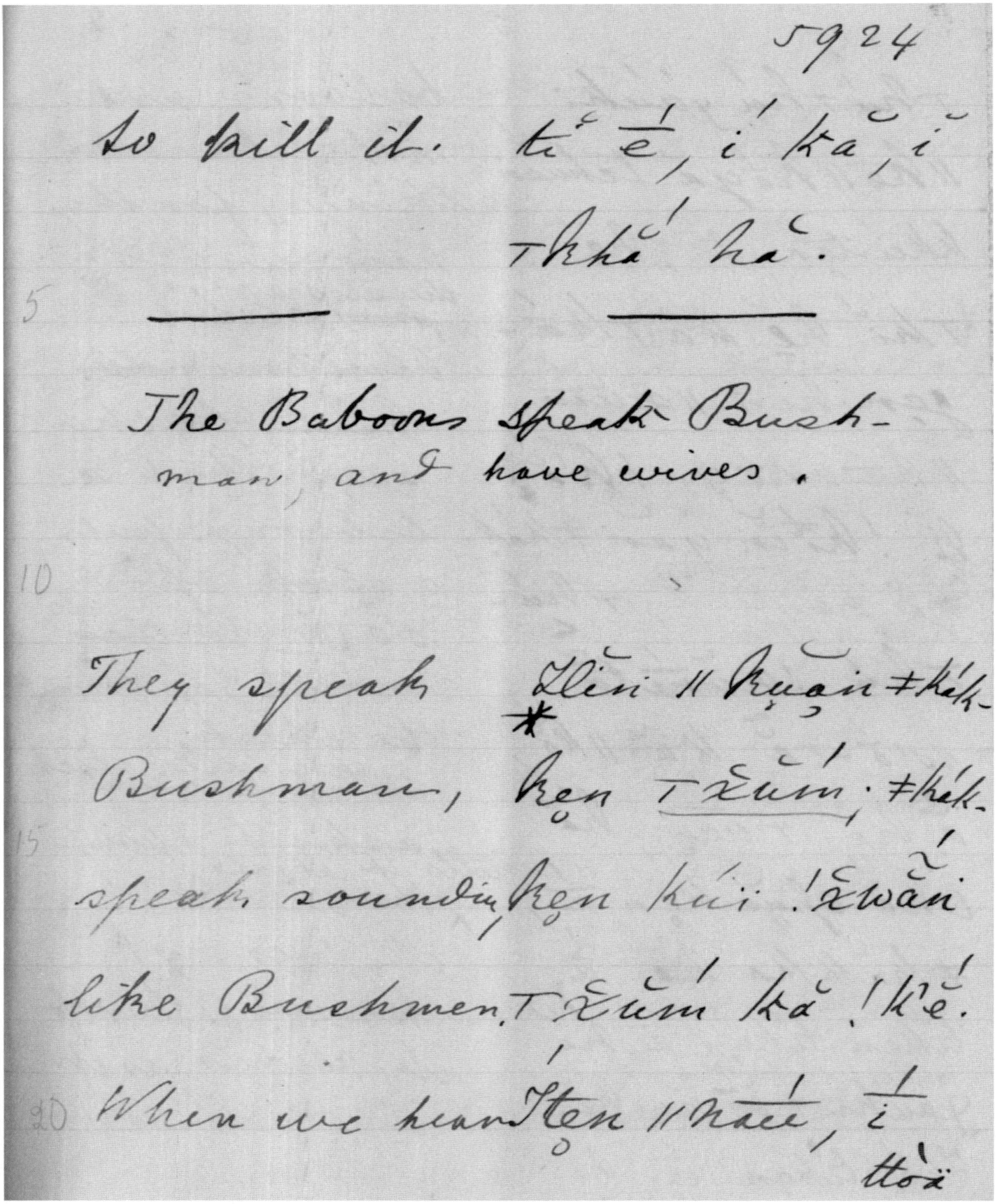
5924

to kill it. ti ē, i ka, i
ǂkhă ha.

The Baboons speak Bushman, and have wives.

They speak Bushman, speak sounding like Bushmen. When we hear — Tĭ ||kuan ǂkĕk- ǩen ǂxūm; ǂkĕk- ǩen kúi !xwăn ǂxūm ka !kē. ǩen ||naeē, i ttoä

Notebook page from the narrative 'Baboons speak Bushman'

PART I
BABOONS

Baboons are not like other things.
– Diä!kwain: 'Baboons speak Bushman' –

The |Xam called baboons (*Papio ursinus*, the Chacma baboon) the 'people that sit upon [their] heels' (Bleek & Lloyd 1911: 17) – they look like people, they have wives, and they speak and sing like |Xam people (see 'Baboons speak Bushman'; 'A baboon acts like this …'; 'Baboons were once people'). But although baboons may be like people, they are 'strangers', 'people who are different' (L.VIII.11: 7077-7078). The reasons for their difference go back to the time of the Early Race when all the animals lived together, gathering and hunting much as the |Xam did (Hewitt 1986: 105; see also 'Special speech').

Baboons and the Early Race

Like all the animals at this time, baboons were considered to be people but, by |Xam standards, their behaviour was shocking. They were the 'stereotype of undesirable in-laws' (Hewitt 1986: 109); for instance, the baboons killed and ate an Early Race woman who lived with them 'because she was not a little fat' (L.V.24: 5992). Another baboon entered the hut of a menstruating girl and seduced her (L.VIII.18: 7608-7625). A band of baboons waylaid the son of |Kaggen, the |Xam trickster-deity and beat him to death with their fists (Bleek & Lloyd 1911: 17-36; 254-259). Baboon behaviour was outrageously anti-social.

Matters came to a head when the first Bushman people cursed the baboons for violating meat-sharing practices – the baboons offered them human flesh, saying that it was gemsbok meat (L.V.24: 5974-5991). In response to this gruesome insult, the people caught a baboon and pressed his buttocks onto red-hot stones. The fire burnt off all his buttock hairs and made his tail kink and shrivel into its present crooked shape. Along with these physical characteristics, the incident entrenched the antipathy between humans and baboons, forever 'fixing' the habits of baboons. Since then the baboon 'does not eat much meat because he remembers that the fire once burnt off for him his tail tip' (L.V.24: 5991).

There may be an ecological component to the |Xam's and other Bushman peoples' negative characterisation of baboons – hunter-gatherers and baboons both subsist on wild plants and they may have competed for food at times (Vinnicombe 1976: 223). Similarities in diet, together with the similarities in looks and behaviour that the |Xam teachers mention, may thus account for the ways that Diä!kwain and

|Haŋ‡kass'o portray baboons as closely related but dangerous creatures that the |Xam 'respected'.

Baboon potency

In whatever way these attitudes developed, the |Xam believed that baboons possessed potency, known variously as *!gi:*, */ko:ode* and *//ke:n*. (For more about potency, see Lewis-Williams 1981; Introductions to Parts I-VIII and 'Special speech'). The baboons' potency gave them supernatural powers, what Dorothea Bleek called 'sorcery'. For example, a baboon always kept a stick of a plant known as *ʃo-/õä* in its left cheek – this plant spoke to the baboon, warning it off and protecting it from unseen dangers (see 'Baboons speak Bushman'; and Part VIII for human use of the same plant). As a result, baboons were immune to all but the strongest sickness (*taŋtaŋ*). The |Xam believed that many illnesses were shot like arrows into a person by spirits of the dead and by sorcerors (see Part VII). The fact that baboons do not get sick may therefore imply that, with the help of the *ʃo-/õä* plant, they are able to fight off such attacks and therefore have a great deal of potency.

|Haŋ‡kass'o interweaves several beliefs about the potency of baboons in a narrative called 'Girl, of the Early Race of People, who married a Baboon' (L.VII. 18: 7608-7625). He links baboons to a powerful substance, *//hara* (black specularite), a much prized, glittering mineral. People dug it out of mines guarded by sorcerors (*!gi:tən*), and then mixed it with fat. They used the mixture to anoint their heads, making themselves 'handsome' *(ắkken* alternatively *akkən or a:kən)* (L.VIII.18: 7608; Bleek & Lloyd 1911: 375-379). When a young girl of the Early Race mentions drawing a baboon with a piece of *//hara*, a male baboon – out of earshot and in his own village behind the hill – sneezes at the mention of his name. Knowing that the sneeze meant his name had been spoken, and possibly as a result of the power of the *//hara* itself, the baboon makes his way to the 'hut of sickness', where the girl has been secluded because she is experiencing her first menstruation (see Part IV, 'Omens, wind-making, clouds' for more about sneezing; Part V for more about the 'new maiden'). He 'marries' the girl, a word that |Haŋ‡kass'o and the other teachers may sometimes have used as a euphemism for sexual intercourse (Guenther 1996: 90). The baboon uses sorcery to transform the girl into a baboon. At every visit he sings a song about her head; eventually her head becomes baboon-like and, finally, she throws away her kaross and climbs up the rocks and over the hill with her baboon husband.

The narrative is thus full of details about baboons and their supernatural powers. Typically, baboon's powers are negative. The baboon's (human) mother-in-law shouts '*/nu !kwi a*' – 'you are a bad person' (L.VIII.18: 7620) – at him as he and her daughter disappear. The translation of */nu* as 'bad' in this context is misleading, however – */nu* also means 'dead', 'spirit' and 'angry' (Bleek 1956; Hollmann 2002; see also Part VII). The */nu !kˀe* or 'spirit people', for instance, are sorcerors who have died but who continue to use their powers (see Part VII,

'Sorcerors'). The mother-in-law is therefore not simply scolding the baboon for eloping with her daughter, but is accusing him of sorcery.

Respecting baboons

There is another strand in |Haŋ‡kass'o's narrative: why does the baboon sneeze at the mention of his name? Sneezing (*/khamma*) is a reaction to a significant event taking place far away, in this case the mention of the baboon's name (see Part IV for more about sneezing). But what is it about the baboon's name that is so important? To answer this question we need to know more about hunting beliefs, more particularly, the observances known as *!nanna-se* (Bleek & Lloyd 1911; Vinnicombe 1976; Lewis-Williams 1981; see Part III) and translated as 'hunting observances showing respect' (Bleek 1956: 473).

Everybody had to *!nanna-se*, not just hunters; women and children back at the camp could jeopardise the chances of a hunter by saying or doing the wrong thing (see Part III, 'The eland's story'). Respecting the names of certain animals, including the baboon's, was an important aspect of *!nanna-se* behaviour. In order to *!nanna-se* an animal's name, a person used an alternative word or phrase – 'people speak as if its [the baboon's] name were not what they were talking of, for they want the baboon to think, people are not speaking to it' (see 'The baboon's name').

What happened if a person did speak the animal's name? No matter how far away it was, the animal instantly became aware that somebody was using its name and, therefore, was not respecting it. Such disrespect was tantamount to mockery and led to negative consequences, the nature of which depended on the kind of animal it was. If it were a wounded eland, then |Kaggen would intervene and allow the eland to escape death from the hunter's poisoned arrow (see Part III, especially 'The eland's story'). A lion, however, would go and confront the person who had used its name in vain (see Part II, 'The lion'). The baboon's reaction to disrespectful behaviour was disastrous for the hunters – 'the place at which I hunted would resemble a burnt place' (L.V.24: 5904). Diä!kwain thus seems to be saying that the baboon would destroy the resources of the hunting-ground, the plant food as well as the game. He also mentions another power of the baboon – its *!k"augən* or 'death influence' (Bleek 1956: 508). A man who has shot a baboon has to put 'the baboon's teeth … on [his] bow' (see 'The baboon's death influence'). Only baboons have such wide-ranging powers to devastate the hunting ground.

I pointed out earlier that Pat Vinnicombe has suggested that baboons and human beings who live a subsistence way of life in southern Africa compete for resources. A troop of baboons within a Bushman band's *!xoe* or 'place' (Bleek 1956: 500) could conceivably deplete resources on which the people were relying. Since they could not permanently eliminate the baboons from their territory, the |Xam had to accept the baboons' presence and devise means of co-existence between humans and baboons. The beliefs about baboons that Diä!kwain and |Haŋ‡kass'o discuss are part of this world view.

Baboons speak Bushman

Narrator: Diä!kwain
Source: 'My father was the person who told me that baboons speak Bushman …'
Dictation dates: 1 February (probably); 6 February; 13 February 1876
Notebook reference: L.V. 24: 5924-5926; 24: 5923 rev., 5925 rev.; 5957-5973
***Bantu Studies* reference:** Vol. 5 (1931), Part I: 167-170

Baboons are exceptional creatures – not only do they speak the /Xam language, but they use the same plant medicines as Bushman people. Dorothea Bleek consolidated three separate narratives from Diä!kwain's twenty-fourth notebook to make 'Baboons speak Bushman'. The first of the original narratives is called 'The Baboons speak Bushman and have wives'.

❑

/hu/hu -//kwaŋ ≠kakkən /xam, ≠kakkən ku:i !xwãŋ /xam-ka-!k'e.	Baboons speak Bushman, speak sounding like Bushmen.
Itən //nau, io ˉtoä he, o he: ≠kakkən //na, itən ka, i siŋ ˉ≠ĩ:, ti e: !kˀe kwitən e: /au //na, o i: k''auki ≠enna he.	When we hear them talking there, we are apt to think that other people are to be found there, though we did not know of them.
Ti e: i /ne /nĩ: he ĩ:, hiŋ e: i //k'oen, ti e: /hu/hu ˍoä ˍdɔä e:, //kakkən ku:ï !xwãn !k'e.	When we catch sight of them, then we see that they were baboons talking like people.
ŋ o:ä kaŋ a: siŋ ≠kakka ke, ti e: /hu/hu ≠kakken /xam.	My father was the one who told me that baboons speak Bushman.
ŋ !kõïŋ !xu:gen-dikən //xam siŋ ≠kakka ke, ti e: /hu/hu ≠kakkən /xam.	My grandfather *!xu:gen-dikən* also told me that baboons speak Bushman.
Haŋ //xam ≠kakka ke, ti e: /hu/hu k''auki //ke://ke:ja tʃwɛŋ kwiten, ta: hɛ /ki hɛ-ka /ka:gən; hiŋ //xam //ke://ke:ja !kˀe.	He also told me that baboons are not like other things, for they have their wives; they also resemble people.
N !kõïŋjaŋ ≠kakka ke, ti e: /hu/hu !num tã: sˀo:-/ã-ka //kha o ha ˍ/wain; ha ʘho-ʘpwakən a: ≠kakka ha ã: tikəntikən e:, ha k'' auki ≠enna he.	My grandfather told me that a baboon holds a stick of *sˀo:-/ã*(1) in its mouth; this little stick tells it about things which it does not know.

He tikən e:, ha ka |kuı !xwãŋ ha: ≠enn akka, o ha sʔo-|ã-ka ||khakən |kuı e: ≠kakkən ha ã:.

That is why it seems to understand them well, because that stick of *sʔo:-|ã* has talked to it about them.

He tikən e:, ha ≠enna ĩ:.

These things are what it knows.

|xam-ka |kʔe kaŋ ke: |ki |hiŋ |hu|hu-ka sʔo:-|ã, e: ha tã: he o ha _|wain, he se |ki|ki he.

Bushmen always take out the baboon's *sʔo:-|ã*, which it has laid in its cheek, that they may keep it.(2)

Ta he |ki |k'e:, ti e:, si |nõ k''au ||k'oen, ti e:, |hu|hu ||nau, ha _|kamainja ha: sʔo:-|ã-ka ||kha, haŋ k''auki tã: ha; ha k''auki tã:, ti e: ha tãŋ ; o ha: ||kha, haŋ a: |kʔõäse ha o tikəntikən e: ka he di ha; ha: sʔo:-ã|-ka ||khakən e: ≠kakka ha ã:, |a: a: |kəm sa ha.

For they say, do we not see that when a baboon is carrying that stick of *sʔo:-|ã*, it does not feel pain ; it does not feel when it is ill, for that stick is what protects it from the things which want to attack it ; that stick of *sʔo:-|ã* tells it that danger is approaching it.

He ha ||xəm |ne tã: ha !kauügən ĩ:; ha !kauü kaŋ |ne di kui taŋ, ha _!hamĩ , o sʔo:-|ã-ka ||khagən e: |ki si _!hamĩ_!hamĩ ha.

And it also feels its body because of this ; its body feels as if it were afraid, because the stick of *sʔo:-|ã* has taught it fear.

Ta: ha !kauügən |kuı taŋ _!hamĩ o ||k'e: a: a, ha !kauü kaŋ k''auki taŋ , ti e:, he ta |kwẽ:ĩ tã, ĩ:.

For its body feels afraid at that time, its body does not feel as it is wont to do.

Ta: ha !kauũgən ||nau, tã:-tã: a:, ha tã-ĩ: ha !kauükən ã:, tikən |kuı taŋ, ti !ko!õĩŋ se _tai ||kaitja, o ||köiŋ ka ti e.

For when its body has this feeling, something is happening, something ugly will walk past on that day.

Ta: ha !kauügən |kuı k''auki tã ti e:, he ka |kwẽ:ĩ tã. ĩ: ; ta ha k''auki tã ≠hannũ ha ≠kauũgən, o ||k'e:a.

For its body does not feel as it usually feels, it does not feel comfortable at that time.

Sʔo:-|ãŋ |kuı a: |kwẽ:ĩ |kwãŋ di ha !kauügən, o sʔo:-|ãŋ |ki ≠enn≠enn ha, ha se ≠enn.

The *sʔo:-|ã* is doing this to its body, in order to teach it to know.

He tikən e:, |hu|hu e tsʔa a: k''auki ka ha se |kuı |ku:kən.

Therefore the baboon is a thing that does not want to die.

Ta: ha |km ≠enna, ti e: he kië: se sé ha; haŋ |kuı ||nau, |ku:kən, haŋ

For it knows what is coming to it, it feels like this about death, it

Baboons speak Bushman

/kuu ≠enna ha ; ta: ha /ki k''auki ka ha se /kuu !ku:kən.

knows it ; for it is not willing to die.

Hɛ tikən e:, mama-gu ka siŋ //nau, /hu/hu !xa-ka /kukən, mama ≠nau, si: /na taŋtaŋ, mama /k'e: tata, mama kuku, mama /k'e:ja tata ã:, tata kwaŋ //a //k'oen, ti e:, ha /nõ k''au se /nĩ /hu/hu ; ha se /kha /hu/hu, ha /ki sa: mama ã: /hu/hu /khuu, mama se //hiŋ !ki /e: he o /nũĩ, si se !kha: //kho ha, o /hu/hu /khuuwa: /e: ta: !nũĩ.:

Therefore our mothers used to say this of a baboon's mane hair, if our heads ached, mother called father, mother spoke, mother told father to go and look if he could see a baboon, he must kill the baboon, he must bring mother the baboon's hair, that she might tie it up with sinew, for us to put (the string) on with the baboon's hair in it.

Mama se da: si ã: ≠kann, si se/kha: //kho /hu/hu /khuu ; ta: /hu/hu e ts'a a: k''auki taŋtaŋ; ta:, ha ka-≠uŋ o ha //na, o ha k''auki tã: taŋtaŋ.

Mother would make us a charm of it for us to wear the baboon's hair, for a baboon is a thing that does not feel ill ; for it lives long where it is without feeling pain.

Ta, ti e:, he: da: ha, /kuu e:, ha ka /ne /nĩ taŋtaŋ, ĩ:. Haŋ e tsʔa a: //nau, ha /nĩ: taŋtaŋ, itən /kuu ≠enn akka, ti e:, taŋtaŋ a: k''auki ta //kaitən ha a:, ha /nã: ha.

But when illness attacks it, it is very ill. It is a thing of which we know well that if illness seizes it, that illness will not be lifted, but will get it.

He tikən e:, ha -≠//kwaŋ /ku:kən ĩ:.

Then it will die.

Ta:, ha /ki e tsʔa a: o k''auki siŋ /kuu tã:ĩ: taŋtaŋ; ta, ha ka /kuu //na, o ha k''auki tã: ha ti e:, ha eŋeŋjã: taŋ; ta:, ha ka /kuu //na, o ha: k''auki tã: taŋtaŋ.

For it is a thing which usually does not feel ill ; for it lives without its body feeling pain ; it lives without suffering illness.

Ta, ti e:, taŋtaŋ /ne /nĩ: ha, ĩ:, hɛ e:, i -//kwaŋ ≠enna, ti e:, ha //khoä /nã taŋtaŋ -!kerri.

But when illness does seize it, then we know that it is a severe illness.

Hɛ tikən e:, ha -//kwaŋ /ne -ku:kən.

Therefore it dies.

Hɛ tikəu e:, tata-gu ka siŋ //nau, o he: /nã: /hu/hu, o ha: -/ku:kən ta:, he //nau, o he /k'e: ja he /ka: gən ã:, he kuku, he tu: tu he

Therefore our fathers do this when they have seen a baboon lying dying, they talk to each other about it, they ask each other,

Baboons speak Bushman

|ka: gən, ts?a ˍka: a: da: |hu|hu, he ha ⁻|ku: kən ta: ti e: ã ?

"What can have happened to the baboon that it lies dying there?

⁻||ka ! |hu|hu e ts?a a: ˍdɔä |ku:kən.

See! The baboon is a thing that can die.

Ta:, ti e:, ha |nã: taŋtaŋ a: |gi: ja, he |kɯ e:, ha ka |ku: ken, ĩ:.

For when it gets a bad illness, then it dies."

Notes

16-17 *... baboons are not like other things*: Here the word *tʃwaŋ*, translated as 'things', means 'animals'. Baboons, in other words, are exceptional; they are different from other animals (see Introduction).

20-21 *My grandfather told me that a baboon holds a stick of* s?o:-|ã *in its mouth ...*:

([1])*s?o:-|ã* is a plant with a red top and long roots which grows in sand, in or near dry river beds; it is used as a medicine or charm.

The word for this plant is also spelt *ʃo-/ õä* (Bleek 1956: 182). Part VIII includes narratives about this important plant and how the Xam used it.

29 *These things are what it knows*: A better translation of the phrase *he tikən e:* is perhaps 'That is why it knows'. The statement refers back to the stick of *ʃo-/ õä* as the reason why the baboon knows things.

30-31 *Bushmen always take out the baboon's* s?o:-/ ã *...*:

([2])*Diã!kwãin's* father, *xaä-tiŋ*, told him that the *s?o:-|ã* lay in the baboon's left cheek.

The ability to store food in the cheeks is a characteristic of the Cheek-Pouch monkey family, *Cercopithecidae*, to which baboons belong (Kingdon 1997). Their cheek pouches can hold as much food as their stomach, an adaptation that enables a baboon to collect food and then move on to eat it somewhere safer (Apps 1992).

37-39 *... that stick is what protects it from the things which want to attack it*: The 'things' (*tikəntikən*) are probably 'harms' things or */kha/kha-tʃeŋ* (L.VIII.20: 7758), sent to kill the baboon (see Part VII, 'Sorcerors').

50-51 *... something* **ugly** *will walk past on that day*: The word *!ko!kõiŋ* may also be translated as 'bad' or 'evil' (Bleek 1956). In this context, 'evil' is probably a better translation; the stick of *s?o:-/ã* is warning the baboon of approaching danger.

61-62 *... for it is not willing to die*: '[Xã:ätiŋ's (Diäkwain's father – ed.) story ends here]' (5964 rev., note omitted).

A baboon acts like this ...

Narrator: Diä!kwain
Source: 'Xã:ätiŋ, the father of Diä!kwain, related this to the latter'
Dictation date: 2 February 1876
Notebook reference: L.V. 24: 5927-5929
***Bantu Studies* reference:** Vol. 5 (1931), Part 1: 170

Baboons know things about people they have never seen before.

❑

|hu|hu kaŋ ka |ku ||nau, ha: k"auki |na: i, ha |ku ||nau, ha |na: i, ha |ku !kwi: i |kẽ.	A baboon acts like this, though it has not seen us before, yet when it catches sight of us, it calls our names.
Tija |ku |xwãŋ, ha ≠enna i |kẽ, o ha: |na io.	It seems as if it knows our names, when it sees us.
Ha k"auki siŋ |na i, ta: ha |km a: ≠enna i kẽ.	It has not seen us, but it knows our names.
Han |ku ||nau, itə n ki _tai, |kãã !ɑhá: hɛ́: ti, haŋ ||nau, haŋ |k'e: ja !kˀe kwitən ã:.	When we merely walk past here, it does this, it tells others about it.
Haŋ kuï, "!kwi a: |kẽ |kwẽ: ĩ-da, ha kaŋ kië: |ke: !ɑhá.	It says, "The person whose name is so-and-so is passing there.
Haŋ ||khoä !kuïtən ||a: o ha-ka neiŋ."	He seems to be returning home."

❑

Talking to baboons

Narrator: Diä!kwain
Source: 'Xã:ätiŋ, the father of Diä!kwain, related this to the latter'
Dictation date: 30 January 1876
Translation dates: 6 February 1876 (5902-5909)
Notebook reference: L.V. 24: 5902-5910
***Bantu Studies* reference:** Vol. 5 (1931), Part 1: 170-171

People should not talk to baboons ...

❑

ŋ oä kaŋ siŋ ≠kakka ke, ti e:, ŋ //nau, !gauë-tukən, o ka: ki tu:ï /hu/hu, o /hu/huwa /k'e:-ã ki !ɑhá: o ŋ, ŋ ˍkɔ-ɔ̈ k''auki ≠kakkən hĩ /hu/hu; ta: ŋ //khoä kaŋ ˉ≠i:, tĩ k''au ka, siŋ //nau, o ka: ≠kakkən hĩä /hu/hu, tikən /kɯ ka, tıja siŋ k''wãŋ, ti !kauro, ti e:, ŋ !hɑn /kɑm //a: hɛ.

My father used to tell me, that if in the early morning I heard a baboon calling to me as I went past, I must not talk with the baboon, for I should think that the place would not be as it had been before I talked with the baboon, the place at which I hunted would resemble a burnt place.

Ta: /hu/hu /ki k''auki e //ẽ:ĩ !kwi, o i ≠kakkən hĩ ha, o !gauë tukən, o itən /kɑm //a: !kauxu.

For a baboon is not a good person, if we talk to it in the early morning, as we go to the hunting ground.

Ta:, i-g //nau, i: ˉtoä /hu/hu, o ha: /k'e:-ã /ki ɑhá: o i, itən //nau, i: /k'e:ja !kuko: ã:, itən /kɯ ï: kuku:i, itən /k'e:ja ha ã:, "!khou !ɑhí ta: ˉ!k'au, ha kaŋ !xwã: //na ti e: ã ; ta:, a /kɯ a: tu:i, ti e: hɛ !kẽ: ã //na ti e: ã."

So if we hear a baboon speaking to us as we go past, if we tell another about it, we merely say to him: "Hipbone is sitting on the saltpan, is making a noise there, for thou canst hear them chattering there."

I /kɯ-g //nau, i: /k'e:ja !kuko: ã:, i k''auki //xã:. i ≠kakkən /ki/ki ha /kẽ, o iten ki tu:i ha,; ta:, i /kɯ k''wãŋ, i k''auki tu:ï ha, o ha /k''e:-ã /ki !ɑhá: o i.

When we have told the other about it, we do not again mention its name, although we hear it, but we act as if we did not hear it speak to us as we pass.

Ta: i /kɯ tauko ˍtai, o haŋ ki /k'e:-ã /ki !ɑhá: o i.

We walk past, even if it speaks to us as we pass.

Ta:**, **tsˀa a: k''auki ka ha se o |nĩ i, ha se ||k'oen xu: tu i, ha |ki ϵ ; ta:, ha ||nau, ha |nĩ: i haŋ |kɯ, ≠kakkən hĩ i,o ha |na: i ; o haŋ ka, i se ≠kakkən hĩ ha.

For it is a thing which does not merely want to see us, to look and leave us ; but if it catches sight of us, it talks to us as long as it sees us, for it wants us to talk to it.

Hϵ tikən e:, ha ≠kakkən-ĩ: i,o ha |na i.

Therefore it is talking to us whenever it sees us.

Haŋ ||ke||keja !khwã: ʘpwa a k''ẽĩjã, ha xarra ka !||nau, ha: |na: i,ha |kɯ k''ẽnk''ẽn i ; ha xarra k''wẽã i, o ha: k''wẽ !kerru i.

It is like a little child who teazes, it always does so when it sees us, it mocks us ; it always goes on like that, as if it were deceiving us.

Notes

11-12 *For a baboon is not a* ***good*** *person ...*: There is an alternative translation of what Diä!kwain said. *//ẽ:ĩ* also means 'lucky' (Bleek 1956: 520). Literally translated, the sentence would then be: 'because a baboon makes not to be lucky a person if we talk to it in the early morning, when we go to the hunting ground'. In other words, Diä!kwain is re-emphasising what he had said about the baboon's power to sabotage the hunter's efforts to find food.

18-19 *'**Hipbone** is sitting on the saltpan'*: *!khou* is a 'respect' word that people use rather than saying */hu/hu,* the usual word for baboon. The idea of 'respect' (*!nanna-se*) is central to |Xam culture (see Introductions to Parts I-VIII and 'Special speech').

The baboon's name

Narrator: Diä!kwain
Notebook reference: L.V. 24: 5905 rev.-5906 rev.
***Bantu Studies* reference:** Vol. 5 (1931), Part 1: 172

The baboon's name is a powerful thing.

❑

|hu|hu a: !ɑhí ||khoã kunno o ha !khou xu, itən _!hamĩ, i |kwẽ:ĩ ku, i |k'e:, o intən ta: ||ka ti e: i ||nau, o i: !kwi: ja ha |kẽ e:, ha |ki kunno, o ha !khou, o i |k'e: ja, '|hu|hu: !khou-ka _≠nwa:', haŋ |kɯ ≠enna, ti e:, i |k'e: ha !khou.

When the baboon puts its paw (?) to the front of its hipbone, we are afraid to speak, for we know that if we say the name (of the thing) which it is touching, if we say, " the end of the baboon's hipbone," it knows that we are speaking of it, the baboon, that we are speaking of its hipbone.

He tikən e:, !kˀe ka |kɯ !kwi: kuï !xwãŋ, ha |kẽ k"auki e:, !kˀe !kwi: he, o haŋ ka, |hu|huwa: siŋ ka, ha: ˉ≠ĩ:, ha-ha k"auki a:, !kˀe |k'e: ha.

Therefore people speak as if its name were not what they were talking of, for they want the baboon to think, people are not speaking of it.

Ta:, !kˀe |kɯ ≠kakkən tʃweŋ e: |xara, !kˀetən _||kwaŋ |k'e: ha, ha a: |hu|hu, o !kˀetən ta: ||ka ti e:, he-ka ≠kakkən e:, he !kwi |k'i |hu|hu |kẽ ĩ:, ti |kɯ ka, tija siŋ k" waŋ |hu|hu ˉtoä, ti e: i ≠kakkən |ki ha.

For people mention different things, although they refer to it, the baboon, for the people know that if their talk mentions the baboon's name, it seems as if the baboon hears that we are talking of it.

❑

Notes

15-17 *For people mention different things, although they refer to it, the baboon …*: People use another word or a phrase rather than saying *|hu|hu* (baboon). Otherwise the baboon would know that people were talking about it (see 'Talking to baboons'). In 'Baboons speak Bushman', speaking the baboon's name causes it to sneeze (see Part I, Introduction). Many of the other *Bantu Studies* narratives mention *!nanna-se* ('respect') behaviour, but in different contexts.

Baboons and dogs

Narrator: Diä!kwain
Source: 'Told to Diä!kwain by his father Xã:ätiŋ'
Dictation date: 4 February 1876
Notebook reference: L.V. 24: 5948-5956
***Bantu Studies* reference:** Vol. 5 (1931), Part 1: 172-173

What /Xam people say to a baboon that has caught one of their dogs.

❑

I e: /xam-ka !kwi, i kaŋ //nau, !kwiŋ!kwiŋ //khauka /hu/hu, hiŋ /ne //aŋ //xarra //kho /hu/hu o !kau.

/hu/hukən /ne ¯//kau siŋ !xuru, o haŋ ka !kwiŋ!kwiŋ k''auki se /ka-ã ha, o haŋ dattən !kwiŋ !kwiŋ.

Ha se //nau, !kwiŋja ka ha //kaitən !ke //e ha, ha se /kã-ã !kwiŋ ha se !kən txeri ho !kwiŋ tũ:.

I //nau, i //k'oen, ti e:, /hu/hu-_!karrokən !kwiŋ, i ku, "!kwi-/a-ka !kwiŋjaŋ tuko /kɯ /ke, a _!karrokən /ke."

/hu/hu /kɯ //nau, ha: ¯toä, ti e:, i ≠kakka ha ã:, ti e:, !kwi-/a-ka !kwiŋ e, haŋ k''auki se //xã: ha _!karrokən !kwiŋ.

Ta:, ha /kɯ-g /ne k''wãŋ ha _!hamĩ !kwiŋ, haŋ k''auki //k'oen //k'oen //wẽ:ĩ !kwiŋ.

Ta:, ha /kɯ !kwaitən tau //k'oen !kwiŋ, haŋ k''auki //k'oen//k'oen //wẽ:ĩ !kwiŋ!kwiŋ; ta:, ha /kɯ k''wãŋ !k''werritən !kwiŋ!kwiŋ, o ha ¯toä ti e:, i ≠kakka ha ã, ti e:, /kwi-/a-ka !kwiŋ e.

We who are Bushmen are accustomed to do this when the dogs chase baboons and drive them away from the mountain.

A baboon sits on a boulder, thinking that the dogs will not catch it, if it deceives them.

It will wait until the dog comes up to it, it will catch the dog and tear off the dog's skin.

When we see that a baboon has seized a dog, we say, " It is a girl's dog that you have seized there."

When the baboon hears us say that it is a girl's dog, it does not seize the dog again.

For it seems to be afraid of the dog, it does not look straight at it.

For it looks sideways at the dog, it no longer looks straight at the dogs ; for it seems to be ashamed of them, when it has heard us say, that is a girl's dog.

Ha |kuı ||koä:kən _!hamĩ xu tu !kwiŋ, o ha ¯toä, ti e:, !kwi-|a-ka !kwiŋ _hã e.

It is very much afraid and leaves the dog alone, when it hears that it had been a girl's dog.

Itən |kuı daudau ha, o itən ka, ha k''auki se !kən txeri |hiŋ !kwin, o ha tũ:.

We deceive it, because we do not want it to tear off the dog's skin.

Haŋ _||kwoŋ !hum i, o i ≠kakka ha a:.

It believes us when we speak to it.

Haŋ ||nau ha _!karrokən-ĩ: !kwiŋ, haŋ |kuı i: daudau !kwiŋ; haŋ k''auki ¯≠ĩ:, ti e:, ha ka ha |kha !kwiŋ; ta:, ha |kuı ĩ: !he |ki |hiŋ-tuï !kwiŋ o ha, !kwiŋ k''auki se sé ha.

It pretends that in snatching at the dog, it is merely playing, it does not mean to kill the dog, for it is just holding off the dog, not letting it come too near.

Tija siŋ k''wãŋ, ha-ká ha |kã-ã !kwiŋ, o haŋ |kuı ĩ: |ki-si _!hamĩ _!hamĩ !kwiŋ, o haŋ ka !kwiŋja siŋ _!hamĩ ha.

Although it seems to seize the dog it is merely making the dog afraid, for it wants the dog to fear it.

Haŋ |kuı k''wãŋ ha ¯||ã !kwiŋ, kaŋ |km ||k'i-||k'i-ĩ: !kwiŋ.

It seems as if it smelt the dog, it laughs gently at the dog.

Notes

11-13 *When we see that a baboon has seized a dog, we say, 'It is a girl's dog that you have seized …'*: A 'girl's dog' (*!kwi-/a-ka !kwiŋjaŋ*) was probably a dog that belonged to her father and which she had to 'protect' (*!koa-sse*) so that the dog would hunt well (see Part V, Introduction, for discussion of the potency of a 'new maiden'). Diä!kwain explains elsewhere how exactly a girl protects a hunting dog (L.V.20: 5592-5604, published in Lewis-Williams 2000: 269-270).

19 *For it looks sideways at the dog*: 'looks angrily at the dog – only looks a little at the dog because he does not make the dog angry' (5951 rev., note omitted).

The baboon's death influence

Narrator: Diä!kwain
Source: 'Xã:ätiŋ told this to Diä!kwain'
Dictation date : 31 January 1876
Notebook reference: L.V. 24: 5911-5916
***Bantu Studies* reference:** Vol. 5 (1931), Part 1: 174

Certain things have to be done after killing a baboon to avoid its death influence (!kau:gən).

❑

Tata kaŋ ≠kakka ke, ti e:, ŋ //nau, o ka: /ka: /hu/hu, ŋ //nau !gwara, ŋ syritənsyritən //kho twitwi:tən-⊙pwonni o ŋ-ka /hau !nu!nuntu.

Father used to tell me that when I had killed a baboon, I must take an arrowhead and cut fine lines round the points of my bow.

Ta:, tata /ki /k'eja ke, ti e:, /hu/hu //khẽĩ//kheĩ(3) e:, ŋ didi //kho he o /hau, /hu/hu //khẽĩ//khẽĩ-jã: siŋ //na /hau.

For father used to say, that the baboon's teeth(3) were what I was putting on my bow, the baboon's teeth would be on my bow.

Ta:, tata /ki ≠kakka ke, ti e:, /hu/hu //nau, o ka: k''auki syritən-syritən //khoä twitwi:tən o /hau, ha ts?axáu-ka //kaurukən /ku /e: tiŋ i-ta /hau, o i: /ka: ha.

For father used to say that if I did not cut fine lines round the bow, the baboon's eyehollow would be in our bows, when we had killed it.

Hɛ tikən e:, i //kho//kho twitwi:teŋ o i-ta /hau o itən ka /hu/hu ts?axáu-ka //kaurukən se /hiŋ tu i-ta /hau.

That is why we cut lines on our bows, for we wish the baboon's eyehollow to leave our bows.

Ta:, tata /ki ≠kakka ke, ti e:, /hu/hu-ka !k''augən /ku //nei//nei: i-ta /hau, o i: k''auki ˍtaba /hiŋ toä he, o i-ta /hau.

For father used to tell me, that the baboon's death would live in our bows, if we did not cause it to leave them.

Ta:, tata /ki ≠kakka ke ã:, ti e:, ŋ /nõ k''au //k'oen, ti e:, /hu/hu ka //nau, o i ka: ha, haŋ ˍ/kwa:gen(4) //ke//ke: ˉ!kwi, o haŋ ta: //ka ti e:, ha /ku //xəm ˉoä e ˉ!kwi?

For father said to me about it, did I not see that a baboon acts like this, if we kill it, its clouds(4) resemble a man's, because it feels that it too was once a man ?

Hɛ tikən e:, ha-ka didi: |kw !naunko ||ke||ke:ja ⁻!kwi, o haŋ ki e |hu|hu.

Therefore its actions are still like a man's, although it is a baboon.

Notes

6-7 … *the baboon's teeth*:

(³)*!gwãĩn ||xam ĩ:ja. Itən ||xam ||nau, i |ki: !gwãĩ, itən ||xam didi ||kho twitwi:tən-ka !kaukən, o itən di, |ki |hiŋ-tu:i !gwãĩ-ta ||k'o:äkən o i-ta |hau, o itən ka !gwãĩ-ta didi:ja: k''auki siŋ ||na i-ta |hau.*

(³)With the hyena it is the same. When we kill a hyena, we also put little lines, in order to take the hyena's curse off our bows, for we want the hyena's actions not to be on our bows.

19-20 … *the baboon's* **death** *would live in our bows*:

Note by D.H. Feb. 1/76. It is like what we say to anyone whose actions are not nice (*ǂhannũwa*). The things he does are not agreeable (*ǂhannũwa*) so we are angry with him, we curse him (*//k''ao*). We say 'Do you think what you are doing is nice (*ǂhannũwa*) that you treat me so?'

(5913 rev. note omitted)

The word *!k''augən*, translated here as 'death', has other nuances. Several translations are given in the *Dictionary* – 'death news, misfortune, death influence' (Bleek 1956: 508). The word may be identical with *!kau:kən*, which appears in Part III, 'Hunting after the death of a friend'. |Haŋǂkass'o explains in this narrative that the death of a friend has a 'death influence', which makes them unable to hunt springbok successfully. In another unpublished instance, a man comes under the death influence when he encounters a dead animal on the hunting ground (L.V.11: 4850). After this encounter, he is unable to find game to hunt.

22 *For father said to me about it …*:

(⁴)Compare *Specimens of Bushman Folklore*, p. 397. Men make clouds when they die.

How a baboon shows respect

Narrator: Diä!kwain
Source: 'Xã:ätiŋ told this to his son Diä!kwain'
Dictation date: 1 February 1876
Notebook reference: L.V. 24: 5917-5924
***Bantu Studies* reference:** Vol. 5 (1931), Part 1: 174-175

How baboons respect the potency or ǀko:ode *of young women (see Part V, Introduction).*

❑

|Xam	English
O !kwi |xa: |hu|hu o !nwa:, haŋ ||xɑm ¯≠i:, ti e:, ha ka ha ||xɑm |ka !kwi; ta:, |kwi ˍ||kwoŋ ||khoä ka !kwi |ka ha.	When a man shoots a baboon with an arrow, it thinks it would also like to kill the man, because he seems to be trying to kill it.
Haŋ ||nau, !nwa: a: i |xã: ha ã:, !nwa:ŋ |ne ||keŋ sˀo ha.	It takes the arrow with which we shot it, which is sticking in it.
Haŋ ≠ke: |hiŋ !nwa: o ha, he ha !kɑn ¯||kau tẽ !nwa o ha !kauru.	It pulls out the arrow from itself and lays it on its forearm.
!nwa:-ka ti ko:kən ||khoï ta: ha |k'a: ko:.	The other part of the arrow lies in its other (right) hand.
Haŋ || nau, ha |k'a: k''ɑm haŋ ˍ|kaö ¯||kau tẽ o ha !kauru, he !nwa: |ku k''wãŋ !nwa: |hiŋ |hau; !nwa:ŋ |ku swe:ŋ ||a: i.	It crosses its right hand over the forearm, and the arrow seems as if it were leaving a bow; the arrow goes flying towards us.
Tikən |ku k''wãŋ ha |xĩ: i o |hau.	It seems to be shooting at us with a bow.
Tata-gu:kən ≠kakka ke ŋ ˍkɔ¯ɔ se ||nau ka: ||k'oen, ti e:, |hu|hu ≠ke: |hiŋ !nwa: o ha, haŋ !kɑn ||k'i: o !nwa:, ha kɔ: !kwe!kwe ||a: ŋ, ŋ ˍkɔ:¯ɔ se oroko |k'e: ha, ŋ se |k'e:-ja ha ã:, ti e:, !kwi-|a-ka !nwa: |ku e: ha !kɑnna, o ĩ:.	The old men told me, that if I saw a baboon pull an arrow from itself and hold it fast as if it were aiming at me. I must speak to it quickly and tell it, that it was a girl's arrow that it was holding.
Haŋ |ku se ||nau, o ka: |k'e:ja ha ã:, ti e:, !kwi-|a-ka !nwa: ϵ, haŋ |ku se tẽ: !nwa:.	Then it would do this, when I had told it that it was holding a girl's arrow, it would lay the arrow down.

Tija kɔ: |kɯ k''wãŋ ha !k''werritən, ha _kɔ:¯ɔ |kɯ !kɑn |ki ||kho: ë ha |na:, ha ¯ko: |kɯ k''wãŋ ha !k''wer-ritən i, o i: |k'e:ja ha, ti e:, |kwi-|a-ka !nwa: ɛ.

It would seem to be ashamed, it would hang down its head as if it were ashamed before us, when we told it that it was a girl's arrow.

Ha _kɔ:¯ɔ |kɯ ĩ: di !go: ë, tija: kɔ: k''wãŋ, ha kaŋ ¯≠ĩ:, ha _||kwaŋ |kɯ se á hi ã:, i se _||kwa |kɯ |ka ha.

It would merely make a sign as if it thought that it ought to let us kill it.

Ta:, i _||kwaŋ ||khoã ¯≠kauwa, ti e: i ka, i |ka ha.

For we had seemed to want to kill it.

Notes

11-12 *It crosses its right* **hand** *over the forearm*: *!kauru* also means 'finger joints' (Bleek 1956). The point seems to be that it looks as if the baboon is shooting the arrow back at the person.

20-22 *I must speak to it quickly and tell it, that it was* **a girl's arrow** *that it was holding*: A girl's arrow (*!kwi-|a-ka !nwa:*) probably refers to an arrow reserved by a girl's father to kill an animal for her: nobody except the girl, her mother and other older women may eat this meat because it is full of !Khwa:'s potency (*|ko:ode*) and is therefore extremely powerful and dangerous (see 'Baboons and dogs'; Part V, Introduction).

27 *It would seem to be* **ashamed**: A better translation of the word *!k''werritən* is 'show respect'. The baboon is not hanging its head in shame. Rather, not looking is a way of respecting the potency of the girl's arrow (see Part III, 'The eland's story' for situations where respect requires the avoidance of doing and saying things). Compare this with 'Baboons and dogs', where the baboon respects a dog that a girl has 'protected' (*!kõa se*) with her potency or *|ko:ode* (for more about girls and *|ko:ode*, see Part V, Introduction).

Baboons were once people

Narrator: Diä!kwain
Source: 'Diä!kwain heard this from his mother ǂKămmi-ăn'
Dictation dates: 26, 27 January 1876
Notebook reference: L.V. 23: 5881-5890
***Bantu Studies* reference:** Vol. 5 (1931), Part 1: 175-177

Baboons still have certain habits and characteristics from the time long ago when they, and the other non-human species, were all people (see Part I, Introduction). The /Xam play a game that they learnt from the baboons long ago.

Mama-gu kaŋ ≠kakka ke, ti e:, /hu/hu _hã: ˉoä e ˉ!kwi, o //k'e: a: i-i e: /ne e !kˀe, i k''auki _oä //na, ã:.

My parents used to say to me, that the baboons were once people at the time when we who are people were not here.

Ha //k'hwi //xɑm ˉoä e /kwi ã:, haŋ a:, /hu/hu: ˉoä //xɑɯ e !kwi ã:, o ha: //k'e:.

When the quagga also was a person, then the baboon was likewise a person.

Hɛ tikən e:, si //k'oen, ti e:, /hu/hu: !kou-tu /kwããja //k'hwi,o haŋ ta: //ka ti e:, hɛ /ki ˉoä e !kˀe, hɛ ko //k'hwi.

Therefore we see that the baboon's belly resembles the quagga's, for they feel that they were once people, they and the quagga.

Hɛ tikən e:, hɛ-ka tikəntikən _/kwããja !kˀe, o hiŋ ta: //ka ti e:, hɛ ˉoä e !kˀe. Hɛ tikən e:, hɛ-ka tikən-tikən _!kwããja !kˀe, ĩ:.

Therefore their parts resemble humans, for they feel that they are people. That is why their parts smell of people.

Mama-gukən ≠kakka si ã:, ti e:, si-g /nõ k'au tu:ï, ti e:, /hu/hu: di kuï !xwãŋ !kˀe o ≠gebbi-gu, hiŋ !gum: kuï !xwãŋ /xam-ka !kˀe, e: !gum: /ki ≠gebbi-gu, o hiŋ ta: //ka ti e:, /xam-ka !kˀe /ki /kɑ /ne !gum //ke://ke: /hu/hu:; ta: /hu/hu: /ki /ka a: //xa://xa: !kˀe o ≠gebbi-gu.

Our parents asked us, did we not hear that baboons make a noise like people in the *≠gebbi-gu* game, they call sounding like Bushmen who call making a *≠gebbi-gu*, for they think that Bushmen always call like baboons because it was a baboon who taught people the *≠gebbi-gu* ;.

Hɛ tikən /ne e:, /xam-ka !kˀe /ne ≠enna ≠gebbi-gu, ĩ:, o hiŋ ta: //ka ti e:, /hu/hu: /ki e:, !gum:

That is how Bushmen come to know the *≠gebbi-gu*, because the baboons used to call teaching

||xa:||xa: hϵ o ≠gebbi-gu, o ||k'e: a: to:ï ||xɑm-oä !gum: ≠gebbi-gu ã:.

Ha ||k'e:tən a:, |hu|hu: ||xɑm-oä !gum: ≠gebbi-gu ã:. ˍ||khã: ||xɑm ˉoä !gum: ≠gebbi-gu; ti e:, ˍ||khã: |ne ˉ||ki: txəri to:ï ||hattən-tu, hiŋ e:, hϵ |ne xu: tuï ≠gebbi-gu, hϵ k''auki |ne -≠na: k'um: ≠gebbi-gu, ĩ:, hϵ hϵ |ne k''auki |ne !kuttən kuï !xwãŋ ti e:, xam-ka !kˀe |ne |kwẽ:ï dakən !kuttən ĩ:; o ˍ||khã:, hϵ ko to:ï e: da: ≠gebbi-gu-ka |a:.

Hϵ tikən e:, hϵ |ne |kɑ ||koäkən ||nau, ˍ||khã da: toï ã: |a:, ≠gebbi-guwa: |kɑ ||koäkən |kiŋ tu hϵ, he, hϵ |kɑ-g |ne ĩ:, di: ʘpwaitən, o ti e:, hϵ kwãŋ di: ≠gebbi-gu-ka |a:, ĩ:.

Hϵ tikən e:, |hu|hu: !naunko ˍ||kwakkən ||ke||keja !kwi. Hϵ tikən e: |hu|hu: !naunko ≠kakkən, haŋ di kuï !xwãŋ !kwi.

them the *≠gebbi-gu*, at the time when the ostrich also called the *≠gebbi-gu*.

At that time the baboon also called the *≠gebbi-gu*. The lion also called the *≠gebbi-gu* ; then the lion kicked(5) the ostrich tearing his——, then they left off the *≠gebbi-gu*, they no longer danced the *≠gebbi-gu*, and they no longer sang it as the Bushmen are used to sing it ; because the lion and ostrich had fought over the *≠gebbi-gu*.

So when all this had happened, when the lion had fought the ostrich, the *≠gebbi-gu* (tunes) left them and they became animals, because they had fought over the *≠gebbi-gu*.

That is why the baboon still understands like a man. That is why the baboon still speaks, he sounds like a man.

❑

Notes

8-10 *Therefore we see that the baboon's belly resembles the quagga's* …: Dorothea Bleek incorporated only part of this informative note about non-human animals and the time of the Early Race, dictated by Diä!kwain on 29 January 1876. Here it is in full:

The quagga and the baboon they have no 'pens' (i.e. stomach – ed.), they do not resemble other things, for they verily possess a *!hu, cloaca maxima*, ['Dick derm'] (large intestine – ed.), of which they make a stomach (*|xoä* – ed); because they think they are not game. Because they once were people. That is why they still resemble us who are people, because they know that they once were people. That is why their organs (*tikən-tikən* – ed) still smell of people because they know that once they were people. That is why their organs still smell of people although they are game.

Part I Baboons

Baboons were once people

Unlike most grazing and browsing animals, quagga – and as Diä!kwain mentions, baboons and humans – do not have additional, ruminating stomachs with which to soak and soften their food. Diä!kwain explains that this anatomical distinction attests to the fact that long ago, quagga and baboons were people.

17-19 *... baboons make a noise like people in the* ǂgebbi-gu *game*: 'A game or dance with peculiar calls, said to have been learnt by the Bushmen from the baboons' (Bleek 1956).

33-34 *... then the lion kicked the ostrich ...*: 'When the lion scratched the ostrich tearing his *//hattən-tu* then they left off the *ǂgebbi-gu'* – part of this note was left out by Dorothea Bleek. The *Dictionary* gives *//hattən-tu* as 'throat' (Bleek 1956: 540).

39-41 *The lion and ostrich had fought over the* ǂgebbi-gu: The story 'The lion jealous of the voice of the ostrich' in Bleek and Lloyd's *Specimens of Bushman Folklore* (1911) concerns this fight and is based on the similarity, at a distance, of the ostrich's booming call to the lion's roar. The lion had challenged the ostrich to call the *ǂgebbi-gu* and see which the women liked most. They prefer the ostrich's call and so the jealous lion attacks the ostrich.

Baboons and the *ǂgebbi-gu*

Narrator: Diä!kwain
Source: 'Diä!kwain heard this from his father Xã:ätiŋ'
Dictation dates: 19 February; 22 February; 22 February (evening) 1876
Notebook reference: L.V. 25: 5998-6007
***Bantu Studies* reference:** Vol. 5 (1931), Part 1: 177-178

Baboons imitate human games, especially the ǂgebbi-gu*,*
a once popular call-and-response game.

❑

|hu|hu: kaŋ ka ||nau ||ga:, hɛ ||keo||ke ti e:, |xam-ka !kʔe xarra ka di hɛ, he hɛ ka ||nau ||ga:, hɛ di ≠gebbi-gu o ||ga:.

The baboons are accustomed at night to imitate what the Bushmen used to do, when they used to play the *≠gebbi-gu* at night.

|hu|hu:kən ||ke||ke:ja |xam-ka !kʔe, he _tai ||k'e:, o ti e:, he kiё !gum: |ki|ki ≠gebbi-gu, ĩ:.

The baboons imitate the Bushmen, they come together at the place where they mean to call the *≠gebbi-gu.*

He |ne di ≠gebbi-gu; itən ka, i: siŋ ka, i: ¯≠ĩ:, |xam-ka !kʔe e: di |ki ≠gebbi-gu, i e: k'auki ≠enna, ti e:, |hu|hu _||kwaŋ ¯≠enna ≠gebbi-gu, haŋ ||xɑm di ku:ï !xwãŋ |xam-ka !kʔe, o hɛ di |ki ≠gebbi-gu.

They hold a *≠gebbi-gu*; we should think that Bushmen were holding a *≠gebbi-gu*, if we did not know that the baboon also knows the *≠gebbi-gu*; it also acts as Bushmen do when they hold a *≠gebbi-gu.*

Hiŋ _||kwaŋ ¯!kuttən ku:ï !xwãŋ |xam-ka |ka: gən.

They sing sounding like Bushman women.

|hu|hu:gen e ts'a a: ||nau, |xam-ka !kʔe ||neinjã _oä !hiŋjã o !kau a:, he _oä ||na ha; hiŋ kiё se ||nau, he: ¯toä ti e:, |xam-ka !kʔe siŋ di |ki ≠gebbi-gu, hiŋ tum-ĩ: ≠gebbi-gu a: |xam-ka !kʔe siŋ ¯!kutta; hiŋ |xɑm |ne ¯!kut-tən ≠gebbi-gu a: |xam-ka !kʔe siŋ ¯!kutta, hiŋ |ne ¯!kuttən kuï !xwãŋ ti e: !kʔe siŋ |kwẽ:ĩ dakən ¯!kuttən ≠gebbi-gu, ĩ:.

A baboon is a thing which acts like this when Bushman huts are near the rock where he lives; they come to watch the Bushmen holding the *≠gebbi-gu*, they listen to the tune which the Bushmen sing; they also sing the tune which the Bushmen have sung, they sing sounding as if it were people singing the *≠gebbi-gu.*

Hiŋ -//kwaŋ tu:tu: he /ka:gən, o ti e: !k?e /nõ siŋ te: dakən ⁻!kutten ≠gebbi-gu ?

They ask each other whether people are not singing the *≠gebbi-gu* ?

/hu/hu: kɔ:gən -//kwaŋ /ne ⁻!kutta !k?e kuitən ã:, ti e:, !k?e siŋ !kwẽ:ĩ dakən ⁻!kuttən ≠gebbi-gu, ĩ:.

One baboon sings to the others as people do when they sing the *≠gebbi-gu*.

Han /ne ⁻!kuttən !kauŋ-siŋjã /hu/hu: kuitən, o haŋ ka, /hu/hu: kuitən se ⁻!kuttən !kuŋ-siŋ ha, he se ⁻!kutten ku !xwãŋ, ti e:, !ku ko: /kwẽ:ĩ dakən ⁻!kuttən ≠gebbi:gu, ĩ:.

He sings before the other baboons, for he wants the other baboons to sing after him, that they may sing as he does when he sings the *≠gebbi-gu*.

Ta: /xam:ka !k?e /ki //xam ĩ:ja, !kwi /aitji kɔ:, haŋ //na, haŋ -mai-i haŋ ⁻!kutta !k?e kuitən ã:, o haŋ ka, !k?e kuiten se ⁻!kuttən !kuŋ-siŋ ha, o !k?e kuitən ta: //ka ti e:, ha /ki a ≠enna ≠ge≠gebbitən-gukən-gukən:

For Bushmen also do this, one woman stands there and sings first, she leads the others as she wants them to sing after her, for the others think that she is one who knows the *≠gebbi-gu* tunes.

Hɛ tikən e:, ha !kum:, haŋ ⁻!kutta !k?e kuitən, o haŋ ta: //ka ti e:, !k?e kuitən /ki k''auki ≠enna, ti e:, hɛ se /kwẽ:ĩ/kwẽ hɛ ⁻!kuttən ≠gebbigu //ka -//kãũĩŋ, ĩ:.

That is why she first sings to the others, for she thinks that the others do not know how they ought to sing the change of the *≠gebbi-gu*.

Ta: /xam-ka !kwi-/aitji kɔ: /ki ka //na, ha: //xa://xa: !k?e kuitən o ≠gebbi-gu.

For one Bushman woman is always there to teach the others the *≠gebbi-gu*.

❑

Notes

24-25 *… they also sing the tune which the* **Bushmen** *have sung*: The notebook translation has 'women' (6002).

47-49 *… they ought to sing the change of the* ‡gebbi-gu: '*/ki:* – D.H. says that the farmers use this word for the *‡gebbi*-gu' (6006 rev., note omitted).

A woman called Natta

Narrator: Diä!kwain
Notebook reference: L.V. 25: 6006 rev.-6007 rev.
***Bantu Studies* reference:** Vol. 5 (1931), Part 1: 178-179

This woman was admired for her participation in the ǂgebbi-gu.

!kwi-|aitji a: !kˀe ¯oä !kwi: ha |kẽ o Natta, ha kaŋ ¯oä ¯!kuttən kuï !xwãŋ, ti e: !gei ||kwa||kwarra ka |kwẽ:ĩ da ĩ:, o hɛ ˍ||gauë !gei-ta !kaukən.

A woman whom people called by the name of Natta used to sing calling as the ewes do when they seek their lambs.

Tija: ¯!kẽĩ ||au, hɛ !xwãŋ !gei ||kwa||kwarra ha: !xwãŋ ti e !gei ||kwa||kwarra ka |kwẽ:ĩ da, ĩ:, o hɛ: ˍ||karrokən |kɑm ||a: !khwa:.

It really sounded just like the call of a ewe that is hurrying to her young.

Ha ˍdɔm-ka ti kɔ:¯wa !xwãŋ ti e:, kɔttən ka |kwẽ:ĩ da, o hɛ: |kwaija, o hɛ: ka hɛ k''wã.

Another part of her throat sounded as partridges do when they go in flocks to drink.

Haŋ a: ¯oä ||xa:||xa: !kˀe.

She was the one who taught the people.

PART II

THE LION

From material collected by
Dr. W.H.I. BLEEK and Miss L.C. LLOYD between 1870 and 1880,
edited by D.F. Bleek

Photo: Roger de la Harpe, Courtesy of Africa Imagery

The lion 'knows he is a great thing. His eyes resemble fires that give light ... They resemble fire.'

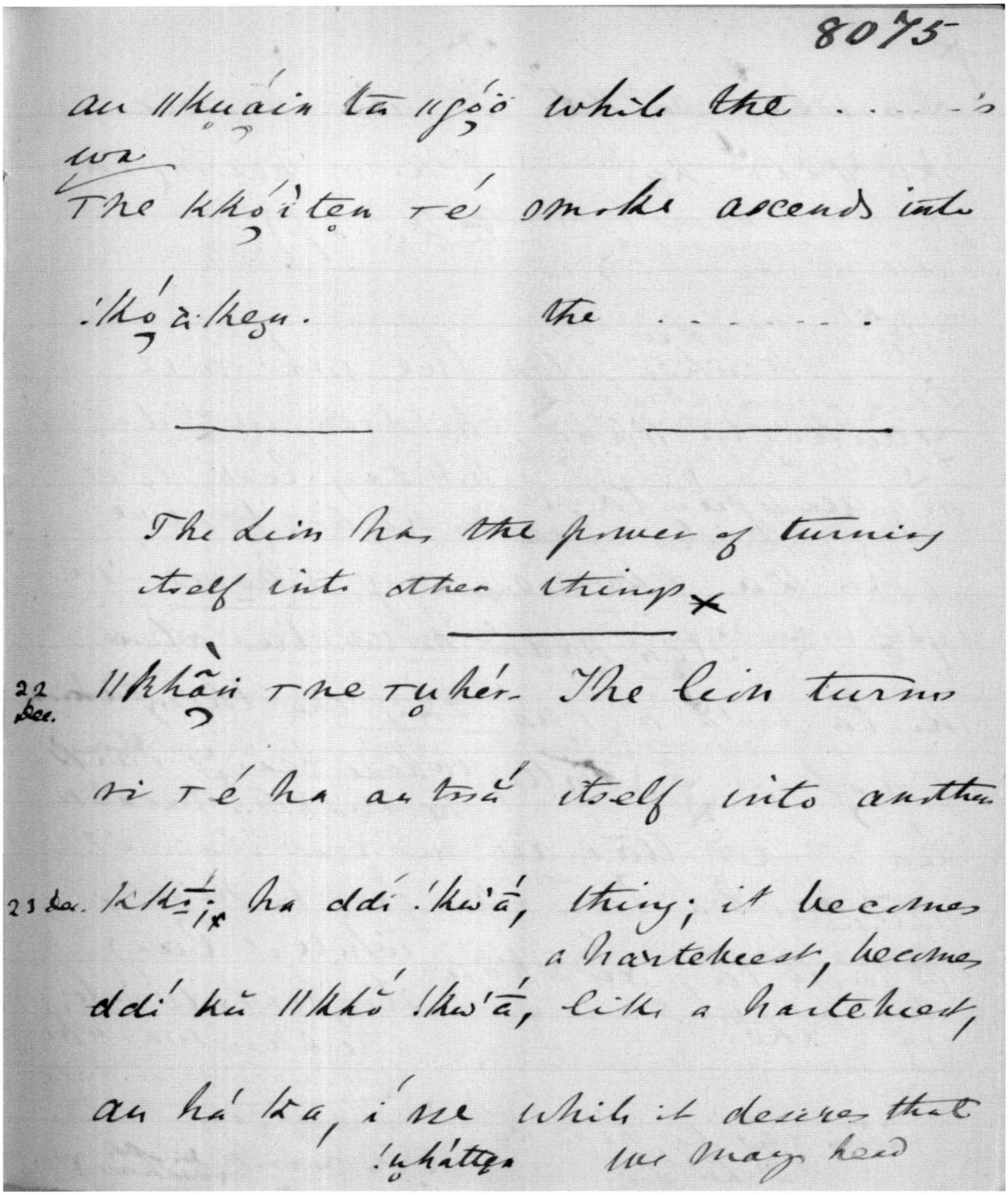

8075

an ||khuáin ta ||gōō while the .... 's
wa
The kkhōïten ‡é smoke ascends into
!khō ā-!kegn. the ......

The Lion has the power of turning
itself into other things ×

22 Dec. ||khãu ‡ne ‡uhér. The lion turns
ri ‡é ha autsá itself into another
23 Dec. kkhī ha ddí !khwá, thing; it becomes
a hartebeest, becomes
ddí hū ||khō !khwá, like a hartebeest,
an há ka, í ne while it desires that
!ghátten we may heed

'The lion … becomes a hartebeest' manuscript page from the narrative 'The lion's transformation (3)'

PART II
THE LION

The lion … makes things happen which we do not understand
– Diä!kwain: 'Lions and waterbags' –

People in Africa have always had to contend with lions (*Panthera leo*). These large predators are superbly equipped for killing, especially at night; their eyes are perfectly adapted for night vision and their massive strength allows them to overpower the strongest prey. They are intelligent too: they devise strategies appropriate to the kind of prey they are hunting. Lions take anything, from tortoises and porcupines to elephant and buffalo (Mills & Harvey 2001). They also kill people.

These natural historical details about lions would, of course, have been common knowledge to |Xam people, who had lived with lions for generations (see Thomas 1995 for a fascinating analysis of the relationship between lions and the Ju|'hoansi of the Kalahari). For the |Xam, however, these feline behavioural characteristics spoke of the lion's powers. The Part II narratives detail many of these extraordinary abilities.

Lions are people too

The |Xam saw certain similarities between themselves and lions. Many of these parallel the observations that both humans and lions are hunters and that sorcerors (*!gi:tən*) and lions are nocturnal. Diä!kwain mentions two further likenesses in behaviour: neither humans nor lions eat game where they have killed it, and both groups remove the animal's stomach contents before eating their prey (see 'Respecting the lion'). According to ||Kabbo, lions have the same family structure as humans, with families of grandparents, mothers, fathers and grandchildren. People can identify the family status of an individual lion by the amount of hair on its body and its colour, as well as by how, where and what the particular lion hunts (L.II.18: 1638-1646; 1650-1653). Furthermore, lions understand human speech (Lewis-Williams 2000: 176) and are able to imitate it (see 'The owl at sunset'). They also speak to each other (L.II.16: 1554-1555), something which their prey, the eland (*Taurotragus oryx*), hartebeest (*Alcelaphus buselaphus*) and gemsbok (*Oryx gazella*) rarely, if ever, do. Lions, in ||Kabbo's words, 'are also people' (L.II.16: 1551).

However, like baboons (see Part I), lions are 'people that are different'; and, moreover, they are 'things which are angry' (L.II.16: 1552) because they kill and eat people. This fundamental attribute of lions figures large in |Xam thought, and understandably so; few things can be more terrifying than being carried away at night and eaten by a great carnivore. ||Kabbo narrates a whispered conversation between two lions that discuss how best to kill a handsome man in a black kaross sleeping inside a hut (L.II.16: 1554-1555). The lions drag him away screaming as his neighbours throw burning logs at them in a hopeless effort to save his life. Soon the man is quiet – he is dead (see 'The lions and the tortoise' in 'Special speech'). Lions therefore feature strongly as the 'ancient dark enemies of human beings' (Biesele 1996: 149).

The enmity between humans and lions goes back to the Early Race times (see Special speech' for a discussion of the Early Race). In one *kum* or 'story' (Bleek 1956: 106), a man of the first |Xam people steals a lion cub to help him hunt gemsbok. His plan is a failure – the young lion kills the man and takes the dead gemsbok that the hunter had shot. The lion cub's family trace their missing child's spoor back to the |Xam village and, consequently, the hunter's bereaved wife and children must flee to her parents' house for safety (Lewis-Williams 2000: 174-205). In another story, a lioness raises a baby girl that she discovers in the womb of a pregnant woman she has ambushed and killed at a waterhole (L.VIII.24: 8084-8169, 8171-8172; L.VIII.25: 8173-8176). When the girl has grown up, she conspires with her human husband-to-be – they wait until the lioness has killed a gemsbok and then stab her to death. The people then take the gemsbok meat for themselves.

These two *kukummi* (plural of *kum*) are corollaries of each other – in one the lions kill the people, take the meat and put them to flight; and in the other, the people win through. Both *kukummi* contain the same fundamental truth: lions and humans are in competition for meat and cannot live together; one will inevitably destroy the other. Many of the Part II narratives describe how the |Xam established symbolic boundaries between themselves and lions, and how these were maintained by observing a particular code of *!nanna-se* or 'respect' behaviour.

The extraordinary powers of lions

Before examining the *!nanna-se* beliefs themselves, however, we first need to know about the extraordinary powers of lions and how these affected the |Xam. Many of these attributes are detailed in the Part II narratives.

Lions have a special relationship with owls, crows and flies, which they send out as 'spies'. These creatures tell the lions where people are sleeping and what they are saying about them (see 'The owl at sunset'; 'The owl and the black crow'; 'Respecting the lion'; 'The lion's name'; 'Lions and waterbags'; 'Owls, flies and lions'). The owl follows people, and then attacks them. An owl can cause the sun to set quickly as it flies off to tell the lion where the people may be found (see 'The owl at sunset'; 'The owl and the black crow'). The behaviour of the black crow is seen as evidence of its relationship with the lion – it flies over people, calling the lion – '*wa wa*', lands in front of them, then flies off to call the lion (see 'The owl and the black crow'). The 'lion's flies' live in its armpit (see 'Owls, flies and lions'), a potent part of the anatomy associated with healing rites (see Part VII), and then go out to eavesdrop on people (see 'Respecting the lion'; 'The lion's name'; 'Lions and waterbags', 'Owls, flies and lions'). The smell of fire, which lions fear, protects the people: often it is an old man who keeps the fire smouldering all night (see 'Tending the fire'). The lions fear to approach because they think people are awake and will shoot them (see 'The owl and the black crow').

Lions (presumably invisible) were believed to attack the waterbags of people on their way to collect water: the delay caused by having to repair the hole in the bag gave the lions a chance to run ahead and ambush the person at the waterhole (see 'Lions and waterbags'). Lions have the ability to experience vivid dreams and to remember these later when they wake up (see 'Respecting the lion'). They can project their */hu/hunta* or 'image (Bleek 1956: 291) to a place before they have arrived there, and they use this ability to trick people (see 'The lion's head'). Most frightening, perhaps, is the ability of the lion to take on the forms of other animals – humans, in one case (see 'The lion's transformation (1)'), and antelope in another (see 'The lion's transformation (3)'). Wild cats that have been killed by |Xam hunters may turn into lions and come and drag people away at night ('The lion's transformation (2)').

Now that we know more about the extraordinary powers of lions we can see how the *!nanna-se* or 'respect' behaviour took these into account.

Respect for lions

Several of the narratives mention situations which demand *!nanna-se* or 'respect' (see Introductions to Parts I, III, IV and V). This involves not saying or doing certain things in order to avoid harm. Thus, children should not say the lion's name, *//kha* – they should say */kukən*, which means 'hair' (see 'The lion's name'), or simply make the sign of the lion's paw with one hand (see 'Respecting the lion').

Other respect words for 'lion' are */kerre-/e:* , 'lighting in', and 'thing whose head's darkness it is' (see 'Avoiding the lion's name'). If children do not respect the lion's name, the lion's flies will know about it and report it: the lion either goes to the little boy's hut immediately (see 'The lion's name'), or waits until the child is old enough to go to the hunting ground before confronting it (see 'Respecting the lion'). Other *!nanna-se* behaviour concerns hunters who have chased a lion away from a kill that it has made – the hunters must leave a portion of the prey for the lion, otherwise the lion will follow the hunters' spoor home and claim a man in compensation (see 'Respecting the lion').

But perhaps the most pervasive use of lion symbolism amongst Bushman and Khoekhoe people is in the supernatural realm, in which *!gi:tən* (translated by Bleek and Lloyd as 'sorcerors') and lions are compared and equated with each other (see Parts VII and VIII).

Lions and sorcery

The |Xam teachers often drew attention to physical similarities and metaphoric links between sorcerors and lions, and many of their observations were published in *Bantu Studies* (see Parts VI, VII and VIII). I summarise them here:

- Both lions and sorcerors are *?ga ka ttss'a* or 'darkness's things' (L.II.18: 1661) that live in holes in the ground (Bleek & Lloyd 1911: 379; L.II.16: 1549). *!Gi:tən* go about at night, either looking for people to kill or, like the sorceress Tãnõ-!khaukən in Part VII, protecting ordinary people from harm inflicted by malevolent *!gi:tən*.
- Their eyes burn red at night, looking like the fires of other people far away (L.II.18: 1671).
- They 'walk on hair' – this is a reference to the hairy footpads of lions. When used of a *!gi:xa*, it implies that he or she has taken on the form of a lion (see Part VIII, 'The sorceror !Nuiŋ-|kuïtən').
- They are angry folk, impatient and irritable. An angry *!gi:xa,* full of dangerously strong *!gi:* (potency), could become a lion, growing hair on his back and running around trying to bite people (see Part VII, 'About the toorman' and 'All about sorcerors'; Part VIII, 'The sorceror !Nuiŋ-|kuïtən'). Lions, like powerful *!gi:tən*, are dangerous and unpredictable.

The Part II narratives make it clear that, as the foremost of the *//khe//khe* (beasts of prey), lions epitomise danger and death. By contrast, the |Xam teachers explain in Part III that game animals have positive associations.

The owl at sunset

Narrator: Diä!kwain
Source: 'This story was related to Diä!kwain by his sister |A-kkŭm, when he was still a boy'
Dictation dates: 1, 2 July 1875
Translation dates: 4869-4870 translated 2 July 1875
Notebook reference: L.V.II: 4869-4889½
***Bantu Studies* reference:** Vol. 6 (1932), Part II: 47-50

Diä!kwain's sister was far from home when the owl saw her. Fortunately, she knew what the owl was going to do and so, when an unknown voice called her name out of the darkness, she knew who it was.

The following story dictated by *Diä!kwain*, a Bushman from the Katkop hills, was related to him by his sister */a:kum* when he was still a boy.

!hũ!hũ: kaŋ //nau ŋ //kaxai /a: kum, o haŋ /hiŋ !kau-/nũnu,(1) !hũ!hũ:wã //nau, haŋ sa: o kammaŋ, o !hũ!hũ: //k'oen ti e:, //kõïŋ ta, //kõïŋ se /e:, !hũ!hũ: _!karrokən-ĩ: ha, !hũ!hũ: ka, ha: /kã/kã ĩ ha.

An owl did as follows to my elder sister /a:kum as she was leaving Kenhart,(1) when she was half way the owl saw that the sun was about to set and snatched at her, it tried to catch her.

Haŋ kaŋ /k'e:, "//kõïŋ //nau !hũ-!hũ: !kwẽ:ĩ k''o, ã /ki //a: ã:, //kõïnjaŋ k''auki dí: //k'e:, ta: //kõïŋ /kɒ o: se /e:. Hɛ !hũ!hũ: //k'oen, ti e: //kõïŋ _//kwaŋ /ne /e:, hɛ !hũ!hũ: xu:wa, ï:, o !nau-tukən."

She said, " The sun behaves as if the owl were doing this, making it set, for the sun does not keep time, but is just setting. And the owl sees that the sun is setting and leaves at dusk "

Hɛ ha //nau, !hũ!hũ: ká ha xu:-wa, haŋ k''auki _hã: tym-⊙pwa /ne !hymmi, hɛ ha _hã: /ne kukú:ï, haŋ ≠ĩ:, "Mama kaŋ ka siŋ ka: ≠ka-ka ke, !hũ-!hũ: _hã: //nau, //k'e: a:, ha /ne ≠en-na, ti e:, //khe//khe: /ne !hiŋja, haŋ /ne xu: i."

And when the owl started to leave her, she was not a little frightened and considered and thought, " Mother used to tell me that the owl acted like this when it knew that a beast of prey was near, it left us."

Hɛ ha _hõ: /ne kukúï, haŋ ≠ï: "ŋ kaŋ se /ki //ka, ti e: a; ŋ se

And she considered and thought, " I will light a fire here, I will

||ke: ||wẽï, ŋ se-g ||nau, |ija ||ka ||na, ŋ se _ta:i. Tsˀa a: |hũ!hũ: siŋ di:ja ha _saŋ ká ha ≠ĩ:, ŋ-ŋ a: ||ke: sˀo: o |ija |kɒ a: ||ka ||na; ŋ se !kú:ĩten, o ha |xuerri _||gauë |ki ŋ, o-g |i!"

make a big fire, so that when the fire is burning I can go. The thing for which the owl was acting so will think I am sitting warming myself at the fire ; I will go home while it is stalking me at the fire."

Hɛ ŋ ||kaxai _hã: ||nau, haŋ _tai, xu: tu |i ; haŋ |auwi _||khã, o _||khãŋ ||khɔ ||kau ʃo: ||xau. Hɛ ha _ha: ku_ku:i, haŋ ≠ĩ:, "Hɛ: tí, hɛ _||kwaŋ e:, ŋ siŋ |k'e: hɛ, o ti e! !hũ!hũ: |kɒ _!karrokən-ĩ ŋ, o ha ||k'oen, ti e:, ||kõ:ïŋ |ne |e:, haŋ |kɒ _!karrokən-ĩ ŋ. Hɛ tikən _||kwaŋ e:, tsˀa gwai á a, ha _||kwaŋ |ne a:, !kã: ||kau sˀo: o-g ŋ."

And as my sister was going to walk away from the fire, she caught sight of a lion sitting up on the Brinkkop. And she considered and thought, "I should have suspected this, when the owl was snatching at me, when it saw that the sun was setting. It must have been because of this great creature that was lying up there in wait for me."

Hɛ ŋ ||kaxai _hã: ||aŋ !xĩ:ja o ha, o haŋ sˀo:. Hɛ _||khã: _hã: sa: |i, ĩ:; hɛ _||khã: _saŋ !ko: ha, o |i. Hɛ _||khã: |kã-ĩ: ha !nwa, ĩ:, hɛ _||khã: !yhí-tiŋ hɛ, ĩ:. Hɛ ha _hã: ||nau, haŋ ||a:, haŋ tú:ï -||khã:, o -||khã:ŋ k''wa:_||gauë |ki ha.

And my sister went evading him as he sat there. And the lion came to the fire and missed her at the fire. And the lion found her footprints and followed them. And as she went along she heard the lion roaring as it sought her.

Hɛ ha -hã: kukúïtən ≠ï:, "Ti taŋ k''auki ≠ka: ka:, ŋ se !ka:gən !kúï:tən ; ta: _||khã: ka ha _saŋ ||nau, ka: !karr̄a, ŋ ||a:, _||khã:ŋ _saŋ !xaitji ||e ŋ. Ta: tí |kɒ ka ≠khãĩ ; ŋ se !ka:gən ||kaitən !kau, ŋ se ||a |ũŋ ||kau-siŋ !kau |nã:-tsi."

And she thought, "The place is not open enough for me to go home in the dusk, for if I still walked on the lion would follow me. But the place is steep (?), I will climb onto a rock in the dusk, I will go to lie down up on the ridge of rock.

Hɛ ha _||kwaŋ _hã: |ne !ka:gən ||kaitən !kau, ĩ:. Hɛ ha |ũn !kau, ĩ:, !kau |nã:-tsi, ĩ:. Hɛ ha |ka:-si taŋ ha ʘpwoiŋ ; hɛ ha !ko:, ĩ: ; hɛ ha tú:ï _||khã: tu:tu: e:, ha !khou-ã _||gauë |ki ha !nwa, ĩ:.

And she climbed up onto the rock in the dusk, and she lay down on the ridge of rock. And she lay waiting, she slept ; then she awoke, and she heard the lion's calls with which he was seeking her footprints.

The owl at sunset

Hɛ ha ˍhã: kúï, "Hɛ tí, hɛ ˍ//kwaŋ e:, ŋ siŋ /k'e: hɛ, ti e:, ˍ//khã: ká ha se /kã-ä ŋ !nwa."

And she said, " This, I suspect, must mean that the lion is trying to follow my footprints."

Hɛ ˍ//khã: //aŋ //nuŋ //a ha o !kau, ĩ:. Hɛ ˍ//khã: ˍhã: kúï, "/a:kum-we, a xa de?" Hɛ ŋ //kaxai ˍhã: kukúïtən ≠ĩ:, "!kwi taŋ k''auki ˍdóä a:, !kwi: //gauë ŋ; ta: ˍ//khã: ˍdóä e. Haŋ //nau, ti e:, ha ka ŋ́ siŋ ≠ĩ:, ti e:, !kwi a !kwi: ŋ, ŋ se //e ha,. Hɛ tikən e:, ha !kwi: kúï !xwãŋ !kwi ĩ:. Ta: mámagu ka síŋ ka, hɛ ≠kaka ke, ˍ//khã: ˍhã: ka !kwi: kúï !xwãn !kwi, o há ka i: se wέ ta. Hɛ tikən e:, há !kwi: kúï !xwãŋ !kwi, ï:, o háŋ ka, i se /k'e:ja ha ã:, ti e:, i //nã he. Hɛ tikən e:, ha !kwi: kúï !xwãŋ !kwi, ï:."

And the lion traced her scent to the rock. And he said, " O /a:kum where are you ? " And my sister considered and thought, " It cannot be a person who is calling seeking me, it must be the lion. He is doing this because he wants me to think that a person is calling me, and go to him. That is why he is calling like a man. The old women have often told me, that a lion will call sounding like a man, when he wants us to answer. Then he calls sounding like a man, for he wants us to tell him where we are. That is why he calls sounding like a man."

ŋ //kaxaitən ˍhã: kukúïtən ≠ĩ:, "A kaŋ ˍ//kwaŋ /kɑ se !kwi //na-//ná, ti /ke: a, ta: a !xwã; kaŋ ≠ĩ, ŋ k''auki ≠en-na, ti e:, á ka ŋ /k'e:ja ha ã:, ti e:, ŋ //na hɛ."

My sister considered and thought, " You may go on calling there at a distance, for you seem to think, that I don't know, you want me to tell you where I am."

Hɛ ˍ//khã: ˍhã: kúï, "/a:kum we, a ˍká: //na tí dé, o ti e:, a !nwa /kɑ //gwi-siŋ ti é? A xa /kam //a tí dé, hɛ-g ŋ k''auki /nĩ: aˀ /k'e:ja ki ã:, ti e:, a sˀo //nã hɛ. Ta: ŋ ˍ//kwaŋ /kɑ ≠ĩ:, ti e:, a ˍ//kwaŋ /kɑ sˀo //na ti e; ta: a sˀo ˍdóä //kaitən !kau. ˍDóä /ki !ke !hóä ŋ. Tsˀa di xa a:, a akke ŋ !kwi: ˍ//gauë /ki/ki a, o ti e:, ŋ ˍ//kwaŋ ≠ĩ:, ti e:, a ˍ//kwaŋ /kɑ sˀo //na ti é:?"

And the lion said, " O /a:kum, where can you be for your footprints vanish here ? Where have you gone, that I do not see you ? Tell me where you are sitting, for I thought you were sitting here, you must have climbed up the rocks. Do pull me up. Why do you let me call seeking you, when I am sure you are sitting there ? "

Hɛ ŋ //kaxai ˍhã: kukúïtən ≠ï:, "!kwi taŋ k''auki ˍdóä a: !kwi: /ki ŋ; ta: ˍ//khã: /kɑ sˀo ˍdóã e. ŋ

And my sister thought, " It cannot be a man who is calling me, but it seems to be the lion. I

k''auki se /k'e:ja ha ã:, ta:, ha //nau, ti e:, há ka ŋ /k'e:ja ha ã:, ti e:, ŋ //nã hɛ."

Hɛ ŋ //kaxai ˍhã: kukúïtən ≠ĩ:, mama ka siŋ ≠kaka ha ã:, ˍ//khã: ˍhã: ka !kan //khóë tẽ ha !khwi, o ha tu, ha !kwi: ˍ//gauë i, o ha /khwijã: //khóë ta: ha tu, o ha ka, ha: siŋ !xwãŋ !kwi, i k''auki siŋ túi ti e:, ha e ˍ//khã:. Hɛ tikən e:, ha //khóë tẽ ha !khwi o ha tu, ĩ:

will not answer him, for he is doing this in order to make me tell him where I am."

Then my sister remembered that mother had told her that a lion will put his tail into his mouth and call seeking us with his tail in his mouth, when he wants to sound like a man, so that we do not hear that he is a lion. That is why he puts his tail into his mouth.

❑

Notes

Sigrid Schmidt discusses this story as an example of a legend disguised as an actual historical event (1996: 118-120; see Part VIII, 'The old woman and the chameleon', for another example).

2–3 … *as she was leaving Kenhart*: Dorothea's note reads:

(1)*!kau-/nũnu kaŋ óä //nau, //k'e: a -//khã: ¯óä /kwẽ:ï /kwã:ŋ dí ŋ //kaxai ã:, /hũ:-ka //nei//nei k''auki ¯óä !naunko //na !kau-/nunu. Ta /xam-ka !kˀe /ka e: ¯óä //an-ĩ: !kau-/nunu.*

(1)As to Kenhart, at the time when the lion acted like this towards my sister, the White men's houses were not yet there. But Bushmen were living at Kenhart.

The |Xam name used for Kenhardt in the notebook is *!kau-/nũnu* (4869).

The owl and the black crow

Narrator: Diä!kwain
Source: 'Told by Diä!kwain, who had it from his mother and father'
Dictation dates: 7, 10 May 1875
Translation dates: 9, 10 and 14 May 1875
Notebook reference: L.V. 9: 4689-4706 1/2
***Bantu Studies* reference:** Vol. 6 (1932), Part II: 50-52

The lion controls the owl and the black crow.

Mama-gukən kaŋ ≠kaka si ã:, ti e: !hũ!hũ: e tsʔa a: ka ||nau, ha: ≠enna, ti e:, _||khã: se !ku:-ïtən-í, !hũ!hũ: sa k''wa: !gwesiŋ í ; ha-g ||nau, ha: k''wa: swe:nja, ha ||xau ú, ha sa _!karrokən í-ta ||neiŋ-ka ||xou||xou, o há: ka _||khã: se sá, |kã-ã |hiŋ i, o ⊙pwoin.

Our parents used to tell us that the owl is a thing which acts like this when it knows that the lion is returning to us. it comes to scream opposite to us ; when it has sat screaming, it flies up, it comes snatching at the bushes of the hut for it thinks the lion will come and catch us asleep.

Hɛ tikən e:, mama-gu kaŋ ≠ka-ka si ã:, si _kóö se !hɑmmi kwɔkwãŋ, o !hũ!hũ:wã: _!karroka |ki ||a: o si, o ||kõïŋ |etən|etən, si _kóö ≠enna, ti e: _||khã: a: !hũ!hu: da: si ã: ha, ha |kwẽ:ï k''o ã:.

Therefore our parents used to say that we had reason to be afraid, if an owl snatched at us in passing at sunset, we should remember that it is a lion which causes the owl to behave like this.

Hɛ tikən e:, mama-gu kaŋ ≠ka-ka si ã:, si _kóö se ||nau, si: ||k''oen, ti e: !hũ!hũ: |kwẽ:ï k''o, haŋ di:, si _kóö k''auki se |ũ:ŋsiŋ, ti e:, !hũ!hũ: siŋ |kwẽ:ï k''o, haŋ dí si ĩ:, o ti e:, si síŋ ka, si |ũ:ŋ he; si _kóö se ||nau, si kí siŋ ≠ĩ:, ti e:, sí ka si |ũ:ŋ hɛ: ti, si _kóö se ||nau, !hũ!hũ:wa !ke sa sí, o si di akən |ki ti e:, si ka si |ũ:ŋ he, si _kóö se ||nau, si ||k'oen ti e:, !hũ!hũ: |kwẽ:ï |kwãŋ di: o si, si _kóö se hɔ:

Therefore our parents used to tell us, that if we saw an owl acting like this, we must not lie down at the place where the owl had behaved thus to us, the place at which we had meant to sleep ; although we had planned to lie there, yet if the owl came to us as we were preparing the place for sleeping, when we saw it going on like this, we should take up our things and leave the spot at which

si-ka tʃweŋ, si se _tai xu: tu ti e:, !hũ!hũ: siŋ !ke sa si-si, ĩ: ; si se //a /ũ:ŋ ti e:/xarra, o si k''auki /ũ:ŋsiŋ ti e:, !hũ!hũ: siŋ !ke sa si ĩ:.

the owl had come to us ; we should go and lie down at a different place, not at the place to which the owl had come.

Ta: si kɛ́: se //nau, si /kwi/kwitən ã: !hũ!hũ:, si _kɔ́ɔ̈ /ne /ũ:ŋ ti e:, !hũ!hũ: siŋ /kwẽ:ï /kwã: ha: di si, ĩ:, _//khã:ŋ á: ká ha se !ke se si, ha _kɔ́ɔ̈ sa /kã-ã /hiŋ si o ʘpwoiŋ.

For if we paid no heed to the owl and slept where it had come to us in this way, the lion would come to us and seize us while we were asleep.

Hɛ tikən e: mama:gu kí:se si o _//hóë, hé ko !hũ!hũ:, ta: mama-gu /ki ≠kaka si ã:, ti e: _//hóë he ko !hũ!hũ:, tʃweŋ e: da: hi _//khã: hɛ é. _//hóë a: /hóäka haŋ a: mama-gu ≠kaka si ã:, si siŋ !hammi //wĩ: ha. Ha kaŋ ka '_wã:, _wã:', ha //ke: a:, ha da hi _//khã: ã:, haŋ a: ha ka '_wã:, _wã:' ã:, o ha //xau //kau ho //a: i ; ha /kwẽ:ï da, ha-g /ne !ahí siŋ //e i, o ha: //xau !kai /hiŋ //a: i. Hɛ ha-g /ne //nau, ha: //k'oen, ti e: i _tai //xĩ: i o ha, ha _kɔ́ɔ̈ //xã:, ha //xau ú, o ha ka '_wã:', ha _kɔ́ɔ̈ //nau ha: k''wa:, ha /kɔ́ɔ̈ !e!éttən ã: //kũ://kũ, o ha: //xã: ha //xau //kau ho //a: i.

That is what our parents taught us about the crow and the owl, for they said that the crow and the owl are things which warn us of the lion. The black crow is the one which our parents told us to fear very much. It calls "*wa, wa,*" when it warns us of the lion, it says "*wa, wa*" as it flies over us ; it goes to sit in front of us, when it has flown right over us. And if it sees that we walk past it, it will fly up again as it cries "*wa,*" and while it cries it flaps its wings and again flies over us.

Hɛ tikən e:, i-g //nau, i: //k'oen ti e:, he /kwẽ:ï k''okən di: o i, ítən k''auki //nẽĩ //nẽĩ ti e:, he siŋ /kwẽ:ĩ/kwẽ, he di i, ĩ:, ta: i _tai xu: ti e:, he siŋ /kwẽ:ĩ/kwẽ, he dí: i, ĩ:, i se //a //na//na ti e /xarra, hɛ !hu-!hu: k''auki siŋ /kwẽ:ĩ/kwẽ ha di, i, ĩ:.

Therefore when we see them behaving like this to us, we do not stay at the place at which they acted in this way to us, but go away, leaving the spot where they went on like this, and going to stay at another place, at which the owl had not acted towards us like this.

Mama-gu, hiŋ kaŋ /k'e:ja si ã:, si se //nau, si: //a ũ:, ti e: /xarra, si _kɔ́ɔ̈ k''auki se ã:, /i se thu:, si siŋ /ki ta: o /i /kwʔãĩ, si se //nau,

Our parents used to tell us that when we went to sleep at a different place, we must not let the fire go out, we must lie down in

si: ⊙pwoinja, si se ||k'oen ti e: |i thu:, si se hɔ: |i |u, si se ||gum |e: ha o |i, si siŋ |ki ta: o |i _|kwˀãĩ, o si ≠ĩ:, ti e: !hũ!hu: siŋ sa: si, o ||kõĩŋjaŋ !khe:.

the scent of the fire, so that while we were sleeping we should notice if the fire died down, then we should take a log and thrust it into the fire ; we must lie down in the scent of the fire remembering how the owl had come to us while the sun was high.

Hɛ: ||khe||khe: a: !hũ!hũ: siŋ di:ja, ha se ||nau, ha ≠ĩ:, ti e: ha ká: ha sa |kãã |hiŋ si o ⊙pwoiŋ, ha se !khou |i _|kwˀãĩ, ha se ≠ĩ:, ti e: !kwi _o:ä |kɒ !naunko !kˀauwa. |i _|kwˀãĩn |kɒ e:, ||khe||khe: ≠ĩ:, ti e: !kwi !kˀauwa ; !kwitən |kɒ ⊙pwoin ||na, |i _|kwˀãĩn |kɒ e: taŋ !kwi ||ke: sˀo.

Then when the beast of prey of which the owl had warned us thinks that it is going to catch us asleep, it will smell the scent of the fire and will believe that a person must still be awake. The fire's smell will make it think that someone is awake, the man will be sleeping there, but the scent of the fire will make it seem as if he were sitting keeping it up.

Hɛ tikən e:, mama-gu ≠kaka si ã:, o |i ĩ:, o hiŋ ta: ||ka ti e:, ||khe-khe: e: tsˀa a: k''auki ká ha se sé ||neiŋ a: ha !khou |i _|kwˀãĩ ã:, ta: ha !hammi:, ha sé ti e:, ha !khou |i _|kwˀãẽ, ĩ:. Ta ha ||xam ≠ĩ:, ti e !kwi _saŋ |nĩ ha, o ha: |xwerri sa o !kwi ; o ha ≠ĩ:, ti e: !kwi ⊙pwoinja, !kwija _óä |kɒ !kˀauwa, !kwi _kɔ́ɔ̈ _óä |ne |xã ha, o ha ≠ĩ: ti e: !kwi ⊙pwoinja.

That is what our parents used to tell us about fire, saying that a beast of prey is a thing which will not come to a hut at which it smells the fire's scent, for it is afraid to come when it smells the fire's scent. For it also thinks the man would see it, if it came stealing up to him thinking he was asleep, if he were awake, then he would shoot it while it thought that he was asleep.

Hɛ tikən e:, mama-gu ≠kaka si, ĩ:, o ti e: ||khe||khe: k''auki ká ha se |ku sé ti e: |i _kwˀãĩ ||aŋ, ĩ:, ta ha !hammi: he, ha |kɒ se: he ; haŋ k''auki ka ha se sé, ti e: |i _|kwˀãĩ |aŋ, ĩ:.

That is what our parents told us, that a beast of prey will not come up to a place at which there is a smell of fire, for it is afraid to come to it ; it does not like coming to a place where there is a smell of fire.

Notes

6-8 … *it comes snatching at the bushes of the hut* …: '[He flies over the top of the house, making a snatch at the top of it, without touching it, D.H. says]' (4689 rev., note omitted).

12 … *if an owl snatched at us* …: '[without touching us]' (4690 rev., note omitted).

14-15 … *it is a lion which causes the owl to behave like this* …: 'We had thought that [it] was an owl, while [it] was a lion; it wanted us to think that [it] was an owl, while it was a lion.' (4690 rev., note omitted).

16-17 *Therefore our parents used to tell us*…: 'that we must take care and do the following' (4692, text omitted).

25-26 … *when we saw it going on like this* … : A more accurate translation is: 'that we must take care should we see that an owl did this, acted like this' (4694).

32-33 *For if we paid no heed to the owl* …: '[i.e. If we thought that the lion deceived us, and were not afraid, and slept at the place where the owl did thus, then]'… (the lion would come to us – ed.) (4694 rev., note omitted)

37-38 *That is what our parents taught us about the crow* …: 'This is a crow which is altogether black, D.H. says.' (4695 rev., note omitted)

39-41 … *the crow and the owl are things which* **warn us** *of the lion*: Literally, *da:* means 'work for' (Bleek 1956: 19).

61 *Our parents used to tell us* …: '… when we had gone away from the place at which the owl had come to us' (4699, text omitted).

66-67 … *we should notice if the fire died down* …: '[i.e. if we awoke]' (4699 rev., note omitted).

67-69 … *then we should take a log and thrust it into the fire* …: '[a stump of firewood that was not in the fire, but lying near it, ready for use]'; '[under the ashes so that it must smoke but not burn away quickly]'(4699 rev., notes omitted).

71-72 … *the owl had come to us while the sun was high*: 'Therefore, we had taken care of our fire, that we might not allow the fire to go out. For, we had been thinking about the thing which the owl had done.' (4701, text omitted)

Respecting the lion

Narrator: Diä!kwain
Source: 'D.H. was taught this by his mother ǂKămmĕ-ăŋ'
Dictation dates: 5, 6, 7 April 1875
Translation dates: 6, 13, 15 and 17 April 1875
Notebook reference: L.V. 8: 4527-4562
***Bantu Studies* reference:** Vol. 6 (1932), Part II: 53-57

Lions have spies everywhere, listening to and watching what people do. Lions are like humans in certain ways and people must know these things so that they can understand and respect (!nanna-se*) them.*

❑

|xam-ka !kˀetən ãŋ !naŋŋa-se _||khã:, o hiŋ ta:, ||ka ti e:, !haukən! haukən tum-ĩ, ti e:, he |kwẽ:ï-da o _||khã:, ĩ:.

Bushmen avoid the name of the lion, because they think that the flies are listening to what they are saying of it.

!haukən!haukakən ||aŋ ||xou |e: _||khã: !nuntu, ĩ:. Hɛ !haukən-!haukən ≠kaka _||khã:, ĩ, ti e:, !kˀe |kwẽ:ï-da o ha, ĩ:.

The flies fly away into the lion's ear. And the flies tell the lion what people have been saying about it.

Hɛ _||khã: |kɒ-g ||nau, o ha: ʘpwoin ta:, haŋ |kɒ !k''abbe |hiŋ ; tija kə: |kɒ k''waŋ !kwi a: |k'e: |hiŋ ha o ʘpwoin.

And as the lion lies asleep, it starts up ; it seems as if a man were calling it out of its sleep.

Hɛ tikən e:, si e: !kaukən, si k''auki ka !kwˀi: _||khã: |kẽ ; ta: si |kɒ !hammi si !kwˀi: _||khã: |kẽ; ta: mama-gu |ki e: kaŋ ≠kaka si ã:, !haukən!haukən ka ≠kaka _||khã: ã:, o !khwã: ʘpwa: !kwˀi: _||khã: |kẽ ; _||khã: |ne _!k''wãïn ti e: !kaukən !xwã: ke: ||gwitən o ha |kẽ.

Therefore we children do not mention the lion's name ; for we are afraid of doing so ; for our parents have told us that the flies tell the lion, if a child says its name ; the lion is angry because the children seem to be playing with his name.

Hɛ tikən e:, _||khã: ||nau !haukən!haukən ≠kaka ha ã:, ha |kɒ te:n |ki |e: ||kõ:ïŋ, o ti e: !haukən-!haukən siŋ ||aŋ ≠kaka ha ã, ĩ:. Ha |kɒ ||nau ||kõ:ïŋ |e:ja, ha |kɒ

Therefore when the lion is told of this by the flies, he lets the sun set where the flies have come to talk with him. When the sun has gone down, he goes in the

Part II
The Lion

!ka:gən //neiŋ a:, !kaukən ⊙pwõnni e:, siŋ !kwʔi:ja ha /kẽ, ha //neiŋ a:, !kaukən //nã ha, o !kʔetən /kɒ ⊙pwoiŋ //na ; o haŋ ka : ha se //a _!no:ä:_!no:ä !kʔe, !kʔe se ≠enn, ti e:, ha a: e //khe://khe:, ha /kv a: !kaukən //gwitən //na o ha /kẽ.

dark to the hut where the little boys who have mentioned his name are living, while the people are asleep there ; for he wants to frighten them, that they may know that he is a beast of prey, with whose name the children made free.

Hɛ tikən e:, mama-gu k''auki ≠kauwa si: !kwʔi: _//khã: /kẽ, ta mama-gu kaŋ /k'e:ja si ã:, si se //nau, si tã: _//khã: !nwa, si se //nau, sí ka si˙se /k'e:ja he ã:, si /kɒ se kukú, si !kun si /k'a:, o sí: ka si ≠kaka he ã:, ti e: si siŋ́ /nã: _//khã: !nwa.

Therefore our parents did not want us to say the lion's name, but used to tell us that if we caught sight of a lion's footprints when we wanted to tell them about it, we should hold our hand like this([2]) to let them know that we had seen a lion's footprint.

Ta: he _//kɒaŋ ké: se ≠enn, ti e: si /kwẽ:ï-da he ã:, ĩ:, o sí: ki sá: //ne:ja hi ã:, si /k'a: ; ta: he _//kwaŋ siŋ ≠enna tsʔa a:, sı ≠kaka he ã: ha, há si tã: ha !nwa.

For they would know what we meant to tell them when we came merely showing them our hand ; for they would have recognized the thing, about which we were telling them, that we had seen its spoor.

Ta: _//khã: ká: ha se //nau, si e: !kaukən, sí: tã: ha !nwa ; o sí: sa: mama-gu, si _kóä /ne kuku, si /k'e:-ja he ã:, si kaŋ siŋ tã: _//khã: !nwa, _//khã:ŋ ká ha se se, /kã-ã si !nwa, e: si siŋ ≠kerre /ki ha !nwa, ĩ:, ha _ko:ä /ne !gauökən /ki !ke se si !nwa o //neiŋ, hɛ ha-g /ne _saŋ /kãã /hiŋ si o ⊙pwoin, o si: /e:ta: ⊙pwoin.

For a lion acts like this when we children see his footprints ; if we go and tell our parents that we have seen them, then the lion picks up our footprints where we had found his, and follows them up to our home in order to catch us asleep, as we lie in slumber.

He tikən e:, mama-gu kaŋ /k'e:ja si ã:, si _kɔ́:ɔ̈ //nau, si /nã: _//khã: !nwa, si _kɔ́:ɔ̈ k''auki se !khe: tiŋ, si se /k'e:ja si /ka:gən ã:, o _//khã: !nwa, si se /kɒ //nau _tai a:, si siŋ _tai //a: ã:, si se /kv //nau si: /nã: _//khã: !nwa, si se /kv ĩ: !kwe!kwe !khe tẽ o si /ka:gən, o sija /kɒ tauko _tai, o si k''auki !khe, si se !khe tau /au _//khã: !nwa.

Therefore our parents told us that if we saw a lion's footprints, we should not stop to tell each other about the lion's spoor, we should walk on as we had been walking when we caught sight of the spoor, we should merely look at each other as we walked on without stopping to stand and look at the spoor.

Respecting the lion

Part II
The Lion

Ta: si |kɒ ĩ: ≠kaka si |ka:gən o si tsaxáitən, ti e: ˍ||khã: ˍ||kwaŋ ||khóä a: siŋ ˍtai |kĩjã ||a:, ti e:. Si tsaxáitakən |kɒ e:, si |kwẽ:ï-da, sitən ≠kaka si |kagən ĩ:, o sitən k''auki kú:ï, '||kaŋ ||k'wã:, ˍ||khã: kaŋ ||kho: siŋ |kãã ||a: ti e.'

For we should merely tell each other with our eyes that it was a lion which had walked along there. Our eyes should be our means of speaking to each other, we should not say, "Look my friend, a lion seems to have passed here."

Mama-gu kon kaŋ |k'e:, si ˍkɔ́:ɔ̈ k''auki se |kwẽ:ï ku, ta: ˍ||khã: e tsa a: k''wãŋ ha tú:ï, ha e. !gauxe a:, i k''auki |nĩ: ha ã:, haŋ |kɒ ≠enna, ti e:, í siŋ |kwẽ:ĩ-da, o ha, ĩ:; haŋ |kɒ tú:ï, ta: !haukən!haukən |ki a: ≠kaka ha ã:, ti e: í siŋ |kwẽ:ï-da, o ha, ĩ:, itən ≠kakən o ha, ĩ:.

Our parents used to say, we must not speak thus, for the lion is a thing which seems to hear. Although we do not see him, he knows what we have been saying about him, he hears, for the flies tell him what we have been saying about him, when we speak of him.

Mama-gukən kaŋ ≠kakən, ti e: tsʔa a: |kɒ ||nau, haŋ ⊙pwoin ta:. haŋ |kɒ ||khabbo-ĩ:, ti e: !kʔe siŋ tã: ha !nwa, !kʔetən siŋ !kwʔi: k''e:nk''e:n |ki ha |kẽ. Haŋ ka ||nau, o ha ||khabbo-ã:, haŋ ka |kɒ !hom ha-ka ||khabbo.

Our parents used to say that he is a thing which dreams when he lies asleep that people have seen his footprints, people have made free with his name. Whenever he dreams, he believes his dream.

Mama-gukən kaŋ |k'e:ja si ã:, si-g |nõ k''au ||k'oen, ti e: ˍ||khã: ka |kwẽï |kwï-|kwé, ĩ:, o ha: |kha: ⊙pwai, ha ka ||khe||khe: !kwi; haŋ k''auki tá ha se ||nau, ha: |kha: ⊙pwai, haŋ k''auki ká ha se hã: tẽ ha o ti |ke:, ha |kha tã: tsʔa ĩ:.

Our parents used to ask us if we did not see how a lion behaves when he kills game, he acts like a man; he will not eat the game he has killed at the place where he has killed it.

Respecting the lion

Ta: ha ká: ha se ˍ||gwai ||khe-||khe: !kwi, ha ˍkɔ́:ɔ̈ thum tsʔa-ka |khara, thum ||kho he, o ti |ke:, ha |kha tã: tsʔa ĩ:. Ha ˍkɔ́:ɔ̈ ˍ|kammain tsʔa, o ha k''auki hã tsʔa. Ti e: ha |ki ||a: tsʔa o ⊙ho, ĩ:, hiŋ e: ha-g |ne hĩ: tsʔa, ĩ:. Han k'auki ká ha se hã: tẽ tsʔa o ≠ka:, ta: ha ká: ha se hã: |ki|ki tsʔa o ⊙ho !kerri, ha: ha ˍ|kammain |ki |e:ja tsʔa ã:, haŋ a:, ha ká ha se hã: bai tsʔa ã:, o tsʔa a |kɒ ||na ⊙ho.

For he is used to open it like a man, so that he may bury the contents of the stomach where he has killed the thing. He will carry off the thing without eating it. When he has taken it to a bush then he eats it. He will not eat it in the open, for he wants to go on eating it under the large bush to which he has carried it, that is where he means to eat it up, under the bush.

Hɛ tikən e:, mama-gu kaŋ ≠kaka si ã:, si ˍkɔ́:ɔ̈ se //nau, sí: /nã: ts?a a: ˍ//khã: /kha ha, sí: ka si /ã ts'a, si ˍkɔ́:ɔ̈ , "auki ˍ/kammain ts'a-ka ku:, si ˍkɔ́:ɔ̈ se kwe:ja ˍ//khã: ã:, ts?a-g /nã:, he kɔ ts'a !xã, tʃweŋ e: !ku:, he /ke, hiŋ e:, si kwe:ja ˍ//khã: ã he, o ts?a /khara, ha se sa /nĩ he, o ts?a /khara.

Then our parents used to tell us, that if we see anything the lion has killed and want to cut it up, we must not carry the whole thing away, we must leave its head for the lion and the upper backbone (?), these two things we must leave for him at the spot, so that he sees them where he left the thing.

O si !he: /ki ˍtaija ha, si ˍkɔ́:ä /ne /ã ts?a, o ha: k"auki //ka, si se-g /ne /ã bai ts?a. Mama-gukən kaŋ /k'e:, si ˍkɔ́:ɔ̈ k"auki se -/kamme:ŋ ts?a-ka eŋ-ka ku:, si se xu:wa ˍ//khã: ã: hã:, o ts?a /khara, si se //xou he, o ʘho:kən e: si siŋ /ã: //kau tã: ʘpwai, ĩ:, ha se sa /nĩ he. Ta: há e ts?a á: ka !gauökən i, o í xa xu:wa ha ã: hã: kuitən.

When we have driven him away, we must cut up the thing in his absence and finish cutting it up. Our parents used to say that we must not carry off all the meat, we must leave food for the lion at the place of the kill, we must cover it with the bushes on which we have laid the meat we cut, so that he finds it. For he is a thing which will follow us, if we do not leave him something to eat.

Mama-gukən kaŋ /k'e:, ˍ//khã: e ts?a a: ká ha se //nau, ts?a !xãka !kwa kí sa: e, haŋ ká ha se se, ts?a /khara, ha se sá k"ãõuŋ he, ha ˍkɔ́:ɔ̈ /kɑ //nau, ha k"ãõuŋ baija he, haŋ /kɑ se ˍtai, ˍ//gauë ts?a a: /xara, há ha ká ha /kha ha. Ti e:, ha //k'oen, ti e: í /kɑ ˍ/komme:njã ts?a-ka eŋ-ka ku:, hiŋ e:, ha ≠ĩ:, ti e:, i ˍkóä k"auki ≠ï:, ti e: ha //xam //kaŋ-a. Ta: i k"auki /ne //khóä ≠ĩ:, ti e:, ha ˍ//kwaŋ a: /kha: ts?a, ta, i /kɑ-g /ne ˍ/kamme: //nts?-ka eŋka ku://gwai.

Our parents used to say, the lion is a thing which acts like this, even if only the bone is left, he keeps coming to the place of the kill to crunch it, and when he has finished crunching it, he will go away and look for something else to kill. If he sees that we have carried off all the meat of the thing, then he thinks that we have not remembered that he is also hungry. For we do not seem to have considered that it was he who killed the thing, for we have carried off every bit of the meat.

Mama-gukən kaŋ /k'e:, ˍ//khã: ka //nau, o há sa !ko: hã:, o ts'a /khara, háŋ ka-g /ne ˍ!kwãĩn, hɛ ha /ne kukú:ï, ha ≠ĩ, '/ne ≠kam-ʘpwa u; o u ˍ//kwaŋ //khóä ˍ/kamme:ŋja ke hã:-ka ku:, ŋ káŋ siŋ /ne //nau, u /kwẽ:ï /kwãŋ dí: ŋ, ŋ kaŋ se /kãã

Our parents used to say that if the lion did not find food at the place of the kill, he would be angry and would say to himself, " Just you wait a bit ; because you seem to have carried off all my food, I will do as you have done to me, I

Respecting the lion

u !nwa, ŋ se ||a |kãã |hiŋ u-ka !ku-ko:, o ⊙pwoin, ŋ se hã: ha. Ta: u _||kwaŋ k''auki ||khóä ≠ĩ:, ti e: ŋ _||kwaŋ ||xam ||kaŋ-a.'

will follow your footprints, I will go and seize one of your men in his sleep and eat him. For you don't seem to have remembered that I too am hungry."

Hɛ tikən e:, mama-gu kaŋ ≠kaka si ã:, si _kɔ́:ɔ̈ k''auki se _|kamme:ŋ tsˀa a: _||khã: |kha ha, ha-ka eŋ-ka ku:, si se |ku:wa _||khã: ã:, eŋ kuitən, o tsˀa |khara, ha se sá |nĩ he, o há sa:. Ta, ha |ki e tsˀa a: ka ||nau, i !he: |ki _taija ha, haŋ ka ||a ||na||na he: ti, o ha !kã: ||kõïŋjã: se |e:ja ha ã:, ha se ||a ||k'oen a ||ga:, ||k'oen, tï e: i |nõ k''au |ku:wa ha ã: hã:.

Therefore our parents used to tell us that we must not carry off all the meat of anything the lion has killed, we must leave some for the lion at the place of the kill, for him to find when he comes. For he acts like this when we have driven him away, he goes to another place and waits till sunset to go in the dark and look whether we have left him something to eat.(3)

Hɛ tikən e:, mama:gu ≠kaka si ã: si k''auki se _|kamme:ŋ tsˀa-ka eŋ-ka ku:, ta: _||khã: ká ha se !gauökən si, o si _|kamme:ŋja tsˀa-ka eŋ-ka . u: gwai.

Therefore our parents told us not to carry off all the thing's meat, for the lion would follow our spoor if we carried off the whole of the meat.

Notes

21-23 ... *he lets the sun set where the flies have come to talk with him*: 'i.e. at the place at which he was when the flies came to tell him [what the child said]' (4528 rev., note omitted).

37-38 ... *we should hold our hand like this*: '[The narrator here held up his right hand, with all fingers and the thumb extended, like a claw]' Dorothea Bleek's note 2 (4531 rev.).

'They hold up the right hand with fingers and thumb extended; and then the parents know that it is the lion's spoor which they [the children] have seen.' (4531 rev., note omitted).

54 ... *as we lie in slumber*: 'i.e. [when we were fast asleep]' (4535 rev., note omitted).

84-85 *Whenever he dreams, he believes his dream*: '[i.e. believes just as if some one had told him the thing, in this instance, D.H. says].' (4542 rev., note omitted).

93-94 ... *so that he may bury the contents of the stomach* ...: '[what is in the animal's stomach grass, etc.]' (4544 rev., note omitted).

Several observers of lions have commented upon this behaviour of lions (see George Schaller's (1972) classic study on lions, *The Serengeti Lion*).

102 *... that is where he means to eat it up ...*: 'He would not be willing to eat laying down the things on a bare place, he would intend to be eating the thing by a large bush that to which he had carrying, put in the thing, it is the one at which he would intend to eat up the thing, when the thing was at the bush.' (4546-4547, text omitted).

109-110 *...the upper backbone [?]*: *!kha* in the notebook, given as *!xã* in *Bantu Studies.* Diä!kwain explains the word as 'cam bein' (4548 rev., note omitted).

120-121 *...we must cover it with the bushes ...*: '[so that other animals should not eat it]' (4550 rev., note omitted).

162-163 *... look whether we have left him something to eat*:

(3)Sometimes a lion who is a rogue appears to go away, but comes stealing back when the people are cutting up the meat, in which case he kills them. So the narrator's mother said that they must cut up the meat quickly and leave the place where he had killed the game.

Dorothea Bleek translated the Dutch/Afrikaans word 'schelm', the term used by Diä!kwain in his narrative as 'rogue' (4558 rev.)

(Omitted text: 4560-4561)

He would, [if] he saw, that, we had not left food for him, he would trace our spoor, if he had missed food; he would go, catching us out from sleep, he would eat us; because he wished that we should know because we did not seem also to think, that, he also was hungry.

The lion's name

Narrator: Diä!kwain
Dictation date: 9 April 1875
Notebook reference: L.V. 8: 4563-4573
***Bantu Studies* reference:** Vol. 6 (1932), Part II: 57-58

Parents teach their children how to talk about the lion without the message getting back to him. This narrative was originally entitled 'The children taught to use another name for the lion'.

❑

Mama-gu kaŋ kí:se si, si se //nau, //k'e: kɔ:, o si: tã: _//khã: !nwa, sí se //nau, sí: ka, si se ≠kaka he ã:, si se kukú, si !kwˀi: _//khã: /kẽ kɔ:, si se ku '/kukən' ã: /kẽ, o si ≠kaka he ã:, ti e: si síŋ tã̰: '/kukən' !nwa o ti é: a, hɛ /hiŋ ti é: a, hiŋ kɔkóä a, /kam //a: ti e.

Our parents used to teach us that on another occasion when we had seen the lion's spoor and wanted to tell them about it, we might mention his other name, we might say " hair " for his name telling them that we had seen " hair's " spoor at such a place, coming thence in this direction.

Ti é: máma-gu e: /kwẽ:ĩ-da: si ĩ:, o hiŋ ta: //ka ti e:, si e /kau-kən, si k''aukì /kɒ ka '_//khã:'. Ta si k''auki e !ke!kerritən, si siŋ /kɒ !kwˀi: _//khã: /kẽ. Ta: _//khã: ká: ha se !ho ki: si, si se /ne _tai !kauxu, he _//khã: /ne /nĩ: si, ĩ:, _//khã: /ne //xou ≠ka:, o há: ka, si se-g /ne /nĩ ha, ha á:, si é !kau-kən sí ka !kwˀi: k''e:nk''e:n o ha /kẽ; ha tuko /ne á:, //xou ≠ka: si ã:, si se-g /ne //k'oen ha, ti e:, ha tuko _dɔ́ä á: a, ha sí é: !kaukən, sí ka //gwitən//gwitən-ĩ: o ha /kẽ.

That is what our parents said to us, for they wanted us children not to say " lion." For we were not grown-up, so that we might mention the lion's name. For the lion would wait until we were big enough to go to the hunting ground, then he would see us there, he would become visible, because he wanted us to see him, with whose name we children had been making free ; he would really appear to us, so that we might see him, that it was really he with whose name we children had been playing.

Hɛ tikən /ne e:, ha-g /ne ká ha, /ki !khe /ho si, si se //k'oen ha, ti e:, ha-g /nũ e //gwitən-ka tsˀa, si se-g /nĩ ha, si se //k'oen ha, ti e:, ha /nũ //kho //gwitən-ka tsˀa.

That is why he wanted to stand in front of us, that we might look whether he were a plaything, that we might see him and look if he resembled a plaything.

Hɛ tikən e:, mama-gukən |k'e-ja si ã:, ‗||khã: e tsˀa á: ||nau, ɩ e !khwã: ⊙pwa, ɩtən !kwˀi: k''e:n-k''e:n-ã: |kẽ, !haukən!haukakən ||aŋ ≠kaka ha ã:, he ‗||khã: kukú:ï, haŋ |k'e:, '|ne ≠kam ⊙pwa, hɛ taŋ ‗||kwaŋ se kiki:tji, he se |ne tai !kauxu, he ‗||kwaŋ e:, ŋ kaŋ se |ne ˌnĩ he, ĩ:, o he |ne kiki:tji ; ta: he k''auki !naunko ‗tai !kauxu ; ta: he |kɑ ||na ||neiŋ ; hiŋ ‗||kwaŋ kɛ: se kiki:tji, he se-g |ne ‗tai !kauxu.'

Therefore our parents told us that if we being little make a mock of the lion's name, the flies go and tell him about it, and the lion says, " Wait a bit, when they are grown they will go to the hunting ground and I shall see them, when they have grown ; for they don't go there yet, they stay at home ; they will soon grow up and go to the hunting ground."

Notes

12-13 *For we were not grown-up ...*: '[a grown-up person may use the lion's name]'

(4564 rev., note omitted).

39-41 ... *they will soon grow up and go to the hunting ground*:

'[That is why our parents taught us about it. Because they knew that once the lion used to wait [until] a little child had grown up, when a little child had, when he small, he [been] playing with the lion's name. Our parents used to say to us about it, did we not see what a lion did to Xwerri-kau on account of it?*]'

(4571-4573, text omitted)

***He had [D.H. says], played when a child with the name of the lion. He did not respect [?] [*!hummi*] the lion's name.**

(4572 rev., note omitted)

Lions and waterbags

Narrator: Diä!kwain
Dictation date: 2 July 1875
Notebook reference: L.V.11: 4869 rev.-4876 rev.
***Bantu Studies* reference:** Vol. 6 (1932), Part II: 58-59

Lions use a combination of magic and trickery to lure children into danger.

Mama kaŋ kaŋ |k'e:, ti e:, _||hhã: ||nau, ||k'e: a:, ha ká ha hã: i, haŋ ||nau, ||kʔõïŋ kí-saŋ !xo:wa, haŋ |kɒ di: ||kˀõïŋ o ha-ka didí:, ||kˀõïŋjaŋ |kɒ |e:, kúï k''wã |kwa-|kwainja, o há ka ha hã: i.

Mother used to tell us what a lion does when he wants to come up to us, although the sun is still high he influences the sun by his doings, the sun sets quickly, because he wants to come to us.

Hɛ tikən e:, mama ka siŋ ka: ≠kaka si ã:, si se ||nau, si |kwen-ja !khwa:, a: ||na ||khwetən, si se ||k'oen ⁻!kaba a: si |kwenja ha, si se ||nau, ha: txérija, si se _||k'auwa há-ka ti e: txérija, ha _kɔ́ɔ̈ ||nau, o si ||hiŋja ha-ka ti e:, siŋ |kuruwa, ha _kɔ́ɔ̈ ⁻||xã: ha |kuru tí e: |xara, mama-gukən kaŋ ≠kaka si ã:, ti e: _||khã: ã: tsi: |ku|kuru ⁻!kaba, o haŋ ka, ha se !kˀai !ke se si, o !khwa:, o si k''u |ki ⁻!kaba.

Then mother used to tell us that if we were fetching water from a distance, we should watch the waterbag in which we were fetching it, if it tore we should mend the place which was torn, but if when we had tied up the place which was torn, it should tear again in another place, then our mothers said that it was a lion biting and tearing the waterbag, because he wanted to overtake us at the water, while we were mending the waterbag.

Hɛ tikən e:, mama ka sin ka: ≠kaka si ã:, o _||khã:-ka didí:, hiŋ e: mama ≠kaka si ã hɛ, o tikəntikən e: _||khã: dí:hɛ, o ||k'e: a:, ha ká ha |kha i ã:, haŋ a:, ha |kwẽï k''o ã:.

That is what mother used to tell us about the lion's doings, that is what she said about them, about the things which the lion does when he wants to kill us, then he acts in this way.

Mamaŋ kaŋ |k'e:ja si ã:, si se ||nau, si: ||k'oen, ti e:, ⁻!kaba k''auki k''waŋ, si ||kwaŋ ||hiŋja, si _kɔ́ɔ̈ se ||nau, ⁻!kaba ki-sa: ≠nai, si

Mother used to say to us that if we saw that it did not seem possible to mend the waterbag, although the waterbag kicked, we

_kɔ̈ɔ̈ se _tai xu: tu !khwa:, si se //a !hau, si _//k'auwa, o si _am _tai /hiŋ tu !khwa:. O !gauxe a: si ¯//ka ã:, si _kɔ̈ɔ̈ _am tai, o si k''auki ≠ĩ:, ti e:, !khwa: kwãŋ //ka:-//ka: si, si _kɔ̈ɔ̈ k''auki /kwẽ:ï-da si ≠ĩ:, si se tai, o !khwa: ki-sa: //ka:-//ka: si.

should go away from the water, we should mend it later, when we had walked away from the water. Although thirst consumed us, we must first walk away and not think about our longing for water, we must not think about it at all, but go on, however thirsty we were.

Ta: !khwa:-ka ¯//ka k''auki se !kha si. Ta: //khe//khe: a tsi /ku-/kuruwa si ã: ¯!kaba, ha a: ká ha se /kha si; !khwa:gən kauki se /kha si.

For the thirst for water would not kill us. But the beast of prey who was biting holes in the waterbag would kill us; the water would not kill us.

Mama kaŋ /k'e:ja si ã:, !hau-kən-!haukən /kɑ ≠kaka _//khã: ã:, o ha: /kɑ //na hɛ: ti. Haŋ /kɑ di kúï k''wãŋk''wãŋ ha tóä ts'a, o hɛ: ti, o !haukən!haukakən /kɑ a: ≠kaka ha ã:, ti e:, !kui ká ha se !xu !khwa:, o //kˀõïŋ ta tí é.

Mother used to tell us that the flies tell a lion about what happens there. He acts as if he had heard things here, because the flies have told him about it, that a person is going to the water to-day.

Hɛ tikən e:, mamagu ka siŋ ka, hɛ: ≠kaka si ã:, ti e:, _//khã: e tsˀa a:, ha ká ha se //nau, ha: ká ha /kha i, haŋ da: hi ã:, tikən-tikən e: i k''auki ≠enna hɛ, o haŋ ka, ha se /nĩ i, o i: dí /ki hɛ́: ti.

So our mothers used to tell us that the lion is a thing which acts like this when he wants to kill us, he makes things happen which we do not understand, because he wants to catch us while we are working here.

Dorothea Bleek left out the last three pages of this story, which are given here (4877 rev.-4879 rev.):

Our mothers used to tell us about it, we should do this when we went down to the water, we should walk far we should walk approaching the water. We should walk looking about us for the lion there also comes up to the water, when we too go to the water, it also approaches the water. That is why our mothers told us that when we went to the water we must not play at the water. We must behave like this when we reached the water to which we were going, we must dip up (water), we must quickly walk away from the water.

❑

Notes

5-6 … *because he wants to come to us*: This should read 'because he wants to come to **eat** us' (4869 rev.)

9-10 … *we should watch the* **waterbag**: The word *!kaba* was originally translated as 'waterstomach'; in the *Dictionary* it is translated as 'waterbag made of buck's stomach' (Bleek 1956: 402).

16-17 … *it was a lion biting and tearing the waterbag* …: Presumably the lion must have made itself invisible in order to do this without the person carrying the bag seeing the lion.

29-30 *Although the waterbag* **kicked:** The original translation of *ǂnai:* was 'leaked', which makes more sense here. Dorothea Bleek seems to have confused this word with *ǂnai,* which means 'kick' (Bleek 1956: 670).

Owls, flies and lions

Narrator: |Haŋ‡kass'o
Dictation date: 22 December 1878
Notebook reference: L.VIII.23: 8058 rev. and 8060 rev.; 8078-8079
***Bantu Studies* reference:** Vol. 6 (1932), Part II: 60

These three creatures have a special relationship.

Dictated by *|haŋ≠kass?o*, a Bushman from the Strontbergen.

ŋ !kõïŋ _Tsatsi ||kwaŋ ka siŋ ≠kakən, ti e: !hũ!hũ ka sé i, au _||khã se sí i, au ha |hiŋ sa _||khã !kha:, au _||khã se sé.

My grandfather Tsatsi used to say that an owl usually comes to us when a lion is coming to us, for it comes out in front of the lion, when the lion is coming.

Hɛ tikɛn e:, ŋ !kõïŋ ta siŋ !gabbetən-ã !hũ!hũ au |i, au !hũ!hũwa sá !kúï, ha !gabbetən-ã !hũ!hũ au |i, au hiŋ tati hĩ ta !hũ!hũ se ||e, !hũ!hũ se ||a ≠kaka _||khã, ti e: !k?e |kʌ |kaŋ-i ha. Au ti e: ŋ !kõïŋ siŋ |kuẽïda, ĩ:.

Therefore my grandfather used to throw fire at the owl, if it came at twilight, he threw fire at it, because they (he and the other old men) wanted the owl to go and tell the lion that people had thrown fire at it. This is what grandfather told us.

Haŋ ||xâmki ĩja au !houkən!houkən. Haŋ ≠kaka si, ti e: !khwã ʘpwa k''auki ta kú, " hmm, hmm, k''a,"[4] *au !houkən!houka !kauŋ siŋja ha |nunu ; ta !houkən!houkən |ké ta ||a ≠kaka _||khã ti e: !khwã ʘpwa |kʌ _!k''ó-e _||khã, hiŋ e:, !khwã ʘpwa k''ak''aŋ-ĩ _||khã |k'wãĩ.*[5]

He also spoke about the flies. He told us that a little child should not exclaim, " *hmm, hmm, ka*,"[4] if a fly sat in front of his nostril ; for the fly always went and told the lion, that a little child had been insulting the lion, that is to say it had been complaining of the lion's bad smell.[5]

He tikən e:, _||khã _ha ka |ne ku, " Há xa te: u? " !houkən!houka _ha |ne kúï, " !khwã kaŋ |kʌ e." He _||khã _ha |ne kúï, " Ha xa -kija? " !houkən!houka _ha |ne kúï, "Ha káŋ |kʌ -!humma." He _||khã _na |ne kúï," |ne |ka ha, ha se -ki."

Then the lion exclaimed "How big is he ? " The fly said : " He is a child." And the lion said, " Is he big ? " The fly said, " He is little." Then the lion said, " Leave him alone, he will grow big."

He tikən e:, í ta !kɒ |ne ||nau, i |ne e ¯!kerri, i |kɒ-g |ne _tai ||kaitən _||khã, au _||khã ta:. He tikən e:, i tú ka |kɒ-g |ne |hóäka au !hɒmmi, au _taitən, _!kauäkən. I túwa k''auki |ne k''wi: au _taitən.

Therefore it happens when we are grown-up, we come unexpectedly upon a lion which is lying down. Then our mouth is black with fear, with terror, with alarm. Our mouth is not light on account of our terror.

Notes

15-17 … *a little child should not exclaim, 'hmm, hmm, ka'*: Dorothea included the following note:

(⁴)Shutting the mouth tight and forcibly expelling the breath through the nostrils.

21-22 … *it had been complaining of the lion's bad smell*: Dorothea included the following note:

(⁵)The fly was a lion's fly. They came from the lion. The fly in question had sat under the lion's armpit.

The lion's head

Narrator: |Haŋ‡kass'o
Dictation date: Between 21 March 1878 and 7 April 1878
Notebook reference: L.VIII. 6: 6576 rev.
***Bantu Studies* reference:** Vol. 6 (1932), Part II: 61

/Haŋ‡kass'o hints at yet another of the extraordinary powers that lions possess.

Au _||khã: |kɒ _naunko sa:, _||khã: |nã |hu|hunta |kɒ |hiŋ se !xwe ; hĩ |kɒ-g |ne ||khóä hãhá, hi |kɒ-g |ne ||khóä _||khã: kwokwáŋ. Ha |nã: |hu|hunta, au hi daudau i.

When the lion is still coming, his head's reflection comes in sight before him ; it resembles him, it looks like a real lion. His head's reflection (it is) with which he deceives us.

Avoiding the lion's name

Narrator: |Haŋ‡kass'o
Source: '|Haŋ‡kass'o from Tssatssi and !Kuä (or Ttarro–hho) Bartman Bastard'
Dictation date: 28 December 1878
Notebook reference: L.VIII.23: 8075 rev.-8076 rev.; 8078 rev.
***Bantu Studies* reference:** Vol. 6 (1932), Part II: 61

There are many ways of referring to lions without their knowing.

❑

Ī e !kaukən, ítən k''auki ta _//khã ã: au //ga: ; tá i /kɑ ka '/kɛrre-/e:' ã. Itən //xɑmki ta ' ts?á a: /na: _/hokən e,'(⁶) au itən tati ha /ke -ta:ï au //ga:, au há siŋ /kɑ ʘpuoin ta:, au //k?ǒïŋja !khe:.

We who are children do not say " lion " to it at night ; but we call it " lighting in." We also say " thing whose head's darkness it is,"(⁶) for we feel that it walks at night after lying asleep while the sun was up.

!kaukən //kwaŋ /kɑ ka /kɛrre- /e: ã:, au //kõïŋ !khe:. Hiŋ //nau au //ga:, hiŋ //xɑmki /kɑ ka ' kɛrre-/e:' ã: ; au hiŋ tatí e, ha /ke _ha ka ka, /kwi/kwíja a:, !kaukən ʘpwonnija !kwi ha /kẽ ã ; au há-ka /kwi/kwí:.

Children call it " lighting in " when the sun is up. When it is night they also say " lighting in " to it, because it (the lion) might think it an insult, if little boys called it by name as if insulting it.

He tikən e:, !kauka: ka _/ khã ã:. He tikən e:, i ta /kɑ ki, ki, ki kí, i /kɑ di ⁻!kerri ; au i k''auki /ne /nĩ ha. He tikən e:, i t /kɑ-g /ne au i /ne e ⁻!kerri, i /kɑ-g /ne _tai / kai-tən ha. He tikən e:, ha ka /kɑ /ne //kw?etən i, ha /kɑ-g /ne /kwẽï /ki, ha !nóë ⁻sɑ au i.

It may happen that children say lion to it. Then we grow, grow, grow, grow, we become grown-up without seeing it. Then, when we are grown-up, we come right upon it. Then it attacks us, it does thus, it comes to fight with us.

❑

Notes

3-5 *We also say 'thing whose head's darkness it is'*: Dorothea Bleek noted as follows –

(⁶)Hiŋ /né ta, hahá-ka _!k?an e.

(⁶)They say that (the darkness) is its shadow.

The lion's transformation (1)

Narrator: |Haŋ‡kass'o
Dictation date: 21 October 1878
Notebook reference: L.VIII.18: 7630 rev.
***Bantu Studies* reference:** Vol. 6 (1932), Part II: 61

The lion's magical powers enable it to take on the shapes of familiar things …

❑

Haŋ ka di ˉ!kwi, ha ˉ||kautẽ ha !khwi ã: |na:, au ha ||khouka |kwi:, au |kwi:ja hã |ki wai.

It (the lion) often turns into a person (male or female), it puts its tail over its head when it goes to vultures eating a springbok.

Ha ||ne !kˀattən kúï k''waŋ !kwi, au ha !kˀatta |kwi:, au ha tati ha ||khóä ˉ!kwi kwokwaŋ.

It trots (along) like a man, as it trots up to the vultures, for it feels like a real man,

❑

Notes

1-2 *It (the lion) often turns into a person (male or female) …*: In the notebook it says that 'It [the lion, both male and female] makes itself into a man (7630 rev).

The lion's transformation (2)

Narrator: |Haŋ‡kass'o
Source: '|Haŋ‡kass'o from his maternal grandfather Tssatssi'
Dictation date: 24 December 1878
Notebook reference: L.VIII. 23: 8080-8083; 8082 rev.
***Bantu Studies* reference:** Vol. 6 (1932), Part II: 62

Another transformation …

ŋ !kõïŋ _Tsatsi |kɒ á: ka siŋ |kwẽ:ï da, ti e: _||gwatən _há ka !xuɔnni |e: ha au _||khã. Hŋ́ _||gwatən(7) e:, i siŋ |kha: tiŋ, ĭ:,(8) au ||kˀõïŋ¯jã !khe, hé _||gwatən ¯hĭ |kɒ-g |ne !xuɔnni |e: hi au _||khã, au ||kˀõïŋ-jã ka: |e:, tí |ne dí: ||ga:.	My grandfather *Tsatsi* used to tell me, that a wild cat will turn itself into a lion. Those cats which we killed when the sun was high, turn themselves into lions when the sun sets and it grows dark.
Hí |kɒ |ne sá: |xai ¯ho i, au í ¯ʘpwoin ta:, au hi |kɒ !xuonni |eja hi au _||khã. He hĭ |kɒ-g |ne sá: !xai hó i, au í ¯ʘpwoin tá:, au i tati e:, í k''auki _dóä |ni: _||khã !nwa.	They come to drag us away as we lie sleeping, when they have turned themselves into lions. Then they come to drag us away as we lie sleeping, because we have not seen a lion's spoor.
He tikən e:, i |kɒ |ne ¯ʘpwoin ||na, au í k''auki |ne ||khau-ĭ; i |kɒ |ne ¯ʘpwoin ||na. He tikən e:, _||khã |kɒ |ne sá: !xai hó i, au i |kɒ |ne ¯ʘpwoinja, au i tati, í k''auki _dóä |ni _||kha, í siŋ |ne ||khau-ĭ.	That is why we are sleeping there and do not lie listening ; we are fast asleep there. Then the lion comes to drag us away while we are asleep, because we had not seen a lion, to make us lie listening.

Notes

Title This excerpt was originally entitled 'A wild cat, when many have been killed by a person, changes itself into a lion, and kills the slayer'.

3-5 *Those cats which we killed when the sun was high …:*

(7)*_||gwatən a: !kwai, i k''auki |ni: _||khã ã:.*	(7)We do not see a lion on account of one cat.
(8)*!kwiŋ!kwiŋ _||kwaŋ |kɒ é: |khi: _||gwa_||gwara, au hiŋ tati e:, hĭ |kɒ e: !khou!khou hó hi.*	(8)Dogs are those which kill cats, because they track them by scent and rouse them.

Tending the fire

Narrator: |Haŋ‡kass'o
Source: '|Haŋ‡kass'o from his maternal grandfather Tssatssi'
Dictation date: 24 December 1878
Notebook reference: L.VIII.23: 8082 rev.
***Bantu Studies* reference:** Vol. 6 (1932), Part II: 62

One sure way of surviving the night ...

Tati i k''auki ¯⊙pwoin au ˍ||khã ; tá |nuk''o ka |kɷ ˍkɔ́äŋˍkɔ́äŋ úï, ha |kɷ |kɩ|kí ||ki: |i, he há |ne téŋ, au |ija-g |ne ||ka sˀo. He ha |ne ||xã, ha ˍkɔ́äŋ úï, ha |ne ˍ||ko¯etən !ho ⊙ho-|u, au há ka, hi siŋ kɔ́¯itən. He tikən e:, ha ka-g |ne ¯⊙pwoin ta:, au ||kˀõïŋ¯jã !khe.

For we do not sleep for a lion ; but an old man keeps getting up, he makes a fire, then he lies down when the fire is burning. Then he gets up again and pushes a tree stump into the embers, because he wants it to smoke. Then he will lie and sleep when the sun is high.

The lion's transformation (3)

Narrator: |Haŋ‡kass'o
Source: '|Haŋ‡kass'o from Tsatssĭ, and !Kuï [or Ttarro-khŏ] 'Bartman Bastard'*
Dictation dates: 22, 23 December 1878
Notebook reference: L.VIII.23: 8075-8077
***Bantu Studies* reference:** Vol. 6 (1932), Part II: 62-63

Here the lion, a pawed creature, changes into its conceptual opposite, an antelope (a hoofed creature). This extract was originally entitled, 'The lion has the power of turning itself into other things'.

-||khãŋ |ne |ɒhérri |e ha au ts?a kɔ:; ha di !kw?a:, dí ku ||kho !kw?a:, au ha ka, í se !ɒhattən ha. He há |kɒ-g |ne ||nau, au í: |ne |xwɛrrija ha, au í |kɒ-g |ne !ga, !ɒhita: ha, há |kɒ-g |ne ||nau, há |ne |khe sa i, ha |kɒ-g |ne dí -||khã:.

He tikən e:, !kauäkən ka |kɒ-g |ne |khi: i, ĩ:, au í |kɒ-g |ne ||k'oen ti e:, -||khã: |kɒ-g |ne á:, -tai !khe sa i; he í k''auki |ne ¯|ki, ti e: í se |ne |kwẽ:ï |ki, ĩ:; au ítən tatti, ha |ke k''auki k''wã ≠hannũwa, au ha |na: i, ta ha ka |kɒ |kha i.

The lion turns itself into some thing else; it becomes a harte-beest, becomes like a hartebeest, because it wants us to head it. And when we hunt it, when we lie in front of it, then as it comes up to us, it turns into a lion.

Then terror nearly kills us, when we see that it is a lion that is walking up to us, while we have nothing with which we can do anything; for we know that it will not act nicely if it sees us, it will kill us.

Notes

**Bartman Bastard:* 'Ttarro-khŏ was his youthful name, his grown up name [*!kerritən-ddi ta ha | kĕ*] is !Kui !kaxu. Ttain-aŋ threw fire at him when he wished to marry her (the word 'marry' was often used as a euphemism for sexual intercourse (Guenther 1996: 90), so it may be that he tried to rape her – ed). This is how he obtained the name !Kui !kaxu, having been badly burned. He is said to be a bad man.' (8074 rev.)

'*|ku-|koru* – the name given by the Bushmen to a lion who does not understand, and who comes to the huts to kill people' (8074 rev.).

2-3 … *it becomes a hartebeest* …: 'it also becomes like a person in a kaross' (8075 rev., note omitted).

PART III

GAME ANIMALS

From material collected by
Dr. W.H.I. BLEEK and Miss L.C. LLOYD between 1870 and 1880,
edited by D.F. Bleek

Photo: Jeremy Hollmann

Game 'does not talk with its mouth, but a man who understands can see.' Engravings from the Vanwyksvlei District, Northern Cape Province.

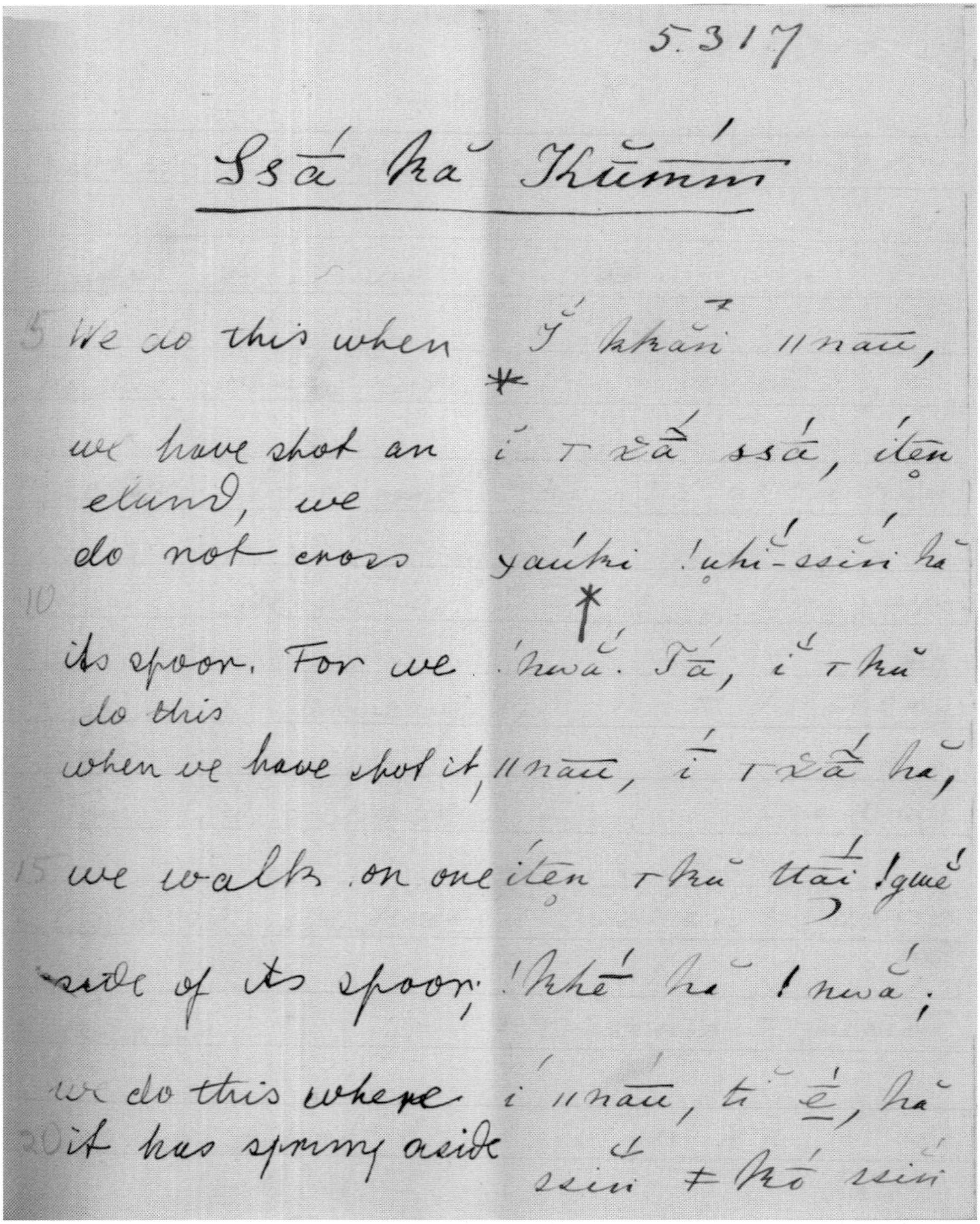
5.317

Ssá ká Kumm

We do this when — Í kkán ||nau,
we have shot an eland, we — í ǂ xá ssá, íten
do not cross — yauki !uhi-ssin há
its spoor. For we do this — !nwá. Tá, í ǂ kú
when we have shot it, — ||nau, í ǂ xá há,
we walk on one — íten ǂ kú ttai !gue
side of its spoor; — !khé há !nwá;
we do this where — í ||nau, ti é, há
it has sprung aside — ssin ǂ kó ssin

'The eland's story': This narrative details how people should respect the eland.

PART III
GAME ANIMALS

(Game) is a thing which smells from afar; that is why it knows all things.
– Diä!kwain: 'The springbok's story'–

In 1930 Marion How interviewed Mapote, the son of the Sotho chief Moroosi, about rock paintings made by Bushman people with whom he had grown up (How 1962). Mapote agreed to demonstrate his knowledge of painting and requested two important components. One was *qhang qhang* or red haematite, much valued as a ritual substance and paint pigment. The other was the fresh blood of an eland. Mapote wanted eland blood because 'the Bushmen of that part of the country were of the eland' (How 1962: 38).

Mapote's words go right to the heart of Bushman hunter-gatherer culture (see Vinnicombe 1976; Lewis-Williams 1981, 1988) – of all the game animals, the eland is central to ceremonies and hunting activities that mark the recognition of adulthood and marriage (Pager 1975; Vinnicombe 1976; Lewis-Williams & Biesele 1978; Lewis-Williams 1981). A boy attains manhood when he kills an eland (see 'The eland's story'), and when the Ju|'hoansi celebrate womanhood they dance the Eland Dance in which they move like eland cows to celebrate 'strength, health, fatness, plenty [and] well-being' (Marshall 1999: 199). Even in everyday conversation, people alter the way they speak when mentioning the eland and other game animals: 'they [the Ju|'hoansi] do so in a highly stylised, almost rhapsodic fashion... The effect it conveys is of a dream landscape dotted with an impossible plenty' (Biesele 1993: 60-61; see Alan James (2001) for similar |Xam 'incantations' (Bleek 1873: 4)).

Whilst gathered *veldkos* (edible roots, grass seeds, bulbs, tubers, insects, tortoises, birds and small mammals) typically contributes the most calories to the diet of Bushman people, it is meat (and therefore hunting) that they value most. Metaphors of hunting underlie relationships between the sexes (McCall 1970; Biesele 1993). Men are like carnivores because they 'hunt' and 'eat' women, just as they do game animals.

In a vivid comparison used by the Ju|'hoansi, women are like meat (Biesele 1993). But women like to eat meat too and few things give greater cause for joy than the sight of men 'carrying', that is, of men returning from the hunt carrying meat. Meat-sharing creates and sustains bonds among people, although it is also the cause of flaring jealousies that have to be soothed at healing dances (Marshall 1969, 1967, 1968).

Respecting the game

Killing one of the big meat animals was, of course, no easy matter. They were |Kaggen's *tʃweŋ* (literally 'things', but meaning game animals in this context). |Haŋ‡kass'o said that |Kaggen 'does not love us, if we kill an eland' (L.VIII.23: 8033). |Kaggen would not let an animal die from a poisoned arrow wound unless the hunter and his family at home had followed the intricate 'code' of behaviours called *!nanna-se* or 'hunting observances showing respect' (Bleek 1956: 473; Bleek & Lloyd 2001: 271-285; Vinnicombe 1975: 388-391, 1976: 178, 180; Lewis-Williams 1981: 55-67). Many of these observances are detailed in the Part III narratives, especially in 'The eland's story'.

Not surprisingly then, the odds were usually against the hunters in any encounter. Sometimes, to save the life of one of his *tʃweŋ*, |Kaggen transformed himself into an insect to trick people into destroying him – if a man disturbed the insect or killed him, |Kaggen would tell the wounded animal to get up and eat because 'people have not respected you' (L.V.17: 5270). ||Kabbo, Diä!kwain and |Haŋ‡kass'o gave many other examples of the tricks that |Kaggen used to cheat hunters out of their prey (Bleek 1924: 10-12; Lewis-Williams 2000).

Now that we know how the |Xam and other Bushman groups incorporated game animals into their thinking, we are better prepared for what Diä!kwain and |Haŋ‡kass'o say in the Part III narratives about the extra-ordinary powers of game animals and how people tried to use these to their advantage.

The potency of game animals

All of the Part III narratives emphasise the potency (*/ko:ode*) of game animals. It is the same potency (referred to elsewhere as *!gi:* and *//ke:n*) that the *!gi:tən* use in their work of making rain, controlling game, and healing (Lewis-Williams 1981).

In a real sense, game animals were extensions of people's senses; by observing the behaviour of animals, the |Xam transcended the limitations of their own sense perceptions and tapped into those of other species. As a contemporary researcher points out, the animals that the |Xam teachers spoke about so much – eland, hartebeest, gemsbok, and springbok (*Antidorcas marsupialis*) – have such acute senses that people not familiar with scientific thinking may believe that these animals have extra-sensory perception. As Apps (1992: 13-14) wrote:

> Antelope often seem to be in a continual state of nervous tension because their senses are so acute that they respond noticeably to stimuli too faint for most humans to detect. Their sensory abilities allow non-human mammals to communicate, navigate, find food and avoid enemies by signals that humans cannot even detect.

The |Xam teachers certainly believed that antelope behaviour told them important things. Just as the game animals were aware of the presence of predators, so too could they smell death in the air before it happened on the ground (see 'The springbok's story'; 'What the springbok and the gemsbok did …'; see also the Part IV narratives). Any behaviour that was out of the ordinary was a sign that an animal was either a spirit creature, or it was reacting to impending events that were literally still in the wind (see Part IV, 'Omens of death'). For instance, when a wounded springbok chewed its leg, bleated, ate and urinated (see 'What the springbok and the gemsbok did …'), Diä!kwain and his wife knew that some great change was coming. As Diä!kwain puts it, '[game] does not talk with its mouth, but a man who understands can see' (L.V.9: 4640 rev.). Knowledge of animal behaviour thus made it possible to know things and to make things happen beyond the limitations of personal time, space and perception, using the */ko:ode* of the game.

Another major legacy of the Bushman peoples is their rock engravings and paintings. These are linked to Bushman beliefs about game animals (Vinnicombe 1976; Lewis-Williams 1981).

The eland's story

Narrator: Diä!kwain
Source: 'Related by Diä!kwain, who had it from his father, Xã: ätiŋ'
Dictation dates: 26 September 1875 (5338-5351); 27 September 1875 (5351-5363); 30 September 1875 (5364-5372); 4 October 1875 (5372-5373)
Notebook reference: L.V. 17: 5317-5353 and 18: 5354-5363; 5359 rev.-5361 rev.; 5364-5373
***Bantu Studies* reference:** Vol. 6 (1932), Part III: 233-240

Just before dictating this passage, Diä!kwain spoke about how /Kaggen tries to protect a hartebeest dying of arrow poison. Now he explains that when a man wounds an eland, one of /Kaggen's favourite creations, the hunter makes a link between himself, his people, and the eland. /Kaggen does his best to break that link and set the animal free. Here Diä!kwain explains the complex set of 'respect' (!nanna-se*) behaviours that people must follow to maintain the link so that the animal may die. The importance of these beliefs is underlined by the fact that Diä!kwain devoted almost one and a half notebooks to this topic. There are astonishing similarities between the customs Diä!kwain describes here and those from the Kalahari (Lewis-Williams & Biesele 1978).*

❑

Sa:-ka kum.

I kaŋ ||nau, i |xã: sá:, itən k''auki !ahí siŋ ha !nwa. Ta: i |ku ||nau, i: |xã: ha, itən |ku _tai !gwe !khe: ha !nwa ; í ||nau, ti e: ha siŋ ≠ko: siŋ !.ϵ, o itən ka, i |xã ha, í |ku ||nau, i |nĩ: ||kabbakən ta:, í: |ku k''auki ho: ||kabba.

Ta: í |ku xú: ¯||kabba, i _am ≠xamma |gum, o itən ka, i se ho: ||k'e: !nwa: o |gum, o itən ka !nwa: siŋ ||khóë tã: |gum. I |ku ||nau, !nwa:ŋ ||khóë ta: |gum, i !kan ||khóë tã ha, o !nwa: kuitən, o itən ka !nwa: a:, i |xã: sa: ã:, ha siŋ ||khóë ta: !nwa: kuitən, o itən ka !khwe k''auki se |nĩ ha; i se |ki ||e ha o ||khwai, o !khwe k''auki |nĩ ha, i se |e !ho ha o ||khwai.

The eland's story.

When we have shot an eland we do not cross its spoor. But when we have shot it we walk on one side of its spoor ; if it has sprung aside at the place where we think we shot it, when we see a bone arrowhead lying there, we do not pick it up.

We leave the arrowhead, we first fetch a leaf (?), for we want to pick up the arrow together with the leaf (?), lying on the leaf (?). When the arrow is lying on the leaf (?), we lay it on another arrow, for we want the arrow with which we shot the eland to lie on another arrow, for we do not want the wind to see it, so we try to get it to the quiver and put it in without the wind seeing it.

!kwija: |kə ||nau ha |e !hóä !nwa:, o ||khwai, ha: |ku !əhai !ho ||khwai, ha: !kúïtən ||neiŋ. Haŋ ||nau, ha !kúïtən ||a:, haŋ k''auki -|nuabba, ta: ha |ku təmse -tai; haŋ k''auki !kauru-ĩ:, ta: ha |ku təmse ||k'oen ti e: ha ||k'oen hɛ, o haŋ ka, sa: k''auki siŋ ||k'oen kúï k''wãŋ ha-há, sa: siŋ ||k'oen kúï k''wãŋ, ti e:, sa: -||kwaŋ tã:, ti e:, ha |ĩ: k''auki taŋ !həmmĩ. Ta: -!gauökən !kan !khi: ha |ĩ:, haŋ k''auki |ne ≠enna, ti e:, ha siŋ !həmmĩ.

When the man has put the arrow into the quiver he slings it on and returns home. On his way back he does not hurry, but goes along quietly; he does not look around, but gazes quietly at what he sees, for he thinks that otherwise the eland would not look as he does, but look as if it felt that its heart were not afraid. For the poison is killing its heart, it does not know that it is afraid.

!kwija |ku ||nau, ha |kə: ||a: o ||neiŋ, ha |ku !gwe siŋ ||neiŋ. |nu|nuk''okən e: ɛ !ke!kerritən, hɛ́: |ku ||nau, o hɛ ||k'oen, ti e:, ha -saŋ !gwe siŋ ||neiŋ, hɛ: |ku |kəm ||e ha, o !kaukən k''auki ||na hɛ. |ka:kaŋ k''auki ||na hɛ, ta: hɛ e: |kˀe-ta tukən !ke!kerritən |ku e:, ||a: !kwi a: |xã: sa: ; o hiŋ ka, hɛ se ||a tú, tsˀa a:, ha k''auki ká ha sé ||neiŋ ã:.

When the man arrives at home he stands opposite the hut. As soon as the old men, the heads of the family, see him standing opposite the hut, they go out to him and the children are not with them. Neither are the women with them, for only the grown-up men go to the man who has shot the eland; for they want to ask him why he has not come to the hut.

Hɛ hɛ !ke ||a ha, hiŋ tu:tu ha, ti e:, tsˀa de |nõ a:, dá: ha, hɛ ha k''auki ká ha |ne ||e ||neiŋ, !kwi a: |xã: sa:, ha-g |ne kukú, há: ≠kaka |nu|nuk''okən ã:, o haŋ k''auki ≠kakən ||wẽ:ï, ta: ha |ku ≠kakən kú:ï !xwaŋ ha taŋ ; haŋ |ku təmse ≠kaka hɛ ã: ; haŋ |k'e:ja hɛ ã:, ti e:, ʘho -dóä a: ||kenjã ha !nwa ; hɛ tikən e:, ha -sáŋ sue:ŋ, ĩ: ; o ha: k''auki kukú, ha: |k'e:ja !ke!kerritən ã:, 'ŋ kaŋ |xã: sa:.' Ha k''auki |kwẽ:ï ku, ta: ha |ku ĩ: ≠kaka hɛ ã:, ti e:, ʘho a: ||kenjã ha, hɛ tikən e:, ha k''auki taŋ, ha ká, ha ||e ||nein, ĩ:.

So they go up to him to ask him what has happened to him that he does not want to come to the huts. The man who shot the eland talks to the old men, but does not speak loud, he speaks as if he were in pain; he speaks quietly to them; he tells them that a bush must have pricked his foot, that is why he must sit down; he does not say to the old men, "I have shot an eland." He does not do that, but merely tells them that a bush has pricked him, and that is why he does not feel able to enter the hut.

!ke!kerrita: |ku ||nau, ha |kwẽ:ï ku, ha: ≠kaka hɛ ã:, hɛ́ |ku -≠kerre ||khwai, o híŋ ka hɛ ||k'oen,

When he says this an old man says to the others, that they must look into the quiver, for they want

tsʔa a: ha |xã: ha, ha |khu, o ⁻||kabba. ||xaukən e: ||nã ⁻||kabba,

to see the hair of the thing which he has shot on the arrow shank.

hiŋ e:, !ka!kanna o tsʔa-ka |khukən. hɛ |khukaŋ e:, hɛ ⁻≠kerre ₋||gauë hɛ, hɛ se ||k'oen ts'a a: |khu ɛ, hɛ se ≠en tsʔa a: !kwi |xã: ha.

The blood on the shank holds some of the thing's hair, that is what they seek, to see what animal's hair it is, to know what the man has shot.

Hɛ́ hɛ |ku ||nau, hɛ k''auki ≠ke: |hiŋ !nwã: o ||khwai, hɛ |ku tɒmse !kwai!kwai ≠ke:≠ke: |hiŋ !nwã:, o hiŋ ka, hɛ se ||k'oen. Hɛ́ hɛ |ku ||nau, hɛ ||k'oenjã ⁻||kabba, hɛ |ku ||k'oen, ti e: sa: ₋óä a:, !kwi |xã: ha, hɛ́ hɛ |ku ||xã:ŋ |ki e: !nwã: o ||khwai.

Then they do not pull the arrows out of the quiver, they pull them a little one by one, in order to look at them. And when they have looked at the shank and seen that it was an eland that the man had shot, then they put the arrow into the quiver again.

!kerri ko:, ha: ||nau !kwi-ka ||ɒhí:, ha: xɒmmi, |ki |e: hɛ o ||kɔroko. !ke!kerritaŋ kaŋ ≠kaka ha ã:, ha: k''auki siŋ ||khu||khu ||wẽ:ï, ta: ha ||nau, ha: ||khu||khu ||wẽ:ï, sa:gən ||xɒm ||khu||khu ||wẽ:ï, ti e:, ha ||khu||khu |ki !kwiŋ, ĩ:, hiŋ e:, sa: ||xɒm k''auki ||khu-||khu ||wẽ:ï, ĩ:.

Another old man takes the man's apron and rolls it up sticking it into the belt (?). The old men tell him that he must not pass water freely, for if he did so, the eland would also pass water freely, if he passed water with difficulty (?), then the eland too would not pass water freely.

Ta:, ti e:, ha ĩ:ja, ĩ:, hiŋ e:, ₋!gauökən !kɒn |khi: sa:, ĩ:, ta: ₋!gauökən !kɒn !haŋ-a sa: ||khuru-kən, hɛ ha k''auki ⁻|ki ti e:, ha se ||khu ĩ:.

For if he acted so, then the poison would hold and kill the eland, for the poison would hold its bladder shut, and it would not open to pass water.

Hɛ !ke!kerritən |ku da: !kwi ã:. ||neiŋ, o ti e: |xarra, hɛ !kaukən k''auki !ke!ke sa: ha, ĩ:, !kauka: siŋ ||kerri-ĩ ha, ĩ:. |nuk''o ko: |ũŋ hĩ !kwi a: |xã: sa:, o ha: ka, ha: siŋ di akka ha ã:, |i. !kwija: |km k''wãŋ ha: taŋ, !kwi !kerrija: !kʔõä-se kúï k''wãŋ !kwija: taŋ, o há: ka, há: siŋ ||ke:ja !kwi ã: |i.

Then the old men make a hut for the man at a different place, to which the children do not come to make a noise. An old man sleeps with the man who shot the eland, for he means to look after the fire for him. The man seems to be in pain, the old man takes care of him as if he were ill, for he warms him at the fire.

The eland's story

Ta: |kaggən |ki k''auki se ⁻ã: !kwi se ʘpwoin; ta: ha ká ha siŋ tsí:-ĩ: !kwi, o há: ka, !kwi se ₋dar-

For the Mantis will not let the man sleep, but keeps biting the man, because he wants him to *rakən, sá: se ||xaəm _darrakən. ||k'e: ko:, haŋ dí kúï taŋtaŋ ʘmuiŋ a: tsí: !kwi. !kwitən ||nau, haŋ ki tã:, ti e:, tí taŋ, ʘmuiŋ a: tsí: ha, haŋ k''auki |kwaïïtən, ta: ha |ku təmse kɔrokən ha !kauügən e:, ha tã:, ti e: tʃweŋ tsí:-ĩ ha.*

move, that the eland may also move. Sometimes he appears as a louse that is biting the man. Even if the man feels that a louse seems to be biting him, he does not scratch, but gently wriggles his body a little where he feels that something is biting him.

Haŋ ≠enna, ti e:, ʘmuiŋ k''auki é, ta: |kaggən |ku á:, dí si kwɔkwaita, ha ã:, o |kakakən ka, há: síŋ ka, ha: ⁻≠ĩ:, ʘmuiŋ e, ha se |kã-ã ʘmuiŋ, ha se |kha ʘmuiŋ, o há: ka, há: ⁻≠ĩ:, ʘmuiŋ e. O ti e:, |kaggən |kwẽ:ï k''ɔkən dí:, ĩ:, o haŋ ka, sa: se _koãŋ |hiŋ o !kwija |kha: ʘmuiŋ, o haŋ ≠enna, ti e:, ʘmuiŋ e |kerri. He tikən e:, há ka ⁻!kwi se |kha ʘmuiŋ, ʘmuiŋ !gau se ||na-||na ⁻!kwi |k'a|k'a, e: ha siŋ !kənna o !nwã:, ĩ:, haŋ |xĩ: sa:, ĩ:, ʘmuiŋ !gau se |e: !nwã:, hɛ se di ku tã serritən o _!gauökən.

He knows that it is not a louse, but it is the Mantis who is trying to cheat him, for the Mantis wants him to think it is a louse and to catch it and kill it, thinking it to be a louse. When the Mantis behaves like this, he wants the eland to get up as the man kills the louse, and he knows that the louse is vermin. So he thinks the man will kill the louse, its blood will be on his hands with which he grasped the arrow when he shot the eland, the blood will enter the arrow and cool the poison.

!kerritən ||nau, ha ||k'oen, ti e:, ti k''waŋ |kaggən ||k'werre ⁻i, haŋ ||ke: |i, o hán ka, |i se ||xarra |kaggən, |kaggən k''auki se ||k'werre ⁻i, ha: tsi:ĩ: i tsaxaitən, i-ka tikəntikən e:, ha dí si ||k'oen||k'oen o í, ĩ:. Ha: ||nau, i-ka tikəntikən-ka ku:, ha: tsi:-ĩ: hɛ, o há ka, í: se |kã ã, hɛ:, i-ka ti e:, ka ≠enna, ti e:, í ka, í se ||nau, í: |kã-ã: hɛ, sa: kɔ:ɔ̈ ⁻!kˀau. Ha: ||ki:-ĩ ⁻i, o ha: |a, í: siŋ |kã|kã-ĩ:, i-ka ti é:, i tã:, ti e:, ti taŋ, tsˀa tsí: hɛ, ta: i tũ: _||kwaŋ taŋ. Itən ||nau, itən ki tã:, ti e:, i tũ: ki taŋ, itən k''auki |kã-|kã-ĩ: í-ka ti e:, i tã:, ti taŋ, tsˀa tsi: hɛ.

When the old man sees that the Mantis seems to be teasing us, he makes up the fire, for he wants it to drive the Mantis away, so that he may not teaze us, he is biting our eyes, with which he makes us look about. He bites all parts of us, for he wants us to take hold of that part, he knows that if we do so then the eland will live. He pricks us for he wants us to catch hold of that part of our body where we feel that something is biting us, because our skin smarts. Even if we feel our skin smarting, we must not touch that part where something seems to bite us.

|nuk''owa-g |ne ||nau, !gauë !khwaija, ha: |k'e: |nuk''o ko:, ha kukú, ha |k'e:ja ha, ã: 'A kɔɔ̈: hɔ: |i, a se ||a |ki ||ka, ti |ke:, ta: ŋ kaŋ tɑmse !khãũ i ||kã: á:-a.' !kwija |ku ˍtai kúï k''wãŋ ha: taŋ; ha: |ku ||a||appəm kɔ ˍtai, o haŋ ka, sá: siŋ ||xɑm ||a||appəm, sa: k''auki siŋ !kõä!kõä ||kho, o ||khwe-tən, sá: siŋ |ku ≠k''am kɔ ˍtai.

When day is breaking the old man speaks to another old man and says to him, "You must take a brand and go and light a fire over there, for I want to cook a little for our brother there!" The man walks as if he were ill; he limps, for he wants the eland to limp too, not to trot far off, but to stumble along.

!kˀe ||nau, hɛ: ˍtai !ɑhí sˀo: sa: !nwa, hɛ k''auki ˉa: !kwi a: |xã: sa:, ha siŋ !ɑhí sˀo: sa: !nwa. Ta: ha |ku ˍtai |ki |kɔ: ||a: !kˀe, o ti e:, ha siŋ xu: sa: !nwa, ĩ:. Haŋ |ku kukúï, haŋ |k'e:ja !kˀe ã:, 'U kaŋ se ˍtai ||e, o ti |ke: ã, u se ||k'oen, ti e:, u-g |nɔ̃ k''au se tã: sa: !nwa, o ti |ke: ã; ta: ŋ ˍ||kwaŋ sin xu: sa: !nwa, o ti |ke: ã.'

The men going to follow the eland spoor do not let the man who shot it follow the spoor. But he takes the men towards the place where he left the eland's spoor. He says to the others, "You must go in this direction to see whether you cannot find the eland's spoor over there, for I left the eland's spoor over there."

!kwi ||nau, ha: |kwẽ:ï ku, ha |k'e:ja !kˀe kuitən ã:, ha |ku ˍtai ||xĩ: !khe o ti e:, !kwi !kerri kɔ: ˍtai |ki ||a: ha, ĩ:. !kˀeja |ku ||a, ˉ|kã-ã sa: !nwa; hɛ |ku !ɑhí tiŋ hɛ, o !kwi a: |xã: sa:, ha: k''auki ||e||e sa: !nwa. Ta:, !kˀe kuitən |ku e:, !kɑnnã o sa: !nwa, hɛ |ku ||e ti e:, sa: ˉ!ku:kən ta: hɛ; o !kwi a: |xã: sa:, ha: k''auki ||e||e !kˀe e: !ɑhí sˀɔ: sa: !nwa.

When the man has told the others about it, he walks back to the place to which the other old man has gone. The men go on picking up the eland's spoor, while the man who shot it does not follow. But the others hold to the spoor, they go to the place where the eland lies dead; while the man who shot it does not go with them.

!kˀe |ku ||nau, hɛ: |na: sa:, o sa: ta:, hɛ |ku ˉã: !kwi a: |xã: sa:, ha |ku kaŋ sue:ŋ, o ha: k''auki se sé ti e:, !kˀe |ã |ki sa:, ĩ:. Ta:, ti e:, !kˀe |ne |ã |khu|khurru sa:, ĩ, hέ hɛ |ã |hiŋ sa: |ĩ:, ĩ:, hɛ e:, ha |ne ||a:, !kˀe e: |ã |ki sa:, ĩ:, o sa: |ĩ:jã: e: |hã: ; o hiŋ !hɑmmĩ:, ti e: sa: ɛ tsˀa a: |ki ˍ|kɔ:öde, ha |ki é.

When the men see the eland lying there, the man who shot it is sitting (at home), and does not come to the place where they are cutting it up. When they have cut it to pieces and cut out the heart, then he joins the men who are cutting it up, after the heart is out because they are afraid that it is a thing which has (?).

The eland's story

Ha |kwãin e:, hє !hammi: hє o sa:, ti e:, hє k''auki ka, ha |kwãi se ||na||na sa:, o sa: k''auki |ã |khu-|khurruwa. Ta: hє ≠enna, ti e:, |kaggən ||na sa:, o sa:gən ki ˉ|ku:kən ta:. Tikəntikən e:, |xam-ka !kˀe dí: hє, hє́ hє !nař̃ra-se tsˀa, o híŋ ka, tsˀa a siŋ ˉ||kˀuwa. Ta:, tsˀá |ki ||nau, háŋ ki ˉ|ku:kən ta:, i ˍ|kwãĩn ||ne||ne: ha, i ˍ|kwãĩn |ki ˍkɔ̃ãĩŋ ha.

It is his scent they fear for the eland, so they do not want his scent to come near it till it is cut up. For they know that the Mantis is with the eland as it lies dying. These things Bushmen do to show respect for the things, for they want it to be fat. But when anything lies dying, if our scent comes to it, our scent makes it lean.

|xam-ka !kˀetən ||nau, o hє: k''auki |ã sa:, hiŋ |kɯ ||nau, o sa:gən !naunko ≠urru, o hє k''auki |khau !ho, o sa:, hє ˍam, ˍmai-i hє |khau |kɑm sa: !khwi. Hє ||nau sa: !khwi, hє: !kaukən-ã sa:, o sa: !khwi. Hiŋ ||nau, hє !kaukən-ĩ: sa: o sa: !khwi, hiŋ !xwãŋ hє !gwi:, o ti e: hє !gwi, ti e:, hє ˍsaŋ |kwẽ:ï da, hє !gwi, ĩ: ; o hє hã: sa:-ka sweŋ, hiŋ e:, hє |kwẽ:ï dakən !gwi:, ĩ: ; ta: hє |ki !kaukən ||kuwi sa:, o ha !khwi.

Before the Bushmen cut the eland, while it is still whole and they have not opened it, they first just cut off the eland's tail. They take the tail and beat the eland with the tail. When they beat the eland with his tail, it seems to sigh just as they are used to sigh ; when they eat eland's fat then they sigh like that, so they beat the eland with its tail to fatten it. (The man who beats the eland with its tail, puts down the tail, takes a knife, cuts the eland open and says :)

'||k'oenjau, sa: e:, ú siŋ kaŋ |k'e:, ha ˍkõãĩŋ, ti e:, ha-g |ne |kwẽ:ï ú, ĩ:. Ta:, u síŋ ka, ha ˍhã: ˍkõãĩŋ, o-g ŋ |k'e:ja hu, ti e:, ha |kɯ a: !kwẽ:ï u, haŋ ˉ||kˀuwa ; ukən |ne ≠nwãĩ ŋ, o-g ŋ |k'e:ja hu, ti e:, sa: ˍdoa ˉ||kˀuwa. Han |kɯ ||nau ti e:, ha !harrowa, hє tikən e:, tí ||khóä ha ˍkõãĩŋ, ï:.'

" Look, the eland which you said would be lean is like this. For you said it would be lean, while I told you it would be fat like this ; you contradicted me when I said that the eland was fat. Because its sides looked hollow, it seemed to be lean."

O í-ka ||gáuä||gáuä ˉ||kau tiŋ tsˀa, itən go:ä tsˀa. I-ta ||gáuäkən |ki ˍkõãĩŋ tsˀa. Hє tikən e:, |xam-ka !kˀe ka ||nau, hє: |nã: tsˀa, o tsˀa ˉ|ku:kən ta:, hє |kɯ ||nau, hє k''auki ||e tsˀa, o hє ta |nĩ ha e:

If our shadow falls on anything we hurt (?) it. Our shadow makes it lean. Therefore when Bushmen see anything lying dead, they do not go up to it as soon as they see it ; but they lay their things down

ta:, hɛ |ku ˍsaŋ tẽ: hɛ-ka tʃweŋ, o ti e: |xarra. !kwi a: !kwai, haŋ |ku a:, !ke ||a tsʔa.

somewhere else. Only one man goes up to the thing.

Haŋ ||nau, ha: k''auki |hiŋ ti e:, ||kõ:ïŋ !khe: hɛ, ta:, ha ĩ: |hiŋ tsʔa ||kã:xu e:, ||kõ:ïŋ k''auki !khe hɛ. Han !ke ||a tsʔa, o haŋ ka, ha |nã: ˍ!kʔantara se ĩ: ||na||na tsʔa ||kã:xu e:, ||kʔõïŋ k''auki ||nã hɛ, o ka, ha se ˍam ˍ!kʔãĩ ˍ||gauë sueŋ o tsʔa, o há-ka ||gáuä k''auki ˉ||kau tiŋ tsʔa. Ha ˍ!kʔãĩ tsʔa, o !kʔe kuitaŋ k''auki ||na.

He does not draw near from the side on which the sun stands, but from the side on which there is no sun. He goes to it so that his head's shadow is only on the side of the thing on which there is no sun, for he wants to approach and sit looking without his shadow falling on it. He approaches it, while the others do not come near.

!kʔe kúitaŋ |ku ||nau, !kwi kɔ: ˍ!kʔãĩ |ki sa:, o ha ká ha ||k'oen ti e:, sa:-g |nõ k''au ˉ||kʔuwa, hiŋ |ku ||k'oen |ki, ti e: |xarra, hiŋ k''auki ||k'oen, ti e:, !ku kɔ: ˍ!kʔãĩ |ki sa:, ĩ:. Ta:, hɛ ki !hammĩ:, ti e:, hɛ tsaxau ||k'oen ˍkõãĩŋ sa:. Hɛ tikɔn e:, hɛ ||k'oen |ki, ti e: |xarra, ĩ:, o hiŋ ka, !kwi á: ˍ!kʔãĩ |ki sa:, ha se ˍmai; i ha ||k'oen, ti e: sa: |kwẽ:ï u, ĩ:

Men do this, when one of them approaches an eland to see whether it is fat, the others look in a different direction, they do not look at the place where he is approaching the eland. For they are afraid that their eye might by looking make it lean. Therefore they look away, for they want the man who goes up to the eland to see first how it is.

Ha-g |ne |nau, !kʔe kúitjaŋ k''auki ||k'oen, ha:-g |ne ||nau, ha ||k'oen, ti e:, sa: ˍ||kwaŋ ˉ||kʔuwa, ha-g |ne ||nau, há: k''auki kukú, ha: |k'e:ja !kʔe kúitɔn ã:; ta: ha |ku ||nau, ha ||k'oen, ti e:, sa: ˍ||kwaŋ ˍ||kʔuwa, ha: |ku ||nau, haŋ ka, !kʔe kúitɔn se sá, ||k'oen, sa:-ka sweŋ, ha: |ku kukú, ha: |k'e:, 'U ˍka: kaŋ ≠ĩ:, sa: a: k''auki ||khɔ, í se hã: ha; ha kaŋ |ku á: a, ta:, ha |ku ˉ!kouwi.'

He looks while the others are not looking, he sees that the eland is fat, he does not speak and tell the others about it; but when he sees that the eland is fat and wants the others to come and look at its fat, he speaks and says, "You thought that this eland did not seem as if we should eat it; it is here, but it is lean."

Haŋ k''auki kukúï, haŋ |k'e:ja !kʔe kúitɔn ã:, '||k'oenju, sa:-ka sweŋ.' Ta:, ha |ku ĩ: |k'e:ja !kʔe kúitɔn ã:, ti e:, sa: ˍkõãĩŋ, o haŋ

He does not say to the others, "Look at the eland's fat!" But he tells the people that the eland is lean, and does not tell them that

k''auki |k'e:ja: !kˀe ã:, ti e:, sa: ¯||kˀuwa. Ta, ha |kɯ ĩ: ≠kaka !kˀe kúitən ã:, ti e:, sa _kõ:aiŋ, o háŋ ka, !kˀe kúitən se ||ĩ: hɛ ||k'oen, ti e:, sa: |kwẽ:ï u, ĩ:.

the eland is fat. He just tells them that the eland is lean, because he wants them to see for themselves what it is like.

Hɛ !kˀe kúitən ||nau, háŋ ka, ha |kwẽ:ï kú, ha |k'e:ja !kˀe kúitən ã:, !kˀe kúitjaŋ !ke ||a: sa:, o hiŋ ka, hɛ se ||k'oen, ti e:, !kẽï ||ou |ːõ a:, ha |k'e:ja, há ka sa: _kɔ̃ãĩŋ. Haŋ |ne !khe |hiŋ ||a:, o háŋ ka, !kˀe kúitən se k'oen, ti e:, sa: kwẽ:ï u, ĩ:.

And the other men do this, when he has spoken to them in this manner, they go up to the eland, for they want to see if it be truth that he has spoken, that the eland is lean. He walks away for he wants the others to see what the eland is like.

Hɛ !kˀe !kúitən kukúï, hiŋ |k'e:, '||k'oenju, sá: a:, i ||kã: ≠kaka hi ã:, ti e: ha _kɔ̃ãĩŋ, ||k'oenju, ti e:, sa: á: a, há-ka sweŋ |kwẽ:ï u, ĩ:, o !kˀetən k''auki _saŋ hã: ¯ã:, o sa: á: a. Ta:, sweŋ !kwˀĩ |kɯ e:, hɛ _saŋ hã: hɛ.'

Then the other people say, "Look at the eland which our brother said was lean, look, this eland's fat is such that people will not eat meat of this eland. For pure fat is what they will eat.'

❑

Notes

79-81 *Another old man takes the man's apron and rolls it up sticking it into the belt.* Dorothea Bleek edited the following five notebook pages extensively, probably to clarify the meaning, but also perhaps to omit the frequent repetition of *//khu*, to urinate. In the editing process, however, detail and meaning have been lost. I therefore give pages 5332-5338 below, as translated in the notebook:

… for he does not want the apron to touch him. He should not handle the apron. He ought to pass water; for these were the matters that the old men took care of, for they thought that he would not himself take care, when he required to pass water, he would pass water without holding it well aside, he would act just as he thought, without handling it, he would pass water. The old men told him that he must not pass water freely (*//weï* can also mean 'strongly' or 'much' (Bleek 1956: 630) – ed.), for if he did so, if he passed water freely, the eland would also urinate freely, if he passed water with difficulty [?], *!kwiŋ*, not in the *Dictionary* – ed.), then the eland would also not pass water freely. For, if he acted so, then the poison would hold and kill the eland; and the eland would not want to urinate if he felt that he did

not have to urinate. For the poison held the eland's bladder so that it did not open in order to pass water. The man should do the same there, then the eland would not pass water and the poison would hold its bladder shut.

There is a problem with the translation of this |Xam phrase '*ŏ haŋ kă //§hiya yauki ssiŋ //xarra hă*' on page 5332. The word *//xarra* means 'to drive, drive away, keep away from' (Bleek 1956: 632), not 'touch' or 'impel' as translated in the notebook. If I am correct, then the sentence should be translated as: 'so that it (i.e. the apron) should not drive it (i.e. the eland) away.'

81-83 *The old men tell him that he must not pass water freely …*: Patricia Vinnicombe, whose work on the rock paintings of the southern Drakensberg is published in *People of the Eland*, has suggested that painted images of men with bars drawn across the penis may symbolise this, or a similar practice (Vinnicombe 1976: 258).

115-116 *… it is the Mantis who is trying to cheat him …*:'[Explanatory note by D.H. Dec. 12/75] The Mantis imitates what people do also, when they want us who do not know Guy Fox to be afraid. They change their faces, for they want us who do not know, to think that it is not a person. The Mantis also does something cheating to make the man move or scratch … that we may not know it is he.' (5341 rev., note omitted)

122-123 *… he knows that the louse is vermin*: ' "*slechte ding*" (bad thing)' (5343 rev., note omitted). Dorothea Bleek seems to have missed the point here by translating */kerri* as 'vermin', a translation which is followed in the *Dictionary* by a question mark – the 'louse' is not a louse, it is |Kaggen himself, trying to sabotage the hunter's kill. The original notebook translation, 'bad thing' (5344), confirms the sense of this translation.

129-130 *… the Mantis seems to be teasing us …*: 'Note added 12 Dec/75. The substance of this was told to D.H. both by !Xugen-ddi [*tata oä*] and by Xã:ätiŋ, D.H. explains.'

My grandfather told me that the Mantis would pinch those of our members which he knew that we should not leave off feeling, of which he knew that if he bit them we should touch them. These parts he bit, to see whether it was true that we respected the eland; for he thought that if we, when we felt him biting that part which we did not want him to bite, we should catch him and kill him; if we have not killed him, we shall have taken hold of him; we should have picked him up. He arises when we have made him get up, he goes to the eland and says: 'Get up out of this, walk away; why art thou needlessly writhing there when thou seest, the man who shot thee does not pass water; get up out of this and go'. This is what people know that the Mantis does when he wants us to do so to him, that the eland may get up. Therefore the man who shot it acts as if he were really ill, for he wants the Mantis not to see that he does not show respect for the eland. That is why he pretends to be ill. When he

feels that his skin smarts, he does not act as if it smarted; for he knows that it is the Mantis who is playing with him like this.

(5345–5348 rev., note omitted)

185-186 ... *they are afraid that it (the eland) is a thing which has* **|ko:ode:** This word means 'magic power' (Bleek 1956) and is therefore an unequivocal statement that the eland possessed magical power.

187-188 *It is his scent they fear for the eland* ...: Smell and scent were important components in several other contexts – the smell of burning *sã:* or buchu calmed angry rain (see Parts V and VI), as well as angry sorcerors (see Part VII). The smell of a sorceror's blood helped to keep evil spirits away (see Part VII).

204-206 ... *it seems to* **sigh** *just as they are used to* **sigh** ...: *!gwi:*, translated here as 'sigh', also means 'break wind, hiccough, smell bad' (Bleek 1956: 393). On the following page of the notebook (5363), *!gwi:* is translated as 'breaking wind'.

279-280 ... *people will not eat meat of this eland*: 'He's amper pir fat' ('it's almost pure fat'– ed.) (5372 rev., note omitted).

The springbok's story

Narrator: Diä!kwain
Dictation dates: 20, 21, 26, 27 April 1875
Translation dates: 26, 28 and 29 April 1875
Notebook reference: L.V. 9: 4619-4651
***Bantu Studies* reference:** Vol. 6 (1932), Part III: 240-243

What happens if a hunter tracks a wounded springbok after sunset.

❑

Mama-gu hiŋ kaŋ kí:se si, ti e:, whai ká ha se ||nau, _||khã: _óä !hi:ŋjã, ha _kóä |ki !ku:xe i, o hέ ti e:, _||khã: ta: he. Ha _kóä |ne ||nau, o ha |ne ≠enna ti e:, _||khã: _||kwaŋ ka, ha _saŋ |ne tu ha, ha _kóä |ne di |ku:kən, o ha ka i' se |ne !ke ||e ha, o í: ka, ise-g|ne _!kaitən |kha ha, o !kau. Haŋ ká ha se ||nau, ha: ||k'oen, ti e:, i |kɐm !kau, í se |ne _!kaitən |kha ha, haŋ k''auki ka: ha se tɐmse _!kwãna, o há ka _||khã: se tu ha.

Our parents used to tell us what a springbok would do when a lion was near, it would take us running to the place where the lion lay. As soon as it knew that the lion was where it could hear, it would act as it if were dying, because it wanted us to go up to it, to kill it by throwing a stone. It meant, as soon as it saw us pick up a stone, to throw at it, to bleat hoarsely, for it wanted the lion to hear it.

Hέ tikən e:, mama-gu kaŋ ≠kaka si ã:, si se-g |ne ||nau, si tú:ï, ti e:, whai k''auki tɐmse _!kwãna, si kɔ: !gõä ĩ: ; ta: si ||kho: kaŋ ≠ĩ:, ||khe:||khe: a:, há ||kau sa:, ha ka sá !khe:, o ha |nĩ:, ti e:, !kwija ||na whai.

Therefore our parents used to tell us that if we heard a springbok bleating hoarsely, we ought to look around ; we seemed to think that the beast of prey which was coming to the sound would stop if it saw a man with the springbok.

Ta:, há ka |ku ||nau, sesé a:, ha sa: ã: haŋ ka |ku ||nau, i ki-sa: |k'e: ha !xwõnni, haŋ k''auki tá ha se !xwõnni. Ta:, ha _||kwaŋ ka: ha se sé i, o í ki-sa: |k'e: ha, ha _kɔ̃ɔ̈ sa ||xãũ |ha: hi ã: whai.

But it would come with a rush, and even if we ordered it to turn back, it would not turn back. For it would persist in coming to us, even if we called to it, it would come to take the springbok away from us.

Hϵ tikən e:, mama-gu kaŋ ≠kaka si ã:, si se ||nau, si ||k'oen, ti e:,

Therefore our parents used to tell us that if we saw the sun setting

||kõ:iŋ |e:, o si ||k'oen ti e:, whai !nau si, si ˍkóö xu: whai, o si: siŋ ||k'oen, ti e:, whai |kwẽ:ï k''o ĩ:.

Ta, si ||kho: kaŋ ≠ĩ:, whai k''au e ts?á a: ka ||nau, ha: dí: í-ta !k''augən, haŋ ká ha se ||nau, í kisá: ||k'oen, ti e:, ha ˍ||kwaŋ k''wãŋ ha ka ha |ku:kən, haŋ ká ha se ||nau, o ha ||k'oen, ti e:, í kíë, i ||xarra ha, o !k?au a: ha !ge: ã:, haŋ ká ha se ú, ha ˍkóä ||xã: ha !kuxe, ha ˍkó:ö |ne ||nau, ha: !əhí hóä í.

O ha: ||k'oen, ti e:, i ||kho, i-g |ne ||nẽĩ||nẽĩ ha ts?ĩ:, ha ˍkó:ö ||xã:, ha te:ŋ, o há ka i se kukú, i ≠ĩ:, 'ŋ kaŋ k''auki ˍdóä se xu: tu whai á a; ta:, ha ˍ||kwaŋ ˍdóä k''wãŋ ha ká ha |ku:kən; ta ha ˍ||kwaŋ |ku a: ||xĩ: ||a ha o-g ŋ; haŋ |ku a: te:ŋ ha á; he ŋ ˍdóä k''auki se xu:wa ĩ:, ta: ha ˍ||kwaŋ ˍdóä k''waŋ ha ká ha |ku:kən.'

Mama-gukən kaŋ |k'e:ja si ã:, si ˍkó:ö ||nau, o si ||k'oen, ti e:, whai |kwẽ:ï k''o, haŋ dí:, si ˍkó:ö se xu:wa. Ta:, whai a: |kwẽ:ï k''o, ha dattən |ki |kəm ||a: si, o ||khe:-||khe:, ha se-g |ne !kuxe !ke ||e ||khe:||khe:. O ha !ke ||a ||khe:-||khe:, hiŋ e:, ha |ne !haugən |ne di: |ku:kən kwokwãŋ, ĩ:, o há |ne ||na ||khe:||khe:, o ||k'e: a:, ha |ne ≠enna, ti e:, ||khe:||khe: ˍ||kwaŋ ˍsaŋ |ne |nĩ e, o í: |ne dí |ki há-ka |kha|kha:, ||khe:||khe:tən |ne !kun ||kau tẽ í o whai.

Hɛ tikən e:, mama-gu kaŋ kí:se si, si se ||nau whai |ke:, si |xĩ:ja, o ||kõĩŋ |etən|etən, o si: siŋ ||k'oenja, ti e:, ha k''auki k''wãŋ si se |kha ha, o ||kõĩŋjã !naunko !khe:, si se xú: tú ha, o si ||k'oen, ti e:, ||kõĩŋ

while the springbok resisted[1] us, we should leave it when we found it acting like this.

Though we seemed to think that a springbok is not a thing to cause our destruction, yet even when we see that it appears to be nearly dying, it will act like this when it finds that we want to drive it away from the "pan" to which it keeps going, it will get up and run on again until it has passed in front of us.

When it sees that we seem to be behind its back, it will lie down again, for it wants us to think, "I ought not to let that springbok go, for it really seems to be going to die; it is the one which just went past me and has lain down there; so I ought not to leave it, for it looks as if it were dying."

Our parents used to tell us that when we saw a springbok behaving like this, we should let it alone. For the springbok was luring us towards the beast of prey, it would run up to it. When it had reached the beast of prey, then it would really die close to the beast of prey, as soon as it knew that the beast of prey could see us as we were killing it, and would throw us down by the springbok.

Therefore our parents taught us to be careful about any buck which we shot at sunset, if we saw that it was not likely that we could kill it while the sun was still up, we should leave it, when

|e:. Ta: whai |ke:, si |xĩ:ja, o |kõĩŋ |etən-|etən, si ||khóä kaŋ ≠ĩ:, ||eiŋ-ka whai kaŋ k''auki e. Ta:, whai a: |ki |kəm ||a si, o si-ka |ku:kən, há é.

we saw the sun setting. Though we seemed to think that a springbok shot at sunset was not a bad one, yet a springbok which leads us to our death it is.

Hϵ tikən e:, sí-ka !kˀe ki:se si, si siŋ ≠enna, ti e:, ⊙pwaitən |kwẽ:ĩ k''o, ĩ:, hϵ-ka didí: e:, hϵ dí: he, o ||k'e: a:, hϵ ≠enna, ti e:, i !gau kϵ: se |hiŋ.

This is what our people taught us that we might know what the game does, its actions when it knows that our blood will flow.

Hiŋ kaŋ |k'e:ja si ã:, ti e:, ⊙pwai e tsˀa á: ka |ku ≠enna í-tya |ku:kən, ||k'e: a:, i se |ku:kən ã:. Mama-gukən kaŋ |k'e:ja si ã:, si |khɔ: kaŋ ≠ĩ:, ⊙pwai k''au e tsˀa á: ká: ha siŋ ≠enna, ||k'e: a:, í-ka !kwi |ku:ka, ã:; haŋ ká ha se ≠kaka hi ã:, ti e:, í-ta !kwi |ku:ka. Ta: ha |ki e tsˀa a !khou, haŋ !khou ||khwe:tən; hϵ tikən e:, ha ≠enna tikəntikən-ka kú:, ĩ:, o haŋ tá:, ||ka ti e:, ha |ki e tsˀa a: !khou.

They used to tell us that the game is a thing which knows of our death, the time at which we shall die. Our parents used to say to us, that we seemed to think that the game is not a thing which knows of our person's death; yet it really tells us when our person is dead. For it is a thing which smells from afar; therefore it knows all things, because it feels that it is a thing which has a keen scent.

Hϵ tikən e:, ha !khou, ti e:, dí tenja tí e: |xara. Hϵ tíkən e:, mama-gu kaŋ ≠kaka si ã:, ti e:, si |nõ k''au ||k'oen, ti e:, whai ka ||nau, !kwija: |ku:kən teŋja hϵ́: ti, si-g |nõ ka ||k'oen, ti e:, whai ka !kwã: |kãä ||e, ti é:, !kwija: |ku:kən teŋja hϵ? Whaitən k''auki ká ha se !kwã: |kãä ti e:, !kwi |ku:kən teŋja hϵ. Ta:, whai |ku ka, hϵ́ se kwã!kwã |kãã !kou a |xara; hϵ ˍkɔ́:ɔ̈ |ku !k''wãŋ, he ≠enna, ti e:, di teŋja hϵ́ ti. Ta tsˀa a: !khou ha |ku e.

Therefore it smells what has happened at a distance. That is what our parents used to say to us, did we not see how the springbok acts when someone lies dead there, did we ever see the springbok travel towards the place where the person lies dead? The springbok will not travel towards the place where someone lies dead. But the springbok keep going along a different road, they seem to know what is lying at that place. For a thing which smells it is.

Hϵ tikən e:, ha |ku ≠enna, ĩ:, ti e: se dí, haŋ |ku ≠enna hϵ; hϵ í k''auki ≠enna hϵ, haŋ |ku a: ≠enna hϵ, ti e: kϵ: se di ten kϵ́: ti.

Therefore it knows what is going to happen, it knows that; what we do not know, it knows, what is going to befall at that place.

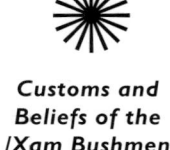

The springbok's story

Notes

6-7 ... *it would act as if it were dying* ...: 'it would now become weak so that the hunter would go up to it' (4619 rev., note omitted).

14-16 ... *if we heard a springbok bleating hoarsely* ...: 'if we heard that a springbok not a little bleated' (4622 rev., note omitted).

28-29 ... *if we saw the sun setting while the springbok resisted us* .. : Dorothea Bleek's note:

[1] *i.e.* would not be driven in the direction we wished.

76-77 ... *its actions when it knows that our blood will flow*: 'These things are those about which our people talked to us, that we might know.' (4637, omitted text)

80-81 ... *the time at which we shall die*: 'These things are those about which our parents talked to us, that we might know, about the pursuing (*//gămmă-ssĕ*) with which we pursue game; that we might attend to the things which the game do, their actions which they do. They are those about which our parents talked to us.' (4638-4640, omitted text)

85-86 ... *it really tells us when our person is dead*: 'D.H. says that it does not talk with its mouth, but that a man who understands can see [know from its actions].' (4640 rev., note omitted)

91-92 *Therefore it smells what has happened at a distance*: 'it is the one who knows it because it knows that it is a thing which smells.' (4642-4643, text omitted)

96-98 ... *did we ever see the springbok travel towards the place where the person lies dead?*: 'It is used to seem as if it knew ([This stands for a whole troop, D.H. says] 4643 rev., note omitted) that a man lies dead [at] that place. Because it knows that it is a thing which smells that which has been done [at] that place, it knows it.' (4644-4645, text omitted)

104 *For a thing which smells it is*: Dorothea Bleek cut the narrative at this point. The remaining pages are given in full here:

These things are those about which it knows. The thing which shall be done, it knows it, that which we do not know, it is the one who knows it, the thing which shall be done at that place. These things they are now those which I now see that truth really must have been that which my parents long ago said to me, about the actions of things. And I now see that the thing looks like that which they long ago thus said, they talked to me about it. Because I now myself, I see that which the thing has done about it. Because the things look like that which they, long ago, they thus said. They talked to me about them. These things they are those which I now see that truth must have been that which they long ago said it to me, about the doings of things. These things they are those to which I now give my assent.

(4648-4651)

What the springbok and the gemsbok did when they knew that Diä!kwain's wife would die

Narrator: Diä!kwain

Source: 'Told by Diä!kwain about his first wife "Mietje" daughter of Kkoä-ken and |Ku|ku [the latter being her mother]. They lived at "Spreet" in the "Zak Rivier" [or |Kubbu]. D.H. explains that they lived in the land of the "Zak Rivier", not *in* it.'

Dictation dates: 29 and 30 April, 4 May 1875

Translation dates: 5 and 6 May 1875

Notebook reference: L.V. 9: 4653-4688

***Bantu Studies* reference:** Vol. 6 (1932), Part III: 243-248

Springbok and gemsbok have uncanny abilities.

❑

!kwi-|aitji á:, ŋ sin _mai-i, ŋ |haŋ s?o: ha, ti e:, whai |kwẽïï |kwã:, whaija: dí, ĩ:, o whai tuko _ó:ä ta:, ||ka ti e:, whai ≠enna, ti e:, ha se |ku:ki. Whai a: ŋ _!kaitən !kwa: ha ¯!kwa, ha ||nau-g ŋ ||khauka ha, ŋ |kha: ha, ha _kõ:äŋ |hiŋ; tíja k''waŋ ha ¯!kwa e: ŋ _!kaitən !kwa: hɛ, ha ||nau, ŋ ã: |ko: sa:, ha hɔ: ha xu, ha !kwe-se ŋ́, ha _!kwãna, ha ||khu, o ha ||k'oen |ki tí e: |xara, ha dí ku k''wãŋk''wãŋ, ha: hã: ||na. Ha ||k'oen ti e:, ŋ ã ||kho: saŋ ||xara ha, ha _kõäŋ |hiŋ, ha !kuxe, ha ||a te:n. Ŋ _||kwaŋ |ne !ke ||a: ha, ŋ ne |khi: ha, ŋ |ne _|kammeŋ |ki !kúïta o ||neiŋ.

It was about the woman[2] whom I first married that the springbok acted like this, when they felt that they knew she would die. A springbok[3] which I hit, breaking[4] its leg[5], did as follows when I chased it in order to kill it, it got up ; it seemed to eat its leg which I had broken, and when I approached, it raised its head and looked at me, then bleated, while it looked away; it seemed to be eating there. It saw that I was trying to drive it back, it arose and ran on, it lay down. Then I went up to it, killed it and carried it home.

Ŋ |ne ≠kaka ŋ |ha ã:, ti e:, whai |kwẽ:ï |kwẽ, há di, ĩ:. Hɛ-g ŋ |ha |ne kukúï, haŋ |k'e:ja ke, ts?a-de |nõ a:, ŋ k''auki siŋ _dóä xu: túï whai ã:?

I told my wife how the springbok had behaved to me. And she answered, asking me why I had not left that springbok alone ?

Hɛ-g ŋ kukúï, ŋ |k'e:ja ha ã:, ŋ ˍ||kwaŋ ||nau, ti e:, ŋ ||k'oen, ti e:, whai ˍ||kwãŋ k''waŋ ha ká ha |ku:kən, hɛ tikən ˍ||kwaŋ e:, ŋ k''auki káŋ xu tu ha, ĩ:.

And I told her that I had seen that the springbok seemed to be going to die, that was why I would not leave it.

Hέ ŋ |ha kukúï, haŋ |k'e:ja ke, ŋ |nõ k''auki ˍdóä ||k'oen ti e:, whai e:, ŋ ˍdóä ˍ!kai:tən |ki he, ti e:, he ˍdóä |kwẽ:ï k''o, ĩ:, ti e:, ŋ ˍ||kwaŋ ka, sa ≠kaka ha ã:, ti e:, whai-ja ˍ||kwa: k''wãŋ, ha: se |ku:kən, hɛ-g ŋ |nõ k''au ˍdóä ||k'oen, ti e:, |k''au-gən ˍdóä é? "Itən ˍ||kwaŋ kɛ:, í se tu kum, o whai á: a, ha-g |ne !kwẽ:ï |kwãŋ dí o á." Hɛ-g ŋ ||nau, ŋ |haŋ ka: ha|kwẽ:ï kú ha |k'e:ja ke, ŋ ≠gou.

Then my wife said, had I not noticed that the springbok which I had recently[6] shot had behaved like this, as I had been telling her, that they had often looked as if they were going to die, and did I not see that this must mean a foreboding of death? "We may be sure we shall hear news, because this springbok acted so to you." When she stopped speaking I was silent.

Hɛ-g ŋ !hənn, ĩ:, o-g ŋ |haŋ |ku twai, ĩ:, o haŋ k''auki taŋ. Hɛ: ŋ ||aŋ ¯|ũ: ¯siŋ ĩ:, hɛ-g ŋ |nĩ: !khwai, ĩ:, o !gauëtən ka: ha !kwai; hɛ-g ŋ ˍ||kwaŋ |xwerri !khwai, ĩ:. !khwaitən !ku k''wãŋ hɛ ≠enna, tí e:, ŋ ||nã: he, hɛ-g ŋ ˍ||kwaŋ |xwerri !khwai ĩ:. !khwaitən |ku ||k'oen ti e:, ŋ ˍdóä |xwerri |hiŋ hɛ, !khwai-ta ku: gwai, hiŋ |ku ˍdóä ||k'oen |ki, ti e:, ŋ ˍdóä |xwerri |hiŋ hɛ. Hiŋ k''auki |nĩ: ŋ, ta:, hɛ |ku e: k''waŋ hɛ ≠enna ŋ, ti-g ŋ ˍdóä |xwerri |ki hɛ.

Then I went hunting when my wife was well, ailing nothing. Then I went to sleep and caught sight of gemsbok when the day had broken, so I began to steal up to them. The gemsbok seemed to know that I had seen them as I was stealing up to them. They looked towards the place from which I was stealing, all the gemsbok kept looking at the place where I was. They could not see me, but they seemed to know that I was coming.

Hɛ he ˍ||kwaŋ k''wãŋ, he tã:, ti e:, ŋ |kə: sa:, hɛ he |ku ˍtai !kˀũ:ï, ĩ:, hiŋ |ku ˍtai.

They seemed to feel that I had come near, for they retreated, they went away.

What the springbok and the gemsbok did ...

Hɛ-g ŋ |ne kukúï, ŋ ≠ĩ:, ŋ kaŋ́ se ˍam ||xã:, ŋ dí ||k'oen, ŋ se ||k'oen, ti e:, he se |kwẽ:ï |kwẽ|kwẽ, ĩ:. Hɛ-g ŋ ˍ||kwaŋ ||aŋ, ||nũŋ ||a:-g ŋ o ||xãũ, o kaŋ ≠ĩ:, ti e:, ŋ kaŋ |xwerri he o !khwirri a:, he kerre !ke ||a ha. Hɛ-g ŋ ˍ||kwaŋ tattən ||khóë !khwirri, ĩ:, hɛ-g ŋ ||an |xwerri kerre !ke ||a: ĩ:, o kaŋ

Then I thought to myself, I will first take another look to see what they are doing. So I went back round behind the Spitzkop, meaning to steal up to them at the (dry) river-bed, as they went along there. Then I descended into the river-bed, and I stole along it, thinking that I would creep along

≠ĩ:, ti e:, ŋ kaŋ /xwerri !ke:ŋ //e !khwai, o kaŋ -//kwaŋ //k'oen, ti e:, !khwai -//kwaŋ hã:ã kerre !ke sa: !kwirri.

to meet the gemsbok, for I saw that they were going grazing along the river-bed.

Hɛ !khwai /ku k''wãŋ, hɛ tã:, ti e:, ŋ //na !khwirri, híŋ /ku /hiŋ tu:ï !khwirri, híŋ /ku -tai !ke //khɔ !khwe ; hɛ-g ŋ /ku-g /ne //kóä:kən //k''oen //khóë siŋ !khwirri, ĩ:, o kaŋ kaŋ /ne -am //k''oen tsʔa a:, !khwai /ne /kwẽ:ï k''o ã:.

Then the gemsbok seemed to feel that I was in the river-bed, they left it, they went up into the wind ; and I watched closely sitting in the river-bed, for I wanted to see why the gemsbok were going on in this manner.

Hɛ !khwai /ne k''waŋ hɛ /ku ≠enna ŋ, hɛ: !khwai /ku !kuxe, ĩ:, o hɛ k''auki /nĩ ŋ ; ta: hɛ /ku e: //au se !kuxe, o hɛ k''auki /nĩ ŋ. Hɛ-g ŋ /ku kukúï, ŋ ≠ĩ:, ŋ /ku se /kã: !khwai ã:, !khwai se /ku !kwã: -tai.

Then the gemsbok seemed to know about me, and ran on, although they did not see me ; yet they ran for no reason, although they did not see me. Then I thought I would leave them, let them escape.

Hɛ-g ŋ /ku -kóäŋ /hiŋ, ĩ: ; ŋ /ku /kam //a: Sũ:-!kúïtən-ta:, ĩ:, o ti e:, ha sʔo ko //k''oen ŋ, ĩ: ; ti-g ŋ /kwẽ:ï k''okən /xwerri !khwai, ĩ:. Hɛ-g ŋ -//kwaŋ !ke //a ha, ĩ:, hɛ ha tu:-tu:-g ŋ, ĩ:, ti e:, ŋ /nõ -dóä te: k''okən /xwerri !khwai. Hɛ-g ŋ -//kwaŋ k''e:ja ha ã:, ti e:, ha-g /nõ k''au -dóä //k'oen, ti e:, !khwai /kwẽ:ï k''o, ĩ:, hɛ-g ŋ /k'e:ja ha ã:, ti e:, si -dóä se kúïtən //neiŋ, si se //a //k''oen //neiŋ.

So I rose up and went up to Snore-white-lying[7] where he sat watching me as I stalked the gemsbok. As I approached him, he asked me how I had got on with hunting them. Then I said, had he not seen how the gemsbok were behaving, and I told him we ought to go home, to see how things were at home.

Hɛ si-//kwaŋ !kúïtən //neiŋ, ĩ:, hɛ-g ŋ /ku xu: we, ĩ:, o hiŋ /ku !naunko sa:, ŋ /ku !kúïtən //neiŋ, hɛ-g ŋ /ku //a: //neiŋ, ĩ:. Ŋ /ku //nau, o kaŋ tũ:ŋ /e: //neiŋ, ŋ /ku /auwi ŋ /ha, o haŋ //khó:ë ta: //neiŋ, o haŋ k''auki təmse taŋ, o haŋ k''auki təmse tu: ; ta ha /ku tu: -//gauë ha /ĩ:, o haŋ ta: //ka ti e:, ha k''auki tu: /nĩ: ha /ĩ:.

So we started for home, and I left the others to come on behind, I went home, went to the hut. As I entered the hut, I saw that my wife who was lying in the hut was not at all well, but was breathing very badly, she was breathing as if she were seeking her heart, panting, for she felt as if she could not perceive her heart when she breathed.

Hɛ-g ŋ tu:tú: ha, ti e:, tsʔá de /nõ á: dá: ha, hɛ ha /kwẽ:ï k''okən

And I asked her what had happened to her to make her

thu:. Hϵ ha |k'e:ja ke, ĩ:, ti e:, ha tã: tsʔa a: !kauŋ !khe: ha ||kwa-||kwan, haŋ _||kwaŋ a:, ha |kwẽ:ï k''okən thu:, ã:, hϵ tikən e:, ha k''auki ≠enna tsʔa a dá: ha, hϵ tsʔa |ne !kauŋ !khe: ha ||kwa||kwan ĩ:. Hϵ ha |k'e:ja ke, ĩ:, ti-g ŋ ||khóä kaŋ ≠ĩ:, ha ||kũŋ||kũŋ taŋ, ha ká: !kɔn ¯kwakkən !khwã:. Ta: Trúɜ |ku a: !kɔn!kɔn !kauŋ !ho !khweitən o !khwã: tu.

breathe like this. And she told me that she felt as if something were sticking in her neck hollow and making her breathe like this, but she did not know what it was that had hurt her, sticking in her neck hollow. And she told me that I must not think that her arms were strong enough to hold and suckle the child. For *Trúɜ* (their eldest daughter) had held the breast to the child's mouth

Hϵ Sũ:-!kúïtən-ta: _||kwaŋ |ne sa:, ĩ:, haŋ |ne |k'e:ja ke, ti e:, ha _||kwaŋ siŋ _dóä ≠kaka ke, ti e:, kϵ́: se dí tıŋ si ||neiŋ, hϵ _||kwaŋ _dóä e:, tʃwen |kwẽ:ï k''o, ĩ: ; hϵ whai e: ŋ _!kaitji, hϵ _||kwaŋ _dóä ≠enna, ti e:, kϵ: se di tiŋ si ||neiŋ. Hϵ tikən e:, ŋ _||kwaŋ |ne ||ĩ: ŋ ||k'oen, ti e:, ŋ |haŋ |ne |kwẽ:ï k''okən thu:, ĩ:, o há siŋ ≠kaka ke, ti e:, si _||kwaŋ ka, si se !naunko |nĩ, ti e:, kϵ́: se di.

And Snore-white-lying came, (he lived at the same place); he said that he it had told me something would happen at our home, and that was why the creatures were acting like this; those springbok which I had hit must have known that something was happening at our home. How I myself saw that my wife was breathing in this way, after telling me that we should soon see that something would happen.

Hϵ-g ŋ kukúï, ŋ |k'e:ja Sũ-!kúï-təŋ-ta: ã:, ŋ xá se tϵ́: |ki, ŋ dí ŋ-ka !kwã:, o xɔro k''auki ||na: ka:, ti e:, ŋ se |ki kwaka o xɔro-ka !khweitən. He Sũ:-!kúïtən-ta: ku-kúï, haŋ |k'e:ja ke, ' A kaŋ _||kwaŋ |ku se xú:, i se ||k'oen, ti e:, |ha se |kwẽ:ï |kwẽ, ha dí, ĩ:, o ti e:, ha |nõ k''au se twaitən.' Hϵ ŋ |ha ||nau, o ||kõïŋjaŋ ká: ha |e:, haŋ |ku:kən.

And I asked Snore-white-lying what I should do about my baby, as no cattle were at hand, that I might let it drink cow's milk. [His father-in-law had given him a cow and bull, but they had run away]. And Snore-white-lying said, " Wait and see whether your wife will not get better." But when the sun was setting, she died.

Hϵ́ Sũ-!kúïtən-ta: kukúï, haŋ |k'e:ja ke ã:, ŋ se ||a |k'e:ja ŋ ||ka-xai-ka !khwã:, ã:, ha se sé, ha se sá: |ki kwáka ke !khwã:. Ta: ŋ _||kwaŋ ŋ ||ẽĩŋ ||k'oen, ti e:, !khwã: a: k''auki kí:ja, há |ku é ; haŋ k''auki hĩ: ; ti e:, ha síŋ sin hĩ:, ĩ:, hiŋ e:, si siŋ se |ki hã: ha, o eŋ, ĩ:, haŋ

And Snore-white-lying said to me, that I must tell my sister's daughter to come in order to suckle the child for me. For I could see for myself that it was still a baby, it could not eat; if it had been able to eat, then we could have fed it with meat, but

What the springbok and the gemsbok did ...

k''auki hĩ:. "Hé tikən e:, ||kaxai-ta !khwã: se sé, há se |ki kwaka ha ã:, !khwã:. Ta: !khwã: |ku se |ku:-kən o ||kaŋ."

it could not eat. "Therefore your sister's child must come to suckle the little one for you. Otherwise it will die of hunger."

Hɛ si -||kwaŋ |ne ||nau, o ŋ ||kaxai-ka !khwãŋ ká ha se, haŋ |ne |ki kwakən !khwã; hɛ si-g |ne !nau ||kho !khwã: xoä, ĩ:.

And when we knew that my sister's child was willing to come to nurse the baby, then we buried the mother. [The child was about two months old. They waited for the niece to come before they buried the mother the day after her death].

Hɛ si-g |ne |ũ:ŋ, ĩ:; he whai |ne ||nau, há: ||ga:, á: si |ũ:ŋ sʔo ã:, whaitən |ne |ku sa:, whaitən |ne -saŋ |ũ:ŋ, ti e:, si siŋ !nau ||khóä ŋ |ha, ĩ:. Hɛ Sũ:-!kúïtən-ta: |ne kukúï, haŋ |k'e:ja ke ã:, '|ne ||k'oenja, tsʔa diŋ a:, whai |ne sa:, ti e:, whai k''auki -dóä |kwei-tən se sé hɛ? Ta: ||ke: á: a, ha |ku-g |ne á:, whai |ne sá: ti é: a, ã:'.

Then we went to sleep; and on that night as we lay sleeping the springbok troop came to lie at the place where we had buried my wife. Then Snore-white-lying said to me: "Look, why have the springbok come to a place to which they never used to come? But on this occasion they have come to this place."

Hɛ-g ŋ |ne kukú:ï, ŋ !k'e:, ŋ k''auki ≠enna; ta:, i-í -||kwaŋ |ku se ||k'oen, tsʔa a: whai |ne |kwẽ:ï k''a ã:, he whai |ne |kwẽ:ï |kwãŋ dí:, ĩ:.

And I said that I did not know; but now we should see why the springbok had behaved as they had been doing.

Hɛ Sũ:-!kúïtən-ta: kukúï, haŋ |k'e:, ŋ -||kwaŋ -dóä siŋ ||k'oen, ti e:, whai ɛ:, ŋ siŋ -!kʔaitən |ki he, ti e:, he siŋ |kwẽ:ï k''o, ĩ:. Hɛ tikən e:, si ||kwaŋ k''auki se ≠xóä, ĩ:; ta:, si |ku se ≠gou.

And Snore-white-lying said, now I could see why the springbok which I had shot had been behaving so strangely. However we should not go on talking about it, but should be silent.

❑

What the springbok and the gemsbok did ...

Notes

Title *What the springbok and the gemsbok did when they knew that Diä!kwain's wife would die*: 'This part relates to what the springbok did which D.H shot, but the whole troop came afterwards by the wife's grave and slept there' (4652 rev., note omitted).

1 *It was about the woman …*:

[2] *Díä!kwain*'s first wife who lived with him at Spreet near the Zak River.

4-6 *A springbok which I hit, breaking its leg …*:

[3] It was a springbok ewe.

[4] He hit it with a ball from a gun.

[5] Compare : *!kwa:* " broke," *¯kwa!* " leg," *!kwa* " bone."

10-11 *…it raised its head and looked at me …*: 'it urinated' (*hã ||khŭi*) (4655, text omitted).

27-28 *The springbok which I had recently shot …*:

!ka!kauru a: !kwai, ha kaŋ́ |ku a:,ŋ _dóä |kwẽ:ï k''okən ||k'oen whai, ã:, ha whai k''auki ka, whaija |ku:ka ke, ã:. Ta: whai _||kwaŋ siŋ ||nau, _maïï_maïïda, whaitən _||kwaŋ siŋ |ku:ka ke, o-g ŋ _!kaitən |ki whai o _maïï_maïïda. ||ke: a: a haŋ |ku-g |ne a:, ŋ k''auki |ne ≠enna ts'a a: di:, he whai |ne |kwẽ:ï k''o ã:.

[6] For one month I had noticed this, that the springbok did not fall down dead for me. For the springbok had previously always fallen down dead when I shot them with ball. During this period I did not know what was the matter with the springbok that they acted like this.

40 *Then I went to sleep …*:'[in the veldt]' (4662, text omitted).

40-41 *… caught sight of gemsbok …*: '[about 20 gemsbok, D.H. says]' (4661 rev., note omitted).

77 *… yet they ran for no reason …*: 'hol vorniet' (i.e. run for no reason – ed.) (4667 rev., note omitted).

81-82 *So I rose up and went up to Snore-white-lying …*:

D.H. gives me the following information about his *'maat'* (i.e. friend – ed.), a Bushman, whose Dutch name was 'Witbooy'. He died at the Breakwater, he went there before Diä!kwain. The latter thinks that he stole a sheep. He was older than D.H., but not an old man.

(4669 rev., note omitted)

[7] This friend of *Dä!kwain's* was a somewhat older Bushman. The name Snore-white-lying was given him by his mother, a medicine woman who used to cure people by " snoring " them, lying by them without her kaross. Medicine men usually " snored " people lying covered by their karosses, but this woman, whose skin was very light, did not. People blamed her for this, so she gave the name to her son.

91-92 … *I left the others to come on behind* …: '[because he thought that things seemed to be not right at home]' (4671 rev., note omitted).

Ssũ !kuï-ten tta's child Sănnă was there. Also ǁKu-ăŋ, a Bushman woman, whose Boer name was 'Dortje', said to be still alive. She brought up a child of D.H.'s, after the death of his wife.

(4671 rev., note omitted)

156-157 *They waited for the niece to come* … 'The niece lived near, and D.H. went to fetch her on the morning which followed his wife's death' (omitted from the end of this note on 4683 rev.).

Hunting after the death of a friend

Narrator: |Haŋ‡kass'o
Dictation dates: Sometime between 8 July and 12 August 1878
Notebook reference: L.VIII.14: 7281-7286
***Bantu Studies* reference:** Vol. 6 (1932), Part III: 248-249

After a friend has died, certain things need to be done before people may resume hunting activities.

❑

|xam-ka !kʔe ˍ||kwaŋ ka k''auki |ne |khi: wai, au hi |ke: ko:wa ˉ|kuka, au hĩ di !kuko: !k''aukən. (I |ku-g |ne k''waŋ ≠kuɛrrə.) Hi k''auki |khi:, hi |ku ˍtaŋ-ĩ wai. Waija k''auki ||xamki ˉ|kukən, wai ˉtsi-ĩ twi:, au i !k''auka !kuko; waija |ku k'waŋ, wai a: ˉ!kauwa; waiˉja |k''auki k''waŋ ha |ki twi:.

Bushmen are not wont to kill springbok, if their friend has died, while they are mourning (?) the other. (We seem to be bad shots). They do not kill, they miss the springbok. It also does not die, it bites the wound, when we are mourning someone; it seems to be like a live springbok; it does not seem to be wounded.

He tikən e:, !kʔe-ta |kagən ka kəˉïta hi !nwa:, au ˉsã, au hĩ ||ka ||khóä ˉsã; he hĩ |ne |ã !ho au i ||kã-|na:. Hi |ne ˍkuom i !gau, hi |ne ||kuarre||kuarre ˉ|e hĩ, au wai ||kẽĩ. He hí |ne ||nau wai ||kẽĩ |ne ˉ!kauŋ-a au i !gau, hĩ |ne ||ka ||kho ˉsã, hi |ne ||ka ˉ||kau ||kho i !gãu au ˉsã, au hĩ ta, waiˉja siŋ te:ŋte:ŋja hi:.

Therefore the women smoke arrows for us with buchu, putting the buchu to burn; then they make cuts on our shoulder (with a sharp arrowhead). They suck our blood, they spit it out into a springbok horn. When the horn is full of our blood, they put buchu to burn, they put our blood to burn on top of the buchu, for they want the springbok to lie down (to die) for us.

Hi |ne |xũŋ i |na:-ka tikəntikən e: a, i xu !koukən!koukən-ka tikəntikən e: a; kukúï hi |xũŋ |xũŋ tẽ au i |na-ka tikəntikən e: a; au hĩ ta wai siŋ ||xam !nõë-ĩ i; ta: waiˉja k''auki ĩ:ja; ta: waija |ku ||xĩ:||xĩ wai au í; í |ku ˍ!kaüŋ-ĩ wai, au wai k''auki !hĩŋ.

They shave these parts of our head, our temples lines here, (showing direct lines from the temples backwards); thus they shave paths on our heads, for they want the springbok to run straight to us, as they have not been doing, for they have been passing to the side ; we have been shooting at them when they were not near.

He tikən e:, hi ta |xũŋ akkən i |na:, au hĩ ˍtabba akkən i, au hĩ ta, wai se !nõë ã i.

Therefore they shave our heads nicely for they want the springbok to run straight up to us.

Notes

Title This excerpt was originally entitled 'Unsuccessful springbok hunting after the death of a companion. Means employed to make it more fortunate'.

3 *... while they are mourning [?] ...*: Literally, 'they do the other man death influence' (*hi di !kuko: !k"aukən*) (7281). The meaning of the word *!k"augən* ('death influence'), of which *!k"aukən* is probably a variant spelling, is discussed in Part I, Introduction.

5–6 *They do not kill, they miss the springbok*: 'We resemble a bad shot [i.e. a person who shoots badly]' (7280 rev.).

11–12 *Therefore the women smoke arrows for us with buchu ...*: This procedure seems to counteract the 'death influence' (*!k"augən*) that the dead person has over his living comrades (see Part I, Introduction).

27–29 *... for they want the springbok to run straight to us ...*: Dorothea Bleek cut the narrative short here. The omitted lines are

... while they feel that the springbok pass on our sides, while they wish the springboks to come straight up to us. Therefore they shave nicely our heads while they desire that the springboks may come straight up to us.

(7286, text omitted)

The slaying of a white springbok will cause all the other springbok to disappear

Narrator: |Haŋ‡kass'o
Source: '|Haŋ‡kass'o from his maternal grandfather Tss'atssĭ'
Dictation date: Between 31 October and 17 November 1878
Notebook reference: L.VIII.22: 7994
***Bantu Studies* reference:** Vol. 6 (1932), Part III: 249

There are three different colour variations in springbok: normal, in which the back is bright cinnamon-brown; black, in which it is dark chocolate brown; and white, in which the back and side stripe and legs are varying shades of brown-white (Kruger et. al. 1979; Skinner & Louw 1996). White is the scarcest of the variations – perhaps its rarity and the fact that this colour is associated with much !gi: *(supernatural power) made the white springbok a special creature.*

Wai a ⁻!kuïta, !kˀetən k''auki |khi: ha ta !kˀe |ku ||k'oen áu ha ; au !kˀetən tatti e:, wai |ké ta |ku ||kóäkən ||gwi ; wai k''auki |ne se sé au ti é:, wai ã ⁻!kuïta, ha |kukən téŋja hĩ, waita ⁻ku |ku ||kóäkə̃n ˍta⁻ï. He tikən e: !kˀe ta |ku ||k'oen au wai a ⁻!kuïta, há ki !hiŋja au hĩ.

People do not kill a white springbok, but merely look at it ; for they know that the springbok would disappear altogether ; they will not come to a place at which a white springbok has lain dead, but all the springbok go quite away. Therefore people merely look at a white springbok, even if it is near them.

Notes

3-4 *... the springbok would disappear altogether ...*: In a previously unpublished note dated 27 July 1878, |Haŋ‡kass'o explains that the converse is also true – where there is a white springbok, there are many springbok:

When the *//xuai* is thus, they [the Bushmen] say, "Oh Beast of Prey the *//xuai* throat is really that which comes here [i.e. meaning the coming of the springbok themselves]; and my ears are deaf on account of it." The people say that the springbok resembles the Milky Way when a white springbok is there. That is why people say *!ki-gusa* so

it [i.e. to the white springbok]. They also say that the number of the springbok resembles the stars. Also say *!guarra!guarra* **to it. Therefore they say "Oh Beast of Prey! I have espied a** *!guarra!guarra* **(i.e. a white springbok – ed.) at the place to which I ran [after a wounded springbok] at this place I went [and] espied a white springbok, a white springbok went forward." Because this other man, he, when he assents to the other man, he says "Oh Beast of Prey these things they are those which the springboks which come to us here, they have not that which I should possess arrows on account of it; as if my arrows were always numerous; they [the springbok] have not that which we go away as, with [?] arrows. For, we go away, as with the bow alone." [On account of the great number of the springbok, their arrows will be exhausted.]**

(L.VIII.14: 7242 rev.-7244 rev.)

PART IV

OMENS, WIND-MAKING, CLOUDS

From material collected by
Dr. W.H.I. BLEEK and Miss L.C. LLOYD between 1870 and 1880,
edited by D.F. Bleek

Photo: Jeremy Hollmann

'Therefore I want this child to go out and pick up asbos to make a shelter for the hut ...'
Asbos (*Psilocaulon* species) in the foreground and brosdoring (*Phaeoptilum spinosum*) in the background.
Kenhardt District, Northern Cape Province.

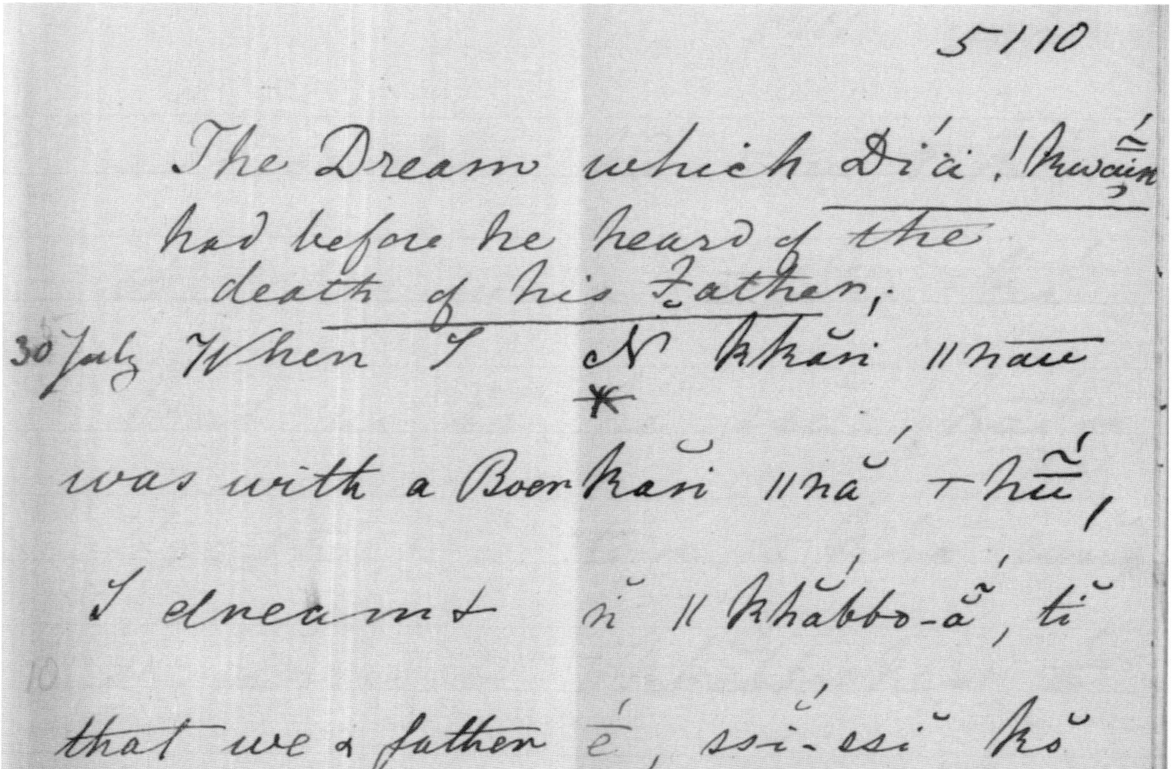

5110

The Dream which Dïä !kwāĩn had before he heard of the death of his Father.

30 July When I — N ǀǀkhăń ǀǀnau

was with a Boer — kăń ǀǀnă ⊤hū,

I dreamt — ń ǀǀkhăbbo-ā, ti

that we & father — ē, ssi-ssi kŏ

were cutting — tăta, ssi hā

up a sheep. The — ⊤ā !gei. ⊤hŭń

Boer came up — hā ⊤ně !kě-ssā

to us, as we — ssi-ssi, ō ssiten

were cutting it up, ⊤ā !gei. Hē ⊤hū

Manuscript page L.V.15: 5110, the first page of the narrative 'Omens of death'

PART IV
OMENS, WIND-MAKING, CLOUDS

The wind is one with the man.
– |Haŋ‡kass'o: 'Wind and stars'–

Much of what we see and hear about Bushman people's relationship with 'nature' is based on what outsiders have to say about it – some of it is insightful and well intentioned; much of it, however, is based upon ignorance and self-interest. The narratives in Part IV replace these misunderstandings with the beliefs of real |Xam people in their own words – and in all their complexity.

The three narrators – ||Kabbo (one narrative), Diä!kwain and |Haŋ‡kass'o (five narratives each) – reveal the subtle, often invisible, connections between people, and also between people and the weather, wind and animals, specifically springbok.

The first link or omen is /*khamma* (sneezing), an apparently telepathic response to the conversation of other people who are emotionally close but physically far away. Like *houŋ*, the 'presentiments' that Diä!kwain talks about in Part VII, and the dreams and conversations that ||Kabbo has with his absent wife and family (Lewis-Williams 2000: 131-132), sneezing connects people who are eager for news and contact with their families. Sneezing also affects the relationship between the hunter and his wounded prey, as well as other animals (see Parts I and III for sneezing in other contexts). The hunter's behaviour and that of the wounded animal are intimately linked – disrespectful and inappropriate behaviour such as sneezing, which startles the game, could sever that connection and thus set the animal free.

But the most sensitive and pervasive relationships are those between people, the weather (especially the wind), and the behaviour of springbok.

Relationships with the wind

A little over half of the Part IV narratives concern the wind and its intimate relationship with humans. Diä!kwain's account of his father's death brings several different beliefs into play about the relationship between people, their environment, and the unseen links between them. Since some of these elements feature in all the Part IV narratives, they require some explanation here.

Dreaming, like sneezing and presentiments, is a way of knowing things about people far away. In the dream, Diä!kwain's father winks at him (*dabbadabba*); then his father dies and the rain wind (*!khwa:-ka !khwe*) from the north comes up, bringing rain. Diä!kwain goes to look for his father and learns from his mother that his father has indeed died, and that a wind from the north had come up, driving a multitude of springbok in front of it. Diä!kwain hears the rain wind calling him (*ta-a*) and realises that it is his father's wind, one that always blew when his father had shot springbok.

The significance of this chain of events can only be guessed at unless one is familiar with two key concepts: the significance of winking, and the relationship between an individual and his or her wind. The meaning of winking is discussed first, before examining more closely what |Haŋ‡kass'o meant by saying that the 'wind is one with the man'.

Winking

The act of winking seems to activate *!gi:*. David Lewis-Williams (1996) points this out in an analysis of a narrative by ||Kabbo, 'A visit to the lion's house'. Here |Kaggen, who is hiding inside a bag, winks twice at a little lion through a hole. ||Kabbo explains that the little lion knew that by winking at him, |Kaggen was trying to bewitch (*tsweiten tsweiten*) him. The little lion therefore cries for his mother, who angrily pulls |Kaggen out of the bag. |Kaggen quickly 'gets feathers' (*/ki ‡gerri*, L.II.5: 539) and flies up into the sky. Lewis-Williams argues that this example of winking, as well as the winking of Diä!kwain's dying father and the subsequent rain, is related to the work of *!gi:tən*.

There is certainly more to winking than is first evident; in another instance of winking, this time in a narrative by |Haŋ‡kass'o (see Part IX, 'The young dog'), one of the Quagga's children winks out tears onto a cooking pot containing her mother's remains, thus causing the pot to split in two. Here the word used for wink is *tsˀunn*, but although this is a different word, the act of winking nonetheless still has similar magical results. It thus seems that the act of winking was another, currently little understood, mode of manipulating *!gi:*.

The wind

Whatever the links between winking and *!gi:* , the death of Diä!kwain's father causes the north wind to blow. The wind, in turn, brings the rain clouds and causes the springbok to behave unusually. They come to his father's hut and play there before moving off downwind. |Haŋ‡kass'o explains in 'Wind and stars' that individual hunters are each linked to a particular wind, and that a man's wind blew when he had killed an animal – the wind, in short, was 'one with the man'. |Haŋ‡kass'o's wind, like that of Diä!kwain's father, was from the north and was warm and pleasant. Others, like the sorceress |Xar̃raŋ|xar̃raŋ, had a 'cold' wind that blew up dust (see 'Notes on |Xar̃raŋ|xar̃raŋ').

But what was the significance of the links between a person, the wind, and the weather? To understand more about the |Xam beliefs linking people to different winds, we need to be aware of a similar set of beliefs held by the Ju|'hoansi, who live in the Kalahari today. Known as *n!ow* (Marshall 1957; 1999), or *n!ao* (Biesele 1993), the wind '… is the force … [that] interacts with and influences the weather most strongly' (Marshall 1999: 168). Good *n!ao* brings rain, and bad *n!ao* brings cold and dryness. Most significantly for understanding the death of Diä!kwain's father and the subsequent rain-bringing wind, Marshall reports that when a person dies, his *n!ao* influences the weather in the same way that it did when he was alive (Marshall 1957).

Like the |Xam, the Ju|'hoansi believe that the *n!ao* of a hunter interacts with that of his prey. A favourable interaction is called *ǂgani* in Ju|'hoansi, and means that good weather follows the killing of an animal; an unfavourable, *!/ghui* interaction brings cold and dry weather. Not all animals have *n!ao* – in the Kalahari, giraffe, eland, gemsbok, kudu, hartebeest and wildebeest are considered to have *n!ao*. Marshall's Ju|'hoan teachers said they did not know whether or not springbok had *n!ao* – these animals occurred too rarely there and thus were seldom killed. We know from Diä!kwain's testimony, however, that springbok were plentiful where he lived, and they possessed the |Xam equivalent of *n!ao*. Furthermore, we know from the statement that the springbok came to the dead man's hut to play, that Diä!kwain's father had something like *ǂgani n!ao*, the favourable *n!ao* that brought the north wind and rain.

The burning of animal horn to avoid a 'fight' of rain, mentioned by |Han‡kass'o in the Part IV narrative 'Clouds', is another example of the similarities between |Xam culture and the world-views of other Bushman groups. The Ju|'hoansi use the horns of game that they have shot in a similar way (Marshall 1957: 239).

The correspondences between Bushman societies separated in time and space are, as David Lewis-Williams has argued, 'too good not to be true' (Lewis-Williams 1998: 86). They suggest that beliefs about the weather, wind and animals are ancient and widespread.

Sneezing (1)

Narrator: ||Kabbo
Dictation date: 13 October 1871
Notebook reference: L.II. 6: 634-637
***Bantu Studies* reference:** Vol. 6 (1932), Part IV: 323-324

Sneezing was one of the ways that //Kabbo felt he could keep in touch with his relatives who were far away in /Xam-ka !aũ.

ŋ ≠i:, *ti e:, |haŋ≠kassˀo |na: !kwɔba-aŋ, ŋ ≠i:, ti e: |haŋ≠kassˀo |na: Swɔba-||ken.* ŋ ≠*i: ti e: !kwɔba-aŋ !kwi: ŋ |kẽ:; ŋ ≠i:, ti e: Swɔba-||ken !kwi: ŋ |kẽ:; ŋ ≠i:, ti e: ||gɔ́ɔ̃-ka-!kwi !kwi: ŋ |kẽ:, haŋ toto: Kerru au ŋ |kẽ. Haŋ toto: Kerru, " ||khabbowakən ||na tí dé?" Kerruwakən ≠kaka ha, " ó: ä kaŋ ||ná ha-ka gau-k''au." Ha xóäkən toto: ha, haŋ ≠kaka ha xóä, " |ha kaŋ ˍhã: ||na ha-ka gau-k''au."*

I think that *|haŋ≠kassˀo* has seen *!kwɔba-aŋ*, (*||khabbo's* wife), and has seen *Swɔba-||ken*. I think that *!kwɔba_aŋ* calls my name; I think that *Swɔba-||ken* calls my name; I think that *||gɔ́ɔ̃-ka-!kwi* (*||khabbo's* son) calls my name, he asks *Kerru* about me. He asks *Kerru*, " Where is *||khabbo?*" *Kerru* answers, " (Your) father is with his master." His (the son's) mother asks him, he says to his mother, " (Your) husband has stayed with his master."

ŋ *|kwẽ:- da, ŋ ≠i:, ŋ ≠ĩ: ti e: |haŋ≠kassˀo |na: Swɔba-||ken ; ŋ ≠i:, ti e: Swɔba-||ken !kwi: ŋ |kẽ, ta: ŋ |kamma.* ŋ ≠*i:, ti e: ŋ |ha !kwi: ŋ |kẽ, ta: ŋ |kamma.* ŋ ≠*i:, ti e: ŋ ʘpwɔŋ !kwi: ŋ ≠kẽ, ŋ ≠i:, ti e: m ʘpwaxai !kwi: ŋ |kẽ, ŋ |kwẽ:-da, ŋ ≠i:, ta ŋ |kamma.*

This is what I think, I believe that *|haŋ≠kassˀo* has seen *Swɔba-||ken;* I think that she has called my name, because I sneeze. I think that my wife calls my name, because I sneeze. I think that my son calls my name, I think that my daughter calls my name, I think so, because I sneeze.

ŋ ≠*i:, ti e: m ʘpwaxai |ha ≠kaka m ʘpwaxai, ti e:, " Óä-ka burke tan é: a, ha-ka gau-k''aukən a: á ha, ã:, ha-ka gau-k''aukən |ne ≠kaka ha, ti e:, ha si akke: hi."* ŋ *|kwẽ:-da, ŋ ≠i:. Ha xóäkən toto: ha, " Óä-ka burke xa |ke: á?" Ha*

I think that my daughter's husband says to my daughter: " These are father's trowsers which his master gave him telling him to give them to me." That is what I think. Her mother asks, " Are those father's trowsers?"

⊙pwaxai |haŋ ≠kaka ha, "|ha-ka burke taŋ e: a, he ha a akka hi." ŋ |kwẽ:-da, ŋ ≠i, ta ŋ |kamma.

Her daughter's husband says to her, "They are (your) husband's trowsers which he gave me." I think so, because I sneeze.

ŋ |haŋ toto: ha, "⊙pwai |hi-ta burke xa |ke: a?" Haŋ ≠kaka ha ⊙pwaitente, "|ha kaŋ óä ka, ŋ siŋ sá ≠kaka ha, ŋ si ||e ha, ta: ha ||óä:kən ||na ha-ka gau-k''au; ŋ |kwẽ:-da, ŋ ≠i:, haŋ óä ≠kaka ke, ti e: ha ⊙pwɔŋ _hã: si ¯||óä:kən ||na hí ŋ-ŋ, si si ||é ha." ŋ |kwẽ:-da, ŋ ≠i:, ta: ŋ |kamma.

My wife asks him, "Are those (your) father-in-law's trowsers?" She says to her daughter-in-law, "Husband seems to want me to come and talk to him, for he is staying with his master; I think he is telling me that his son has been staying with me, we will go to him." I think so, for I sneeze.

Notes

6-7 *I think that ||góö-ka-!kwi ||Khabbo's son* ... In the notebook, his other name, 'Smoke's man', is also given.

7-8 ... *he asks Kerru about me:* In the notebook, Kerru's other name, 'Sopɔi', is given.

Sneezing (2)

Narrator: |Haŋ‡kass'o
Dictation dates: Sometime between 21 September and 12 October 1878
Notebook reference: L.VIII.18: 7594 rev.-7595 rev.
***Bantu Studies* reference:** Vol. 6 (1932), Part IV: 324

When someone utters a person's name, that person soon gets to know about it, even if they are far away.

|khammaŋ¯aŋ é. Ha !kwi-|a a: ıŋ ¯!kwi: ha |kẽ, hé e:, ha |ne hamma, ĩ:. He ti hiŋ e:, |xam-ka ʔe ta ||nau, hĩ |khamma, hi ¯ku, '|khe||khe-wɛ:, ||kã kaŋ a: !xwa kwi ŋ |kẽ, ta: ŋ ˍdɔ́ä |kɯ |khamma na."

It is sneezing. That girl has spoken his name, therefore he sneezes. This is what Bushmen do when they sneeze, they say, "O beast-of-prey, our brother must have called my name, for I am sneezing here."

!kuko: a:, ha ¯ku, "I ||kɛnni |kwaŋ ˍdɔ́ä |kɯ |k'e: ŋ, ta:, ŋ ''auki ˍdɔ́ä |khamma, ta |khamaŋ a:, siŋ k''ó:ä, ha |kɯ-g |ne 'xuonni, ŋ k''auki |ne |khamma ıiŋ ha."

The other answers, "Our brothers seem to be speaking of me, for I do not sneeze, but the sneeze which threatens will not turn aside, I do not sneeze it away."

Notes

1-2 *That* **girl** *has spoken his name …*: Dorothea Bleek translated the term *!kwi-|a a:kaŋ* as 'girl', but the term in fact refers to a 'girl who is new', a girl experiencing her first menses. Lloyd and Bleek generally translated the term as 'new maiden'. A new maiden was potentially dangerous if she did not respect and take care of her family and the community (see Part V, Introduction).

Sneezing and how it affects the game

Narrator: Diä!kwain

Source: 'Note by D.H. who heard it from his parents, and experienced it in person also, he says'

Dictation date: 6 December 1875

Notebook references: L.V. 21: 5654 rev.-5655 rev.; 21: 5654-5659; 21: 5658 rev. and 5657 rev.

***Bantu Studies* reference:** Vol. 6 (1932), Part IV: 325-326

In the first two narratives, sneezing seems to keep people in touch with each other when they are out of sight and earshot. Here Diä!kwain talks about the rather different effect it has on game animals.

❑

|khammaŋ ϵ ||k''ó:äkən. Itən ||nau, i |khamma, itən |khamma hɔ ⊙pwai. Ta, mama-gu |ki ≠kaka si ã:, o !gauë-tukən-ka |khammaŋ, hϵ k''auki á: kən, o itən |khamma o !gauë-tukən.

Sneezing is unfortunate. When we sneeze we drive the game away. Our mothers used to tell us that sneezing in the early morning is not good, if we sneezed in the early morning.

Ta mama-gu ka ||nau, si: ko: úï, si-g |ne |khamma, mama-gu |k'e: si, ti e:, ts?a de |nõ a:, si ta |khamma ã:, o si: !ko: úï? Si ||khóä kaŋ ¯≠i:, !gauë-tukən-ka |khammaŋ k''au ϵ !kho:xa:.

If we sneezed when we woke up, our mothers used to ask us, why we were sneezing as we woke up? We seemed to think that sneezing at daybreak is not a bad omen.

O i |khamma o !gauë-tukən, itən |ne ˍkɔ̃aŋ |hiŋ, itən ˍtai !kauxu, itən k''auki ka, í se |kɒm !gɔ́ë, o i: |khamma o !gauë-tukən. !nãũŋ k''auki ta, !nãũ se ú !ɒhí u í, o !gauë:tukən-ka |khammaŋ. Ta, mama-gu |ki ≠kaka si ã:, ti e: si |khamma ||k''óäkən !kau a: si !hɒn !khe tiŋ ha.

If we sneezed at daybreak and got up and went to the hunting ground, we should not get a tortoise because of our sneezing early. The hare would not come out in front of us because of the sneezing. For our mothers said that by sneezing we cursed the ground over which we were hunting.

Mama-gukən ||xɒm ≠kaka si ã:, o |khammaŋ. O tʃweŋ ϵ: mama-gu ≠kaka si ã: hϵ, o ||k'e: a:, si |xã: ⊙pwai ã:, haŋ a: mama-gu

Our mothers also spoke to us about sneezing. Among the things they said was this, when we had shot game, then we must remember

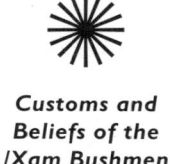

|k'e:ja si, ã:, ||khóä kaŋ ¯≠ĩ:, |khammaŋ ϵ ĩ hĩ-ka tsʔa. Ta:, i-g ||nau, i |khamma, o ⊙pwai-ja: twi:ja, ítən |khamma |kabbakən hɔ ⊙pwai, o í: |khamma |e:ja !kwi a: |xã: ⊙pwai ha !nu!nuntu.

⊙pwaitən ||nau, ha ¯to:á: i-ta |khamma|khamma, ⊙pwaitən ||xam |ku dí kúï k''waŋk''waŋ ha tu:i i, o itən |khamma, o !kwi a: |xã: ha, haŋ |ku a: ¯tó:ä i-ka |khamma |khamma ; haŋ |ku kaŋ su:kən ú:ï.

Hϵ tikən e:, mama-gu ka siŋ ||nau, si: ≠na:, si- |ne |khamma, mama-gu |k'e: si, si |ki |e: si |k'a: o si tu, si se ˍkwɔbbo: |khammaŋ, |khammaŋ k''auki se ˍtai ; si se ˍkwɔbbo ||gwi ||khóë ||khɔ |khammaŋ o si |nũnu, |khammaŋ k''auki se ˍtai

I ||nau, i tã:, ti e:, ti taŋ, i ˍsáŋ |khamma, itən !kan ||kau ||kho i |k'a: o i |nũnu, i se ˍkɔrokən ¯|ku:-kən |khammaŋ.

that sneezing effects our thing. For if we sneezed when game was wounded, we startled it by our sneezing, if we sneezed into the ears of the man who shot the game.

If he heard our sneezing, the game would also act as if it heard us sneezing, because the man who had shot it had heard us sneeze ; it would spring away.

Therefore our mothers said that if we forgot and were sneezing, we should put our finger (first of right hand) into our mouth and rub the sneeze away, not letting it come out ; we should rub till it vanished from our nostrils without coming out.

If we felt that we were going to sneeze, we should put our hand over our nostrils, we should destroy the sneeze. (The first finger of the right hand is put into the mouth and pulled out against the left cheek, making a noise ; the right hand is then put over the nose and mouth and rubbed about a little).

❑

Note

1 *Sneezing is unfortunate*: The word *//k"ó:äkən* is variously translated as 'to curse' or 'make unfortunate' (1956: 606).

Omens of death

Narrator: Diä!kwain
Source: 'Told by Diä!kwain'
Dictation dates: 30 July; 2, 3, and 4 August 1875
Notebook reference: L.V.15: 5110-5146
***Bantu Studies* reference:** Vol. 6 (1932), Part IV: 326-330

Potency, known by the /Xam as !gi:, |ko:ode, *or* ||ke:n, *is behind every remarkable occurrence in this moving story. It was originally entitled 'The dream which Diä!kwain had before he heard of the death of his father'.*

❑

N kaŋ ||nau kaŋ ||na |hũ:, ŋ ||khabbo-ã, ti e: si-si ko ta:ta, si _hã: |ã: !gei. |hũ:n _hã: |ne !ke. sa: si:si, o sitən |ã !gei, hє |hũ:-hã: |ne |k'e:, ti e:, ha ká ha se _!kaitən |kha si.

When I was with a farmer I dreamt that my father and I were cutting up a sheep. The farmer came up to us, as we were cutting it up, and said that he intended to beat us to death.

||khabbokən a: |kwẽ:ï-dakən ≠ka-ka ke, hє ŋ _hã: |k'e:ja |hũ:, ã:, |hũ: _am k''auki |kha si, ha ĩ: ¯a si, si _tauïta ha ã:, o ha k''auki |kha si.

The dream told me that I asked the farmer not to kill us at once, but just to let us work for him for it instead of killing us.

Ta-g ŋ k''auki ≠kauwa ha |kha ŋ ó:ä, ta: ŋ kaŋ se a: _tauïtən ŋ óä-ka _tauïtən e: ha siŋ |kha: !gei, ĩ:; ŋ se _tauïtən ||k'e hì, ŋ-ka _tauïtən, o-g ŋ õä-ka _tauïtən.

For I did not want him to kill my father, but I wanted to work off what my father owed for the sheep; I would work off what I owed and what my father owed.

Hє ||khabbo ≠kaka ke, ĩ:, ti e:, ŋ _hã: ||k'oen ŋ óä, o haŋ |ku:kən |ko:||ta:||gu||gu. Hє ŋ _hã: k''wa:, ĩ:, o káŋ kaŋ ||k'oen, ti e: ŋ ó:ä ɔ́ɔ̈ !kẽĩ ||ou haŋ |ku:kən. Hє-g ŋ _hã: kukúï, ŋ |k'e:ja |hũ: ã:, Tsʔa-de |nõ a:, |hũ: k''wãŋ tsʔa !kerri a: si |kha: ha, haŋ |ne |kwẽï |kwãŋ dí:, o ti e:, ha |ku siŋ se ¯a si ã: _tauïtən, o ha k''auki |kwẽï |kwẽ, ha dí? ŋ |ne ||khabbo-ĩ, ti e:, |hũ: _hã: _swaija si-si ko ta:ta, o sitən

And the dream told me that I saw my father lying dead in the sun's heat. And I cried when I saw that my father had really died. And I spoke, I asked the farmer, Did he think that it was such a big thing which we had killed that he had acted in this manner, when he could have let us work it out and not have acted as he did? I dreamt that the farmer drove us before him, and we carried the sheep's

-hã: -/kammɛŋja !gei-ta eŋ, o /hũ:ŋ -hã: -swai /ki !kúïtən si o /hũ:-ka //neiŋ.

body, while the farmer drove us back to his house.

Hɛ-g ŋ //nau, !gauëtən ka ha !khwai, ŋ -kɔãŋ /hiŋ, ŋ ≠kaka ŋ /ha ã:, ti e: //khabbo ≠kaka ke, ti e: si -hã: /ã: /hũ:-ka !gei. ŋ //k'oen ta:ta, o tatakən /ku:kən !khai !khe. ŋ /k'e:ja ha ã:, ti e:, ha /kho: kaŋ ≠ĩ:, si k''au ka si se tú kum, o //khabbo /kwẽï kúïtən ≠kaka ke?

Then when day broke I arose and told my wife that a dream had told me we were cutting up a farmer's sheep. I saw father standing dead there. I asked her, did she not think that we should hear news of that which the dream had told me?

Hɛ !khwe !kuŋ-sin, ĩ:; hɛ-g ŋ /k'e:ja ha ã:, tí e:, ha /nõ k''au //k'oen, ti e: -!gwa:xu /kwẽï u, ĩ:, tikən //khóä !khwa: se kãũ, o //khabbokən ka ha ≠kaka ke ã:, ⁻!kˀãũ-wãŋ !ahitiŋ -!gwa:xu. Hɛ tikən e:, ŋ kaŋ se -tai, ŋ se //k'e//k'e:ja /hũ: ã: //xɔro, ŋ se //k'oen, ti e:, tsˀa-de /nõ a:, ti /kwẽï //khauwi ã:, o káŋ kaŋ //khabbo-ã ta:ta, ti e: /hũ: -hã: /kha: si. //khabbokən /ku ≠kakən ku:ï !xwãŋ-a ka:, !kwi a: ≠kaka ke. Hɛ tikən e:, í kíɛ̈: se: !kúïtən, i se //a tum-ã //na//na //neiŋ, i se //k'oen, ti e:, í /nõ se tu: kum.

Then the wind was in the north, and I asked her if she did not see how the sky looked, it seemed as if rain would fall, as the dream had shown me, covering the sky. Therefore I would go and talk to the farmer about an ox, to find out what was happening, what had made me dream of father, of the farmer killing us. The dream spoke just as if a person had told me. Therefore we will go home, we will go and listen at the house and see if we do not hear news.

***Hɛ ta:ta tsaxáu -dabba-dabba /ku //nau, ŋ́ ã: k''auki -tai,** hiŋ /ku dí kúï k''wãŋ !khwa: se !kẽï //ou, ha kãũ, !khwa: //ki e: k''auki ≠en, hiŋ /ku //khóë//khóë; hɛ-g ŋ /k'e:ja ŋ /ha, ĩ:. ŋ kukúï, ŋ /k'e:ja ha ã:, " Akən k''au //k'oen, o ŋ siŋ ≠kaka ha, ti e:, ŋ //khabbo:ĩ ta:ta, akən k''au //k'oen, ti e:, !kwi tsaxáu -dabba-dabba -//kwaŋ e: ã. !kwi a: //kho: /ku:ka, ha tsaxau -dabba--dabbakən -//kwaŋ e: ã.*

Then father's eye blinked at me before I had started, it acted as if rain were going to fall, rain water in quantities would come down; so I had told my wife. I spoke saying to her, " You did not look when I told you that I had been dreaming of father, you did not see that someone's eye was blinking there. It was the eye blinking of a person who seemed to be dying.

" Hɛ tikən e:, a -//kwaŋ ka, a se -//k'oen, o !khwa: //ki e: ã, hɛ /kwẽ:ï /kwãŋ //kho:e. Ta:, a //kho: kaŋ ≠ĩ:, ŋ-ka //khabbo k''au ≠ka:, ŋ ka /nĩ tsˀa a:, //khabbo-ã siŋ ≠kaka

" Because of that you are going to see rain water which will pour down like this. For you seem to think that my dream was not clear, that I should see the thing which

ká ha, ŋ́ ka |nĩ ha. Hɛ tikən e:, a -||kwaŋ ka, a se ||k'oen, o a k''auki !hum ŋ, o-g ŋ ≠kaka ha ||khabbo, ti e:, ||khabbo |kwẽ:ï-da: ka:, ĩ:.''

the dream told me I should see. Now you will see, although you would not believe me, when I told you what the dream showed me.''

Sitən |ne !kúïtən ||neiŋ a: si ||na |hũ: ã:, hɛ si ||nei||nei o ||ga||ga e !ku: ; hɛ mama ||nau, o ||ga: ko:, mamaŋ sá: si, ĩ:. Hɛ-g ŋ tu:tu: mama o ti e:, tsˀa-de |nõ a: !khwa:-ka -|kwa:gən |ne |kwẽï u, ã:, hɛ !khwa:- ka -|kwa:gən ĩ-||ɑhá||ɑhá: !kuŋ-tiŋ, hɛ !khwa:-ka -|kwa:gən ||kho, ti e:, !khwa:-ka -|kwa:gən ka kwẽï u, ĩ:, o ta:ta ≠kaka:, ti e:, !khwa: se kãũ.

We returned home to where we lived with the farmer, and we stayed there two nights ; and on the second night mother came to us there. Then I asked her what was happening to the rain clouds that were coming up in front there, the clouds were acting as they used to do when father said that it was going to rain.

Hɛ tikən e:, ŋ -||ki, ĩ:, ti e:, tsˀa-de |nõ a:, !khwa:-ka -|kwa:gən |ne |kwẽï u ã:. !khwetən |ne tʃu kúï táŋ-a ka:, ti e:, !khwe ta |kwẽï tã, ĩ:, o-g ŋ -dóä ||khabbo-ã ta:ta, ti e: |hũ: -hã: |kha: si, o si -hã: |ã: |hũ-ka !gei, |hũ:ŋ |ne |khi: si o !gei ta k''wa:. ||khabbokən a: |kwẽï-dakən ≠kaka ke.

Therefore I wondered what was going to happen, when the rain clouds acted like this. The wind blew as if it were begging from me, just as the wind had done, when I was dreaming of father, that the farmer killed us when we cut up this sheep, when the sheep bleated. The dream had told me this.

Hɛ mama |ne kukúï, haŋ ≠kaka ke, ŋ -ɔ̃ɔ̈ sˀɔ́ |ne ≠nwãĩ ||khabbo, ŋ |ne -ɔ̃ɔ̈ sˀɔ́ kaŋ ≠ĩ:, ŋ kaŋ se ||xã:, ŋ |nĩ ta:ta, ta: ||khabbo -||kwaŋ a: ≠kaka ke, ti e:, ŋ k''auki kaŋ se |nĩ ta:ta. Ta:, hɛ ti hɛ -||kwaŋ e:, ŋ |nĩ: mama, ĩ:, o mamaŋ siŋ ka, ha se sá ≠kaka si-si ã:, ti e:, tata -||kwaŋ |ku:kən xu:wa si. Hɛ tikən -||kwaŋ, e: si ||k'oen, ti e:, !khwa: |khu k''auki |hiŋ tóä -!gwa:xu, hɛ !khwa: |khu -||kwaŋ |ku ||na -!gwa:xu.

And mother said to me, I seemed to have disbelieved the dream and to have thought I should see father again, though the dream had told me that I should not see him again. But now I saw her and she had come to tell us that father had died leaving us. That was why we saw that the rain's hair (the clouds) did not come out of the sky, but stayed in the sky.

Hɛ-g ŋ |ne tu-tu: mama, ĩ:, o ti e:, tsˀa-de |nõ a: da: ta:ta. Hɛ mamaŋ |ne ≠kaka ke, ti e:, ha ||k'o:ë é:, há ka |kwẽïtən ≠kaka si

Then I asked mother what had happened to father. And mother told me that it was because of his back, about which he had long

ã hɛ, hɛ -||kwaŋ ɛ́:, ha |ku:kən ta: hɛ.

been complaining to us, that he had died.

Hɛ mama kukúïtən |k'e:ja ke, ŋ ||kho: kaŋ ≠ĩ:, whai k''au |ku ||nau, tata |ĩ||⁻!kˀõ:ä, whaïïtən k''auki k''wãŋ whai -||kwaŋ ||k'oen si, o ||neiŋ; ta: whai |ku !hau, !gwe ta: ||neiŋ, whaïïtən k''auki k''wãŋ hɛ !hammĩ. Mamaŋ k''auki ≠enna, ti e:, whai |hiŋ hɛ, hɛ whai k''auki tymse |k'waija; whaïïtən |ku-g ||nau, o whai sa:, whaïïtən |ku tauko ||gum, o whai gauwa ||neiŋ a:, ta:ta |ku:kən ta: ha.

And mother said to me, I seemed to think the springbok had not known when father's heart fell, and had not acted as if they saw us at the hut; but the springbok just afterwards had passed opposite the hut as if they were not afraid. She did not know where they came from, and they were not a few; the springbok were playing as they came along approaching the hut where father lay dead.

"Whaïïtən k''wãŋ whai ||kóä:kən !kwã: ||a:, o !khwe tuko a: tʃu !kuŋ-sˀo:. Há !khwetən a:, whai !ke ||khóä ha. Há ó:ä-ka !khwe tuko -||kwaŋ é, hɛ a -||kwaŋ |ku ||ï:, akən tã:, ti e: !khwe |kwẽï tä, ĩ:. A -||kwaŋ |ku ≠enna, ti e:, óä -||kwaŋ xarra ka siŋ ||nau, ha: |xã: ʘpwai, há-ka !khwejã: |kwẽï tã."

"The springbok appeared to be moving away and the wind really blew following them. They were running before the wind. It was really father's wind, and you can feel yourself how it is blowing. You know that whenever father used to shoot game, his wind blew like that."

Hɛ-g ŋ |ne |k'e:ja mama ã:, ĩ:, ti e:, ŋ -||kwaŋ tã: !khwe, ti e:, !khwe |kwẽï tã, ĩ:. Ŋ -||kwaŋ |ku ≠enna, o-g ŋ tã: !khwe, o !khwa: ||ki e: siŋ tattəntattən ||kóë siŋ !kˀãũ. Hiŋ -||kwaŋ e:, ŋ siŋ ||nau, o káŋ kaŋ ||k'oen hɛ, ŋ |ku |ne ||kóä:kən |kwẽï |kwãŋ tã: !khwe, o káŋ kaŋ ||k'oen.

Then I told mother, that I had felt the wind, that it was blowing like that. I had understood, when I felt the wind, when the rain water had fallen on the ground. It was while I was seeing things that I had really felt the wind, as I looked.

Omens of death

Ŋ |ne |k'e:ja ŋ |ha ã:, ŋ |ne kukúï, ŋ |k'e:ja ha ã:, ha ||kho: kaŋ ≠ï:, ŋ k''au tã: ŋ ||kaië; hɛ tsˀi:ï:, o !khwe a: siŋ -dóä tʃu !kˀũ:ï, ŋ |ne -dóä tã: ti e:, ŋ ||kaië |ne -dóä tsˀi:ï:. Haŋ ||kho: kaŋ ≠ĩ:, ŋ k''au ka ||nau, ŋ-ka !kwija -óö é: |ku:ka, ŋ |kwẽï |kwẽ, ŋ ||kaië taŋ-taŋ, o ŋ́-ka !kwija -óä é.

I had spoken to my wife about it and asked her whether she thought I was not feeling my inside; it was biting (aching), as the wind was blowing past, I felt that my inside was biting. She seemed to think that I did not feel when one of my people was dying, my inside always ached when it was one of my people.

Notes

3-6 *The farmer came up to us, as we were cutting it up, and said that he intended to beat us to death*: There is an autobiographical element here – Diä!kwain was imprisoned for killing a white farmer who had accused Diä!kwain of theft and threatened Diä!kwain's family. It is rumoured that Diä!kwain, who disappeared without trace after returning home, was murdered by friends of the dead farmer (Deacon 1986).

12-14 *… I wanted to* **work off** *what my father owed for the sheep*: The phrase in the original translation is 'work out' (5112), not 'work off' as appears in *Bantu Studies*. The same mistake is made in the next sentence 'I would work off …'

38 *Then the wind was in the north …*: This is the direction from which rain comes in |Xam-ka !aũ (see Part V, The rain).

47-49 *The dream spoke just as if a person had told me*: Dreams and dreaming were valued by the |Xam (see Part VI, 'Where a rain-maker dreams rain to fall'). In Diä!kwain's dream, several signs alert him to his father's death.

52 *Then father's eye* **blinked** *at me …*: The word translated as 'blinked' (*dabbadabba*) is associated with dying, dreaming rain, and bewitchment – and therefore with sorcery (see Part IV, Introduction).

86-88 *The wind blew as if it were begging from me*: The wind here was that of Diä!kwain's father – he explains this in the final paragraph of this narrative.

102-104 *… the rain's hair… stayed in the sky*: 'And mother asked me, did I not see that the dream I had dreamed had spoken the truth? We now saw what had made me dream it. So the dream I had told her about had not deceived me.' (5134-5136, text omitted)

111-115 *I seemed to think the springbok had not known when father's heart fell, and had not acted as if they saw us at the hut …*: Diä!kwain describes how springbok and gemsbok can sense a person's death by scent (see Part III, 'What the springbok and the gemsbok did …').

129-131 *… whenever father used to shoot game, his wind blew like that*: The idea of a person 'owning' a wind is discussed in the Introduction.

142-143 *… my inside, it was biting*: Diä!kwain refers to 'biting' (*ts*ˀ *i:ï*) sensations and an aching (*taŋtaŋ*) inside his body because his father's wind is blowing away.

The wind an omen

Narrator: Diä!kwain
Translation dates: 8 and 9 January 1876
Notebook reference: L.V. 23: 5841-5845 and 23: 5847-5857
***Bantu Studies* reference:** Vol. 6 (1932), Part IV: 330-332

Strong wind summons up 'things which walk about'. The notebook title of this narrative is 'The crying of the wind is considered an omen of evil'.

❑

Mama-gu ka //nau, o hɛ: tóä !khwcja: k''wa:, hɛ kukú, hɛ /k'e:, "‾Aũwi !khwe ≠gou, ta, u //khóä kaŋ ‾≠i:, !kẽï a !khwe /kwẽï-da ã:, ta !khwe k''wa: //ke//ke: ti e:, !kˀe ˍsaŋ /kwẽï-da, hɛ k''wa:, ĩ:, o !kukɔ:, o ha: /ku:ka. Ta: !khwe k''wa: hi, i se ‾≠en, ti e:, i /ke: kɔ: ká ha se /ku:kən. Hɛ tikən e:, !khwe k''wa:, ĩ:, o haŋ ta: //ka ti e:, i ˍsaŋ k''wa:."

When our mothers used to hear the wind cry, they used to say, "Let the wind be silent, for you seem to think good will come of it, but the wind cries as the people are going to cry when someone dies. For the wind cries for us, that we may know that another friend is dying. Therefore the wind cries, as it feels that we shall cry."

Hɛ tikɛn e:, mama-gu ka siŋ //nau, hɛ: tóä !khwe, hɛ /kɯ ku, "/ki !haŋ u !khwe, !khwe k''auki siŋ /kwẽï-da ; ta:, i //neiŋ kíë: se /ki/ki, ti e: k''auki twai-ĩ:. Ta: hɛ ti hɛ e:, !khwe /kwẽï-da, ĩ:, o haŋ dá hi ã:, ti !kɔ!kõïŋ se //na-//na í-ka //neiŋ. Ta: !khwe k''wa:, o ha /kwẽï-da."

Therefore when our mothers used to hear the wind, they said, "Make the wind still, (i.e. move the mat when the wind is blowing there), that it may not do this ; for our home will suffer misfortune. For the wind acts like this when it is bringing evil to our home. The wind cries as it does so."

Mama-gukən /k'e:ja ke, ti e:, !khwe //nau, ha !xwãŋ ha k''wa:, haŋ k''wa: /ki //kkóë hɔ ha-ka k''wak''wa: o !khwe. T∫weŋ e: ˍtaiˍtai xa ta:, hiŋ tú:i !khwe, o !khwetən !kẽä //na i //neiŋ. Hɛ //khetən//khetən k''wãŋ hɛ ≠en, ti e:, i //na hɛ, o hiŋ ta: //ka ti e:, hɛ tu:ï !khwetən ‾!kwi /ki hɛ.

Our mothers told us that when the wind sounds as if it cries, it is sending its crying on the wind. Things which walk about hear the wind as it sweeps past our hut. Then the beasts-of-prey seem to know where we are, for they hear the wind calling to them.

Ta: mama-gu /ki ≠kaka ke, ti e:, //khe//khe: //nau, ha ˍtai-ã-tiŋ,

For our mothers used to tell me, that when a beast-of-prey walks

haŋ k''auki ||au-se _tai-ã-tiŋ o !khwe, ta ha _tai-ã-tiŋ hĩ !khwe. ||k''e: a: !khwe tsu ||wẽï ã:, haŋ a: ||khe||khe: _tai-ã-tiŋ ã:, o haŋ ka, i k''auki siŋ tu:ï tʃweŋ e: _tai-ã-tiŋ, ||khe||khe: se sá |kãä i, o !khwe ||kaië, o !khweja: tsu ||wẽï, i siŋ !xe: ta: !khwe ã:, o i: tã:, ti e:, !khwe k''auki ta ||kaitən. Haŋ _tai |ki sa: o tʃweŋ e: !xwãŋ hϵ k''wa:, hϵ tʃweŋjaŋ e: !kwi: ha, hiŋ ≠kaka ||khe||khe: ã:, ti e: i ||na ti ϵ. Hϵ ||khe||khe: |kɯ |kɒm ||a: i, ĩ:, haŋ ||aŋ |khi: i, o !khwe a: ≠kaka ha ˉã:, ti e: i ||na hϵ.

Hϵ tikən e:, mama-gu ka siŋ ||nau, hϵ tú:ï, ti e:, !khwe k''auki tymse tʃúï, hϵ kukú, hϵ |k'e:, " U kaŋ ˉ≠ĩ:, _||khã: k''au ka ||nau, ||k'e: a:, ha ká ha se sa, |kãä |hiŋ i, o ʘpwoin, !khwetən k''auki tymse tʃúï, o haŋ ka, ha se !ke se í, i í: !hymmĩ ta: o !khwe, ha se |kãä |hiŋ i o ||neiŋ, ha se tsi: |kha i."

Mama-gukən ≠kaka ke ti e:, !khwe ||nau, ≠k'e: a: _||khã: ká ha se sé i ã:, !khwetən k''auki tymse tʃúï, o haŋ ka !khwiŋ k''auki se tú ha, o ha: gauwa i. Hϵ tikən e:, mama-gu ka siŋ ||nau, o hϵ: tã:, ti e:, !khwe k''auki tymse tʃúï, hϵ kukú, hϵ ≠kaka si ã:, "||k'o:kən sauwi hi ã:, i se |ki tẽ:n |i _|k'wãĩ. Ta:, ú |kɯ e: tã:, ti e:, !khwe |kwẽ:ĩ tã, ĩ:. Tã:, !kˀe !ke!kerritən ka síŋ ≠kaka si ã:, ti e:, _||khã: ||nau, ||k'e: a:, ha ka ha se !kúïtən, i-ka ||neiŋ ã:, haŋ dá: hi !khwe, o haŋ ka, i k''auki se ≠enna ||k'e: a:, ha sa: i ã:."

about, it does not walk against the wind, but with the wind. At the time when the wind blows strongly, then the beast-of-prey walks about, for it does not want us to hear anything moving, so that it may seize us while the wind is blowing hard, so that we are lying in shelter because the wind is not light. It comes up when things sound as if they were crying, calling to it, telling it that we are here. Then the beast-of-prey goes towards us, to kill us, because the wind has told it where we are.

Therefore when our mothers heard the wind blowing strongly, they said, " You do not seem to know that when a lion is coming to us to snatch us from our sleep, the wind blows strongly, because it (the lion) is approaching us as we lie in fear of the wind, to snatch us from our hut and bite us to death."

Our mothers told me that at the time when the lion means to come to us, the wind blows strongly, for the lion does not want the dogs to hear it as it approaches us. So when they heard the wind blowing strongly, they said to us: " Bring firewood for us, that we may lie in the smoke of the fire. For you feel how the wind is blowing. For the old folk used to tell us that when a lion wants to come to our hut, it makes the wind blow, because it does not want us to know the time when it comes to us."

Part IV
Omens,
Wind-making,
Clouds

The wind an omen

Note

16-17 ... *for our home will suffer misfortune*: The original translation in the notebook, 'our home shall get a thing which is not good' (5844), is perhaps better because Diä!kwain means that a 'thing' (i.e. an evil thing) will enter their house.

Wind-making (1)

Narrator: Diä!kwain
Notebook reference: L.V.23: 5842 rev.-5846 rev.
***Bantu Studies* reference:** Vol. 6 (1932), Part IV: 332-333

Here is an old woman who, like the sorceress !Kwara-aŋ in Part VII, feels that the people ||am *or underrate her.*

❑

|nu-tara a:, !kˀe ¯óä !kwi: ha |kẽ o ˍ≠náä-aŋ, ha |kẽ kɔ ɛ |xar̃r̃aŋ-|xar̃r̃aŋ, ha kaŋ ka siŋ ||nau, !kˀeja: ≠kwãĩja ha, ha-g |ne ˍk''wãĩn !kˀe. Ha-g|ne ≠kaka !kˀe ã:, ti e:, |kˀe ||khóä káŋ ¯≠ĩ, !khwe k''au a: ka ha se tsú, ha se xarra ti tsutsú, |ki |e: !kˀãũ o !kˀe tsaxáitən. Ta: !kˀe tuko ||kwaŋ ˍdóä |kɯ ta: ||ka ti e:, hɛ ||kwaŋ ˍdóä |kɯ |u: ha. Hɛ tikən e: hɛ ka |kɯ ˍ≠kwãĩ |ki ha, ĩ:.

An old woman whom people called ¯≠*náä-aŋ*, her other name being |*xar̃r̃aŋ|xar̃r̃aŋ*, used to get angry with people if they scolded her. She said to the people that they seemed to think the wind was not going to blow as it does when it blows dust into people's eyes. But now they had felt that they disliked her, that was why they had kept scolding her.

!khwe-g ||nau, o ha: |kwẽĩ kú, ha |k'e:, !khwe |kɯ ku !khu !k'ũ, !khwe |kɯ tsú |ki |hiŋ, ti e:, i k''auki |ki ti e:, i se !gõã-ã, ĩ:. Ta: i |km ||nau, í ka, i ˍhã: !gõã¯ĩ:, !khwetən |kɯ tsutsú |ki |e: !káuökən o i tsaxáitən, i k''auki |ki ti e:, i se ||k'oen, ĩ:, o ha ˍ!k''wãĩnja í. !khweja: |kɯ tsutsú hóä !kˀe ã: ˍ||ka: e: hɛ !xwarra !xwarra tã: hɛ, !khweja |kɯ ˍ!gabbetən-ã !kˀe ã: hɛ, o ha: ˍ!k''wainja !kˀe.

The wind arose as she spoke, it blew so that we were not able to see the place, and look around. For when we wanted to look about us, the wind blew stones into our eyes, so that we could not see, because she was angry with us. The wind blew away the people's mats on which they had been lying, the wind threw them at the people, because she was angry with them.

Hɛ tikən e:, !kˀe ta siŋ ||nau, hɛ: túï, ti e:, !kˀeja !xwãŋ, !kˀeja ˍ≠kwãĩ ha, !kˀe |kɯ ɔróko kukú, hɛ |k'e:, " U ¯kaŋ k''auki se ||xã:, u ˍ≠kwãĩ |nu-tara |ke: ã. Ta i ˍsaŋ ||xã:, i tẽ:ntẽ:n ¯≠ka:, o !khweja ˍgabbetən-ã: hi ¯ã: tʃweŋ, o há: ˍ!k''wãĩnja ĩ."

Therefore whenever people heard that someone seemed to be scolding her, they quickly said, "You must not scold the old woman again. For we shall be laid bare again while the wind throws things at us, if she is angry with us."

Hɛ tikən e:, ŋ !kõ:ïŋ !xugəndi ka siŋ //nau, o ha: tã:, ti e:, tsʔu-tau k''auki tymse //kɛ:n-ĩ: ha, ha kukú, "/xarr̃aŋ/xarr̃aŋ wɛ́:, !kan bo:kən !hóä ki, a-ka !nuiŋ //xã:xu, !khwe _am ¯tsu:wa ke, tsu-tau se _taija ke. Ta:, tí taŋ, ŋ k''auki se ⊙pwoin, o tsu-tauwa //ke:n-ã /ki ŋ. Ta: tsu-tau /ku sũ:, hɛ tsu-tau k''auki tymse /k'waija. Ta: tsu-tau /ku //xau //ke:ŋ-ĩ: ŋ tsa-xáitən, hɛ tí /ku taŋ, !gauë _saŋ /ku !khwai, o tsu-tauwa: //ke:n-ã /ki ŋ."

That is why my grandfather, *!xugəndi* used to say when he felt mosquitoes biting him badly, "O */xarr̃aŋ/xarr̃aŋ*, pull the side of your kaross open for me, so that the wind may just blow on me and the mosquitoes leave me. For it seems as if I should not sleep, for the mosquitoes are biting me. For the mosquitoes sting, and they are many. The mosquitoes are also biting my eyes, and it looks as if dawn will break while they are biting me."

!khwe //nau, ŋ !kõ:ïŋjã: /kwẽï ku, ha /k'e:, tíja /ku k''wãŋ ha: túï ŋ !kõ:ïŋ, !khwe /ku ¯o: se tsu /ki _tai tsu-tau.

When my grandfather spoke thus, it seemed as if the wind had heard him, for the wind blew the mosquitoes away.

Notes on |Xar̃r̃aŋ -|xar̃r̃aŋ

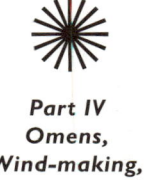

Narrator: Diä!kwain
Dictation dates: 10, 11 and 12 January 1876
Notebook reference: L.V.23: 5858-5861, 23: 5860 rev.–5861 rev. and 23: 5862–5371
***Bantu Studies* reference:** Vol. 6 (1932), Part IV: 333-335

More about what seems to be something of a |Xam stereotype – the old sorceress, powerful, fearsome and bad-tempered (see Part VII, 'The sorceress !Kwara-aŋ').

❑

|nu-tara |xar̃r̃aŋ|xar̃r̃aŋ |na: kaŋ k''auki óä _|kwãĩja, i e: !kʔe kuitən, i |na: ; ta: ha |na: ʘpwa |kɯ ¯oä taurutauru, hiŋ _|kwãĩja tó:ï. Ha ||kaurukən _|kwãĩja tó:ï, ha |na:-ka |kukakən k''auki _|kwãĩja i-i kuitəŋ |na: |ku, ta: ha |na:-ka |kukən ||kho ti e:, tó:ï |na:-ka |kukən ka |kwẽĩ u, ĩ:.

The head of the old woman, *|xar̃r̃aŋ-|xar̃r̃aŋ* was not like the heads of us others; for her little head was steep (?), it resembled an ostrich. The back of her head was like an ostrich, her head's hair was not like that of us others, it was like an ostrich's head's feathers.

Haŋ ka siŋ ||nau, ha: _tai ||a:, ha: _tai kúï k''wãŋ ti e:, tóï ka |kwẽĩ k''o, ha _tai, ĩ:. Ha k''auki _tai ||kabba, ta: ha |kɯ _≠kanxa-ko_tai, o ha _tai ||a. Haŋ k''auki _tai _||kabba, ta: ha ka síŋ |kɯ k''wãŋ, há ka ha !kuxe !kʔũ, o ha-ka _tai |kɯ e: |kwẽĩ ú. Hɛ tí ||khóä, ha ká ha !kuxe !kʔũ, o ha-ka _tai |kɯ e: |kwẽĩ ú.

She used when she went about to walk as an ostrich does. She did not walk quietly, but danced (?) along as she walked. She did not walk quietly, but she seemed as if she were running away, when her walk was like this. It seemed as if she wanted to run away, when her walk was like this.

ŋ siŋ |ha:ŋ-sʔo |nu-tara |xar̃r̃aŋ-|xar̃r̃aŋ ʘpwɔŋ ʘpwaxaitən e:, ŋ siŋ |ha:ŋ:sʔo hɛ. Hɛ tikən e:, ha ʘpwɔŋ a:, ŋ siŋ dá ŋ ʘpwai-|hĩ ã:. Ha |kauru siŋ ||xam _!kwãĩja ha xoä |xar̃r̃aŋ|xar̃r̃aŋ, ha ||kauru !khwitən k''auki ||na. Ta:, ha ||kauru |kɯ ≠khi≠kerre, ha ||kauru-ka ti e:, !kʔe: kaŋ |k'e: !nãũ ||neiŋ, ĩ:, hiŋ k''auki ó:ä ||na. Ta: ha ||kauru ka siŋ |kɯ ||kho, i xu, hɛ |kɯ ≠khi≠kherri.

I married the daughter of the son of the old woman, *|xar̃r̃aŋ-|xar̃r̃aŋ*. Therefore it was her son of whom I made my father-in-law. The back of his head was like his mother's, the bulge at the back of his head was not there. For the back of his head was flat, the part that people call the hare's house was not there. For the back of his head was flat like our foreheads.

Hɛ tikən e:, hă o:ä //ke//ke:ja ha xoä, /xar̃r̃aŋ/xar̃r̃aŋ. Há-ka didi:-tən /ku k''wãŋ ha xoä. Hɛ tikən e:, !kˀe ta siŋ //nau, hɛ: //k'òenjã ti e:, ha:ka didí: k''auki a:kən, !kˀeja: k''auki /k'e: ha. Ta:, !kˀe /ku //k'oen-ã:, hɛ k''auki ≠kaka.

In this way he resembled his mother, /xarraŋ/xar̃r̃aŋ. His doings were like hers. Therefore when people saw that his actions were not good, yet they did not scold him. For they merely looked at him, they said nothing.

Ha siŋ //na !gerri, a: sí siŋ //na ha. ŋ -//kwaŋ ¯oä /na: ha, hɛ tikən e:, ŋ -//kwaŋ ≠enna, ti e:, ha ¯oä /kwẽï k''okən dí:, ĩ:. Hɛ tikən e:, ŋ -//kwaŋ ≠enna há-ka didi:. //k'e: a:, ŋ !naunko e !khwã: ã:, ha kaŋ a:, ha ¯/ku-ka ã:. ŋ kaŋ siŋ /km -/ka:gən dí: k''au-dɔro, /nu-tarakən /ku:kən -tai.

She lived at the "*Zak* Rivier," where we lived with her. I used to see her, so I knew how she acted. Therefore I knew about her doings. While I was still a child she died. I had just become a youth, when the old woman passed away.

!kˀetən ka siŋ //nau, haŋ ki /ku:-ka, !kˀe !kwi: ha /kẽ, o !kˀetən ta:, //ka ti e:, !khwe ka /ku //nau, o hɛ: ¯!kwi:ja ha /kẽ, !khwe /ku tʃˀu. Tíja /ku k''wãŋ !khweja: tüï, ti e:, i ¯!kwi: ha /kẽ. Ta:, ha /ki ka siŋ //nau, !kˀeja: //xarra /k'e: ja ha, ha-g /ne -!k''wãïn, ha-g /ne k''wa:, tíja taŋ !khweja: k''wa: hĩ ha, o ha tsaxáu-ka !khweitən e: /hiŋ.

Although she was dead people used to call her name, for they believed that if they called her name, the wind would blow. It seemed as if the wind heard when we called her name. For she had been used to get angry whenever people scolded her, and to cry ; it seemed as if the wind cried with her, when her tears fell.

Hiŋ e:, !khwe k''auki ¯≠kauwa, hɛ se /hiŋ, ta:, !khwe k''auki ta síŋ ka, ha kwãŋ k''wa:. Ta: !khwe ka siŋ /ku //nau, ha ka k''wa: é, !khwe /ku tsˀu, o !khwe-tən k''auki ¯≠kauwa, ha tsaxáu-ka !khweita: se /hiŋ. Ta: tí /ku //nau, ha k''wa:, tikən k''auki //khou akən, ta: !khwe /ku k''wãŋ, !khwe tsˀu-ta: !kˀãũ. ʘho:kaŋ k''auki tymse -darakən, o !khwe tʃu:ï, o ha k''wa:. Tíkən k''wãŋ, !khwe a: /waita ha ã:, !kˀe e: /k'e: ha.

Then the wind did not want them to fall, for it was not willing she should cry. For the wind used to blow whenever she cried, because the wind did not want the tears from her eyes to fall. So when she cried the place became unpleasant, for the wind seemed to blow the earth away. The bushes were much shaken when the wind blew because she cried. It seemed as if the wind were avenging her on the people who scolded her.

!kˀe-g /ne //nau, !kˀeja: //k'oen ti e:, !khwe k''auki tymse tʃú:ï, !kˀe-g /ne kuku, he /k'e:, " Tsˀa-de xa a:,

When people see the wind blowing strongly, they say, "Does not */xar̃r̃aŋ/xar̃r̃aŋ* seem to be

|xar̃r̃aŋ|xar̃r̃aŋ ||kho ka ha kwãŋ |kɯ ||kóä:kən !k''wain i? He ha k''auki ka-g |ne ka ha kwãŋ !kan !haŋ-a hi ã: há-ka !nuiŋ ||xã:xu e: !khwe ||xĩ: sa: !khwe, ĩ:. Hɛ há ka |kɯ̀ ||kóä:kən |ne |dí |ɷhá: o í, o há k''auki |ne k''wãŋ ha: ||kwa: e !kerri. Ta: ha ka |kɯ k''wãŋ ha ||khou||khouka !kˀu !kõä, hɛ ha k''auki ta-g |ne k''wãŋ ha: ||kwa: |ki ha ||khou||khougən.''

very angry with us? For she does not seem to want to hold the sides of her kaross together for us in which the wind hides itself. She is really doing harm to us, and she does not seem to be altogether grown up. For she acts as if her thoughts had gone astray, and she does not act as if she really had all her senses.''

Notes

3-4 … *for her little head was* **steep** *[?]*: The word *taurutcuru* is given in the *Dictionary* as meaning the opposite, 'flat [?]' (Bleek 1956: 195). Given what Diä!kwain says later about |Xar̃r̃aŋ-|xar̃r̃aŋ's son, 'flat' seems to be a better translation than 'steep'.

11-13 *She did not walk quietly, but danced [?] along as she walked*: This is not a close translation of the |Xam text – the original translation reads, 'She used when she walked about to walk like an ostrich does when it walks' (5860).

13-14 *She did not walk* **quietly …**: The original notebook translation of *||kabba* is 'leisurely' (5860).

45-46 *Although she was dead people used to call her name …*: The living would call on the 'dead people' (*|nu !kˀe*) to help them to bring rain, heal sickness and influence the behaviour of game animals (see Parts V, VI and VII).

79-81 … *and she does not act as if she really had all her* **senses:** The original notebook translation gives the word *||khou ||khougən* as 'thinking strings' (Bleek 1956: 577).

Wind-making (2)

Narrator: |Haŋ‡kass'o
Dictation dates: 23 and 24 April 1878
Notebook reference: L.VIII.8: 6725-6728
***Bantu Studies* reference:** Vol. 6 (1932), Part IV: 336

|Haŋ‡kass'o explains how the /Xam used the wind to their advantage. This extract was originally entitled 'Windmaking and springbok hunting'.

Si _//kwaŋ ka /kuɯ !kaukən-ã ⊙hokən, au sí ta, !khwe se !kkwi, si !kaukən-ã ⊙hokən au //kha. Sí ta, " Oëja, ŋ kaŋ síŋ ta, !khwe se antau !khweija ¯hi, i se antau //nuŋ //e í, au _/ká:ö-ka ti e:. Ta:, a /kuɯ a //k'oen, wai e: _tai sa hi é ; hiŋ /kuɯ //khóä i k''auki saŋ /ki/ki !nwa:, ta:, ⊙hokən k''auki //na. Ta:, a /kuɯ a //k'oen, ⊙hokakən k''auki //na, ta: wai eŋeŋ /kuɯ e: _tai sa, hi e. Hɛ a /kuɯ a //k'oen, !kʔãũŋ _//kwaŋ /hiŋ ĩ:.

We are wont to beat the bushes when we want the wind to blow hard, we beat the bushes with a stick. We say, " Listen, I want the wind to blow quickly for us, that we may quickly get behind the hill there. For you see these are springbok which are coming towards us ; it looks as if we had not enough arrows, for the bushes are not visible, only the bodies of oncoming springbok are there. And you see the dust getting up.

" Hɛ tikən e:, ŋ síŋ ta, i //kã: a:-ka !khwe ta !khwi !kuŋ siŋ, ha !kaukən-ã ⊙hokən, i se antau !ɑháttəŋ. Ta:, í ta //nau, au i _!kwɔmmaiŋ-ã, !nwãŋ ka !xi:ta ¯hi, au !nwa: ¯//kou//kou tẽ wai /na:ŋ. Hɛ tikən e:, ŋ síŋ ta, i se /xwerri wai, ta: ŋ-ka !nwa: k''auki /k'waija, ŋ siŋ _!kwɔmmaiŋ-ã."

" Therefore I want our brother whose wind blows hard from the north to beat the bushes, so that we may head them quickly. For if we shoot them running, the arrows keep breaking for us, when they hit the springbok's heads. Therefore I want us to lie in wait for the springbok, for I have not enough arrows to shoot them running."

Notes

3-4 … *we beat the bushes with a stick*: 'With a stick [with a man's stick]' (6724 rev., note partially omitted).

10-11 *... for the bushes are not visible...*: 'For the bushes are not there [i.e. the springbok are so numerous that the bushes are not visible]. For, thou art the one who beholdest the bushes are not there; for it is the springbok bodies which are coming.' (6726-6727, text partially omitted)

14-16 *Therefore I want our brother whose wind blows hard from the north to beat the bushes ...*: There may be special significance in choosing a man who has the north wind, because this is the rain-wind (several narratives in Part V mention the north wind as the one that brings rain). In the summertime, the season during which rain is most likely to fall, the springbok move around in smaller groups, following the isolated thundershowers as they fall over |Xam-ka !aũ. Animals tend to move into the wind and so, if a north wind were blowing, the springbok herds would head north into the wind towards where the rain would fall. This is probably why it was desirable for a man who had the north wind to beat the bushes – it was the wind most likely to attract the springbok.

17-18 *For if we shoot them running ...*: 'to shoot the springbok when the springbok are running, we are shooting the arrows in among the springbok.' (6727 rev., note omitted)

The winds

Narrator: |Haŋ‡kass'o
Notebook reference: L.VIII.1: 6096-6101 (dictated sometime between 10-28 January 1878); L .VIII.13: 7196 rev. (dictated sometime between 29 June-7 July 1878)
Bantu Studies reference: Vol. 6 (1932), Part IV: 336-337

Each wind has its own name and set of characteristic weather patterns.

!khwe a ts?u !kuŋ ʃo:.

!khwe a !kuŋ ʃo:, he ti hiŋ e: -|kwa:gən e: |wérri:ja, hiŋ |ne sweŋ ||a, ti e:, au hiŋ tati e:, !khwe dóä !kuŋ ʃo. He ti hiŋ e:, -|kwa:gən e: |wérri:ja, hiŋ |ne sweŋ ||a ti é; au hiŋ tati e:, !khwe !kuŋ ʃo:.

The north wind.

The wind blows underneath, therefore clouds which are strong go floating there, (to the south), because the wind blows underneath. That is why strong clouds go floating there, because they feel that the wind is north.

Wyrri.

!khwe a: ta: wyrri, haŋ a: |kɯ ts?u |ki -|ua: ||a !khwa:-ka -|kwa:-gən. He ti hiŋ e:, !khwa:-ka -|kwa:gən |kɯ-g |ne ĩ: te-n ||a ti é.

The west wind.

The wind which lies in the west is that which drives the rain clouds back. Then the rain clouds go quite over there (to the east).

!khwe a ts?u ||kau !khe.

!khwe a: a, haŋ a: te?u ||kau !khe. He ti hiŋ e:, haŋ |ne |kɑm !k?ãũ, ĩ:, ha !khwe, ha ts?u ||kau khe.

The south wind.

This wind blows down from above. Therefore it raises dust, for it blows down from above.

-!káuä.

!hhwe a: ta -!káuä, haŋ k''auki tym ʘpwa ts?üï, haŋ a: ta -!káuä, ha -k''aö. He ti hiŋ e:, |xam-ka !k?e ta |kɯ-g |ne |kuïta, |kúïta ʘhokən. Hiŋ |kɯ-g |ne |kúïta, hiŋ |kɯ-g |ne ||ké:ï |i, hiŋ |kɯ-g |ne kuŋ ʃo:. He ti hiŋ e:, hi ta |kɯ-g |ne |kúïtən ʃo:, i:, |kúïtən !a ʃo ʘho, hi |kɯ-g |ne ||ké:ï |i, hi |kɯ-g |ne kuŋ ʃo:.

The east wind.

The wind which lies in the east blows very hard, it lies in the east, it is cold. Therefore the Bushmen make shelters, shelters of bushes. They make shelters, they light a fire, they sit warming themselves. That is how they sit sheltered, the shelters are close to the bushes, they make a fire and warm themselves.

!khwetən *ˍdɔ́ä* *siŋ* *ta:,* *ˍ!káuä* *||kẽĩ.*

The south-east wind (which lies on the east wind's horn).

!khwetən *|ne ta: ||k'hwi ˉ||xũï.*

The north-west wind (which lies in the quagga's knuckle).

!káuökən.

The north-east wind (so-called because it blows from the mountains).

❑

Notes

Title *The winds*: This short narrative was entered on the contents page of notebook 13 as 'Rainmaking, when the wind is in the north'.

2 *The wind blows underneath …*: The idiomatic phrase *!khwe a !kuŋ ʃo:,* literally 'the wind is underneath', was translated by Dorothea Bleek as 'the wind is north' (6097).

16 *Therefore it raises dust …*: 'That is why it raises the dust; this wind blows standing above' (6099, text omitted).

20 *… blows very hard …*: Literally translated, 'does not a little blow' (6099) – this is a characteristic way of expressing superlatives in Xam.

20 *… it lies in the east …*: 'That wind does not a little blow; it is the one which lies in the east …' (6100, text omitted).

Wind and stars

Narrator: |Haŋ‡kass'o
Source: '|Haŋ‡kass'o from his maternal grandfather Tsatsi'
Dictation dates: 1, 2 June 1879
Notebook references: L.VIII.28: 8458 rev.-8465
***Bantu Studies* reference**: Vol. 6 (1932), Part IV: 337-339

There is a strong association between a person, the stars and the wind.

!xam-ka !kʔetən |né ta, !khwe |ne |kó:äkən, au !khwe k''auki |ne tʃúï, hiŋ ||xɑmki ||nau, au !khwe a tʃu ¯||wẽï, hĩ ta, !khweja ||gõũ||gõũ.

The Bushmen say, the wind is still when it does not blow, they also say, when the wind blows strongly, that it blows a gale.

Au !khwe siŋ tʃúï, he !khwe |ne ¯|kukən, !khwe |ne dí kúï tã |í, au há tati, ||kõĩŋjã |ne dí kúï tã |i ; he ||kõïŋ tsaxáuwa |ne ||kóä:kən ||ka||ka siŋ, ĩ:.

When the wind has blown and dies away, it feels warm, because the sun feels warm, the sun's eye is burning.

He |xũ-de |ku-g |ne |hiŋ, he ||kõïŋ tsaxáuwa |ku-g |ne ||kóä:kən ||ka||ká siŋ ; tí |ku-g |ne ||kóä-kən di kúï tã |i, au híŋ tati, |xũ-de e ||kwar̃r̃a-ka tʃweŋ, ka ˍ|kwaˍkwa-tən.

Then the Pleiades come out, and the sun's eye is burning; the whole place becomes quite warm, because the Pleiades are summer's things, (summer's) stars.

!kwi a:, ha ||nau, ha |khi: tʃweŋ, ha ¯k''ao, há-ka !khweja ¯k''ao. !kwi ||nau, !kwi |khi: tsá, !kwitən ¯k''ao, tsá-ka !khwetən k''auki tym ⊙pwa ¯k''ao. He tikən e:, !kʔe kwitən ta kú, " I ||kã a: a, ha-ka !khwe taŋ ˍdóä |kwẽ:ï tã, au ha |khi: tʃweŋ, ha-ka !khwetən k''auki ˍdóä tym ⊙pwa k''ao."

When one man kills things, he is cold, his wind is cold. When he kills anything, he is cold, for the thing's wind is not a little cold. Therefore people are wont to say, " Our brother there, his wind feels like this when he kills things, his wind is not a little cold."

Háŋ a ka ||nau, ha |na: ˍ|kwat-tən, ˍ|kwatta: |ne ¯k''ao, ˍ|kwattən-ta !khweja k''auki ¯tym ⊙pwa ¯k''ao au hĩ tati, !kwi a: hã a: |na: -|kwattən, há ¯k''ao, au ha |khi: tʃweŋ. Au ha |khi: tʃweŋ, ha-ka

When he sees a star, the star becomes cold, the star's wind is very cold, because the (wind of) the man who looked at it is cold, when he has killed things. When he kills things, his wind is cold ; it

!khweja ⁻k''ao ; hĩ ⁻//khou-ĩ, au ha /khi: tʃweŋ. !khwe a !kwai, há _//kwaŋ /kuı, hiŋ !kwi. He tikən e:, _/kwattən ta /ne k''ao, ĩ:, au há /na: _/kwattən, _/kwattən-ta !khweja k''auki /ne ⁻tym ʘpwa tʃúï.

blows up dust, when he kills things. The wind is one with the man. Therefore the star grows cold, when he looks at it, the star's wind blows strongly.

!kuko:, a:-ka !khweja ⁻twai-ĩ, haŋ a: ka //nau, ha /na: _/kwattən, //k'óägu, //kõĩŋ tsaxáu //ka siŋ, he tí /ne //kóä:kən /karrakən. He tikən e:, !kˀe kúïtən tá ka, " I //kã á -ka !khwe kaŋ _dóä /kwẽĩ tã, hĩ k''auki twaitən //ka: hĩ, hĩ /kuı ⁻tym ʘpwa bébéï, au hi k''auki tʃu //wẽ:ï, au haŋ tati, há-ka !khwe /ke ta /kwẽĩ tã, au ha /kha tsa, ha_ka !khwe /kuı bébéï, au hĩ tati e:, tí di kúï tã /i."

When another man whose wind is pleasant sees a star, Canopus, the sun's eye is burning, and the place gets very warm. Therefore people say, " Our brother's wind feels like this, there is no other as nice as it, it blows softly, and does not blow hard, for his wind always feels like this when he kills anything, his wind blows softly, and then the place grows warm."

_/kwagən _//kwaŋ é, !kˀe /ne ta, !kwi //nwaŋ ⁻ã e, au _/kwagən e: /hó⁻aka, au !khwe ta: ⁻wyrri ; !khwe /ne ⁻k''ao, au !khwe ta: ⁻wyrri. He tikən e:, !kˀe ta /ne ta, !kwi-ta !khwe⁻ja é.

They are clouds, people call them a man's liver, because the clouds are black, when the wind is in the west ; the wind is cold when it is in the west. Then people say, it is a man's wind.

!kuko: a ⁻hã _!kauä, ha-ka !khwe-ja k''auki tã !ke !khe, au ⁻hi ta: _!kauä, ha ⁻hã e _!kauä.

Another one goes to the east, his wind does not feel as if it stands still, when it is in the east, it is eastwind.

ŋ-ka !khwetən k''auki twaitən //ka hĩ, au ⁻hĩ ⁻!kuŋ⁻sˀo:, ta: hĩ /kuı tã /i, au hĩ ⁻tsˀuwa úï _!kauä, hiŋ /ne ⁻!kuŋ-siŋ, au ŋ /khi: tóï. Hiŋ k''auki /ne twaitən //ka hĩ, hĩ /ne tym ʘpwa tsúï. Hiŋ /kuı-g /ne tym ʘpwa bébéï ⁻!kuŋ-sˀo:. He tikən e:, ŋ́ ka /kuı-g /ne //khóä !nwiŋ, au ka: tati, !khwe /kuı-g /ne tã /i. ŋ a /kuı-g /ne //khóä ⁻!nwiŋ, au ka tati, !khwe /kuı-g /ne ⁻kuŋ-sˀo:, !khwe k''auki /ne twaitən //ka: ha.

My wind has no equal in pleasantness, as it is the north wind, for it feels warm when it blows the east wind away, after I have killed an ostrich. There is no wind so pleasant as it, it blows gently. It blows softly from the north. Then I put my kaross down, because the wind feels warm. I lay it down when I feel the wind in the north, than which there is no wind more pleasant.

❑

Notes

3-4 ... *the wind blows strongly ... it blows a* **gale**: The word *//gõũ//gõũ*, translated as 'gale' in *Bantu Studies* and as 'hard' in the original notebook, is not in the *Dictionary*. It may be a variant spelling of *//go//go* or 'whirlwind' (Bleek 1956: 534). Whirlwinds are often associated with !Khwa: (see Part V, Introduction), the personification of rain / water, and with other supernatural events.

9 *Then the Pleiades come out* ...: This is the time that the */xo e* (the Pleiades or 'Seven sisters', a cluster of stars in the constellation of Taurus) come out. The Pleiades are visible in summer and are associated with the heat of summer.

14-15 *When one man kills things, he is cold, his wind is cold*: 'i.e. the killed thing's wind is cold, not the man himself' (8459 rev., note omitted). The Ju|'hoansi in the Kalahari call the idea that human beings and certain antelope cause specific changes in the weather *n!ao* (see Part IV, Introduction).

23-24 ... *the star's wind is very cold* ...: '[that is] the star's wind' (8460 rev., note omitted).

25 ... *the man who looked at it is cold* ...: 'that is, his wind is cold, not his body' (8460 rev., note omitted).

27-28 ... *it blows up dust* ...: 'has dust ... A man throws up dust. The wind is that [of] which they are wont to say, it is blowing up dust' (8461 rev., note omitted).

Clouds

Narrator: |Haŋ‡kass'o
Source: '|Haŋ‡kass'o from observation' and 'from his maternal grandfather Tsatssī'
Dictation dates: 25-28 November; 4 December 1878
Notebook reference: L.VIII.23: 8018-8029 and 8030-8031; 8026 rev.
***Bantu Studies* reference**: Vol. 6 (1932), Part IV: 339-342

What people do when they see 'jackals' on the horizon, and a remedy for dispersing dangerous storm clouds.

❑

Hĩ |né ta 'kɔro' au |kwa:gən e |hóäka. He tikən e:, hĩ ta |né ta, '||khe||khe-we:, akən tuko se di akka ¯hi ||neiŋ, ta a |kɯ a ||k'oen, kɔro a: ¯teŋ, a: ¯||kou ¯teŋ. Haŋ ||nau, ha |kwẽ:ï |kĩ, haŋ ¯teŋ ||a, háŋ ka ha se ¯||kou |hiŋ. Ha koá |ne ko¯kóä, au há tati, ha |ne ¯!kuítən ||a:. He tikən e:, a ||k'oen, haŋ tẽ ||a: kɔro. Haŋ ||nau haŋ |ne ¯||kou |hiŋ, ítən k''auki |ne se té: |ki ha. Ta, ŋ |kɯ-g |ne ||xwe:, ta, ŋ́ a k''auki |ki ¯!nwiŋ. He tikən e:, a _dóä se di akka ¯hi ||neiŋ.'

They say "jackal" to clouds which are black. Therefore they are wont to say, "O Beast of Prey, you must make the hut nice for us, for you can see the jackal lying to the south. When it (the rain) goes along like this, it will turn back (to the north-east whence it came). It turns, because it goes back. Then it lays down (jackal clouds), as you see. When it turns back, we shall not know what to do. For I am cold, because I have not got a kaross. Therefore you must make the hut nice for us."

!kwi gwaïtən ta, '|khe||khe-we:, akən tuko se di akka ¯hi ||neiŋ.' !kwi |aitikən a: ka, 'ŋ |hã-we:, akən tuko se |kɛ|kɯm se ⊙hokən, a se ||khou ¯|kúïta ¯hi ||neiŋ. Ta, ŋ siŋ _|ka:ti tɔtɔro, ŋ k''auki taŋ ŋ siŋ ||xã ŋ tɔtɔro. Ta, !khwa: ||ki k''auki tã ≠hãnũwa, au í ||ka:. Ta, ti e:, i kwe: ¯||kowa, ĩ:, hĩ, e:, ti twaï, ĩ:.'

The man says (to his wife) "O Beast of Prey, you must make the hut nice for us." The woman says, "O my husband, you must bring bushes to cover the hut in for us. For I was drenched lately, I do not want to be drenched again. The rain drops do not feel nice when we are wet. When we are comfortably dry, then it is pleasant."

|nukən|nukənk''au hiŋ tá ka, '||khe||khe-we:, akən |kɯ a ||k'oen,

Old men are wont to say, "O Beast of Prey, you see it is a white

-!guru e: teŋ ||a, hĩ e.' He kuko-g |ne kúï, '||khe||khe-we:ja, haŋ ||nau, ha |kwẽï |ki, haŋ teŋ ||a, haŋ ka ha se ||khou |kóäkən. He ti hiŋ e:, ŋ ka, !khwã a, ha se ú, ha se hohó se _!kwa:, ha se ||khou -|kuĩtən.'

|nutara ku, ' Oëja, ŋ káŋ ka ŋ |k'e:, a se ú, a se ||khou -|kuïtən, ta, ŋ |ke á a, ha |ha |ku !kwai, hĩ k''wãŋ k''aodəro, hiŋ |ku ||khou -|kuïtən |ki ||neiŋ, au !khwetən ts?u ||khóëta ŋ-ka ||neiŋ -||kaië, au akən kwaŋ |ku ||kerri ||na au !khwa:, au akən k''auki kəä akən ||khou -|kuïtən, au a -xu óä ≠kakən≠kakən. Ta, a ||k'oen, kərowakən ||khõä se -teŋ.'

!kuko: a: ku, ' A _||kwaŋ ||k'oen, tikən ||khou |hóäkən, tí |ke -!kuŋ, hiŋ kaŋ ||khou |hóäkən, au hiŋ tati e:, ts?a a: !əhí siŋ -||a, ha ||khóä, ha se _mai-i ha !khe:. Ta, ha kwəŋ, |kwẽ:ï _|kwãĩ, haŋ ||khóä, ha se !khe:, ha ;kwa se |hiŋ. Ta, ha kwəŋ |kwẽ:ï _|kwãĩ, haŋ ||khóä, ha se tẽ: ||kəroko. Ta, ha kwəŋ ||khóä, ha ká ha ||khou |hóäkən, u ha k''au |ku _|ka:ti sweŋ -||a.'

He ti hiŋ e:, |nuk''o á a, ha ka |ne -ku, ' ŋ |ke ta ha |kwẽ:ï |ki, !kaukən _saŋ ||k'oen, -ko: !ho, ta wai saŋ !k?attən -|ko !khe se. He tikən e:, !kaukən sa |ku ||k'oen -|ko !hóä; ta, !kwi a _|ka:ŋ-a !khwa:, ha e, ha _saŋ !k?attən -|ko !khe se, au hã ka, ha se _tái tau k''oã.'

He tikən e:, !kaukən _sa ||k'oen, -|ko !hóä, hi _saŋ -||kãũï ha, au hi

cloud that is floating along here." And another says, "O Beast of Prey, when it floats along like this, it is going to turn black. Therefore I want this child to go out and pick up 'asbos' (Mesembrianthemum micranthum) to make a shelter (for the hut)."

The old woman (the second man's wife) says, "Stop, I say you should go out and make a shelter; this my friend's husband works alone like a young man, putting up a shelter for the hut, while the wind is blowing through the inside of my hut, while you are screaming there about the rain, instead of building a shelter and leaving off talking. For you see a jackal cloud seems to be coming."

Another (old man) says, "You see it is getting black, the part underneath is growing black, because the thing (cloud) which goes outside seems as if it would soon stop. For it behaves as if it were going to stop, that its leg may come out (the rain). It appears to be letting its apron fall. It seems to be going to turn black, as if it had not just been going along."

Then this old man exclaims, "I always want it to do so, that the children may look up the valley, for the springbok will come trotting. Therefore the children shall look up the valley; for it is a being that loves the rain, it will come trotting up in order to drink as it goes along."

Therefore the children go to look up the valley and surround

_|kɔ́ɔ̈ !ɑhí tã: ã ; he hi |ne _swai, !kʔa: ||kho ||a ha, au _!kóäkən, au hĩ ta, hi _sa: |kɯ-g |ne te¯ten ta:, au há |ne ¯|hiŋ _!kóäkən. Ha ká: |ne !kuxe ¯||khóä !khe ||a:, he hi |ne ¯!kitən-ã hi |ka:gən ã, au hĩ tã, hi se |xã|xã ¯!hiŋ ||kho, au hi k''auki ¯!nou hi |ka:gən.

it, sticking ostrich feather brushes in the ground outside it ; then they drive it (the springbok) towards the brushes, for they mean to lie in wait for it, as it retreats from the brushes. It runs to leeward, and they beat for each other, for they wish to shoot from near at hand, so they do not let the game pass their mates.

Hi _||kwaŋ ka ||ke: ||ke:¯ĩ||ke:-¯ĩ-ka ||kɔro, au hĩ ta, !khwa se ¯|khuru, au hĩ ||k'oen, ti e:, há !khwa, ha ||khóä há se di |a:, hiŋ e:, ha-ka _|ho:¯a |kɯ ||khóä ||ga:, há |ne ||khou _|ka¯in.

They (the Bushmen) burn the outer covering of horns, when they want the rain to disperse, when they see that the rain seems to be bringing danger, because its darkness is like night, it (the cloud) is turning green.

He tikən e:, hĩ ta |ne ||ke: ||kɔro, au hĩ ||k'oen, ti e:, !khwa ||khou _|ka¯in, hi |ne ku, "Ukən tuko se ||ke:ja hi ||kɔro, !khwa: á a, ha se |ki:ja ¯hi, tá, ha kwɔŋ ||khou _|ka¯in.' Hi _|k'wãï _||kwaŋ ɛ, he k''auki tã ≠hanũwa, hiŋ e:, hĩ ta, ||kɔro-ka _||gɔ́ɔ̈ se _kóïtən ¯!kʔa siŋ _!gwaxu, _|kwagən se |khuru.

Therefore they burn horn when they see that the raincloud turns green, they say, "You must really burn horn for us, that the raincloud may disperse for us, for it is turning green." Its scent does not smell pleasant, therefore they want the horns' smoke to rise up into the sky, that the rain-clouds may disperse.

Hiŋ !hɑmmi !khwa:, au hĩ ||na ¯!kauxu, hiŋ |kɯ !hɑmmi kwokwáŋ !khwa:, au hĩ ||na ¯!kauxu. Au hĩ ||na ||neiŋ, hiŋ k''auki !hɑmmi !khwa, ta:, hi |kɯ ko:ka !khwa:.

They are afraid of the rain when they are on the hunting-ground, they are very much afraid of it there. If they are at home they are not afraid of the rain, but they love it.

❑

Notes

10-11 *Then it lays down (jackal clouds) …*: The parenthesis is incorrect here: it should read 'Then it lays down jackals [i.e. cloud]' (8019).

34-35 … *I want this child to go out and pick up 'asbos'…*: 'They [the farmers] make soap with it [i.e. its ashes are used in soap-making]' (802[illegible] rev., note omitted).

This plant is probably a *Psilocaulon* species (*Mesembryanthemaceae*), (Le Roux et. al. 1994: 198-199).

39-41 *say you should go out and make a shelter ...*: 'The woman tells the man to leave off the sending of the child ... (two or three illegible words – ed.) ... that he may get up, that he may pick up ...' (the 'asbos', presumably – ed.) (8021 rev., note omitted).

45-46 *... while you are screaming there about the rain ...*: 'The man is the one who talks about the rain [instead of silently sheltering the house with bushes]; that is why the woman reproves him.' (8022 rev., note omitted)

'|Kana. The name of a Bushman woman who lived at */itten /hiŋ* [the Strandberg mountains south east of the Bitterpits]. Her husband's name was *//Gweten//gweten*. She was very short-tempered.' (8022 rev., note omitted)

48-49 *For you see a jackal cloud seems to be coming*: 'Jackal-like clouds [the tops of the clouds are those to which the people say jackals]. Jackals [i.e. jackal-like clouds] seem to be coming' (8023 rev., notes omitted).

50-51 *You see it is getting black ...*: 'while they feel that the rain is falling [there, in the distance where it looks so dark]' (8023 rev., note omitted).

55-56 *For it behaves as if it were going to stop ...*: 'Nett nou ons xa rain' (Afrikaans, literally, 'just now we will rain' – ed.) (8024 rev., note omitted).

63 *I always want it to do so*: '[in order that] the springbok may come' (8025 rev., note omitted).

65-66 *... for the springbok will come trotting*: 'the springbok; the springbok are those of whom he speaks' (8026 rev., note omitted).

71-74 *Therefore the children go to look up the valley and* **surround*** *it, sticking* **ostrich feather brushes**** *in the ground ...*:

***[they] intend that they may shoot the springbok.**

(8027 rev., note omitted)

****ostrich feather brushes they are; male ostrich feathers. They do not a little smell; from the things with which they work the feather brushes, then the springbok are afraid of the feather brushes.**

(8027 rev.-8028 rev., note omitted)

81-82 *... they do not let the game pass their mates*: 'Letting alone [?] is that on account of which the springbok pass [between the people] while they [the people] let alone for each other' (8028 rev., note omitted).

83-84 *They ... burn the outer covering of horns ...*: see Part IV, Introduction.

86-87 *... when they see that the rain seems to be* **bringing danger** *...*: The notebook translation is 'that rain seems as if it would *make war*' (8030). The phrase in question, *di /a:*, can also be translated as to 'make a fight'. !Khwa: is thus bringing a 'fight', i.e. a violent thunderstorm.

PART V

THE RAIN

From material collected by
Dr. W.H.I. BLEEK and Miss L.C. LLOYD between 1870 and 1880,
edited by D.F. Bleek

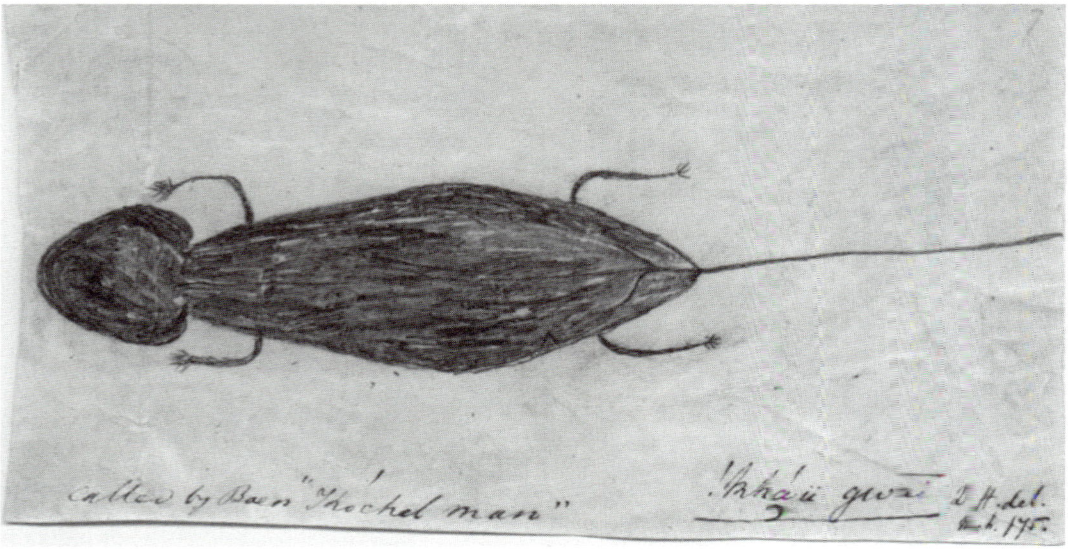

'[T]he male agama … lies up on the thorntree, it keeps its head toward the place where the north wind blows and bewitches the rain clouds'. Drawing by Dia!kwain of a male Agama lizard.

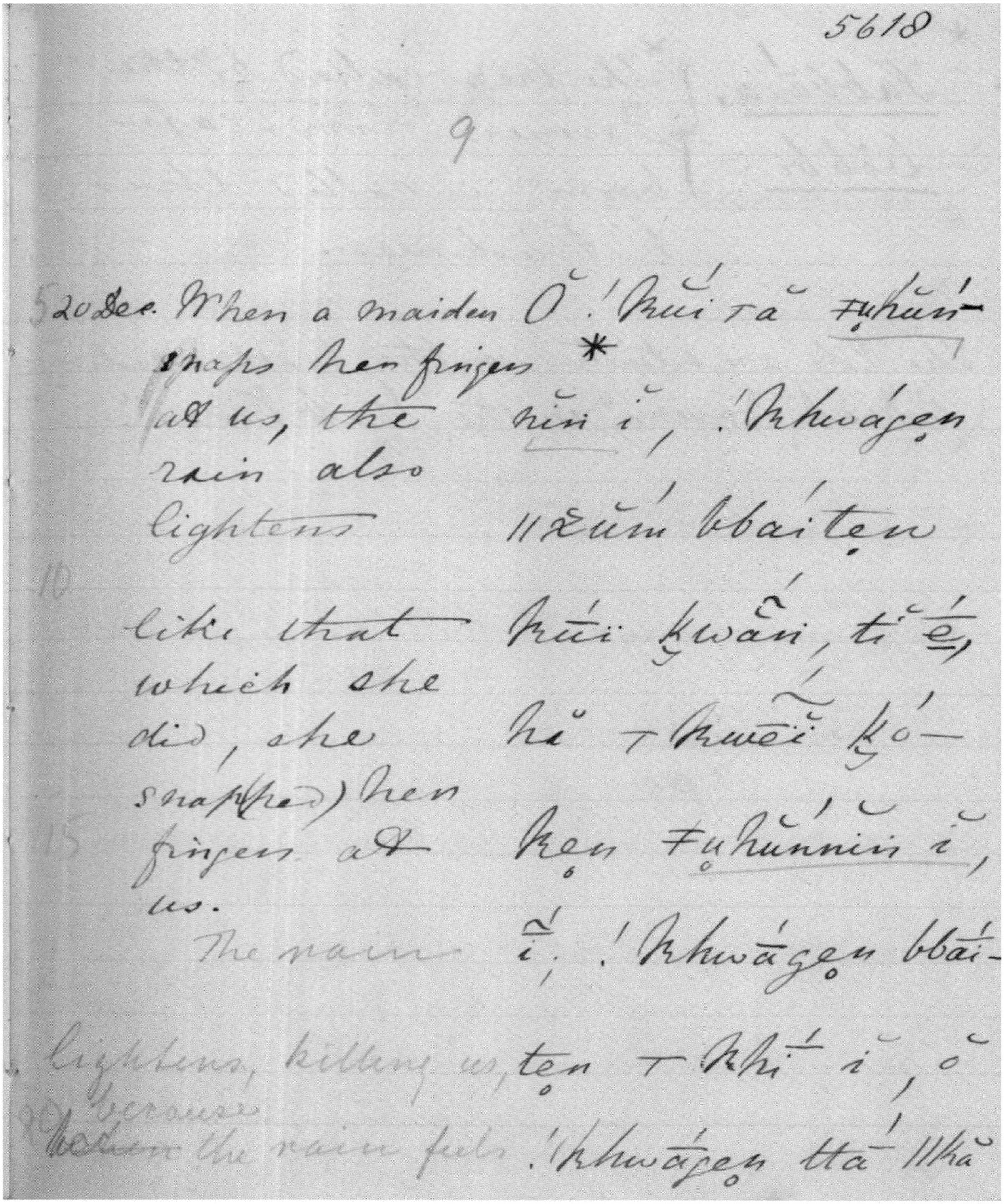
5618

9

20 Dec. When a maiden snaps her fingers at us, the rain also lightens

like that which she did, she snap(ped) her fingers at us.

The rain

lightens, killing us, because the rain feels

‘When a maiden snaps her fingers at us, the rain also lightens’: manuscript page from the narrative ‘When a girl snaps her fingers’

PART V
THE RAIN

The /Xam say 'rain liquid'
but Europeans say 'rain' to water falling out of the clouds.
– |Haŋ‡kass'o: '!Khwa: and rain liquid' –

When he said this, |Haŋ‡kass'o was emphasising to Lucy Lloyd that Europeans and the |Xam had different ideas about the nature of rain. For Lloyd and the others, rain was 'precipitation' – the condensation of water vapour in the atmosphere and its descent to the earth in drops; for the |Xam, 'rain liquid' was only one aspect of *!khwa:*, the word commonly translated as 'water' or 'rain'. There are further distinctions that need to be made, which are discussed below.

The |Xam teachers must have thought it essential for Bleek and Lloyd to know about *!khwa:* – they dictated hundreds of pages of anecdotes in which *!khwa:* plays a central role. Dorothea Bleek later selected many of these narratives for inclusion in *Bantu Studies*. A large number of these extracts are about the special relationship that *!khwa:* had with women and how *!khwa:* was involved in the bringing of rain.

There are three main aspects to *!khwa:*, although it is sometimes not easy to distinguish them from each other. One emphasises *!khwa:* as H_2O, the chemical compound. This aspect is sometimes, but not always, qualified by the phrases *!khwa: //ki* ('rain liquid'), or as 'rain's rain' (*!khwa: ka !khwa:*). The second manifestation of *!khwa:* is as 'rain-cattle' (*!khwa:-ka xoro*), which were captured by rain-makers and led to the places where rain was needed (Hewitt 1986). A third aspect of *!khwa:* emerges clearly in the Part V narratives about women – here *!khwa:* appears as a conscious being, personifying rain / water and the natural forces associated with it, such as clouds, wind, thunder and lightning. This is what I call *!Khwa:* with a capital 'K'*. The two other aspects already mentioned – *!khwa:* as precipitation and *!khwa:* as rain-cattle – are under the control of this last manifestation of *!khwa:*. In order to emphasise this distinction, I use !Khwa: from this point on when referring to this powerful personification.

!Khwa: and the rain

In an arid, semi-desert environment with 200 mm (8 inches) or less of rain per year, it is not surprising that water was a central concern in the lives of the |Xam. Rain in |Xam-ka !aũ falls in scattered thundershowers, refreshing plants and attracting animals to the fresh growth in some places, and leaving other places dry. 'Rain-cattle' (*!khwa:-ka xoro*) were a conceptualisation of this weather pattern: where they walked, they shed their blood and milk that fell as rain. People always asked for a female rain (*!khwa: /aiti*) to walk over their place because it was gentle and deep-soaking. But when !Khwa: was angry, a male rain (*!khwa gwai*) brought strong winds, thunder and lightning, pouring down floods of water, killing people and destroying their homes.

The riders of the rain

'Dead people' (the */nu/nukən !kʔe*), or spirits of dead rain-makers, rode the rain-animal to the places where people hunted and gathered. Living 'rain's men' (*!khwa:-ka !ke*) could also call on !Khwa: to let it rain – these men all seem to have been 'grandfathers' (*!kõĩŋgu*), that is, older men, perhaps because it needed skill and experience to catch a rain-animal (see Part VI, 'Rain-making', for texts about capturing rain-animals). There are no records of women 'owning' rain, perhaps because !Khwa: was involved in women's lives in a different and potentially dangerous way.

!Khwa: and women

From her first menstrual period until the time she married, a woman's 'waters' (*//kitten ka !khwa:*) magically connected her to !Khwa: , and she shared his */ko:ode* ('magic power'). A girl experiencing her first menstruation was a *!kwi //kaŋ* or 'new girl', translated by Lloyd and Bleek as 'new maiden'. During this time her power was especially dangerous, and she lay secluded in a small hut, the *!kaukən-ka //neiŋ* or 'house of illness', until the new moon. Her mother and the other, older women (*xoakengu*) looked after her and advised her about how to behave. Much of what a new maiden learnt was about how to respect (*!nanna-se*) !Khwa: and protect (*!koa-se*) the family and community from !Khwa:'s anger.

Respecting the rain

Respecting !Khwa: meant 'fearing' (*!hammi*) his magic power (*/ko:ode*), as well as the */ko:ode* that a girl possessed in her own right. The new maiden's anger provoked !Khwa: to react angrily towards the people (and the girl too), particularly if she had violated any of the taboos during her stay in the 'house of illness'. Many of the narratives in Part V are 'sensational' cases of girls in puberty who did not respect !Khwa: and became angry with others – with disastrous results.

In addition, girls had to use alternative 'respect' words for certain reptiles – these were considered to be !Khwa:'s 'things'. The girls learnt how to behave respectfully towards these 'things' to avoid !Khwa:'s anger.

Adolescent females also showed respect for !Khwa: by performing ceremonies at waterholes and springs – some of these involved the strewing of *sã:* (aromatic herbs believed to possess magical properties) onto the water, and 'darkening' (*/ho:*) the water with powdered red haematite (*to:*) to calm 'new' rain. New maidens were uniquely suited for this kind of magical intervention because of their particularly close relationship with !Khwa:.

Taking care of the community

!Khwa: was jealous of girls in puberty and became violently angry when he smelt a girl's scent (*/k"wai*) on other people, especially males. This behaviour, and a reference to !Khwa:'s genitals ('Old men insult !Khwa:'), suggest that !Khwa: was a masculine being. Girls were expected to *!koa-se* (protect) their relatives by 'fumigating' (*ho:§itja*) them, and anybody else (particularly young men) with whom they came into contact, by burning *sã:* (aromatic herbs). This fragrant mixture masked the girl's smell and had a soothing effect on !Khwa:. A girl would also paint zebra-like stripes of red haematite on the young men to protect them from lightning

A new maiden's water and her magic power also affected the success of men in hunting. A glance from a menstruating girl made the game behave unfavourably. Any contact with a hunter and his weapons made it impossible to hunt and attracted !Khwa:'s anger. To avoid contamination, the girl's father reserved certain arrows to kill animals for his daughter – only the old women shared this food with her.

!Khwa: in perspective

For the |Xam teachers who committed their beliefs about the rain to paper some 115 years ago, !Khwa: was a conscious, gendered being who controlled where and how the rain fell. His behaviour was largely determined by people's behaviour – when they respected him, he favoured them with 'female' rain and harmonious social relationships; when people (especially young unmarried women) did not respect him, !Khwa: became angry and destructive. Every member of the community had their own relationship with !Khwa: which, in turn, affected everybody else. Most important for men was their ability to bring female rain to where it was needed. Women seemed to have a physiologically-based relationship with !Khwa:, focused upon menstruation, which gave them !Khwa:'s magic power. Thus, beliefs about !Khwa:, the nature of the rain, and how people influenced it, were an important part of the |Xam world-view.

❑

Note

[*] Folklorist Megan Biesele (1975: 131) compares !Khwa: with ||Gauwa, the lesser god of the Ju|'hoansi who live in the Kalahari Desert. Like !Khwa:, ||Gauwa is 'generally thought of as the destroyer' (1975: 131), but he performs both good and evil deeds.

When a girl snaps her fingers …

Narrator: Diä!kwain
Source: 'Díä!kwain heard this from Xã:ätiŋ (his father)'
Dictation dates: 20 and 21 December 1875
Notebook reference: L.V.20: 5618-5624
***Bantu Studies* reference:** Vol. 7 (1933), Part V: 297-298

When a girl snaps her fingers at somebody, the rain will 'shoot' that person.

❑

O !kwi-|a ≠ɑhuńniŋ i, !khwagən ||xɑm baitən kúï k''wãŋ, ti ε:, ha |kwẽ:ï k''okən ≠ɑhuńniŋ i, ĩ:. !khwa:gən baitən |khi: i, o !khwa:gən ta: ||ka ti ε:, ha |ki a: ≠ɑhuńniŋ-ĩ i, o haŋ ε !kwi-|a ˍ||ka:ŋ. He tikən e:, mama-gu k''auki ka, si se ˉã: !kwi-|a se ≠ɑhuńniŋ si. Ta: ||ẽiŋ k''auki a: !kwi-|a da: sija, ta: ha da: si ã:, !khwa: se |kha si.

Mama-gukən |k'e:ja si ã:, ti ε:, !khwa: ||nau, si ||k'oen, ti ε:, !khwa: k''wãŋ !khwa: k''auki tɑmse kãũ, si ˍkóä: |ne |k'e: !khwa:, !khwagən k''auki se !hɑm si, ta:, !khwa: ||nau !khwa: tú:ï, ti e:, si ≠kakən hĩ !khwa:, tikən kïẽ: siŋ !xwãŋ, !khwa: |ku ˍ!k''wãiŋ si-ta ≠kakən ε:, !khwa: tú:ï hε, hε si ≠kakən hĩ !khwa:, ĩ:.

!khwa: ˍkɔ́:ö !ka!karrakən-ã si, !xwãŋ ha k''auki ≠kauwa si-ta ≠kakəŋ. Haŋ txi: si-ta ≠kakən, o haŋ ||xɑm txi: ||ke||ke:, ti ε:, !kwi-|a da: he, o haŋ ta: ||ka ti ε:, !kwi-|a |ki a: txi: si. He tikən ε:, !khwa: ||xɑm txi: si, ĩ:.

When a girl snaps her fingers at us, the rain also lightens, doing as she does when she snaps her fingers at us. The rain lightens killing us, because she has snapped her fingers at us as a new maiden. Therefore our mothers do not want us to let a girl snap her fingers at us. For she does not do so from friendship, but to make the rain kill us.

Our mothers told us that when we saw that the rain seemed as if it were not falling gently, if we therefore spoke to the rain, it would not listen to us, but when it heard that we were speaking with it, then it would sound as if the rain were angry about our speech, which it heard when we addressed it.

The rain would thunder at us, as if it did not like our speech. It would shoot at our speech, for it also shoots just as a girl does for it feels that a girl is accustomed to shoot at us. Therefore the rain also shoots at us.

❑

Note

21-23 *The rain ...would* **shoot** *at our speech*: Wilhelm Bleek, Lucy Lloyd and Dorothea Bleek were not entirely sure that they had understood what *txi:*, translated here as 'shoot', meant – there is a question mark after this translation (Bleek 1956: 245). The word seems to have been recorded only in this single instance. Perhaps it was reserved to describe the unique power of !Khwa: to throw thunder and lightning at people, or perhaps it was not a 'word', but rather an onomatopoeic sound that Dia!kwain improvised to describe the sound of !Khwa: 'shooting' somebody.

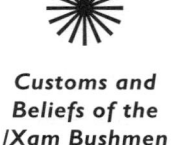

A girl and the rain's bolts

Narrator: Diä!kwain

Source: 'Diä!kwain heard this from his mother ǂKămmĕ-ăŋ and says that 'Jan Roundebout's mother !Kwárra-ăn also knows it'

Dictation dates: 17, 18 December 1875

Translation dates: 19, 20 December 1875

Notebook reference: L.V.20: 5608-5617

***Bantu Studies* reference:** Vol. 7 (1933), Part V: 298-299

Diä!kwain explains what happens when a pubescent girl (new maiden) becomes angry and curses somebody (see Introduction).

!khwa:-ka !k''abbe, hɛ ||nau ; !kwi-|a k''auki ka, i: ≠kaka, ha |kɯ ||nau, i: |k'e:ja ha, ha ||kɯ ||kha, ||kóë siŋ i tu, o i: |k'e:ja ha. Tʃweŋ e: |kwẽ:ï u, hiŋ e: _|gwãĩn i ; hiŋ ||nau, o hɛ k''auki _|gwãĩnja i, tʃweŋ e: |kwẽ:ï u, hiŋ tattən-tatten |hiŋ, ¯||k'e: !khwa: ||ki, o hiŋ ta: ||ka ti e:, !khwa: |waitən i. He tikən ɛ:, !khwa:-ka !k''abbe ||na !khwa: ||ki, ĩ:, o !khwa:gən ta: ||ka ti ɛ:, ha ká ha |kha i ; he tikən ɛ:, !k''abbe ||na !khwa: ||ki, ĩ:, o !khwa:gən ta:, ||ka ti ɛ:, !khwa: |waitən i. !khwa:gən ||xɑm ||ke-||ke:ja ti e:, !kwi-|a da: hi ã: hɛ. He tikən e:, !khwa: k''auki |ki i, ĩ:, o haŋ ta: ||ka ti ɛ:, !kwi-|a a: k''auki ta i ≠kaka. He tikən ɛ:, !khwa: k''auki |ki i, ĩ:.

The rain's bolts (?) do this; when a girl does not want us to talk to her, if we speak to her she curses our mouth with which we have spoken to her. Things like these enter us; or if they do not enter us, things like these fall (from the clouds) together with the rain water because the rain is angry with us. Therefore the rain's bolts (?) are with the rain water, because the rain feels as if it wants to kill us, that is why the bolts (?) are with the rain water, because the rain feels that it is angry with us. The rain behaves to us just as the girl does. Therefore the rain does not like us, because it feels that the girl does not want us to talk. Therefore the rain does not like us on account of it.

Ta:, mama-gu |ki ≠kaka ke, ti ɛ:, !kwi-|a a: _hã ¯oä ɛ !kwi-|a, haŋ _hã: ||nau, ha xóãkən-gu |k'e: ha, ha k''auki |kwẽ:ï k''o, ta: ha ɛ |kwi-|a _||ka:ŋ, haŋ _hã: k''auki

For our mothers used to say to me, that there was once a girl who, when her parents said that she must not speak like this, because she was a new maiden, would not

túï ha xóäkən-gu, hɛ |k'e: ha. Ha _hã: |kɯ ||nau, ha xóäkən-guwa: |k'e:ja ha, ha |kɯ ≠ɒhuńniŋ ha xóäkən-gu, o há: ka há ≠ɒhuńniŋ ha xóäkən-gu, ' U _ka: kaŋ ¯≠ĩ:, ŋ kaŋ se tú u, o ú: ki:sa: |k'e: ŋ?' Ha |kɯ ||nau, o ha: ≠ɒhuńniŋja ha xóäkən-gu, ha |kɯ dí-a |hiŋ, o ʒu:, o ha: |kwẽ:ï ku, ha |k'e:ja ha xóäkən-gu ã:.

!khwa: _hã: ||nau, o !khwa:gən |wuitən ha, !khwa: _hã: _||ɒha:, !khwa: _baitən hɛ, !khwa: |kɯ _baitən ||khóë siŋ hɛ. !khwa: _hã: |kɯ ||kóä:kən _baitən ||kho ≠hauru, o ti ɛ:, hɛ ||na hɛ; hɛ-ta ku: gwai _hã: |kɯ ||kóãkən |e: ≠hauru, o !khwa: _hã: |kɯ _baitən |ki |e:ja hɛ, o !kˀãũ; !kˀãũ _hã: |kɯ ||kóäkən di: _≠k''wara, o ti e:, hɛ |e: hɛ, !kˀãũwã _hã: |kɯ ||kóäkən ||kau tiŋ hɛ.

listen to them, when they spoke to her. As they were talking to her, she kept snapping her fingers at them (saying as she did so), "Do you think that I will listen to you, even if you order me to do so?" As she snapped her fingers at them, she went springing away on one foot and then the other, while she spoke like this to her parents.

Then the rain became angry with her, the rain gathered its clouds and lightened on them (her parents and others who were with them), lightened among them. It lightened making a waterpit at the place where they lived; they all disappeared in the waterpit, for the rain lightened putting them underground; the ground became black mud where they went in, it covered them entirely up.

Notes

1 *The* **rain's bolts** *(?)*: Dorothea Bleek was not sure exactly what *!khwa:–ka !k''abbe* were, but there is a note on the rain's bolts in the Bleek and Lloyd Collection which describes them as black pebbles thrown by !Khwa: (Hewitt 1986: 284).

3-4 *... she curses our mouth ...*: *//kha,* translated here as 'to curse', was also an exclamation of anger (Bleek 1956: 572).

'D.H. explains this that she will not have you talk to her, and will not wait for you to do so, and become angry and scolds us' (5607 rev.-5608 rev., note omitted).

5-6 *Things like these* **enter** *us...*: Diä!kwain means things like the *k''abbe*, the things that fell with the rain. The word */gwãĩn*, translated here by Dorothea as 'enter', has a more specific and significant meaning. It means 'to get into the flesh, take possession of' and is associated with 'magic' (Bleek 1956: 285). See Part VII, 'The sorceror's heart (more about sorcerors)' for another context in which the word */gwãĩn* is used

What the rain does to people and their things when he is angry

Narrator: |Haŋ‡kass'o
Source: |Haŋ‡kass'o, from his mother |Xabbi-aŋ, who thinks that she probably had it from her mother "Kammi
Dictation date: 9 September 1878
Notebook references: L.VIII.16: 7418-7429
***Bantu Studies* reference**: Vol. 7 (1933), Part V: 299-300

In this richly detailed account, |Haŋ‡kass'o talks about !Khwa:'s extraordinary power to transform people and their possessions. He describes how girls soothe angry, 'new' water in waterholes.

Hĩ _||kwaŋ tati e:, !ke!ketən e: ta, !khwa: ka |kha i, au !khwa |waita i. !khwa: !nu: hó: ||neiŋ, he !gweja-g |ne _!kˀaitən-ĩ i, he !gweja-g |ne _!kˀaitən ¯|kɑm úï ¯||nei-||nei, he ¯serreja |ne ¯|e !kˀe, ĩ:.

This is what the old people say, the rain wants to kill us when it is angry with us. The rain attacks the hut angrily, and the hail beats down on us breaking down the huts, and the cold wind gets in to the people in consequence.

Ha |ne |kɯ swai tau hohó !kˀe ; he !kwi a:, hã a:, !khwa: a: |waitən !kˀe ã:, hã |ne a:, ¯serreja |ne _maïi, ha |ne hó ha, ha |ne |ki ¯||kaitən ha au _!gwaxu. He ha |kɯ-g |ne k''uwa !a: tiŋ _!gwaxu, he há |kɯ-g |ne |hiŋ, !a: |hiŋ _!gwaxu, he ha |kɯ-g |ne ||a: ¯|e _tsaxukən, he há |kɯ_g |ne ¯|e _tsaxukən, há |kɯ-g |ne dí ¯!gã.

It drives out the people ; and the man, because of whom the rain is angry with the people, is the one whom the wind first lifts up, and blows up to the sky. Then he goes floating about in the sky, then floats out of the sky and drops down into a pond, then he stays in the pond and becomes a frog.

He !kˀe |kɯ-g |ne u-úï, !kˀe |kɯ-g |ne ||kaitən¯||kaitən _!gwaxu, ¯serreja |kɯ-g |ne |ki|ki ¯||kaitən hi au _!gwaxu. Hĩ |kɯ-g |ne |hiŋ-|hiŋ, ¯!a |hiŋ, hĩ |kɯ-g |ne |e¯|e tsaxukən, au hĩ |kɯ-g |ne e ¯!gã.

Then the people one after another go out and fly up into the sky, the cold wind blows them up into it. Then they keep coming out of it, floating down and falling into the pond, where they become frogs.

Au hı-ta !nwi!nwi |kɯ-g |ne ˉdi wai, hĩ |kɯ-g |ne ||gwaka ||e toukən, hĩ |kɯ-g |ne |kwẽĩ |ki, hĩ |kɯ-g |ne !ku!kurukən |kẽï a: ; au ||khaita |kɯ-g |ne dí ʘhokən, hiŋ |khwetən ; au !nwa: ˉã |kɯ-g |ne ||kóäkən !khe tiŋ, ||khwai||khwai ˉã |kɯ-g |ne ||xɑm ki !khe tiŋ. ||khwai||khwai-ta tũ e: !kˀe siŋ !xumma ||khwai-||khwai ĩ:, hĩ |kɯ-g |ne di wai, au ||khwai||khwai |kɯ-g |ne !khe tiŋ, hĩ |kɯ-g |ne |ki|ki hi !nu!nuntu:, au !khwa: |kɯ-g |ne ||kóäkən di ˍtsa-xukən, au hĩ tati, !khwa: eŋeŋjã |kɯ-g |ne ||khóë siŋ.

Meanwhile the karosses become springbok which lie down and roll, thereby shaking out (the water from their skins), while the sticks and branches (of the hut) become bushes; then the arrows (or reeds) just stand about, and so do the quivers. The skins of which people have made the quivers turn into springbok, as the quivers stand about there, they get ears; meanwhile the rain turns altogether into a pond, because its body goes into it.

Há !khwa:, haŋ a:, ka |waitən i, au há tati, !khwa: ˍ||ka:ŋ ã é, ha |waitən i, au í !kai!kai ha. He tikən e:, !kwi-|kagən k''auki ta !kai!kai ˍtsaxukən, ta:, í e !ke!ketən, í |kɯ e: ka |kwenˉĩ. He tikən e:, !kwi-|a ||nau, ha |ne se !kˀai !khwa:, ha |ne ≠kɑmʘpwa |kɯ kãũ, he, ha |ne ˍkərokən ˉsã, ĩ:. He tikən e:, ha |ne ||nau, ha |ne !kˀai ˍtsaxu-kən, ha |ne ˍ|gɔm |hiŋ ˉsã, ha |ne ˉ||kou !khwa: au ˉsã.

That is the water that is angry with us, because it is new water, it is angry if we throw stones at it. That is why the girls must not throw stones at the pond, as we, who are old people, have told them. Therefore when a girls approaches the water and it is raining gently, she grinds buchu. Then as she approaches the pond, she scoops out the buchu and strews it on the water.

Ha |ne ||nau, au há ˉ||kouwa !khwa: au ˉsã, há |ne sá |ho: !khwa:-ka tikəntikən e: !a:, au ˉto, au hiŋ tati e:, !khwa: k''auki tɑm ʘpwa ˉkoka ˉsã, ta: ˉsã e:, ha |ne ||ã: ĩ:. Haŋ |kɯ-g |ne kwe: ˍdauökən ki sˀo:, au haŋ tati e:, ha ˉ||ã:, au tʃweŋ e:, |k'wai k''auki twaitən ||ka hĩ. He e:, í ta ||a: |kweŋ, i akən xa se |hiŋ !khwa:. Ta:, ha |ke |kɯ ||nau, au !kwi-|a |kɯ !k'aija ha, au |kwi-|a k''auki ˍtaba aka, ha |kɯ !kwerritən, au ˍ|kwaka: k''auki ||na.

When she has strewn the water with buchu, she comes and darkens the parts of the water which float on top with red haematite, because the rain loves buchu very much for buchu is what it smells. It glides quietly along when it smells things which are unequalled in scent. Then if we go to dig up, we take the water out nicely. But if a girl approaches it without acting nicely, it happens that then it thunders, though clouds are not there.

❑

Part V
The Rain

What the rain does to people ...

Notes

3-4 *The rain attacks the hut angrily …: hó:* is translated here as 'attacks'. The *Dictionary* translation, 'to take, lift, pick up' (1956: 62), suggests rather that !Khwa: picks the house up and blows it away, exposing the people inside to the hailstorm.

6-7 *… and the cold wind gets in to the people in consequence*: 'wind it is. It resembles a whirlwind.' (7418 rev., note omitted). Whirlwinds are commonly associated with !Khwa: when he is angry, as well as with other supernatural phenomena.

14-15 *… and drops down into a pond …*: The word translated as pond is *tsaxukən*, used here instead of the more usual word *ǂhauru* (Bleek 1956: 651). In other contexts, *tsaxukən* is translated as 'eye' or 'berry' (Bleek 1956: 213). Perhaps |Haŋ‡kass'o used the word to mean *oog* (eye), the Afrikaans word for a spring of water.

37-38 *That is the water that is angry with us …*: It is a girl who performs the rituals necessary to pacify the new water (*!khwa: //ka:ŋ*). In all likelihood the girl, like the rain, is new (*//ka:ŋ*, the same word used to describe new water [Bleek 1956: 556]) – her state as a new maiden or newly developed girl meant that she was most suited to pacify the rain (see Part V, Introduction).

49-52 *When she has strewn the water with buchu, she comes and darkens the parts of the water which float on top with red haematite …*: The significance of *sã:* (aromatic herbs) and haematite are discussed in Part V, Introduction.

Drought

Narrator: |Haŋ‡kass'o
Source: |Haŋ‡kass'o from his maternal grandfather, Tsatsi
Dictation date: 14 September 1878
Notebook reference: L.VIII.16: 7449-7451
***Bantu Studies* reference**: Vol. 7 (1933), Part V: 301

The killing of a creature associated with water causes drought that drives away two important food sources. People are forced to eat 'famine food', which makes some of them sick.

❑

|xam-ka !kʔe ̠||kwaŋ k''auki |khi ̄!gã, au hiŋ tati e:, !khwa: |ke k''auki ta |ne kãũ, au i |khi ̄!gã. He |khuruwa |ku-g |ne te:ŋ, au i |khi ̄!gã, au !khwa: k''auki |ne kãũ, he ti |ku-g |ne ̄||ko:.

Bushmen do not kill frogs, because the rain does not fall if we kill frogs. A drought comes if we have killed frogs, and the rain does not fall, and the place becomes dry.

He ti hiŋ e:, |xam-ka !kʔe ta |ne ̄!kauwi ĩ:, au !khwa: a: k''auki |ne kãũ, he waija k''auki |ne ||na, ĩ:, !houwa k''auki |ne ||na. He !houwa |ku-g |ne ||gwi:, waija ||xamki |ku-g |ne ||gwi:. |xam-ka !kʔe |ku-g |ne ̄hĩ ̄|kuï, he e: |k'a ka ||na. !kouwi |k'akən |ku ||gwisiŋ, ̄|kuïtən e:, |k'a ka ||na.

Then it is that the Bushmen grow lean, because the rain does not fall, and the springbok are not there, and the locusts are not there. Then the locusts vanish, the springbok also vanish. The Bushmen eat gambro (a sort of melon), the plants of which are there. The (?) plants vanish, only the gambro is there.

̄|kuïja-g |ne ||xamki ̄||ko:. He ti hiŋ e:, ̄|kuï ta-g |ne |khi i, ĩ:, í |ne ̄!gwe. !kʔe kuitakən ̠||kwaŋ ̄|kuï |khi hĩ. He tikən e:, í ta |ki !xo |uru-ka |k'un, au i ta, i siŋ |ne |ki|ki |hiŋ hi, í siŋ !khou hi, he e:, ̄|kuï k''auki ta di-ĩ i, ĩ:. !kʔe kuitəŋ ̠||kwaŋ ̄!gwe au ̄|kuï.

The gambro also dries. Then the gambro poisons us, we are intoxicated by it. Gambro harms some people, therefore we take out the skin of the porcupine's tail, for we want to have it out in order to smell it, then the gambro will not injure us. Other people are intoxicated by gambro.

|khuruken a: tí ta ||khou ̄!kuïtəŋ ã:, ʘhokən |ku-g |ne ̄||ko:, au |khuru. Au !khwa: |kwẽ:ï k''wã, !khwa: kãũ, au hã ̄ã se ||khou

Drought is that which makes the country grow white, the bushes dry up in the drought. When the rain falls like this, a Cape

|k'wai, he tikən e:, !kˀe ta |ne ta, !khwa: kãũ tẽ !xu:, he !kˀe k''auki |ne dí akən !hou, hiŋ kóä wai.

winter), food will be plentiful, then people say, the rain falls bringing plenty, and people are not careful of the locusts and the springbok.

Notes

10 *... the locusts are not there*: The |Xam relied on locusts, probably the brown locust, *Locustana pardalina* (Robert Toms, email communication, 25 July 2002), as an important seasonal *veldkos* (Deacon & Deacon 1999: 144). Locusts are particularly nutritious during certain phases of their development and are roasted before they are eaten. An early Dutch traveller in South Africa reported seeing Bushman people waiting for locusts to settle on a bush at dusk before setting fire to it and then collecting the roasted insects the following morning (Mossop 1935). The |Xam believed that locusts possessed their own magic power (*/ko:ode*) and that they were controlled by *!gi:tən* (sorcerors), who kept them underground and released them through a hole that was covered by a stone (see Part VII, 'Sorcerors, locusts and locust birds').

12-13 *The Bushmen eat gambro ...*: The gambro is a uniquely southern African plant (genus *Fockea*, in the Milkweed family). It grows widely in arid areas and is an important water source for the Kalahari Bushman groups living to the north of the |Xam. The plant has a large underground tuber, with thin, creeping branches above the soil. People often have to dig holes of a metre or more deep, using digging sticks, in order to get the tubers out. They peel the tuber and cut it into pieces before eating the white watery flesh (Van Wyk & Gericke 2000).

24-25 *Other people are intoxicated by gambro*: Elsewhere |Haŋ‡kass'o describes the symptoms that some people develop when eating too much */kuï* – 'Our heads are like to split with gambro, and our ears sing from the gambro, because the gambro is killing us' (L.VIII.7: 6679 rev.).

32-33 *... people are not careful of the locusts and the springbok*: The word *a:kən* (alternatively *akkən*) has a wide range of positive meanings – 'to be nice, good, handsome, beautiful, to do nicely, well' (Bleek 1956: 7). Here it may mean that when things are abundant, people do not behave properly, that is, respectfully. Their disrespectful behaviour brings about drought and scarcity of the things that they abused. (See the Introductions to Parts I–III and V for more about *!nanna-se* or respect behaviour.)

The west wind

Narrator: |Haŋ‡kass'o
Notebook reference: L .VIII.1: 6102-6106
***Bantu Studies* reference:** Vol. 7 (1933), Part V: 301-302

The west wind was unwelcome and unpleasant. It heralded a time when hunting and gathering became extremely difficult.

❑

O !khwe |kɯ-g |ne te:ŋ wyri, he !khwa:-ka _|kwagən |kɯ-g |ne ĩ: kukúï, he sitən |ne ||õ:ïŋ, ï:. O !khwe |kɯ-g |ne teŋ wyri, he !khwa:-ka _|kwagən |kɯ-g |ne ĩ: !xwɔnni ; o !khwa:gən sin _||ɑ-hɑ:, he !khwe |kɯ-g |ne teŋ wyri.

He si |kɯ-g |ne |a: !khe o ||õïŋ, he ti hiŋ e:, !kaukən |ne |kwenja si _tsa:xukən, ĩ:, o híŋ tati e:, si |a: !khe ||õïŋ, o hiŋ ta, sí se k''wã. He e:, sitən |ne saŋ k''wẽ:ï, ĩ:, o !kaukən |ne |ki sa si !khwa: ; sitən |ne saŋ k''wẽ:ï, o sitən tati e:, si ||k'wa: taŋ.

He tikən e:, si k''auki ⊙puru ʃo: o !khwa:, o sitən tati e:, si ||kaŋ-a. He ti hiŋ e:, si k''auki ⊙puru ʃo o !khwa:, o hã:ŋ k''auki ||na !khwa:. He ti hiŋ e:, si-g |ne ||enna ti e:, |kú:ï ||na he, o sitən tati e:, hã: k''auki ||na !khwa:.

When the wind is in the west, then the rain clouds turn back, and we are thirsty in consequence. When the wind is in the west, then the rain clouds really turn back; the rain always passes away when the wind is in the west.

Then we stand half killed by the sun, so the children dip up water for us at the pond (a long way off) because we are half killed by the sun, for they want us to drink. Then we shall drink, when the children bring us water; we shall drink while we feel that we are hungry.

That is why we do not stay near the water, because we feel that we are hungry. So we do not stay near the water, for there is no food near the water. That is why we live where the gambro is, because we know, that food is not at the water.

❑

Notes

1-2 *When the wind is in the west, then the rain clouds turn back*: '... because the rain clouds do verily turn back, and we are thirsty on account of it' (6101 rev., text omitted).

4-5 *... the rain clouds really turn back ...*: '... because the wind is in the west, because the rain has passed across in front and the wind is in the west' (6103, text omitted).

9-10 *... so the children dip up water for us ...*: 'K.J. (i.e. Klein Jantje – ed.) explains that the children go to a distance [such as from here to the Breakwater] to fetch water for them' (6103 rev., note omitted).

This distance from Mowbray, the suburb of Cape Town where the Bleeks, Lucy Lloyd and the |Xam teachers lived, to the Breakwater – the prison nearby Cape Town harbour – is about ten kilometres.

Lizards and rain

Narrator: |Haŋ‡kass'o
Dictation date: 13 February 1878
Notebook reference: L.VIII.3: 6232 rev.-6234 rev.; 3: 6259-6261
***Bantu Studies* reference:** Vol. 7 (1933), Part V: 302-303

The territorial behaviour of the agama lizard is believed to influence the coming of rain.

Sitən |ne ||nau _!kháü gwai, sitən ta, !gɔmma-gɛrri ã:. Há ka ¯||kau ta !nabba, haŋ |ne !khe ta ti e:, !khwe a: tsʔu !kuŋ ʃo:, au ha !hau !khwa:-ka _|kwagən. He ha |ne ĩ-kwa ã |na:, o ha k''u ||kau ta !nabba, haŋ |ne ĩ:-kwa ã |na:,.

We do this to the male agama, we say noisy rejoicer to it. It lies up on the thorntree, it keeps its heads towards the place where the north wind blows and bewitches the rain clouds. Then it nods its head lying on the thorntree.

He ti hiŋ e:, sí ta ku, _!khaügən tuko _k''óä a:, ||kau ta !nabba, ha í se |xã-ã: ha, ha se ú ||khóë ; au i |xã-ã: ha, ha se ú ||khóë ; ta:, ha _k''óä _dóä a:, ¯||kau ta: ʘho. He ti hiŋ _k''óä dóä e:, !khwa: k''auki ta !khwa: ||ɑ_ha:, ĩ:, o haŋ _k''óä _dóä a:, ¯||kau ta: !nabba. He ti hiŋ e:, i se |xã-ã ha, ha se ú ||khóë o i |xã ã ha.

Therefore we say, the agama must really be lying on the thorn tree, we will shoot at it, to make it come down; when we shoot at it it will come down, for it must be lying on the bush. That must be why the rain will not come up, because it must be lying on the thorntree. So we will shoot at it that it may come down.

O ||gɛrre e: ta k''wa:, ha se ú ||khóë, ta:, ha _k''óä _dóä a:, ¯||kau ta !nabba. He ti hiŋ e:, i se _|kwai-ïtən ã, o ||gɛrre e: ta k''wa:, ha se ú ||khóë. |khu|khu a: _saŋ |hiŋ, ha _saŋ kwe: |hiŋ se, |khukən ʘpwa _saŋ tsʔu sweŋ ||a hé ti e. !khwa: ʘpwa _saŋ !hau !kheja hí, ti e: a, o ha tati e:, |khukən ʘpwa siŋ tsʔu swen ||a ti é.

When the arrow feather whizzes, it will come down, for it must be lying on the thorntree. Therefore we will startle it, as the feather whizzes, it will come down. The hairs (of the feather) will come out gently. A little hair will blow along here. A little rain will come later and stand here, because the little hair blew along here.

Notes

1-6 … *the male agama* … **bewitches** *the rain clouds*: *!hau* also means 'to frustrate' (Bleek 1956: 396). In other words, the agama bewitches the rain clouds by frustrating, or preventing, them from forming. Janette Deacon (1988: 134) has pointed out another connection between agama lizards and the topography of |Xam-ka aũ – the Strandberg is a series of three hills, said to be the remains of an agama lizard that was squeezed and broken into pieces when it tried to pass through the mountains. The |Xam made rock engravings on top of all three hills, but most were made on the 'head' of the lizard, the northernmost hill which faces directly into the rain wind, the wind from the north.

6-7 … *it nods its head lying on the thorntree* …: The Southern Rock agama (*Agama atra*) occurs in the areas where |Haŋ‡kass'o and the other |Xam teachers lived. A dominant male agama perches on the highest point of his territory, nodding his brightly coloured head as a signal for other males to keep away (Branch 1998).

15-16 … *because it must be lying on the thorntree*: 'That must be why the rain will not come up for he must be lying on the Driedoorn tree' (6259, text omitted).

16-17 *So we will shoot at it that it may come down*: '… because we shoot at him' (6259, text omitted).

18 *When the arrow feather whizzes* …: The whizzing sound of the arrow feather apparently startles the lizard out of the tree. A little hair from the feather falls out and floats on the breeze. In response, a little rain will come to the place where the arrow feather fell.

In Part VIII, '*ʃo-õä*, a vegetable medicine or charm', //Kabbo says that 'an arrow that flies well makes a tearing sound through the air'.

The rain's animals

Narrator: |Haŋ‡kass'o
Dictation date: 12 September 1878
Notebook reference: L .VIII.16: 7431 rev.
***Bantu Studies* reference:** Vol. 7 (1933), Part V: 303

!Khwa: keeps certain animals for his own use.

||khwı, hiŋ tau kóä !gukən, hiŋ _!góë, hiŋ ||go:. Hé t∫weŋ, hiŋ e:, !khwa: ⁻|kuwa hi, ã:, au !khwa: eŋeŋ. He ti hiŋ e:, |xam-ka !kˀe k''auki təm-⊙pwa !həmmi hi. He t∫weŋ, hiŋ e:, !khwa: ka _!gabbetən-ĩ í, ĩ:, au haŋ tati tsˀá a: |gija ha é.

The cobra, and the puffadder, and the tortoise (Testudo geometrica), and the water tortoise (Testudo leopardis). These things the rain puts aside as its meat. Therefore Bushmen fear them greatly. With these the rain pets us, because it is a strong thing.

The rain behaves differently with different people

Narrator: |Haŋ‡kass'o
Source: 'My grandfather Tsatsi was the one who thus told me, as well as my elder female relations'
Dictation dates: 6 March 1879
Notebook reference: L.VIII.26: 8303-8309
***Bantu Studies* reference:** Vol. 7 (1933), Part V: 303-304

Young men and women have to respect !Khwa:'s 'things' or face the consequences. |Haŋ‡kass'o *explains that people try to influence the way that !Khwa: behaves. The rain responds to each person differently, for reasons that are given here.*

ŋ *!kõïŋ _Tsatsitən á ka siŋ |kwẽï da: ke, hiŋ kóä ŋ !kó:ëtukən. Hiŋ e: ta, !kwi-|a: k''auki ta ⁻hĩ _!góë, hiŋ kóä k''aodəro; ta: !khwa: |ké ta he t∫weŋ, hĩ |ke é:, !khwa: ka-g*

My grandfather Tsatsi told me this, also my grandmother and aunts. They said that a girl does not eat the tortoise, neither does a young bachelor; for the rain

|ne !kwerritən _||gauë hĩ, he !kwi-|a: siŋ ¯hĩ hĩ, au !kwi-|a: e !kwi-|a. He tikən e:, !khwa: k''auki ta-g |ne tã !khe!khe, ĩ:.

He tikən e:, !kwi a: |ĩ twaïï, ha a: ka |k'e: !khwa, au !kuko:wa kóä, '||khe||khe-we:, akən tuko se |k'eja hi !khwa á, ta, ha k''auki tamʘpwa battən-ĩ. Ta !khwa: ka ||nau, ŋ́ a |k'e:ja !khwa:, !khwa k''auki tamʘpwa !kwerritən, di ku !xwã !khe-!khe, au ŋ́ a |k'e:ja !khwa. Ta:, a á ka !khwa: ka tamʘpwa ¯kãũ, au á |k'e:ja !khwa:, au á-ka !khwagən tati, a k''auki ≠kakən au ||kakən. He tikən e:, a-ka !khwa ka an!au ¯xu-u !kwerritəŋ, au hiŋ tati e:, hĩ k''auki |ne battən-ĩ, he hi |ne tamʘpwa ¯kãũ. hĩ |ne ¯kãũ ĩ: ||ki, au hi k''auki |ne !kwerritən.'

owns these things, it seeks them thundering, if a girl has eaten them as a girl. Then it is that the rain becomes wrathful.

Therefore a man with a good heart (who does not scold) addresses the rain, while another man says (to him), "O beast of prey, you shall address this rain for us, for it is lightning badly. For when I am the one who addresses the rain, it thunders loudly and sounds angry at my addressing it. But you make the rain fall gently, when you speak to it, for your rain feels that you do not speak hastily. Therefore your rain quickly leaves off thundering and falls gently, it only rains liquid rain and does not thunder.

The rain and rain liquid

Narrator: |Haŋ≠kass'o
Source: 'My grandfather Tsatsi was the one who thus told me, as well as my elder female relations'
Dictation date: 6 March 1879
Notebook reference: L.VIII.26: 8307 rev.
***Bantu Studies* reference:** Vol. 7 (1933), Part V: 304

|Haŋ≠kass'o observes that /Xam and Europeans have different ideas about what 'rain' is (see Part V, Introduction).

|xam-ka !kˀetən e: |né ta '!khwa ||ki', au ¯|hũ |né ta 'rain', au !khwa: e: ¯kãũ !a: |hiŋ _|kwagən.

He tikən e:, |xam-ka !kˀe ta |né ta, !khwa: !xwã xokən¯xokən, au ha tati, há |ne !kwerritən ¯!a tã au _!gwaxu.

Bushmen say "rain liquid" when Europeans say "rain" to the water which falls from the clouds.

That is why Bushmen say that the rain sounds hollow, when it thunders lying along in the sky.

Old men insult the rain

Narrator: |Haŋ‡kass'o
Source: 'My grandfather Tsatsi was the one who thus told me, as well as my elder female relations'
Dictation dates: 6 March 1879
Notebook reference: L .VIII.26: 8304 rev.-8305 rev.
***Bantu Studies* reference:** Vol. 7 (1933), Part V: 304-305

Old men are asked to persuade the rain to fall. They, in turn, approach others that have the power to influence the rain. Diä!kwain describes how old men insult !Khwa:.

❑

ŋ !kõïŋ -//kwaŋ ka siŋ /k'e: !khwa:.

My grandfather used to address the rain.

The rain is addressed in the following manner by the old men:

/nu/nukən !kʔe e: //na !khwa:.

first they speak to the dead men who are with the rain.

' ⁻Kauüü wɛ,
⁻Kauüü wɛ,
U kaŋ k''auki ta /ne ⁻≠enna au ŋ́,
U k''auki /ne ⁻k''waŋ u ⁻≠enna ŋ-ka //neiŋ.'

" O gallopers,
O gallopers,
Do you not know me?
You do not seem to know my hut."

Then they speak to the rain itself,

' A siŋ ⁻kwaŋ /ne //kabbeta a,
Ta !kwi /ka⁻ka //k'oen//k'oen sauro a,
A siŋ ⁻kwaŋ /ne //kabbeta !kaukən ã: a.'

" Thou shouldst put thy tail between thy legs,
For the women are looking shocked at thee,
Thou shouldst put thy tail between thy legs for the children."

He tikən e:, !khwa: ka /ne !kwerritən dí ku !xwã ⁻≠ẽrri:, au há tati, ha /ne !kwerritən ⁻!a tẽ, au -!gwaxu. He tikən e:, há /ne !xwã ⁻≠ẽrri, ĩ:, au há tati ha /ne ⁻xu úï battən-aŋ, há /ne /ku ĩ: /k''əm.

Then the rain thunders sounding little, because it thunders lying along in the sky. Therefore it has little sound, because it leaves off lightning, it only lightens distantly in sheets.

Note

13-14 *Thou shouldst put thy tail between thy legs*: Dorothea Bleek omitted a note from the original notebook:

'Explanation: the women see the *!khoa !kweiten*' ['rain penis'] (8305 rev.).

The rain animal seems to be compared to a four-legged animal with a tail. When the tail is raised, its genitals are visible – when scolded, it tucks its tail between its legs (obscuring the genitals) and flees. Bushman people in the Kalahari are known to insult the spirits of the dead with phrases like 'hyena / elephant / lion penis', 'thrown away penis' and 'filthy [i.e. shit] face' (Marshall 1969: 376). It seems that the |Xam also braved the power of spirit beings by throwing insults at them.

Dead men that ride the rain

Narrator: |Haŋ‡kass'o
Source: '|Haŋ‡kass'o from Tsatsi, ‡Kămmi-ăn and Tuai-aŋ'
Notebook reference: L.VIII.27: 8399 rev.-8400 rev.
***Bantu Studies* reference:** Vol. 7 (1933), Part V: 305

A rain-maker goes to find the dead men that ride the rain.

❑

|nu|nukən !kˀe: e |hiŋ !kˀãũ jakən e:, ŋ !kóïŋ-gu ka síŋ ta, hi _ha e: !kabbi !khwa:, au hiŋ tati e:. !hôũ-!hõũ e: hi |ki hi, hi ||ke||keja bara-ka !hõũ!hõũ, hiŋ ||hiŋ !khwa:. He tikən e:,·hĩ e !kabbi !khwa:, au hiŋ ta ti e:, hĩhĩ e: |ki !khwa:.

Dead people who come out of the ground are those of whom my parents used to say, that they rode the rain, because the thongs with which they held it were like the horse's reins, they bound the rain. Thus they rode the rain, because they owned it.

He tikən e:, !kˀe ta |ne ku, au !khwa: á:, há !kwija, hĩ |ne ta, !gita _ha ||a ¯kwerre !hõũ. He tikən e:, !khwa |ne ||a kãũ, ||khou !kwi:, au !khwa: !kwa: ¯a siŋ ≠ẽr̃i ki ||a:. !khwa ||ki e: |hiŋ _|kwagən. !khwa ||ki _||kwaŋ |ku e, e: !kˀe |ne ta, !khwa: !kwa:, ĩ:, au !kˀetən tati e:, ha k''auki kãũ tikəntikən-ta¯ku.

Therefore people say, when there is a big rain, that the sorcerer has gone to loosen the thong. Then the rain falls and increases, where first a little rain leg had passed by. The rain liquid it is which comes from the clouds. It is that that people call the rain's leg, when it does not rain everywhere.

❑

Note

16-17 … *when it does not rain everywhere*: 'The rain liquid which comes out of the clouds' (8400 rev., note omitted).

Drizzle and lightning

Narrator: |Haŋ‡kass'o
Dictation date: 8 May 1878
Notebook reference: L.VIII.9: 6813 rev.-6815 rev.
***Bantu Studies* reference:** Vol. 7 (1933), Part V: 305-306

Two kinds of rain are described in the first paragraph, one good and the other dangerous. |Haŋ‡kass'o describes the special precautions that people take with their children when they see that a dangerous kind of rain is coming. They fear one particular aspect of the 'angry' rain most of all.

❑

⊙pwɔ⊙pwɔ̃nnu : !khwa: a ||kija k''auki ||na, ha ||ki ⊙pwɔnni e: ||khóë, hi |ne ≠ẽr̃ri ≠ẽr̃ri au hĩ ||khóë. He ti hiŋ e:, si ta-g |nė ta, hi ⊙bu:kən !kˀãũ. Au !khwa: a: !khwa !kwija, haŋ a:, si ta |né ta, 'A ̠||kwaŋ |kɯ a ||k'oen, ||khugən e: ||khóë e. Ta:, ha |ne ||khõä se tẽ: kɔro. He tikən e:, a ||kwaŋ |kɯ a ||k'oen, ||khukən e: ||khóë !ɑhí úï, ha ⊙pwurru a: tattən !khe.'

A drizzle : it is not liquid rain, its little drops which fall are tiny, very tiny as they fall. Therefore we are wont to say, they fall gently on the ground. When the rain is a great rain, we are wont to say " You ought to see that a stream is falling. For it seems to knock down the jackal. Therefore you ought to see the stream pouring down from above, it knocks things down."

He tikən e:, si ta ka, !kaukən ̠kɔ́ä: se !xe:, ta:, !xóë ta ti e, hi ta !khwa: ̠dɔ́ä battən-ĭ, hiŋ k''auki ta !ke!ke, ta: ha ˉoä battən ||k''abbi !khou ||khóä-si, au ti e. Ta: he !xóë ta tí, hĭ ̠dɔ́ä é: a, hi-ta !khwa: k''auki ̠dɔ́ä ta !ke!ke. He tikən e:, ŋ ka, !kaukən se !xe:, ta:, hĭ sˀo ka, !kwi a: kaka, ̠!kãũwa e, ha k''au á.

Therefore we say, the children ought to hide, for the rain seems to be lightning at this place, it is not quiet, but it has lightened strongly, growing larger here. For this place must be the one at which the rain does not fall gently. That is why I want the children to hide, for it seems not to be a being that is willing to fall gently.

He tikən e:, ha ka |kɯ ˉ|arro i, au í k''auki ≠enna, ha ka |kɯ ˉ|arro i, au !khweitən a: ̠hóäka, há i k''auki |ni ti sá ha.

Therefore it will strike us without our knowing it, it will strike us in the dark, while we do not see it coming.

❑

Notes

7-8 *You ought to see that a* **stream** *is falling*: Dorothea Bleek translated the word *//khugən* as a 'stream'. In fact, the word means 'to make water' or 'urinate' (Bleek 1956: 577). The downpour of rain is therefore being described by |Haŋ‡kass'o as a strong stream of (the rain's) urine

21-22 … *it seems not to be a* **being** *that is willing to fall gently*: The rain is referred to as '*!kwi*', which is usually translated as 'person' (Bleek 1956: 466). Here Dorothea translates it as 'being'. The use of this term to describe rain / water suggests that in the |Xam world-view, !Khwa: was capable of conscious thought and action (see Part V, Introduction).

Young unmarried women and girls must be silent and hide from the rain

Narrator: |Haŋ‡kass'o
Source: From his maternal grandmother, Kammi
Dictation dates: 6 December 1878
Notebook reference: L.VIII.23: 8032-8031 rev.
***Bantu Studies* reference:** Vol. 7 (1933), Part V: 306

'New maidens' and unmarried menstruating women must be taught how to respect !Khwa:. This extract describes one example of respectful behaviour and explains who teaches the girls what they need to know.

!kwi|kagən ₋||kwaŋ ka |kɯ ≠gouwa, au hĩ tati hĩ |kɯ !xeja au !khwa:, hi |kɯ ||gwitən ||na, au !khwa: k''auki sa:, au hiŋ tati e:, hi xóäkəngu e: ta, hi koa: se ⁻!xe:, au !khwa: ⁻!naun sa:. He !khwa: |kɯ-g |ne sa:, au hĩ |kɯ !xe:ja te⁻ten ta:, ta !khwa: ₋saŋ |waitən hĩ, au hĩ ₋taija !ahí tiŋ !khwa:, au !khwa: sa:. He tikən e:, hi |kɯ se !xe:, au !khwa: ⁻!naunko sa:.

|nutarakən ₋||kwaŋ a: ≠kakən ; háŋ ka, haŋ ≠kaka !kaukən, ã:, ha ka síŋ |kɯ |e:ta ||neiŋ, au há e !kwi|a.

Girls must be silent when they are hiding from the rain, though they have been playing there when no rain was coming, as their mothers have told them to hide, when the rain is just coming. Then the rain comes, while they lie hidden, for the rain would be angry with them, if they walked about in front of it, as it came. Therefore they must hide while it is yet coming.

An old woman is the one who speaks ; she tells the children about it, how she used to go into the hut when she was a girl.

Note

1 *Girls must be silent*: |Haŋ‡kass'o actually said 'young unmarried women and girls must be silent' (8032).

The rain-maker

Narrator: ||Kabbo
Dictation dates: 29 November to 11 December, 1872
Notebook reference: L.II.24: 2213-2226 and 25: 2227-2262 (shortened by Dorothea Bleek)
***Bantu Studies* reference:** Vol. 7 (1933), Part V: 306-312

Originally entitled 'The story of the old man who makes rain', this long and intriguing text has all the attention to detail that is so characteristic of //Kabbo's style. In the story, a man visits his grandfather, a rain-maker, and tells him why he wants rain to fall. The old man explains that the people have driven the rain away by their own actions. Two kinds of rain are described – one feared, the other welcome. The old man explains where he finds the rain and how he makes it fall. Using a series of dramatic comparisons, //Kabbo describes the build up and eruption of a rainstorm over the plains of the Karoo. After the rain, two of the animals that the /Xam hunted arrive on the hunting ground. //Kabbo describes their appearance and behaviour in great detail. All of the missing text and notes have been included.

❑

!kwi a: a, haŋ ≠ĩ:, ti e:, ha _saŋ |a ≠kakən, !khwa: se kãũ, au haŋ ati e:, haha-ka !kwi é: e !khwa:-ka kwi. Haŋ |ne |ũ:ŋ, ha |haŋ |ne ≠kaka ha, '||a: ≠kaka !kõïŋ, !kõïŋ se |ki kãũwa hi: !khwa:. I se k''wã !khwa _||ka:ŋ ||ki, e: ||kau siŋ !kˀãũ, he _|ka:ti kãũ. I se !həm !kwã xo-u ||nɛiŋ tʃɔrokən, au i tati e:, i-g |ne !kwã |kəm ||a !khwa _||ka:ŋ ||ki, e: twaïï ; ta, i dóä |kɯ k''wã |ki |u:.'

This man thinks that he will go and talk, so that rain may fall, because his relation is a rain man. He sleeps, his wife says to him, "Go and talk to the old man, that he may make rain fall for us. We will drink new rain water lying on the ground which has recently fallen. We will travel away from the old hut and travel to the new water which is sweet, for we have been drinking bitterness."

Ha |haŋ !hom ha, '!gauë ka:, ŋ _saŋ _tai ã ; ŋ ||kã: ⊙pwa _saŋ ||na hĩ ŋ ; si _saŋ ||a toto: ha !kõïŋ, !khwa se kãũ |ki _|ua: sa si whai.' Ha |haŋ !hom ha, ' ŋ ||kwaŋ |kwẽ: da.'

Her husband agrees with her "To-morrow I will go about it ; my younger brother will go with me ; we will go and ask that old man that rain may fall, bringing us back the springbok." His wife assents, " Yes."

Hiŋ |ũ:ŋ, hiŋ !ka:gən kau _tai. Hiŋ ||a ha !kõïŋ, hiŋ toto: ha !kõïŋ, 'A xa k''auki _dóä ≠ĩ:, ti e:, !khwa: se kãũ?' Ha !kõïŋjaŋ ≠kaka hĩ, 'Tsa de ba a:, u-g |ne toto: ŋ ã:?' Ha ||kã: ⊙pwakən ≠kaka ha !kõïŋ, 'ŋ !kõïŋ-we, ŋ kaŋ ka, a |ki kãũwa ke !khwa:, !khwa: se kãũ kwerrekwerreja ke !kʔãũ. Ta, ŋ |nu|nuäde ||ka k''ɔrrokən, an !kʔãũ e: ta |i, au ŋ |xwerri tóï; he ti hiŋ e:, ŋ sa á, ĩ:, ŋ se ≠kaka ha:.'

They sleep, they go out early. They go to the old man and ask him, "Do you not think that rain will fall?" The old man says, "What are you asking me about?" The younger brother says to him, "My grandfather, I want you to make rain fall for me, to cool the ground for me. For my knees are burnt from the ground which is hot, where I crawl after the ostrich; that is why I have come to talk to you."

Ha !kõïŋjaŋ ≠kaka hã, ha ||kãŋ tum-ĩ. Ha !kõïŋjaŋ ≠kaka hã, 'ŋ káŋ ka:, !kõïŋ-gu se |ki kãũwa hi: !khwa:, !kʔãũ se kwerreja hi:'. Ha ⊙pwa⊙pwaidikən ≠kaka ha, 'ŋ _dóä ka, á se e |ki kãũwa ke !khwa:.' Ha !kõïŋjaŋ ≠kaka ha, 'ŋ káŋ tuko a: _!k''wainja, ti e:, !kʔe ta bu: |e |i, au !khwa: _tai sa. He e:, !khwa:-gən |ne |ki:, ĩ. He ti hiŋ e:, !khwa k''auki ta-g |ne |kãũ akkən !kʔãũ, ĩ:.

The old man speaks to him, his brother listens. The old man says, "I think that the old men will make rain fall for us, to cool the ground for us." His grandson says, "I thought you would make the rain fall for me." The old man says, "I am angry, because the people make fire, when the rain comes. That is why the rain disperses. That is why the rain does not fall properly on the ground.

'He ti hiŋ e:, kammaŋ ko: ka-g |ne ||ko:wa, ĩ:, au !khwa |kɯ-g |ne kaŋ kãũ akkən !kʔe-ta !xóë. He e;, ka ⊙hokən ha-g |ne kerruwa, ĩ:, au ti e:, ŋ́ a ʃo: hĩ, hĩ-ku ⊙hoka |ne ||ko:wa, ú ŋ a k''au á: |ki kãũwa !khwa:. !khwa: |kɯ-g |ne ĩ: kãũwa !kʔe, au !khwa:-g |na: |i, a ha !ɑhí !khe: !khwa:, au |kʔe !hɑmmi !khwa:-ka _!kʔan, au hĩ: |ne ≠ĩ:, ti e:, |ka-|ka: ||khõä |kɯ e.

"Therefore the middle part is dry, while the rain is falling nicely at the place of yonder people. Their bushes are green, while the bushes of the place where I live are dry, as if I were not the one who makes the rain fall. The rain was really falling for the people, when it saw the fires standing in front of it, because the people were afraid of the rain's shadow, thinking it seemed to portend death.

(Omitted text: 2223-2225)

As if they did not live in a place that has trees. There are big trees, they have thick trunks that the wind blows past, and the thick tree trunks stand firm. And then the wind blows [as they] stand firm. Because the wind feels that

their trunks are in the earth. The tree is tall; the house stands quiet below, because the wind cannot blow the house away, [the house stands fast in a large tree, J.T. explains, and is not shaken by the wind].

Then the house is warm because the house stands under a huge tree trunk, that is why the house stands quiet.

'ŋ ˍ//kwaŋ siŋ dá: ha, a se-g /ne //k'oen ; a se k̓''auki /ne bu: -/e: /i, au a-g /ne !hammi ˍ!k²an, au á: fo ka dum-mo k''au /ku é, he /ku e !k²an, au hiŋ tati e:, ˍ/kwagən !kerri é. /a:gən k''auki ˍdóä é. Ta, ≠gou /ku é, ʘho:kən se kerru.'

"I will make it (rain), for you to see; you must not make a fire, when you are afraid of its shadow, for you seem to think it is darkness, but it is shadow, because the clouds are big. It is not danger, but it is peace, that the bushes may become green."

Ha ʘpwaʘpwaidikən ≠kaka ha, 'A ˍkwa: k''auki se //k'warre: ˍ/k'a:-xa, ta, a se /ku ˍtabba !khwa: /aiti, ha k''auki ˍ!kwa, ha se tamʘpwa kãũ, au hã tati e, !kwəbba /ku e. Ha a: tamʘpwa kãũ ˍt²ain !k²ãũ, !k²ãũ se //ka//ka: ki /e: au !k²ãũ //kaië. Ta, !k²e ta /ne !hammi !khwa: gwai, au !k²e tummĩ hã, au há /ne !kwerri:ta sa:, au ha tati e, ha /ki ha !kwa !kwagən.

His grandson says to him, "You must not arouse a rain-bull, but you must make a she-rain, which is not angry, which rains gently, because it is a slow shower. It is one that falls gently, softening the ground, so that it may be wet inside the earth. For people are afraid of a he-rain, when they hear it come thundering, as it gets its legs.

'!k²e: /ne ≠ĩ, ti e:, /kukən-ka //kõïja //khõä é. Hiŋ e: !kaugən /naŋ/naŋ-a: /ne /kwẽ:ï ú, au !k²anna /ku é ; /a: k''auki é. Ta:, !khwa: gwai ka !ahí //kóä !k²ãũ ã:xu. Ha siŋ ˍtai //kõë hóä !k²ãũ. He ti hiŋ e:, !khwe ta /ku ˍmaïi, !khwe ts²u /kam ú //neiŋ, ĩ:. He e:, !k²e /ne bu: /e /i, au !k²e /ne !hammi: ˍ/k'a:-xakən-ka ˍ//xaˍ//xabbakən xa, au ha tati, ha ˍ!kwa:ŋˍ!kwa:ŋ. Au !k²e ≠ĩ, ti e:, //neiŋja ˍsaŋ !k²ũ, he ti hiŋ e:, !k²e /ku ˍmaïi, hĩ bu !ahí !ho /i au !khwa:, au !khwa: !naunko ˍtai sa, !khwa: se !ham !xwonni //e, au hiŋ tati e: //nei//nei ˍsaŋ ts²u !k²ũ.'

"People think that the time of death must be come. Then the mountain tops are covered, but it is a shadow, it is not danger. For a he-rain is passing over the face of the earth. It follows the dust. For a wind goes first, the wind blows the hut away. Then the people light fires, because they fear the rain-bull's wrath, when it is angry. When people think that the hut will be caught up, then they light fires in front of the rain so that as the rain comes up, it will turn back in fear, for they think the huts may be blown away."

(Omitted text: 2232-2233)

For the darkness is very dark on the Brinkkop's summit. The rain's darkness is black because the clouds are black. Therefore the darkness is black. Therefore the people do first, they fear; because they think that the houses will blow away.

Ha !kõïŋjaŋ ≠kaka ha ʘpwa-ʘpwaïdi, " A ˍkwɔŋ k"auki ˍsaŋ bu |e |i, ta, i-ta !xóẽ-ka ʘhokən ||ko:wa ; á se !ke!kɛja hi: !khwa:. Ta, ŋ se |ã !khwa: |aiti, ha |ki !khwaitən, ŋ siŋ tsˀau ha, ha a: ka kãũ ˍtˀain !kˀãũ, !kˀãũwa se ||ka||ka ki !kˀai au !kˀãũ ||kaië. He e:, ʘhokən ka ˍ!kˀɔ:ŋ, ĩ, ʘho ka: se kerru akən, he e:, whai ta ˍ||ka:rokən sa ĩ:. Whai se !kaukən !xóëtən!xóëtən-ka ku:, !kˀe-ta ku: se |xãä. Ta: !xóë-ta ku: e: ||ko:wa, ta: ˍ!gwa:xu ˍ||kwaŋ kwerri:ja, haŋ kwerri: ʃo:. He ti hiŋ e:, !khwa ˍ||kwaŋ se kãũ !xóë-ta ku:, ta: ŋ se tsˀau !khwa |aiti, he é:, ŋ |ne |í ha, í, ŋ siŋ |ã|ã tɔrro !ho !khwa:-ka ||xaukən, !khwa: !gau se !kau tiŋ !kˀãũ. Whai se ˍdauko kwˀã !khwa: !gau, au whaija ˍ||kabbe ||a:, au whaija tati, whai |ku-g |ne ||ke:n ||a:, ta !khwa |aiti á ka kãũ kwerri siŋ, au há ka, há se ||ka||ka !xwetən!xwetən-ka ku:.'

The old man says to his grandson, " You must not make a fire, for the bushes of our place are dry ; you must wait quietly for the rain. For I will cut a she-rain which has milk, I will milk her, then she will rain softly on the ground, so that it is wet deep down in the middle. Then the bushes will sprout and become nicely green, so that the springbok come galloping. They will travel to all parts, and all the people will shoot. For all places are now dry, because the sky is clear, it is round. Therefore rain must fall on all places, for I will milk a she-rain, I will cut her, by cutting her I will let the rain's blood flow out, so that it runs along the ground. The springbok will drink the rain's blood as they go, they will gallop about, they will feel that they can leap about, because the she-rain has fallen everywhere for she means to make all places wet."

Ha ʘpwaʘpwaidikən ≠kaka ha, ' ŋ ˍdóä |kwẽ:-da, ta: !khwa: |aiti á: ka |ki ha tutu:, he e: ta ||kóä |kum ; akən se ĩ: ||a |ã tẽ !khwa: au !khwa:-tu !kerri e ˍ|xarra, e: ||kóë ʃo !kaugən.'

His grandson says to him : " I understand, for the she-rain is drawing her breath which resembles mist ; you must please go and cut the rain at the great waterpits which are on the mountain."

Ha !kõïŋjaŋ ≠kaka ha, " ŋ kaŋ |kú se ĩ: |ki ||kaitən !khwa: au !kau, !kau a: ŋ |kwaitən |ã|ã ||kau tẽ !khwa ã:. Ha !xo:wa, !khwa:-ka ||xaukən se !kˀattən ||kóë, ta Swa:-ka !kˀe ||anna !kˀãũ. Hé ka ≠ĩ, ti e:, hĩ se !hammi:, ti e: |ku:ka |ku

His grandfather says to him: " I will really ride the rain up the mountain on top of which I always cut the rain. It is high, so the rain's blood flows down, for the Flat Bushmen live on the plains. They think they should be afraid, for I

a:, ŋ a di: ha, ta ŋ a //khõä /ku di /ki: hĩ. He ti hiŋ e:, hĩ ka-g /ne bu:-ã /i ĩ, au hĩ ≠ĩ ti e:, /ka/ka: á: a, ŋ a di: ha. Ta: _!gwaxuwa-g /ne /kwẽĩ _/kwãĩ, hĩ k''auki /ne /ni: !kaugən /naŋ/naŋ.

seem to be bringing death to them. That is why they light fires for they think that I am causing danger. For the sky is angry, they cannot see the mountain tops.

" Hĩ /ne di /kurru !khwa:, !khwa:-ka _/kwa:ka se /kurru, au hĩ /ne tã-ĩ //kaŋ, au hĩ tati, hĩ !xe!xe /e:ta //neiŋ. Hĩ /ne //kaŋ, au hĩ /ku-g /ne /kã:, au hĩ k''auki /ne _tai //gauë hã, au hĩ tã:-ĩ _k''ao ; hĩ /ku-g /ne kuŋ //na, au hĩ tã //ka//ka ti e:, hĩ !go:ëja !nwi!nwi. Hĩ /ne _//kao /ki ʃo:, au hĩ k''auki /ne _tai_tai úĩ, hĩ se-g /ne _tai //kóë ho !khwe, au !khwa-ka !khweja-g /ne _k''ao.

" They disperse the rain, (with fires), the rain clouds disperse, although they feel hungry as they hide in the huts. They are hungry as they sit waiting and do not go out to seek food, because they feel the cold ; they warm themselves (at the fire), feeling they lack karosses. They remain sitting and do not leave it to walk in the wind, for the rain wind is cold.

" Hĩ //ka, hĩ /ki hã:, hĩ ka !khwa: kãũ. Hĩ /ne di /kurru !khwa:, au hĩ e ≠kaka, ŋ /ne !hom hĩ, ŋ /ne /ki kãũwa hĩ !khwa:. ŋ ka ≠ĩ:, ti e:, ŋ a se /ã !khwa: //kwarra, ha /ki !khwaitən, ha a //ki tʔain, ha-ka !khwetən //ko:wa. Haŋ tym⊙pwa kãũ, au han tati e:, ha-ka _/kwagən tʔain, au han tati e:, ha /kú /ku e, ha eŋeŋ k''auki e, ta !khwa /kú /ku e.

" They fail to get food, they want rain to fall. They make the rain disperse, though they asked for it and I assented, I make the rain fall for them. I think that I will cut a mother rain that has milk, she moistens softly, her wind blows gently. She rains gently, because her clouds are soft, for they are her hair, they are not her body, for they are the rain's hair.

" !khwetən tsʔu //ko //a !khwa /ku, au hiŋ tʔainja. Hiŋ /uerri:, hiŋ di: _/kwagən. !khwetən tsʔu //kau //ko //a: /kukən ko:, haŋ //xã:, haŋ di _/kwa:gən. Haŋ /ne //khau /hóäkən, au han tati e:, ha /ne /ki !kʔan. Ha se-g /ne /ki /hiŋ !khwa: !kwa!kwa-gən, hĩ se-g /ne !khe!khe, hĩ se-g /ne kãũkãũwa !kũ //e.

" The wind blows the rain's hair along when it is soft. It hardens, it becomes cloud. The wind blows another hair along, it also becomes cloud. It turns black, because it holds darkness. It (the rain cloud) puts out the rain legs, that they may stand and advance raining. (The rain as it streams down is the rain's legs, it walks along on them).

" Ha se-g /ne !kuŋ tẽ tũŋ !kerri, au _!gwaxu /u. Ha /hóä:ka, ha á: /ne !ka:gən sa, au !kʔe /ne ⊙poinja, ha se-g /ne //ka: totorro !kʔãũ.

" It will lay the great skin along the horizon. It is black, it is that which comes in the dark while people sleep, to pour down wetting

The rain-maker

!khwa !kwa!kwa:kakən e: |hiŋ ||a !xwe:, he e: ||ka||ka: |hiŋ ||a !xwe:. !kʔãũ kuitakən !naunko ||ko:wa. Tũ !kerrijakən te:ŋ-a sa:, ha |uerri:-ja. Ha a: tati e:, ha kãũwa sa, au !xóë-ka ku:, !khwã se !kʔattən kérre !khe !kwirri!kwirri. Hĩ se !kʔattəŋ-!kʔattən |e: !khwaitən!khwaitən tu:, hĩ se !xau!xau ||kóë siŋ, hĩ se !xau-!xau ||ʔwi:.

the ground. The rain legs go out first, to moisten it first. The rest of the ground is still dry. The great skin comes in a lying position, it is hard. It comes and rains on all the places, so that the water flows along the 'Har Rivier.' It flows into the waterpits, to lie in them and fill them up.

"*He e whai se _dauko k"wã hĩ, au whaija !kwã: ||a:. Tői se ||xam _dauko ||erri hĩ eŋeŋ, ta tői siŋ |ku hãhã !khe:. Tői se-g |ne !kwã: ||kóë ho whai, !kʔe siŋ |ne |xwərri ||k"e: tői au whai, ta tői a: ka _maĩ, ha ||kóë ho !khwa:, ha se _dauko ||erri: ha, ha _!nwəmmaŋ ||kóë hóä !khwa: ||ki, au ha: !kwa |hiŋ ||a !xwe. Ha a !kwã |hiŋ ||a: whai !ka:, au !khwa ||kitən _|ka:, whaiïtən |ne _tai sa !khwa ||kitən |ko|kowa. Whai sin |ne _dauko hĩ: kerru-ka !kaukən, he _|ko:ti |hiŋ.*

"Then the passing springbok will drink from them, as they travel along. The ostriches will also go to wash their bodies as they stand eating. They travel with the springbok, so people hunt them together, for the ostrich enters the water first, to wash himself as he passes; he wades through the running water, as he starts out first. He goes ahead of the springbok while the running water makes the ground wet, the springbok comes when it has dried off a little. The springbok go along eating the young green that has just come out.

(Omitted text: 2254-2257)

The springbok travelling swallow them – those that the rain brought out so that they may grow; because the rain felt that the bushes were dry. Them and the grass. They all spring up [out of the ground] and then the young bushes grow, so that everything becomes green; for the rain did fall cooling it, because the rain feels that, a great rain [it] was which was cut. It is a mother rain. It has milk, which I milked so that the rain would make rain streams (*!khwa //ki*), knowing that the rain mother is not angry, it is one that rains silently (*ǂgeowwa*). It is not angry. She pours laying her streams on the earth, but she is silent as she rains, bringing the springbok, so that the springbok will be everywhere.

"*!kʔe se !kagən-ã whai, !kʔe se |xãã whai-ta |ka:gən, he e:, |ku ka akən, au !khwa a ||errija hĩ. Hĩ |ne !ku!kurrukən |hiŋ ||e |kukən tsʔərokən, |kukən ||ka:ŋ a: se !ku, he*

"People will go out in the dark to shoot the springbok ewes whose hair is beautiful, for the rain has washed it. They shake off the old hair, so that fine new hair may

a:kən ; he e, //hau-ka /kukən. He e:, !k?e //k'oen hĩ, !k?etən /ne /ni: whai e akən, whai-ta /kagən e: /ku a:kən, !k?etən /ki: hĩ. He e_maïï, hiŋ //ku//ku:ka, au hiŋ tati, hĩ e _maïï hĩ /kukən a:kən, he ti hiŋ e:, hĩ //kúï, ĩ, au whai-ta gwai /kuwakən !naunko !xwĩ. Au hiŋ tati e:, hĩ !kuwa //kwanna-ka /kukən, hĩ se _/ka:ti !ku //hau-ka /kukən. He e: /ne kiki:tən au !na:.

" Hiŋ /ne a:kən, au hiŋ tati e:, !na: e, au hiŋ tati, whai-ta gwai /ne //kúï. Hĩ /kukən !ne !kúïta, au hiŋ tati e:, !k?auä se /ne /e: se, au whai-ta tukakən /ne //kóäkən //kúï, au hiŋ tati e:, //k'õïŋ /ne //kóäkən di kúï ta /i. He e: /ne //ka //ko:wa whai /ku, au hiŋ tati e:, whai /ku siŋ !ki:ja, au !na: e, au whaïïtən tati e:, whai e _/kõä. He ti hĩŋ e:, whai /ku !naunko !ki:ja, au hiŋ tati e:, /kukən _/ka:gən /hiŋ //a. /kukakən /ne !kúïta, au /kukakən tati, /kukən !kett!kettən /ne e, he //k'õïŋ /ne ta /i ĩ:."

grow, the autumn's hair. Then people see them, see that the springbok ewes have fine hair, and kill them. They are the ones that get fat first, just as they first get fine hair, so they get fat, while the male springbok are still ugly. These have grown summer's hair, later they will grow autumn's hair. That will grow long in winter.

" They are handsome when it is winter, because the male springbok are fat then. Their hair is white when spring is coming, then the male springbok get quite fat, when they feel the sun growing really warm. Then the springboks' hair bleaches, which was red in winter, when they were lean. Then the springbok hair is red, when the old hair falls out. The (red) hair turns white as it grows long, while the sun shines warmly on it."

❑

Notes

22-23 *Do you not think that rain will fall?*: A better translation is: 'Do you not think that rain **should/must** [*se*] fall?' The man is asking the rain-maker if he does not agree that the rain-maker should fetch rain now because of the drought.

30 *… where I crawl after the ostrich …*: 'They lie on the ground J.T. says, and crawl on all fours' (2216 rev., note omitted).

43-45 *That is why the rain does not fall properly on the ground*: 'J.T. says that the rain is "bank fier groote fier"' (the rain is scared of a large fire – ed.), (2213 rev., note omitted).

56-57 *… thinking it seemed to portend death*: 'J.T. explains that they feared being made dead by the rain, and so make large fires. They think that their houses are only little ones.' (2221 rev., note omitted)

78 ... *it is a slow* **shower:** 'J.T. translates here, "mooi rain", but I think that the word means something a little different' (2226 rev., note omitted).

The word *!kwobba* is given in the *Dictionary* as 'fine rain' (Bleek 1956: 468).

90 *It follows the dust*: In the notebook this is translated as 'it must walk in the dust', which emphasises that male rain falls down violently, spattering the dust, as opposed to the female rain he has just described, which falls gently.

118-119 ... *because the sky is clear, it is round*: The *Bantu Studies* translation is puzzling – there are no words on the notebook page (2236) that can be translated as 'clear' or 'round'. The translation in the notebook reads 'because the sky is very big, it [the sky] sits'. In the context this suggests that there is a huge, dark mass of clouds covering the horizon.

140-141 *It* (i.e. the mountain – ed.) *is high, so the rain's blood flows down* ...: '*Kamm xhară kă !kạŭ* is the name of the high mountain, at Wittberg, which rain is made at. It is not in Bushmanland, Jantje has not seen it, but Stoffel has – Kafirs (sic – ed.) live at the water near it.' (2238 rev., note omitted)

206-207 ... *the springbok comes when it has dried off a little*: 'the earth being still wet within' (2252 rev., note omitted).

224 ... *the autumn's hair*: The notebook reads 'Then the autumn's hair dies' (2258).

230-231 *These have grown summer's hair*...: Here ||Kabbo seems to mean that the female springbok become beautiful in summer because they shed the old 'autumn's hair' and grow fat on new green plant growth that has sprung up as a result of the summer rains.

234-235 *They are handsome when it is winter* ...: In contrast to female springbok which, according to ||Kabbo, pick up weight and develop fine pelage early on in the summer, the males' condition only improves later, so that they are at their peak in (early) winter.

240-241 *Then the springboks' hair bleaches, which was red in winter*...:'The young short hair is red, J.T. says' (2261 rev., note omitted).

PART VI

RAIN-MAKING

From material collected by
Dr. W.H.I. BLEEK and Miss L.C. LLOYD between 1870 and 1880,
edited by D.F. Bleek

Photo: Jeremy Hollmann

'I will really ride the rain up the mountain on top of which I always cut the rain'. One of the many *bruinkoppe* in |Xam-ka !aũ. On top of these hills the |Xam made engravings and called for rain. Kenhardt District, Northern Cape Province.

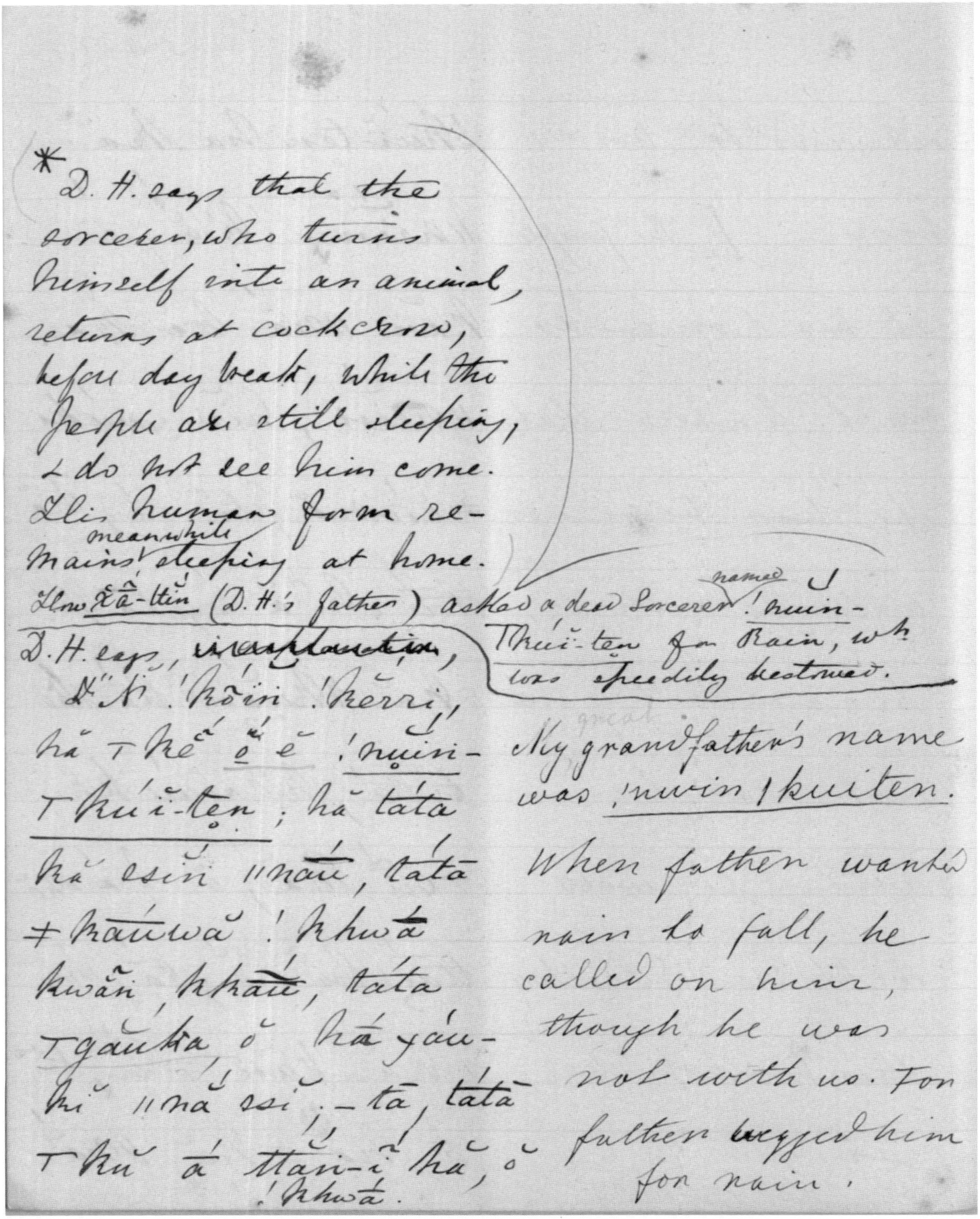

* D. H. says that the sorcerer, who turns himself into an animal, returns at cock crow, before day break, while the people are still sleeping, & do not see him come. His human form re-mains meanwhile sleeping at home.

How Xā-ttin (D. H.'s father) asked a dead sorcerer named !nuin-|kui-ten for Rain, wh. was speedily bestowed.

D. H. says, ~~in explanation~~,

D" Ñ !kōin !kerri, hă |kĕ ō ē !nuin-|kui-tĕn; hă tāta	My grandfather's name was !nuin |kuiten.
hă esin ||nau, tāta ‡kauwā !khwā kwān |khau, tāta |gaukka ō hă yau-hi ||nă ssi -tă, tāta |ku ā ttan-i hă, ō !khwā.	When father wanted rain to fall, he called on him, though he was not with us. For father begged him for rain.

'How Diä!kwain's father asked a dead sorceror for rain from '!Nuiŋ |kúitən, a rain medicine man': manuscript page L.V.14: 5068 rev.

PART VI
RAIN-MAKING

|Kããnũ was a rain's man
– ||Kabbo, 'More about |Kããnũ' –

Rain-makers are probably the kind of *!gi: xa* (sorceror) most often mentioned in the *Bantu Studies* narratives (see Parts V, VI, VII and VIII). One likely reason for their pre-eminence is the nature and frequency of rain in !Xam-ka !aũ – the annual rainfall is extremely low, averaging 200 mm a year, and long droughts are common. Rain occurs in the form of localised thunderstorms that bring relief to some parts of the country, but leave others dry. After the rain, the Karoo shrubs or *bossies*, and the plants that lie dormant underground, sprout rapidly. It was then that the |Xam people harvested *veldkos* and hunted the springbok that came to eat the fresh vegetation. The job of the *!khwa:- ga:!kʔe* (water's or rain's people) was thus vital; they were responsible for bringing the rain to the people's *!xoe* (territory) so that they could find food.

Fetching the rain

In Part V we saw that, in certain contexts, people thought of precipitation as a rain-animal; the Part VI narratives describe how the rain's sorcerors (*!khwa:-ga !geitən*)* 'worked magic' upon these *!khwa: ka xoro* (rain-cattle) so that rain would fall where the people needed it. Rain sorcerors could *ǂxamma* the rain in several ways. The word *ǂxamma* is given as 'fetch' or 'seek' (Bleek 1956: 678), but these translations do not convey the supernatural connotations associated with this activity – it was first translated as to 'work magic' (B.XXVII: 2545 in Part VI, 'Leading out the rain-animal'; Lewis-Williams 1992).

One way of fetching the rain-animal was to ambush it at the waterhole in which it stayed during the daytime. The rain-animal, like hippopotami, grazed at night. People waited downwind for its return, slipping a thong (*!hãũ*) over its neck and pacifying it with the smoke of burning herbs (*sã:*). The thong was not merely a strip of leather, however. In 'The breaking of the thong', Diä!kwain explains that, when a thong broke, it vibrated – sounding like a musical instrument. Paintings of lines often surround paintings of rain-animals in the south-eastern mountains, sometimes with fish and people attached to them. These paintings, together with the descriptions of the string (*!nuiŋ*) in Part VIII (see 'The sorceror !Nuiŋ-|kũiten' and 'What Xã:ätiŋ used to sing'), suggest the likelihood of the thong also being a metaphysical concept based upon sensations experienced by ritual specialists in dreams and other altered states of consciousness. (Bradford Keeney's book, *Ropes to God* (2003), has more detail about these experiences.)

Sound was also an important element of a second technique used to summon rain – in the narrative '|Kãũnũ, a rain-maker', |Haŋ‡kass'o explains that some people brought rain by striking a bow string (*/hou-ka !nũĩ*). A third method of finding a rain-animal was to dream (*//khabbo*) it. |Haŋ‡kass'o describes an instance when a group of rain-makers dreamt rain to come (see 'More about |Kannu'). Shortly afterwards, a thunderstorm arrived.

Besides rain-making techniques, however, there was another important dimension to rain-making – the places at which rain-making activities were performed.

Hilltops – places of power

The |Xam teachers lived in a landscape of vast flat plains, punctuated with hills and mountains that were covered with dolerite boulders. The teachers used two words, *//xaũ* and */ka§o,* to describe a particular feature of the countryside that Lucy Lloyd and Dorothea Bleek translated as 'the Brinkkop'. Janette Deacon (1986, 1988, 1997) argues that the word Brinkkop is in fact a misspelling of *bruinkop,* an Afrikaans word meaning 'brown hill', a name that refers to any hill made up of dolerite boulders.

The importance of the *bruinkoppe* and their significance as rain-making places is hinted at in a narrative by ‡Kasiŋ (see Part VIII, 'How an old woman asked a chameleon for rain'). In this story, an old woman who has asked for rain to fall** goes and sits on top of a hill. Sure enough, her child smells the rain in the wind shortly afterwards. There is also more direct support for the idea that the *bruinkoppe* were linked to rain-making. Many of the boulder-strewn hills have engravings on them of rain bulls and other animals that are symbolically linked to water, such as eland and elephant (Deacon 1986, 1988, 1997). Finally, the fact that ||Kabbo, Diä!kwain and two others called themselves 'Brinkkop men' suggests that they had taken part in a ceremony or vision quest conducted on one of the hilltops in |Xam-ka !aũ. Certain hilltops or *bruinkoppe* were thus chosen by rain-makers and other *!gi:tən* as important ritual places at which they performed ceremonies and other activities associated with their work.

Another aspect of rain-makers that the |Xam teachers mention – their irritability and 'angry' behaviour – is discussed below.

Angry rain-makers

Throughout the *Bantu Studies* narratives, there are references to the anger of rain-makers: ||Kunn punishes his people by withholding rain; |Kannu, another rain-maker, becomes angry when requested to make rain; and |Kãũnũ was much feared by people (see '|Kãũnũ, a rain-maker'), as was !Nuiŋ-|kúïten (see 'The sorceror !Nuiŋ-|kúïten'). The anger of rain-makers and people's fearful attitudes towards them seem puzzling at first – rain-makers, after all, were believed to perform a vital function, so why were relations between the rain-makers and 'ordinary' people characterised by tension?

There were two important reasons for this state of affairs. First, rain-makers were caught in a double bind. When rain fell, and *veldkos* and animals were plentiful, people tended to forget about the rain-makers and did not give them credit for their work. But when it did not rain, then people were quick to scold (*!kʔəjə*) them, holding them directly responsible for the drought, even though in some cases the people themselves had driven the rain away, for example by making fires (see Part V, 'The rain-maker').

The second reason for the rain-makers' anger towards people is less obvious but equally, if not more, important. Rain-makers, like the other *!gi:tən*, possessed *!gi:*. This supernatural potency was the source of the *!gi:tən* 's anger. Lorna Marshall, who worked with the Ju|'hoansi of the Kalahari for many years, found that they had a concept of supernatural potency called *n/um* (now spelt *n/om* [Biesele 1993]) (Marshall 1969, 1999). Marshall's observations (1969: 351) about *n/om* assist in understanding the *!gi:tən's* angry behaviour:

> It seemed to me that *n/um* had several attributes similar to those of electricity. Like electricity, *n/um* is powerful and invisible, capable of beneficent effects, but highly dangerous if too strong. Referring to the strength of *n/um*, the !Kung [i.e. the Ju|'hoansi] call it a 'death thing'.

Marshall's vivid comparison of potency with electricity gives us an idea of just how strong *n/om* is – at times it becomes too strong and is deadly. For this reason, rain-makers and other *!gi:tən* were irascible and dangerous people – the *!gi:* they possessed made them behave in this way.

The |Xam and the Ju|'hoansi also express their beliefs about potency in terms of animal symbolism. In the Part VII narratives, *!gi:tən* grow lion's hairs on their backs and have to be restrained from attacking other people. Such lion-like behaviour was described as 'angry' behaviour (see Part II, Introduction), the sort of transformation that could happen to any *!gi:tən*, rain-makers included. Their anger was also seen in the kind of rain they brought, either heavy downpours accompanied by lightning (see the 'angry rain' in 'More about |Kannu'), or gentle, soaking showers (see Part V, Introduction, for discussion of male and female rain).

❑

Notes

* Three different terms are used interchangeably to describe those people who fetch the rain – *!geitən* ('medicine men'), *!khwa:-ga !kʔe* ('water's people'), and *!khwa:-ga !geitji* ('water's medicine men').

** This is the only instance in the BLC that I know of where a woman acts as a rain-maker.

Leading out the rain-animal

Narrator: Diä!kwain
Dictation date: 21 June 1874
Notebook reference: B.XXVII: 2540-2554
***Bantu Studies* reference:** Vol. 7 (1933), Part VI: 375-376

The underground stems or corms of !kauï *were* |Xam-ka !kˀe-tu ha: *('/Xam food'), a reliable* veldkos *or bush food that could be gathered only once it had rained – then the corms sent out green leaves that the people could see. Rain in the form of a 'water-bull' had to be brought to the places where the people gathered. Fetching the rain, bringing it home and making it fall was the work of* !khwa:-ga !kˀe *(rain's people).*

❑

Ma:ma siŋ ká haŋ ˉ|k'e:, ti e: !kˀe !kan |hiŋ !khwa:-ka xɔro, hiŋ ke: |ki _tá:ïja ó hi-ka !xó:ë, !khwa: se ||a kãũwa he ã: he-ka !xó:ë, !kauï |k'a: se |hiŋja he ã:, hɛ se !au!augən. He _saŋ ||nau, !khwa: xa kãũwa, he _kóä _saŋ ˉ!khouwi.

Mother used to say, that people pull out the water-bull in order to lead it over their place, that the rain may fall upon their place and the wild onions (Jock uintjies) sprout there, so that they may live. If the rain did not fall, they would starve.

Hɛ tikən e:, !geitən se ||a ˉ|ka: tĩ !khwa:-ka xɔro au hɛ-ka !xó:ë, ti e:, hɛ _tá:ï ||nai !kauï |k'a:, hɛ hĩ se ||keŋ _ha:ï o !kauï. Au !khwa: k''auki kãũwa, he _kwa k''auki |ni !kauï ˉ|k'a:, ta hɛ tsˀoëŋ e: !kau!kaunka ĩ, hɛ ka ||keŋ hĩ hɛ ĩ:. Hɛ tikən e:, hɛ ka !khwa: kãũwa hɛ ã.

Therefore the medicine men shall go and kill the water-bull on their land, where they walk to be near the wild onion leaves, in order to dig up and eat the wild onions. If rain does not fall, they cannot see the wild onion leaves, for these things are bulbs which they dig up and eat. Therefore they want the rain to fall.

Hɛ tikən e:, hɛ ka !khwa:-ga !kˀe |ki kãũwa hɛ a: !khwa:, hɛ̃ si ||keŋ _ha: hĩ, au !khwa: kãũwa !kauï ˉ|k'a:, ta hɛ tsˀóëŋ _dɔa e:, hɛ ˉhĩ:, |xam-ka !kˀe-tu hã:. Hɛ

That is why they want the water's people to make rain fall for them, that they may dig and feed themselves when rain falls on the wild onion leaves, for these are what they

tikən e: hɛ taŋ-ĩ !khwa:-ga !geitən, hɛ si |ki kãũwa hɛ ã: !khwa:.

eat, the Bushman's food. So they beg the water's medicine men to make rain fall for them.

Hɛ tikən e:, hɛ kaŋ ||e !khwa:-ga !geitji ≠xamma hɛ ã:, !khwa: se kãũwa hɛ ã:, hɛ si |ni ˍha:. Hɛ tikən e:, !khwa:-ga !kˀe |ne ˍtá:ï ĩ, au hiŋ |ne ke: a ≠xamma !khwa:, hiŋ |ne se |ki se !khwa:, ta !kˀe ||kwaŋ |gaukən ti e:, hɛ ka !khwa:-ga !geitən |ki kãũwa hɛ ã: !khwa:, hɛ xoákən-gu se ||keŋ ˍha: hĩ-ka !kauki, hɛ kya !kaukən ||keŋ ˍha: hĩ.

Then the water's medicine men fetch it for them, that the rain may fall for them, that they may see food. Then the water's people walk about fetching the water, bringing rain, for the people are asking that the rain medicine men may make rain fall for them, that the mothers may dig up food for their children and the children dig up food for themselves.

Hɛ tikən e:, hɛ ¯|k'e: !geitən ĩ:, !geitən ||xum hɛ, !geitjaŋ kan |ne !keiŋ ||au-g |ne |ki kãũ-wa hɛ ã: !khwa:. Hɛ tikən |ne e:, hɛ |ne ||aŋ ˍ|k'o: !hãũ o !khwa:-ga xɔro ||kẽĩ-||kẽĩ, hiŋ |ne ≠kɛi |hiŋ !khwa:-ga xɔro, hiŋ |ne |ki ˍta:ïja, o hiŋ kɛ ˍ|k'o: !hãũ o ha ||kẽĩ||kẽĩ. Hɛ |ne |ki ||a:||aŋ |khi:ja au kamaŋ, hɛ !khwa:-g |ne kãũ. Hɛ-g |ne |ĩ:ja, hɛ |khwa:-g |ne kãũ au hɛ́ ti e:, hɛ |ka ta !khwa: ĩ:.

Therefore they speak to the medicine men about it, and these promise that they will really make rain fall for them. Then they go and sling a thong over the water-bull's horns, they lead it out, they make it walk when they have slung the thong over its horns. They make it walk along and kill it on the way, that the rain may fall. They cut it up, and rain falls at the place where they threw it down.

Leading out the rain-animal

Hɛ !khwa:-g |ne ˍóäkən kãũ, hɛ-g |ne ||nau !khwa: ; au !khwa:-ga eŋ-jaŋ !hauwa, au !khwa:-g |ne kãũwa sˀa: !gáokən ||a ĩ:, o hiŋ !kúïtən ||a: ; !khwa:-g |ne kãũwa !kuŋ sˀo:, hiŋ |ha: !xwe:. !kˀe e: siŋ taŋ-a !khwa:, hiŋ !kwẽ:ï óë ||k'oen !khwa:-ga ˍ|kwa:gən. (!khwa:-ga) !kˀe ||a: ||neiŋ, hɛ ≠kaka !kˀe e: siŋ ||na ||neiŋ, ti e: !khwa: kaŋ ka se kãũ, hɛ !kˀetən |ne kukúïtən |k'e:, ti e:, hɛ siŋ ˍdóäka !khwa: !keiŋ ||auwa |kwẽ:ï |kwĩ, ha kãũwa he ã:

Then the rain does fall, they compel it; where the water's flesh is put down, there rain falls following them as they return home; the rain falls behind them, they come on first. The people who have asked for rain can really see the rain clouds. The (rain's) men reach home and say to the people who are at home, that the rain is going to fall, and these answer that they see rain is truly going to fall for them.

Notes

1-2 *... people pull out the water-bull ...:* The original notebock translation for this phrase (*!khwa:- ka xoro*) is 'water-cow' (2540 passim).

Commenting on this statement, Wilhelm Bleek noted that: 'It appears to me not a literal translation; the sense is apparently the reverse' (2540 rev., note omitted). In other words, Bleek suspected that the business of pulling the water-bull out did not take place in the material world, but rather in the spirit realm.

5-6 *... the* **wild onions** *... sprout there ...:* '*!kauï* an edible plant, similar to an onion' (2539 rev., note omitted).

The plant is probably the sedge *Cyperus fulgens*, the most widely distributed and economically important southern African wild 'onion'. The corms are easy to dig out and can be eaten raw, roasted or boiled (Van Wyk & Gericke 2000: 86).

27-28 *Then the water's medicine men fetch it for them ...:* The word *ǂxamma* was originally translated in the manuscript as 'work magic' (2545). (See the Introduction.)

Further notes

Narrator: Diä!kwain
Dictation dates: 14, 15 January 1875
Translation dates: 14, 15 January 1875
Notebook reference: L.V.3: 4078-4085
***Bantu Studies* reference:** Vol. 7 (1933), Part VI: 377-378

What sorcerors do with a rain-bull once it has been caught. Here we learn how people can see that the rain's men are really doing their job and why they will not always make rain fall.

!gitaŋ |ne |ĩ: !khwa:-ka xɔro, hiŋ |ne |kwãĩ-ĩ: !khwa:-ka xɔro-ka eŋ. Hiŋ |ne ||nau, !khwa:-ka xɔro-ka eŋ kuitje, hiŋ |ne _!gabbetən-ĩ he, ti e: !khwa: se |kwẽ:ï |kwi ha kãũ, ĩ:. !khwa:gən |ne ||nau, ti e: he |ka tã: !khwa:-ka xɔro, ĩ:, !khwa:gən |ne !kˀattən-ĩ. He !kauï |k'a: _||kwaŋ |ne |ha: !kˀe ã:, he !kˀe _||kwaŋ |ne ||ke:n hĩ: he o !kauï, ĩ:.

The medicine men cut up the water-bull, they broil its flesh. They treat the rest of its flesh this way, they throw it away on the places where they want the rain to fall. The rain does as follows, where they kill the water-bull, there rain runs along the ground. Then the wild onion leaves sprout for the people, and these dig and feed themselves with them.

!kˀe e: ||na ||neiŋ, he |auwi !khwa:-ka _|kwa:gi, ĩ:, he he ku-kúïtən |k'e:, '!gitən taŋ _||kwaŋ ||khóä |k'a|k'a swe:nja !khwa:-ka xɔro, ta:, u _||kwaŋ |ne ||k'oen, ti e:, !khwa:-ka _|kwa:gən _||kwaŋ |ne swe:ŋswe:ŋ sa:. Ta: !khwa:ka _|kwa:gən _||kwan a:ki, he tí _||kwaŋ ||khɔ, he se !kẽ:ï ||ou, he |ki kãũwa hi ã: !khwa:.' Hé he |auwi ti e:, !khwa: _baitja sa:, he he kukúïtən |k'e:, '!khwa: kaŋ _oä se !kẽ:ï ||ou ha kãũ, ta: u _||kwaŋ |ne ||k'oen, ti e:, !khwa: |kwẽ:ïk''o, haŋ _baitən-ĩ, ĩ:.'

The people who are at home see the rain clouds and say to each other, "The medicine men really seem to have their hands upon the rain-bull, for you see that the rain clouds come gliding along. For the rain clouds are fine, and it looks as if they are truly going to make rain fall for us." Then they see that the rain comes with lightning, and they say to one another, "Now rain is really going to fall, for you see that the rain is lightning."

He !khwa:-ka !giiən !kúïtən sa:, ĩ:, hé he kukúï, hiŋ |k'e:ja !kˀe ã:,

Then the rain medicine men return and say to the people, that

ti e:, he ‗//kwaŋ /ki kãũwa !kˀe ã: !khwa:, !kˀe se-g /ne dí ti e:, hé ka dí he, he ta //nau !khwa: kãũwa, he-g /ne k''auki !kõäse he /ka:gən, ta:, he ta-g /ne di: tikəntikən !ko!kõ:-ïŋ, o he k''auki /ne ‗//gauë hĩ: he; he he-g /ne di: /a:, o he //ku//ku:ka, o !khwa: kãũwa he ã:. O he-g /ne !kau!kauüka, he-g /ne //ku//ku:kən, he he-g /ne k''auki ≠ĩ:, he siŋ ‗//kwa: taŋ-ã: !gitən o !khwa:. Ta: hé ti he e:, !gitən k''auki ta: he kwaŋ /ki kãũwa he ã: !khwa:, ĩ:.

they have made rain fall for them, and now the people will act as they always do, when the rain falls, they do not take care of one another, for they do evil actions and do not seek food for them; then they fight when they have grown fat, after rain has fallen. When they are prosperous they grow fat, and do not remember how they have been begging the medicine men for rain. That is why the medicine men will not always make rain fall for them.

❑

Notes

1-2 *The medicine men cut up the water-bull ...*: 'The water-bull's blood is water' (4077 rev., note omitted).

16-17 *... rain clouds come gliding along:* 'For the rain's clouds now look as if the sorcerors seem now truly they fetch some rain for us.' (4081 rev., note omitted)

22-23 *Now rain is really going to fall ...*: 'D.H. translates here "It is true that it will rain."'(4081 rev., note omitted)

The breaking of the thong

Narrator: Diä!kwain
Source: 'Told to D.H. by his father'
Translation date: 16 January 1875
Notebook reference: L .V.3: 4086-4089
***Bantu Studies* reference:** Vol. 7 (1933), Part VI: 378

Diä!kwain describes how people far away could hear that rain's men had lost control of the rain-animal they were trying to catch.

❑

Ta:ta kukúïtən ≠kaka si ã:, ti e:, Kɔkɔro _hã: kukúï, haŋ ≠kaka ha ã:, ti e:, !hãũ hã: a: he ||khóä ha o !khwa:-ka xɔro ||kẽĩ||kẽĩ, !hãũ _hã: |kɯ ||nau, o hiŋ ke: ≠ke: |ki !xwɔni !khwa:-ka xɔro o !khwa:, e: ha ká: ha |e: he, !hãũ |kɯ-g |ne !kwa:, he xɔro |kɯ |e:, ĩ:.

He !hãũ _hã: |kɯ di kúï !xwaŋ-!xwaŋ !kummi, ĩ:, o ha !a: hóä _!gwa:xu, ha se !kúïtən, !kˀe se ≠en, ti e:, he tã: a !khwa:-ka xɔro, ta: hé ti hi e:, !hãũ |kwẽ: da, ĩ:. Ha _||ka_||kãũïŋ, ha !xwã !góïŋ!góïŋ a: !a: hóä _!gwa:xu. Ti e: Kɔkɔro |kwẽ: dakən ≠kaka ta:ta ã:, ĩ:, ti e: !hãũ _hã: ka |kwẽ: da, ĩ:, o há: !kwa: óä xɔro ||kẽĩ||kẽĩ, _hã: !xwaŋ !kummi-ka !nũiŋ.

Father told us that Kokoro, (a very old Bushmen), had told him about the thong which they placed on the water-bull's horns, how once when they tried to turn the water-bull back from the water into which it wanted to go, the thong broke and the bull went in (to the water).

Then the thong sounded like a *!kummi*, (a musical instrument played by women), as it passed along above in the sky returning home, that men might know they had lost hold of the bull, that was why it sounded. It vibrated (with a ringing noise), as if a bull roarer were crossing the sky. That is what Kokoro told father that if the thong broke off from the bull's horns, it sounded like a *!kummi* string.

❑

Notes

Title This extract was originally entitled 'What happened when the thong (with which they were pulling at the water-bull) broke'.

1 *Father told us that Kokoro ...:* 'This was an old Bushman, who could not speak Dutch; who died when David and Rachel were young children, and told his father many things.' (4085 rev., note omitted)

9-10 *Then the thong sounded like a* !kummi ...: Sound was an important accompaniment to certain supernatural events in the ǀXam's world. Here the sound of the breaking thong used to catch a rain-animal is compared to two musical instruments, the *!kummi* and the *!góïŋ !góïŋ*. Sound also plays a role in other narratives in *Bantu Studies – a !gi:xa* called ǀKãũnũ plucks his bowstring to summon up rainclouds ('ǀKãũnũ, a rain-maker'); singing helps a sorceror to recover after his return from a magic expedition (see Part VII, 'A sorceror's blood vessels'); a star falling into a waterpit makes a noise 'like a quiver', and the heart of a dying sorceror thunders (see Part VII, 'Stars and sorcerors'); the sound of the 'string' (*!nũ:iŋ*) used to lead out rain-animals is heard no more after the death of the sorceror !Nuiŋ ǀkúïteŋ (see Part VIII, 'The sorceror !Nuiŋ ǀkúïteŋ': 'What Xã:ätiŋ used to sing').

13-14 *... they had lost hold of the bull ...:* '"*tta*" is used when a thing gets loose or free "raak frei"' (4087 rev., note omitted).

15-16 *It vibrated (with a ringing noise) ...:* 'it made a noise (a whirring sound) like a *!góïŋ!góïŋ*' (4088, text omitted).

16 *... bull-roarer ...:* 'A *!góïŋ!góïŋ* is made thus: a little stick is cut flat, and attached by a string to another stick. Then it is held in the hand, and whirled round, and it makes a whirring, buzzing sound.' (4087 rev., note omitted)

The ǀXam associated this sound with the buzzing of bees and used the instrument to make the bees leave their hives: 'the people beat the *!góïŋ!góïŋ*, when they desire that the people's bees may go into the other people's places, so that the people may cut honey, that they may put honey away into bags' (Bleek & Lloyd 1911: 354-355). Bees and honey are potent, magical things (see Lewis-Williams 1981).

A rain story

Narrator: Diä!kwain
Source: 'Told to D.H. by his father Xã:ätiŋ or "Jacob" '
Dictation dates: 16, 17 January 1875
Translation dates: 18, 19 and 20 January 1875
Notebook reference: L.V.3: 4090-4121 (shortened by Dorothea Bleek)
***Bantu Studies* reference:** Vol. 7 (1933), Part VI: 378-382

Diä!kwain explains in detail how sorcerors of the rain (!khwa:-ka !gi:tən*) go about the risky business of stalking and capturing a rain-animal. People are quick to criticise one of the sorcerors when he lets a rain-animal get away.*

❑

He !kʔe !hi:ŋ ||a: o ti e: !khwa: ʃo: he, ti e: he ≠enna ti e: !khwa: e:, !khwa:-ka xɔro |e: ta: he. He he tã: ti e:, !khwe sʔo ʃo:we, !khwa:-ka xɔro xa se !khou he, he se ||e !khwa:, o xɔro a k''auki ≠enna he; he se |xwerrija, ha se |kwã:, he se ||e !khwa:, o ha kaŋ |kwã: ||na.

The men go near the place at which there is water (a spring in a deep hole), for they know that the water-bull is in that water. Then they feel where the wind is, lest the water-bull smell them, they mean to go to the water without its being aware of them; they will lie in wait till it goes to graze and approach the water while it is grazing.

He se !kã: |kiseja, he se ||kho: !hãũ o ha |nã:, o ha: sa:; ta: he kíë ≠ni:ja |ki ˍtaija. He tikən e:, he kíë !ke!ke akka, ha k''auki se ≠en, ti e:, !kʔe |xwerri |kija, ta: ha ˍsaŋ ||nau, ha ≠enna, ti e:, !kʔe ˍóä |xwerri |kija, haŋ k''auki ˍsaŋ |hiŋ o !khwa:, !kʔe |k'a|k'a se swe:nja. Ta, hé ti he e:, !kʔe kíë !ke!ke akka ĩ, ha k''auki se |nĩ !khwetən, he se ≠ni: |ki ˍtaija.

They will wait its return to put a thong over its head as it comes, for they want to catch it and lead it away. So they try to approach quietly without its knowing that anyone is lying in wait for it, for if it knew that men were waiting to catch it, it would not leave the water, so that their hands might seize it. That is why people approach quietly, that it may not notice anything, so that they may take it away.

Ta: tsʔa a: ˍtai o ||kwɔnna, ha k''auki e, ta: ha |ku ˍtai o ||ga:. He tikən e:, !gitən ka |ku ≠ni:ja o

For it is not a thing that walks by day, but by night. Therefore the medicine men catch it at night

||ga: a: ha |kwã: ã: ; he tikən e:, he se !kõ:äse ||ke: a: ha se ˍtai ã:, ha se |kwã:. He ha ˍ||kwaŋ ˍtai, ĩ:, he !kˀe !kã: o !khwa:-ka xɔro ||neiŋ, ha se |kwã: ||na||na, ha se sé; he se |kã-ã, he se |ki ˍtaija.

when it is grazing; that is why they watch the time at which it goes to graze. And when it has gone out they wait at its home while it grazes there, for it to come back, to catch it and take it away.

!kwi a:, ha e !khwa:-ka !gi:xa !kerri, ha ≠enna, ti e:, !kˀe |kwẽ:ï k''o, hiŋ ˍtauïtən hĩ !khwa:-ka xɔro, ĩ:, ha se !kãũŋ siŋ, !kˀe e: ha ||ka-||ka: he, he se !kuŋ siŋja. He !kɔn-na o !hãũ |em, he se hérribija, o ||ke: a: ha ||khóä !hãũ o !khwa:-ka xɔro ||kẽĩ||kẽĩ ã: ; o ha: |ki |e:ja !hãũ o xɔro |nã:, he se ≠ke: |ki !xwɔnni ha, o he k''auki ã: !khwa:-ka xɔro se |e: !khwa:. He tikən e:, he se ˍbai, o há: !naunko !uhí ||na, he se !kɔn ||k'e: ã:, he se ||óäkən |ki|kíja, o ti e: !uhí, ha k''auki se |e:, he se ≠ni: |ki ˍtaija.

A man who is an old rain medicine man and knows how people work with the rain-bull will lead, the men whom he teaches will follow. They hold the end of the thong to help him when he has thrown the noose over the water-bull's horns; when he draws the thong tight on the bull's head, they will pull it back and not let it enter the water. That is why they must be quiet while it is still outside there, in order to take hold of it together, to catch it quite outside, so that it cannot go into the water and they can lead it away.

!hãũ |kɯ-g |ne ||nau, !kwi a:, ha ká ha ||kho: !hãũ, o !khwa:-ka xɔro ||kẽĩ||kẽĩ, he !kˀe ˍ||kwaŋ ke: hérribi !kwi a: ||khóä |hãũ o xɔro ||kẽĩ||kẽĩ, !hãũ |kɯ-g |ne !kwa:, he xɔro |kɯ-g |ne |e:, ĩ:. He !kˀe kukúïtən |k'e:, '!hãũ ti xa á:, u |ki|kíja á: a, ha !kwa: xuwa hi ã xɔro á: a?'

Once when a certain man wanted to put the thong over the water-bull's horns, and people were ready to help the man who was putting the thong on its horns, the thong broke, and the bull went in (to the water). Then the people said, "What sort of a thong have you been using, that breaks and lets the bull go from us?"

He !gixa !kerri |ne kukúïtən |k'e:, ti e:, ha ˍ||kwaŋ k''auki ≠enna, tsˀa de |nõ a dí: !hãũ, he !hãũ |ne !kwa: xuwa he ã: !khwa:-ka xɔro, o ti e:, ha ˍ||kwaŋ siŋ ka, haŋ ≠ĩ:, ti e: !hãũ |gi:ja, o !hãũ ˍóä |kɯ k''auki |gi:ja. Ta: he ˍ||kwaŋ |kɯ se-g |ne xu: tu !khwa:-ka xɔro, he se ˍ||kwa: |kɯ !kúïtən ; ta: tsa de ˍ||kwaŋ k''auki da:, ta he ˍ||kwaŋ |kɯ tã:ä !khwa:-ka xɔro. Ta: !kˀe e: ||na ||neiŋ, he ˍsaŋ !kã: |ki|ki he, o hé ka: he ≠ĩ:, he k''auki ||a, ti e:

Then the old medicine man said, that he did not know what was the matter with the thong, that it should break, letting the water-bull go, when he had thought that it was strong, but it could not have been strong. Now they would have to let the water-bull be and return home; for there was nothing they could do after loosing hold of the water-bull. Moreover the people at home would be waiting for them and would think they had not gone

!khwa:-ka xɔro //na he; he se ã: !kʔe se ≠en, ti e:, he -//kwaŋ /kɯ tã:ä xɔro.

to the place at which the bull was; they must let these know that they had lost hold of the bull.

He he -//kwaŋ !kúïtən //a:, ĩ:, o he ≠kaka !kʔe ã:, ĩ:, ti e: !hãũ -//kwaŋ tuko a: !kwa:, he tikən -//kwaŋ e:, he /kɯ-g /ne //ause !kúïtən, ĩ:, o he k''auki /ne /ki sa: o !khwa:-ka xɔro, ĩ:. Ta, he -//kwaŋ siŋ //nau, !hãũwa xa a: !kwa:, hiŋ -//kwaŋ siŋ se /ki se !khwa:-ka xɔro. !hãũ -//kwaŋ a: /ne !kwa: xuwa he ã: !khwa:-ka xɔro.

So they returned home and told the people that it was the thong which broke, causing them to come back empty-handed without bringing the water-bull with them. For if the thong had not broken, they would have had the water-bull. It was the breaking of the thong which caused them to loose hold of the water-bull.

(Omitted text: 4106-4108)

This was now why, they returned empty-handed, because they wanted the people at home to know. Because the people at home were waiting for them, to see if they had been to the right place to find the water-bull, so that the people at home might know that they had seen the water-bull, but that the thong had been the thing which had caused the trouble. That thing (i.e. the thong) did not seem as if their hands had now been upon the water-bull. For, their hands had now been upon the water bull. The thong had now been that which broke letting go for them the water-bull.

He !kʔe kukúïtən !k'e:, tsa de /nõ a:, he /ki/kí !hãũ a: k''auki /gi:ja ã:? He !gi:xa !kerri /ne kukúï, haŋ /k'e:, ti e:, ha -//kwaŋ siŋ ≠ĩ:, ti e:, !hãũ /gi: akka, o !hãũ -óä /kɯ k''auki /gi: akka; ta: !hãũ /kɯ-g /ne //aŋ !kwa: xu:wa he ã: !khwa:-ka xɔro.

Then the people said, why had they taken a thong that was not strong? Then the old medicine man said, he had thought that thong was strong enough, but it had not been strong enough; for it had gone and broken, letting the bull go.

He !gi:xa kɔ: /ne kukúï, haŋ /k'e:, ti e:, !kuko: /nõ k''auki -dóä ≠enna, ti e:, tsʔa ʘpwa k''auki e, he ha /ki-/ki !hãũ a: k''auki /gi: akka; ha-g /nõ k''auki -dóä ≠enn, ti e: !khwa: /ka:xa -dóä e. Ha k''auki ta //kaitən, ha /gi:ja. He tikən e:, ha sin se /ki -tai !hãũ a: /gi: kwɔkwɔŋ-a.

Then another medicine man, (who had been at home), asked the other, if he had not known that it was not a little thing, that he had taken a thong which was not strong enough; had he not known that it was a fierce bull? It was not a weakling, it was strong. Therefore he ought to have taken a really strong thong.

Ta: ha -//kwaŋ ≠enna, ti e:, ha -//kwaŋ ka ha /e !khwa:. Ha -hã: e !khwa:-ka !gi:xa, ha -hã: -//kwaŋ siŋsiŋ, kwaŋ /ku ≠enna, ti e:, ha: se /kwẽ:ï /kwẽ, ha dí, ĩ:.

For he had known that it would try to go into the water. He had been a rain medicine man before, so he ought to have known how he should act.

'Hé ha ka /ku k''wɔŋ !khwã:, ti e:, ha -am ka ≠kaka ke, ti e:, ha -hã: -//kwaŋ e !khwa:-ka !gi:xa ; he tikən -//kwaŋ e:, ŋ kaŋ //k'oen, ti e:, !kẽ:ï //au /nõ a:, ha ≠kaka ke:ja, há ka ha -hã: e !khwa:-ka !gi:xa. Hé ha ka /ku k''wɔŋ !khwã: ʘpwa, ti e:, ha -//kwaŋ /ne a: //aŋ ã: !khwa:-ka xɔro -//kwaŋ /ne !kau-wi:, ti e:, ha //kwaŋ k''auki ta /kwẽ: da. Ta:, ha -//kwaŋ ka !xwɔŋ ha e !khwa:-ka !gi:xa kwɔkwɔŋ, o ha: ≠kakən s?o:wa ka:. He tikən //kwaŋ e:, ŋ siŋ ka ha /ne ≠xamma !khwa:, ĩ:, ŋ siŋ /ne //koen, ti e:, !kẽ:ï //au /nõ a:, ha ≠kaka keja, ŋ se-g /ne //koen. Haŋ -//kwaŋ !kẽ:ï ta:, ha k''auki e !khwa: ka !gi:xa.'

"He has acted like a child, though he told me that he had been a rain medicine man, that was why I wanted to see whether he had told me the truth, when he said that he had been a rain medicine man. He has acted like a little child by letting the water-bull live, which was not what he had promised. He spoke as if he had been a real medicine man, when he sat talking with me. That was why I let him fetch the water, in order to see whether he had been telling me the truth. It is now clear that he is not a rain medicine man."

(Omitted text: 4116-4117)

Because he would have done this, if he were a rain's sorceror, he would not have allowed the rain to escape from his hands. He could not get it, he is not a rain's sorceror.

He ha /ne kukúïtən /k'e:, ' Ts?a -ká: a:, a-g /ne !xwɔŋ ŋ /k'a/k'a k''au -//kwaŋ swe:nja !khwa:-ka xɔro ã:? !hãũ -//kwaŋ /ku a: !kwa: xu-wa ke !khwa:-ka xɔro. He tikən /ne //khɔ, ŋ tã:ä, ĩ:, ta: ŋ siŋ se k''auki tã:ä, !hãũ -//kwaŋ /ku a: !kwa: ke, he ti-g /ne //khɔ ŋ tã: ha, ĩ:. Ta ŋ -//kwaŋ siŋ se /ki seja, o !hãũwa xa !kwa: xu: túä ka: ha. He tíkən -//kwaŋ e:, tíkən /ne //khɔ, ŋ tã:ä ĩ:.'

Then the other replied, "**Why do** you talk as if my **hands had not** been upon the rain-bull? The thong it was that broke, letting the water-bull get away from me. That made it seem as if I had lost it, but I should not have lost it, if the thong had not broken, making it seem as if I had lost it. For I should have brought it, if the thong had not broken. That made me seem to have let it go."

He !kuko: kukúïtən /k'e:, ' A xa k''auki -óä s?o -dóä ka //nau, a: dí

Then the other said, "You do not seem to have remembered when

!khwa:-ka ≠ni:≠ni:, a kwɔŋ dí akka tʃweŋ o sã: ; a se ã: !kˀe e: |xãũ ||ne hĩä a, o sã:, he siŋ kwɔŋ |ki sã: _|kwˀãĩ.'

you were seizing the water, that you should put *buchu* on the things; you should have given the men who crept up with you *buchu*, so that they smelt of *buchu*." (If the bull had smelt *buchu*, it would have been calm and gone quietly without struggling.)

Notes

8-9 *... they will lie in wait till it goes to graze ...*: 'They do not try to catch him as he goes out, but as he comes back.' (4090 rev., note omitted

8-11 *... they ... approach the water while it is grazing:* 'The men go near the water while he is away from it.' (4090 rev., note omitted)

22-23 *... that it may not notice anything ...*: '*|ni !khwe-ten* to notice, or to be aware of, anything.' (4092 rev., note omitted)

30-31 *And when it has gone out they wait at its home ...*: 'he is accustomed to go by night [?]' (4094 rev., note omitted)

34-35 *A man who is an* **old** *rain medicine man ...*: Age, size and status are all positively associated in the word *!kerri* – an older *!gi:xa* is also more likely to be more experienced than a younger one.

35-36 *... people* **work with** *the rain-bull: tau§itən*, which is translated as 'work with', is also listed in the *Dictionary* as 'to work magic with' (Bleek 1956), probably a better translation in this context.

41-42 *... he draws the thong tight on the bull's head ...*: 'The thong is made into a noose, and put loosely over the animal's head, then afterwards pulled tight.' (4096 rev., note omitted)

70-71 *... and would think* **they** *had not gone to the place ...*: 'the sorcerors' (4102 rev., note omitted).

145 *Then the other said ...*: In this page and a half of notebook text, Dorothea Bleek's translation leaves out interesting details about the capturing of the water-bull, the use of *sã:* (aromatic herbs) and its supernatural context. I provide a closer version of the notebook translation here for comparison:

When you took the rain by force you didn't treat the things properly – the rope and the men who helped should have been sprinkled

> **with fine-powdered *sã:*, you should have given *sã:* to the people who went with you on a magical expedition, so that they would have the scent of *sã:* on them.**
>
> (4119 rev.)

In an omitted note, D.H. says:

> **... if the water-bull had smelt the scent of the *sã:* , he would have been calmed, and would have gone quickly with the men (without struggling to get away from the noose).**
>
> (4118 rev.)

Another note, also omitted, says: 'When the sorceror goes away while the other people lay sleeping, the Bushmen call it */khau ttai,* D.H. says.' (4118 rev.)

No appropriate translation of */khau* appears in the *Dictionary,* but the similar-sounding word */xãu* does appear – it is translated as 'to go on a magical expedition' (Bleek 1956: 363).

!Nuiŋ |kúïtən, a rain medicine man

Narrator: Diä!kwain
Dictation date: 25 July 1875
Notebook reference: L .V.14: 5068 rev.-5079 rev.
***Bantu Studies* reference:** Vol. 7 (1933), Part VI: 382-385

Diä!kwain explains how the living could call upon their dead ancestors in times of need. A father scolds his son for talking about things that should only be looked at, not spoken about.

ŋ !kóïŋ !kerri, ha |kẽ ó e !nuiŋ-|kúïtən ; ha táta ka siŋ ||nau, táta ≠kauwa !khwa: kwãŋ kãũ, táta |gauka ; o há: k''auki ||na si, ta: táta |ku a taŋ-ĩ ha o !khwa:. O tátakən ta: ||ka ti e:, ha |ku túï táta, o táta |gauka, ha |ku e !gi:xa.

My greatgrandfather's name was *!nuiŋ-|kúïtən* ; father called on him, when he wanted rain to fall ; although he was no longer with us, yet father used to beg him for rain. For father believed that, being a rain medicine man, he would hear father when he called.

Hɛ tikən e:, táta ˉóä ||nau kaŋ !naunko e !khwã:, o !kwetən-ta-||ke:njaŋ !naunko ≠ãnni ; táta |gauka, o !khwa:, o ŋ ||xẽĩ-|ha |k'e:ja táta, táta ˍam |gaukən, hɛ se !kúïtən hέ-ka !xóë, !khwa: se kãũwa hɛ ã:, ta:, ||kwɔnna k''auki tym ⊙pwa ta |i ; !kˀãũ se ˍam di ku tã serrika hɛ ã:, !kou a:, hɛ kíɛ̈: |kã-ã ||e ha.

That was what father did when I was still a child and (my sister) *!kwetən-ta-||ke:n* was still small ; father prayed for rain when my brother's wife begged him just to pray, that they might return home, that rain might fall for them, for the sun was burning not a little that the ground be made cool for them, the hill which they had to pass.

Hɛ táta ||nau, ŋ ||xẽĩ-|haŋ ka ha |k'e: táta, tátakən kukúïtən |k'e:ja ŋ ||xẽĩ-|ha ã:, tsˀa de |nõ a:, ŋ ||xẽĩ-|ha |ne |kwẽï kú:ï ã:? ha-g |ne !xwãŋ !kʰwa:-ka !khwa: se kãũ ?

When my brother's wife spoke thus to father, he answered, asking her, why she did so ? did it seem as if rain were likely to fall ?

Hɛ ŋ ||xẽĩ-|ha ||nau, tátakən ká ha |kwẽï kóä ŋ ||xẽĩ-|ha ã:, ŋ ||xẽĩ-|haŋ kukúï, ' ŋ ⊙pwai-|hĩ-wɛ:, a kaŋ k''auki se |kwẽï ku ; ta: a |ku

Then my brother's wife said to father, after he had answered her in this manner, "O my father-in-law, you should not say that ; but

se ˍam /gaukən //k'waiŋ, ti e:, !khwa: /khu /nõ k''au se swe:ŋ seˍ!gwa.xu, tí se xarra, ti di ku tã serritən, o ˍ/kwa:gən-ka dummo.'

you should first pray and try, whether a rain hair will not come gliding over the sky, that the place may be cool again with the clouds' shadow."

Hɛ tátakən kukúï, haŋ /k'e:, '/ne ú ki //kaitən //xau, i /ne //a //kau siŋ //xau, i /nɛ sˀo ko !gõä-ã ˍ//gauë whai,' Hɛ táta kukúïtən /k'e:, táta ˍ//kwaŋ ≠enna, ti e:, ŋ //xẽĩ-/ha-gu ˍ//kwaŋ ≠umma, o hiŋ //na ti e: ã. Hiŋ ˍ//kwaŋ ≠kauwa hɛ !kúïtən hɛ-ka !xóë. Tátakən ˍ//kwaŋ //xam ≠kauwa, ti e:, hɛ kíɛ̈: !kúïtən hɛ-ka !xóë. Hɛ si //kau siŋ //xau, ĩ:, o //kõïŋjaŋ //kau !khe:.

Then father answered, "Go out and climb the Brinkkop, let us go and sit up on the top of the Brinkkop and look about for springbok." And father said that he knew that my brother's wife's people were waiting where they were. They wanted to return home. He also wanted them to return to their home. Then we climbed up the hill, when the sun stood above it.

Táta ≠kakən ĩ:, hɛ táta kúï, '!nuiŋ-/kúïtən-wɛ, /ne ˉã !kaukən /ne !kúïta //xwa:gən-tẽ ã:, ha se /nĩ !kaukən; ta: ha ˍ//kwaŋ sˀo ≠ĩ: !kaukən. Ta: !kaukən //kwaŋ ≠umma, o hiŋ //na ŋ. Hẽ tikən ɛ:, a se ˍam serritənserrika hɛ ã:, !kˀãũ ɛ:, hɛ kíɛ̈ !kúïtən /kãã //a hɛ.'

Father spoke and said, "O *!nuiŋ-/kúïtən*, let the children return to *//xwa:gən-tẽ*, (their father), that he may see the children, for he seems to sit thinking of them. But the children are waiting here with me. Therefore do please cool for them the ground which they must pass on their return."

Hɛ táta kukúïtən /k'e:, 'A á: //kho !nuiŋ-/kúïtən, a kaŋ ka síŋ ka á: ≠kaka ke, a ˍhã: se //nau, //k'e: a: a /ku:ka ã:, ha-g ŋ /gauka a ã:, akən ˍhã: se /xum ŋ, a se ˉã !khwa: se kãũwa ke.' Hɛ !khwa: /ku //nau, tátakən sˀo ko ≠kakən, !khwa:-ka ˍ/kwa:kakən /ku swe:ŋ sa:, !khwa:-gən k''auki //uhá: //kabba, ta: !khwa:-ka ˍ/kwa:gən /ku ≠ka-≠kãĩn ˍ!gwa:xu.

And father said, "You who seem to be *!nuiŋ-/kúïtən*, you used to say to me, that when the time came that you were dead, if I called upon you, you would hear me, you would let rain fall for me." And when father spoke thus, the rain clouds came gliding up, the rain did not pass over, for the rain clouds covered the sky.

Hɛ ŋ kukúï, ŋ /k'e:ja táta ã:, 'Táta-wɛ, /ne //k'oenja, !khwa:ka ˍ/kwa:gən kaŋ /ku /ki !haŋ ˍ!gwa:-xu.' Hɛ táta kukúï, haŋ /k'e:ja ke, ŋ xu: tu /kwẽĩ ku, ŋ /ku ≠gou, si se /ku //k'oen, o si tsaxáitən, o si: k''auki ≠kakən !khwa:-ka ˍ/kwa:-gən. Tátakən ˍ/kwã:ŋ ŋ, ti e:, ŋ

Then I said to father, "O father, look, the rain clouds are covering the sky." Then father told me, that I must stop talking and be silent; we should look with our eyes and not talk about the rain clouds. Father was angry with me for speaking like that and not

kwãŋ |kwẽĩ da, o ŋ k''au |ku ≠gouwa. Tátakən kukúï, haŋ |k'e:ja ke, ti e:, i k''auki ta kwẽĩ da, o !khwa:-ka -|kwa:ka |ne swe:ŋswe:ŋ sa:, ta:, í ta |ku ĩ: ||k'oen !khwa:-ka -|kwa:-gən o i tsaxáitən, o í k''auki ≠kake.

Hє !khwe |ku ||nau, o tátakən sʔo ko ≠kaka ke, !khwetən |ku ĩ: !kuŋ siŋ sa:. Hє táta kukúïtən |k'e:, 'ŋ ʘpwaxãĩ-|ha-wє:, á kaŋ ||kho kaŋ ≠ĩ:, !nuiŋ-|kúïtən k''au ka siŋ ka há ||khau ŋ, ti e:, ha -hã: ka ||nau, ||k'e: a: ha-g ≠ni: !khwa: ã:, haŋ a: !khwe tʃʔu !kuŋ siŋ ã:. Haŋ ka siŋ |kwẽĩ da, ha: ≠kaka ke; ŋ a: tã:ã sʔo o !khwe. Tikən taŋ !khwe ĩ: tʃʔu !kuŋ siŋ, hє !khwe |ku ĩ: tʃʔu ki |hiŋ ti e:, !khwe |ku ĩ: tã serritən, ĩ:. !khwa: -|k'wãĩn |ku ||aŋ sa: hĩ !khwe, !khwa:-ka |hãũ e: sa: hĩ !khwe.'

Hє táta kukúï, haŋ |k'e:, 'U hi ||kóë ||neiŋ, i se ||a sʔo ko ||k'oen siŋ ||neiŋ, i se ||k'oen tsʔa a: !khwe tʃʔu kúï: taŋ !khwa: -saŋ kãũwã:.' Hє si ||khóë ||a: ||neiŋ, ĩ:, hє: si ||nau, o sí ka swe:ŋ tã:tã: é, hє !khwa: -tsʔam-ĩ si:, hє !khwa: !gãũ ĩ:.

Hє táta kúï, 'Du-||hũ, a kaŋ -||kwaŋ !xwã: |k'e:ja ke, ŋ se tú a, ti e:, a -||kwaŋ |ne !kúïtən. Ta ŋ -||kwaŋ |ne tu:ï, ti e:, a -||kwaŋ |ne !huru ||kho, o !kʔãũ.'

Hє !khwa: |ku ||nau, !khwa:gən ka ha |kwẽĩ ku, ha !gãũ, hє |ka-|hiŋ kukúï, haŋ |k'e:ja táta ã:, '≠gwãĩ-|k'a-wє, tóä! Ti kaŋ !xwãŋ !khwa: a: kãũwa |hiŋ sa: ||xau, ta: ha -||kwaŋ xaitən. Ŋ -||kwaŋ -ɔ: se !kúïtən ŋ-ka !xóë.'

being silent. Father said, that we ought not to talk when the rain clouds were floating along, but merely to look at the rain clouds with our eyes, without speaking.

Then the wind came, while father sat talking to me, a following wind. Then father said, "My daughter's husband, you seem to think that *!nuiŋ-|kúïtən* has not heard me, because at the time at which he brings rain, he lets the wind blow following it. He is doing as he promised me, it was I who begged for the wind. The place needs a following wind, and the wind is only blowing so as to cool it. A smell of rain comes with the wind, it is the rain's scent which is with the wind."

Then father said, "Do you enter the hut, let us go and sit watching in the hut, to see whether the wind is blowing as if rain will fall." Then we went into the hut, and as we sat waiting the rain poured down on us and broke (?).

Then father said, "*Dú-||hũ:*, I think you told me that you were returning home. I heard that you were seated (?) on the ground."

Then the rain acted as if it would break (?), and *|ka-|hiŋ* said to my father, "*O≠gwãĩ-|k'a*, stop! It sounds as if rain were falling coming from the mountain for it is drizzling. I will now return to my place."

!Nuiŋ |kúïtən, a rain medicine man

Notes

5 ... *father used to* **beg** *him for rain:* The word used here, */gauka,* translated as 'to beg for, call on, pray' (Bleek 1956: 276) may have been a respect word used when asking the dead for rain.

94-96 ... *as we sat waiting the rain poured down on us and* **broke** *[?]*: The word *!gãũ* is given in the *Dictionary* as 'to resound, make a noise like the rain, rumble' (Bleek 1956: 378).

The rain-maker ||Kunn

Narrator: Diä!kwain
Dictation dates: 26, 27 December 1875
Notebook reference: L.V.22: 5743-5754
***Bantu Studies* reference:** Vol. 7 (1933), Part VI: 385-386

In this extract Diä!kwain expresses a theme to which he and |Haŋ≠kass'o often referred – tension between !gi:tən *(sorcerors) and the rest of the group. When people became angry with a* !gi:xa, *he in turn became angry and used his powers to punish them (see Part IV, 'Wind-making' and 'Notes on |Xarraŋ|xarraŋ'; Part VI, '|Kannu, a rain medicine man'; Part VII, 'The power over ostriches possessed by |uhére'). This particular narrative ends in the same way as Diä!kwain's anecdote in Part IV about |Xarraŋ|xarraŋ, who held the wind inside her kaross – the* !gi:xa's *angry behaviour is recalled at every reoccurrence of the same unfavourable circumstances for which the* !gi:xa *was originally responsible.*

❑

||kunn kaŋ ka ||nau ; o !kˀɛja |ki _!kwain_!kwainja ha, ha-g |ne |k'e:ja !kˀe ã:, ti ɛ:, !kˀe ||khóä kaŋ ¯≠ĩ:, !khwa: ka !khwa: se kãũ, ta !khwa: ka !khwa: se _am ¯ã ⊙hoken se ¯||ko:, !kˀe se ||k'oen, ti ɛ:, tʃweŋ |nõ se _tai, o ⊙hoka: ¯||ko:wa. Ta:, ti e: !khwa: kãũwa, ĩ:, hɛ e: ⊙hokən ka ||khou akən ĩ:. Tʃweŋ |ne _tai, o _hɛ. tá: ||ka ti e:, hɛ !khou, ti e:, ⊙hokən _|kwˀãĩ ||aŋ. Hɛ |ne tai, o hɛ: tá: ||ka ti e:, hɛ !khou ti e:, ti tãŋ ⊙hokən kaurruwa, hɛ |ne _tai-ã tiŋ.

||kunn used to do as follows; when people were angry with him, he told them, that though they seemed to think that the rain meant to fall, yet it would wait till the bushes were dry, that they should see whether any game would come while the bushes were withered. For when rain fell, then the bushes became nice. Game came, because they smelt that the scent of the bushes was sweet. They came, because they smelt that the bushes seemed to be sprouting, they walked about.

||kunn ||nau, ha: |kwẽï ku, ha |k'e:, ha _tai xu: tu !kˀe. !kˀe ||nau, !kˀeja ||k'oenjã ti e:, ||kunn _óä !k''wain kwɔkwãŋ !kˀe, !kˀe |ne ||e ||kunn, hɛ |ne |k'e:ja ||kunn ã:, ti e:, tsˀa de |nõ a:, ha ka |kwẽï |kwẽ, ha dí, ã:. Ha ||khóä k''auki ka ¯≠ĩ:, ti e:, ha-ka !kaukən ||kwaŋ ka ||xɒm

When ||kunn had said this, he walked away leaving the people. When they saw that he was really angry with them, the people went to ||kunn and asked him why he had acted like this. He seemed not to think, as his children were thinking, that they were hungry,

¯≠ĩ:, ti e:, hɛ _//kwaŋ ¯≠kauwa, ti e:, hɛ ka !kauï /k'a: se /hã hɛ ã:, hɛ se //ke:n hã: hɛ o !kauï.

that they wished the wild onion leaves to sprout for them, so that they might dig and feed themselves with the wild onions.

//kunn /ne //nau, !kˀeja /kwẽï ku, hɛ /k'e:ja ha ã:, ha-g /ne ≠kaka !kˀe ã:, ti e:, ha _//kwaŋ k''auki ≠enna, tsa a: !kˀe k''auki ka tymse /k'e: ha. Ha _//kwaŋ /kɯ a:, ha ¯≠ĩ: ha, o ti e:, !kˀe _//kwaŋ ka !xwãŋ ha /ki kwɔkwãŋ-a !khwa:. Hiŋ _//kwaŋ ka //nau, hɛ: //k'oenjã, ti e:, !khwa: k''auki ta !khwa: kãũ, hɛ _//kua: kuku, hɛ /k'e: //kunn, //kunn kwãŋ /ki kãũwa hɛ ã: !khwa:. Hiŋ ka //nau !khwa: /ne kãũwa, hɛ k''auki /ne ¯≠ĩ:, ti e, hɛ _//kwaŋ ka /k'e: ha, ha kwãŋ /ki kãũwa hɛ ã: !khwa:.

When the people scolded //kunn in this way, he answered saying, that he did not know why they did not speak gently to him. He had thought to himself that the people sounded as if they believed that he really owned the rain. Whenever they saw, that rain was not going to fall, they talked about it, they scolded him, saying he must make rain fall for them. Then when rain fell, they did not remember that they had asked him to make it fall.

Hɛ tikən e:, mama-gu ka siŋ //nau, hɛ: //k'oenjã, ti e:, !khwa:-ka _/kwa:-gən /kuẽï k''o, ĩ: ; hɛ //nau, hɛ: ≠kaka hɛ /ka:gən ã:, hɛ kuku, hɛ /k'e:, '!kˀe kaŋ //khóä /k'e:ja //kunn, ta:, ú /kɯ e:, //k'oen, ti e: !khwa:-ka _/kwa:gən /kuẽï-u, ĩ:, ta: !khwa:-ka _/kwa:gən _//kwaŋ ka a:gən. Tikən _//kwaŋ ka //kho !khwa: se kãũ kwɔkwãŋ. !khwa: /kɯ-g //nau, o i: _//kwa: ≠ĩ: kuɔkwãŋ, ti e:, !khwa: se kãũ, !khwa:-ka _/kwa:gən /kɯ _tsˀóäkən !kum, o !khwa: k''auki kãũ. !kˀɛtən //khɔ: e: _≠kwaija //kunn. Hɛ tikən e:, !khwa:-ka _/kwa-gən /kwẽï k''o, ĩ:, Ta:, tí ka !kẽĩ ta:, !kˀeja /k'e:ja //kunn, o tíja /ne /kwẽï u, !khwa:-ka _/kwa:ka /ne /kwẽï u.'

This is what our mothers used to say whenever they saw the rain clouds gathering like this; they told each other about it and said, "People must have scolded *//kunn*, for you can see that the rain clouds are coming this way, the clouds are beautiful. It looks as if rain is really going to fall. Then when we really think it is going to rain, the clouds disperse and no rain falls. Some one must have contradicted *//kunn*. That is why the rain clouds are acting like this. For it is true, that when people scold *//kunn*, the consequence is that the rain clouds act in this manner.'

Note

The following note by Diä!kwain provides additional information about ||Kunn:

||Kunn, or 'Koos Groot oog', the name of a Bushman referred to in connection with this relation (i.e. Xã:ätiŋ, Diä!kwain's father); he is now dead. He lived at *!khai /ku* 'Rooicass Pits'. The place is called by the latter name by the farmers, on account of one '*Rooicass*' tree which stands by the Pits. The Pits are situated on the farther side of '*Dick Doorns*', in the Sak Rivier.

(L.V.21: 5617 rev.-5618 rev.)

More about ||Kunn

Narrator: |Haŋ‡kass'o
Dictation date: 15 October 1878
Notebook reference: L .VIII.20: 7746-7749
***Bantu Studies* reference:** Vol. 7 (1933), Part VI: 387

Here |Haŋ‡kass'o tells what he knows about the rain-maker //Kunn, mentioned by Diä!kwain in the previous extract.

ŋ *-||kwaŋ óä ||k'oen ha; ŋ -||kwaŋ ||k'oenja !khwa: a, ha |ki kãũwa ha. Haŋ ka siŋ |ki kãũ !khwa:. Ha-ka !khwa:gən ¯ĩ kãũ-kãũ |hiŋ ¯wurri:, hi |ne ¯ĩ ||kó:ë, au haŋ tati, há e ti é-ta !kwi, !kou sˀo !kui |ku é. Sí-ta !kwitən -||kwaŋ e. Hiŋ ||nau, ti e:, hi |ku ¯ĩ: ||na ti é, sitən |ku ¯ĩ ||na ti é, ti e: ||kõïŋ |hiŋ hi.*

I have seen him; I have seen the rain which he caused to fall. He used to make rain fall. His rain came streaming from out of the west there, it went to the north, because he was from that part, he was a mountain Bushman. He was one of our family. When they lived over there (north), we lived there (east), where the sun rises.

ŋ *!kõïŋ -||kwaŋ e ¯||kunn.* ŋ *!kõïŋ kwɔkwãŋaŋ k''auki e. Hiŋ e:, k''auki óä tym⊙pwa ko:ka ŋ.*

//kunn was my grandfather. He was not my real grandfather, (but a relation of my maternal grandfather). He loved me dearly.

ŋ *k''auki ≠enna ¯||kunn óä, ŋ k''auki ≠enna hi, hiŋ kóä ¯||kunn xóä, ŋ k''auki ≠enna hĩ. ||kunn-aŋ |ku !kerritən kwɔkwáŋ-a, |ku-g |ne*

I did not know *//kunn's* father nor his mother; I did not know them. *//kunn* was quite an old man, he was a very old man, when

!kerritən tɔ_tɔ́roka, au ŋ́ |ku siŋ !naunko e !khwã. Haŋ |ku siŋ |ne _dóä !kerritən tɔ_tɔ́roka; he tikən e:, ha _ku-g |ne ⁻|kukən, ĩ:.

I was still a child. He must have been very old then, so he is dead now. (He was alive when *|han-≠kass?o* came to Cape Town, about 1870, but dead when he went home about 1873.)

How rain is made

Narrator: |Haŋ‡kass'o
Dictation date: 21 January 1878
Notebook reference: L.VIII.1: 6093-6095
***Bantu Studies* reference:** Vol. 7 (1933), Part VI: 387

How the rain's sorcerors make it rain.

!khwa:-ka !gitən |ne !kan !kwa: !khwa:-ka !kãũ!kãũ. Hiŋ |ne ku-kúï, hiŋ hərruki ||a hi, o !khwe a ĩ: ta: ti é:a, ha !khwe, ha e !khwa:ka !khwe; he ĩ: ta: ti é: a. Ha !khwe ha ts?u !kuŋ ∫o, ha !khwa:-ka !khwe. He ti hiŋ e:, !khwa:-ka _|kwa:gən |ne |hiŋ sa:, ĩ:. He ti hiŋ e:, !khwa:-g |ne ||kóäkən _||uhá:, ĩ:. o !khwa:gən tati e:, !khwe _dóä ||kun ∫o:.

The rain's medicine men seize and break the rain's ribs. Then they throw them along, when the wind lies over there (north), that wind is the rain wind; it lies over there. That wind blows from the north, that rain wind. Then the rain clouds come out. Then the rain passes in front of it, for the rain feels that the wind is from the north.

Notes

4-5 ... *that wind is the rain wind ...*: |Haŋ‡kass'o mentions in more than one narrative that the rain wind (*!khwa:-ka !khwe*) in |Xam-ka !aũ comes from the north.

|Kannu, a rain medicine man

Narrator: |Haŋ‡kass'o
Dictation dates: Sometime between 15 March and 15 May 1878
Notebook reference: L.VIII.7: 6639 rev.-6646 rev.
***Bantu Studies* reference:** Vol. 7 (1933), Part VI: 388

In this extended note to another longer narrative about locusts, |Haŋ‡kass'o relates how tensions arise between a rain medicine man and an old man who petitions him for rain on behalf of the people.

❑

|kannu, haŋ a óä |ki !hou, haŋ |ki !khwa:. Hé ti hiŋ e:, ŋ !kõïŋ ta siŋ |ne |kwe:nja, haŋ ¯ku. '||kha||khawɛ, akən tuko se_!hamma ¯|auwa¯hi, ta, ti ta |kwẽ, hi k''auki ≠hannuwa, au hi ¯||kowa, au ⊙hoka ¯||kowa ; tija |kwe, hi k''auki ≠hannuwa, au hĩ ¯!kuïta, au ⊙hoka ¯||kowa. Ti se kwaŋ _!ham ¯||ka, ⊙hoka se ||khou akən. Ta:, ti ta a:kən, au tí a ¯kɛrruwa, au !kauëgən |naŋ|naŋaŋ |ne ¯|kainja.'

|kannu possessed locusts and rain. Therefore my grandfather used to fetch water and say, "O beast-of-prey, you must please really listen to us, for the place here is not pleasant, for it is dry, for the bushes are dry; the place is not pleasant, because it is white, for the bushes are withered. Please let it be wet, that the bushes may grow beautiful. For a place is beautiful when it is sprouting, when the mountain tops are green."

Hé ti hiŋ e:, |kannu ka siŋ |ne ku, '||khe||khauéja, á kaŋ ¯a, sa-g |né ta, |a ¯a, au ⊙hokakən ¯||kowa.'

Then |kannu would answer, "You beggar, (?), you come and talk of danger because the bushes are dry."

Hé ti hiŋ e:, ŋ !kóïŋ ta síŋ |ne ku, 'A _dóä se dá hi¯!kwɔbba, ha á ka ¯sitən, ta: !khwa: !kwa!kwagən k''auki ta !xwã !ke!ke. Ta: ŋ́ a k''auki |ki ||neiŋ, ta:, ŋ |ku ||nau, ti e:, ti ta |kwẽ, hi k''auki ≠hannuwa, au tíja ¯||kowa. Hiŋ e:, ŋ ta ≠kaka ha, au kakən tati, !kˀe ta |kwẽï da, hĩ ta, ŋ ¯kwaŋ ≠kaka ¯ha, ú hi k''au e:, ta dí ¯|khuru !khwa:,

Then my grandfather would reply, "You should make a cloak (of rain) to give to us, for the rain legs do not seem to stay. For I have no hut, that is how I am used to live when the place is not comfortable, when it is dry. Then I speak to you, because the people are talking so, saying that I must speak to you, as if they had not

au a //ka://ka: hi, ã ti. Hi ⁻!ku, //khóë //na//na !khwa:, au tí e, ŋ ₋//kwaŋ xara ka kwe:ja, au ŋ k''auki dí /khuru !khwa:. ŋ a ₋//kwa tʔam ʃo ⁻!ki ta tí, ₋//kwa tʔam /ko: ʃo hi; ŋ ₋//kwa ⁻//ka tɔtɔ́ro, au ŋ a tati, ŋ ã ₋//kwa k''auki /ki //neiŋ. He ŋ ã ₋//kwa /ne /hiŋ ⁻!kuŋ, au há /ne kúï, //nwɔbbo !kʔũ //a:. ŋ a ₋//kwa /ne ⁻bu !ho /i, ŋ a ₋//kwa /ne //ke:, !kerrukən!kerrukən ŋ.'

dispersed the rain, when you wet them there. They hid away from the rain, whereas I kept quiet, I did not disperse the rain. I just covered myself with a piece of kaross, gently put it over me; I became very wet, because I had no hut. Then I came out from underneath, when it passed over. I lighted a fire, I sat by the fire drying myself."

Notes

1-2 *|kannu possessed locusts and rain:* There is a natural connection between rain and locusts – swarms of locusts often emerge after good rains, when plant food is abundant (Skaife 1987: 72-73). These insects are highly nutritious and were a valued *veldkos* (see Part VII, 'Sorcerors and locusts', 'Sorcerors, locusts and locust birds'). The word translated as 'possession', */ki,* has two meanings here – in one sense, */ki* means 'possession' or 'ownership', much as Bushmen in the Kalahari refer to people as 'owning' supernatural potency (Marshall 1999). In the second sense, */ki* means 'to cause to do'. |Haŋ‡kass'o was therefore saying that |Kannu had the power to make rain and to control locusts, two valuable resources for the people of the arid |Xam-ka !aũ.

|Kannu 'was the maternal grandfather of "Klaas Streep" or ||Kóäken !khe'. (6639 rev., note omitted).

16-17 *... you come and talk of danger ...:* The phrase, *a kaŋ a, sa-g /ne ta, /a a,* as translated, does not make sense here – what 'danger' is being referred to? The original notebook translation is also unclear: *'You are the one who will call out "danger"'* (6641 rev.). */a,* the word which is translated as 'danger', is given in the *Dictionary* as 'fight' or 'curse' (Bleek 1956: 267). The statement may be literally translated as *'you are coming wanting fight'*. |Kannu may be warning |Haŋ‡kass'o's grandfather not to fight or curse him because the bushes are dry, meaning perhaps that |Kannu is telling the man not to hold him responsible for the drought.

20-21 *You should make a cloak (of rain) to give us ...:* The word *!kwobba* is translated here as 'cloak', but in the *Dictionary* only a single meaning, 'fine rain', is given (Bleek 1956).

37 ... *when it passed over:* The *Bantu Studies* translation obscures the fact that it is |Kannu himself who orders the rain to move off – this is clearly the case in the original notebook translation which reads 'when he says go forward' (6646 rev.). This also explains why |Haŋ≠kass'o's grandfather told |Kannu that he did not try to make the rain go away, that it was other people who tried to disperse the rain.

More about |Kannu

Narrator: |Haŋ‡kass'o
Source: 'From his mother, |Xabbi-an'
Dictation dates: 22-23 November 1878
Notebook reference: L.VIII.23: 8005-8010
***Bantu Studies* reference:** Vol. 7 (1933), Part VI: 389

|Kannu, the rain-maker, 'dreams' rain.

❑

ŋ -//*kwaŋ* /*kw* /*k'e:* /*nukən*/*nu-kənk''ao*, /*kannu-gu*, *hé e: siŋ ĩja.*

I am speaking of the old men, /*kannu* and his friends, this is what they did.

Hĩ -//kwaŋ /kw //khabbo-ĩ, ti e:, !khwa: se-kãũ. He e:, hi /ne≠kaka !kˀe kuitən, ti e:, hi //khabbo-ĩ, ti e: !khwa: se -kãũ. He !khwa: /ne //uhá, ĩ:. !khwa:-ka /kwa:kakən /ne -/hiŋ, au hiŋ tati, !khwe -!kuŋ ʃˀo, hiŋ /ne /hiŋ. He tikən e:, !khwa: /ne -kãũ.

They had been dreaming that rain would fall. Then they told the other people that they had dreamt that rain would fall. Then the rain came up. The rain clouds came out, because the wind was in the north, they appeared. Then the rain fell.

Hi /né ta, '//khe//khe-we:, itən tuko se antau !kúïtən, ta:, ŋ -dóä siŋ //khabbo-ĩ, ti e:, !khwa: -kãũwa, há !khwa:, há ŋ siŋ //khabbo-ã ha, ti e:, ha -há k''auki ta !khe!khe; ta:, ha k''auki -tym⊙pwa battən-ĩ. Ta:, ŋ /kw //khabbo-ĩ, ti e:, ha -há /kw battən -//k''abbi í, itən -há /kw-g /ne -!xe:ja, au !khwa: !kwaitən.

They said, "O beast-of-prey, let us now return home, for I have been dreaming about rain falling, the rain I dreamt about was an angry rain, for it lightened not a little. For I dreamt that it lightened very strongly at us, so that we hid from the thunderstorm.

' -!koãŋ -ha /e:ja i, ŋ //khabbo-ĩ, ti e:, ŋ -há //keŋ /ki -!koã, au -!koã -ha /e:ja ŋ, au //neiŋjaŋ -ha /kw-g /ne -!kauŋ-a. ŋ há -≠k''anna //na, au ŋ́ ka, !kwa: se di kú tã //garra-kən//garraka ke. Tá, //uhá -ha /kw /ki !haŋ-a -//nei//nei, ŋ-ka //neiŋjaŋ -ha /kw-g /ne !kˀúï, au hiŋ tati, hi /kú-g /ne //ka: kúï tu-tunnuŋ-a.

"Running water came in among us, I dreamt that I dug a channel for the water, when it came into my hut, till the hut was full. I called (to the rain), for I wanted it to fall gently for me. But the rain storm shut out the huts, my hut fell down, because it became wet through and through. There-

He tikən e:, ŋ ̠há |ne ¯≠k''anna, ĩ:, au ŋ́ ka, !khwa: se dí ku tã ||garakən||garakən. Ta ||uhá |kɯ |ki !haŋ ||neiŋ.'

fore I called (to the rain) about it, for I wanted the rain to fall gently. For the storm was shutting out the huts.''

❑

Notes

4-5 *They had been* **dreaming** *that rain would fall:* The word *//khabbo,* (also spelt *//kabbo*), and translated as 'dreaming', is used actively here – the |Xam believed that people could cause things to happen by dreaming them (see Lewis-Williams's 1987 discussion in 'A dream of eland'). In this case it seems that |Kannu and friends had caused the rain to fall by dreaming it.

12 *They said,* **"O beast-of-prey"** ...: According to a note that Dorothea left out, the 'beast of prey' (*//khe//khe-we:*) was 'a man who had dreamt about the rain' (8005 rev.), i.e. |Kannu. 'Beast-of-prey' was a term sometimes used to address sorcerors (Hewitt 1986; Lewis-Williams 1981).

19 *... we hid from the thunderstorm:* 'on account of the lightning' (8008 rev., note omitted).

21-22 *... I dreamt that I dug a channel for the water ...:* 'with a stick tipped with horn, but without a perforated stone' (8008 rev.). This note was mistakenly included as the final paragraph of 'Explanation of *ǂk'anna*'.

29 *I called (to the rain) ...:* |Haŋǂkass'o explains how |Kannu and friends do this in 'Explanation of *ǂk"anna*'.

Explanation of *ǂk"anna*

Narrator: |Haŋ ǂkass'o
Source: 'From his mother, |Xabbi-an'
Dictation date: 23 November 1878
Notebook reference: L.VIII.23: 8008 rev.
***Bantu Studies* reference:** Vol. 7 (1933), Part VI: 390

Here, instead of insulting !Khwa: and ordering rain to fall (see Part V, 'The rain's animals'), a different approach is adopted.

❑

_||kwaŋ ¯!kwi: !khwa:, _||kwaŋ !kwi¯!kwi ||khóë ||kho au !khwa:. Hiŋ né ta, ' ¯Kou-we, ¯Kou-we, ¯Kou-we, |ne !kɒn kóä ta, ||garakən-||garaka ki !khwa: ||ki,' au hĩ ta, !khwa: se tym⊙pwa ¯kãũ.

Call out to the rain, keep calling standing in the rain. They say, "O friend, (?), O friend, O friend, hold still, rain gently for me' when they want a little rain to fall.

They dug with a stick tipped with horn, but without a perforated stone.

❑

Notes

Title *ǂk"anna*: This word is translated in the *Dictionary* as 'to call to the rain' (Bleek 1956: 668).

6-8 *They dug with a stick ... a perforated stone*: This paragraph was mistakenly added to this narrative, presumably during the editing or typesetting process. It is in fact a note in the previous extract (see 'More about |Kannu').

|Kãũnũ, a rain-maker

Narrator: |Haŋ≠kass'o
Dictation dates: Sometime between 10 August and 21 September 1879
Notebook reference: L.VIII.31: 8743 rev.; 8748 rev.; 8759-8762
***Bantu Studies* reference:** Vol. 7 (1933), Part VI: 390-391

This rain-maker had an unusual way of calling up the rain.

❑

!gixa kwɔkwáŋaŋ e. !kwi ¯!kerri _||kwaŋ é, |xam-ka !kwi, !kauökən !kwi. Haŋ _dóä |kɯ |kuka, !kaukən-ka-|a: |kha ha, ¯!khou tã ha au !nwa:. ¯|kãũnũ ⊙pwɔŋwaŋ e: ≠ko:-!khwa:, ≠ko:-!khwa: ¯⊙pwɔŋ |ne e: !kaukən-ka-|a:, !kaukən-ka-|a: !kõïŋ kwɔkwáŋjaŋ e: ¯|kãũnũ.

A real medicine man he was. An old man he was, a Bushman, a mountain Bushman. He is now dead, *!kaukən-ka-|a:* killed him, knocking him down with an arrow. *|kãũnũ's* son is *≠ko:-!khwa:*, *≠ko:-!khwa:'s* son is *!kaukən-ka-|a:*, *!kaukən-ka-|a:'s* paternal grandfather is *¯|kãũnũ.*

|nuk"o a: tsaxáitən óä |kɯ ||khóä ¯!hú!hũ. Há a: !kˀe k"auki tym-⊙pwa !hɑmmi ha ; ta, ha tsaxaitən |ké |kɯ ||ke||ke:ja ¯||khe¯||khe: ; _||gwattən tsaxáitən |kɯ ≠ente. Ha tsaxáitakən |kɯ ||khóä to:ï. Há |kɯ óä _|ka:ti ¯!khue:tən.

(He was) an old man whose eyes were like an owl's. He was one whom people were much afraid of, because his eyes used to shine like a beast-of-prey's (eyes); a cat's eyes were small (in comparison). His eyes were like an ostrich's. He early became grey.

_|kãũnu _||kwaŋ ka siŋ |kɯ !koukən |hou-ka !nũï, he _|kwaka: |kɯ-g |ne ¯|hiŋ, au si |kɯ ¯⊙pwoinja. He !kˀe |kɯ-g |ne !kho: au _|kwa:ka: |kɯ-g |ne |ki !haŋ-a tí, au !kˀe |kɯ ¯⊙pwoinja. He !kˀe |kɯ-g |ne !kho:, au _|kwa:ka: |kɯ-g |ne |ki !haŋ-a ||k'õïŋ.

¯*|kãũnũ* used to strike the bow-string, and then clouds came up while we were asleep. Then the people awoke, when the clouds had shut in the place while they were asleep. The people awoke, when the clouds had shut out the sun.

He !khwa: |kɯ-g |ne dí !kwɔbba, ha |kɯ-g |ne ¯kãũ ||na, ¯kãũ ki¯|e ||k'õïŋ: !gauë |ne ¯!kwai, au !khwa: ¯kãũ ||na, he ||k'õïŋ |ne¯||xã, ||k'õïŋ |ne¯||xã, ||k'õïŋ ¯|e:, he !khwa: |ne

Then the rain made a cloak (of rain), it rained there, poured down until the sun set. Day broke while it rained there, and the sun set again, then at earliest dawn the

//nau, !gauë !kha!khatu, !khwa: /ne ¯/khuru. He, há /ne //kóäkən ₋/khuru, au ha k''auki ¯//xã, ha /ne ¯kãũ.

rain broke. Then it broke altogether, and did not rain again.

Si /ku ¯⊙pwoinja ; ha /ku s?o ¯ho /hou, au si /ku ¯⊙pwoinja. He si /ku-g /ne ¯!k''wɔr̃r̃in, si /ku-g /ne túï !nũï, au ha !koukən //na.

We were asleep ; he sat and took up the bow, while we were asleep. Then we turned over, we heard the bow-string as he was striking it there.

Note

10-14 *(He was) an old man whose eyes were like an owl's ... his eyes used to shine like a beast-of-prey's (eyes) ...*: The |Xam believed that owls and lions were in constant communication with each other about the movements and behaviour of humans (see Part II, The lion). Both owls and lions were considered to be dangerous things and therefore people greatly feared |Kãũnũ.

More about |Kãũnũ

Narrator: ||Kabbo
Notebook reference: L.II.25: 2263 rev.-2264 rev.
***Bantu Studies* reference:** Vol.7 (1933), Part VI: 391

This feared rain-maker had two nicknames. He died under tragic family circumstances.

❑

|kãũnu was a Rain's man. His names were also *!khwa:-ka |kãũnũ* and *|kãũnũ !kwa:*. The first name means "Rain's new grass," the second "New grass leg." The man so named had his leg once injured by new grass (pierced by it). He was *||khabbo's* father's "person," and after the death of the father he was *||khabbo's* "person."

|kãũnũ was shot by his grandson in the dark. *!kaukən-ka-|a:* was the name of this grandson, a "Wittberg's man." He was angry with the old man. Some of the women were scolding each other, and the old man went out of his hut to tell his wife, who was one of them, to leave off and be still. He was returning to his hut when he was shot by his grandson.

❑

Notes

This narrative was not taken down in |Xam – Lucy Lloyd compiled the notes directly in English.

1 *|kãũnũ was a Rain's man:* 'J.T. was sitting with him on one bed, in his [|Kannu's] house' (2263 rev., note omitted).

3 *The man so named had his leg once injured ...*: ǂ'Kó !khwa was the son of the above, and the father of !Kaukən ka |a. J.T. had gone to visit him there (2263 rev., note omitted).

5 *... he was //Khabbo's 'person'*: 'J.T. says that he has been of years dead [. had been the previous year to see him]' (2264 rev., note omitted).

7 *... a 'Wittberg's man'*: The Witberg (*Kamm xhară kă !kaŭ*) is the name of a high mountain outside the area, with which ||Kabbo was familiar, where rain is made (L.II.25: 2238 rev.). A Witberg man may be, as Janette Deacon (1988, 1997) has suggested for the term 'Brinkkop man', a person with the power to make rain.

An eclipse of the sun

Narrator: |Haŋ‡kass'o
Source: '|Haŋ‡kass'o from personal observation'
Dictation date: 24 May 1879
Notebook reference: L.VIII.28: 8438-8441
***Bantu Studies* reference:** Vol. 7 (1933), Part VI: 391-392

When the sun 'goes into the sky', people try to get it to come out again.

❑

||kõïŋ |kɯ ¯|e: ˍ!gwaxu.

Hi |ne !koukən-ĩ ||khaitən, au hĩ ta, ||kõïŋjã se |hiŋ. Hi ||xamki !koukən¯ĩ !ku!ku, au hĩ ||k'oen, ti e:, ||kóïŋjã ||khou ≠enniŋ; hi |ne !koukən-ĩ !ku!ku, au hi ta ||kõïŋjã se |hiŋ, he ||kõïŋjã |ne ||khou !kwi:, au ||kõïŋjã tatti, ||kõïŋjã |ne |hiŋ, ||kõïŋjã |ne !uhí !khe ˍ!gwaxu. He hi |kɯ-g |ne di kautẽ.

Si ˍ||kwaŋ k''auki tym⊙pwa !hammi ||kõïŋ, au sitən tati e:, si |kɯ ||na ¯!kouxu, he ||kõïŋ |kɯ ˍsaŋ ||nau, au ||kõïŋja |e:ja, ||ga ˍkóä |kɯ |ne |ki !haŋ si au ||neiŋ. Ta, ha-ka tí |kɯ ||ke||keja |kum, au ha |e:ja ˍ|gwaxu.

The sun goes into the sky.

They strike sticks (upon each other), because they want the sun to come out. They also beat shoes together, when they see the sun getting small; they beat the shoes because they want the sun to come out, until it gets big, until it comes out, and stands outside in the sky. Then they leave off.

We fear the sun not a little, for we know that if we should be on the hunting-ground and the sun were to go in, darkness would shut us out from home. For its shadow is like a mist, when it goes into the sky.

❑

Note

1 *The sun goes into the sky*: '[the Bushman mode of describing an eclipse of the sun]' (8437 rev., note omitted).

PART VII

SORCERORS

From material collected by
Dr. W.H.I. BLEEK and Miss L.C. LLOYD between 1870 and 1880,
edited by D.F. Bleek

In part VI of Customs and Beliefs of the |Xam Bushmen, published in Vol VII No 4 of Bantu Studies *reference has been made to the 'Medicine men' of the Bushmen. The term was used by me, as I think it is the word most generally employed to designate a worker in magic whose object is the cure of illness or any other beneficient activity. The word used by Miss Lloyd is 'sorceror', whether the actions described are helpful or harmful; the |xam only use one word in both cases. On the advice of Professor Maingard I am following the first translation as closely as possibly, am therefore using only the word 'sorceror' in this number.*

At Professor Maingard's request I am also adding to this and any future |xam texts the reference Nos. corresponding to those published in A Brief Account of Bushmen Folklore *by W.H.I. Bleek and* A Short Account of further Bushman Material *by L.C. Lloyd. The letters L. or B. show whether the piece was written down by Lloyd or Bleek, the following Roman numeral shows which Bushmen dictated it, the Arabic numerals mark the notebook and pages in the MS.*

Original note by Dorothea Bleek (Vol. 9 (1935) Part 7:1)

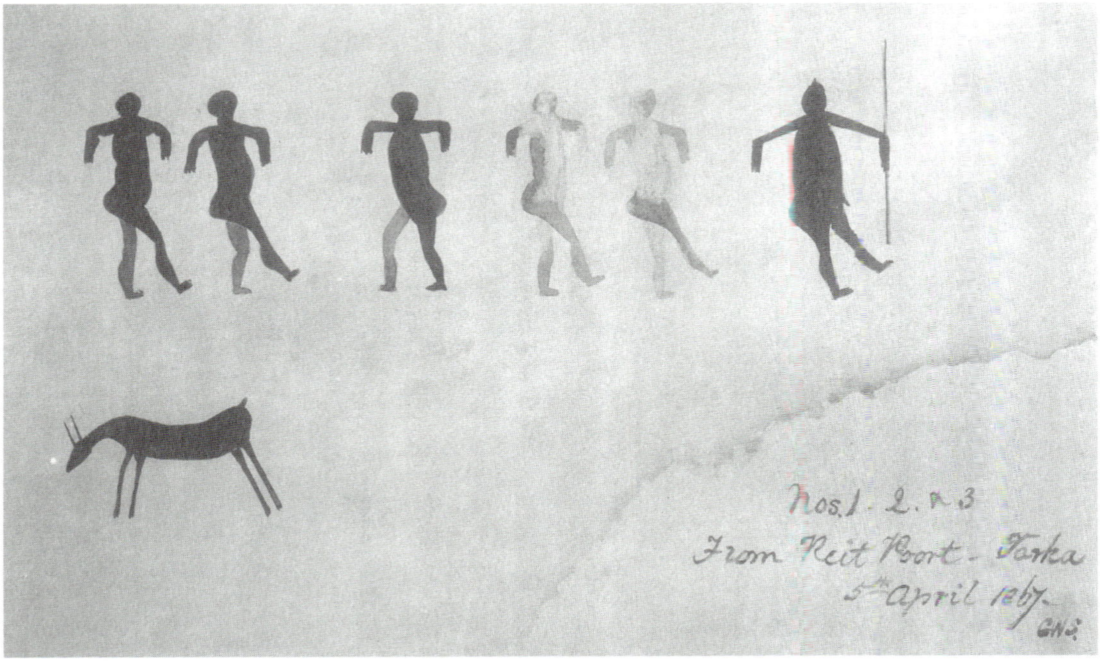

'They seem to be dancing, for they stand bending their knees.' Diä!kwain gave a detailed explanation of these Bushman paintings copied by George Stow, and published in *Rock paintings in South Africa* (Stow 1930).

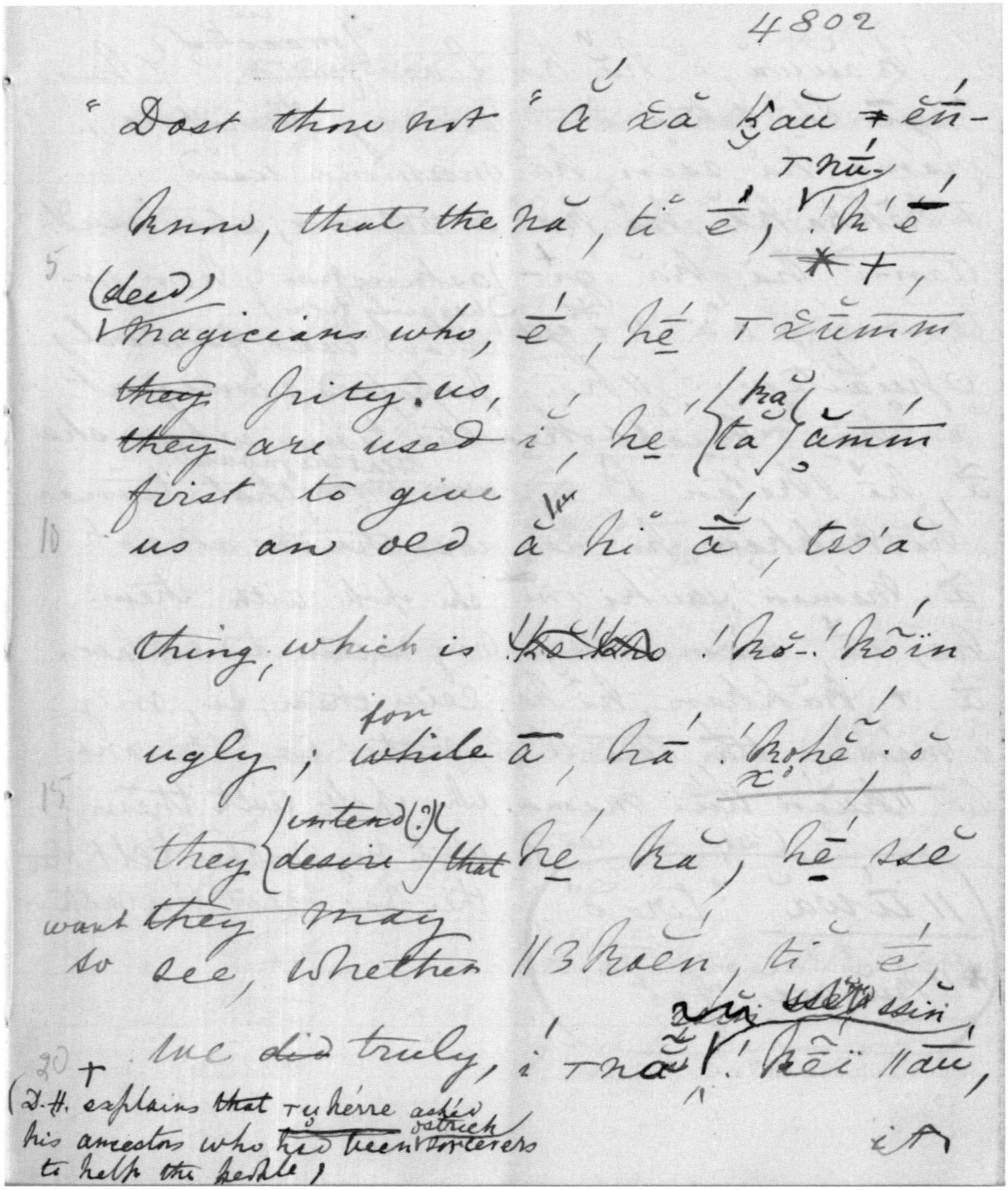
4802

"Dost thou not 'ā xā kau ǂ ēn-
know, that the nā, tí ē, !nū !nʹē
(dead) magicians who, ē, hē ǂxummi
~~they~~ pity us, í, hē {ka / ta} ǂamm
~~they~~ are used
first to give
us an old ā hī ā, tsʹa
thing, which is !kō-!kōin
ugly; while (for) ā, ka !kohē ō
they {intend(?) / ~~desire~~} ~~that~~ hē ka, hē sse
want ~~they may~~
so see, whether ||kaen, ti ē,
we ~~did~~ truly, í ǂnā !kēi ||au,
(D.H. explains that ǂuhérre asked his ancestors who had been ostrich sorcerers to help the people)
it

Notebook page from the narrative 'The power over ostriches possesed by |ʊhére'

PART VII
SORCERORS

... these are not people who are like other /Xam people ... they are sorcerors
– Diä!kwain: 'Mr Orpen's picture' –

Of all the narratives that Dorothea Bleek gathered together for *Bantu Studies*, Part VII is the richest single source of insight into |Xam cosmology. The ideas, concepts and beliefs presented here about *!gi:*, *//ken* and */ko:ode** characterise the |Xam world-view and parallel those of every group of Bushman people, both in the present, and over the past several thousand years. These beliefs underlie every other facet of the |Xam world described in the *Bantu Studies* series, from the significance of baboons in Part I to the speech of animals and the Early Race people in the last part 'Special speech'.

Not surprisingly, Part VII has the most narratives and is also the longest of all the parts Dorothea Bleek prepared for *Bantu Studies*. Presented by the three main |Xam teachers – ||Kabbo (one narrative), Diä!kwain (thirteen), and |Haŋ‡kass'o (five) – they are rich in the detail of healing practices that people of Bushman and KhoeKhoe descent will recognise and appreciate as part of their own background.

Others, however, may find the ideas strange and difficult to understand because they have no precedent for them in their own culture. I therefore outline certain concepts and beliefs expressed by the narrators concerning the experience of altered states of consciousness by *!gi:tən*, before moving on to highlight descriptions of relations between *!gi:tən* and ordinary people.

The anatomy of sorcery

The narrators in Part VII talk about anatomical and physiological aspects of altered states of consciousness, describing in detail how the experience of *!gi:* (potency) affects the body. Significantly, the word *!gi:xa* (the |Xam word translated by Bleek and Lloyd as 'sorceror') emphasises the powerful, all-embracing effects of *!gi:* – the word is compounded from *!gi:* 'magic power' and the suffix *-xa* 'full of', that is, 'full of *!gi:*'. *!Gi:* was literally and figuratively in the blood – it was carried in a sorceror's */xuttən /xuttən*, translated as 'blood vessels', 'arteries', and 'senses'. Diä!kwain mentions a particular artery, the *!kháũä* – the so-called 'vertebral artery' – that was an important conduit of *!gi:* (see the note in 'A sorceror's blood vessels').

The */xuttən /xuttən* are closely associated with *!kaukən* or trembling. *!kaukən* causes the *!gi:xa*'s veins to rise up (*u:ï*). Sometimes the rising up of the veins caused lion's hair to grow out of the *!gi:xa's* back – a *!gi:xa* so overwhelmed could turn into a lion that would chase people and try to bite them. Other people helped the *!gi:xa* to get his *!khãũä* and the other */xuttən /xuttən* to lie down by giving him burning *sã:* (aromatic herbs) to smell, and by rubbing him with fat, and singing and dancing. These activities are an integral part of the curing dances held in the Kalahari today.

Trembling or shaking is common to ecstatic healing practices in many cultures (Keeney 1994). For the |Xam it was also linked to a state of being in which *!gi:tən* would */xãu:* ('go on a magical expedition'). David Lewis-Williams has identified */xãu:* as the sensation of 'out-of-body travel' (Lewis-Williams 1981), and suggests that it was an important resource that had 'direct economic and social consequences' for the community (Lewis-Williams 1982: 436).

Things like */ko:§o-de* or 'magic things found in the body causing illness' (Bleek 1956) could enter the */xuttən /xuttən*, and malignant *!gi:tən* roaming around at night would 'walk over' the arteries to test the apparently sleeping *!gi:xa*'s ability to detect their presence and warn them off. People's arteries were also vulnerable to inexperienced or ill-intentioned *!gi:tən*, who could kill a person by severing their blood vessels with their noses. Older and more experienced sorcerors would *sũ:* magic power into the veins of younger *!gi:tən*. The word *sũ:* is often translated as 'snore', but the early European travellers who initiated this translation had no cultural equivalent for *sũ:*. They probably based their translation on the sounds that a *!gi:xa* made when removing sickness from a patient. *Sũ:* is performed using the nose or */nũnu*, a word that may also be translated as 'snoring power', the power to sũ:. A *!gi:xa* can *sũ:* out things such as */koken-tiken* (magic sticks), butterflies, and even an evil *!gi:xa* who had invaded another man's body.

The detailed descriptions of the role of the */xuttən /xuttən* in containing *!gi:* and the significance of *!kaukən* and */xãu:*, give us valuable insights into what the *!gi:tən* experienced when they entered the states of altered consciousness associated with the presence of activated *!gi:*, a central component of the |Xam religious experience.

Relations between *!gi:tən* and ordinary people

The narratives in Part VII provide a unique perspective on relations between *!gi:tən* and the rest of society. Many of the narratives in Parts VI, VII and VIII emphasise that *!gi:tən* of whatever kind – healers, rain-makers and game specialists – were feared by ordinary people, and for good reason (see Part VI, Introduction). Many of the *!gi:tən* mentioned in the narratives are unpleasant people; they are 'angry' in the |Xam sense of the word – anti-social, even murderous. Some sorcerors were like lions, prowling about at night, snatching away people and eating them (see Part II, 'The lion'). No doubt the narrators might, if further questioned on the matter, have conceded that many of these negative attributes would have applied more to strange and unknown *!gi:tən* than to the *!gi:tən* with whom they were familiar. Nevertheless, the *!gi:tən*'s control over valued resources – health, the rain, and game – led to tensions and violence breaking out between *!gi:tən* and their public (see 'The sorceress !Kwara-aŋ', 'Luck in hunting'). *!Gi:tən* were held accountable for the state of things because they could choose to manifest their magical abilities in positive or negative ways (see Part VI, Introduction). *!Gi:tən* who violated the social contract were chastised, refused payment, or even beaten.

For their part, the *!gi:tən* in the narratives complain that when they are successful in their work, the benefits they bestowed are not acknowledged; but, when disaster strikes, people hold the *!gi:tən* responsible. The narratives thus provide us with an inside view of the relationship between *!gi:tən* and the rest of society, one that describes in detail how and why tensions arose between them.

The /*nu !k*ˀe, the spirit people

Perhaps the most powerful of all the *!gi:tən* were the */nu !kˀe*, translated as 'dead' or 'spirit' people. These were *!gi:tən* who had died and taken their *!gi:* with them (it is not clear whether other, ordinary people also became */nu !kˀe* when they died). The living would */gauka* (a word translated as 'beg for, call on, pray' [Bleek 1956: 276]) the invisible spirit people to do things for them. In Part V |Haŋ≠kass'o describes how his grandfather called upon the 'dead men who are with the rain' (Part V, 'Dead men that ride the rain') to make it rain. In Part VI, another old man calls on !Nuiŋ |kúïtən, a deceased rain-maker, to bring rain. People also called on dead people who were *opwaitən-ka !gi:tən*, or game sorcerors (see Part VII, 'The */nu-!kˀe*', 'The power over ostriches possessed by |uhére' and 'Luck in hunting') to help them find and kill game. Living sorcerors too called on the */nu !kˀe* for the same purpose (see Part VII, 'The power over ostriches possessed by |uhére'). People feared the */nu !kˀe*, as they did living *!gi:tən*, and for the same reasons – fear of their power to inflict sickness and bad luck. Diä!kwain mentions that, when a *!gi:xa* died, he or she would sometimes try to take people away (see 'Falling stars and sorcerors'). The */nu !kˀe* may also have been more powerful than living *!gi:tən* because they existed in spirit form and were not subject to the same physical constraints. Workers in the Kalahari have observed similar beliefs amongst the Ju|'hoansi – dead healers, and those who live far away are credited with more supernatural potency than living ones and those living nearby (England 1968: 416-417; Lee, 1968: 46; Marshall 1969: 358, 378).

Whether or not there was a loose hierarchy of *!gi:tən* in which the */nu !kˀe* were superior, the Part VII narratives are complex and detailed testimonies that show how *!gi:* is manifest in the body and manipulated by experts who use it to do vital work for society.

❑

Note

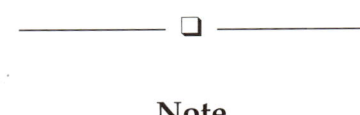

* All three words are variously translated as sorcery, magic power and magic doings.

'About the toorman (sorceror)' or 'The Bushman witchdoctor'

Narrator: ||Kabbo
Dictation dates: 14-16 June 1871
Notebook reference: L.II.1: 273-275
***Bantu Studies* reference**: Vol. 9 (1935), Part VII: 1-2

//Kabbo's description of a transforming !gi:xa *is an ethnographic 'classic' that has made it possible to understand the significance of certain motifs in painted and engraved Bushman images all over the southern African subcontinent.*

❑

Haŋ |ne tʃũ: !kwi au ha |nunu, au !kwitən ta: ; he ti hiŋ e: haŋ |ne !kaukən-ĩ:. Haŋ |ne tsi:ï !kˀe au ha ||ke||ke ; au haŋ tati e:, !kˀe kuitən |kei|kei-ĩ ha, au hi |k'a|k'a, he ti hiŋ e:, haŋ |ne tsi:ï !kˀe kuitən ĩ:. !kˀe kuitakən |ne !kɑn tẽ ha, hiŋ |ne !gwi ha tsi:nxu au swiŋ, au haŋ !kaukən. He ti hiŋ e:, haŋ |ne xo úï !kaukən!kaukən-ĩ:, au haŋ tati e:, ha e: !gi:xa ; he ti hiŋ e:, ha !kaukən-ĩ:, au haŋ ka: sũ: !kwi au ha |nunu.

-||khã: |khukən |ne |hiŋ ha tsi:nxu, !kˀetən |ne !gwi hi au swiŋ, hiŋ |ne !gwi turru hi. He ti hiŋ e:, !kwitən |ne xo úï !kaukən!kaukən-ĩ:, au -||khã: |khukən ka ||gwi au ha tsi:nxu. Hiŋ |ne !gwi turru hi, he ti hiŋ e:, -||khã |khukən |ne ||gwi ĩ:.

He ti hiŋ e:, !kwitən |ne kóäŋ |hiŋ, ĩ, au han tati e:, ha |ne twaïï. Haŋ |ne swe:ŋ, au haŋ twaïï, haŋ |ne ʃo ko ≠kakən, au haŋ |ne twaïï. Hiŋ |ne ʃo ko k''we ĩ:, haŋ |ne tẽ:ŋ, au haŋ twaïï.

He (the sorceror) sniffs at a person with his nose, as the man lies ; then he beats (? the air). He bites people with his teeth ; when other people seize him with their hands, then he bites the other people. The others hold him down and rub his back with fat, as he beats. Then he leaves off beating, because he is a sorceror ; that is why he beats when he is snoring a person with his nose, (to cure the person).

Lion's hair comes out on his back, people rub it off with fat, they rub pulling the hair out. Then the man leaves off beating, when the lion's hair has come off his back. They rub it off, so that the lion's hair falls off.

Then the man (the patient) gets up, because he is well. He sits down because he is well, he sits talking because he is well. They sit drinking there, he lies down, for he is well.

Note

3 … *then he beats* …: Dorothea Bleek did not appreciate the role that *!kaukən* (shaking or trembling, but here translated as 'beat') plays in the healing rituals of many cultures (see Introduction).

All about sorcerors

Narrator: |Haŋ‡kass'o
Dictation dates: 17, 18, 19 and 20 October 1878
Notebook reference: L.VIII.20: 7757-7759; 7752 rev.-7753 rev.; 7753-7756; 7759-7762 and 7768-7774
***Bantu Studies* reference:** Vol. 9 (1935), Part VII: 2-5

|Haŋ‡kass'o describes how the /Xam sorcerors or !gi:tən *that he knew (see 'What sorcerors eat' for a list of names that he gives) were able to extract sickness from the body.*

❑

ŋ -//kwaŋ /ne //k'oen !kʔe, !gitən e: /ne /a:-/wanna.

I have seen these people, sorcerors who are now dead.

!gixa -//kwaŋ ka //nau, !gixa gwai, hiŋ !gixa /aiti, au ha ¯sũŋa !kwi, he ha /ne /ki /hiŋ -//khã, he ha /ne ¯tsi:ĩ !kʔe. !kʔe /ne !kou ha, !kʔe /ne !kɑn //wĩ: ã, ná se k''auki /hiŋ, há se ¯!kuxe /hiŋ.

A sorceror acts like this, a sorceror or sorceress, when he snores a person, he takes a lion out (of the patient), and then he bites people. The people seize him and hold him fast, so that he cannot escape and run away.

He !kʔe /ne !khouwa ha au ¯sã, he ha /ne /khamma /hiŋ -//khã, ĩ:. He ha /ne wai /kha/kha-ka tʃweŋ. Hiŋ /né ta !kʔɔkən-tikən, ĩ, au tʃweŋ e: //ke//keja ʘho. Hiŋ k''auki akən //ka hi, au ŋ óä //k'oenja hi. He e:, ha akənxa se /khamma/khamma /hiŋ hi.

Then people give him *buchu* to smell, and he sneezes the lion out. Then he takes out harm's things (from the other person). They call them bits of wood, for the things are like sticks. They were very pretty when I used to see them. These he sneezes out nicely.

He !kwi /ne twaitən, ĩ:. !kwi /ne /ku kwe:, !khe tau !uháttən, au wai ja //na.

Then the person recovers in consequence, he goes quietly to hunt, if the springbok are there.

Tʃweŋ é: a, hiŋ e: //xamki e /kha-/kha-ka tʃweŋ, hiŋ e: /kha-ĩ i.

These things (pointing to a cat) are also things which bring illness, which harm us.

ŋ -//kwaŋ //k'oen !kʔe e: taŋtaŋ, *he !kwi a:, ha a: ¯sũwa !kwi, ha /né*

I have seen people who were ill, and the person who snored the

ta, da_dabassija a:, ¯/kha !kwi: da_dabassi a ¯!kuïta.

sick man said, that a butterfly was killing him; a white butterfly.

Da_dabassi _//kwaŋ ka /kha /e: i eŋeŋ, he !gixa /ne _sũ i, ha /ne wai hĩ; ha /ne /khamma/khamma /hiŋ hĩ au ha /nunu, au hĩ e: /kha-ã i, he i /ne taŋ¯taŋ, ĩ:; !gixa /ne -sũ i.

Butterflies hurt us by entering our bodies, then a sorceror snores us, he draws them out; he sneezes them out of his nostrils, because they have been hurting us so that we were ill; the sorceror snores us.

I _//kwaŋ k''auki ¯tã hĩ, itən k''auki //xamki /nĩ /nĩ ki sa: hĩ, ta: !gi:-ta tʃweŋ /ke /kɯ. Itən k''auki //xamki ta !kauka _!kaitən-ĩ hĩ, /xam-ka !kˀe, ta: taŋtáŋ /ki ta te:ŋ, au !kauka _!kaitən-ĩ hi, hĩ /kha-ĩ hĩ. Au tija e:, dí kóä tã /i, he //kõïŋja k''auki /né ta !khe!khe, he taŋtaŋ ¯ã /ne te:ŋ. !kˀe /ne !kou, au !kˀe taŋ, !kˀe ta ¯kuwa e taŋ.

We do not feel them, nor do we see them come, for they are magic things. We also do not let children throw stones at them, we Bushmen, for illness occurs if children throw stones at them, to kill them. When the place is getting warm, while the sun is not high yet, then the illness comes. People get up feeling ill, all the people are ill.

Ŋ k''auki ≠enna, ti e:, ha ĩja, ta:, ŋ /ne ¯tã, ti e:, ŋ !nuntu /kɯ-g /ne ¯taŋ, ŋ !nuntukən k''auki tym-ʘpwa ¯taŋ, he ŋ /na: /kɯ-g /ne taŋ, ŋ xu ¯/kija. Ŋ /naŋ k''auki /ne taŋ, ŋ ka: -!kwa-!kwai !khe, he ŋ /kɯ-g /ne ta:.

I did not know what had happened, for I felt that my ear was sore, my ear hurt not a little, and my head ached, my face smarted. My head did not feel as if I should be able to stand, so I lay down.

He /xu-aŋ /ne ¯sũ ŋ !nuntu, ĩ:. Haŋ /ne /ki /hiŋ da_dabassi, haŋ /ne ≠kakən, ti e:, da_dabassi e a: /kha /eja ŋ !nuntu. Haŋ /ne /kwẽ ï da, he ŋ /ne ¯tã, ti e:, ŋ !nuntu /ne twaitən, au ŋ /na: e: siŋ taŋ, ŋ xu e: siŋ taŋ, hi /ki:ja, hiŋ /ne twaitən. He ŋ /ne !uháttən, ĩ:.

Then /xu-aŋ snored my ear. She took out butterflies, she said that butterflies were hurting me in my ear. She did this, and then I felt that my ear was healed, while my head which had been aching, and my face which had been aching, smarting, were well. Then I went hunting.

!kwi gwai _//kwaŋ ka e !gi:xa, !kwi /aitija k''auki e !gixa, ha-ka gwaija e !gixa. Au !kwi gwai á: a, ha /ha e !gixa, !kwi /aiti, !kwi gwaija k''auki e !gixa. !kuko á: a, há e !gixa, !kwi gwaija e !gixa, ha-ka /aitija //xamki e !gixa. Hĩ !ku: e

Sometimes a man is a sorceror and the woman is not a sorceress, her husband is the sorceror. Another man's wife is a sorceress, the man is not a sorceror. Another is a sorceror, the man himself, his wife is also a sorceress. They are

!gitən, !kwi /aitija e !gixa, !kwi gwai-ja e !gixa. Hiŋ ĩ:ja /xam-ka !kʔe.

both sorcerors, the woman is one, the man is one. This is the custom among the */xam* Bushmen.

Ha /ne !xwaŋ !hũ!hũ:, ha /né ta, '¯hŋhŋ, ¯hŋ:,' au ha /ki /hiŋ !hũ!hũ au !kwi. He ha /ne //a !khamma /hiŋ ha. Ha /ne sa ¯sũ !kwi, ha /ne wai //khaitən, ha /ne /khamma-/khamma /hiŋ hĩ.

He makes a noise like an owl, he says, '¯hŋhŋ,¯hŋ', when he extracts an owl from a person. Then he goes to sneeze it out. He comes to snore the person, he draws sticks out, he sneezes them out.

Ha _//kwaŋ ka //xamki !xwaŋ _//khã, ha ka, 'haŋ-a:, haŋ-a,' au haŋ tati, _//khã ĩ:ja, _//khã ka, 'haŋ-a:, haŋ-a:.' He há /ne ta, '¯hm_m, ¯hm_m.' He !kʔe kuita /ne !kouwa ki //a ha, he hi /ne //a, /ki /hiŋ ¯sã:, hi /ne !khouwa ha au ¯sã:, he ha /ne /khamma /hiŋ _//khã.

He also makes a noise like a lion, he says, '*haŋ-a:, haŋ-a:,*' because a lion does so, it roars, '*haŋ-a:, haŋ-a:.*' Then he says, '*¯hm_m, ¯hm,_m.*' Then the other people hear him and follow the sound to him, then they take out *buchu* and give it to him to smell, then he sneezes out the lion.

He ha /ne taŋ, sa:; ha /ne sa ¯sũ !kwi. Ha /ne ¯!hou, ha /ne wai tʃweŋ e: //khaitən, he e:, ha /ne akənxa se u-úĩ, ha /ne //e//e, ha /ne /khamma/khamma /hiŋ hi. He ha /ne sa ¯sũ !kwi, ha /ne !ko:¯ĩ !kwi, he ha /ne sweŋ _kó:äŋ úĩ, he ha /ne kúĩ, ha-ka sũsũ kaŋ k''auki te: tã, ta: ha //nau, ti e:, _//khã a: /kha ha, ta: ha-ka sũsũ _//kwaŋ k''auki te: tã, ta: ha-ka sũsũ _//kwaŋ taŋ, ha _san di ku k''wã ≠hannũwa, ta: ha sũsũ k''auki te: tã. He !kwi /ne twaitən, ĩ:

He is wont to come; he comes to snore a man. Afterwards he extracts things like sticks; these he draws out nicely, then he goes out and sneezes them out. So he comes and snores the man, he wakes him up, so that he sits up and says, that the other's snoring will not let him lie down, though he feels as if a lion were killing him, yet the snoring will not let him lie down, for it feels as if he should get well, for it will not let him lie down. Then he recovers.

He tikən e:, !kʔe ta ka, 'ŋ kaŋ ka, !kõĩŋ ¯kwaŋ aroko /auwa ¯hi, ta:, ha ka //nau, ha ¯da í-ta tí, ha di akən hĩ, he í /ne _ta:-_i, ĩ:.

Therefore people say, 'I want the old man to help us quickly, for when he treats our illness, he does so nicely, and we walk away.'

!kwi a:, ha taŋ kwɔ¯kwaŋ-a, haŋ a:, !kʔe ta //nau, hi sũwa ha,. !kwi a: ha e !gixa, ha /né ta, 'Taŋtaŋ kaŋ /ku_tso:wa i //kã, haŋ /ku taŋ kwɔ¯kwaŋ-a. Haŋ k''auki taŋ, ha se antau twaitən, ta:, ha /ku taŋ

When people are snoring a man who is really ill, the man who is a sorceror says, 'Illness has taken hold of our brother, he is really ill. He does not seem to be going to recover soon, he is really ill, he

kwɔ¯kwaŋ-a, ta:, ha taŋ ha sa: !naunko ˍ/ko:ë ¯ĩ; ha-ka sũsũ k''auki taŋ, ha se antau twaitən.'

feels as if he were going to suffer; his snoring does not feel as if he were going to recover soon.'

Notes

32-33 *... because they have been hurting us ...*: The word *ǀkha* was originally translated as 'killing' (7753).

41-45 *When the place is getting warm, while the sun is not high yet, then the illness comes. People get up feeling ill, all the people are ill*: This translation of these phrases is not accurate. The original translation reads: 'Then they (i.e. the butterflies – ed.) make it warm while the sun is not yet high, then the illness comes; the people are well, then they are ill, all the people are ill.' (7753 rev.).

71-77 *He makes a noise like an owl ... He also makes a noise like a lion*: For more about lions and owls, see Part II, The lion.

Part VII
Sorcerors

All about sorcerors

Invisible arrows and their cure

Narrator: |Haŋ‡kass'o
Source: 'By |Haŋ‡kass'o, from his mother |Xabbi-aŋ'
Dictation dates: 12, 13 August 1878
Notebook reference: L.VIII.14: 7287-7288 and 15: 7289-7295
***Bantu Studies* reference:** Vol. 9 (1935), Part VII: 5-6

Here |Haŋ‡kass'o explains how it is that people become sick without knowing why.

!gitən ˍ||kwaŋ ka |xã !kwi ; hĩ-ta !nwa:, itən k''auki |ne |ni ti sá hĩ. Ta:, í ta |kɯ ˉtã, he í-ta tí, hĩ |kɯ-g |ne taŋ: he i k''auki |ne dí kúï tã ≠hannũwa, í |ne taŋ, i ||ˀu: wa.

Sorcerors are wont to shoot a person ; we do not see their arrows coming. But we feel pain, and some part of us aches ; then we do not feel well, we feel tired.

He ti hiŋ e:, !kuko: ka ku, ha |k'e:, 'Tsara i ||kã xau ˍdóä k''wã ≠hannũwa ã? He ha k''auki ˍdóä ˍdarrakən?' He !kuko: a, ha |ne kúï, 'ŋ kaŋ k''auki ˍdoä tuˉtuwa i ||kã, au ha-ka tí e:, sˀo ˍdóä e, ta:, ha dóä k''waŋ ha taŋ. Ta, ha k''auki ta |kwẽ:ï k''wã ; ta:, ha k''auki ˍdoä ˍdorrakən, ta, ha ˍdóä siŋ |kɯ ta:, au haŋ k''auki dá ti e:, ha á ka ˍmaiï ha !kho, ha |ki ||ka |i. Ta:, ha ˍdóä siŋ |kɯ ta:. !khwãŋ |kɯ a: siŋ |ki ||kéï |i, au haŋ k''auki dá ti e:, ha |kɯ a: ka ˍmaiï ha !kho. ||kõïŋjaŋ |kɯ-g |ne |hiŋ, au haŋ ta:. Haŋ ˍdoä k''waŋ ha taŋ. He tikən e:, ŋ́ ka ha se ≠kakka ke, ha-ka ti e: sˀo ˍdoä e.'

Then someone asks us, 'Why does our brother not seem well ? And why does he not stir ?' And another answers, 'I have not asked our brother what part of him is affected, but he seems to be ill. For he never used to act like this, he does not stir, but keeps on lying down and does not get up as he always used to do, to be the first to make the fire. But now he just lies still. This child has made the fire, because he has not been the first one to get up. The sun rose, while he was still lying down. He seems to be ill. That is why I want him to show me what part of him is affected.'

He tikən e:, !kuko ka-g |ne ku, ha |k'e, '||ke||ke-we:, a -koá ka, ŋ ka ti e:, k''au dóä e, e: k''auki tym ʘpwa taŋ ?'

Then the other, (the invalid) answers, 'O Beast of Prey, do you think that there is any part of me which does not ache a little !'

He !kuko: a: |xara, ha |ne kúï, 'ŋ |ké ta, !kõïŋ -saŋ ≠kakka !kóïte, ˍ!kóïte ˍsaŋ |auwa ha, ha saŋ |kym ˉoä há tsa. Ta a kwaŋ k''auki k''wã ≠hannũwa, u siŋ ˉkwaŋ kwe:, k''wã twaïï; ta a kwaŋ k''auki k''wã ≠hannũwa. Ta !kóëtukən ka |kwẽ, hĩ k''auki ta, hi kwaŋ aroko dí ti.'

He tikən e:, |nu|nutatən ka |ne sũ, ī:, hi |ne wai tʃweŋ au ˉi, tʃweŋ e: hĩ |khaˉã ˉi, au hĩ sũwa i. Hi |ne |kiˉ|ki |hiŋ tʃweŋ. Hĩ |ne ta, 'A ˍkoa: ka, tsa k''au ||nau, ti e:, tsa |kha ˉkoä kũ, au á-ka ti e? Ta: ha ka sũsũ ˍ||kwaŋ k''auki ˉte: tã, ta, ha ˍ||kwaŋ se ˍ|kati, di ku k''wã ≠hannũwa, haŋ k''auki ˍsa !kãnna ha |kwã: ï k''wã.'

Then another says, 'I wish Grandfather would speak to Grandmother, and get her to doctor him, to take that thing away. For you are not comfortable, so that you can lie quietly, because you are not well. For the old women have not been willing to act quickly.'

Then the old women snore and extract things from us, the things which are hurting us when they snore us. They take these things out. They say, Do you think this has not been hurting like a blow on that part? Now this snoring does not feel nice, but later it will make him feel comfortable, he will not feel bad again.'

Notes

17-18 *This child has made the fire …*: [the child of the sick man] (7290, text omitted).

38-39 *… the things which are hurting us …*: 'The thing lies inside [?] (*‡nu[illegible]nu ttiŋ*, not in the *Dictionary* – ed.) that part of us' (7293 rev., note omitted)

41-43 *Do you think this has not been hurting like a blow on that part?*: 'O Beast of Prey, a stone struck [me] a blow on this part of me. Then a bruise came out there' (7293 rev., note omitted).

The fate of good-looking people

Narrator: |Haŋ‡kass'o
Source: '|Haŋ‡kass'o, from his mother |Xabbi-aŋ'
Dictation dates: Sometime between 13 August and 28 August 1878
Notebook reference: L.VIII. 15: 7296-7303
***Bantu Studies* reference:** Vol. 9 (1935), Part VII: 7-8

In this extract |Haŋ‡kass'o explains why good-looking people often become unaccountably sick and die, despite the fact that people are taking care of them.

❑

Au !kwi a:, ha akən, haŋ ka taŋtaŋ, he tikən e:, ha ka-g |ne ¯||ko:sa, au hĩ tati e:, ha akən. He tikən e:, |nu|nutatən ta !né ta, 'ŋ kaŋ tati e:, !kwhã a, ha |ke ˍdóä e ¯||ko:sa. He tikən e:, ŋ ka, ú se ¯kwaŋ |kweŋ, ha siŋ ¯kwaŋ kwe: sˀo:, ta:, ŋ k''auki taŋ, ŋ ká |ketən ha, au !khwa:. Ta:, ha ka ˍ|kóë ã, au ha |kweŋjã. He tikən e:, ŋ́ ta ka, ha siŋ ¯kwaŋ kwe: ¯sˀo, ta, ŋ k''auki taŋ ha ka : |kweŋ-ĩ.'

When a person who is good-looking is ill, he is always taken care of, because he is good-looking. Therefore the old women say, 'I think this child must be taken care of. So I want you to go and fetch water, that he may keep quiet, for I do not want to send him to the water. For he might be worse, if he fetched water. So I want him to keep quiet, I do not want him to fetch water.'

!gitən ˍ||kwaŋ ||ke||keja ˍ||khã. Hi tsaxaukən ka ||ke: ||ke: au !kwi a: akən ; he tikən e:, ha !kwi ha a:, ka |ne taŋtaŋ, he ha |ne ¯|kukən, ĩ:. ||k'oen||k'oenjaŋ e, ti e:, !gixa ka ¯ĩ ta ||k'oen |ki !kwi a:, ha a:kən ; hi ¯ĩ ||k'oen |kija. He tikən e:, ha !kwi a: ka-g |ne taŋ¯taŋ. He tikən e:, !kˀe ta-g |né ta, '¯||ko sa, ã.'

Sorcerors resemble lions. Their eyes look like (a lion's) at a person who is good-looking ; then that person gets ill and dies. A look it is with which a sorceror takes a person who is good-looking, holds him with a glance. Then that man falls ill. Therefore people say, 'take care of him.'

Hi |ne ¯|kẽï ha, ĩ: ; he tikən e: !kwi ta ¯|kukən, ĩ:, au !gitən e: ¯|kẽï !kwi. He tikən e:, !kˀe ta ka, '!kwija ||xã, !kwija taŋ¯taŋ, !kwija kõä !kou, au !kwija ||xã, ha taŋ¯taŋ. He tikən e:, !kwi ta-g |ne ¯|kukən, ĩ:, au hĩ e: |xãũŋ|xãũŋ !ke sa !kwi.'

They seize him ; therefore the person dies, because the sorcerors are seizing him. Then people say, 'that man is ill again, the man gets better, then he gets ill again. Then the man dies, because they keep coming to shoot him.'

He tikən e:, !khwiŋ!khwiŋ k''auki ta ¯⊙pwoin, au hĩ bɔkən ||na, hi bɔkən |kˀe e:, hi |xãũŋ sa:. He hĩ |xãũŋ-a !kwi a:, ha taŋ. He tikən e:, !kwi ta |kɯ-g ||nau, tsˀa _||ka:ŋ, a: !khe !kwi, !kwitən |kɯ-g |ne ¯|kukən ã:, !nwa _||ka:ŋ, a hĩ |ne |xĩ !kwi ã. Hiŋ |kɯ-g |ne |xã ¯||kˀɔro, hiŋ |kɯ-g |ne -!kou tẽ !kwi.

He tikən e:, !kˀe ta |kɯ-g |ne ||nau, au hĩ |ne sũ !kwi, !kwija |kɯ ||nau, hi ¯ku siŋ, hĩ wai tʃweŋ, !kwija |kɯ-g |ne taŋ kwɔ¯kwaŋ ; ha k''auki |ne ¯k''waŋ !kˀeja wai tʃweŋ, au !gita |kɯ-g |ne |xã |e: tã ha, au !kˀe |nu|nutu, hiŋ |xã-ĩ !kwi a: !kˀe sũ: hã. He tikən e:, !kwi |ĩ: ka |kɯ-g |ne !kˀũ ĩ:, !kˀe ki sũ hã, ha |ĩ: |kɯ-g |ne !kˀũ.

Then the dogs do not sleep, but are barking there, they bark at the men who are coming to shoot. Then these shoot at the man who is ill. When this new thing strikes the man, he dies of it, of the new arrow with wich they shoot him. They shoot to kill, they strike the man dead.

That happens while people are snoring the man, although they are taking things out of him, yet he is very ill ; he does not look as if people were taking anything from him, for sorcerors shoot into him under the people's noses, they shoot the man whom people are snoring. Then his heart falls, although they are snoring him, his heart falls down.

Notes

13 *Sorcerors resemble lions*: This is a pervasive Bushman belief (see Part II, Introduction).

29-30 *Then the dogs do not sleep, but are barking there ...*: Apparently dogs could detect the presence of the sorcerors who keep returning and shooting arrows of sickness into the dying man.

43-45 *... for sorcerors shoot into him under the people's noses ...*: 'J.T. says that sorcerors see a handsome person and shoot; for they eat' (7302 rev., note omitted).

What sorcerors eat

Narrator: |Haŋ‡kass'o
Source: '|Haŋ‡kass'o heard this from ||Khabbo, !Kuobba-aŋ, |Guï-aŋ, ||Kuen-aŋ and also Guï-aŋ's mother Kkebbi-aŋ, who were all *!gi:tən*'
Dictation dates: Sometime between 13 August and 28 August 1878
Notebook reference: L.VIII.15: 7304-7306
***Bantu Studies* reference:** Vol. 9 (1935), Part VII: 8

This passage describes a shocking differençe between !gi:tən *and ordinary people.*

❑

ŋ -//kwaŋ túï, ti e:, !kˀe ta, !gitən kuitən hĩ !kˀe ; !gitən kuitakən e: hĩ !hou, he e:, !gitan kuitən !khuwa hĩ !hou, -//kwaŋ /ki si hĩ hĩ. He e:, !kˀe kuitakən !khuwa !kˀe kuitən ã !kˀe, au !kwi ¯/kukən. Hiŋ /ne /ki si hĩ !kwi, au !kwi-ta ¯ã. Hiŋ //xamki /ki si hĩ /kwi, au !hou, hiŋ tau kóä !houkən!houkən. He tʃweŋ hiŋ e:, hi /ki si hĩ !kˀe, ĩ:. !kwi a:, ha !kuka, hiŋ e:, hi /ki si hĩ !kˀe ĩ:.

I have heard people say that some sorcerors eat people ; there are others who eat locusts which others collect for them and make them eat. Others collect human beings for the others, when a man has died. They make them eat the man, of his flesh. They also make the man eat locusts and flies. These things are what they make people eat. A man who dies they make people eat.

❑

Notes

5-7 *Others collect human beings for the others, when a man has died*: This is perhaps one of the reasons why evil sorcerors kill people – for 'food'.

8-9 *They also make the man eat locusts and flies*: See the following two narratives for more about the symbolic and economic importance of locusts.

Sorcerors and locusts

Narrator: |Haŋ‡kass'o
Dictation dates: Sometime between 19 and 21 August 1879
Notebook reference: L.VIII.31: 8756-8758 and 8754-8756
***Bantu Studies* reference:** Vol. 9 (1935), Part VII: 8-9

/Xam sorcerors controlled other important natural resources besides the rain and game animals.

❑

_||kã̃ũnu-ka ≠kakakən |kɯ e, ‘!hou ˉ|hiŋ̈,’ ĩ:, au ha ka _||gauru si ||na||na, ||naˉ||na !kaukən; he !hou |ne ˉ|hiŋ̈. He !hou |ne |hiŋ̈, au há a: ka _!gauruwa se ||naˉ||na !kaukən. !hou-ka tukən e:, !kˀe ta ka _||gauru, ĩ:; au ||kerrija e: -maiˉĩ, hi |hiŋ̈, he !hou |ne ˉ|hiŋ̈ ĩ:. He !kˀe |ne ||ki: !hou, ĩ:.

!kaunu's (see Part VI) saying was, ‘locusts come out,’ when he wanted to drive them there, drive them among the children; and the locusts came out. They came out as he drove them among the children. Male locusts are the ones that people drive, while the locust bird comes out first, then the locusts come out. Then people grab the locusts.

He !hou |ne ||khou |k'wai, !hou ka tíja |ne ||khóä ˉ!kˀauˉkˀau, au !hou |ne |hiŋ̈ |k'wai. He !kˀe |né ta ˉ!xu, au ˉhĩ tati !hou !ne !k'waija.

And the locusts are numerous, part of them are like dust, and many locusts come out. Then people say there is plenty, for the locusts are many.

Si _||kwaŋ ka siŋ |kɯ _!kaita |ki ˉ!hou. ŋ !kõĩŋja |ne |kˀe: ŋ, ŋ kwaŋ k''auki _!kaitən-ĩ ˉ!hou. ||hóäkən!khe !kõĩŋja |né ta, ŋ !kõĩŋ kwaŋ |kɯ |ka:, si kwaŋ |kɯ kwe: ||gwitən ||na; ta: ŋ́ a ||gwitən ˉhĩ ha ⊙pwa⊙pwaïdi, ha hã a: ||gwitən !hou. Si |ne |kẽˉ|kẽï !hou, au !houwa ||khouwi; si |kɯ ||gwitən akən ||na. Si |kɯ ||gwitən akən ||na, si ||gwitən |ki !hou, au si _!kaita |ki !hou, si |kẽˉ|kẽï !ḥou.

We used to throw stones to kill locusts. My grandfather told me not to throw stones at locusts. ||hoaken-!khe's grandfather said my grandfather should let be, we should play there quietly; for I was playing with his grandson who was playing with locusts. We were catching locusts as they flew past; we were playing nicely there. We were playing nicely there, playing at killing locusts, throwing stones to kill them, we were catching them.

Notes

1-2 *!Kaunu's saying was, 'locusts come out':* !Kãũnũ is the *!gi:xa* mentioned in Part VI, '|Kãũnũ, a rain-maker', who possessed rain and locusts. He probably used the saying 'locusts come out' as part of his ritual to make the locusts swarm.

2-4 *... he wanted to ... drive them (the locusts) among the children...*: It seems that it was the |Xam children who did most of the harvesting of locusts for food.

8-9 *... the locust bird comes out first ...*: For more about the locust bird, see the next narrative 'Sorcerors, locusts and locust birds'.

Sorcerors, locusts and locust birds

Narrator: Diä!kwain
Source: 'Tannă !Kauken was the one who told mother about it, then mother talked to us about it …'
Dictation dates: Between 21 November and 15 December 1875
Notebook reference: L.V.21: 5708-5719
***Bantu Studies* reference:** Vol. 9 (1935), Part VII: 9-11

Diä!kwain points out that a special relationship exists between sorcerors and locusts.

The *||kerri* is a bird rather smaller than a dove, with a black back and white breast. It travels with the flocks of locusts, but in more or less numerous parties, not alone. It is only seen when locusts are about. It is called by the farmers 'sprinkaanvoël'.

*Mama-gukən ≠kaka si ã:, ti ɛ:, ||kerri ɛ ts*ʔ*a a: k''auki |kɯ ˍtai |hiŋ, ta ||kerri |kɯ ||na !hou. ||k'e: a:, !gitən |ki bɔ:kən !ho !kau a:, hɛ !ku: !kãũŋ !hõä ha, o ti ɛ:, !hou ||nã hɛ, !hougən |ne |hiŋ, !hougən |ne ||khouï. Hiŋ |kɯ ɛ:, ||kerri ka, ||kerri se ||xaɯ |hiŋ, ĩ:, hɛ ||kerri |ne ˍtai, hĩ !hou, ĩ:. Ta: ||kerri k''auki ka hɛ se ˍtai, o !houwa k''auki |hã:.*

*Ta: ||kerri ||xam ||ke||ke:ja !hou, haŋ ||xam !kã: ||k'e: a: !gitən se !nwerri ˉ|kym tu !kau a:, !gitən !ku: !haŋ-a !hou ã:. Ha !kaukən |kɯ a:, hɛ !kã: ha, !gitən se |kym tu ha. Hɛ, hɛ |ne ˍtai, ĩ: ; ta: hɛ ||ke||ke:ja !k*ʔ*e ɛ:, i |ki |e: tã hɛ, o ti ɛ:, hɛ k''auki se |hiŋ, o i: xa ≠kaka hɛ ã:, ta: hɛ |kɯ ĩ: !kã: ||k'e: a: i se |k'e:ja hɛ ã:, haŋ |kɯ a:, hɛ !kã: ha.*

Our mothers told us that the locust bird is a thing which does not go away, for it keeps with the locusts. At the time when the sorcerors remove the stone which they have put on the place where the locusts are, the locusts come out and fly. Then the locust bird also wants to come out and go with the locusts. For it will not go about before the locusts have come out.

For the locust bird is like the locusts, it also awaits the time when the sorcerors will roll off the stone with which they have shut in the locusts. That stone is what they wait for, till the sorcerors take it off. Then they go out, for they are like people whom we have shut up so that they can't get out unless we tell them to do so ; for they merely await the time when we shall speak to them; that is what they wait for.

Ta hɛ /ki //xam //ke//ke:ja ti ɛ:, i i da: hɛ, itən ¯!kõäse !kukɔ:, o itən ka !kukɔ: k''auki se /kɯ ˍtai. !gitjaŋ //xam ĩ:ja !kau a: hɛ !ku: !kãũŋ !hóä ha, o ti ɛ:, !hou //nã hɛ. I ɛ: k''auki ɛ !gi:xa, itən k''auki ka, i se //a /kym ha, o !hou. Ta: i /kɯ //nau, o i: //a /kym ha, i ɛ: k''auki ɛ !gi:xa, itən /kɯ ka, i se ¯/ku:kən, o i: ka, i: ¯≠i: i ka i /kym tu !kau a: ¯!kãũŋ !khe: !hou-ka !kó:ä-tu. Ta:, mama-gu /ki ≠kaka si ã:, ti ɛ:, !kau a: !kãũŋ !khe ti ɛ: !hou //na hɛ, haŋ //ke//ke:ja !gi:xa a: //na, ti ɛ:, !hou //na hɛ. Ta, !gitən /ki //nau, hɛ kiɛ //a /ki /hiŋ !hou, hiŋ /kɯ ˍtabba hɛ, o //ke:n-ka didí:. Hiŋ /kɯ //aŋ /ki /hiŋ !hou, o hɛ /kɯ /xarrase da: hɛ.

For it is like what we do when we are taking care of someone and do not want him to walk about. The sorcerors do the same to the stone with which they shut in the place where the locusts are (i.e. place a spell or it). We who are not sorcerors dare not go and take it off the locusts, for if we who are not sorcerors went to take it off, we should die when we tried to lift off the stone which stands upon the mouth of the locusts' hole. For our mothers used to tell us that the stone which stands over the place where the locusts are, is as if a sorceror were at the place where they are. When the sorcerors mean to take out the locusts, they charm them with magical doings. They go and take out the locusts as they have always done.

Hɛ tikən ɛ:, mama-gu, kíɛ: se //nau, hɛ: /nã: ti ɛ:, si /kym !kau, sitən ˍ!kaitən !hou, mama-gukən k''auki ka hɛ se tym ʘpwa /k'e: si; ta: hɛ kĩɛ̃ se kukú, hɛ ≠kaka si ã:, si //khóä kaŋ ¯≠ĩ:, !hou //ouse ˍtai-ã tiŋ, o ˍ/kɔ́:ɔ̈de. Ta: !hou /ki ˍ/kɔ́:ɔ̈de. !hougən //nau, i: ˍ!kaita !hou, o !kau, !hou-ka !gitjaŋ //k'oen i, o i ˍ!kaitən !hou o !kau. Itən /kɯ tã: i, o !gitən ɛ: /xĩ i, o hɛ ˍ!k''wain, ti ɛ, i ˍ!kaitən-ĩ !hou, o !kau. Hiŋ /kɯ ¯ã ˍ/kɔ́:ɔ̈dekən /kɯ /khi: i, o hiŋ ˍ!k''wain; ti ɛ:, hɛ siŋ ¯≠ï:, ti ɛ:, hɛ /ki ˍtaija hi ã: !hou, i se akənxa se hã !hou, o i: k''auki //k'werre !hou. Itən /kɯ /ku:kən, o i //k'werre !hou.

Therefore if our mothers saw us take a stone to throw at the locusts, they used to scold us severely: they used to say to us, that we ought to remember, that locusts only go about because of magic doings. For locusts have magic powers. If we throw stones at the locusts, their sorcerors see us throwing stones at the locusts. We find this out when the sorcerors are shooting at us, because they are angry with us for throwing stones. They let magic things kill us, because they are angry; for when they have made the locusts go about nicely for us, we should eat them nicely and not play with them. We die, if we play with the locusts.

Notes

Title This narrative was originally entitled '*//kerri*', the /Xam name for the 'locust bird'.

The *//kĕrri* or locust bird is probably the Blackwinged Pratincole, *Glareola nordmanni*. These birds are migrants and travel between Eurasia and the grasslands of southern Africa. They arrive in southern Africa in the summer and prey on locust hoppers that have hatched out as a result of the summer rains (Anonymous 1999).

5 *Our mothers told us ...* : In an important reverso note, Diä!kwain explains how sorcerors magically create locusts out of *to:*, red haematite, a substance that figures in many dealings with supernatural powers such as !Khwa:, the rain. Here is the previously unpublished note in full:

Tannă !Kauken was the one who told mother about it, then mother talked to us about it, for she felt that she [T.K.] had told her about it that she might keep us away from the locust bird. For mother seemed to think that the locust bird and the locust were not pleasant things (*tchuēŋē twai*). For they are things which bring illness. For they do not travel alone; for sorcerors are with the locusts when these travel. Because she used at the time when people who possess locusts (i.e. sorcerors who have supernatural control over locusts – ed.) roll away the stones with which they have shut the locusts up. She [T.K.] was with others when they open the hole for the locusts to come out. Mother seemed to think that the place feels light (*ti e ta //kaiten*) from which the locusts come. But it is a charmed (*/giya*, strong – ed.) place. For people who go to take out the locust they make them of *to:* which is the stuff they make them of. These things seem to bring danger (*Hĕ tĭ kwăŋ hĕ di /ā, i* or a 'fight', 'harm' or 'curse' – ed.). Because they are fighting things (*/ā kĕ di-di* – ed.). When they make the locusts act in this way, that is what they think.

(5707 rev.-5709 rev., note omitted)

The //ke:n dance and sorcerors

Narrator: Diä!kwain
Dictation dates: Between 21 December 1875 and 3 January 1876
Notebook reference: L.V. 22: 5755-5775
***Bantu Studies* reference:** Vol. 9 (1935), Part VII: II-14

Diä!kwain's comments are about as close as a rock art researcher can get to interviewing the makers of Bushman imagery from long ago. In these twenty manuscript pages, Diä!kwain provides the key to recognising the motifs in the Bushman's paintings and engravings by linking them explicitly to the work of sorcerors.

Hɛ kaŋ //khóä hɛ !kˀõä //na, ta: hɛ !khe ≠ka≠kauroka, hɛ !kwa!kwa:-gən. !kwi á: a, ha !khe: !xwe:, tikən k''wãŋ, ha a: !kˀõä !kˀe ã:, !kˀe se !kˀõä; hɛ tikən e:, ha !kanna //kha, ĩ: o haŋ ta: //ka ti e:, ha ɛ !kwi ⁻!kerri. Hɛ tikən e:, ha !kanna o !kˀõä!kˀõä-ka //kha, ĩ:, o hiŋ ta: /ka ti e:, ha /ki a:, ˍmai-i, haŋ !kˀõä !kˀe ã:, hɛ !kˀe /ne !kˀõä !kuŋ sin ha, ĩ: o !kˀetən ta: //ka ti e:, ha /ki a:, !kum haŋ !kˀõä, o haŋ ta:, //ka ti e:, ha /ki ɛ !gi:xa ⁻!kerri. Hɛ tikən e:, ha ˍmai-i, haŋ !kˀõä, ĩ:, o háŋ ka, !kˀe e: //xá://xa: hɛ o !gi:-ta didi:, hɛ se !kˀõä !kuŋ siŋ ha. Ta:, ha /ki a:, !kˀõä /ki /e: !gi:-ta didi: o !kˀe. Hɛ tikən e:, ha !kum, haŋ !kˀõä' ĩ:, o haŋ ka, !kˀe e: //xá://xa: hɛ, hɛ se !kˀõä ku k''waŋ ti e:, ha /kwẽ:ĩ k''okən !kˀõä, ĩ:. Ta: !gi:xa /ki //nau, ha //xá://xa: i, haŋ ˍmai-i, haŋ !kˀõä //ke:n, hɛ !kˀe e: //xá://xa: hɛ, hɛ /ne !hau, hiŋ !kˀõä, o há a: !kˀõä hɛ ã:.

They seem to be dancing, for they stand stamping (?) with their legs. This man who stands in front seems to be showing the people how to dance ; that is why he holds a stick, for he feels that he is a great man. So he holds the dancing stick, because he is the one who dances before the people, that they may dance after him, for the people know, that he is the one who always dances first, because he is a great sorceror. That is why he dances first, because he wants the people who are learning sorcery to dance after him. For he is dancing, teaching sorcery to the people. That is why he is dancing first, for he wants the people who are learning to dance as he does. For when a sorceror is teaching us, he first dances the *//ke:n* dance, and those who are learning dance after him as he dances.

!gi:xakən //nau, ha //xá://xa: i, haŋ //nau, ha /nũnũ-ka: //xaukən

When a sorceror is teaching us, when his nose bleeds, he sneezes

|hã:, o ha |nũnũ, ha: |xamma !ɑhí ||kho ha |nũnũ-ka ||xaukən, o ha |k'a:, ha: !khou tã: hi, ha |nũnũ -ka ||xaukən o haŋ ka ha |nũnũ-ka ||xaukən ˍ|kwʔãĩ, hɛ se |e: i !kãũä, i !kãũä se dí ku taŋ, hɛ ˍkóäŋ |hiŋ o ha |nũnũ-ka ||xaukən e: |ki ˍkóäŋ |hiŋ i !kãũä. Hɛ i |ne ||nau, ha |nũnũ-ka ||xauka: |ki ˍkóäŋ |hã: i !kãũä, i !kãũäŋ |kɯ-g |ne dí kúï tã serritən, tikən |kɯ tãŋ !khwa: e: ˍk"áö, hɛ e:, |e: ta: i !kãũä. Ta:, !gi:xa |ki ||nau, tikən ki tã |i, ha |nũnũ-ka ||xaukən, hiŋ |kɯ taŋ !khwa: e: tã serritən, o ha ɛ !gi:xa, hiŋ |kɯ ˍk"áõ'

the blood from his nose into his hand, he makes us smell the blood from his nose, for he wishes its scent to enter our gorge (?), that our gorge may feel as if it were rising, because the blood of his nose is making it rise. And when his blood has made our gorge rise, our gorge feels cool, as if water which is cold were in it. For however hot a place may be, the blood from a sorceror's nose feels like cold water, because he is a sorceror he is cold.

Hɛ tikən e:, i ||nau, !gi:xa !khouwa hi, o ha |nũnũ-ka ||xaukən, itən |kɯ ˍ|xammoŋ úï, o i !khouwa ha |nũnũ-ka ||xaukən ˍ|kwʔãĩ. Itən |kɯ ˍ|xammoŋ úï, ta: i !kãũä |kɯ taŋ, hɛ su:kən úï ; itən |kɯ-g ne ||kóäkən !kouky, o itən |ne ta: ||ka ti e:, hɛ: ||xaukən hɛ-ka ˍk"áö e: |e: ta: i !kãũä, hɛ !gi:xa ||kaŋ. Hɛ tikən e:, i |kɯ-g |ne ˍk'áö. He tikən e:, !kwi a: !gi:xa, ha ka ha se ||nau, tïja ki sa:, tã |i, haŋ k"auki se ||kho: haka !nwiŋ, o ha: ta: ||ka ti e:, ha tã, ti e:, tí k"auki taŋ, ti ˍ||kwaŋ tã |i ; ta:, ha ||kaië |kɯ ˍk"áö. Hɛ tikən e:, ha |kɯ ||nau, ha: ||khóä !nwiŋ, haŋ |kɯ !koukŋ, haŋ |kɯ ˍk"áö, o ha ||khóä !nwiŋ. Ta: ||ke:n-ka didí: |ki k"auki ta ||kaitən.

Therefore when a sorceror makes us smell the blood from his nose, we shudder away, when we smell its scent. We shudder away, for our gorge feels as if it would jump up ; we shiver all over, for we feel that this blood, the cold of which is in our gorge, is fresh from a sorceror. Therefore we are cold. Therefore a man who is a sorceror will not lay down his kaross, even if it is hot, because he knows that the place will not seem hot to him, for his inside is cold. Therefore if he put the kaross down, he would shiver, he would be cold. For the doings of sorcery are not easy.

Ta: !kwi a: ɛ !gi:xa, ha !kõäse ha, o há !gi:xa ; haŋ k"auki |kɯ dí ||ka ti e:, ha |kwẽ:ï dakən ¯≠ĩ:, ĩ:. Ta: !gitən kuitən ka hɛ se |kha ha, o ha: k"auki !kõäse ha, o ti e: ha |ki hɛ. Ta:, !gitən kuitən ||nau, hɛ ≠enna, ti e:, !gi:xa ko: ||na hɛ́: ti, hiŋ |xãũ |kɑm ||a ha, ti e:, hɛ

A man who is a sorceror takes care of himself, because he is a sorceror ; he does not act as he pleases. For other sorcerors will kill him, if he does not take care of himself, when he meets them. For when other sorcerors know that another sorceror is at that

Part VII Sorcerors

The ||ke:n dance and sorcerors

≠enna, ti e:, ha //na hɛ. Hiŋ /kw //nau, haŋ /e: ta: ⊙pwoin, hiŋ /kw !ke //a: ha, o haŋ ⊙pwoin //na. Haŋ /kw //nau, haŋ ¯⊙pwoin ta:, haŋ /kw !koukŋ, o !gitən kuitən e: gauwa ha, hiŋ e:, ˍtai hɔ ha-ka ≠xuru.

place, they hurry towards him, as soon as they know where he is. As he is lying asleep, they come upon him sleeping there. He shivers in his sleep, because the others are seeking him to walk over his veins.

Hɛ tikən e:, i ka //nau, //ga:, i tu !gi:xa, o há: !koukŋ ; o //k'e: a: !gitən kuitən sa: ha ã:, haŋ a:, ha !koukŋ ã:, o !gitən kuitja kíë sa //k'oen, ti e:, ha-ka ≠xuru /nõ !naun-ko !kauwa ; hɛ /ne //k'oen, ti e: !kuko: ˍ//kwaŋ ≠en /ki sa: hɛ. Hɛ /ne ¯//xã: hɛ ˍtai, o hɛ //k'oẽnjã, ti e:, !kuko: ˍ//kwaŋ ˍóä //khou, ĩ:, o ha ⊙pwoin //na, ta: ha ˍ//kwaŋ /ne ≠en /ki sa: hɛ. Hɛ, hɛ //kwaŋ /ne //k'oen, ti e:, !kuko: ˍ//kwaŋ ˍóä ɛ !gi:xa ¯!kerri, ta: ha ˍ//kwaŋ /ne ≠en /ki sa: hɛ. Ti e: hɛ sa: ha hɛ /ne /kw //nau, !kuko:, hɛ /kw !xãũ ha, o hɛ: kiё /xãũ /kəm //e ti e: /xa-ra, hɛ se //xəm //k'oen, ti e:, hɛ /kwẽ:ï-u, ĩ:.

That is why we sometimes hear a sorceror shivering at night ; when other sorcerors come to him, then he shivers, because the others want to see whether his veins are still alive ; that they may see whether the other knows they are coming. They go away again, when they have seen what the other has become as he sleeps there, for he knows of their coming. Then they see that he really is a great sorceror, for he has known of their approach. When they come to him, they do this, they smell (?), for they want to hurry to another place, that they may see as they are wont to do.

I e: k''auki ɛ !gi:xa, itən, k''auki ≠enna o hɛ /kwẽ:ï k''o //na ; ta hɛ e: !gitən, hɛ /kw e: ≠enna hɛ /ka:-gən, ti e:, hɛ /ka:gən /kwẽ:ï k''o //na, ĩ:.

We who are not sorcerors do not know what they are doing there, but those who are sorcerors know their mates and what their are doing.

Notes

Title Originally this narrative was called 'Mr G. Stow's Picture, No. 3'.

1-2 *They seem to be dancing, for they stand stamping …* : The original translation was 'they stand [?] bending their knees'. The 'stamping' action is a characteristic of the healing dances of many Bushman groups and involves the bending of the knee (see Introduction).

3-4 *This man who stands in front …* : 'The first figure to the right of the beholder of the picture' (5754 rev., note omitted).

27 *… when his nose bleeds …*: The |Xam teachers frequently mention sorcerors having nose bleeds (see Part VIII, 'How an old woman asked a chameleon for rain', about the possible use of the 'springbok bush' to induce nose-bleeds).

30-31 *… for he wishes its scent to enter our gorge …*: The smell of blood and its effect on the 'gorge', often associated with physical revulsion, also kept away harmful things.

47-48 *… we shiver all over …*: The word used is *!kaukən*, which describes the trembling of people who are entering an altered state of consciousness in the healing dance (see Introduction).

51-53 *…a man who is a sorceror will not lay down his kaross …*: Rock art researchers have used this information to identify rock art images of humans and human/non-human combinations as images of Bushman sorcerors, or shamans (Lewis-Williams 1996).

78-80 *… because the others want to see whether his veins are still alive …*: '[it means all his veins here, D.H. says]' (5771 rev., note omitted).

88-89 *When they come to him, they do this …*: This translation is awkward and does not make sense – neither does the manuscript translation, which reads:

they do this they lie down to sleep for him for they want to hurry reach another place, that they may also see what they are wont to do.

(5774-5775)

This is another puzzling instance where the English translation does not correspond with the |Xam text (see Part V, 'The rain-maker', for another example). Based on the original |Xam text, and with the context in mind, I put forward the following translation of the sentence:

- **|Xam text:**

  !kuko he /ku !xau ha, o he kie /xau /kum //e ti e /xara, he sĕ //xŭm //§koen tĭ ē, hĕ /kwēï-ũ, i

- **Literal translation:**

  another they do carry away him because they try shoot with magic arrows close go place which different, they must do also see place which they are like to do

- **Idiomatic translation:**

  They carry another person away because they stop trying to shoot him with magic arrows (i.e. the vigilant sorceror): they must go and look for some other place to try the same thing there.

Picture of Mr Orpen's

Narrator: Diä!kwain
Source: 'Diä!kwain heard this from his mother ǂKămmi-ăn'
Dictation date: 20 February 1876
Notebook reference: L.V.25: 6008-6013
***Bantu Studies* reference:** Vol. 9 (1935), Part VII: 14-15

Again Diä!kwain links rock art and sorcery, this time to paintings from the Maluti mountains in Lesotho, hundreds of kilometres east of the paintings he described in 'The ||ke:n *dance and sorcerors'. Diä!kwain was looking at copies of rock paintings made by Joseph Millard Orpen when he spent time in these mountains in the 1870s. Orpen's report about his conversations with a Maluti Bushman called Qing in the* Cape Monthly Magazine *of July 1874 has become another ethnographic 'classic' in the interpretation of Bushman engravings and paintings (Vinnicombe, 1976; Lewis-Williams 1981).*

❑

Tsa kaŋ _|kwãĩja tsa a:, !kˀe ||nau, ||k'e: a:, he di: ||ke:ŋ-ka di, hiŋ |ki ha, o hiŋ ka, he se !khouwa !kˀe kuitən e: |ku:kən o ||ke:ŋ, he k''auki !naunko |gi: akka. Hiŋ e:, he kíë: hɛrribe he, he se ||xã: he se dí ||ke:ŋ ; o hé tʃweŋ e: |e: ta: hé tʃweŋ, o he |gi|gi:ja he-ka |xuttən-|xuttən.

The thing (held by the first man on the right) is like the thing which people take when they are practising sorcery, for they mean to let other people, who are dying of sorcery, smell it, those (learners) who are not strong enough yet. This will help them to practise sorcery, for these things are in the things with which they strengthen their senses.

Ta: !kˀe e: ||ke:||ke:ja |xam-ka !kˀe kuiten, he |ki k''auki e. Ta: he |kɯ e !gitən, he i e: k''auki ||ke:-||ke:ja he, i |kɯ ||nau, o i: ||a: he, itən |kɯ ||nau, i: xarra _tai, ||nuŋ hóä he ||k'ó:ë, tikən |kɯ k''wãŋ tsa a: ||ke:n tẽ i, o hé ka !gitən |kɯ e:, ||ke:ŋ tẽ i. Itən |kɯ |ku:kən, o i k''auki tã:, ti e:, i taŋ.

For these are not people who are like other Bushmen. For they are sorcerors, and if we who are not like them go to them, though we always walk behind their backs, it seems as if something bewitches us, for these sorcerors bewitch us. We die without feeling ill.

Ta: !gitən e:, |kuu |ki tʃweŋ e: !kau!kauüka, he |ki |kuu e. Tʃweŋ e:, he |ki he, hiŋ |kuu k''wãŋ he ||k'een. He tikən e:, !gi:xa |kuu ||nau, he: tʃweŋ, o he: k''wãŋ, he |na: ti, o !gi:xakən k''auki ≠enna, !gi:xa |kuu tã:, ha-ka |xuttən|xuttən, ti e:, he taŋ, ti di te:ŋja hé: ti.

For these are sorcerors who have things whose bodies they own. These things enable them to appear to see. So it happens that when these things have seen anything which the sorceror does not know, he perceives by his magic what is happening.

❑

Notes

1-2 *The thing (held by the first man on the right)* ...: '[the thing held by the first man to the right of beholder in Mr Orpen's picture in the *Cape Monthly Magazine* for July 1874]' (6007 rev., note partially omitted).

9-11 *... for these things are in the things with which they strengthen their senses*: */xuttən/xuttən*, the word translated as 'senses', in fact means 'arteries' (Bleek 1956). Diä!kwain is referring to the belief that the blood vessels contain *!gi:* or 'magic power', at least some of which is put inside the blood vessels by older, more experienced *!gi:tən* (sorcerors). See 'A sorceror's blood vessels' for more on this point.

12-13 *For these are not people who are like other Bushmen*: Again Diä!kwain emphasises the difference between *!gi:ten* and ordinary people – sorcerors have the ability to 'bewitch' (*//ke:n tē*), literally to 'throw magic' – while others do not.

26-27 *... he perceives by his magic what is happening:* The notebook says 'the sorceror feels in his senses [?] that something is happening' (6013). The word for 'senses', however, also means 'blood vessels', in which a sorceror's *!gi:* was carried. See Part VII, Introduction for more about a sorceror's blood vessels.

The sorceror as a jackal or bird

Narrator: Diä!kwain
Dictation date: 22 July 1875
Notebook reference: L.V.14: 5055-5078½
***Bantu Studies* reference:** Vol. 9 (1935), Part VII: 15-19

!Gi:tən *have the power to change themselves into other animals.*

Koro á: e !gi:xa, ha kaŋ //nau, !kwi á: e !gi:xa, ha kɔ́:ka i ; itən siŋ //na ha, itən /ne _tai xu: túï ha, haŋ //nau, haŋ kaŋ //na, ti e:, i siŋ _tãi xu: túï ha ĩ:, haŋ /kɯ dí: ha o koro, o haŋ ka, ha se tauko !kˀõäse i, ha se //k'oen, ti e: i /nõ akkənxa se !kúïtən i-ta //neiŋ, o i: twai-ĩ //ke//ke:ja ti e:, í siŋ //na ha, ĩ:. Itən //nau, //kõïŋ !xo:wa, itən k''au-ki /nĩ: ha, ta: //k'e: a:, //kõïŋ /ne !khe !xwɔ̃nni ã:, ha-g /ne a:, i /nĩ: ha ã:, o kwerrekwerre-ka //k'e:, haŋ a:, i /nĩ: ha a:, o haŋ ta: //ka ti e:, //kõïŋ /ne di: /e/e:.

A jackal who is a sorceror does as follows, when the man who is a sorceror loves us ; we have lived with him, we go away and leave him, while he continues to live at the place we have left, he turns himself into a jackal for he wants to go about taking care of us, that he may see whether we reach home safely, and are as well as we were when we lived with him. When the sun is high, we do not see him, but when the sun has turned back, then we see him in the evening, when he feels that the sun is just going to set.

Hɛ tikən e:, ha-g /ne //xou ≠ka:, ĩ:, i se /nĩ ha, ha se //xɑm //k'oen, ti e:, i-ta _tai /nõ !naunko //xwerrita, ha se !kˀóäse i, o //ga:. Ha //nau, o ha //k'oen, ti e: //kõïŋjã: ka ha //kau siŋ //e !hum, ha //nau, ti e:, í ka, i //a swe:ŋ hɛ, o i tã: ti e:, i taŋ i //kˀɩ:wa, o _tai a:, i siŋ _tai sa: ã:, ha i !kwa!kwa:gən _//kwaŋ taŋ o _tai. Hɛ tikən _//kwaŋ e:, i ka itən ≠ĩ:, i ta i _am swe:ŋ, i !kwa!kwa:gən se dí ku tã ≠hannũ-wa ; ta: hɛ _//kwaŋ taŋ, o _tai a:, i siŋ _tai sa: ã:.

Then it is that he becomes visible, so that we may see him, and he may also see, whether we are still going on well, and may take care of us by night. He does this when he sees that the sun has just set behind the mountain, when we are going to sit down, for we feel that we are tired from the walk which we have taken, which has made our legs ache. Therefore we think that we will rest a bit, that our legs may get rested ; for they are aching from the walk which we have taken.

Ha //nau, i ¯sã:¯sã: sˀo: o i, há: //kho !gwe ʃo i, ha sˀo kõ bɔrro kúï !xwãŋ koro. I ka ≠ĩ:, ‘koro a: a, há xa ka, ha te: /ki ŋ, hɛ ha bɔrro !gwe ʃo ŋ?’ I e: k’’auki ≠enna, ti e:, koro a: !kˀõäse, i ha e, itən kíë se /kwẽï ku, i ≠ĩ:; i ko //nau, i ≠enna, ti e:, !kwi a: siŋ e !gi:xa, ha e, ha í siŋ //na ha, ha e, o í: ≠enna, ti e:, ha _//kwaŋ a:, tu:tu: i, ti e:, í /nõ !naunko taŋ, ti e:, i siŋ /kẽï tã, ĩ:, o í /hiŋ ha.

As we sit resting ourselves, he sits up opposite us, he sits barking like a jackal. We think, ‘why does this jackal want to come to me to sit barking opposite me?’ We who do not know that he is a jackal that takes care of us, think this; when we realise that he is a person who used to be a sorceror, with whom we used to live, then we know that he is asking us whether we are still as well as we were when we left him.

Itən //nau, i ≠enna, ti e:, ha _//kwaŋ tu:tu: i, ti e:, i /kwẽï tã, ĩ:, itən ≠kaka ha ã:. Haŋ k’’auki //na i, ta:, ha /kɯ kaŋ !gwe ʃo i, itən ≠kakən kúï !xwãŋ ha sˀo hĩ í. Itən kukúï, itən /k’e:ja ha ã:, ‘ŋ kaŋ_//kwaŋ k’’auki te: tã, ta-g ŋ _//kwaŋ /kɯ !naunko taŋ, ti e:, ŋ siŋ x̀u: á, ĩ:.’

When we understand that he is asking us, how we are, then we answer him. He is not close to us, for he continues to sit opposite us; we speak as if he were sitting by us. We say, ‘There is nothing the matter with me, for I am still feeling as I did when I left you.’

Ha-g /ne ≠gou, o i /kwẽï ku, i /k’e:ja ha ã:; ha-g /ne /kɯ _kõãŋ /hiŋ, ha /kɯ /kɑm //e ti e: /xarra, I ka: ≠ĩ:, ha: //kóä:kən _tai xu: i, o ha: /kɯ _//kwa:, ta: //ka ti e:, ha: túï, ti e:, i _//kwaŋ _óä /kɯ !naunko twai-ĩ:. Hɛ tikən e:, ha /ne _tai, xu: túï i. Haŋ //nau, itən ≠ĩ: ti e:, ha /kɯ sˀo //na, ti e:, i siŋ /nĩ ha, ĩ:, itən //xã:ŋ /auwi ha, o haŋ !kˀattən !gwe !khe: i; o haŋ k’’wãŋ ti e:, !kwiŋ kă dá: hɛ, hɛ: ha xarra ka !kˀattən !gwe !khe i, i-g /ne //a /ũ:ŋ siŋ hɛ: ti.

He is silent, when we have spoken to him; he gets up and goes to another place. We think that he is leaving altogether, as soon as he has heard that we are still well. That is why he goes away from us. When we think that he is sitting where we last saw him, we catch sight of him as he is trotting past us, for he acts as a dog does, and it always trots past us where we lie down to sleep.

Ha //nau, !khwa:gən e:, í siŋ _kwarre ta hɛ, i /ne _!gabbetən_!gabbetən tẽ: tóä hɛ. Ha-g //nau, i: ʘpwoiŋ //na, ha se, ha sa k’’ãũŋ hɛ, í siŋ _!gabbetən_!gabbetən tẽ: tóä hɛ. Ha k’’wãŋ !kwiŋ, ti e:, !kwiŋ xarra ka /kwẽï k’’o ĩ:, hɛ !kwiŋ xarra ka

He waits for the bones which we throw down when we have gnawed them. When we are asleep there, he will come to crunch what we have thrown down. He acts like a dog, does what a dog always does, and a dog always crunches the

Part VII
Sorcerors

The sorceror as a jackal or bird

k''ãũŋ !kwa:gən e:, i: tẽtẽ tóä hɛ. Ha //nau, i: !ke sa:, i //neiŋ, ha //kho !gwe siŋ i-ta //neiŋ, o ha: ka, há se //k'oen, ti e:, i /nõ akkənxa se !ke //a i-ta !kʔe, e: i siŋ _tai, xu: tóä hɛ. Ha-g /ne //nau, ha: //k'oen, ti e:, i: _//kwa: //na, i-ta !kʔe, ha /ne !kúïtən ha-ka //neiŋ.

bones we throw down. When we reach home, he is sitting opposite the hut, for he wants to see whether we arrive safely among our people, whom we have left. As soon as he sees that we are really among our people, he returns to his home.

!kʔe e: kaŋ //na ha-ka //neiŋ, hiŋ k''auki ≠enna, ti e:, ha _tai hĩä i, ta:, hɛ /ku _//kwaŋ ta: //ka ti e:, hɛ k''auki /nĩ: ha, o ha /ne _tai hĩ i, ta: hɛ /ku kaŋ ≠ĩ: ti e:, ha /ku //na hĩä hɛ, o haŋ k''auki ĩ:ja. Ta:, ha /ku /ahérri /e:ja ha o koro ; haŋ /hu _tai hĩ i, o haŋ /ku e koro. !kʔetən /ku //k'oen /ki ha eŋeŋ e:, ha e !kwi, ĩ:, hɛ //na //neiŋ ; hiŋ /ku e: !kʔe //k'oen /ki hɛ. !kʔetən k''auki ≠enna ha eŋeŋ e: _tai hĩä i, !kʔetən k''auki ≠enna hɛ.

The people who are at his home do not know that he walks with us, because they are not able to see him when he is walking with us, so they think that he is with them, although he is not there. For he turns himself into a jackal ; he walks with us when he is a jackal. The people still see his body, in which he is a man, that is at home ; that is what people see. They do not know the body in which he walks with us, that they do not know.

(*Díä!kwain* says that the sorceror who turns himself into an animal returns at cockcrow, before daybreak, while the people are still sleeping and do not see him come. His human form remains meanwhile sleeping at home).

Ta:, ti e:, ha !kúïtən ; //a:, ĩ:, hé /ku e:, ha-g /ne ≠kaka !kʔe ã:, ti e:, !kwi a siŋ //na hɛ, ha _//kwaŋ kaŋ !kúïta há-ka //neiŋ. Haŋ _//kwaŋ k''auki te: /ka:, ta, ha _//kwaŋ /ku twai-ĩ, haŋ /kãä //a: !kau a: ha siŋ /kãã //a ha. Tsʔa a: !humma, haŋ k''auki _//kwaŋ //xe:ja ha, ta: ha _//kwaŋ /ku akkənxa se !kúïta há-ka //neiŋ, o haŋ k''auki _//kwaŋ te: k''o.

But when he returns, then he tells the people that the man who used to live with them has now returned to his home. Nothing has happened to him, for he has gone in safety along the path which he was taking. No mishap has befallen him, for he has arrived nicely at his home without any accident.

The sorceror as a jackal or bird

Ha //nau, i: taŋ e: ≠na: ha, ha di k''ãnĩ o //k'e: kɔ:, ha sa //k'oen i, ha /ku //nau, i: ʃo:, ha /ku //xou se, ha /ku sa, //kau siŋ i /nã:. O

At some other time, when we are liable to forget him, he turns into a little bird, he comes to see us where we live and flies about our

//k'e: kɔ:, ha: //nau, ha: //kau s²o i /na:, ha s²o ko kənniŋ-ĩ i, ti e:, i /nõ !naunko //kho, ti e:, i siŋ xu: túï ha, ĩ:. Ti e: /xarra, hɛ /nõ k''au s²o da: i, o //k'e: á:, ha siŋ //aŋ //na há-ka //neiŋ ã:, haŋ á: ha ≠ĩ:, ti e:, ti s²o dá: i, o haŋ //aŋ kaŋ //na. Hɛ tikən e:, ha -saŋ //k'oen i, ĩ:. Itən //nau, í e !kwi a: -//kwakka, o i ≠enna, o i //k'oen ti e:, ha -saŋ //kau siŋ i, ha s²o ko kənniŋ-ĩ i, itən //nau, itən /k'e:ja ha ã:, ti e:, í -//kwaŋ k''auki te: tã, ta:, i -//kwaŋ !naunko -twai-ĩ; itən -//kwaŋ /ku !naunko taŋ, ti e:, i siŋ /kwẽï tã, ĩ:, o í /hiŋ ha.

heads. Sometimes he sits on our heads, he sits peeping at us to see if we are still as we were when we left him. If there is a difference, (he wants to know) what has happened to us since he went to his home, for he thinks something has happened since he left. That is why he must look at us. If we are wise people, if we recognize him when we see him sitting above us peeping at us, then we talk to him and tell him, that nothing has happened to us, for we are still well; we still feel as we used to do, when we left him.

Haŋ s²o ko tum-ĩ i, o i /kwẽï da, itən /k'e:ja ha ã:. Haŋ //nau, ha: tóä, ti e:, i -//kwaŋ ≠kaka ha ã: ti e:, i -//kwaŋ k''auki taŋ, haŋ //xou ú:ï, haŋ /e: i-ta //neiŋ, haŋ ≠kerre-ĩ:, i-ta tʃweŋ e: !hau //kóë ta:, i-ta //neiŋ. Haŋ //nau, ha: //k'oenja, ti e:, í-ta //neiŋ -//kwaŋ !naunko a:kən, haŋ //xou ú:ï. Haŋ //nau, ha //xou ú:ï, haŋ k''wa: kúï !xwãŋ!xwãŋ k''ãnĩ, o ha: //xou ú:ï.

He sits listening to us as we tell him this. When he has heard what we have told him, that we are not ill, he flies up and enters our hut, he inspects our things which are about in our hut. When he has seen that our hut is still nice, he flies away. As he flies away he chirps, just as a little bird does when it flies away.

Haŋ /ne /k'e:ja hi ã:, ti e:, ha -//kwaŋ /ne !kúïtən há-ka //neiŋ, ti e:, ha siŋ ka ha se sa, //k'oen i, hɛ tikən e:, ha siŋ sa:, ĩ:. Itən //nau, í: e !kwi a: -//kwakka, itən //nau, í: tú:ï, ti e:, ha /kwẽï kú:ï, o ha //xou ú:ï, itən /k'e:ja ha ã:, o ha: ki sa: tauko //xouwi, itən kukúï, itən /k'e:ja ha ã:, '/ne !kúïta, ta ŋ -//kwaŋ ≠enna, ti e:, a -//kwaŋ a:, siŋ saŋ //k'oen ŋ; ŋ -//kwaŋ ≠enna, ti e:, k''ãnĩ -//kwaŋ k''auki e, ta a-á -//kwaŋ e. ŋ -//kwaŋ ≠enna, ti e:, a-á -//kwaŋ e, a: siŋ -saŋ //k'oen ŋ.'

He tells us that he is returning to his home, that he had just wanted to come and see us; that was why he had come. When we who are wise people hear him chirp like this as he flies away, we speak to him, although he is flying along, we say to him. 'Return, for I knew it was you who had come to see me; I knew that it was not a little bird, but it was you. I knew that you were the one who had come to see me.'

The sorceror as a jackal or bird

The sorceress !Kwara-aŋ

Narrator: Diä!kwain
Source: 'She talked to D.H.'s mother, when she cured him'
Dictation dates: 23, 25, 26 and 27 January 1875
Notebook reference: L.V.3: 4132-4161½ and 4: 4162-4199 (shortened by Dorothea Bleek)
***Bantu Studies* reference**: Vol. 9 (1935), Part VII: 19-22

This account was originally entitled 'The tale of a sorceress/wise person, what she said, when she talked with us' (4132):

This, D.H. says, happened to himself, when as big as Edith (who is 11 years old). !Kwara-aŋ was still living, on this side of Calvinia, with her children, when D.H. came down with Klaas and Rachel in 1874. 'Mietjie' is her Boer name. Her husband was shot by the Boers in the year that Klaas and David came to the Breakwater, but before they were taken prisoners. Mietjie can only speak a little Dutch. She was living on a Boer's land, when D.H. came last down. She came from Hartebeest Rivier, and has only later learnt a little Dutch, since she came among the Boers. She is middle-aged; and when they went home after their stay at the Breakwater (and here), they found her married again; but now to a Grass Bushman. The name of the husband whom the Boers shot was ǂGĕrrĭ-ssĕ, or 'Jan Roundabout'. D. says that when the Boers shot him (and a young son of his) he was doing nothing; and had been away from home getting poison to prepare his arrows for shooting springbok.

(L.V.3: 4131 rev.-4133 rev., note omitted)

Diä!kwain's account is rich in detail and epitomises the way that stories are related in oral cultures. To people from alphabetic cultures, Diä!kwain's performance may appear long-winded and repetitive (Dorothea Bleek omitted 23 notebook pages in her Bantu Studies version). Nonetheless, the way that Bleek and Lloyd recorded the narratives verbatim is precisely what makes the Bleek and Lloyd Collection such a valuable resource.

❑

!kwara-aŋ ||nau ha sũ:wã ŋ, ha |ne |ki |hiŋja tsˀa o ŋ ||nwaŋxu. Ha-g |ne ˍ!ko:äŋ |ki |hiŋ ||a tsˀa, ĩ:, he ha-g |ne ||a ˍ!ɑhá tiŋ o tsˀa. Ha-g |ne ||xã:, haŋ kaŋ ˍ!kõ:äŋ ˍ|ua: sa:, o haŋ ka: ha se dun-na

!kwara-an when she snored me, took something out of my liver. Stooping she took the thing outside, then she went to lie down outside with it. She came back again stooping, for she meant to

ke ti e:, ha siŋ /ki /ha: ts?a, ĩ:, ka twi:, a: ts?a siŋ s?o: ha, o haŋ ka twi:ja xa siŋ ʃo:, o //xaukakən /hiŋ o ha /nũnu.

heal for me the place from which she had taken the thing, the hole in which it had been because she did not want the wound to stay open, while blood came from her nose. (She cut the thing out of her nose when she went outside).

He ha //nau, //xaukən e: ha siŋ /kama /hiŋ hĩ ts?a, ĩ:, haŋ /ne !gwi: ŋ, ĩ:, o haŋ ka, ŋ se /ki/ki he: //xaukən, he ˍ/kw?ãĩ. Ha: dá: !gi:xa, ha-g /nũnu-ka //xaukən ˍ/kw?ãĩ se //na//na ŋ, ŋ se twaitji. Ha-g /nũnu-ka //xaukən ˍ/kw?ãĩ siŋ //na ŋ, tʃweŋ se k''auki //xã: he ˍ/gwain ŋ. Hɛ tikən e:, ha dí: ŋ o ha !gau, ĩ.

She took the blood which she had sneezed out with the thing and rubbed me with it, for she wanted me to have that blood's scent. She being a sorceress, the scent of the blood from her nose should be on me that I might recover. The blood scent must be on me, that things might not get into me again. That was why she rubbed me with her gore.

(Omitted text: 4136)

She wished that her blood scent (*!gau /kwai*) should be upon me; she who is a sorceress, her blood scent should be upon me.

Haŋ /ne kúïtən /k'e:ja ke, ti e:, !gitən kuitən ˍdóä e: ≠ni:ja ŋ, he kïï /ki -/tai ŋ ; he tikən e ; ŋ taŋ-taŋ, ĩ:. Hiŋ síŋ se, o ha: xa o:-ruko sa:, !gitən kuitakən síŋ se ≠ni: /ki ˍtai ŋ, ta he kië ≠ni:ja /ki ˍtai ŋ o mama-gu. Ta:, mamaˍgu k''auki ke: ã he ã: ŋ¯ŋ, ŋ se //na-//na he, ŋ se k''a: se: he. He tikən e:, he-g /ne kaŋ /k'e:, he-g /ne se ≠ni: ŋ ; ta:, mama k''auki ta ha !kau xú ŋ. He tikən e:, he se-g /ne ≠ni: ŋ, ĩ:, o //ke:ŋ-ka didí.

She told me, that other sorcerors had been seizing me, they wanted to take me with them ; that was why I was ill. If she had not come quickly, the other sorcerors would have taken me away with them, for they wanted to take me from my parents. For my parents were not willing to give me to them, to live with them and seek food for them. That was why they had said they would seize me, for mother would not give me away. So they tried to seize me by sorcery.

!kwara-aŋ /ne kukúï, haŋ /k'e:, ti e:, ha /khuru:wa, ĩ:, he ˍ//kwaŋ /ku e:, he-g /ne se tuko ˍ//kwa ≠ni: ŋ, ĩ:, ta:, he siŋ se //nau, o há: //ke//ke:ja ti e:, ha óä dá he, o

!kwara-an said that she was not so strong as she had been, that was why they had nearly taken me away. For they would not have done so, if she had been as she used

ha e !gi:xa -||ka:ŋ, !k?etən k''auki síŋ se ≠ni: mama ã ŋ, o ha: xa siŋ |khuru:wa, o dí-aŋ a: gwai óä dí-ĩja ha ã:, haŋ a: ha |khuru ã:. Ta:, ha óä ||nau, !gitən -|ka:gən ||xa:||xa: ha, haŋ ka siŋ sũ:ŋ ho !kwi a: ha: ta: |kukən ã:, haŋ ka siŋ sũ:ŋ ho ha. Haŋ tuko -||kwaŋ |ne a: |khuru:wa, haŋ k''auki ta |ne o:ruko !khou |ni ti e:, ts?a s?ɔ ʃɔ: he, o haŋ ta:, ||ka ti e:, ha -||kwaŋ tuko a: |ne |khuru:wa. He tikən e:, ha ka ≠um, o ha: sũ: -||gauë |ki ts?a, ti e:, ts?a: s?ɔ: ʃɔ: he; o| |xaukən e: gwai óä di-ĩja ĩ:, hiŋ tuko -||kwaŋ e:, |e:ja ha |nã:. He ||xaukakən -||kwaŋ e:, ha |khuru te:nja he.

to be when she was a new sorceress, the people would not have seized me, if she had not been weakened by the fight she had had with her husband, that had made her weak. For when the sorcerors had newly taught her, she had been used to snore up a man who lay dying. Now she had become weak, she could not smell out quickly where the mischief seemed to be, because now she felt weak. That was why she was slow when she snored seeking the spot where the thing was, because when her husband had been fighting her, the blood had gone to her head. That blood was what was making her feel weak.

(Omitted text: 4146–4148)

And it seemed as if she did not 'snore'. And the people were used to say that she did not 'snore' a person well, that she had become weak. This was why it seemed that she could not 'snore' a person well, although she was a sorceress that used to be able to 'snore' and rise up a person who had been lying dying for a long time, somebody whom the others had not thought would live. She had been able to 'snore' him up because she was single. She became weak.

He tikən -||kwaŋ e:, !k?e |ne ||am ha, ĩ:, he |ne ka ka:, he |k'e:, ti e:, ha k''auki -dóä sũsũ: akən !k?e e: ha dóä sũ: he. !k?etən |ne ka hiŋ |k'e:, ti e:, ha -hã: ka |kɯ ||nau, o ha: sũ:ŋ-a !kwi, ha -hã: |kɯ ĩ: hĩ: !kwi, o ha k''auki sũ: akən

That was why people underrated her, they kept saying that she did snore nicely those whom she had to snore. The people kept saying that when she had snored a man, she had really eaten him, and had not snored him nicely.

(Omitted text: 4150-4151)

She acted thus because her nose is that which had become weak. That is why the people said that she was not a sorceress who snored people nicely.

!kwi. He tikən e:, !kˀe kaŋ |k'e:, he k''auki kwaŋ ||kwi:ja ha ã: o ha: sũ: !kwi.

That was why the people said that they would not pay her when she had snored a person.

He tikən e:, ha -||kwaŋ |ne |khuru, ĩ:, o haŋ ta:, ||ka ti e:, !kˀe k''auki ka ||kwi:ja ha ã:, o ha: sũ həwa !kwi. Ha k''auki hĩ: tʃweŋ !ko!kõ:iŋ, ta:, ha !kóäse tʃweŋ e: ha hĩ hẽ; ha xa siŋ ha: ||k'e: !kú:ï, ĩ:, ta: ha ka: ha se ||nau, ha: hĩ: tʃweŋ e: k''auki a:kən, haŋ se |khuru, ha-g |nunu -kóä u.

This was why she was weak now, because the people would not pay her, when she had by snoring raised up a man. She did not eat bad things, but was careful as to her food, lest she eat ashes with it, for if she ate things which were not clean, she would become weak, her snoring power would leave her.

(Omitted text: 4152-4154)

This was why she had become weak, because she knew that she had been able to snore up a person who had lain down for death ['i.e. the people had not thought that he would recover' (4152 rev. note omitted)]. That was why the people had seen her [doings] ['This was why the people used to know where she lived. But people did not think that she used to 'snore' people up. When they saw that a person was ill, then they knew where she lived. But they did not know her' (4152-4153 rev., note omitted)]. The people had been used, when a person was ill, they then knew the place which she was when the person was ill ['D.H. explains, when the people were ill they knew where she lived, but when well they knew nothing of her' (4153 rev. note omitted)].

He tikən e:, ha -||kwaŋ ka ||nau, !kˀeja ki sa: !khwi:ja, ha kwaŋ sa sũ: !kwi, ha -am |ku ka: ha: ≠ĩ:, ti e:, !kˀe -||kwaŋ ka ||nau, o he xa taŋtaŋ-a, he k''auki !khwi:ja |kẽ, he: |ku ≠gouwa. Ti e:, he-g |ne tã:-a he tũ:, ĩ:, hiŋ e:, he ka |ne ≠en ha ĩ:; ta he k''auki ta ≠en ha, o he: xa taŋtaŋ-a. Hiŋ k''auki ke:, he kwaŋ ||khwi:ja ha ã:.

That was why, when people came to call her to snore someone, she merely thought that if they were not ill, they would not call her name, but would be silent. If they felt pain, they remembered her, but they did not know her if they were not ill. They were not willing to pay her.

(Omitted text: 4157-4180)

And this was why her snoring-power (*|nunu*) had become weak; once she had been a sorceress who could snore up a person, she could smell the thing out quickly. Now she felt that her snoring power was broken and that was

why people were saying that she could not snore well. And so she had thought that the things old are the people did not pay her for it. She now she first thinks that a person does like this when she snores him up, he does not remember that he had just been in pain, he had been moaning and restless. That is why from now on I want them to think on these things. Because they seem as if their skin does truly ache strongly. That is why from now on I want them to truly they think it [the pain]; that they may pay me from now on. Because I wish like this when I snore a person, I am thinking that I am the one who snores raising up the person, his people should see him that I am the one who snoring raised him up. That is why I want from now on that they think that my doings, from now on they pay me. Because I intend in future when I come and see that a person seems as if he will die, I will not snore him. I must first see. Because they are used to say I do not allow them to live, that is why I will do like this I come and see that the person really seems if he will die, I will not put my hands on him; for, I shall allow him that he may be the one to himself snore himself, that I see that he will do, he snore himself. Because they are used to do this when I have snored them, they go out, they give me much talk (*kkokkummi e /kwaiya*). Because the people formerly beat me, when I was talking to them that they should pay me; a fight was that which came upon me; when I was telling them that they should pay me. That is why I am afraid on account of it. From now on I am afraid to snore a person, because I continue to sit thinking of the things that they did to me. That is why from now on I will first see how it is because I want that the person must first feel (his) skin because he is used if I snoring raised him up he does not remember that he had been in pain. Because he is used to forget I had raised him up from the place which he had lain in. Now he should be, his skin be really very painful. He is like this because if I make him cool his skin he does not remember that I had cooled his skin. But he forgets that I was the one who made cool his skin. That is why I do not wish that I must make cool their place that they point to. That is why I must continue to look, because I see that they seem their skin aches they must feel, they must know that I was the one who helped them about it their place that they showed it where they ached. That is why I do not do so. He must feel it. Because these things they are those which I always say; that they just do not want to pay me. I will do thus from now on, when I come and see that a person lies at the point of death, I will not help him. But I will looking, leave him, he must himself, he arise. Because are used to do this when I have cooled for them the place which it [the pain] was in it, which had seemed as if they truly their skin ached they do like this when I cool their skin, they carry on making up stories that I do not understand, they always make them about me. That is why I want them to do this, when they feel pain they must not call me that I must come and help them they should look for another *!gi:xa* that she must snore them, because I do not want I must do like this they come and call me that I must come and snore

them, I would not come and snore them. Because they must look for another *!gi:xa*, she must snore them. Because they continue to say that I used to eat them. That is why I will not snore them, because of this. But they must look for a *!gi:xa* who does not eat them. Because they continue to say I used to kill them when I snored them. That is why I would not consent, because of it, for they would do like this should the man die, they would thus speak, they say that I am the one who killed the person. That is why I will not put my hands upon a person, because a person would be ill, because he must continue to look for a person who wants to snore him if he wants that a person wants to snore him. Because the sorcerors are used to say they want to take away my magic power. Because I continued formerly to kill people when I snored them ['she means that this was what people *said* of her' (4179 rev. note omitted)]. That is why the sorcerors were saying that they intend taking away my snoring power that I killed people with. They will taking throw it away.

Haŋ -||kwaŋ ≠en-na, ti e:, !kwi-g ||nau ha xa ka: ||khwi:ja !gi:xa ã:, !gi:xakən k''auki di kúï k''wã ≠hanũ:wa. Ta:, ha-g |ne di: |hõä-gau, haŋ |ne |kɯ ka:, ha ĩ: |khi: !kˀe, o ha sũ:. Ti e: !kˀe kwerekwere ha |ĩ:, ĩ:, hiŋ e:, ha |ĩ: twai-ĩ:, ĩ:, he ha ||nau, o ha sũ: ta: ha o !kwi, ha |ĩ:ŋ twai-ĩ, ĩ:. Ta:, ha |kɯ-g |ne ||nau, o ha sũ: ta: ha o !kwi, haŋ |kɯ-g |ne sũ: ko ≠ĩ: ta:, ti e:, ha |kɯ se sũ: |ka-|kaukən !kwi-ta |xutən|xutən, he ha |kɯ-g |ne di: |kha|kha: o !kwi, ĩ:. Haŋ k''auki |ne ka, ha sũ: akən !kwi, ta:, ha |kɯ-g |ne ≠ĩ: |ɑhá: o !kwi, ti e:, ha |kɯ se sũ: |kha !kwi.

She knew that if a man does not pay a sorceror, that sorceror does not do good work. For he becomes a rascal, he merely wants to kill people when he snores. If people cool his heart (by paying him), then it is comfortable, and when he lies snoring a person his heart is quiet. Otherwise when he lies snoring a man, he keeps thinking that he will snore cutting the man's arteries, that he may bring death to the man. He will not snore the man nicely, for he is thinking evil to the man, that he will by snoring kill him.

(Omitted text: 4184–4187)

For the people would, if he had snoring raised up the person, they have many stories, they do not speak like old people [not like old people, who understand, but like little boys (omitted note, 4184 rev.)]. Because their stories usually continued to be like small children that think that they were like grown-up people when they sat talking. That is why I did this when I sat listening to their stories – they at first seemed as if truth were that which they spoke. I see that truth could not have been that which they spoke to me. Because they did this when I snoring raised up the man, they did truly beat me, because I thought that they must pay me. This was why I then snoring killed the man because of it.

'Ta:, ŋ -//kwaŋ ka //nau ka: /ki /hiŋ ts?a, o !kwi !kauüg∂n, ts?a a: ŋ ã: /ki /hiŋja, haŋ k''auki ta //kait∂n; ta tí ka taŋ ŋ !khãüä ke: /khuru, ta:, ts?a a: ŋ ã: /ki /hiŋ ha, o !kwi, ha /ki -//kwaŋ !k?auwa. He: tik∂n e:, há-ka -!ɑhá-!ɑhá: k''auki ta //kait∂n, o haŋ ta: //ka ti e:, ha /ki -//kwaŋ !k?auwa. He tik∂n e:, ha k''auki tá ha kwaŋ á ke, ŋ se -!ɑhá /hiŋ ha.

'Hé tik∂n e:, ŋ ka !k?eja: kwaŋ ≠ĩ: he, ti e:, ŋ -//kwaŋ ka, //nau ts?a a: ŋ /ki /hiŋja, ŋ -//kwa: //u:. He tik∂n e, ŋ -//kwaŋ ka, !k?e kwaŋ !kẽï //au, he kwaŋ //khwi:ja ke, o

'Now when I take something out of a man's body, that thing which I have taken out is not easy; for it seems as if my vertebral artery would break, for the thing which I have taken out of the man is really alive. Therefore forcing it out (of the nose) is not easy, because it feels that it is alive. Therefore it is not willing to let me sneeze it out.

This is what I want the people to remember, that because of the thing which I have taken out, I am now weary. That is why I want the people really to pay me

(Omitted text: 4191-4194)

for the thing seemed as if my artery would break; for the thing was not easy; for, the thing now seemed as if it would come out at a different place; I now was the one who directed it/drove it away [*?khara*]. And this is why it seemed as if it would come out rightly. I did like this it was I, the *!gi:xa* who had done this/dealt with the sticks they were strong. I took them out. Then they seemed to think that the sticks that I took out were not strong. Because that was why they did not remember that I had snored living myself for the man it ached, I had tired myself when I took the thing from the man.

That is why I really want them to pay me

!kẽï //au, he kwaŋ //khwi:ja ke, o tã:tã: a:, ŋ ka tã: ha, ti e: ts?a ka /kwẽ: tã, ĩ:, o ka: -!ɑhá ʃo a:. He tik∂n e:, ŋ -//kwaŋ ka !gwara kw∂kw∂n ĩ:, o ka: -//kwa: ka, he kwaŋ !kẽï //au, he kwaŋ /ku //khwi:-ja ke.'

for the pains which I suffered, which the thing made me feel, when I was sneezing it out. Therefore I want a real knife, for I am sure they really ought to pay me."

(Omitted text: 4196-4199)

For then my heart is happy, for I feel that they have cooled my heart, and my heart is not angry. Because, that they have made my heart happy, then I am happy. Because I am sure if the harmful things (*/ko:§o-de*) came to me that had been killing them, I should be able to keep them away from them, the harmful things which were killing them, they would not know them. I should see them,

they would not see them. They would have felt like this—bad. Before I consented, they had pain (literally, skin, *tu*). Then it had been that I took care of them. That is why it seemed they did not feel their pain (skins).

❑

Notes

1-2 *She … took something out of my liver:* In the notebook *//nwaǂxu* is translated as 'stomach: i.e. lit. the front of my liver' (4132).

27-28 *… other sorcerors had been* **seizing** *me …* : 'D.H. explains thus for *ǂniya*: They 'take' him, he becomes ill; when he dies, they take him away quite' (omitted note, 4135 rev.).

34-36 *… my parents were* **not willing** *to give me to them … :* Diä!kwain suggested the word 'jammer' (4137 rev., note omitted), meaning 'sorry'. In other words, his mother (not 'parents') felt sorry for him and for this reason refused to give her son to the sorcerors. The word *ko:* in the *Dictionary* is translated as 'to be fond of, cling to' (Bleek 1956: 95).

40-41 *So they tried to seize me by sorcery*: 'Toorman manier (i.e. sorceror's way – ed.)[Toorman manier, i.e. using the sorceror's way of doing things] D.H. says' (4138 rev., note omitted).

62-63 *… when her husband had been fighting her …*: 'He had beaten her head with a knobkerry, D.H. explains' (omitted note, 4143 rev.).

72-74 *That was why people underrated her, they kept saying that she* **did** *snore nicely*: This is a mistake since the word *k:"auki*, meaning 'not', has been omitted from the English translation. It should therefore read: 'they kept saying that she did *not* snore nicely'.

77 *… she had really eaten him …*: 'Later, after she had been used to snore well at first, the people said this' (omitted note, 4149 rev.).

109 *… but would be silent:* 'They forgot her name when not ill, D.H. explains' (4154 rev. note omitted).

174-176 *She knew that if a man does not pay a sorceror, that sorceror does not do good work*: 'becoming angry about the want of payment' (missing note, 4180 rev.).

It seems that payment for services was another way of reinforcing a sorceror's power, perhaps because it was a way of showing appreciation for their work.

202-203 *… for it seems as if my* **vertebral artery** *would break…*: 'The great artery in the back, D.H. says.' (4187 rev., note omitted). See the discussion in the next narrative, 'A sorceror's blood vessels'.

205-206 *Therefore forcing it out (of the nose) is not easy …*: 'as one does to get any obstacle out of one's nose; not *real* sneezing (which is */kamma*)' (4188 rev., note omitted).

206-207 … *because it feels that it is alive*: 'The thing is not willing to come out, and is difficult and makes the doctor's head ache, being in his head, D.H. says. It looks like a little stick, when it comes out, and is as big, or less, than a pencil.' (4188 rev., note omitted)

A sorceror's blood vessels

Narrator: Diä!kwain
Source: 'This was told to D.H. by his mother, and he has also seen it for himself'
Dictation dates: 20, 21 January 1875
Translation dates: 21 January 1875
Notebook reference: L.V.3: 4122-4131
***Bantu Studies* reference**: Vol. 9 (1935), Part VII: 22-24

Along with the other narratives in Part VII, this extract provided South African rock art researcher David Lewis-Williams (Lewis-Williams 1981) with the insights necessary to interpret Bushman rock paintings of figures with bristling hairs and feline characteristics.

❑

O ha !kúïtən |e sa:, o ti e:, ha siŋ |xãũ |kɔm ||a he, haŋ |ne !khauki. He !kˀe-g |ne !khouwa ha ã:, o sã:, ĩ:, o hiŋ ka, ≠xuru se te:nja ha ã:, ta ha !kháüä _||kwaŋ e: ú:ï, o haŋ ta: ||ka ti e:, ha-g |ne !kúïtən |e: sa:. Ha-g |ne !khaukən |ki |e:ja o ||neiŋ, o haŋ ta: ||ka ti e:, ha-ka !kˀe se ≠en, ti e:, ha _||kwaŋ |ne !kúïtən |e: sa:.

When he (the sorceror) returns from the place to which he has gone on a magic expedition, he trembles. Then people let him smell *buchu*, for they want his veins to lie down, for his vertebral artery has risen up while he was returning. He comes trembling into the hut, because he wants his people to know that he has returned home.

He tikən e:, ha !khãũä úï, ĩ:; !kˀe se |ki tˀaintˀainja ha !khãũä, !khãũä se te:ŋ, ta: ha !khãũä tuko _||kwaŋ ú:ï, o haŋ ta ||ka ti e:, ha siŋ _taija tiŋ. Tʃwen e:, ha siŋ dí |ki he, hiŋ k''auki ta ||kaitən, ta:, he |gi:ja. He tikən e:, ha !khãũä k''auki ta ||kaitən, ï:.

Then his vertebral artery stands up ; the people will make it soft, that it may lie down, for the artery has risen up while he was walking about. The work he had been doing was not easy, for it was difficult. That was why his vertebral artery would not give way.

!kˀetən |ne !kutən tẽja ha !khãũä, o !kˀetən ka ≠xuru se te:nja ha ã:, tá:, ha _saŋ k''auki dí ku k''wã ≠hanu:wa, ha _kɔ:ö _saŋ |ne taŋtaŋ, o !kˀeja xa !kutən tã: ha ã: ≠xuru. !kˀe se |auwa ha ã:,

The people by singing make his vertebral artery lie down, for they want his blood vessels to lie down, for he would not be well, he would be ill, if they did not by singing make his blood vessels lie down.

ha !khãüä, ta:, ha -saŋ di -//khã:, o !kʔeja xa !kutən tã: ha ã: ha !khãüä.

The people must look out for his vertebral artery, for he would turn into a lion if they did not by singing make it lie down.

He tikən e:, !kʔe se ɔru:ko heribi ha, ĩ:, ha !khãüä se te:nja ha ã:, ta:, !gi:xa //nau, o ha ≠xuruwa xa te:nja ha ã:, ha /ku !khu /ku:ki, ha !ku-g /ne di //khe//khe:, ha /ku-g /ne ka: ha tsi: ã !kʔe. He tikən e:, !kʔe ta //nau ha !khãüä ó:ä, !kʔe ɔru:ko heribija, o hiŋ ta:, //ka ti e:, he ≠en-na, ti e:, ha !khãüä k''auki ta //kaitən. He tikən e:, he ta ɔru:ko !khouwa ha ã: o sã:, ĩ:, o he: ka, ha xa -saŋ di //khe//khe:; ha -saŋ tsi:-ã /kʔe, o ha -dóä da: //khe//khe:.

This is why people must help him quickly, so that his vertebral artery may lie down, for if a sorceror's bloodvessels do not lie down, he grows hair, he becomes a beast-of-prey, he wants to bite people. Therefore when his vertebral artery has risen up, people help him quickly, for they know that it resists. So they quickly make him smell *buchu* for they do not want him to become a beast-of-prey; he would bite them if he were to become a beast-of-prey.

Ta:, ti e:, !kʔe /ki /e:ja ha, ĩ:, -dóä e, he k''auki ta //kaitən. !gitən ã ha ã: ≠xuru, ha se dí !gi:xa, ha se kwaŋ //nau, !kwija: taŋtaŋ-a, ha se sũ: !kwi. He tikən e:, !kʔe dí:ja ha o !gi:xa, ĩ:; !kʔe //xa://xa: ha, ha se kwaŋ //nau, o !kwija taŋtaŋ-a, ha se sũ !kwi.

For the things which the (old) people have put into him are not facile. The sorcerors gave them into his blood vessels (by snoring), that he might become a sorceror, that when a man were ill, he might snore him. That was why they had made a sorceror of him; they had taught him, so that he could snore a man if he were ill.

Notes

6-7 … *for his* **vertebral artery** *has risen up* …: An omitted note translates *!kháüä* as 'the great vein (D.H. says) which lies inside the backbone. 24 Jan. (1875) vertebral artery, Dr Stewart says.' (4121 rev.) However, in his book *The First Bushman's Path*, Alan James has argued that both of these descriptions are anatomically inaccurate (James 2001: 212) – there are two vertebral arteries, both of which are unlikely candidates for two reasons: the one artery does not lie inside the backbone; the other lies in the backbone, but is not a large blood vessel. James suggests instead that either Diä!kwain may have meant the spinal column itself, which stiffens during trance, or that 'the "great vein" was an accepted cultural fiction instrumental in experiencing trance experience' (James 2001: 212). David Lewis-Williams (1981: 78) has argued that the word *!kháüä* is better understood as the metaphoric use of a verb meaning 'to boil': the 'boiling' probably described the rising sensation that people experience in their spines when entering an altered state of consciousness.

12-13 **Then** *his vertebral artery stands up ...*: In the original notebook translation, 'Then' is translated as 'This is why' and an omitted note explains '... that the people may know that he has come in, D.H. says' (4123 rev.).

20-21 *The people by singing make his vertebral artery lie down*: 'They also dance, D.H. says' (4124 rev., note omitted).

Clearly, Diä!kwain is referring to a ceremony or ritual similar to the healing dances held by Bushman people in the Kalahari today.

23-24 *... he would be ill ...*: 'D.H. explains that the body becomes stiff; and that the blood would 'spring' from the vertebral artery internally [not externally]' (4126 rev., note omitted).

47-49 *The sorcerors gave them into his blood vessels (by snoring), that he might become a sorceror ...*: 'i.e. old sorcerers have "snored" his work into his veins, so that he might become like them' (4129 rev., note omitted).

The note gives us a glimpse of how a *!gi:xa* or sorcerer goes about 'training' a new healer.

The sorceror after death

Narrator: Diä!kwain
Dictation dates: 12 November 1875
Notebook reference: L .V.19: 5506 rev.-5512 rev.
***Bantu Studies* reference:** Vol. 9 (1935), Part VII: 24-26

Dead sorcerors still played an important part in the lives of the living.

!gi:xa ||nau, ha |kɯ:ka, ha |ĩ: |ki ɛ: |hiŋ _!gwa:xu, hɛ ||kho _|kwattən. Ha |ĩ:ŋ ta: ||ka ti ɛ:, ha k''auki !naunko ¯!kauwa; he tikən ɛ:, ha-ka !kauükən |ke:, ha siŋ ¯!kauwa, ĩ:, hiŋ |ke:, dí: _|kwattən, o haŋ ta: ||ka ti ɛ:, ha |ki |kɯ e !gi:xa. Hɛ tikən ɛ:, ha-ka !gi: di _|kwattən, hɛ se ¯|ki _tai ha-ka !kauükən ɛ:, ha siŋ ¯!kauwa, ĩ:. Ta, !gi:xa |ki |kɯ ||k'oen tʃweŋ ɛ:, i-í ɛ:, k''auki ɛ !gi:xa, hɛ i k''auki |nĩ: hɛ.

When a sorceror dies, his heart comes out in the sky and becomes a star. His heart feels that he is no longer alive; therefore his body there, in which he was alive, becomes a star there, because it feels that he used to be a sorceror. Therefore his magic makes a star, in order to let his body in which he lived walk about. For a sorceror sees things which we, who are not sorcerors, do not see.

Haŋ |kɯ a:, ||k'oen hɛ; ta:, !gi:xa |ki ||nau, ||ga: a: !kwˀai, haŋ _tai !xóë ɛ: |kwaija, o ||ga: a: !kwˀai; haŋ !kúï:tən ||neiŋ o há: ||ga:. Tikən k''auki ||khɔ, ha siŋ _taija !xwetən!xwetən e: |kwaija, ta, ti |kɯ ||khóä, ha k''auki siŋ _taija. Itən ¯|kɯ kaŋ ≠ĩ:, ha k''auki siŋ _taija.

He is the one who sees them; for a sorceror is wont to go to many a place, when night has fallen; he returns to his home the same night. It does not seem as if he had gone to many places, for it seems as if he had not been walking about. We always think that he has not been out.

Hɛ tikən ɛ:, !gi:xa ká ha se ||nau, há-ka !kˀe e:, ha ||kaŋ ko, hɛ ha ||na hɛ; haŋ ká ha se ||nau, ha ||k'oen, ti ɛ:, !kˀe k''auki ||khóä, hɛ kíɛ̈ se, o !kˀeja siŋ _taija hɛ́: ti, haŋ ¯|kɯ ||nau, !kˀe kuitja |kɯ ⊙pwoin ||na, haŋ |kɯ _tai _||gauë !kˀe, ||k'oen ti ɛ:, !kˀe _dóä ||na hɛ. Haŋ dí ha o kɔro, haŋ ||aŋ ||k'oen

This is what a sorceror does for his people, with whom he and his brother dwelt: when he sees that the people do not appear to be where they used to go about, then, while the others are asleep there, he walks about seeking them, to see where they are. He turns himself into a jackal, he goes to

!kˀe, han ⁻/ku //nau, o ha: k''auki //e !kˀe, haŋ /ku ˍtai !gwe ho !kˀe. Haŋ /ku !khou !kˀe ˍ/kwˀãĩ. Ha /nũnũŋ /ku ɛ:, ≠kaka ha ã:, ti e:, !kˀe /kweĩ k''o //na, ĩ:. Hɛ: ha /nũnũŋ /k'e:ja ha ã:, tʃweŋ ɛ:, !kˀe dí /ki hɛ. Haŋ ˍóä //nau, !kˀeja /kha: tsˀa, a: ɛ ʘpwai, haŋ !khou tsˀa, a: !kˀe /kha ha ˍ/kwˀãĩ.

look at the people. He does not walk up to the people but walks past them. He smells their scent. His nose tells him where the people are. And his nose tells him, what things they have got. If they have killed any game, he smells the scent of the thing they have killed.

Hɛ ha ≠enna, ti ɛ:, há tsˀa, ha ˍóä a:, !kˀe //na ha. Hɛ tikən ɛ:, !kˀe k''auki ká hɛ !kúïtən, ï:, o hin ˍóä tuko /ã /ki ʘpwai. Hɛ tikən ɛ:, hɛ k''auki ka hɛ !kúïtən ĩ:. Ha //nau, o ha !khouwa, ti ɛ:, há tsˀa, ha ˍóä a:, !kˀe //na ha, ha-g /ne //nau, //k'e: a:, ha ka ha se /ne !kúïtən ã:, haŋ /ne dí kúï !xwãŋ !xwãŋ kɔro, o haŋ tu:tu: !kˀe, o //k'e: a:, !kˀe se !kúïtən ã:.

Then he knows that this is the cause of their staying there. It is because the people do not want to go home, until they have finished cutting up the meat there. That is why they do not go home. He acts like this when he has smelt out why the people are staying there; at the time when he wants to go home, he makes a noise like a jackal, he asks them when they are going home.

Hɛ !kwi a: ˍ//kwakka, ha ≠enna, ti ɛ:, !gi:xa ˍ//kwaŋ a:, tu:tu: hɛ, o //k'e: a:, hɛ se !kúïtən ã:; haŋ /ne /k'e:ja ha ã:, ti ɛ:, hɛ ˍ//kwaŋ ka, hɛ !kúïtən; hiŋ ˍ//kwaŋ //nau, ti ɛ:, hɛ !naunko ⁻//kho:⁻//kho: /ki tsˀa a:, hɛ /kha: ha, ha-ka ⁻èŋ. Hɛ tikən ɛ:, ti k''auki //khɔ, hɛ kíɛ̈ !kúïtən, ï:. Ta, hɛ ˍ//kwaŋ kíɛ !kúïtən, o tsˀa-ka eŋja ⁻//kho:wa.

Then a man with sense knows that it is a sorceror asking them when they mean to go home; he tells him when they are intending to go home; they are still packing up the meat of the game which they have killed. Therefore they do not seem ready to go home yet. But they mean to go home as soon as the meat of the game is packed up.

!gi:xa /ne //nau, o há: ⁻tóä, ti ɛ:, !kˀe ˍ//kwaŋ /k'e:ja ha ã:, ti ɛ:, ⁻eŋ ˍ//kwaŋ ɛ:, hɛ ⁻//kho: ⁻//kho: /ki hɛ, hɛ tikən ˍ//kwaŋ ɛ:, hɛ k''auki kíɛ̈ !kúïtən, ĩ:, ta:, hɛ ˍ//kwaŋ kíɛ̈ !kúïtən, o ⁻eŋjã ⁻//kho:wa; !gi:xa /ne //nau, ha ⁻tóä ti ɛ:, !kˀe ˍ//kwaŋ /k'e:ja ha ã:, ti ɛ: hɛ ˍ//kwaŋ kíɛ̈ se !kúïtən, ha /ku ˍtai, o ha ⁻tóä, ti ɛ: ˍkˀe ˍ//kwaŋ /k'e:ja ha ã:, ti ɛ:, hɛ ˍ//kwaŋ !kúïten.

The sorceror listens to what the people tell him, that it is the meat which they are busy packing up, and that that is why they are not ready to go home, but that they mean to go home as soon as the meat is packed up; when the sorceror hears them say, that they mean to go home, he walks away, as soon as he has heard the people tell him that they are going home.

The sorceror after death

An earthquake

Narrator: Diä!kwain
Source: 'Díä!kwain heard this from his mother ǂKămmĕ-ăŋ or |Kho-ăŋ (l.n.)'
Dictation date: 15 November 1875
Notebook reference: L.V.19: 5531-5536½
***Bantu Studies* reference:** Vol. 9 (1935), Part VII: 26-27

An earthquake occurs at the same time as another dangerous phenomenon.

|khabbakən kaŋ ||nau ||k'e: a:, !gi:xa |ku:ka ã:; haŋ a:, |khabbakən !kʔũ:ĩ ã:, o haŋ ta:, ||ka ti ϵ:, !gi:xa a: |ku:ka. Hϵ tikən ϵ:, !khabbakən !kʔũ:ĩ ĩ:, o haŋ ta:, ||ka ti ϵ:, !gi:xa a: sũsũ |hiŋ tʃweŋ ϵ: !kau!kauüka, há a: |ku:ka.

An earthquake occurs at the time when sorceror has died ; then the earthquake occurs, because it feels that the sorceror has died. That is why it happens, because a sorceror who snored out things which are bodies has died.

Hϵ tikən ϵ: ˍ|kwattən |xĩ:, ĩ:, o haŋ ta:, ||ka ti ϵ:, !gi:xa a:, siŋ ||narro tʃweŋ e: !kau!kauüka, ha tuko a: |ku:ka. Ha-ka !gi:tən ϵ: |xĩ:, o hiŋ ta:, ||ka ti ϵ: ha-ka ≠xuttən≠xuttən, hϵ |ki !kau!kauü-ka. Hϵ tikən ϵ:, hϵ dí: |ke:ŋ-ka di.

Then a star shoots (falls), for a sorceror who has gone about among things which are bodies has really died. His sorcery is shooting, because his spirits (?) have got bodies. Therefore they work magic.

Ta:, |gi:xa |ki |ku ϵ tsʔa a: ||nau, haŋ |e: ta: ʘpwoin, haŋ |ku ≠enna tʃweŋ ϵ: ˍtaiˍtai xa ta:, o ||ga:, hϵ i ϵ: k''auki ϵ !gi:xa, hέ i k''auki ≠enna hϵ. Haŋ |ku a: ≠enna hϵ, ta:, ha |ki ||nau, o haŋ kí saŋ ʘpwoinja, haŋ |ku !kõ:ãse tikəntikən ϵ:, di: o ||ga:; o haŋ ka, há: siŋ ||xarra !kʔe ã:, tʃweŋ ϵ: sa:, hϵ kíë sa ko |khi: !kʔe.

For a sorceror is always a thing which knows while he is asleep, what things are walking about at night, which we, who are not sorcerors, do not know. He is one who knows them, for although he is alseep, he is watching the doings that occur at night, for he wants to protect people from the things which come to kill them.

Hϵ tʃweŋjaŋ ϵ:, ha !kõ:ãse !kʔe ĩ:, o haŋ ta:, ||ka ti ϵ:, !gitən kuitən |ki ˍtai o ||ga:, hϵ kíϵ ||k'werre !kʔe o ||ga:.

Hϵ tikən ϵ:, ha ||khau ĩ: hϵ, ĩ:.

Because of these things he watches over the people, for he is aware that other sorcerors walk by night to attack people at night.

Therefore he protects them from these.

Notes

8 *Then a star shoots (falls) ...* : There are translation problems with this confusing sentence:

- The clause 'because it knows' was left out.
- The word *!kau!kauüka,* translated as 'bodies' in the *Bantu Studies* text, is given in the *Dictionary* as 'to be hale', 'to flourish, to live' (Bleek 1956: 417). The word for body is *!kauukən* (Bleek 1956: 416).

I therefore suggest the following translation: *'Then a star falls because it knows that a sorceror who went about amongst living things has really died.'*

11-13 *His sorcery is shooting, because his* **spirits** *[?] have got* **bodies:** This is another confusing sentence with translation problems:

- The clause 'because it feels that' was omitted.
- There was evidently uncertainty about the translation of the word 'spirits' because there is a question mark after it. The word translated as 'spirits' is given as *ǂxuttən ǂxuttən*, but it is not listed in the *Dictionary*. There is, however, a word */xuttən/xuttən*, meaning 'arteries' (and, presumably, 'blood vessels'), which is important in the context of |Xam healing practices (see 'A sorceror's blood vessels').
- The word *!kau!kauüka* means 'alive', not 'body' (see previous note).

The sentence would then read: *'His sorcery falls because it knows that his arteries are alive'*. This may be a way of saying that, although the sorceror is dead, he still has his arteries – in other words, he retains his *!gi:*. This translation of the sentence is much clearer; it also fits better with the sentence that follows.

Falling stars and sorcerors

Narrator: Diä!kwain
Source: 'Told to Diä!kwain by his mother'
Dictation dates: 3, 6 and 9 November 1875
Notebook reference: L.V.19: 5478-5483; 5481 rev-5483 rev.; 5483-5505
***Bantu Studies* reference:** Vol. 9 (1935), Part VII: 27-31

There is a special relationship between shooting stars, sorcerors and waterholes. Why sorcerors are like dogs.

❑

Mama-gu kaŋ ¯kaŋ |k'e:, ˍ|kwatən ka ||nau, ha tatən !kˀõä ˍ|gwa:xu, ha ||a |e ≠hauru. Ha ||nau, ha: |e: ≠hauru, ha dí ku !xwãŋ!xwãŋ ||khwai, o ha: |e: ≠hauru. Haŋ |k'e:, i ka tu ha, o ha !xwaŋ !khwa: a: !gãũ, o ha: !gãũ |ki |e:ja o ≠hauru, o ha: ıa: ||ka ti ϵ:, ha ¯|ki ||kóë-siŋ ≠hauru.

Our mothers used to say, that when a star falls from the sky, it goes into a waterpit. As it enters the waterpit it sounds like a quiver. She said, we hear it as it sounds like rain pouring down, when it pours into the waterpit, when it divides in the waterpit.

Hϵ tiken ϵ:, |xam-ka !kˀe ka ||nau, o hϵ: |nã: ˍ|kwatən o ˍ|kwata: tatən !kˀũï ˍ!gwa:xu, hϵ ||nau o hϵ: |ki !khwã: a: ≠eni, hϵ ||nau, !khwaitən ϵ:, hϵ siŋ !kwe ||a: ˍ|kwatən, ĩ:, o hϵ: |ki sˀɔ:, ĩ:, hϵ tsˀau |hiŋ tóä !khwã:-⊙pwa ã: hϵ, o hϵ k''auki ¯ã: !khwã:-⊙pwa kwakən hϵ !khwaitən ϵ:, hϵ siŋ ||k'oen ˍ|kwatən, ĩ:. Ta: mama-gu |ki kaŋ |k'e:, !khwã:-⊙pwa ||nau, ha kwakən |hã !khwaitən ϵ:, ha xóä siŋ ||k'oen ˍ|kwatən ĩ:, hϵ !khwaitən hiŋ kúï, tu: u ¯||kau siŋ ||a: !khwã: -⊙pwa |ĩ:, ||ke:||ke: |i a: ||kha ¯||kau siŋ ||a: !khwã:-⊙pwa |ĩ:, hϵ !khwĩ:-⊙pwa |ku:kən, ĩ:.

Therefore Bushman women do this : when they see a star falling down from the sky, if they have a little baby, they take the milk which they have when they catch sight of the star, as they sit there they milk it out away from the baby and do not let the child suck that milk with which they saw the star. For our mothers used to say that if a baby sucked the milk when its mother had seen a star (fall), that milk would be as if a breath had been over the baby's heart, as if a fire had burned (a mark) over the baby's heart, then the baby would die.

Ta: mama-gu |ki kaŋ |k'e:, ˍ|kwatən-ka ≠k''an |ke:, i ||k'oen hϵ, hiŋ ka ||kho |i-ta kwitənkwitən,

For our mothers used to say that the star's lice yonder which we see resemble sparks of fire, and

hɛ kwitənkwitən ɛ: ⁻//kau siŋ khwã:-ʘpwa /ĩ:. Ta: hɛ /ki ⁻/ki /i, hɛ /itən ɛ: di kṹĩ taŋtaŋ //kwɔna, o _/kwatən !kˀũ:ï; _/kwatən-ka ≠xi:≠xi:, hiŋ ɛ: e /i. Hɛ ɛ //aŋ kú:ï tu: u ⁻//kau siŋ !khwã:-ʘpwa /ĩ:

these sparks sit over the baby's heart. For they have fire, and the fire becomes hot when the star falls ; the star's light is fire. That is what goes to breathe over the baby's heart.

Ta mama-gu /ki kaŋ /k'e:, _/kwatən-ka /i -/ki //nau, ha /kũ:ï, hiŋ k''auki ta //kaitən o haŋ ta: //ka ti ɛ:, ha /ki tatən !u: !kũ:ï _!gwa:xu. Haŋ /kam //a ≠nauru a: k''auki ta //kaitən. Hɛ tikən ɛ; mama-gu ka //nau, hɛ: /nã: _/kwatən, o _/kwata: !kˀũ:ï, hɛ /xi: /ki !gaugən hɛ //ki, o _/kwatən. Hɛ //nau, hɛ: /xi: _/kwatən, hɛ kuku, hɛ /k'e:, o hɛ: /xi:ja, hɛ ku, '!kwi /ke //a:, ha ku siri u siŋ //e, ti /ke:, ha !kweritən swe:ŋ //a: hɛ; ha se //a ku siri u siŋ, //e hɛ.' O mama-guken kaŋ /k'e:, taŋtán /k'e:, ha /ki //a:, ĩ:, hɛ ha /i, hɛ se //a dí ku tã siritən, o ha //a: ≠hauru.

For our mothers used to say, the star's fire always falls, it does not rise, for it feels it has fallen from the sky. It goes into a waterpit which does not rise. Therefore when our mothers saw a star as it was falling, they used to spit blood and spittle at the star. As they spat, they spoke, saying, 'May the person who goes yonder go and cool off at that place where he goes thundering may he go and cool himself off there.' When our mothers spoke, the illness there went away, its fire went to get cool in the waterpit.

Ta mama-gu /kí kaŋ /k'e:, !gi:xa //nau, ha /ku:ka, ha /ĩ:ja tatən !a: !kˀũ _!gwa:xu, hɛ //a: /e:≠hauru. Mama-gukən kaŋ /k'e:, _/kwatən //nau, ha tatən !kˀũ:ï, o ha /kam //a: ≠hauru a:, ha ká ha //a /e: ha, haŋ //nau _/kɔ̃ɔ̃-de, haŋ /xã /ki !xwɔ̃ni hɛ, o ti ɛ:, !kˀe //na hɛ. O !kˀe ɛ:, ha ⁻≠kauwa, ha ≠ni: hɛ, o ha-ka //ke:ŋ o ha siŋ ≠ĩ: hɛ, o ha /naunko //na !kˀe.

For our mothers used to say, that when a sorceror dies, his heart falls down from the sky, it goes into a waterpit. Our mothers said, when the star is falling, approaching the waterpit into which it means to go, he takes the magic power, he shoots it back to the place where people are. For the people are those whom he wants to take away with his sorcery, for he thought of them while he was among men.

Mama-gukən kaŋ /k'e:, !gi:xa //nau, ha ⁻/ku:kən, haŋ //xãũ !kˀe ɛ:, ha siŋ kɔ:ka hɛ, o há xa taŋ, ha ká ha /ku:kən, hɛ !kˀetən ɛ:, ha ká ha ≠ni:, /ki !gauöke, o hahá,

Our mothers said, a sorceror does this when he dies, he takes away the people whom he has loved when he feels ill and is going to die, these are the people whom

hϵ se !gauöka. Hϵ tikən ϵ:, mama-gu ka siŋ //nau, -/kwata: !k?õä, hϵ kukú, hϵ /k'e:, '!gi:xa kaŋ //khóä /ku:kən tiŋja, ti ϵ: ã. Hϵ tikən ϵ:, u //k'oen, ti ϵ:, ha /ï:!khũ!khũ ϵ:, !k?ũ:ï, hiŋ !kweritən -tai. Hϵ tikən ϵ:, u ka, u se tã:, ti ϵ:, //kwõnã-ka //kwõnã siŋ kwẽ:ï tã, ĩ:. Ta: //xi:-ka !gi:xa //khóä ϵ: /ku:ka; ta, tí ka !kẽ:ï ta:, !gi:xa a: /ki //xi:, ha a: /ku:ka, o -/kwatən /ne /kwẽ:ï /kwẽ/kwẽ, o !gi:xa a: /ki //xi:, ha: a: /ku:ka, o -/kwatən /ne tatən !k?ũ. Ukən ka, u se tum, ti ϵ: -/kwatən /nõ k"au se !gãũ, o ha: kóä ¯kau u siŋ //e.'

he gets, makes them follow him, that they may go with him. That is why our mothers used to say when a star fell, 'A sorceror seems to have died there. Therefore you see that his heart strings (?) have fallen, they go thundering. Now you will feel what the summer's heat will be like. For a sorceror of illness seems to have died, it is truly a sorceror who brings illness who has died when a star acts in this manner; when a sorceror who brings illness has died, then a star falls down. You ought to listen, whether the star falls straight down as it disappears.'

Itən -//kwaŋ ka, i se tu, ti ϵ:, ha se !gãũ /ki /kam //e ha //ka -//kãũïŋ, ĩ:. Ta:, !gi:xa -//kwaŋ ϵ ts?a a: //nau, ha ¯/ku:kən, haŋ -//kwaŋ ka ha se !gãũ /ki -tai ha-ka !gi:; o ha ka, ha-ka -tauïtən ϵ:, ha siŋ /ki hϵ, hϵ se -tai /hiŋ tu !k?ãũ ϵ:, ha siŋ -tai //na hϵ. Haŋ k"auki ka ha se ¯ã: ha-ka !gi: se //na//na, o ha sín ϵ !gi:xa a: /xãũ. Haŋ ka ha se //nau, ha: ¯/ku:ka, ha-ka !gi:, hiŋ -tai //nẽ hĩ: ha. Ta, !gi:xa /ki //nau, ha /ku:kən, ha-ka !gitən !naunko -tai //na.

We want to hear whether it will fall straight down, taking its vibrations (?). For a sorceror is a being who when he dies, wishes to fall heavily taking his sorcery; for he wishes his work, which he used to do, to leave the earth on which he used to walk about. He does not want to allow his sorcery to stay where he has been a sorceror who goes on magic expeditions. When he dies, he wants his magic to go with him. For when a sorceror dies, his magic power still goes about.

Hϵ tikən ϵ:, mama-gu ka siŋ kukú, hϵ /k'e:, 'Ts?a-di xa a:, i-ka !k?e e: -am ¯oä ϵ !gitən, hϵ //khóä /ku /ku:kən/ku:kən /kam tóä hϵ //kou//kóugən o i-í. Ta, hϵ siŋ se kwaŋ //k'oen, ti ϵ:, i: /kwẽ:ï /kwã:, i: //na, ĩ:. Hϵ se kwaŋ //k'oen //kau tẽ, o í, ta:, hϵ -//kwaŋ ka siŋ ka: /k'e:, hϵ -//kwaŋ -hã: ka siŋ ≠en-na, ti ϵ:, hϵ: di tiŋjã hé: ti. O ti ϵ:, ŋ /ku-g /ne //k'oen, ti ϵ:, hϵ /ku -ó:ä ¯!kẽ:ï

Therefore our mothers used to say, 'How is it that our people who used once to be sorcerors, seem to be dying taking their thoughts away from us? For they ought to look if we are still at the same place. They ought to look down on us, for they used always to say, that they should know about the things which were happening here. Then I should see whether it were true, that in

||ou, hiŋ |ku:kən|ku:kən |ki ˍtaijã hɛ ||kou||kóugən, o i. Hɛ i k''auki ka |ne |nĩ, ti ɛ:, hɛ kíɛ da: hɛ; o hɛ: ka, i se |nĩ hɛ. Ta:, hɛ ||kou||kóugən ˍ||kwaŋ |ne ||khóä |ku !kõ!kõ:ä o i-i, hɛ i k''auki ka-g |ne ||nau, i: |gauka hɛ, itən k''auki ka |ne |nĩ, ti ɛ:, hɛ: kíë |ne da: hi ã hɛ, i se-g |ne |nĩ, ti ɛ:, hɛ ˍ||kwaŋ ˍó:ä !naunko ≠en-na i. Ta:, i ka |ku-g |ne |gaukən !kãũa-ka !ho o hɛ; hɛ k''auki |ne kɛ: |k'e:ja hi ã:, i se ¯≠en.'

dying they took their thoughts away from us. And we do not see what they are doing, though they want us to see them. But their thoughts seem to go away from us, so that when we call upon them, we do not see what they are doing for us, that we may see whether they still know us. For we call without getting an answer from them; they will not talk to us, that we may know!'

Hɛ tikən ɛ mama-gu ka siŋ ||nau, !kwi a: ɛ: !gi:xa, ha-ka tʃweŋ, mama-gu |k'e:ja si ã:, ti ɛ:, si ||khóä kaŋ ¯≠ĩ: !gixa k''au ||nau, ha-ka tʃweŋ, haŋ ká ha: siŋ, sa ko ≠kerre ha-ka tʃweŋ, ti ɛ:, !kˀe |nõ ||ẽ:ï aka ha-ka tʃweŋ. Ha ||nau, ha-ka tsˀa ˍ|gwãĩn i, hɛ |e: i, i ¯|ku:kən, o ha-ka tsˀa ˍ|gwãĩnjã i, o hiŋ ta: ||ka ti ɛ:, ha-ka tʃwen |ki¯|ki ha ˍ|kwˀãĩ. Hɛ tikən ɛ:, ha-ka tʃweŋ k''wãŋ hɛ ¯!kauwa.

Then our mothers used to tell us about the things of a man who is a sorceror, they used to say that we seemed to think that a sorceror would not deal with his things, but he would come to look after his things, whether people were taking possession of them nicely. If anything of his gets into us, so that it is in us, we die, because his thing has entered us, because his things have his scent. That is why his things seem to be alive.

Ta !gi:xa |kí |ku e, ná |ku ˍtai o ||ga:; haŋ |ku ⊙pwoin ʃo: hĩ i, ha-ka ||ke:ŋjaŋ |ku ˍtai-ã tiŋ, o i ⊙pwoin ||na. I ɛ: k''auki ɛ !gitən, itən k''auki ≠en-na, tikən-tikən, ɛ:, ha dí |ki hɛ, o ha-ka ||ke:ŋ, ti ɛ:, ha-g |ne ≠kaka hi ã:, hiŋ |ku ɛ:, i-g |ne tú:ï, ti ɛ:, ha ˍóä ˍdóä siŋ ˍtaija. Ta:, ha-g |ne ≠kaka hi ã:, tʃweŋ ɛ:, ha siŋ ||k'oen ¯|ki hɛ, o ti ɛ:, ha siŋ |xãũ |kam ||a: hɛ.

For it is the sorceror's custom to walk at night; he lies asleep by us, his magic walks about, while we sleep there. We who are not sorcerors do not know the things he is wont to do with his magic, though he told us about it, it was what we had heard when he had been walking about. For he had told us about the things which he had been wont to see, when he was out on a magic expedition.

Hɛ tikən ɛ:, !gi:xa |ku ||nau, haŋ |ku ⊙pwoin ||na, há |ku !khou, ti ɛ:, di tiŋjã hɛ́: ti; hɛ-ka ||xaukən |kwˀãĩ, há |ku hõũŋ hɛ, ó ha

That is how, when a sorceror is sleeping there, he smells what has thing been passing here; the scent of its blood he perceives with

/nũnũ. Ta:, !gi:xa /ki !khou //ke:-//ke: !kwiŋ, haŋ !khou ⁻//khwetən, !khou ti ϵ:, di tiŋjã hέ: ti, o haŋ /kɯ ⊙pwoin //na.	his nose, For a sorceror smells like a dog, smells from far off, he smells what has been happening here, while he is sleeping there.

Notes

3-4 *As it enters the waterpit it sounds like a quiver:* Here is another instance where sound plays an important part in a 'magical' process (see Part VI). The falling of a star into a waterpit is actually the sound of the sorceror's heart.

38-39 *It goes into a waterpit* **which** *does not rise*: This should read 'It goes into a waterpit *and* does not rise' (5482 rev.).

77-78 *For a* **sorceror of illness** *seems to have died:* '"A *Tornar* (i.e. *towenaar*, Dutch for 'sorceror' – ed.) what bring sick". *//xi* is the name for an illness' (5485 rev., note omitted).

83-84 *You ought to listen whether the star falls* **straight down** ... : This meaning of the word *!gãũ:* is recorded in the *Dictionary* as 'to resound, make a noise like rain, rumble' (Bleek 1956: 378). Given that it is the *sound* of the star falling into the waterpit that seems to be important, it is possible that the word has been mistranslated – *!gãũ:* should rather be 'making a noise like rain' or 'rumbling'. This interpretation is borne out by Diä!kwain's comments in 'More about sorcerors', where he says that 'a sorceror's heart's sound makes a noise like rain ...' It is also corroborated by Diä!kwain's use here, in the following sentence, of the word, *//ka§//kãũ§ïŋ*, which is described in the *Dictionary* as 'to vibrate' or 'vibration, sound, change [music]' (Bleek 1956: 565). He uses this word in two other contexts to describe the nature of a particular sound or vibration: the breaking of the thong connecting a rain sorceror and a rain-animal makes this sound (Part VI, 'The breaking of the thong'), as does the sound of the breaking string between the sorceror !Nuiŋ /kuïtən and Xã:ätiŋ, Diä!kwain's father (Part VIII, 'What Xã:ätiŋ used to sing'). In all three cases, the word *//ka§//kãũ§ïŋ* describes auditory phenomena associated with sorcerors and sorcery.

111-112 *Then I should see whether it were true ...*: There are two small differences between the *Bantu Studies* translation and the original, notebook version: 'Then I should see whether it were true that in dying they took their thoughts *of us* with them. And we do not see what they are doing *to us*, though they want us to see them.' (5495–5496, my italics)

128-129 … *we seemed to think that a sorceror would not* **deal** *with his things* …: The original notebook translation of *//nau* makes more sense in this context: 'we should not think the sorceror had *forgotten* his things' (55[illegible], my italics). 'Things' here probably mean things that a sorceror uses to bewitch people.

152-154 … *the scent of its blood he* **perceives** *with his nose* … Diä!kwain's explanation of the word *hõũŋ* is given in the following extract, Note on *hõũŋ*.

Part VII
Sorcerors

Note on *hõũŋ*

Narrator: Diä!kwain
Source: 'Note by D.H.'
Dictation date: 10 November 1875
Notebook reference: L.V.19: 5504 rev.
***Bantu Studies* reference:** Vol. 9 (1935), Part VII: 31

Hõũŋ *means 'to perceive, be aware of' and the word* hõũŋhõũŋ *means 'presentiments'. The /Xam teachers discussed how they experienced presentiments as physical sensations. For instance, //Kabbo interpreted a tapping sensation at his ribs as the black hair on the sides of a springbok – this 'springbok sensation'* (whai-tă/k"*ʌm) meant springbok were approaching the hunting ground. Presentiments were highly valued: //Kabbo explained that these beatings in their bodies were like an alphabet that could communicate information about things happening somewhere else ('Bushman presentiments' in Bleek & Lloyd 1911: 330-339). See Part VIII, Introduction, for more discussion.*

❑

Hõũŋhõũŋ kíɛ̈: tsˀa a:, i tã:, ti ɛ:, hɛ di tiŋja ti ɛ: /xara. Hõũŋhõũŋ haŋ //xɑm //ke://ke:ja //khabo, ti ɛ: i ka //khabo-ã. I xara //nau, o itən ¯!kwai, i !kauükən hiŋ sou, hέ: ti. Tikən taŋ tsˀa //na hɛ: ti; i !kauükaŋ /ki !hɑmi!hɑmi i. I ¯toukən, o i !kauükaŋ ɛ: ≠kaka hi, ti ɛ:, /a: ˍdóä //na, ti έ: ã.

A presentiment is a thing which we feel when something is happening at another place. A presentiment is also like a dream which we dream. Sometimes when we are alone our body starts at some place It seems as if something were there which our body made us dread. We avoid it because our body is telling us, that there is danger at that place.

❑

Note

5-6 *Sometimes when we are alone our body starts at some place*: In other words, the person's body makes an involuntary bodily movement.

The sorceror's heart (more about sorcerors)

Narrator: Diä!kwain
Source: 'Diä!kwain was told this by his mother, ǂKămmi-ăn'
Dictation dates: 11, 12, 13 November 1875
Notebook reference: L.V.19: 5506-5530
***Bantu Studies* reference:** Vol. 9 (1935), Part VII: 31-35

Why people fear falling stars.

Mama-gu kaŋ ¯kaŋ ≠kaka si ã:, ti ϵ:, !gi:xa |ĩ: !khũ!khũ ϵ: !gãũ |ki _tai ha, o hiŋ ta: ||ka ti ϵ:, ha-g |ne |ku:kən _tai. Hϵ tikən ϵ:, ha |ĩ: _!kaitən ||khóë siŋ ≠hauru, ĩ:. Hiŋ |ne !gãũ, o hiŋ ta: ||ka ti ϵ:, hϵ:, |e: ≠hauru, a: ¯!kˀauwa, ha-ka !khwa:. Hϵ tikən ϵ:, hϵ !gãũ, ĩ:, o hiŋ ta: ||ka ti ϵ:, hϵ |e: !khwa: a: ||xɒm ¯!kau, ||ke:||ke:ja há a: !gi:xa. Hϵ tikən ϵ:, ha !gãũ, ĩ:, o haŋ ta: ||ka ti ϵ:, !gi:xa |ĩ: !khũ!khũ |ki ϵ:, |e: !khwa:.

Our mothers used to tell us, that a sorceror's heart's sound makes a noise like rain taking him away, because it feels that it goes away dying. Then his heart falls down into the water-pit. It sounds like rain as it goes into the water-pit which is alive, (into) its water. That is why it sounds like rain, because it enters water which also lives, as does he who is a sorceror. That is why he sounds like rain, because it is the sound of a sorceror's heart which enters water.

Ta, !khwa: a: !gitən ||a ko ≠xama !khwa:-ka xɔro ã:, ha |ki ϵ:, hϵ tikən ϵ:, ha |uaitən !gi:xa-kɔ: _|kwˀãĩ, ĩ:. Hϵ tikən ϵ:, !gi:xa-kɔ: |ĩ: !gãũ swe:ŋ ||a, ĩ:, o haŋ |k'e:ja !gi:xa-kɔ: a ≠en-na ≠hauru, ha ã:, ha se ≠en, ti ϵ:, ha tuko ||xɒm ||a ≠hauru, ha á: ϵ !khwa: ¯!keri.

For this is the water from which sorcerors are wont to fetch water-bulls, so he is displeased by another sorceror's scent. Then the one sorceror's heart comes down like rain, as he tells the other sorceror who knows the waterpit, who he is, that he may know, that he really also goes to the waterpit which is a big water.

Hϵ tikən ϵ:, mama-gu !hɒmi _|kwatən, ĩ:, o hiŋ ta: ||ka ti ϵ:. _|kwatən ϵ tsˀa a: k''auki se ||ause ¯tatən !kˀũ. Ta: ha ≠en-na ti ϵ: da:; hϵ tikən ϵ:, ha ¯tatən !kˀũ:ï, ĩ:.

Therefore our mothers fear the stars, for they feel that a star is a thing which does not fall down for no reason. For it knows what has happened, that is why it falls down.

Ta:, !kʔe ɛ: ɛ !gitən, hɛ ˉ/ki /ku //nau, hiŋ //na !xóë a: /xara, hiŋ /ku /ke:tən hɛ-ka !gi:, o hɛ́: ti; hiŋ /k'e:ja hɛ-ka !gi:, ã:, ti ɛ:, hɛ-ka !gi: se //a /kwẽ:ï /kwẽ, ha dí, ĩ:. !gi-tən !ku ˍtai, ti ɛ:, !gi:xa /ke:tən /ki /kəm //a: ha ĩ:, haŋ /ku //aŋ dí:, ti ɛ:, !gi:xa siŋ /kwẽ:ï da hi ã:, ĩ:.

For people who are sorcerors are wont, when they are at a different place, to send their magic power to this place ; they tell their magic power where to go and what to do. The magic power goes where the sorceror sends it, it goes to do what the sorceror makes it do.

!gi:xakən /ku //aŋ //xãũ !kwi a: ha ≠kauwa ha, o hɛ́:ti. Ha-ka !gi:tən /ku ɛ́:, //aŋ //xãũ ˉ!kwi o hɛ́: ti. Itən /ne kaŋ ≠ĩ:, tsʔa de xa a:, !kwi á: a, ha /ku ˉo: se /ku:kən ã:; o i-í ɛ: k''auki ≠en-na, itən ɛ /kwẽ:ï dakən ĩ:.

The sorceror goes to carry off a person whom he wants from here. It is his magic power which goes to carry off the person from here. We wonder why this person seems about to die ; for we are those who do not know, we who think thus.

!gi:xa-kɔ: a: ≠en-na, haŋ /ku a: ≠en-na, ti ɛ:, !gi:xa-kɔ: a:-ka //ke:ŋ, ɛ: saŋ kɛ: //xãũ !kwi. Haŋ /ku a:, ≠kaka hi ã:, ti ɛ:, i //khɔ-kaŋ ˉ≠ĩ:, taŋtaŋ a: ˉ!kwi /ku:kən ta: ha. Ta: //ke:ŋ a: /khi: !kwi. Hɛ tikən ɛ:, i //k'oen, ti ɛ:, !kwi /ku /ku:kən, ĩ:; hiŋ k''auki siŋ ≠ĩ:, ti ɛ:, !kwi se ˉ/ku:kən.

One sorceror who knows, understands that it is another sorceror whose charm is trying to carry off the person. He says to us, that we seem to think it is illness of which the person lies dying. But it is enchantment that is killing him. Then we see that the man seems dying ; they do not think he will die.

Hɛ tikən ɛ:, !gi:xa-kɔ: ká ha se //nau, o !gi:xa-kɔ:, ha ˍ/gwainja í, !gi:xa-kɔ: ˍkɔ́:ö /ne sũ: /hiŋjã, o i-í. Haŋ /ki //a: ha, o ti ɛ:, ha ká ha //aŋ sũ: /hiŋ ha, ĩ:. Haŋ /khi: !gi:xa-kɔ:, a: ˍ/gwainja í. Haŋ ˍ!kaitən /khi: ha, o ˉ!kou; haŋ //nau, ha ˍ!kaita, haŋ kaŋ /k'e:, '!kwi á, ha ˍtaija tiŋ, há siŋ /khaä tiŋ o !kʔe, ŋ kaŋ /kha /kəm ta ha, ta, ha /ku ɛ /hõ:ä-gause-!kwi. Hɛ tikən ɛ:, ŋ kaŋ /kha ha, ĩ:.'

Then one sorceror will do this to the other sorceror who has bewitched us, he will snore him out of us. He makes the other go from the place out of which he snores him. He kills the other who has bewitched us. He strikes him dead with a stone ; as he strikes him, he says, 'This man has been going about killing people, I will kill him knocking him down, for he is a rascally person. Therefore I will kill him.'

The sorceror's heart ...

Ha //nau, ha: ˍ!kaitən ˍ≠kɔmma ha, ha ˍ/gəm ho //k'e:ja, o !kãũ ɛ:, ha siŋ ˍ!kaitən ˍ≠kəm //k'e:ja ha, ĩ:, ha ˍ!kaitən /ki ˍtai ha. Ha-g

When he has beaten him to make him soft, he scoops him up with the earth on which he has pounded him soft, he beats him

||nau, ha: _!kaitən |ki _tai ha, ha ¯ku', '!kwi |ke: ã, ha |kɒm ||e |nu: !ke: ɛ:, hɛ ka |kweitən |kɯ |kha |ki !kˀe, ĩ:. Haŋ _ó:ä _dóä tuko siŋ ka ha sé ti έ: ã, ha se sa |kha, |ki|ki !kˀe, ĩ:.'

away. As he is beating him away he says, 'May that man go to the spirits who are always killing people. He has only wanted to come here, in order to kill and carry off people.'

Ha |ne ||nau, ha: |kwẽ:ï |kwẽ, ha dí, !gi:xa kɔ: á: ha |ki |hã ha o ¯!kwi, ha kan _!kõ:äŋse !kwi a:, ha _dóä sũ: ha, ha tẽ:n, o há ka, ha se dun-na, !kwi a: taŋ ha ã:, ti ɛ:, !gi:xa-kɔ: siŋ sˀe: hɛ. Ta: twi: tuko _||kwaŋ a: sˀo ti ɛ:, !gi:xa-kɔ: siŋ sˀo: hɛ:. Ta:, ha |ki _||kwaŋ hã: ||khóä ¯twi:, o !kwi-ka ti ɛ:, ha siŋ sˀo: hɛ. Ha twi:tən á:, !gi:xa-kɔ: ka ha dun-na !kwi ã: ha, ha k''auki siŋ bɔ:kən !khe:.

When he has in this manner made the other sorceror come out of the man, he takes care of that man whom he has snored; he makes him lie down, for he wants to cure the man who is suffering where the other sorceror sat. There is a real wound where the other sorceror was. For he had eaten a wound in the part on which he sat. Of that wound the sorceror wishes to cure him that it may not stand open.

Hɛ tikən ɛ:, ha ká ha tˀerija !kwi ã: twi:, o ha |nũnu. Itən k''auki |nĩ: twi:, o !kwi tũ: ɛ: ||kauta:. Ta ha |nũnu |kɯ e:, kaŋ |e: !kwi eŋeŋ, o ti ɛ: ||khó:ë. Ha |nũnũŋ |kɯ ɛ !khou, ti ɛ:, ||khóë, hέ ha _taba ¯!kwi eŋeŋ, ĩ:. Haŋ ||nau, ha |nũnũ, haŋ ≠um !haŋ !kwi-ka twi: tu, ɛ: !gi:xa-kɔ: hã: ||khóä hɛ, o ¯!kwi eŋeŋ ||kaië.

Therefore he is wont to rub the man's wound with his nose. We do not see a wound, for the man's skin is over it. But his nose goes into the man's body to the place underneath. It is his nose which works the spot underneath, where he works on the man's flesh. His nose sews up the mouth of the man's wound, where the other sorceror had eaten of the man's flesh inside.

Ha ||nau, ha: dun kuitja, ha-g |ne ||nau, ||xaukən ɛ:, ha siŋ |xama |hiŋ !gi:xa-kɔ:, ĩ:, ha |õä ¯!kwi a: taŋ, ha ĩ:, o ha !nũnũ-ka ||xaukən, ĩ:. Ha !gwi ¯!kwi ĩ:, o haŋ ka, ha a: !gi:xa, ha |nũnũ-ka ||xaukən _|kwˀãĩ se ||na||na ¯!kwi. Ta:, ha |nũnũ-ka ||xaukən |ki ||ke:||ke:ja ha a: ɛ !gi:xa. Han !gwi: !kwi, o haŋ ka !kwi se ʘpwoin hĩ ha |nũnũ-ka ||xaukən.

When he has finished curing him, he takes the blood in which he has sneezed out the other sorceror, he paints the man who is ill with it, with blood from his nose. He anoints the man with it, for he, being a sorceror, wants the smell of the blood from his nose to be upon the man. For blood from his nose makes one resemble him, a sorceror. He anoints the man,

Part VII
Sorcerors

The sorceror's heart ...

for he wants him to sleep with the blood of his nose on him.

Hɛ tikən ɛ:, ha !gwi: ¯!kwi, ĩ:, o haŋ ta: //ka ti ɛ:, ha !kúïtən ha-ka //neiŋ, ha se //a ʘpwoin, o haŋ ≠ĩ:, ti ɛ:, /kɔ́:ɔ̈-de kwitən ˍsaŋ //xã:, hɛ /kha !kwi. Hɛ tikən ɛ:, ha di: ¯!kwi, o ha /nũnũ-ka //xaukən, o haŋ ka, ha /nũnũ-ka //xaukən ˍ/kwʔãĩ, hɛ: siŋ //na ¯!kwi. /kɔ́:ö-de ɛ: sa:, hɛ kíɛ̈ se /kha !kwi, hɛ se !khou ha /nũnũ-ka //xaukən, hɛ: siŋ !hɔmi ha /nũnũ-ka //xaukən ˍ/kwʔãĩ; o haŋ ta: ti ɛ:, ˍ/kɔ́:ö-de k''auki kíë se sé, ti ɛ:, hɛ !khou !gi:xa:kɔ:-ka //xaukən. ˍ/kwʔãĩ, ĩ:. Hiŋ k''auki kíë se sé, ti ɛ:, hɛ !khou !gi:xa-kɔ: !gau, ĩ:.

So he anoints the man, because he intends to go home and sleep, for he thinks that other magic things may come again to kill the man. Therefore he dabs the man with the blood of his nose, for he wants the scent of it to be on the man. Magic things which come to try and kill the man will smell the scent of the blood of his nose; for he thinks that magic things will not come where they smell the scent of another sorceror's blood. They do not come where they smell another sorceror's blood.

Notes

2-4 *... a sorceror's heart's sound makes a noise like rain taking him away ...*: The sound (*!khũ!khũ*) of the sorceror's heart signals the beginning of its falling into the waterpit (*≠hauru*).

5-6 *Then his heart falls down into the water-pit*: Diä!kwain commented at length on this in a note (5506 rev.–5512 rev.) which Dorothea Bleek published in *Bantu Studies* as 'The sorcerer after death'.

29-30 *... that is why it falls down*: 'Our mothers used to say, a star will not fall for nothing, for it knows what happens, that is why it falls down' (5511, sentence omitted).

48-50 *... it is another sorceror whose* **charm** *is trying to carry off the person*: Here *//ke:ŋ* is translated as 'charm'; it is more often translated as 'magic power' (5515).

52-53 *But it is* **enchantment** *that is killing him*: Here Dorothea Bleek translated *//ke:ŋ* (magic power) as 'enchantment' (5516).

57-59 *Then one sorcerer will do this to the other sorceror who has* **bewitched** *us ...*: For the various meanings of the word */gwainja,* see Part V, 'A girl and the rain's bolts'.

110 *He* **anoints** *the man with it …* : Diä!kwain explains that there are four |Xam words with closely related meanings – *!koirri* and */kac,* meaning 'smear' and perhaps 'stroke'; and *!gwi* and */oä,* meaning 'smear' in the sense of 'anoint'. '[D.H. says that the first two (words) mean the same thing; and the last two a different thing – but there is only one word in Dutch for all the four.]' (5524 rev., note omitted)

The */nu:-!kʔe*

Narrator: Diä!kwain
Source: 'Note by Diä!kwain'
Dictation date: 24, 25 June 1875
Notebook reference: L.V. 11: 4801 rev.- 4809 rev.
***Bantu Studies* reference:** Vol. 9 (1935), Part VII: 35-37

This extract is a clear and unequivocal statement of the /Xam belief in ancestral sorcerors who could be approached for help by the living.

❑

Mamaŋ siŋ káŋ ≠kaka ke, ti ϵ:. /nu:-!kʔe ϵ:, siŋ ϵ ⊙pwaitən-ka !gitən. Hϵ ka //nau, o hϵ /ku:ka, he //khou//khougən e:, he siŋ e !gi:xa, ĩ:, hϵ siŋ di: !gi:, ĩ:, he ta //nau, o he: /ku:ka, i k''auki /nĩ: he; ta:, hϵ-ka !gi:-ka didí: /kɯ e, e: he !naunko _tai //na, ĩ:.

Mother used to tell me that the spirit people were those who had been game sorcerors. When they died their thoughts, with which they they had been sorcerors and worked magic, continued, though they died and we did not see them; still their magic doings went about here.

Hiŋ //nau, he:ta !gi:-ta didí, hiŋ //ke://ke:ja ti e: !kwi xara ka !kʔauwa, hiŋ k''auki //kóä:kən /ku:kən: ta:, ha !naunko !kʔauwa, o ha-ka !gi:.

Their magic doings are like a person who always lives, they do not altogether die; thus he still lives in his sorcery.

Hϵ tikən e:, mama ka siŋ, ká: ≠kaka ke, ha ka taŋ-ĩ: ha-ka !gitən e: óä //ĩ:ja ⊙pwaitən; o //ke: a: ha /kwɔbokən ã:, ha: //ketən a: ha ≠kakən hĩ he, ã:. Mama k''auki /nĩ: he, ta: mama /kɯ a: ≠kakən hĩ he; o mamaŋ ta: //ka ti e:, he _//kwaŋ tú:ï mama. Mamaŋ kí saŋ k''auki //k'oen hϵ, ta: mama _//kwaŋ ≠en-na, ti e:, he _//kwaŋ tú:ï mama, mamaŋ kí saŋ k''auki /nĩ: hϵ. Ta:, hϵ /ki /kɯ e !gitən, hϵ /kɯ ≠en-na tikəntiken o hϵ-ta !gi:, hϵ:, hϵ /kɯ e:, _taba hϵ.

Therefore mother used to tell me that she would beg from her sorcerors who had owned game; when she beat the ground, then she spoke with them. Mother did not see them, yet she talked with them for mother felt sure that they would hear her. Although mother did not see them, yet she knew that they would hear her, without her seeing them. For they had been sorcerors, they had known things by their sorcery, this it was which they worked.

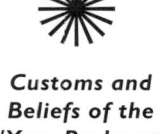

Hɛ tikən e:, mama ka siŋ ||nau, ha: |kwɔbokən, ha taŋ-ĩ: !gitən o ʘpwaitən; mama ||nau, ha: _!kaitən !ho !kau, ha ku, 'ŋ-ka |nu:-!kʔe:-wɛ:, u xa te:-da:kən ≠ĩ: o ŋ́? Hɛ ti |ku k''wãŋ, u |ku tsetsé:ja ŋ, hɛ u k''auki k''wãŋ, u _||kwaŋ ≠ĩ:, ti e:, u _||kwaŋ ka siŋ ||nau, ||ke: a:, u ¯óä !naunko !kʔau!kʔauüka ã:; ukən _||kwaŋ ka siŋ ≠kakən kúï !xwãŋ, u !kẽï ||augən kɔ:ka ŋ. Ta:, tí |ku-g |ne k''wãŋ, u |kukən|kukən |kam tóä u ||khou||khougən o ŋ́. Ukən |ku-g |ne ||khóä ≠nã: ŋ.

Therefore mother used to do this, she beat the ground, she begged the sorcerors for game; as she struck down the stone she said, 'O my spirit people, do you no longer think of me? It seems as if you had turned your backs on me, that you do not seem to think as you used to do, at the time when you still had bodies; you used to talk as if you really loved me. But it seems as if you had in dying taken your thoughts away from me. You seem to have forgotten me.

'Ta:, u k''auki ta-g |ne xara ti _ã: ŋ |ha ã:, tsʔa !ko!kõïŋ a:, ha ka: ha !xwẽ, ha: se |kha: keja, ŋ ã: se hã: ha, o ha: ki sa: !xwẽ. Hɛ ti |ku k''wãŋ u |ku:kən |ki _taija u ||khou||khougən e:, u ka siŋ k''wã twïï, o-g ŋ, ĩ:. Ta:, ŋ |ha siŋ se k''wãŋ ||nau, u dóä !naunko ≠en-na ŋ, haŋ siŋ se k''wãŋ, |nĩ tsʔa !ko!kõïŋ a:, ha ká: e !ɑhára, ha kwãŋ |kha: keja, ha e !ɑhára, ŋ ã se hã: ha.

'For you do not always give my husband some old thing that he can first kill for me, that I may eat of it, although it is the first. It seems as if you had died taking away your thoughts which used to be favourable to me. For while you still knew me, my husband used to find some old thing which he thought was lean, he would kill it for me, it being lean, that I might eat of it.

'Ta:, ŋ _||kwaŋ k''auki se kweritja, ta-g ŋ _||kwaŋ ≠en-na, ti e-, tsʔa !ko!kõïŋ a:, u ¯||kwa: sɔ |xum ŋ ã:, ha _||kwaŋ sɔ e. Hɛ tikən e:, ŋ _||kwaŋ siŋ kwãŋ ≠ĩ:, ti e:, tsʔa a:, u _||kwa: sɔ e: áke ha, ha _||kwa: e. Hɛ tikən e:, ŋ ha se kwãŋ _||kwa: ||nau, ha: |nã: tsʔa a:, ha e !ɑhára, ha se _||kwa: |kha: keja, ŋ se _||kwa: hã: ha.'

'But I used not to complain, for I knew that this old thing must be what you had provided for me. Therefore I just used to think that it must be the thing that you had given me. So whenever my husband sees anything lean, he will just kill it for me and I will eat it.'

Ta:, mama xóä |ki kaŋ |k'e:ja mama ã:, ti e:, mama a |kwẽ:ĩdakən ≠kaka sí-si ã:, ti e:, i-ta !gitən e, hɛ síŋ e !gitən, hɛ ta |ki !khwa: hi ã: tsʔa-ka ti, o hɛ́: ka, i se |nĩ tsʔa, o tsʔa: duru-ã tiŋ, i se |kha tsʔa. Hɛ-g |ne ||nau, hɛ ¯á hi ã:

For mother's mother had told mother, what mother likewise told us, namely that our spirits, who had been sorcerors, were accustomed to break some part of a thing for us, for they wanted us to see the thing limping about, that

tsʔa a:, há e !ɑhára, hɛ-g |ne !hau hɛ ¯á tsʔa a:, há e sweŋ. Hɛ tikən e:, mama ka siŋ ká: ha ≠kaka si ã:, |nu:-!kʔe: ka ˍam ¯á hi ã: tsʔa !ko!kõiŋ, i ˍam hã: ha. Hɛ-g |ne !hau, he ¯á hi ã: tsʔa á:, ha a:kən.

we could kill it. When they had given us a lean thing, they would later give us a fat thing. That is what mother kept telling us, the spirit people would first give us an old thing, we must eat it first, later they give us something good.

Note

Title *|nu:-!kʔe*: Depending on the context of the statement, */nu:-!kʔe* can mean either 'old people', 'spirit people', or 'dead people'. The categories seem to blur into each other: the elders have their many years of experience to draw upon and are generally the strongest *!gi:tən* amongst the living. Spirit people, however, seem to be the most powerful of all and their assistance is asked, or begged for (*/gauken*).

The power over ostriches possessed by /uhére

Narrator: Diä!kwain
Source: 'Told by Diä!kwain'
Dictation dates: 16, 19 and 22 June 1875
Translation dates: 24 June 1875 (4797-4802); 2 July 1875 (4869-4870)
Notebook reference: L.V.10: 4778-4795 and 11: 4797-4807 (originally)
***Bantu Studies* reference:** Vol. 9 (1935), Part VII: 37-40

Violence breaks out when people confront a game sorceror who has power over ostriches.

❑

|ɑhére kaŋ ka ||nau, !kʔeja |ki si ˍ!k''wãĩŋˍ!k''wãĩnja ha, ha-g |ne ˍ!k''wain !kʔe, ha-g |ne |k'e:ja !k'e ã:, ti e:, tői ka tői se ||xɑm ˍ!k''wain !kʔe, o !kʔe |kwẽ:ï k''o o há. Tőïtən ka, tőïja: siŋ kwaŋ |ku k''wãŋ tőïja ≠en-na, ti e:, !kwija: |xweri sʔo: tőï, ĩ:. Tőï kwaŋ |ku ||nau, ha: ˍ||kwa: siŋ |kɑm ||a !kwi, ha se |ku k''wãŋ, ha |nĩ: !kwi, ha se |ku !xwɔ̃ni, ha se |ku |kɑm ||e ti e |xara. !kwija siŋ |ne ka: ≠ĩ:, ˉtőïjá xa dóä |nã ŋ, he tői |ne !xwɔni?' Tőïtən k''auki |nã ha, ta: |ɑhére a: |kwẽ:ï ku, ha |k'e, tőïja siŋ kwẽ:ï k''o, tőïja k''auki siŋ k''wã ≠hanũ:wa.

/uhere used to act like this when people made him angry, so that he was wrath with them, he said to the people that the ostriches would also be angry with them, as they had treated him in this manner. The ostriches would henceforth behave as if they knew where a man was lying in wait for them. An ostrich would act like this, it would be approaching a man, it would seem as if it caught sight of him, it would turn back and go to a different place. The man would think, 'has the ostrich seen me that it turns back?' The ostrich would not have seen him, but */uhere* would have told it to act like this, not to act nicely.

He tikən e:, !kʔe ka-g |ne tu:tú: ha, he-g |ne kukúï, he |k'e:, '|ɑhére-we, tsʔa-di xa a:, a k''auki k''wãŋ a ≠ĩ:, ti e:, si ˍ||kwaŋ |ki !kaukən e: si siŋ ˍ||gauë hĩ: he, e: si ã-á he ã:, hã:, he a |ku k''wãŋ, a ≠ĩ: |ɑhá:, he a |ku-g |ne dí kúï k''wãŋk''wãŋ !khwã:; akən k''auki |ne k''wãŋ !keri a: |ki ha ||khou||khougən, a ˍ||kwaka. Akən

Then the people used to ask him, saying, 'O */uhere*, why is it that you do not seem to think, that we have children for whom we must seek food, that we may give it them to eat, that you seem to think angrily and you act like a child, not like a grown-up person who has sense and understands. You do not seem to realise that

|ne k''auki k''wãŋ a _||kwaŋ ≠en-na, ti e:, ʘpwɔnde _||kwaŋ |ki !kaukən e:, he _||kwaŋ _||gauë hĩ: he; akən se k''auki |kwẽ:ï |kwẽ, a di. Ta:, a se ≠kakən aka !kʔe ã:, o tóï; !kʔe se ||nau, hɛ: |xwerija tóï, tóï se _tai !ke se he, he se |kha tóï, he se ã: he-ta !kaukən ã: hã:.'

the young people have children whom they must seek to feed; you should not act like this. For you should talk nicely to the people about the ostriches, that when the people are lying in wait for an ostrich the ostrich may walk up to them, that they may kill the ostrich, that they may give their children food.'

|ahére |ne kukú, ha |k'e:ja !kwi ã:, ha taŋ-ã: ha, o tóï, '|ne |ku !kúï:ta a-g ||neiŋ, a-g |ne se ||a |ũ:ŋ;, a _saŋ |ne ||nau !gauëja: !khwaija, a se-g |ne ||k'oen, ti e:, a ká a _taija tiŋ he, a se-g |ne ||k'oen, ti e:, tóï á: e _!kãũï-!kwã, ha-g |nu k''au se ã ha, a |nĩ ha, o ha: ||gwi||gwita sa:; ha !xɔhé:nja, a se- |nĩ ha.'

|*vhere* spoke, he said to the man who begged him about the ostrich, 'Return home and go to lie down; then when day has broken you shall look at the place where you intended to walk about, you shall see if an ostrich which is a dwarf will not allow you to catch sight of it, as it comes playing; it is ugly, you shall get it.'

-!kãũï-kwã is an ostrich which never becomes large; it grows up, but remains small. There is always one of these hatched in a brood, it goes in front of the others when they run or walk, being always in front. It is sometimes a male, but generally a female bird. It comes from one of the outer eggs, which stand in a cold place. The old people say, the outer eggs do not belong to the mother. (The little outer eggs are mentioned in the story of the Mantis and *!kaken-!ka-ka !kauï*).

!kwi |ne _tai, ti e:, |ahérejã siŋ |k'e:ja ha _tai |kam ||e he; ha-g|ne |ku ||nau, ha: _tai ||a:, ha |ku |ou tóï, o tóïja: !kuxe |kam sa ha. Haŋ |ne kukú, ha ≠ĩ:, '|ahére taŋ _||kwaŋ ||khóä !kẽ:ï ||au, haŋ |xum ŋ, o !gauë ta ti é: a. Ta:, tóï _||kwaŋ |ne e: ≠hau sa: o-g ŋ; he k''auki siŋ _dóä |kwẽ:ï k''o. Ta: tóï e:, ŋ _||kwaŋ k''auki siŋ ≠en-na he, he _||kwaŋ |ne e: ≠hau sa: o-g ŋ.'

The man went to the place to which |*vhere* had told him to go; as he went he saw ostriches come running towards him. He said to himself, '|*vhere* does really seem to have taken pity on me to-day. For ostriches are coming passing in front of me; as they have not been doing. Yet these ostriches of which I did not know are coming passing in front of me.'

The power over ostriches ...

!kwi |ne tẽ: ha-ka tʃweŋ, ha-g |ne !kuxe ||kam !ho ||e tóï. Tóï |ne ||nau o tóïja: ||k'oen, ti e:, ha

The man laid his things down, he ran to meet the ostriches. When the ostriches saw that he seemed

-||kwa: |ne k''wãŋ ha ká ha ≠hau tőï, tőï |ne ||khou !ke!ke ha. Ha-g |ne kukú, ha ≠ĩ:, 'Tsˀa -ka: a:, tőï e: sa:, he -||kwaŋ, k''waŋ he kïë ||nau, !gauë ta ti é, he -kɔ́:ɔ̈ sé ŋ, ta:, he -||kwaŋ |ku ||nau, he ||k'oen, ti e:, ŋ dí: he-ka ≠hau, hiŋ -||kwaŋ ||khou !ke!ke ŋ.'

to be going to pass in front of them they appeared to wait for him. He said to himself, 'What can have happened to the ostriches which come, they seem to want to come to me to-day, for when they see that I am going to head them off, they seem to wait for me.'

Ha-g |ne ||kəm !ho ||e: he, ha |ne |xãä !khe ||e, ĩ:, ha-g |ne |kha tőï a: ha !xɔhénja, ha-g |ne ||khou !ho: ha, ha-g |ne !kúïtən ||neiŋ,. Ha-g |ne |k'e:ja ||nein-ta !kˀe ã:, ti e:, ha -||kwaŋ siŋ |ñã: tőï, o ||kőïŋ ta ti e. Tőïtən -||kwaŋ ≠hauwa ha, haŋ -||kwaŋ |kha: tőï a: k''auki ||khɔ ha siŋ ||na tőï kwitən, ta: ha |ku -kõãïŋ.

He went to meet them, he shot at them, he killed an ostrich which was ugly, he put it down, he returned home. He told the people at home about it, how he had seen ostriches to-day. The ostriches had passed in front of him, he had hit an ostrich which did not seem to have been with the others, because it was lean.

Ha: |nu-tara a: e |nu-tara !keri, ha |ne kukú, ha |k'e:, 'A kaŋ k''auki se |kwẽ:ï ku, ta:, a -||kwaŋ siŋ ≠kaka ke, ti e:, a -||kwaŋ hã: siŋ |k'e:ja |əhéere, |əhére -am ≠:ĩ, ti e:, ha -ka: ha ≠ĩ: akən, ha se |k'e: tőï, tőï se dí ku k''wã ≠hanú:wa, o !kˀe; hɛ tikən e:, a k' auki se ≠kakən, ĩ:. Ta:, a |ku se |ki|ki !kˀe e: kíë -tai hĩ a, a se ||a |ã tőï, a se -|kame:ŋ |ki se ha. O !gauxe a:, ha -kõãïn ã:, a se |ki sa: (=|ki se ha) !kauka o ||neiŋ, !kaukən se -||kwa: |ku -am hã: ha, o ha ki sa: -kɔ̃ãïn.'

An old woman who was very old spoke, saying, 'You must not talk like that, for you told me, that you had been telling *|vhere* he should please think favourably and tell the ostriches to behave nicely to the people; therefore you should not talk like that. For you should get people who are willing to go with you, and go to cut up the ostrich and carry it. Even if it is lean, you must bring it home to the children, that they may first eat it, although it is lean.'

|nu-tara |ne kukú, haŋ |k'e:ja !kwi ã:, ha siŋ taŋ-ã: |əhére o tőï, ha |ne ku, ha |k'e:ja ha ã:, 'A xa k''au ≠en-na, ti e:, |nu:-!kˀe e:, hɛ: |xum i, hɛ́ ta -am ¯á hi ã:, tsˀa !ko!kőïŋ a:, ha: !xɔhẽ, o hɛ́ ka, hɛ: se ||k'oen, ti e:, í |nõ siŋ !kẽ:ĩ ||au, í: |xwama hɛ. Hɛ |ne ||nau, hɛ: ||k'oenja ti e:, í: -||kwa: |ne hã: -bai tsˀa !ko!kőïŋ, hɛ |ne !nau, hɛ ¯á hi ã: tsˀa a:, ha: ||kuwa.

The old woman talked to the man who had asked *|vhere* about the ostriches, she said to him, 'Do you not know that the spirit people who take pity on us, first give us something old which is ugly, for they want to see if we were in earnest in our prayer. When they see that we have really eaten up the old thing, later on they give us something fat.

The power over ostriches ...

'O hɛ: /ne //k'oenja, ti e:, i k''auki kweritən tsˀa !ko!kõïŋ, /nu:-!kˀe /ne kukú, he ≠xóä he /ka:gən ã:, ti e:, he _//kwaŋ se ã:, tʃwen se di ku k''wã ≠hanu:wa !kˀe ã:, ta: hɛ _//kwaŋ k''auki kweriten tsˀa !ko!kóïŋ. 'Ta ú ka, u se ã:, tʃweŋ se di ku k''wã ≠hanu-wa hɛ ã:, hɛ-ka _//gauë e:, hɛ _//gauë tʃweŋ e:, hɛ kíë _//gauë hĩ: hɛ, ĩ:. He: siŋ ʀ''wã twai-ĩ, hɛ, kwãŋ //nau, hɛ: _taija, hɛ́ ti, he kwãŋ /nĩ tsˀa a:, ha: _tai sa:, hɛ se /kha ha; tsˀa a siŋ kwãŋ k''wãŋ, ha: k''auki !hɑmĩ:, ti e: !kwi _//kwaŋ sˀɔ /xweri /ki ha, ha: kwãŋ di: ≠gou, o ha k''auki di: !hɑmi.''

'If they see that we do not grumble at the old thing, the spirit people mention to each other, that they may now let the things act nicely towards the people, for they have not grumbled at the old thing. 'Now you shall let the things behave nicely to them, on their hunts, for they are seeking things which they want to eat. They shall be lucky when they walk about here, they shall see something coming that they may kill ; the thing will not seem to be a afraid of the man stealing up to it, it shall be quiet and not be afraid.''

❑

Notes

Title '/*υhére's* "little name" was |Kai kwa. He was a Bushman who could not speak Dutch. He was the brother of Diä!kwain's mother' (4777 rev. note omitted).

38-39 ... *that they may give their children food*: '/*υhére* spoke, and said, that he would not do so, for now he did not possess ostriches; for, he did not know why the people behaved like this, they scolded him, they thought that it was his doing. The people made as if he truly possessed ostriches. He had first thought that the people had not spoken as if he were a man; the people had scolded as if he were a little child' (text omitted, 4785-4787).

70-71 ... *he seemed to be going to pass in front of them* ...: The original translation is rather different – 'he seemed as if he were going to jump (*≠hau*) on the ostrich, the ostrich appears to wait for him' (4793).

92-93 ... *you had been telling /υhére he should please think favourably* ...: '[That he must leave off being angry, and think amiably, etc.]' (4798 rev., note omitted).

105-107 *Do you not know that the* **spirit people** *who take pity on us* ...: In the notebook, */nu:!kˀe* is translated as '[dead] magicians' (4802). In an omitted note, '[D.H. explains that /*υhére* asked his ancestors who had been ostrich sorcerors to help the people]' (4802).

Luck in hunting

Narrator: Diä!kwain
Dictation dates: 23, 28 June 1875
Notebook reference: L.V.11: 4807-4828
***Bantu Studies* reference:** Vol. 9 (1935), Part VII: 40-43

A woman uses a !kwe *stone to improve her husband's luck in hunting. This is a continuation of Diä!kwain's narrative about /υhére, who could control the behaviour of ostriches (see 'The power over ostriches possessed by /υhére').*

❑

Hɛ tikən e:, mama ka siŋ //nau, tata ˍtaija, ha-g /ne !kúïtən se, o ha: k''auki /nã ts?a a:, ha ká ha /ki sa:, si ã:; tata /ne sa, ≠kaka mama ã:, ti e:, ha: ˍ//kwa: siŋ //k'oen, tʃwenjaŋ /ku //nau, o ha !xweri tʃweŋ, tʃweŋjaŋ /ku k''wãŋ, hɛ ≠en-na, ti e:, tata ˍdóä //nã he; k''auki təm⊙pwa !gõä:ĩ:, hɛ /ku k''wãŋ, hɛ ˍtã:, ti e:, tata ˍdóä /xweri /ki hɛ.

This is what mother did when father went out and returned without having seen anything that he could bring us; father used to tell mother how he had seen the things behave, when he was stalking them, they had seemed to know where he was; they kept looking round, they seemed to feel that he was stalking them.

Mama /ne kukú, mamaŋ /k'e:, '!k?e e: ka ˍtauwitən //nã, hɛ taŋ ˍ//kwaŋ e:, //xã:, hɛ ts?ére tʃweŋ, hɛ tikən e:, tʃweŋ /kwe:ĩ k''o, ĩ:. Ta, tʃweŋ ta !kẽ:ĩ ta:, !gi:ta: ts?éreja tʃweŋ, ta:, hɛ e:, tʃweŋ ta /kwẽ:ĩ k''o, ĩ:. Ta:, a ˍ//kwaŋ ka ≠kaka ke ã:, ti e:, a ˍ//kwaŋ //k'oen tʃweŋ, tʃwenjaŋ ˍ//kwaŋ /ku e:, k''auki k''wã ≠hahu:wa.'

Mother spoke, saying, 'The people who work magic there, must have bewitched the things again, that they act like this. For the things act as if sorcerors had bewitched them, they behave like that. For you tell me, you saw the things, and they did not act nicely.'

Mamaŋ /ne kukú, ha /k'e:ja si ã:, mama ká ha se /kwɔbokən, ha se ˍdóä //k'oen, ti e:, ts?a-de /nõ ˍdóä a:, tata /ne ˍtai-ĩ, ha !khe tau !hən,ĩ:, tʃweŋjaŋ k''auki k''wã ≠hanu:wa, o ha !khe tau ˍtai. (I //nau, i: /kwɔbokən, itən taŋ-ĩ, !k?e e: /ki ⊙pwaitən; hɛ tikən e:, i /kwɔbokən,ĩ:, ta:, taŋ-ĩ: ha /ku e.)

Mother told us that she would beat the ground (with a stone), to see what could be the matter, that when father was hunting the things did not act nicely as he stood or walked. (When we beat the ground we beg of the people who own game; that is why we beat the ground, for it is a prayer).

(This beating on the ground is done with a round stone called *//ó-:é*, and sometimes with a *!kwe:*.)

Mama /ne kukú, ha /k'e:ja si e: !kaukən ã: '/ki sou itje !kwe:, ŋ _dóä //k'oen, ti e:, tsʔa-de /nõ _dóä ã:, óä k''auki ta /kwẽ:ï /kwã:, ha /ki sa: hu ã:, _!góë /kwe:, u se kwãŋ xarati //ka !ho ha; hɛ ŋ //kwaŋ _dóä !ku //k'oen, ti e:, óä:ka _tai e:, ha !khe kau _tai, ĩ:, hɛ k''auki _dóä k''wã ≠hanu:wa, ta hɛ /ku _dóä k''wã _/kwãĩ:ĩ.'

Mother said to us children, 'Bring us the digging-stick stone, so that I can find out what is the matter, that father does not do as usual, he brings you an old tortoise, for you to put to roast; then I can find out why father's going, his standing and walking is not successful, but is unlucky.'

Hɛ:, si-ka !khwã: ⊙pwa kɔ:, _//kwaŋ /ne ¯á mama ã:, !kwe:, hɛ mama /kã: !kwe:, ĩ:, hɛ mama _tai /hiŋ //a:,ĩ:, hɛ mama swe:ŋ ⊙ho, ĩ:, hɛ mama kukúïtən /k'e:, ha ká ha //k'oen, ti e:, tsʔa-de /nõ _dóä a:, di:, he tata-ka _tai /ne /kwẽ:ï ú, ĩ:. Hɛ mama //nau, o mamaŋ _!kʔaitən !ho !kwe:, o !kʔãũ, mamaŋ kúï, 'U //kau//kautəntu é: ã, u e: /nu:-!kʔe:, u //kau//kautəntu é: ã, u tsetseja ŋ ĩ:, hɛ é.'

Then one of us, a little child, gave mother the digging-stick stone, and mother took it and went out, and sat down by a bush and said, she would see what was the matter, that made father's going like this. And when mother struck the digging-stick stone on the ground, she said, 'The backs of your heads are here, you who are spirit people have turned your backs on me here.'

Mama /ne kukú ha /k'e:, 'Tsʔa-de /nõ _dóä a:? Ti k''auki _dóä k''wãŋ ŋ /ha _dóä !khe tau _tai, o ti é:, ha _//kwaŋ ka //nau, o ha: /hã: !kauxu, ha _//kwa: sa, ≠kaka ke ã:, ti e:, ha _//kwa: /kəm //a: //khwetən. Hɛ tikən e:, ŋ _//kwaŋ !kẽ:ï //au ŋ //k'oen, ti e:, /nu:-!kʔe: _//kwaŋ tsetseja si. Hɛ tikən e:, ŋ _//kwaŋ ka, ŋ se _am /kwɔbokən, ŋ se //k'oen, ti e:, tsʔa-de /nõ a di:, hɛ ŋ /ha-ka _tai, e:, ha !khe kau _tai, ĩ:, hɛ k''auki /ne k''wã ≠hanu:wa; hɛ:g ŋ k''auki /ne ¯≠en-na tsʔa a: di:.'

Mother spoke, saying, 'What can be the matter? It does not seem as if my husband could hunt here; when he leaves the hunting ground, he has to come and tell me, that he has had to go far. Therefore I truly see that the spirit people have turned their backs on us. So I will just beat the ground to see what is affecting my husband's going, his hunting is not fortunate, and I do not know what is the matter.'

Luck in hunting

Mamaŋ /ne /kwɔboken, hɛ si-g /ne !kʔũ //a:, sitən /ne ũ:ŋ. Hɛ tata /ne //nau, !gauëtən ka ha khwai, tataken /ne !hvn; hɛ tata /ne

Mother beat the ground, and we went back, we lay down to sleep. And when day was about to break father hunted; and as he was

|kɯ ||nau, haŋ _tai ||a:, tóïtən |kɯ !kuxe !ɑhí úï ||neiŋ. Hɛ tata kukúï, haŋ |k'e:, ha _||kwaŋ ta:, ||ka ti e:, ha-ka _tai _||kwaŋ ka |kɯ _am |kwẽ:ï u, ta: tóï _||kwaŋ |kɯ-g |ne dau ú:ï, ti e:, ha siŋ _||kwaŋ _dóä !khe kau _tai hɛ.

going along an ostrich ran past the nest. Then father spoke, saying that he felt his going would be just like that, for the ostrich sprang out from the place where he had meant to walk and stand.

Tata |ne ||khúïtən tóï; tóïja-g |ne !kúïtən se tata, o tóïtən |kɯ k''auki tɑm⊙pwa k''wãŋ ha kɔ:ka !kwitən. Ta:, tóï |kɯ ||nau, _tai a:, ha sa: ã:, haŋ |kɯ _tai !ɑhí !khe sa: ||neiŋ. Haŋ |kɯ !khe kau ⊙mwain-ĩ !kwitji, o haŋ k''auki di: !hɑmi. Haŋ |kɯ ||nau, _!ka_kãnõ e:, tata ||khóä ha ã hɛ, haŋ |kɯ !khe sa:, haŋ |kɯ hĩ: he, o haŋ k''auki ≠ĩ:, ti e:, tsˀa-de |nõ a: _!ka_!kãnõ so: ||neiŋ ã:. Haŋ k''auki |kwẽ:ï dakən ≠ĩ:, haŋ |kɯ ≠ĩ:, ti e:, !kauí a: tóï |aitji sˀɔ a: |kha: ha, ha sˀɔ e.

Father made a screen of bushes near the ostrich; it returned to him, for it seemed to love its eggs very much. For as the ostrich walked, it came past to the nest. It stood fondling the eggs and did not seem to be afraid. When father put down whites of egg for it, it came up and ate them, without thinking that something must be the matter, that whites of egg could be at the nest. It did not think of that, it thought that this seemed to be an egg that the hen ostrich had killed.

Hɛ tata _||kwaŋ |ne ||nau, o haŋ hã: |ki _!ka_!kãnõ, tatakən |xĩ: ha, hɛ, ha ≠ko: siŋ, ĩ:, hɛ ha !kuxe ||a:, ĩ:; he ha !khou !khe, ĩ: hɛ ha te:ŋ, haŋ _tai, o tatakən |ne so ko ||k'oen ha, ti e: ha _||kwaŋ k''wãŋ tata |xã aka ã:.

Then while it was eating the whites of egg, father shot it, and it sprang aside and ran along; then it stood still, it lay down, it walked on, while father sat watching to see whether he seemed to have shot it nicely.

Hɛ tata ||k'oen, ti e:, ha |hiŋ ||a: ||xau, hɛ tata kukúïtən ≠ĩ:, ha ká ha se |hiŋ o ||khú:ï, ta: tóï _||kwaŋ |hiŋ ||a:, hɛ ha k''auki _||kwaŋ _saŋ |nĩ· tata. Hɛ tata |hiŋ o ||khú:ï,ĩ:, hɛ tata _|kame:ŋ |ki |e: !kwitən o ||khú:ï, ĩ, hɛ tata _|kamɛ:ŋ !kwitən kwitən.

Then father saw that it went out of sight, and he thought he would come out of the screen, for the ostrich had gone away and could not see him. So father came out of the screen and carried (some of) the eggs into the screen and brought the other eggs (home).

Hɛ mama kukúïtən |ke:, '||k'oen-yau, tsˀa-diŋ a:? Ti ||khóä óä _|kamɛ:ŋja á:.'

And mother spoke saying, 'Look what is happening? It seems as if father is carrying food.'

Notes

13-14 ... *must have bewitched the things again, that they act like this* ...: '[D.H. explains that / *uhére* was angry because the people had beaten him, and talked badly to him, so he had asked his ancestors that things would not do nicely]' (4809 rev., note omitted).

47-48 *The backs of your heads are here*: 'D.H. explains thus: "They will not turn round, that they might look at us, [to see what we want, or what is happening to us], for, the thing must be so, that they sit with their backs towards us; that is why father's going is like this."' (4815 rev.-4816 rev., note omitted)

81-83 *When father put down whites of egg for it* ...: 'The white things, those which are inside the egg, their name is *!kă-!kannõ*. The name for the yellow part of the inside of the egg is *ǂkarriten*, D.H. says.' (4823 rev., note omitted)

87-89 ... *it thought that this seemed to be an egg that the hen ostrich had killed:* Male and female ostriches take turns in guarding the eggs. The male ostrich is eating the egg whites.

91 ... *father shot it* ...: 'Through a little hole in the bush house. This hole is called *tchwai*.' (4824 rev., note omitted)

The sorceress Tãnõ-!khaukən

Narrator: Diä!kwain

Source: 'Told by Diä!kwain about a great Bushman doctress and sorceress who did not understand Dutch. D.H. saw her, and says that she was the height of his sister !Kweiten tã ||keŋ. She has been a long time dead. She died while !Kweiten tã ||keŋ was a child.'

Dictation dates: 14, 15, 17 and 19 May 1875

Translation dates: 21 May 1875 (4707-4709); 28 May 1875 (vi-4710 rev.); 7 June 1875 (4717-4727); 8 June 1875 (4727-4743)

Notebook reference: L.V. 10: 4707-4743

***Bantu Studies* reference:** Vol. 9 (1935), Part VII: 43-47

With the probable exception of rain-making, post-menopausal women in |Xam society possessed supernatural powers equal to those of men (but see Part VIII, 'How an old woman asked a chameleon for rain'). The last three pages of this narrative, omitted from Bantu Studies, *are included here.*

❑

ŋ !kóïte, há ka siŋ |ɷhéri |e: ha o _||khã, ha _||gauë si, o há ka, ha !|k'oen, ti e:, si |nõ !naunko twaïĩ, si ||na. Ha ||nau, ha: !khouwa si ||neiŋ _|kwˀãĩ, ha-g |ne ||nau, há: !gwe ho ||a: si, ha-g |ne k''wã ku !xwãŋ!xwãŋ _||khã, o há ka, si se tu ha, ti e:, ha: _||kwaŋ a: siŋ _||gauë ã sa:, o si. Hϵ tikən e:, ha ka:g |ne |k'e:ja si ã:, ti e:, ha _||kwaŋ a: siŋ _||gauë:ã sa:, o si.

My aunt used to turn herself into a lioness and seek us, as she wanted to see whether we were still well where we lived. When she smelt the scent of our hut she passed before it and roared like a lioness, because she wanted us to hear her, that it was she who had come to look for us. Then (later) she told us about it, that she had come seeking us.

(Omitted text: 4709-4710)

That is why she did as follows [when] we saw her, she told us that she had been the one who had sought for us; she had, calling, sought us, she whom we had heard; she told us about it, that, she had been the one who had sought for us.

|a:gən k''auki a:, ha siŋ ||a: ã:, ta:, ha _||kwaŋ |kɯ siŋ ká ha !|a !|k'oen, ti e:, sí sˀɔ ||nã he, ti e: tata _tai |ki ||nã si, ĩ:. Hϵ tikən e:, ĩ: ti ||khóä ha ||aŋ _tai !gwe hɔ si ||neiŋ.

Fighting was not the reason why she had gone out, for she had wanted to see where we lived, the place to which father had taken us. That was why she had seemed to pass our hut.

Part VII
Sorcerors

(Omitted text and note: 4711-4712; 4711 rev.)

For, she was wont to do so, when she had wanted to see us, the place which father had taken us to live. Therefore, the thing seemed as if she went walking past our house [It had seemed, because she passed by, as if she had been coming to bite them, D.H. explains, i.e. as if she had been some other 'schelm'].

Hɛ mama |ne ≠kaka ha ã:, ti e:, ha -||kwaŋ se kwãŋ ĩ:, o há ka, ha se kwãŋ ||k'oen, ti e:, si: ||nã he; ha siŋ kwãŋ ⁻≠en-na, ha siŋ ≠ĩ: !hóä o sí; tikəntikən e:, hɛ se dí si, ha siŋ ||k'oenja si ã: hɛ. Ta:, ha -||kwaŋ ka ||nau, ha: ≠kakən s?ɔ mama ã:, ha -||kwa: ≠kaka mama ã:, ti e:, ha -hã: -||kwaŋ ka ≠en-na, ti e:, sí: ||nã hɛ. Hɛ tikən e:, ha k''auki se kwãŋ ≠ĩ:, ≠nã: sísi ĩ:. Ta, ha se kwãŋ -||kwa: |ku ||a ||k'oen si.

And mother said to her, that she should do as she liked, she should look at the place where we were staying, to know and remember about us; the things which happened to us she should look at. (To take away evil). For as she had sat talking to mother, she had said that she now knew where we lived. Therefore she would not forget us. For she would keep going to look at us.

Hɛ tikən e:, ha-g ||nau, whai a: tata |kha: ha, há e |kwi-sa, ha ≠kaka mama ã:, ti e:, há-ka whai e, hɛ tata |kha: he. Haŋ |ne |k'e:ja mama ã:, ti e:, ha -||kwaŋ k''auki -!k''wãĩnja tata o whai Hɛ mama |ne |k'e:ja ha ã:, ti e:, K''obo: ||nau, tata |kha: ha: whai, K''obo: a: taŋtaŋ, o ha -hã: hã: whai a: e |kwi-sa. Haŋ |ne ≠kaka mama ã:, ti e:, whai a e: ||hau-gu, ha tuko e; ha: ha ||hau||hau !ho: ha. Hɛ tikən e:, mama siŋ ||k'oen ti e:, whai a: e dɛbi, ha |ku e; hã:-ka whaitən k''auki e. Ta:, ha ʘpwɔŋ-ka whai |ku e.

Then she spoke about a springbok that father had killed, which was a shorthorned one, she said that it was her springbok which father had killed. She told mother that she was not angry with father about the springbok. Then mother told her, that when father had killed the springbok, *K''obo:* (*Did !kwain's* elder brother) had fallen ill, after eating the short-horned springbok. She told mother that it was really a springbok that she kept tied up. That was why mother had seen that it was castrated; it was not a food springbok. For it was her son's springbok.

Hɛ tikən e:, mama |ne |k'e:ja ha ã:, ti e:, mama -||kwaŋ !k?au |ha: ha ã:, whai |nã:, mamaŋ |ne da: ha ã: !khi:, ĩ:, o mamaŋ ta:, ||ka ti e:, mamaŋ -||kwaŋ ||k'oen, ti e:, whai k''auki ||khɔ whai

Then mother told her that she had cut off the springbok's head for her and had made her a cap of it, because mother felt that she had seen that this springbok was not like the others. That was

Hɛ tikən e:, mama ₋//kwaŋ a, ti e:, mama ká ha se tu why she knew, that she would soon hear a story about it.

(Omitted text: 4720-4722)

Therefore, mamma made a springbok head's cap, on account of it; while mamma felt that she saw that the springbok did not resemble the other springbok. Therefore, mamma thought that she would make a springbok head's cap, that she might put it by, that she might listen whether she would not hear the springbok's story.

whai-ta kum. Hɛ tikən e:, ha ₋//kwaŋ /ne tú:ï whai-ta kum, ĩ:, o ha: k''auki !naunko /nĩ /nu-tara, a:-ka whai e; ŋ !ko:ïŋ /ahére, haŋ /ne ≠kaka mama ã:, ti e:, ₋Tãnõ-!khaukən-ka whai e: ha túï, ti e:, tata /kha: he; ₋Tãnõ-!khaukakən ≠kaka ha ã:, ti e:, tata /kha: ha ʘpwəŋ-ka whai.

Then she had heard about the springbok before she saw the old woman whose springbok it was ; my uncle */khere* had told mother that it was *Tãnõ-!khaukən's* springbok that he heard father had killed, *-Tãnõ-!khaukən* had said father had killed her son's springbok.

(Omitted text: 4723-4724)

And she [the old woman] had said to the people about it, that the people should do as follows when they saw mamma, that they should say to mamma about it, that mamma appeared to think that the springbok which father had killed, her [the old woman's] son's springbok was not.

Whai a: k''auki ka !ahí !khe, haŋ e; ta: whai a /kuı /hiŋ !hãũ, ha /kuı e; whai a: k''auki ₋tai₋taija tiŋ há /kuı e. Ta:, whai a: ka /kuı //hau !khe:, ha /kuı e. Ha /kuı

It was a springbok that did not stand outside, but one that was loosed from a thong, a springbok that did not wander about, but was used to stand tied up.

(Omitted text: 4725-4726)

She now did not scold father about the springbok; but she would have, if it had been a different man, he had been the one who had killed the springbok, she would have been angry. For, a springbok which she did not want to die, it was.

kwere: /hiŋ whai, o !hãũ, haŋ /ke:tən /ki //kó:ë hə whai o whai

She had untied it and sent it in among the other springbok, for she

kuitən, o haŋ ka, whai se /ki //a mama ã:, whai kuitən, o ti e:, mama //nã he. Mama a: siŋ taŋ-ã: ha, o whai, whai se //e ha, ha-g /ne se dí //ka ti e:, ha siŋ /k'e: he. Ha siŋ ka, haŋ /k'e:, ha ˍhã: /ki !kwã: ha ã: whai, mama se hã: whai.

wanted it to take the others to mother, to the place where she lived. Mother had been begging for springbok to go to her, that she would do as she had promised. She had been used to say that she would make the springbok travel to mother for her to eat.

Hɛ ha /ne /k'e:ja mama ã:, ti e:, mama ˍ//kwaŋ dí akən, o ha da: ha ã:, whai /nã:-ka !khi:. Ta: tsˀa-de ˍ//kwaŋ k''auki da:, o mama hã: whai; whai /nã:-ka !khi:tən ˍ//kwaŋ e:, ha /kwẽ:ï /kwãŋ ka mama dá: ha ã he. Ta: ha ˍ//kwaŋ k''auki ká ha se ≠kakən o whai.

Then she told mother, that mother had done well when she had made her a cap of the springbok's head. It did not matter, that she had eaten the springbok, for such a springbok's head cap was just what she wanted mother to make her. Now she would say no more about it.

Haŋ /ne /k'e:ja mama ã:, ti e:, mama //kho kaŋ ≠ĩ:, ha k''au ˍ//kwaŋ ≠en-na, ti e:, tata ˍ//kwaŋ a: /kha: whai; haŋ //xamoke ≠en-na, ti e: K''obo: taŋtaŋ-a, o ha hã: whai. Haŋ ˍ//kwaŋ k''auki ˍ!kãĩnja, o whai, ta:, ha /ku ĩ: a: !kaboka, o ha //k'oenja, ti e:, tata /kha: whai. Hɛ tikən e:, K''obo: /ne taŋtaŋ, ĩ:. Haŋ /ne ˍ//kwaŋ ≠ĩ:, ti e:, ha k''auki se /xãũwa mama ã: K''obo:. Ha siŋ se //nau, !kwi a: /xara, há siŋ a: /kha: whai, haŋ siŋ se //xam di taŋ ha /ĩ:, ha se ≠en, ti e:, ha k''auki se /kha whai ã: /kwẽ:ï /kwãŋ /kwãĩja.

She said to mother, mother need not think she had not known that it was father who had shot the springbok; she had also known that *K''obo:* was ill after eating of the springbok. She had not been angry about the springbok, but she had been startled when she saw that father had killed it. That was why *K''obo:* was taken ill. She thought she would not really take *K''obo:* away from mother She would have done so, if anyone else had killed the springbok, she would have made his heart ache too, to let him know not to kill such a springbok.

(Omitted text: 4731-4733)

For he should have done as follows, [when] he saw such a springbok, he should, looking, leave it alone; for it is not one (i.e. not the only one available to shoot – ed.), for springbok are plentiful; and such a springbok, it walks among them. Therefore, he does as follows, [if] he even sees that a springbok is handsome, he looking, leaves it, while he does not shoot it; for, he will shoot a different springbok, while he does not shoot a springbok which is short-horned, even if it be handsome. For, he looking, leaves it alone.

Hɛ |nu-tara |ne kukúï, haŋ |k'e:ja mama ã:, mama -||kwaŋ siŋ |k'e:ja ha ã:, ha |ki !kwã: mama ã: whai, mama se |nĩ hã:. Ta:, mama -||kwaŋ |gauka, ha |xum mama, ha se ã:, whai se !kwã: ha ã:, ha se hã: whai.

Then the old woman said to mother, that mother had been asking her to let the springbok travel, that mother might have food. So as mother had begged, she would take pity on mother and let the springbok come to her, that she might eat springbok.

(Omitted text: 4735-4737)

For, mamma wanted springbok's flesh, mamma wanted that mamma should eat springbok. Therefore, mamma was asking her for springbok; that she [would] first make the springbok to travel for mamma. And the old woman spoke, she said to mamma about it, how was it that mamma seemed [to think] that the springbok would truly, the springbok travel.

Hɛ |nu-tara |ne kukúï, haŋ |k'e:ja mama ã:,

Then the old woman said,

'-≠kame-aŋ-we:, |ne |kã: ŋ-ka !khi: |kwe:, a se |ki|ki he, a se ||k'oen, ti e:, whai |nõ k''au se !gauökən !khi:, ti e:, !khi: ||aŋ ||nã he. A se |kɯ -||kwa: ||a -tai ||na||na, a:ka !xóë e:, á ka -tai ||nã he; a siŋ |kɯ -tai ||nã, a: siŋ |kɯ ||k'oen, ti e:, whai a: !kwai, ha-g |nõ k''au se ||khou ≠ka:, a se |nĩ ha, o ti e: a ||aŋ -tai ||nã he; a se-g |ne |kɯ ||k'oen, ta: a -||kwaŋ |k'e:, ŋ -hã: ã: whai !kwã:, akən |ne !xwãŋ, ŋ sʔo !kẽ:ï ||au, ŋ |ki whai, ŋ |ne e whai-ta !gi:xa.'

'O -≠*kame-an*, take my old cap, keep it and see whether the springbok do not follow the cap to the place to which it goes. You must go and stay at your home, where you usually walk about, you must look whether one springbok will not appear, you will see it where you are walking about; you must keep on looking (for others), for you say, I must let the springbok travel, you believe that I really own springbok, that I am a springbok's sorceress.'

(Omitted text: 4741-4743. These three pages of the text were omitted from *Bantu Studies*.)

And mamma spoke, she said to her about it [that] she [the old woman] should not speak thus; for, she should now think that mamma had little children; they were those of whom she [the old woman] must therefore think; that she should therefore allow that the springbok should travel for the children, that the children might get food from mamma. For, she knew that mamma had no flocks ['*vie*' i.e. means here sheep, goats. N.B. 20/09/1904. I took down what

the narrator said, phonetically, as nearly as I could; but, I see, in the Dutch dictionary, that, *vee* is given for 'cattle']' (4741 rev., note); therefore, she [mamma] wished that she [the old woman] would therefore think that springbok were those which mamma was used to eat, mamma did not possess things which mamma was used to kill, feeding herself with them. For, these springbok, they were those of which mamma made her flocks.

❑

Notes

1-2 *My* **aunt** *used to turn herself into a lioness…*: 'The word (i.e. *!koïte*) stands here for a first cousin once removed. D.H. says that she was his maternal grandmother's niece; her name was *Tãnõ-!khauken*.' (vi, note omitted).

32 *(To take away evil)*: 'i.e. That she might take away evil from them' (4713 rev.).

30-32 *… the things which happened to us she should look at*: (4713 rev., note omitted):

Mamma told us about it that she (i.e. *Tãnõ-!khauken* – ed.) now should therefore, look, seeking us where she wanted that she might therefore look for us at the things which would happen to us, that she might look at us about them. This was why she now should therefore look seeking us.

46-47 *K"obo: (Diä!kwain's elder brother)*: (4716 rev., note abbreviated in *Bantu Studies):*

[whose Boer name was 'Jacob', an elder brother of David's, he was living with Abraham van Wyk at Nieuwe Post in Hantam [?] when D.H. went back to Bushmanland in 1874; but before D.H.'s arrival at Nieuwe Post he had gone with the sheep to Bushmanland for a time.]

106-108 *… a springbok's head cap was just what she wanted mother to make her*: '[She was well satisfied about it, D.H. explains]' (4726 rev., note omitted).

120-121 *She thought she would not really take K"obo: away from mother…*: '[by killing him, in this instance]' (4728 rev., note omitted).

125-126 *… to let him know not to kill such a springbok*: 'Her "heart's" springbok it had been, so she would have made the man who had killed it feel also, had it been a different man who had done the action.' (4729 rev., note omitted)

PART VIII

MORE ABOUT SORCERORS AND CHARMS

From material collected by
Dr. W.H.I. BLEEK and Miss L.C. LLOYD between 1870 and 1880,
edited by D.F. Bleek

Photo: Jeremy Hollmann

'The people speak thus when they describe what she used to do, they say when they have done talking about her name, that they wish the camelthorn tree would hold the woman fast. For she was an old woman who had her nose, she knew things.' Acacia tree, Katkop Hills, Northern Cape Province.

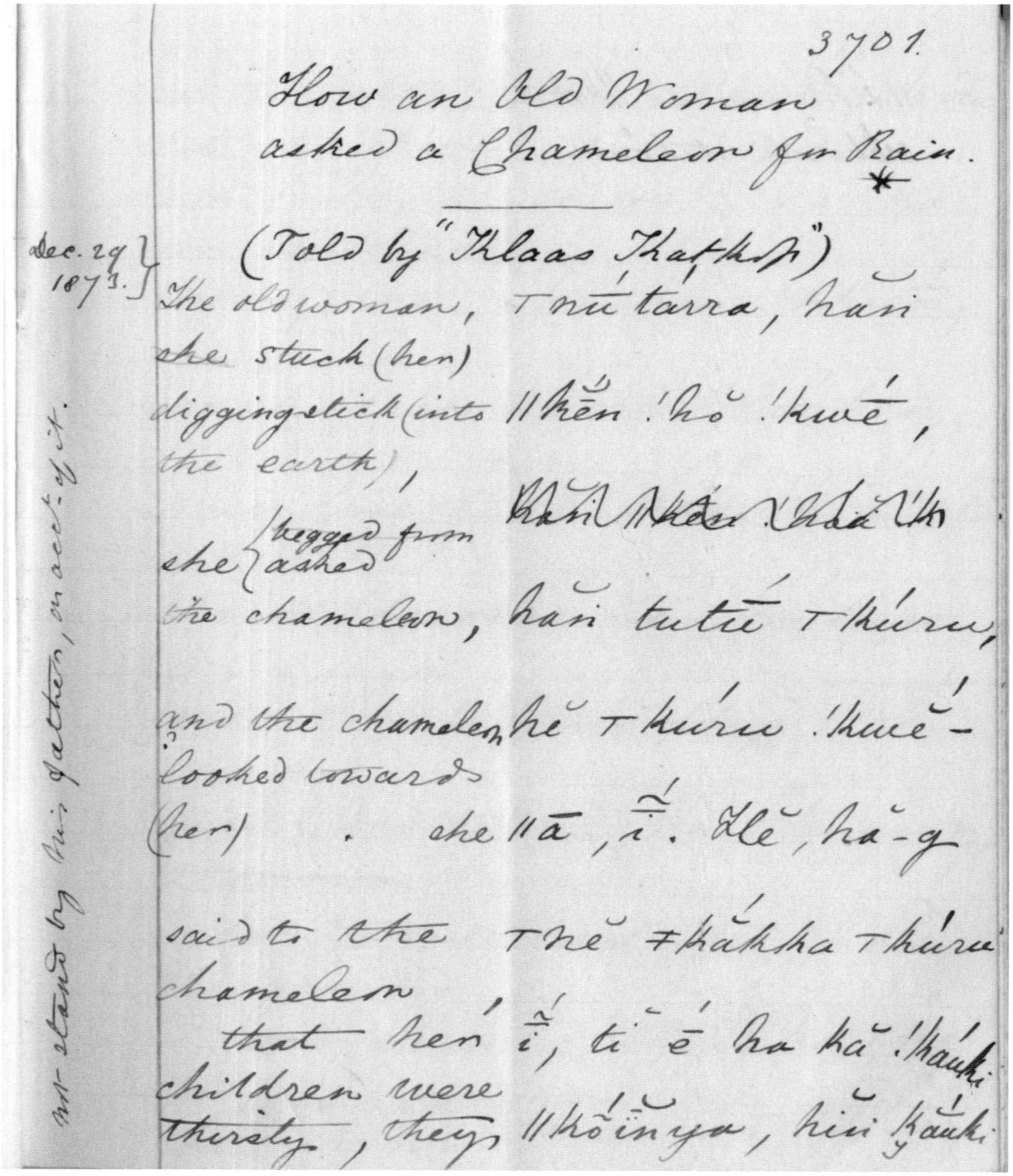

3701.

How an Old Woman
asked a Chameleon for Rain. *

(Told by "Ӏklaas Ӏkaṭkoṗ")

Dec. 29} 1873.} The old woman, ⊤nŭ tarra, hañ
she stuck (her)
digging stick (into ‖kĕn !hō̆ !kwē,
the earth),
she {begged from / asked} hañ ‖kéo !khā ǀk
the chameleon, hañ tutŭ ⊤kúru,

and the chameleon hĕ ⊤kúru !kwē-
looked towards
(her). she ‖ā, ī. ǀlĕ, hă-g

said to the ⊤nĕ ǂkăkka ⊤kúru
chameleon,
that her ī, ti ē ha kă !kauki
children were
thirsty, they ‖kō̆ĭnya, hĭñ kauki

m stands by his father, on acct. of it.

Notebook page from L.IV.3: 3701, 'How an Old Woman asked a Chameleon for Rain'

PART VIII
MORE ABOUT SORCERORS AND CHARMS

People were those, who broke for me the string
– Diä!kwain: 'The sorceror !Nuiŋ-|kúïtən' –

Of the eight parts of |Xam Bushman beliefs and customs published in *Bantu Studies,* three of them – Parts VI, VII and VIII – are entirely devoted to the activities of *!gi:tən*, who make rain, heal and control game. The Part VIII narratives focus on accounts of *!gi:tən*, whom Diä!kwain and |Haŋ‡kass'o knew, an intriguing story by ‡Kasiŋ about rain-making, and descriptions by ||Kabbo of a mysterious plant with potent properties.

Some of the narratives refer to aspects of *!gi:tən*'s behaviour already mentioned (see Parts II, V, VI and VII). For instance, !Gverritən-dé – like the sorceress Tãnõ-!khaukən (Part VII) – is a 'springbok sorceror' (*wai-ta!gi:xa*) and wears a scalp cap made of springbok skin; both *!gi:tən* claim to control the behaviour of springbok. The renowned rain-maker, !Nuiŋ-|kúïtən, like Tãnõ-!khaukən, can turn himself into a feline – they transform into felines and 'go about' (*taiya*) at night (see Part II, Introduction, and Part VII, for narratives about transformation into a lion).

The breaking of the string

In addition to these accounts, Dorothea Bleek included new material in Part VIII. Diä!kwain relates a song about *!nũ:ïŋ*, the string, that his father, Xã:ätiŋ, sang after the death of !Nuiŋ-|kúïtən, his teacher. !Nuiŋ-|kúïtən died at the hands of a Boer commando – the people in the song have 'broken the string' by killing him (see 'The sorceror !Nuiŋ-|kúïtən'). !Nuiŋ-|kúïtən's death changes Xã:ätiŋ's perception of life – the 'place' seems 'open' and it no longer feels *‡hannũwa*, a word variously translated as 'comfortable', 'happy', 'good', 'nice' and 'fortunate' (Bleek 1956: 650). |Haŋ‡kass'o mentions a similar instance in Part III, 'Hunting after the death of a friend' – hunters experience a time when things are not *‡hannũwa* after their friend's death; they miss their aim and the springbok they shoot are not easily wounded.

Xã:ätiŋ used to hear the string 'ringing', *//ka//kauïŋ*, when !Nuiŋ-|kúïtən 'called forth' a rain-animal. After !Nuiŋ-|kúïtən's death, however, he no longer hears the sound of the string in the sky. In addition to hearing the string, Xã:ätiŋ also felt it as 'vibrations', *darrakəndarrakən*, in his body (see 'What Xã:ätiŋ used to sing'). The vibrations stop when !Nuiŋ-|kúïtən dies. The string and its strange properties could be a reference to the thong (*!hãu*) that a rain-maker uses to control a rain-animal. In Part VI, 'The breaking of the thong', people realise that the thong is broken when they hear a 'ringing sound' *//ka//kauïŋ*, the same word that Xã:ätiŋ uses – in the sky. Another narrative relates how a *!gi:tən*'s heart, in the form of a star, makes the same sound when it falls into the waterhole (see Part VII, 'Falling stars and sorcerors').

But how do we explain Xã:ätiŋ's experience of the string vibrating in his body? Elsewhere, ||Kabbo uses the same word, *darrakən*, to describe sensations that he knew foretold the arrival of many springbok, an event subsequently confirmed by children sent up a hilltop to look out for game (Bleek & Lloyd 1911: 330-339). In an effort to explain these presentiments to Bleek and Lloyd, ||Kabbo – himself a *!gi:xa* – said that they were the Bushman peoples' letters. He explained that the 'tapping' of which he spoke was, like writing, a way of communicating things to those who had developed the necessary skills. (Diä!kwain discusses presentiments in Part VII, 'Note on *hõũŋ'*.) The string is thus part of the network that connected *!gi:tən* to each other, as well as to rain-animals and game, in extraordinary ways.

The supernatural properties of the string in Xã:ätiŋ's account – its ringing sound and its vibrations – suggest that they might have their origins in altered states of consciousness, as do the ropes or threads that Ju|'hoansi ritual practitioners in the Kalahari see during the healing dance, and along which they travel to visit God's house (Marshall 1962: 242; Biesele 1993: 72; Katz et. al. 1997: 80-81, 108; Keeney 1999: 61-62, 105). These accounts, in turn, have provided rock art researchers with clues to the meanings of Bushman engravings and paintings of the line motif – the lines link images of *!gi:tən*, rain-animals and game (Lewis-Williams et. al. 2000), thus performing a similar connective function as the string described in the |Xam narratives.

The old woman and the chameleon

Unlike the stories in Part VIII by Diä!kwain and |Haŋ‡kass'o, which concern flesh-and-blood *!gi:tən*, many elements in the narrative 'How an old woman asked a chameleon for rain' by ‡Kasiŋ, Diä!kwain's brother-in-law, suggest that the unnamed characters in this tale were never actual, living people. The narrative belongs, rather, in the category of story in the Bleek and Lloyd Collection that Roger Hewitt argues is similar to that of Western legends (Hewitt 1986: 48). Stories of this kind feature 'human beings and often appear … to be set in an immediate historical past' (see also Schmidt, 1996: 118-120).

To begin with, the story is too densely packed with curious events relating to rain-making rituals and other beliefs about !Khwa: to be anecdotal. Some of these elements are pointed out in the notes to the narrative. But if the people in the story are not real, then who are they? The clue to their identity lies in the ways they do things – their behaviour contravenes |Xam norms. For example, it is an old woman, not an old man, who calls the rain, the only instance in the entire BLC, as far as I am aware, in which a female performs this ritual (see Parts V and VI for stories about rain-making). The episode in which the little children sniff the springbok bush, causing their noses to bleed, is another inversion of conventional behaviour. Adults, not children induce nosebleeds as part of healing activities (see Part VII for more about nosebleeds and healing; Butler 1997 for discussion of the springbok bush and nosebleeds).

These details therefore suggest that the people in the story are indeed *!Xwe:-/na-se-!kˀe*, the 'first-there-sitting-people' or – in Lucy Lloyd's phrase – Early Race people, who predate the |Xam's existence (see Introductions to Parts I and II, and 'Special speech').

Vegetable medicines and charms

Although plants are vital sources of food and medicine, the |Xam teachers say little about them. They mention trees and bushes, as well as staple foods such as the wild onion (see Part VI, 'Leading out the rain-animal') and the gambro (see Part V, 'Drought'). The *!kuisi* plant (an edible bulb), features in an Early Race story in which a girl throws up a handful of their roots, which turn into locusts; in another tale, a man turns into a tree (Lewis-Williams 2000: 271-272, 277). Overall, however, descriptions of plants and their uses are lacking. Under these circumstances, |Kabbo's observations about the *ʃo-/õä* plant, which cover 85 notebook pages, are all the more valuable.

ʃo-/õä was men's medicine, a charm used by hunters to make the springbok 'foolishly afraid', thus making it easier for them to get close to the animals before shooting off an arrow. The use of *ʃo-/õä* also helped an arrow to 'fly well at the springbok' (see '*ʃo-/õa*, a vegetable medicine or charm'). Hunters always carried some *ʃo-/õä* in a band (*!hum*) when the springbok migrated through |Xam-ka !aũ, so that the springbok would smell its scent on the hunters' bodies. Men also used *ʃo-/õä* when fighting each other (see 'When Bushmen are angry ...').

The roots of the *ʃo-/õä* plant are used to make medicine – people dig them out and cut them up into sections about 300 mm (12 inches) long before packing them into an old bag. The roots must not come into contact with meat – people who eat meat contaminated with *ʃo-/õä* die: 'their stomachs swell up and they die because they cannot breathe properly' (see 'More about *ʃo-/õä*'). The plant may therefore contain highly active biological compounds. Since *ʃo-/õä* could apparently not be eaten, it was administered by rubbing the juice of the root on the skin, or by chewing and then spitting out a piece of root, or by introducing it into the bloodstream through cuts made on the arms and face for this purpose.

There were many strictures around the harvesting of *ʃo-/õä* and its subsequent treatment. *ʃo-/õä* roots could only be safely dug out by a '*ʃo-/õä*'s man', someone who 'spoke the *ʃo-/õä*'s language' (see 'The man who misused *ʃo-/õä*'). Women had first to be introduced to recently harvested *ʃo-/õä*, and were required to walk downwind of a hanging bag containing fresh *ʃo-/õä* roots (see 'Women fear the new *ʃo-/õä*').

Remarkably, however, despite its extraordinary properties, the *ʃo-/õä* plant has not yet been identified, even though ||Kabbo provides enough information about the plant's appearance and habitat to make a preliminary identification possible. He reports that the plant grows on the 'Orange River's mountains', often at the base of *haakdoorn* bushes alongside streambanks, as well as under larger trees along rivers (see 'More about *ʃo-/õä*'). The stems, which are green and brittle, scramble into the higher bushes and trees around them and can cover the entire canopy of a tree. The roots of the plant are a reddish colour (see 'More about *ʃo-/õä*').

One plant matches this description of the plant, its habitat and distribution closely; known variously as 'old man's beard' in English, and as 'kleefgras' (clinging-grass) and 'rooivergeet' (literally, red-forget) in Afrikaans, its botanical name is *Galium tomentosum* Thunb. (Rubiaceae) (Van Wyk, email communication 17 July 2002). The plant has a woody rootstock from which sprout several slender, much-branched green stems up to 3 m long; these scrambling stems easily cover an entire tree (Shearing 1997: 144; Puff, 1986: 68-69). The plant's habitat and distribution fits that of *ʃo-/õä* – it occurs in streams and rocky valleys in the mountains south of the Orange River and elsewhere. The plant is used medicinally by Nama people (Archer 1990; 1994), and was reported by Kiewiet Danster, a farm worker of Bushman descent in the Eastern Cape Karoo, to have medicinal properties, being especially useful in remedying backache (Shearing, email communication 31 July 2002).

The name 'old man's beard' refers to the white and fluffy flower stalks that hang from female plants 'like hanks of wool' (Dean & Milton 1991: 83). The name 'kleefgras' comes from an obvious characteristic of the plant which ||Kabbo does not mention – each leaf has a small, backward-curving spine on its tip, which grips onto skin and clothing, and causes the sensation of stickiness (Shearing 1997: 144). ||Kabbo was not a *ʃo-/õä*'s man, however, and he may not have been told about this characteristic; furthermore, the plants vary in their degree of stickiness (Puff 1978: 26), so this may not have been a prominent feature of the plants with which ||Kabbo's informants were familiar. The first part of its other Afrikaans name, 'rooivergeet', probably refers to the red colour of the roots upon which ||Kabbo remarked. The second part of the name, 'forget', is intriguing – does it refer to the same properties that made the springbok foolishly afraid? Having tentatively identified the plant as *Galium tomentosum*, further ethnobotanical and pharmacological investigations are needed to answer these questions.

The sorceror !Nuiŋ-|kúïtən

Narrator: Diä!kwain
Source: 'This was told to Diä!kwain by his father Xã:ätiŋ
Dictation dates: 26, 27 July 1875
Translation dates: 30 July 1875 (5079-5085); 3 August 1875 (5085-5095); 20 October 1875 (5095-5098)
Notebook reference: L.V.15: 5079-5103
***Bantu Studies* reference:** Vol. 10 (1936), Part VIII: 130-134

In this much quoted narrative, Diä!kwain tells us more about this powerful sorceror (see Part VI, '!Nuiŋ-/kúïtən, a rain medicine man'). Before he died of gunshot wounds, he made Xã:ätiŋ, Diä!kwain's father, promise certain things. See the Introduction for more about the 'string' that he mentions.

❑

He was a friend of *Díä!kwain's* paternal grandfather, and was seen by *Díä!kwain's* father, Xã*:ä-tiŋ*, when the latter was a young man. He taught *Xã:ä-tiŋ* about the Rain's things.

Tata kaŋ ka siŋ ka: ≠kaka ke, !nuiŋ-/kúïtən _hã ka //nau //k'e: a: ha dí _//khã: ã:, ha: _tai twãnna o /kukən.

My father used to tell me what *!nuiŋ-/kúïtən* used to do when he became a lion, he walked treading upon hair (lion's hair).

He tikən e:, !kˀe _hã: ka siŋ //nau, he: tã: ha !nwa, hɛ //nau, hɛ: /k'e:ja hɛ /ka:gən ã:, hɛ kukú, hɛ /k'e:ja hɛ /ka:gən ã:, '!nuiŋ-/kúïtən kaŋ //kho: á:, siŋ _tai /kãä //a:, ti é: a; ta: u _//kwaŋ /kɯ e: //k'oen, o ti e:, ha _//kwaŋ _tai o /kukən. Ta: ti _//kwaŋ //kho, ha á: !kerri, ha á: siŋ _tai //a: o ti é. Ha //kho: siŋ _tai //k'oen !xóë, ti e: !xóë /kwẽï u, ĩ:. Ta: há ka !kẽï ta:, há ka ha //k'oen tikəntikən ; o ha-g /ne /kwẽï /kwe/kwẽ, i-g /ne tã: ha !nwa, o há: _tai /kãä //a: hɛ́: ti.'

That was why the people used, when they saw his spoor, to speak to each other about it, they spoke, saying to each other, '*!nuiŋ -/kúïtən* seems to have walked passing along here ; for ye can see that he has been walking upon hair. For it looks as if someone big has gone along here. He seems to have gone to look at the place, to see what the place is like. For he does so, when he wants to look at places; when he acts thus, we see his spoor, as he walks about at this place.'

Tatakən kaŋ ≠kaka ke, ti e:, !nuiŋ-!kúïtən e !kwi á: _tai o //kuõnna, ha k''auki é. Ta: ha /kɯ

My father used to say to me, that *!nuiŋ-/kúïtən* is not a man who walks in the daytime. For he

-tai o //ga:, o haŋ ta: //ka ti é:, ha /ki k''auki e //ẽĩŋ !kwi; o haŋ !hummi, ti e:, ha -óä /ne se /kha !kwi, o !kʔeja /xãä ha. He tikən e:, ha k''auki ≠kauwa, !kʔe se //k'uerre ha, o !kʔeja: /na: ha. He tikən e:, ha -!xẽĩ: ha !kauügən, ĩ:, o haŋ ta:, //ka ti e:, ha-g //nau, !kʔeja: //k'uerreja ha, haŋ -ó:ä /ne /ki taŋ-taŋ !kwi tũ:.

goes by night, because he feels that he is not a patient man; so he fears that he might kill a man, if the people were to shoot at him. Therefore he does not want people to attack him, if they see him. Therefore he hides his (lion's) body, for he feels that if the people were to attack him, he would hurt the people.

Hɛ !kʔe /ne /k'e: ha, ti e:, tsʔa de /nõ a:, ha-g /ne /kwẽĩ /kwãŋ dí: ã:? o ti e:, ha -am ka /k'e:, ti e:, ha k''auki -tai-ã tiŋ, há siŋ dí /a:. Ta:, há /kɯ -taija tiŋ, há siŋ //k'ɔen !kʔe kuitən ɛ́: -taija tiŋ, hɛ́ kɛí /khi: !kʔe; hiŋ /kɯ e:, há ka -tai //k'ɔen-ã tiŋ, ĩ:, o háŋ ta: //ka ti e:, !kʔe kuitən ka //nau, o hɛ́: /nã: !kʔe-ta //neiŋ, hɛ !ke //e hɛ o //ga:, hɛ /kãä /hiŋ !kwi o //neiŋ. Hɛ tikən e:, ha ≠ĩ: hɛ.

Then the people ask him, why he has acted in this manner? because he had been wont to say, that he would not go about in order to fight. For he would go about looking at the other people who walked about; those who wanted to kill people were those for whom he went looking about, for he felt that if they saw men's huts, they would go to them at night, to take someone out of the hut. This was what he thought about.

Hɛ tikən e:, ha ka -tai, ha: siŋ //k'ɔen !kʔe kuitən, ĩ:. Ta: !kʔe kuitən k''auki ka -tai akka tiŋ: ta:, hɛ ka /kɯ -tai dí-ã tiŋ. Hɛ k''auki -tai akka tiŋ hɛ́ se akkənxa se !kúïtən.

This was why he had gone, that he might look at the other people. For these used not to go about nicely, they used to go about doing harm. They did not go about nicely, that they might return peacefully.

Hɛ tikən e:, ha //nau, o ha /xãũŋ-a, há: /ne /nĩ /hũ-ka xɔro, o haŋ e -//khã, ha-g /ne /kha /hũ:ka xɔro. /hũwã: /ne /nĩ ti e:, ha /kha: xɔro, /hũwã: /ne k''ao ha, /hũ: wã: /ne //a: /xã-a ha. Haŋ /k'e:ja tata ã:, ti e:, tata //kho: kaŋ ≠ĩ:, /hũ: k''au !xauru:ka ha. Hɛ tikən e:, ta:ta //kho kaŋ ≠ĩ:, ti k''au taŋ ha se /ku:kən o /xã/xã a: !kʔe /xã: ha ã: ; ta:, hɛ́ ti hɛ e:, ha ≠kaka tata ã:, ĩ:, o haŋ ta: //ka ti e:, ha tã:-ĩ ha.

Then when he was on a magical expedition, he saw a Boer's ox, while he was a lion, he killed the Boer's ox. The Boer discovered that he had killed the ox, and raised a "commando" against him, went to shoot at him. He told father about it, as father seemed to think that the Boer had not wounded him. That was why father seemed to think that it did not look as if he would die of the shots which people had fired at him; but all this he told my father for he felt that he was suffering.

Hɛ tikən e:, ha ≠kaka tata ã:, ĩ:, ta:, ha k''auki ≠enna, ti e:, tata |nõ se ||xã:, tata |nĩ ha; ta:, ti |ku taŋ ha se |ku:kən o tata k''auki ||xã:, ha |nĩ ha. Hɛ tikən e:, ha ≠kaka tata, ĩ:, tata siŋ ≠enna. Ta:, |hũ: tuko ˍ||kwaŋ ˍdóä |xã: ha, hɛ tikən e:, tí taŋ ha xwaitən |ku:ka, o ||k'e: ko:. Haŋ |k'e:ja tata ã:, ti e:, tata ||kho: kaŋ ≠ĩ:, ha k''au |ku durru !kúĩ-ta ha-g ||neiŋ, ta: !kˀe ˍ||kwaŋ siŋ kɛ́: |kha kwɔkwáŋ ha. Haŋ |km ||nau, ti e:, ha a: ||khouken !kˀe: hɛ tikən e:, tí ||kho !kˀe !hammĩ xu: ha, ĩ:, ta:, !kˀe ˍ||kwaŋ siŋ kɛ́: |kha kwɔkwáŋ ha.

This was why he spoke to father about it, for he did not know whether father would see him again; for it seemed as if he would die without father seeing him again. These things he told father, so that father might know. For a Boer had really just shot him, so he seemed likely to die suddenly at another time. He said to father, that father seemed to think he had not limped home, but the people had really tried to kill him. He however had driven the people away, therefore it seemed as if the people had been afraid and left him, for they had really been trying to kill him.

Tá:takən ≠kaka ke, ti e:, ha ˍhã: |kwẽĩ ku, ha ≠kaka tata ã:, o haŋ ˍó: se !kẽĩ ||ou, ha |ku:kən. Ha ˍhã: |kwẽĩ ku, ha: ≠kaka tata ã:, o ||k'e: a: ha ˍó: se |ku:kən ã:, haŋ a:, ha ≠kaka tata ¯ã:, ã: ; ti e:, ha |kwẽĩ taŋ, tã: ha eŋeŋ, ĩ:. Hiŋ e: ha ≠kaka tata ã:, ĩ:; o haŋ ka, tata siŋ ≠enna. Ta ha ≠ĩ, ti e:, ha xwaitən ˍtai xu: tóä tata. Hɛ tikən e:, ha ≠kaka tata ã:, ĩ:, o tã:tã: a: ha tã:-ĩ ha ã:, haŋ |ku a:, ha ≠kaka tata, tata siŋ ≠enna; ta ha ˍdóä tã:-ĩ ha; tikən ˍ||kwaŋ taŋ, o ha tã:-ĩ ha; tikən ˍ||kwaŋ taŋ, ha xwaitən ˍtai, xu: tóä tata.

Father told me that he (*!Nuiŋ-|kúĩ-tən*) had spoken in this manner to father, when he was truly about to die. He said this to father at the time when he was going to die, then it was he told father how he was suffering in his body. That was what he told father about, as he wanted father to know. For he thought that he should soon go, leaving father. Therefore he told father about the pain which he was suffering, that was what he told father, that father might know; for he was suffering; things felt as if he were suffering; things felt as if he must soon go, leaving father.

Ta:, ha ˍ||kwaŋ ka sín ka ha !xãũ tata, ha se ||xa||xa: tata, o há-ka didi:, e: ha di: hɛ. Hɛ tikən e:, tata se ||nau, tikəntikən ɛ́:, ha ¯óä ||xa:-||xa: tata, ĩ:, tata k''auki se ≠na: hɛ, tata siŋ kwãŋ ≠ĩ: hɛ, o ti e: tata ˍtai ||na hɛ. Tata se kwãŋ ||nau, ||k'e: kɔ:, tata se kwãŋ |ku !hãũ !kuttən!kuttən a: ha ¯o: ||xa:-

For he wanted to take father with him, to teach father about his magic, which he worked. Then father would know the things which he had taught father, father would not forget them, father would go on thinking of them, where father walked among them. At another time father must sing the songs

//xa: tata ã:, haŋ a:, tata se kwãŋ !kutta.

which he had taught father, then father must sing about him.

Hɛ tikən e:, tata siŋ //nau, tata !kuttən, tata ka: /k'e:,

That was what father did sing about, father said,

'!kʔe kaŋ ˍdóä e:,
!kən !kwa: ka: !nũ:ïŋ.
Hέ tikən e:,
Tí /ne /kwẽ úä ka:,
ĩ:,
O !nũ:ïŋ a: ˍdóä !kwa: ka:.

'People were those,
Who broke for me the string.
Therefore,
The place became like this to me,
On account of it,
Because the string was that which broke for me.

Hέ tikən e:,
Tí-g /ne k''auki taŋ-a ka:,
Tí ka siŋ /kwẽï tã: ka:,
ĩ.
Ta:,
Tí /ku-g /ne tã bo:kən !kheja ka:,

Therefore,
The place does not feel to me,
As the place used to feel to me,
On account of it.
For,
The place feels as if it stood open before me,

O !nũ:ïŋ a: !kwa: ka:.

Because the string has broken for me.

Hέ tikən e:,
Tí k''auki /ne tã ≠hannũwa ka:,

Therefore,
The place does not feel pleasant to me.
On account of it.'

❑

Notes

6-7 … *he walked treading upon hair (lion's hair)*: '[The hair of the lion's own feet]' (viii, note omitted).

25-26 … *he feels that he is not a patient man* … : 'i.e. he becomes quickly angry' (5083 rev., note omitted).

27-28 … *if the people were to shoot at him*: Diä!kwain is probably referring to other sorcerors, as well as to evil spirits that shoot sickness into people using magic arrows. See Part VII, 'Invisible arrows and their cure'.

33-34 … *he would hurt the people*: The phrase */ki taŋtəŋ*, given as 'hurt', is better translated as 'make the people sick'.

39-41 *For he would go about looking at the other people who walked about* … : !Nuiŋ |kuïtəŋ apparently protected people from other sorcerors who walked about at night.

54-55 *Then when he was on a magical expedition ...* : David Lewis-Williams has argued that the word */xãũŋ*, here translated as 'magical expedition', describes a form of out-of-body travel (Lewis-Williams 1981: 95). See Part VII for more narratives where this technique is mentioned.

61-63 *... father seemed to think that the Boer had not wounded him*: '"*kwess* for [h]im", "*Kwetsen*" to wound' (Diä!kwain used the Dutch word for 'wound' here – ed.). (5089 rev., note omitted).

104-105 *For he wanted to* **take** *father with him, to teach father about his magic*: The word *!xãũ*, here translated as 'take', may also be translated as 'carry away'. It seems that dead sorcerors would attempt to carry off with them those people that they liked (see Part VII; also the story, 'Concerning two apparitions' in Bleek & Lloyd 1911: 364-371).

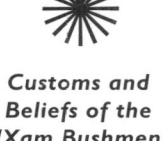

What Xã:ätiŋ used to sing

Narrator: Diä!kwain
Source: 'Diä!kwain tells this about one of the songs which his father used to sing'
Dictation date: 28 July 1875
Notebook reference: L.V.15: 5104-5109
***Bantu Studies* reference:** Vol. 10 (1936), Part VIII: 134-135

Diä!kwain's father is mourning the death of !Nuiŋ/kúïtən, his mentor. He is comforted when !Nuiŋ/kúïtən visits him one night and reassures him of his presence and support. For more about this narrative, see the Introduction.

❑

Tata kaŋ ˉo: kaŋ !kuttən !nũ:ïŋ _dóä a: !kwa:; !nũ:ïŋ a:, ha ka siŋ tú:ï ha, o !nuiŋ-/kúïta: //kãĩ /ki //a:, o !khwa:-ka xɔrɔ. Hɛ́ tikən _dóä e:, tí k''auki /ne taŋ ti e:, ti ˉóä /kwẽï tã, ĩ:.

Father used to sing, that the string had broken; that string was what he used to hear, when !nuiŋ-/kúï:təŋ had called forth the Rain-bull. That was why things were not like they had formerly been.

'Ta:, ti /kɯ-g /ne _!kwãĩ-ĩja ka: ŋ k''auki /ne tú:ï //ka _//kauïŋ a:, ŋ ka siŋ tú:ï ha. N ta: //ka ti e:, !nũ:ïŋ _//kwaŋ tuko _dóä a:, !kwa: xu: tóä ŋ. Hɛ́ tikən e:, ŋ́ ka-g /ne ʘpuoin, ŋ k''auki /ne tã: tsˀa a:, há: ka ha-g /ne /ki _darrakən-_darrakən ŋ, o ka: /e: ta: ʘpuoin.

'For things continue to be unpleasant to me; I do not hear the ringing sound (in the sky) which I used to hear. I feel that the string has really broken, leaving me. Therefore when I sleep, I do not feel the thing which used to vibrate in me, as I lay asleep.

'Ta:, ŋ ka siŋ //nau, o ka: /e: ta: ʘpuoin, ŋ tú tsˀa a !xwãŋ !kwija /k'e: ŋ; há: kú:ï, 'Xã:ä-tiŋ-wɛ́, a xa ʘpuoin _taija, hɛ́ a k''auki /k'e:ja ke, o ti e:, a _//kwan ka ≠kaka ke, ti e:, a _//kwaŋ ka, a kwãŋ _hã: _tai hĩ nˀ O ti e:, ŋ ka /kɯ-g /ne tum-ã _//gauë //k'e: á:, a se kwãŋ /ki !ke !ho ŋ ã:, ŋ se ≠enn, ti e:, a !naunko ˉ!kˀauwa. O ti e:, a _//kwaŋ ≠kaka ke, ti e:, a ká a //kãï !khwa:ka xɔro. Akən !xãã /ne kaŋ ≠ĩ:, á

'For I used, as I lay asleep, to hear something which sounded as if a person called me; it said, '*O Xã ä-tiŋ*, art thou fast asleep, that thou hast not spoken to me, as thou wast wont to talk to me, when thou didst walk about with me? Meanwhile I have been listening awaiting the time when thou wouldst call on me, that I might know, thou art still alive. Then thou wouldst tell me,

ka a se dí ku taŋtaŋ, ti e:, ŋ |kwẽĩ tã, ĩ:.'

whether thou dost lead out the Rainbull. Thou dost sound as if thou dost think of making illness, as I used to do.'

Notes

9-15 *I do not hear the ringing sound … I do not feel the thing which used to vibrate in me …*: See Part VIII, Introduction for more about the ringing sound of the string and its vibration in Xã:ätiŋ's body.

How an Old Woman asked a Chameleon for Rain

Narrator: ǂKasiŋ
Source: 'By ǂKasiŋ the son of a Kora father and a |Xam mother, who heard this from her mother.'
Dictation dates: 29 December 1873; 19 January 1874
Translation dates: 30 December 1873; 19 and 20 January 1874
Notebook reference: L.IV.3: 3701-3737
***Bantu Studies* reference:** Vol. 10 (1936), Part VIII 135-141

What appears at first to be a 'simple' folktale about an old woman and her children turns out to be a rather more complex narrative in which an old woman and a little boy and girl perform a series of rituals to bring rain. See the Introduction for further discussion.

❑

|nu:tara, haŋ ||ke:n !ho !kwe:, haŋ tutú: |kuru, he |kuru !kwe-||a:, ĩ:. He ha-g |ne ≠kaka |huru ĩ:, ti e: ha ka !kauki ||kõĩ:nja, hiŋ k''auki |nĩ: !khwa:, |kuru se á ha-ka !kaukən !khwa:, ha-ka !kaukən se !kou, ta há-ka !kaukən k''auki _dóä |nĩ: hã:.

The Old Woman stuck her digging-stick (into the earth), she begged from the Chameleon, and the Chameleon looked towards her. She told the Chameleon that her children were thirsty, they could not find water, the Chameleon should give her people water, that they might live, for her children could not find food.

He |kuru |ne !kwe-||a: !kˀãũ: ĩ:; he, au ha |ne !kwe-||a: !kˀãũ, haŋ !kwe ||kaitje _!goá:xu, haŋ |ne tá ti !khwa: _||kwaŋ se kãũ, ĩ:. He ha |ne !kwe-||a: !kauki, ĩ:, he ha |ne !kwe-||a: |nu:tara, ĩ:. He !kaukən ⊙puonni k''wẽ-ĩ, ĩ:, tati hi !kwẽ: -ĩ. He |nu:tara !kɔnn |ha: !kwe:, ĩ:.

And the Chameleon looked at the ground, and when it had looked at the ground, it looked up to the sky, it knew that the rain would fall. And it looked at the children, (to see if the Old Woman spoke truly about them), then it looked towards the Old Woman. And the little children laughed, because they rejoiced. And the Old Woman took out her digging-stick (from the ground).

He ha |ne _tai ||kóë ⊙ho:, ĩ:, ⊙ho ha siŋ ||kau !khe ha. Haŋ |ne _tai ||kóẽ-se au ⊙ho, he ha |ne _tai !ahi !khe !kˀãũ, ĩ:; he !kaukən !kuxúï !a: !kheja. He ha |ne ||khou !kúïtje, ĩ:. He !kaukən |ne _|aa: sa:, ĩ:.

And it came down from the bush, the bush on which it had stood. It walked down from the bush and it walked upon the ground; and the children ran along by it. And it became white (like rainclouds). And the children went back. (When they saw that the Chameleon had become white, they knew that it was really going to rain; they were not afraid of the rain but their hearts were satisfied, when they saw that it would really rain.)

He ha xóä |ne _tai, ĩ:, he !kauki |ne _tai hĩ ha xóä. He |nu:tara _tai ||kaitən ||xao ⊙pua, ĩ:, he, ha |ne sue:ŋ, ĩ:. He !khwe ⊙pua ta serritən |hiŋ ti é: tje, ĩ:. Haŋ tʃú:ĩ, he !khwã ⊙pua ko: !khou !khwa: |k'wãï, ĩ:. He ha |ne ǂkaka ha xóã, ti e, ha !khou !khwa: _|kwãĩ; he ha xóä |ne |k'e:ja ha ǂgou, ti e:, ha |ku ka, hi se ||k'oen; he hi |ne _tai u, ĩ:. Hiŋ |ne _tai; he !khwã: |ne |au !ho |kúï ĩ:, ha ||kóë !khe !nabba; he ha |k'e:ja ha xóä, ĩ:. He ha xóä _||kwaŋ |ne sá ||ke:n |kúï, ĩ:. He ha xóä ||ke:n |ha |kúï, he ha _!kaitən !khwi ||ko |kúï au !kˀãũ.

And their mother went away, and the children went with their mother. And the Old Woman climbed up a small hill, and she sat down. And a little cool wind came out from this side. It blew, and one little child smelt the rain smell. And he said to his mother, that he smelt the rain smell; and his mother told him to be silent, because she wanted them to look; and they arose and went away. They went along; and the child (a little boy) saw a 'gambro' creeper in a 'Driedoorn' tree; he told his mother about it. And his mother came to dig out the 'gambro' (root). And his mother dug out the 'gambro', and she threw it down breaking it upon the ground. (Because she had asked the Chameleon for rain she threw the root on the ground, to see if the water from it would wet the ground nicely, then she would believe that the rain would likewise wet the ground. This is not generally done with the root).

He !kaukən ⊙puonni |ne !kuxúï !ke ||a hé: ti, he !kaukən ⊙puonni |ne

And the little children ran up to that place, and the little children

Part VIII Sorcerors and Charms

How an Old Woman asked a Chameleon for Rain

!kwoŋ-ĩ, he hĩ |ne hĩ:, ĩ:. He hĩ |ne ˍtai. He !khwã ʘpua a siŋ !khouwa !khwa: ˍ|k'wãĩ, |kamma |gum, haŋ á ha ||xa ʘpua; he ha ||xa ʘpua |ne !khou |gum, ĩ:, he ha ||xa ʘpua |ne ˍ||gó:ö, ĩ:.

picked up and ate (pieces of 'gambro'). And they went away. And the little boy who had smelt rain picked up a (piece of) springbok-bush, and gave it to his younger sister, and his younger sister smelt the springbokbush and bled from the nose.

!khwã: gwai ʘpua, haŋ |ne |umma ha ||xa ʘpua au ||xauki, au ha-ka ||ahí:, haŋ |umma ho: túä ha ||xa ʘpua au ||xauki, au hiŋ |kuı ||na tsĩ:, au ha xóäkən k''auki ≠enna; he ha xóä |kuı-g |ne !kúïtən, au hiŋ |kuı ||na: tsĩ:.

The little boy wiped the blood off his younger sister with his 'fore kaross', he wiped the blood off his younger sister, while they were behind (the others), and his mother did not know; and his mother returned home, while they stayed behind.

Hiŋ |ne ˍtai sa:; ha ||xa ʘpuakən |au !ho ˍ!gó:ë, ha |ko: !khe !nabba; he ha |ne |ke:tən ha ||ka: ʘpua, ĩ:; ha ||ka: ʘpua se ||a: |ki |hiŋ ˍ!gó:ë; he ha ||ka: ʘpua ˍ||kwaŋ |ne ||a: |ki |hiŋ ˍ!gó:ë, ĩ:. He ˍ!gó:ë a: |kuı-g |ne ||kerri, ĩ:; he !khwã: |ne ˍ!kaitən !ho tóä ha, ĩ:. He ha ||xa ʘpua kaŋ |k'e:, 'T∫a dikən a |kwẽ k''o, akən dí ã:?'

They came along; his younger sister saw a tortoise, it stood under a 'Driedoornbush'; and she told her little brother about it; her little brother should go and take up the tortoise, and her little brother did go and take up the tortoise. And the tortoise screamed, and the child threw it away. And his younger sister (older than he, but having an elder sister at home) said, 'Why do you act like this?'

He ha |ne |k'e: ha ||ka: ʘpua se |kam ˍ!gó:ë, he ha ||ka: ʘpua |ne ||xa:, ha |kam ˍ!gó:ë, ĩ:. He ha ||kaxaitən |k'e:ja, ha !kan ||wẽ:ï ˍ!gó:ë, au ha |k'a|k'a. He ha ||ka ʘpua ˍ||kwaŋ |ne !kan ||wẽ:ï ĩ:. He hiŋ |kuı-g |ne !kúï:tje; tati hĩ k''auki |nĩ: ha xóä, ta ha xóä, |kuı |ne ||na ||neiŋ, au hiŋ |kuı !ku:, ||na||ná tsĩ:.

And she told her little brother to take the tortoise, and her little brother took hold of it again. And his sister told him to hold the tortoise fast in his hands. And her little brother held fast. And they returned, because they did not see their mother, for their mother was at home, while they two were behind.

How an Old Woman asked a Chameleon for Rain

He !khwã |ati ʘpua ˍ||kwaŋ |ne |nĩ: ˍ|kwatti, ĩ:. Haŋ ≠kaka ha ||ka: ʘpua; ha ||ka: ʘpua, haŋ |kuı ≠nwãïja, ti e: ha k''auki |nĩ:

And the little girl caught sight of a little cloud. She told her little brother; her little brother contradicted, that he did not see the little

_|kwatti. Haŋ a |kɒm !nabba !kwa, haŋ a: ||ne:ja ha ||ka: ⊙pua ã:, au !nabba !kwa, ha ||ka: ⊙pua se ||k'oen ki ||kaitje au _!goa:xu ; he ha ||ka: ⊙pua _||kwaŋ |ne |nĩ: _|kwattən, ĩ:. Ha ||kaxai |ne tutú: ha, ti e ha |nu daudáu, he ha ||ka: ⊙pua _||kwaŋ |k'e:, ha k''auki ĩ:ja, ta ha _||kwaŋ ≠kakən !kẽï ||au.

Hiŋ |ne !kúïtən !ke ||a: ||neiŋ, he ha ||ka: ⊙pua hó |i, ĩ:; haŋ ||a ||kei !ɒhí ||ko, he ha ||ka !ho _!gó:ë, ĩ:. _!gó:ëtən ||ka !khe, han sa k''wẽï !khwa:; haŋ ||xã: haŋ |kɒm ||a _!gó:ë, au ha-g |ne k''wã: ; haŋ |ne ||a |ki ||ka: |i, he ha |ne ||k'o:ka tiŋ, ĩ:. Haŋ |ki sa |i, haŋ sa: ||ke:, ||ke: ||kau ||ko _!gó:ë. He haŋ |ne ||xã:ŋ |kɒm ||a ha ||xa ⊙pua, ĩ:, au ha ||xa ⊙pua haŋ ʃo:, ĩ:, he hiŋ ʃo ko |au.

He ha ||xa ⊙pua |ke:tən ha ||ka: ⊙pua ||a |ki |hiŋ _!gó:ë, he ha _||kwaŋ ||a |ki |hiŋ _!gó:ë, ĩ:. Haŋ sa: |ki sa _!gó:ë au ha ||xa ⊙pua, he haŋ _!kʔaitən |kuru _!gó:ë, he ha á ha ||xa ⊙pua _!gó:ë-ta tí ko:, au ha |ki tí ko:. Hiŋ ʃo ko hĩ:; he !khwã gwai ⊙pua ha |auwi !khwa:ŋ baitən-ĩ, haŋ |k'e:ja ha ||xa ⊙pua ã:.

Ha ||xa ⊙pua _||kwaŋ |k'e:, ti e:, ha |kɯ daudáü; he ha |ne |k'e:, ha ||xa ⊙pua se ||k'oen, au ha |ne |k'e: ha ||xa ⊙pua ã:. He ha |ne |kwẽ: da, au ha ||xa: ⊙pua ||k'oen ʃo:, ti e:, ha k''auki ʃo se |nĩ:, au !khwa: baitən-ĩ; he ha ||xa ⊙pua _||kwaŋ |nĩ:, ĩ:, au !khwa:ŋ baitən-ĩ, he ha _||kwaŋ |k'e:, ti e:, ha ||ka: ⊙pua _||kwaŋ ≠kakən !kẽ:ï ||au, ĩ:, ta:

cloud. She broke off a 'Driedoorn' twig, she showed it to her little brother with the twig, her little brother should look up to the sky; and her little brother saw the cloud there. His sister asked him whether she had told stories, and her little brother said, that she had not done so, for she had told the truth.

They returning reached home, and her little brother took a fire stick, he went to make fire outside, and he put the tortoise to roast there. The tortoise stood roasting, he went to drink water; he went back to the tortoise when he had drunk; he went to make up the fire, he went about getting wood. He brought firewood, he came to make up the fire upon the tortoise. And he went back to his younger sister where she sat, and they sat talking.

And his younger sister sent her little brother to take out the tortoise, and he went and took out the tortoise. He came bringing the tortoise to his younger sister, and he broke it in two, he gave his younger sister one piece, while he had the other piece. They sat eating; and the little boy saw the rain lightening, he told his younger sister about it.

His younger sister said that he was telling stories; and he said, his younger sister must look, when he told her to do so. And he did so, whereupon his younger sister sat looking whether she could not see if the rain were lightening; and his younger sister did see, when the rain lightened, and she said, that her little brother had told the

Part VIII Sorcerors and Charms

How an Old Woman asked a Chameleon for Rain

ha ˍ||kwaŋ ||ẽ:iŋ ||k'oen, ti e:, !khwa: baitən-ĩ, he ha ||ka: ⊙pua ˍ||kwaŋ |k'e:, ti e:, !khwa: ˍ||kwaŋ kãũ.

truth about it, for she herself saw that the rain was lightening, and her little brother said, that it was raining.

He ha ||xa ⊙pua tutú:wa ha ||ka: ⊙pua, ti e ha ||ka: ⊙pua se á hĩ ≠kaka ha xóä. Ha ||ka: ⊙pua ˍ||kwaŋ |k'e:, hĩ k''auki se ĩ:, ta ha xóä |ku ⊙puoiŋja. He hĩ k''auki se ĩ:, ĩ. He ha ||xa: ⊙pua ˍ||kwaŋ |ne !humma, au !khwa:gən kãũ sa:. Hiŋ |ku ʃo:, hiŋ k''auki taŋ ⊙puoiŋ.

And his younger sister asked her little brother, whether he would let them tell their mother. Her little brother said, they should not do so, for their mother was sleeping. And they did not do so. And his younger sister assented, while the rain came falling. They sat, they did not want to sleep.

Hiŋ |ku |auwi !khwa:, haŋ ⊙pwuruse baitən-ĩ; he !khwa: ||k'i sue:ŋ ||a !khwã: gwai ⊙pua |k'a; ha ˍtai ||kwe ||a au |i-ta ≠xi:, he haŋ |au ||kóä !khwa: ||k'i, au ha |k'a. Haŋ |ne ≠kaka ha ||xa ⊙pua ã:, he !khwa: |ne !gãũ-ĩ, ĩ:. He ha |ne |k'e:, ha ||xa ⊙pua se á ha !nuiŋ, ha se !nwa:, ta !khwa: kãũ, he !khwa: ||k'i |ku-g |ne xuttən ||kau !khe hi, ĩ:, au ha: |ne kãũ. He hĩ |ne sue:ŋ |e: ||neiŋ, ĩ:, tá ti !khwa: |ne tuko kãũ, he hĩ |ne ||ka: ; he hĩ |ne sue:ŋ |e:, ĩ:.

They watched the rain, it was lightening near by; and a rain drop fell upon the tittle boy's hand; he went to look at it by the fire's light, and he saw the raindrop on his hand. He told his younger sister about it, and the rain thundered. And he said, his younger sister should give him his kaross, so that he might cover himself, for it was raining and raindrops were falling fast upon them, as it rained. And they sat down in the hut, because the rain was falling and they were wet; so they sat down inside.

He ha xóä |ne !k''abbe |hiŋ ⊙puoiŋ, he ha xóä |ne tutú: hĩ, 'Tsa dekən e?' He hiŋ |ku |k'e:, ha xóä se tum-ĩ; he ha xóä túĩ, ĩ:, ti e: !khwa: |kuẽ: da, haŋ kãũ, ĩ:. He ha xóä ˍ||kwaŋ |ne sue:ŋ |hiŋ sa, ĩ; ha se ||k'oen, ti e: !khwa: |ne kãũ ||wĩ; haŋ ˍ||kwaŋ |ne ||ẽiŋ ||k'oen, ti é: !khwa: ˍ||kwaŋ kãũwa, he !kaukən ˍ||kwaŋ se |nĩ !khwa:, ĩ:.

And their mother started out of her sleep and asked them, 'What is the matter?' And they said, their mother should listen; and she heard how the rain was falling. And their mother sat in the doorway to look whether the rain fell much; she herself saw that the rain was falling, and the children could have water.

How an Old Woman asked a Chameleon for Rain

He ha |ne |k'e:ja !khwã: gwai ⊙pua ĩ:, !khwã gwai ⊙pua se ||a |kəm ˍ!gó:ë, ˍ!gó:ë a: hĩ dí kəmmetji, hĩ se k''oãk''oã |hiŋ

And she told the little boy, that he should go and get the tortoiseshell, the tortoiseshell that they used for a cup, that they might

!khwa:. He !khwã _||kwaŋ ||a |kəm _!gó:ë, ĩ. He ha !əhí !ho ||a _!gó:ë, ĩ:, !khwa: se kãũ |e:; he ha |ku-g |ne |e sa ||neiŋ, ĩ:, au _!gó:ëtən !əhí !khe. Haŋ |ku ʃo:.

He ha xóä |ne |k'e: ha, ha |hiŋ ||a:, á ha ã !khwa:, ha se k''õã; ha _||kwaŋ |ne ≠xamma |hiŋ ||a !khwa:, ĩ:. Haŋ |ne |ki sa ha xóä ã !khwa:, ha xóä |ne k''wẽĩ, he ha |ne á !khwã gwai ⊙pua ã !khwa:, ha se ||xəm k''wã. He !khwã gwai ⊙pua |ne ||a te:n, ĩ, ha se ⊙puoiŋ. He ha xóä ||xəm te:n, ha se ⊙puoiŋ, ĩ:. He hiŋ |ku-g |ne ⊙puoinja, au !khwa:gən |naunko kãũwa, ĩ:.

He hi |ne !ka:gən ko !kho úĩ, ĩ:. He !khwã: gwai ⊙pua |ki ||ka: |i, ĩ:, au ha xóäkən ta:. He ha !kwi: ha ||xa ⊙pua, ĩ:, au ha xóäkən |ku-g |ne túĩ !kwikwi:ja, ha !kwija ha ||xa ⊙pua ã hĩ. He ha xóä |ne |k'e:ja ha ã, ti e:, ha se k''auki !kwi: !kabbe |hiŋ ha ||xa: ⊙pua, ha se |ku-g |ne ||ẽiŋ ⊙puoiŋ !kho: úĩ. He !khwã: gwai ⊙pua _||kwaŋ |ne ≠gouwa, ĩ:.

He ha xóä |ne _kóaŋ |ha:, ĩ:. Haŋ |ne tutú: !khwã: gwai ⊙pua tí !khwa: |ne kãũ akka. He !khwã: gwai ⊙pua |k'e:, tí !khwa: kãũ akka. He ha xóä, |k'e:, ha síŋ ka !khwa: se |kwẽ:ï ki |kã, kãũwa !kaukən ã:, !kaukən se-g |nĩ !khwa:, he !kauwi |k'a se |hiŋja !kaukən, ĩ:, he !kaukən ⊙puõnni se |nĩ: hã:, ĩ:.

drink out water. And the child went and got the shell (of a great female tortoise), and put it outside, that rain might fall into it, and he came into the hut, while the shell stood outside. He sat down.

And his mother told him to go out to give her some water to drink; he went out to fetch the water. He brought the water to his mother, she drank, and gave some water to the little boy, that he might drink too. And the little boy went to lie down to sleep. And his mother also lay down to sleep. And they slept on, while the rain was still falling.

And they woke up early next morning. And the little boy made a fire, while his mother lay still. And he called his younger sister, so that his mother heard the call with which he call his younger sister. And his mother told him that he should not call startling her awake, that she should rouse her self from sleep. And the little boy was silent.

And his mother got up. She asked the little boy whether the rain had fallen nicely. And the little boy said that the rain had fallen nicely. And his mother said, she had thought the rain would do so, would fall for the children, that the children might find water, and that the wild onion leaves might sprout for the children, and the little boys might find food.

Notes

Note to the preceding story

ŋ xóä siŋ ≠kaka ke, ti e /kuru /hiŋ: -/goa:xu, he /kuru haŋ é i óä-ka[1] *!kwi. He ti hiŋ e:, ŋ xóä, ka siŋ ≠kaka ke, ŋ k''auki /ka ha, ta: ŋ óä*[2] *ka se !k''waiŋ ŋ, ĩ:; ha k''auki se akke hã:, ĩ:.*

My mother told me that the Chameleon came out of the sky, and the Chameleon is our father's man. Therefore my mother used to tell me not to kill it, for my father would be angry with me; he would not give me food in consequence.

[[1] He says he means God here, he explains that God and his father would both be angry, and that his father would not give him food, and that God would not stand by his father on account of it.]

1-2 *The Old Woman stuck her digging-stick (into the earth)*: This appears to be a ritual action performed before speaking to the Chameleon about bringing rain – after speaking to it, she takes the digging-stick out of the ground again; see Part VII, 'Luck in hunting' in which a woman contacts spirits of the dead by beating on the ground with a bored stone.

11-15 *... the Chameleon looked at the ground ... it looked up to the sky, it knew that the rain would fall*: The chameleon was another one of !Khwa:'s 'things' or animals (see 'Note to the preceding story', as well as Part V, 'The rain's animals'). The chameleon's head movements are interpreted as indications that rain will fall.

18-20 *And the little children laughed, because they rejoiced*: 'They rejoiced, seeing that the chameleon had looked at them, to see if they were hungry, and that it saw that the old woman had spoken the truth, and that it had looked at the old woman assentingly with its eye' (omitted note, 3702 rev.).

38-40 *And the Old Woman climbed up a small hill, and she sat down*: Janette Deacon has suggested that rain-making ceremonies may have been held on top of certain hills in |Xam-ka !aũ (Deacon 1988: 134-135; see Part VI, Introduction). The Old Woman may have climbed up to perform such a ritual herself because, after she sits down, a rain-bearing wind starts to blow.

48-50 *... and the child... saw a 'gambro' creeper in a 'Driedcorn' tree ...*: Notes omitted by Dorothea Bleek read:

'a root of which they compare in size to the Manglewurzel plant (a Eurasian variety of the beet, *Beta vulgaris* – ed.), but say that it is more watery, it is a climbing plant' (3706 rev., note omitted).

'a short thorn bush without real thorns, it has white flowers; the Boers' name for it is "Dree Doorn"' (3706 rev., note omitted).

53-55 *And his mother dug out the 'gambro', and she threw it down breaking it upon the ground*: The reasoning behind digging out and breaking the 'gambro' is explained by the note in brackets that follows. For more about the 'gambro', see Part V, 'What !Khwa: does to people and their things when he is angry'.

68-70 *... the little boy who had smelt rain picked up (a piece of) springbok bush ...*: This and the following paragraph appear to refer indirectly to a rain-making ritual that the boy and his sister perform, and which involves nasal bleeding (Bleek translates *//gó:ö*, 'bleed', as 'nasal bleeding'). Nasal bleeding is strongly associated with states of altered consciousness in |Xam culture. The narrative suggests that springbok bush was used to provoke nasal bleeding (see Guy Butler's 1997 article on the springbok bush).

74-76 *The little boy wiped the blood off his younger sister with his 'fore kaross'*: 'made from the skin of a jackal's neck, Klaas tells me' (3709 rev., note omitted).

82-83 *... his younger sister saw a tortoise ...*: In the notebook, !goië is translated as 'great tortoise'. The tortoise (*!gó:ë*) is one of !Khwa:'s animals and is therefore associated with rain. The girl does not handle the tortoise at all, but instructs her brother about what to do with it, probably because as a girl she may not touch !Khwa:'s things. The relationship between !Khwa: and girls is discussed in Part V, Introduction.

88-89 *And the tortoise screamed*: It seems likely that the 'screaming' (*//kerri*) of the tortoise was a significant part of the narrative – it may have confirmed that rain was soon going to fall.

103-104 *And the little girl caught sight of a little cloud*: There is a connection between this paragraph and a later one – first, the brother tells the sister that she is lying (*daudáu*) about seeing the cloud, but he soon admits she is telling the truth. Then, in a later paragraph, the sister at first disbelieves the brother when he points out the rain and lightning to her. The repetition suggests that this may have been a way of 'respecting' the rain by pretending not to notice its approach. Many of the |Xam narratives involve respect behaviours that require people to be silent, or not to see or do certain things when in the presence of powerful spirit beings (for example Part III,'The eland's story' and 'A person's death foretold by the springbok and the gemsbok').

164-170 *... a rain drop fell upon the little boy's hand ... He told his younger sister about it, and the rain thundered*:

A note omitted by Dorothea Bleek concerning the translation of *!gãu:* reads: 'slaan' (3725 rev.). This Afrikaans word means 'strike' and probably refers to the striking of lightning.

This part of the narrative highlights the different relations of men and women to !Khwa:, the rain. The boy is able to touch the raindrop, but the rain thunders (*!gãu:*) at the mere mention of the girl: this seems to reflect the different, gender-specific roles of men and women in |Xam society (see Part V, Introduction).

176-177 ... *because the rain was falling*: 'the abundant rain drops' (3726 rev., note omitted).

193-195 *And the child went and got the shell (of a great female tortoise) ...*: The use of a tortoise shell to catch the rain is another way in which the tortoise, one of !Khwa:'s animals, is related to the rain (see Part V, 'The rain's animals'). Earlier in the narrative, a tortoise seems to forecast rain – now a large tortoiseshell is used to collect the resultant downpour.

203-204 ... *she ... gave some water to the little boy ...*: 'The little girl drank no water then, as she was already asleep.' (3731 rev., note omitted)

228-229 ... *that the wild onion leaves might sprout ...*: ǂKasiŋ explains that *!kauwĭ* is 'a root something like an onion in shape which is eaten by the Bushmen; the outer skin of it is red; the leafy part of the plant is not eaten, but thrown away' (3735 rev., note omitted).

Notes on the sorceress Tãnõ-!khaukən

Narrator: Diä!kwain

Source: 'Told by Diä!kwain about a great Bushman doctress and sorceress who did not understand Dutch. D.H. saw her, and says that she was the height of his sister !Kweiten tă ||keŋ. She has been a long time dead. She died while !Kweiten tă ||keŋ was a child.'

Dictation date: 28 May 1875

Notebook reference: L.V.10: 4709 rev. and 4710 rev.; 4712-4714 rev.

***Bantu Studies* reference:** Vol. 10 (1936), Part VIII: 142-143

Nobody was safe with this old woman around – she knew what people were up to, even if she was not there at the time.

Ti |ke:, !kˀe kaŋ ||na he, hέ: |nu-tara ||xɑm kaŋ ||na he. Hέ: !kˀe mu: ≠enn |nu-tara, ï:. !kˀe ka ||nau, hέ: kє: ≠xóä, ti e:, |nu-tara ka |kwẽ:ï k''o, ĩ:, hє: ||nau, hέ: |au kara o |nu-tara |kẽ, he kukú, he |k'e:, -||gɔro -kɔ́ɔ̈ sa !kɑn !ho |nu-tara. Ta ha |kɯ e !nu-tara á: |kɯ |ki ha |nũnu, ha ka ≠enna tikəntikən.'

Ha ka ||nau, ti e:, i: !kwi:ja ha |kẽ, ĩ:, haŋ ka sé he, ti e:, í: siŋ !kwi:ja ha |kẽ, ĩ:, o há: ka, ha se sá ||k'oen hє, ti e:, tsˀa de |no a:, í: !kwi: ha |kẽ ã:, ti e:, í-g |nõ k''au ≠enna, ti e:, ha k''auki ka ʘpwoin ʃo: hĩ !kˀe; ta: ha ka |kɯ ||nau, !kˀeja ʘpwoin ||na, haŋ ka |kɯ -taija tiŋ.

Hє tikən e:, ha ka |kɯ ≠enna tikəntikən e: !kˀeja k''auki ≠enna he; o haŋ ta:, ||ka ti e:, ha ka |kɯ

The place there (at |khau-!kãũ.) where the people lived was also where the old woman lived. So the people knew her. The people speak thus when they describe what she used to do, they say, when they have done talking about her name, that they wish the 'camelthorntree would hold the old woman fast. For she was an old woman who had her nose, she knew things.'

She used to come to the place at which we had called her name, because we had called her name there, for she wanted to look at it, to see what was the matter, that we had called her name, whether we did not know, that she was not used to lie sleeping with the people; for she was accustomed, when the people were asleep there, to walk about.

Therefore she used to know things which the people did not know; for she felt that she used,

||nau, !kʔeja ⊙pwoin ||na, há |kɯ _taija ||kau tiŋ !kʔe, o !kʔeja |kɯ ⊙pwoin ||na. !kʔeja ká: ≠ĩ:, há: ||xam ⊙pwoin ||na hĩ !kʔe, o há: |kɯ siŋ _taija tiŋ; ha |kɯ ||k'oenja tiŋ, o tʃweŋ e: !kʔe k''auki ≠enna he, he e: ha ||k'oenja _ã tiŋ, ĩ:.

when the people were asleep there, to go walking about among the people as they lay asleep there. The people thought she was asleep with them, while she was walking about; she was looking about at things which the people did not know, those were what she looked about for.

!kʔe kaŋ k''auki !kwi: ha |kẽ o ||ga:, ta: ||kuonna á:, !kʔe !kwi: ha |kẽ ã:; o hiŋ tá:, ||ka ti e:, ||kuonna é, he tikən e:, he !kwi: ha |kẽ ĩ:. ||kuonnaŋ á:, he ≠enna, ti e:, ha k''auki ká ha se sé, o ||kuonna.

People do not say her name at night, for it is day when people say her name; when they feel that it is day, then they say her name. By day they know that she will not want to come. (Even if she did come she would do no harm and her coming would not matter).

I e: !kaukən, itən k''auki ||gwitən ||gwitən-ĩ, o ha |kẽ; ta: i |kɯ !hammi: ha |kẽ, ta: ha |ki ka ha se ã: |num-se ||keŋ i e: !khwã: ⊙pua, o i: !kwi: ||gwitən||gwitən-ĩ o ha |kẽ.

We who are children do not play with her name; for we are afraid of her name, for she is accustomed to let the beard pierce (killing) us, little children, if we call playing with her name.

Hɛ tikən e:, mama-gu ka siŋ ||nau, hɛ́: tóã, ti e: si: !kwi:ja ha |kẽ, mama-gu |kɯ ho: !hãũ, he |kɯ ||a !kaukən-ã si: hɛ tikən e:, sí e: !kaukən, si |kɯ !hammi:, si !kwí: ha !kẽ.

This was why, if our parents heard that we had called her name, they would take up a strap, they would go to beat us; therefore we children were afraid to call her name.

Ta: mama_gu |ki e: |k'e:ja si ã:, si k''auki ||gwitən||gwitən-ĩ: o ha |kẽ. Ta: ha ká ha se |ki taŋtaŋ si tã:, o há ka si se ≠enn, !kwi !kerri-ta |kwi |kwitənaŋ; si se ≠enn, ti e:, !kaukən ⊙puonni k''auki ta !kwi: ||gwitən||gwitən-ĩ:, o !kwi !kerri |kẽ.

For our parents were those who had told us not to be playing with her name. For she would make us feel pain, because she wished us to learn respect for grown-up people; we should know that young children must not speak playing with a grown-up person's name.

Notes

10-11 … *she was an old woman who had her nose …*: The phrase refers to the |Xam belief that evil and many other things may be detected by means of their characteristic smell (see Part VII, 'More about sorcerers').

46-47 … *she is accustomed to let the beard pierce (killing) us*: Did old |Xam women threaten to rub children with their beard hairs (facial hair is characteristic of post-menopausal women) as a way of frightening them into good behaviour?

58-59 … *she would make us feel pain*: *taŋtaŋ*, the word translated here as 'pain', has connotations of sickness caused by sorcery (see 'The sorceror !Nuiŋ-|kúïtən').

||Khabbo

Narrator: |Haŋ‡kass'o
Dictation date: 29 November 1878
Notebook reference: L.VIII.23: 8033 rev.
***Bantu Studies* reference:** Vol. 10 (1936), Part VIII: 143

An outsider to /Xam culture would be baffled by this description of //Khabbo. However, once we understand that /Xam sorcerors derived supernatural potency from their relationships with other animals, then the meaning of the statement is clear.

❑

ŋ ⊙puai-/hī //khabbo -//kwaŋ óä /ki /ka/kaggən, haŋ -//kwaŋ óä e /kaggən-ka !kwi.

My father-in-law //khabbo had Mantises, he was a Mantis's man.

❑

Note

2 Lewis-Williams argues that the phrase 'Mantis's man' means that ||Khabbo (more commonly spelt ||Kabbo) claimed a special relationship with |Kaggen, the Bushman trickster-deity and Lord of the Animals, which 'allowed him to intervene with the trickster-deity and perhaps thereby secure good hunting' (Lewis-Williams 1996:139).

!Gʋerritən-dé

Narrator: |Haŋ ≠kass'o
Dictation dates: Sometime between 31 October and 17 November 1878
Notebook reference: L.VIII.22: 7974 rev.
***Bantu Studies* reference:** Vol. 10 (1936), Part VIII: 144

This passage, together with the statements contained in Part VII, 'The sorceress Tãnõ-!khaukən', is important for the interpretation of certain Bushman rock paintings of figures with antelope features. There are many Bushman paintings of figures with human heads, arms and legs with antelope-eared caps: these probably refer to game sorcerers like !Gʋerritən-dé and Tãnõ-!khaukən. In many cases, however, figures have antelope heads and feet *and, occasionally, what look like images of antelope are depicted in human postures: these paintings show an even deeper level of identification that is achieved by sorcerors in dreams and trance states, and perhaps by the spirits of dead sorcerors* (|nu !kˀe).

❑

!gɑerritən-déjakən á: óä e wai-ta !gixa, haŋ óä |ki wai, haŋ |kɯ á: ka siŋ !k''áo |hiŋ wai |na:. He haŋ ||xɑmki !k''ao ₋!kãũ, ha |ne kukúï, ha ≠um ₋!kãũ-ka ⁻!khi, já |ne ||khóä ts?a !nu!nuntu, au ha |ne !khija hi. He tikən e:, hĩ ta siŋ |ne ĩ: u, au há s?o:.

!gʋrritən-dé was a springbok sorceror, he had springbok, he used to cut off the springbok head. He also cut off the scalp, he thus sewed a scalp cap, which looked like a thing's ears, when he put it on. Then they (the ears) stand up like this, (holding up thumb and little finger and bending down the three middle fingers), as he sits.

❑

Note

2 *... he had springbok ...: haŋ óä |ki wai.* This statement means that !Gʋerritən-dé had the power to control the behaviour of springbok.

ʃo-/õä, a vegetable medicine or charm

Narrator: ||Kabbo
Dictation dates: 6 and 18 September 1873 (the first date mentioned gives the year as 1872, but this appears to be a mistake – the other date gives the year 1873)
Translation dates: 11-23 September 1873
Notebook reference: L.II.36: 3242-3261
***Bantu Studies* reference:** Vol. 10 (1936), Part VIII: 144-148

In the first of four extracts about this important, but as yet unidentified plant, //Kabbo describes what ʃo-lõä *is used for and how it is applied.*

The ***!kurri-ka !ke*** or Hart River's people call it *ʃo-/õä*, the ***Swa:-ka !ke*** or Flat Bushmen call it *//karrukən//karrukən*, the ***!kuara*** or ***Koranna*** call it */u-ʃõä*.

ʃo-/óä é: a, //ke//ke.ja /k'ĩ:-ta ʃo-/õä.

This *ʃo-/õä* resembles the Orange River's *ʃo-/õä*, (also that of the */**nu:-ka !ke***, who live north of the Orange River).

!ketən e: //keinja hĩ au !kau. !ketən //kein//kein /hiŋ hĩ, au hiŋ //khwe//khwe ta !k?ãũ. Hiŋ /ne /ki sá: hĩ au //neiŋ; hiŋ saŋ //ko: tẽ hĩ, hĩ se /kaukən hĩ au !gwara; hĩ se /ku: hĩ au //ho:; hĩ se /ku: /e tẽ hĩ, hĩ siŋ !k''wobbe hĩ, au hĩ tatti e:, hĩ ka hĩ se twaitən.

Men are those who dig it out of the hill (with a stick). Men dig it up as it stands in the ground. They bring it home; they come and lay it down, to cut it with a knife; they will pack it into a bag; they will put it away in it, in order to rub themselves when they want to be well.

Hiŋ /ĩ: hĩ eŋeŋ; hiŋ //ka !ho ʘho; ʘhokən //ka k''ərrokən; hiŋ !kən tu: ha, au haŋ məmənniŋ; hiŋ k''ó:ẽtən /e: au sweŋ; hiŋ !kãũ hĩ. Hiŋ !k''wobbe //kóë tẽ au /ã/ã, /ã/ã-ka twitwi:tən; hiŋ xuruxuru hĩ, au ʃo-/õä-ka /hóä e: /hóäka. He ti hiŋ e:, /ã/ã-ka twitwi:tən /hóäka, ĩ: au /ã/ãŋ tatti e:, hóä /e/é ta:; hiŋ /ne //ko:, hé e:, /ã/ã /ne //ko: !haŋ; /hóä /ne /hóäkən/hóäkən /e: ta:

They cut their flesh; they burn (a piece of the) wood; it burns to charcoal; they hold it blowing it out where it flames; they dip it smoking into fat; they grind it (between stones). They rub it into the cuts, the wounds of the cuts; they blacken them with the *ʃo-/õä* coals which are black. Then the cuts' scars are black, because the coals are black in them; they become

hĩ-ka tũ:.

dry, then the cuts dry closing up; the coal lies black inside their skin.

!ke e: |xãĩ hĩ |ka:gən, hiŋ e: |ĩ: hĩ ||xwe||xwarritən, au hiŋ ka, hĩ siŋ |xã|xã akən, au hi |ka:gən, au hiŋ tatti !kuirri ʃo !ke |ku é.

People (Koranna) who shoot at their fellows, cut the back of their (left) wrist and hand, when they want to aim well at their fellows, for they are the Hart River's people (from a part near the Orange River).

Hiŋ |ĩ: hĩ ||xwe||xwarritən é: a, au hiŋ tatti e:, hĩ _!gwáĩ hĩ |ka:gən au !kuara-ka _!gwa_!gwa:, au hiŋ ka, hĩ se _!gwa |ku:kən !ku ko:.

They cut the back of their wrist and hand here (right hand), when they want to strike their fellows with the fist, in the Koranna fist-fighting, for they want to strike the other man dead.

!ke e: ||ki: whai, hiŋ e:, |ã !kauŋ ||kóä au hĩ |ka !karrokən tu, !nwa: se ||khou akkən au whai.

People who kill springbok (Bushmen), cut their hand between the thumb and first finger, (the place where the arrow lies) that the arrow may fly well at the springbok

Hiŋ ||ka !ho ʃo-|õä, hiŋ ||ka||ka k''ərokən !ho au hĩ xu !khaukən-!khaukən. Hiŋ |ã|ã !ho ĩ: |na:; hiŋ ||ka !ho ʃo-|õä, ʃo-|õän bu: |e:, au han tatti e:, ha |ku kúï ≠kup; hiŋ !kan tu: ha; hiŋ _k''óëtən ||kau ||ko au !kau; hiŋ _k''ərokən au hĩ |k'a, hiŋ xuruxuru ||kóë tẽ |hóä au |ã|ã. |ã|ãŋ ||kó:; |hóäkən |ne |hóäkən|hóäkən |e: ta: |ã|ã; au |ã|ãŋ |ne ||ko:wa, hĩ |na:ŋ |ne kuerre, he siŋ taŋ.

They burn (the end of a piece of) *ʃo-|õä*, they put it burning to their temples, (for they want the pain to go). They make cuts on their heads, they burn the *ʃo-|õä* on them; it flames up, because it takes fire quickly; they hold it, blowing it out; they put it smoking on to a stone; they crumble it with their hand, they blackening lay the coal into the cuts. The cuts become dry; the coal lies black in the cuts; when the cuts are dry, their heads which had ached become cool.

Hiŋ ≠ĩ:, ti e:, hĩ _saŋ !han, hiŋ |ĩ: hĩ ||kũŋ||kũŋ; hiŋ kúï ≠kup au ʃo-|õä, ʃo-|õä məmanniŋ; hiŋ !kan tu: ha, haŋ kúï tʃup. Hiŋ xuru-xuru hĩ ||kũ-ka |ã|ã. Hiŋ !han, hiŋ ||kaitən _|kao, hiŋ ||ke:, ||kau siŋ _|kao; hiŋ !gõä ||kau siŋ, hiŋ |nĩ: whai.

They think that they will hunt, they cut their arms; they set fire to the *ʃo-|õä*, the *ʃo-|õä* flames up; they hold it and blow it out, it goes out. They blacken their cuts. They hunt, they climb a hill, they make a fire, up on the hill; they look around sitting up there, they catch sight of springbok.

ʃo-|õä, a vegetable medicine or charm

Hiŋ ≠kaka hĩ /ka:gən, hiŋ tutú:, '!ku di xa á: ʃo siŋ /ki _taija ha-ka !hum?' !ku kokən ≠kaka ha, 'ŋ kaŋ k''auki /ki _taija ŋ-ka !hum, ta:, ŋ ka i //kenni se _taba si, whai /ke: _tai sa, hĩ se təm ⊙pua _!kŏäka sí, si se /xã/xã !hi:ŋ //ko.' !ku kokən kuerre /hiŋ ha-ka !hum.

They speak to each other, they ask, 'What man has brought his band (with him)?' The other says to him, 'I did not bring out my band, for I wanted our friends to work for us, upon the springbok coming yonder, that they may gently run round passing us, that we may shoot them from near by.' Another unloosens and takes off his band.

(Note: *!kwitən //aŋ _tan-ĩ whai, haŋ !kúïtən sa, haŋ ≠kakən, ti e:, ha tuko _taŋ_ã: whai, haŋ _dóa !kúïtən sa, ta:, ha !hən xu óä ha-ka !hum au //neiŋ. Ha se sa /ã ha //kũ; !nwa: se //khou akka ha, ta: !nwa: /ku //khou _/k'waĩ-ĩ; !nwaŋ /ku ≠kabe≠kabe:. !nwa:-ka //gɛrre se _/kwaïïtən, ta //gɛrre k''auki /xorokən, ta: ha tuko ≠kóätən-ĩ whai.*)

(Note: A man goes missing the springbok, he turns back, he says that he has really missed a springbok, he had to return, for he had hunted leaving his band at home. He must cut his arm, that the arrow may fly well for him, for it had flown badly. The arrow had turned round in the air. The arrow's feathers should make a tearing noise, but the feathers did not make a noise, for he really missed the springbok.)

(When an arrow flies well, it makes a tearing sound through the air,—*_/kwaitən, xaitən, _txaitən*—, but when it flies badly, it makes a whistling, hissing sound—*≠kóëtəŋ*.)

Haŋ kúï ≠kubbu !ho ⊙ho; haŋ //ne: whai au ⊙ho; whaïïtən _tai sa:. Haŋ ≠kakən, 'ŋ-ka ʃo-/õäŋ /ke:, ŋ //ne: whai e: _tai sa, ĩ:, hĩ se təm ⊙pua _!kŏäkən; ta: ŋ́-ka ⊙ho e: _//kauwa hĩ /ku e.' Haŋ !kən tu: ʃo-/óä-ka /i. Haŋ !əhi !ho /hóä ã /khĩ-tu.

He quickly burnt a stick; he pointed at the springbok with it; the springbok were coming. He said 'My *ʃo-/õä* here I point at the springbok, that are coming, that they may run gently; for my stick which is bitter it is.' He puts out the *ʃo-/õä*'s fire. He makes a line with the burnt wood between his eyebrows.

ʃo-/õä, a vegetable medicine or charm

(He draws a line of burnt powdered wood with his finger down the centre of his forehead and nose, and before he reaches the nose tip, turns aside over the middle of his right nostril to the middle of his right cheek.)

Haŋ ʃo ko /kou whai-ta !nwa:. Hiŋ ≠kaka hĩ /ka:gən, '/nou hi:,

He sits sharpening a springbok arrow. They say to each other,

i-g |ne ||khãũë he whai, i-g |ne |xãä hĩ. Ta: !ke kuitən se ||khãũë ||khãũë !kauŋ ho !khwe; !ke e: se ||kou ho se whai; he e: ˍsaŋ |ne !kuxe !kuŋ siŋ sa whai; au whaija-g |ne ˍ!kóäkən sa:; |ke se |kɯ-g |ne doudou ||k'e: au whai; au whaija-g |ne ˍ!kóäkən !kou |e: !ke-ta kammaŋ, hĩ se |xã: !kou !ho whai au hĩ-ta kammaŋ.'

‘Let us get up, that we may go round the springbok to shoot them. For other people shall go round them under the wind; these will throw (up dust) driving the springbok, they will run behind the springbok as the springbok come running; the people will stooping surround the springbok, as the springbok run in between them, they will shoot as the springbok pass through their midst.’

He e:, whai se ˍ!kõäkən akkən, ĩ:, au whaija tatti e:, whai |na: !khwetən au whai ts'ĩ:; whai siŋ k''auki |ne ˍdaitənˍdaitən !khe, au whaija tatti e:, !ke kuitən !ho!hóä !kˀãũ, au whai ||xã ||xã. He e:, whai se ˍ!kóäkən !kɒn ||k'e:, ĩ:, au !kˀãũ. Ta: whai ˍk'waija, ta: !kaukən |kɯ e:, se ||khou hó se whai, whai se tũ:ŋ akkən, au whaija tatti e:, !khwe ˍ||kwaŋ sirritən au i tsˀĩ:.

Then the springbok will run nicely, for they feel that danger is at their back; the springbok will not stand looking back, because they notice the other people throwing up dust on their flanks. Therefore they will run close together because of the dust. For there are many springbok, but the children are throwing dust, driving them, so that they run straight into the opening, for they feel the wind blowing cool from behind us.

Hiŋ |ki:, !ke kuitakən ||kãũï |kẽï |ɒhóbbakən, au !ke kuitakən |ne ||kãũï |kẽï !khwe-tu; hĩ se !khe: bɔ:kən ||ko !khwe, !khwe se tsu !khou siŋ hĩ-ta kammaŋ, au hĩ |ne !khe bɔ:kən ||kóä !khwe, whai se ˍtã ≠ka: ||ko !khwe, au !khweja-g |ne tsˀu !khou |e: hĩ-ta kammaŋ, au hĩ |ne !khe: ta: !khwe ||xã||xã. Whai se ≠kɒm ⊙pua ˍ!köökən !khou |e:, hĩ se ˍ|kati !kũ!kũ se, au hĩ tatti e:, hĩ ≠ĩ: ti e:, hĩ ˍbaiˍbai-ĩ !xwe:-|na:, au kammaŋ.

They (the men) divide, some run round to leeward, while others run round to windward; they will stand leaving the wind open, that it may blow in between them, as they stand leaving it open, that the springbok may feel the wind clearly, as it blows in between them, while they stand on either side of the wind. The springbok will run through first, the men will advance afterwards, for they mean to race the leaders to the middle.

!xwe:-|na: se !ku:xe !khou |e: ||e kammaŋ a: ≠ɒnni, ha a: hĩ se |xã-|xã !hi:n ||ko ã:, au hĩ tatti e:, !khau ⊙pua ≠ɒnni, ha whai !ku:xe !khou |e: ha. Ha a:, hĩ se teteŋ taŋ, hĩ se teŋteŋ ti |xã-ã, au hĩ

The leaders will run through a narrow gap, where they will shoot at them from nearby, because it is a very narrow path through which the springbok are running. That is where they will lie in wait, that

ʃo-/õä,
a vegetable
medicine or
charm

tatti e:, hĩ /ne /nĩ/nĩ: whai-ta /ka:-gən. He e: /ne !ku!ku:xe ≠ka: !khe, ta. !na: é; ha a: whai-ta /ka:gən /kɯ-g /ne a:kən, au hãhã. Ta: whai-ta gwai kó:ïŋ.

they may lie and shoot, when they catch sight of springbok ewes. These are handsome as they run, for it is winter, when the springbok ewes are beautiful. But the springbok rams are lean.

❑

Notes

57-58 ... *they blackening lay the coal into the cuts*: 'really the burnt wood produced' (3246 rev., note omitted).

72-73 *What man has brought his band ...*: A band of material (probably animal hide), called a *!hum*, could be tied to the body, forming a pouch in which to put *ʃo-/õä*.

'[has brought it out hunting instead of having left it at the house]' (3249 rev., note omitted).

120-121 ... *the people will stooping surround the springbok...*: '[from opposite quarters]', '[many springbok]' (3253 rev, notes omitted).

125-126 *Then the springbok will run nicely*: '[in between them all] in the middle of all of them, J.T. explains' (3254 rev., note omitted).

130-132 *Therefore they will run close together because of the dust*: 'the dust's fear' (3255 rev., note omitted).

135-136 ...*so that they run straight into the opening...*: '[through between the people]' (3256 rev., note omitted).

149-150 ... *for they mean to race the leaders to the middle*: '[the springbok run through and the men run fast together from each side to where the first springbok of the herd (i.e. the "leaders" mentioned in the text – ed.) will pass through, so as to be ready to shoot it]' (3258 rev., note omitted).

159 *These are handsome as they run ... : !kuxĕ ≠ka: !khĕ,* literally 'run near stand'. 'This is an expression the sense (?) of which I cannot understand yet. J.T. says "mooi harteloop"' (3260 rev., note omitted).

***ʃo-/õä*, a vegetable medicine or charm**

When Bushmen are angry …

Narrator: ||Kabbo
Dictation date: 20 September 1873
Translation date: 22 September 1873
Notebook reference: L.II.36: 3262-3268
***Bantu Studies* reference:** Vol. 10 (1936), Part VIII: 148-149

A man uses ʃo-/õä in a fight with devastating effect.

Au |xam-ka !ke !k''wainja hĩ |ka:gən au hĩ ||kho||khougən, au hĩ k''auki !k''wainja au hĩ |ĩ:, hiŋ |kuɯ _!gwa-ĩ hĩ |ka:gən.

When Bushmen are angry with each other in their thoughts, though they are not angry in their hearts, they fight each other with fists.

!ku kogən |ne |ku:kən, hiŋ e:, ha |ne arro:ko herribi !ku ko: |ĩ:, haŋ |nẽ: !ku ko: |ĩ:, ha se |nẽ: |ki _|ɑa:-se !ku ko: |ĩ:, !ku ko: se arro:ko !kwe |hiŋ. Ta: !ku ko: !khaukən, au han tatti e:, ha |ĩ: !kũn ||a: au !ku ko:-ka ʃo-|õä.

The other man faints, then he (the first man) quickly treats the other's heart, he helps the other's heart, that he may help to bring back the other's pulse, that the other may quickly open his eyes. For the other trembled, when he felt his heart fall down because of the first man's *ʃo-|õä* (with which he had rubbed his hands before fighting.)

He ti hiŋ e:, !ku ko: arro:ko |xi: ha xu, ha tsaxdítən se !khe: _||nwar-ritən, ta: !ku ko: !gwirri.

Then the first man quickly spits in the other's face (having chewed *ʃo-|õä*), that his eyes may turn, for the other's eyes had turned up.

Ha tsaxdítən |hum|hum e: |hóäka, hĩ ||nuŋ ||a hĩ au ha tsaxdu tsĩŋxu; haŋ |kuɯ-g |ne tsaxdítən-ta !gwirri !gwirri-de !kúïta.

His eyes pupils which are black had rolled behind to the back of his eyes; he showed his eyeballs' white.

!ku ko: |ne _|kammeŋ úï, !ku ko: |ne sue:n !ke siŋ; haŋ |ne _|kati _tai !kũ ||a:, haŋ |ne sue:ŋ ||a:, haŋ |ne ||ɑhóbbakən !ku ko: xu, au ha _|k'wãĩ; haŋ |ne |ki hiŋ ʃo-|õä

The other starts up, the other sits up opposite; then he (the first man), presently walks away and goes to sit down, he anoints the other's face with his scent; he takes out

e: ha _taba !ku ko: ĩ:, he e: ha |ki !káuï !ku ko: ĩ:.

the ʃo-|õä with which he has treated the other and revived him.

(He rubs himself under the arms, where he had rubbed the medicine before going to fight, and then rubs the sick man's face with perspiration and the scent of the plant together. Afterwads he cuts the man's chest and back and rubs the ʃo-|õä into the cuts; and then afterwards gives the patient the piece of ʃo|õä that he had doctored him with, having more in his own possession.)

!ku ko:-g |ne |ki |hiŋ _!gao!gao-ka !nwa:, haŋ |ne á: ha ã hĩ. Haŋ |ne ||xam |ki |hiŋ hã-ka !nwa:, haŋ |ne á: !ku ko: hĩ; !ku ko:-g |ne |e !ho hĩ au |ku ko:-ka ||khwai, au haŋ |ne _tai |ki u ||a: !ku ko:-ka !nwa:, haŋ |ne ||a ŋ |e !ho hĩ au ha-ka ||khwai.

The other (the patient) took out poison's arrows, he gave him some. He (the helper) also took out his arrows, he gave the other some; the other (the patient) put them into his quiver, while he (the helper) took the other's arrows away, he went to put them into his quiver.

Haŋ |ne |ki |hiŋ !gwarra ʘpua, haŋ |ne |ã !ahí te au !ku ko: !kaxu. Haŋ kúï ≠kup au ʘho ʘpua, haŋ !kan tu: ha, haŋ xuruxuru ||kóö të au |ã|ã, haŋ _tai u ||a:, ≠goukən te:n; au haŋ |kɯ-g |ne ||aŋ sueŋ ha-ka ||neiŋ, au !ku ko:kən |kɯ-g |ne ʃo ko _≠ka_≠kakən. Hiŋ ||kóäkən ≠gou.

He (the helper) takes out an arrow-head, he cuts across the others's chest, he sets fire to the twig, he holds it putting it out, he rubs the burnt powder into the cuts, he goes away, quiet reigns; while he goes to sit at his home, while the other sits talking (with his own people). They are at peace for the future.

Notes

Title The original title of this part was 'Illustrative of ʃo-|õä – How a man fights another [having previously rubbed his hands with ʃo-|õä]. Afterwards restores him by means of it' (3262).

5 *The other man* **faints** ...: 'the other man dies [becomes insensible?]' (omitted text, 3262). In an omitted reverso note, ||Kabbo explains 'nett so he dod (Afrikaans phrase meaning "just like this (i.e. suddenly) he dies" – ed.) cannie bauie dod, betje dood', (i.e. "not very dead, a little dead" – ed.) (3261 rev.).

The death-like state of the man resembles the state of altered consciousness that Ju|'hoansi healers reach during the healing dance, and which they call 'half death' (Lee 1968; Marshall 1969). It is possible that the *ʃo-/õä* plant was believed to have a similar effect on people.

5-7 *he … quickly treats the other's heart…*: *ʃo-/õä* seems to cause a seizure in which the heart stops beating, the body trembles violently, and the eyes roll upwards in their sockets (see 'The man who misused *ʃo-/õä*'). The other people rescue the man by spitting chewed *ʃo-/õä* in his face and by rubbing him with sweat, considered to be medicinal in many Bushman cultures. There is a specific |Xam word, *||Ωhóbbakən*, for this particular therapeutic practice.

18-19 *… for the other's eyes had turned up*: '[the whites being visible, the black part having gone behind]' (3264, text omitted).

'*/nẽ* is the Bushman word for "help"; *herribi* is white man's talk, J.T. says' (3261 rev., note omitted).

25 *… then he (the first man):* The original translation says '[the helper]' (3264).

27-28 *… he anoints the other's face with his* **scent**: '[in this instance it means perspiration and the *ʃo-/õä* smell together]' (3264 rev., note omitted).

36-37 *The other … took out poison's arrows …*: The patient and the helper exchange poison arrows. Whatever other significance was attached to this exchange, it would also create obligations between the two in the future – both men would have to share any game that either of them shot because an animal killed with a poisoned arrow belonged to the arrow's owner not to the person who actually shot the animal (see Marshall 1961 for details of this practice amongst the Ju|'hoansi).

More about *ʃo-/õä*

Narrator: ||Kabbo
Dictation dates: 22 September 1873
Translation dates: 22 and 23 September 1873
Notebook reference: L.II.36: 3269-3278
***Bantu Studies* reference:** Vol. 10 (1936), Part VIII: 150-151

ʃo-/õä – *where to find it, what to do with it and how to respect it.*
Originally entitled 'About ʃo-/õä *[Where to be found]'.*

ʃo:-|õä k''auki ||na Swa:, ta: Swa:-ka !ke |kuɯ ||amma hĩ au !ke e: ||anna !kaogən, au hiŋ tatti e:, he !ke hĩ e:, ||ke:n ʃo-|õä au |k'ĩ:-ta !kaogən.

ʃo-|õä is not on the Flat, for the Flat's Bushmen buy it from the people who inhabit the mountains, for they feel that these people are the ones who dig out *ʃo-|õä* from the Orange River's mountains.

Hiŋ k''auki ||na !xóë a: !kwai, ta: hĩ ||na !xóë-ka ku:-ka !kaogən. Hiŋ ||xɑm ||na !kuirri!kuirri-ka ku:, hiŋ kaŋ ||xɑm ||na !kuirri!kuirri-ka !kaukən, he k''auki |ki !khou, tá hĩ |kuɯ |ki !kwi!kwiŋ e: |k'waija, hiŋ |ki ≠kautən≠kautən.

It is not (only) at one place, for it is on the mountains of the whole place. It is also at all the rivers, it also is at the little streams which have not great thorn trees, but have many thornbushes, they have 'Haakdoorns.'

ʃo-|õäŋ !kɔ:ŋ |hiŋ au ʘho |u, haŋ dou !ketən ˍtai ||a:, hiŋ |nĩ: ha |k'a|k'a e: ˍ|kainja, hiŋ ||k'oen ˍ||gauë ti e:, ha !kɔ:ŋ |ha: hĩ. Hiŋ |hiŋ ha, hiŋ |e tĩ ha au ||ho:.

ʃo-|õä grows out by the Haak-doorn stem (from the earth), it grows tall. People walk along, they see its branches which are green, they look seeking where it is growing out. They take it out, they put it into the sack.

(Having broken the long pieces of root or stem, which were in the ground, into bits about a foot long, they put them into an old bag; they leave the green part which was above behind, having planted some of it (the top with a bit of stem to it) back in the hole that they took the roots out of, so that it may grow again.)

Hiŋ ˍtai úĩ, hiŋ ˍtai kere !khe !kuirri; hiŋ ||xa:, hiŋ |nĩ: ʃo-|õä

They walk on, they walk keeping along the river bed; they again see

ko: |k'a, hiŋ ||ke:n siŋ ||a:, hiŋ ʃo ko ||ke:n. Hiŋ |hiŋ ha, hiŋ ʃuru-tən !kwa |kɑm úï, ʃo-õä |k'a, hiŋ tẽ úï hĩ, hiŋ |e tẽ ʃo-õä !kwa!kwa:gən, hiŋ hó sa ʃo-|õä |k'a, hiŋ |ki |e: hĩ au ||ka tu, hiŋ tum |haŋ hĩ, au !kˀãũ.

the branches of another *ʃo-|õä*, they go to dig it out, they sit digging. They take it out, they twist off the *ʃo-|õä* foliage they lay it down, they put the roots in (the bag), they lift up the foliage, they put it in to the little hole, (out of which they took the root), they close it in with earth.

Hiŋ ||a: ||neiŋ; hiŋ ||aŋ ||hau !ho ||ho:, hiŋ tatti e:, hĩ ≠ĩ: ti e: ʃo-|õä !naunko -|ka:, hĩ se ||kɔ: |e tiŋ ||ho:, au ||ho:wa ||hau !khe ʘho a: !gwe !khe ||neiŋ; au hiŋ tatti ||ho tsˀorokən |kɯ é, há |kɯ ||ko:wa Ha hĩ k''auki |ku: hã: ã:, au hiŋ tatti e:, hĩ !hɑmmi ʃo-|õä -|k'wai au ||ho: -||ka:ŋ.

They go home, they go to hang up the bag, because they think that the *ʃo-|õä* is still damp, it will dry in the bag, when the bag is hanging up on a bush opposite the hut, because it is an old bag which is dry. In that they do not put away food, because they are afraid of the scent of the *ʃo-|õä* for a new bag.

(If they put meat in a bag that has contained *ʃo-|õä*, when they eat it, their stomaches swell up like a bladder, and they die, because they can not breathe properly.)

Hiŋ e:, hĩ |kɯ |ku: ||ho: tsˀorokən au ʃo-|õä, ha a:, hĩ k''uaki |ku: ha au eŋ, ta hĩ |kɯ ĩ: |ku: ||ho -||ka:ŋ au eŋ. Hiŋ |kɯ kaŋ ||hau !hóä ha, !khwa: siŋ |kɯ kãũ !hóä ha, au ha: ||hau !khe:.

Hence they keep an old bag for the *ʃo-|õä*, one which they do not keep for meat, for they verily keep a new bag for meat. They hang it (the old bag) up a little way off, that rain may fall upon it, as it hangs.

Hiŋ |kɯ ≠um !hum, hĩ se |e tẽ ʃo-|õä e: |k'waija, hĩ se-g |ne !hauë-tən tẽ !hum au hĩ !káuükən, hĩ se-g |ne |ki|ki -tai ʃo-|õä.

They sew a band, that they may put plenty of *ʃo-|õä* into it that they may fasten the band to their bodies, that they may take the *ʃo-|õä* with them.

(When hunting quietly they wear the band slung over the right shoulder and under the left arm, but when running after springbok they wear it round the waist.)

ʃo-|õä siŋ |ne ||na hĩ eneŋ; ta: !khwa: -||kwaŋ |ne kãũ ki sa: |xã-an-ka tʃweŋ, he hĩ !ku:xe |xãï hĩ ĩ:. Au hiŋ tatti e, hĩ |kɯ siŋ |ku:wa ʃo-|õä au ||neiŋ, au hiŋ tatti e:, tʃweŋ k''auki !kwã: sa:, ta !kˀãũ

The *ʃo-|õä* must be on their flesh; for the rain has fallen bringing things to shoot, and they run shooting them for themselves. They feel that they had kept the *ʃo-|õä*, at home, when the game

|ku !naunko ||ko:wa. He e:, hĩ siŋ |ku |ku:wa ʃo-|õä au ||neiŋ, hĩ siŋ |ne ˍtabạ tʃweŋ e: hĩ |xãï hĩ. Au hiŋ tatti, tʃweŋ e ˍdarrakən, hĩ ˍ||kwaŋ |ne é.

did not travel, because the earth was still dry. Then they had kept the *ʃo-|õä* at home, they had treated the things with which they shot. For they felt that things which move they are, (i.e. the game is.)

(They put the smell of the *ʃo-|õä* upon the men's bodies, that the game may be foolishly afraid, not strongly afraid, that they may forget what they were afraid of, and run in among the people acting foolishly.)

❑

Notes

Title 'J.T. adds that a certain kind of *ʃo-/õä* [white *ʃo-/õä*] is to be found in the earth' (3268 rev., note omitted).

11–13 *... but have many thornbushes, they have 'Haakdoorns'*: '*ǂkăutĕnǂkăutĕn* (pl.) 'Haak Doorn' [so called because its thorns are curved and catch like the tooth of a rake]' (3270 rev., note omitted).

75–76 *For they felt that things which move they are...* : In the original translation it says: 'While they [the people] feel that, things which have a waving motion, they [the game is] are.' (3278)

Women fear the new *ʃo-/õä*

Narrator: ||Kabbo
Dictation date: 23 September 1873
Translation date: 23 September 1873
Notebook reference: L.II.36: 3279-3283 and 3284-3286
***Bantu Studies* reference:** Vol. 10 (1936), Part VIII: 152-153

How women respect ʃo-/õä.

!ke-ta /ka:kakən //nau, ʃo-õä //hau !khe:, hiŋ k''auki ̠*tai //a: au !əhóbbakən, ta: hĩ /ku* ̠*tai !kauŋ ho !khwe tu, au hiŋ ≠ĩ:, ti e: ʃo-/õä* ̠*//ka:ŋ /ku é, he k''auki !naunko ≠enna hĩ.*

The women act like this when the *ʃo-/õä* is hanging up, they do not walk to leeward, but they walk passing the wind's mouth, because they think that it is new *ʃo-/õä*, which does not know them yet.

(The plant only knows the man who hung it up. When the man is digging up the plant, he bites off a tiny bit of the root, he chews it, he spits out the saliva into the little hole in the ground, while the plant is still in it, and says—so that the plant may know him—,

'ʃo-/õä we, a óäkən e ŋ-ŋ, ŋ /ke: //ke:ŋ ʃo au a, ŋ /ke ; akən ≠enna ŋ, akən dí a óä au ŋ, ta: ŋ /kweitən /ku á:a, ŋ a /kweitən //ke:n u-ú. ŋ a: ʃo-/õä-ka !kwi, ŋ a /kweitən /ku a:, eŋeŋ ̠*//kaowa, au kákən tatti e:, ŋ a: ʃo-/õä-ka !kwi, ŋ /ku e. !kwi a: /xarra haŋ k''auki á.'*

'O *ʃo-/õä*, thy father am I, I here sit digging at thee, I here; thou knowest me, thou dost make thy father of me, for I always am the one to dig ye out. I am the *ʃo-/õä*'s man, I always am the one whose flesh is bitter, for I feel that I am the *ʃo-/õä*'s man, I am he. No on else is that.')

Hĩ ≠enna, ti e: ʃo-/õä ̠*/k'wai* ̠*san* ̠*!kwa:ŋ ; ʃo-/õä* ̠*/k'wai* ̠*kwaŋ //k'uerre hĩ /ĩ:. Ta: ʃo-/õä k''auki !naunko ≠enna hĩ* ̠*/k'wai. He ti hiŋ e:, hĩ !hammi, ĩ:.*

They (the women) know that the *ʃo-/õä*'s scent would be angry; the *ʃo-/õä*'s scent would hurt their hearts. For the *ʃo-/õä* does not know their scent yet. Therefore they are afraid of it.

!kwi gwai se ≠kam ʘpua ̠*taba /ki /e: ʃo-/õä* ̠*/k'wai au ha /ha. He e: ʃo-/õä* ̠*/k'wai /ne //aŋ au ha /ha. He e:, ha se·g /ne* ̠*tai //kóë*

The man will first work putting the scent of the *ʃo-/õä* onto his wife. Then the *ʃo-/õä* scent will go forth from his wife. Then she

!khe ha /ka:gən, ha a: ʃo-/õä _/k'wai //na ha. He e: ha /ka:gən /ne !khou hãhã _/k'wai.

will walk among her companions, she who has the *ʃɔ-/õä* scent about her. Then her companions smell her scent.

He ti hiŋ e:, ha a:, !ke kuitən /ne _tai //a: hĩ ha, há ä: /ki /ka:gən-di-ka ʃo-/õä _/k'wai. He e:, /ke kuitən /ĩ: /kwu twai-ĩ, ĩ:, au hĩ /ne _tai /a: au !ɑhóbbakən, au haŋ tatti e:, hãhã-ka ʃo-/õä e: /ne !kõä-se /ka:-gən kuitən, au hiŋ tatti e:, hãhã a: _/kɑmme:nja /ka:gən-di-ka ʃo-/õä. He e: //xɑm !kõä-se há eŋeŋ, he ti hiŋ e:, ha k''auki _kɔ́ïŋ, ĩ:.

Therefore she is one with whom the other people go walking, she is one who has womanhood's *ʃo-/õä* scent. Hence other people's hearts are comfortable, when they go walking to leeward, for she feels that her own *ʃo-/õä* is taking care of the other women, because she herself is the one who carries womanhood's *ʃɔ-/õä*. That also protects her body therefore she does not become lean.

Women fear the new ʃo-/õä

Au !ke-ta /ka:gən k''auki !hɑmmi: ʃo-/õä _/k'wai, ʃo-/õäŋ /ki: hĩ /ĩ:; hĩ /ĩ:ŋ _kɔ́:ïŋ, hiŋ e:, hĩ /ne _//ɑhái ĩ:, au hiŋ tatti e:, ʃo-/õä _/k'wai /e:ja ʃoʃó:.

If the women do not fear the *ʃo-/õä* scent, the *ʃo-/õä* kills their hearts; their hearts become lean, then they cough, for they feel that the *ʃo-/õä* scent has entered the lungs.

Hĩ eŋeŋjaŋ //khou /hóäkən, au hiŋ tatti, hĩ k''auki //kuwa. Hiŋ tatti, hĩ _kɔ́:ïŋ, //khou /hóäkən. Hĩ xukən //xɑm //khou /hóäkən, au !kwi /aiti-kən tatti e:, ha tsaxáitən-ta !guirri-!guirri-de /kuu-g /ne /kainja, au han tatti e:, ha se _//ɑhái /ku:ka. Haŋ k''auki //kúï tʃweŋ e: ha hĩ: hĩ, au han tatti e:, ha !kaxu /kuu-g /ne //kɔ:, au haŋ _//ɑhái //na; ha tũwã:ŋ /kuu-g /ne //k'i://k'i: kau ta !kwa:gən.

Their flesh becomes black, and they feel that they are not fat. They feel, they are lean, become black. Their faces also turn black, while the woman feels that her eye-whites are yellow, and she feels as if she will cough to death. She does not get fat from the things she eats, because her chest is dry, she is coughing; her skin lies tight over her bones.

Notes

Title The full titles in the original translation are: for 3279–3283, 'How the women fear the new *ʃo-/õä* which has just been brought home' and for 3284–3286, 'The consequences of a woman's smelling fresh *ʃo-/õä*'s scent'.

19 *No one else is that*: Literally, 'A man who is different, he is not here' (3280 rev.).

21-23 *… the ʃo-/õä's scent would* **hurt** *their hearts*: The word *//k"uerre* is not in the *Dictionary* but *//k"were* may be translated as to 'attack' (Bleek 1956: 610).

47-48 *The ʃo-/õä* **kills** *their hearts …* : The word *hĩ:* is usually translated as 'to eat, or feed' (Bleek 1956: 60).

54 *They feel, they are lean…* : '[If they eat, they still are lean, as if they were in the midst of starvation]' (3284 rev., note omitted).

The man who misused *ʃo-/õä*

Narrator: ||Kabbo
Dictation dates: 24, 25, 26, 27 September 1873
Translation dates: 24, 25, 26 and 27 September 1873
Notebook reference: L. I. 36: 3287-3332
***Bantu Studies* reference:** Vol. 10 (1936), Part VIII: 153-160

This foolish man was not a 'ʃo-/õä's man'. He went out to dig ʃo-/õä and told no one. When he did not come back that night they went looking for him …

!kwitən ||ke:n siŋ ||a:, haŋ ʃo ko ||ke:n, haŋ |nĩ: ||khwitən ˍtai sa:, au han tatti e:, ha k''auki ≠kaka, ta:, ha |ku ||ke:n siŋja, au haŋ ≠gouwa. Haŋ |ku ʃo ko ||ke:n ʃo-|õä, au han tatti, !gebbi e, ha k''auki |kweitən ||ke:n ʃo-|õä.

A man went to sit digging *ʃo-/õä*, he saw a snake come, because it (the *ʃo-/õä*) felt that the man did not speak, but sat digging while he was silent. He sat digging *ʃo-/õä*, because he was a foolish person, he did not usually dig *ʃo-/õä*.

He ti hiŋ e:, ha |ku ≠gouwa, haŋ |ku-g |ne ||k'i: siŋ, au haŋ ≠gouwa, au han tatti, ha k''auki !naunko ˍ||kuakka ʃo-|õä-ka ≠kakən≠kakən, ha se-g |ne ≠kakən; au han tatti e:, ha k''auki ≠kaka au ||neiŋ, ha se ≠kakən ≠enn ʃo-|õä-ka !kwi, há a ˍ||kuakka ʃo-|õä-ka ||ke:n-||ke:n. ʃo-|õä-ka !kwi se ||na hĩ hã, ha se ||a:, !kan si ||ke:n||ke:n ha; au ha tatti e:, ʃo-|õä e ˍ!kwa, hĩ é; ≠gou-ka ʃo-|õä k''auki e, ta: ʃo-|õä e: |ki: !ke hĩ |ku e:, ha ||aŋ ||ke:n hĩ.

Therefore he was silent; he sat fastened to the ground, while he was silent, because he did not yet understand the *ʃo-/õä's* language, that he might talk; because he had not spoken about it at home, that he might talk learning from the *ʃo-/õä's* man, who understands the digging of *ʃo-/õä*. The *ʃo-/õä's* man would have been with him, would have gone to help him digging; because it is an angry *ʃo-/õä*, not a *ʃo-/õä* of peace, but one that kills people, that he went to dig up.

||kõĩŋjaŋ |e:, au !ketən !kã: |ki ha. !ketən ≠kakən, '|ne ó hi:, i-g |ne ˍ||gauë i ||kã:, ta. ha ʃo !kau ta: tsˀa !kerri, ta: !khwai |ku a:, ||kõĩŋ ta |e:, au i: !kau ta: ha. I-g |ne se !gauökən i ||kã: !nwa:.'

The sun set, while the people waited for him. The people said, 'Come, let us seek our brother, for he seems to have killed something big, for a gemsbok is that for which the sun sets when we kill it. We will follow our brother's spoor.'

!ku ko: |haŋ ≠kakən, 'U ˍkwaŋ se !gauökən |ke: !nwa e: |hiŋ ||neiŋ, ta: ha siŋ ≠kaka ke, ti e:, ha ˍhã: se ||a: ||ke:n ʃo-|õä.'

The other man's wife said, 'Ye must follow your friend's spoor which goes out of the hut, for he told me, he would go to dig up *ʃo-|õä.*'

ʃo-|õä-ka !kwiten ≠kakən, 'Há xa ˍ||kuakka, hiŋ e:, ha k''auki ≠kaka ka:?'—Ha |haŋ ≠kaka !ku ko:, ʃo-|õä-ka !kwi, '|gebbi |ku é, ha k''auki ˍ||kuakka.'—ʃo-|õä-ka !kwitən tutú: ha, 'Há xa |kweitən ||ke:n ʃo-|õä?'—Ha |haŋ |ku te: ʃo-|õä-ka !kwi, 'k''auki ĩ:ja, ta: ||k'e:||ou |ku |ke: ha ||a: ||ke:n ʃo-|õä ã:, au hŋ !gauë ta ti e:, ĩ !kã: |ki ha ĩ:, hĩ é: a.'

The *ʃo-|õä's* man said, 'Does he understand, that he did not tell me about it?'—His wife said to the other, the *ʃo-|õä's* man, 'A foolish person he is, he does not understand.'—The *ʃo-|õä's* man asked her, 'Is he accustomed to dig up *ʃo-|õä?*'—His wife said no to *ʃo-|õä's* man, '(He) has not done so, for the only time he went to dig up *ʃo-|õä* is this very day, upon which we are waiting for him.'

ʃo-|õä-ka !kwitən ≠kaka !ke kuitən, 'U ˍkőä k''auki se xuxú u-u-ku !hum, ta: u se !hauëtən !kauëtən tẽ u-ka !hu!hummi; u se ˍ||gauë i ||kã:, u se ˍhai tsʔi ha, u se ||a |nẽ:ja ha, ta: ha ˍk''őä ʃo ||aŋ ||k'i: ʃo:. Ta !kwi ta |kwe:ï |kĩ, au ha: ||k'i: ʃo.'

The *ʃo-|õä's* man said to the other men, 'Ye must not leave your band behind, but must fasten on your bands; ye shalt seek our brother, ye shall hasten to him, ye shall help him, for he seems to have gone to sit fast. For a man is like this when he sits fast.'

!ku ko:kən !hum ha. !ku kokən ≠kaka ha, 'Tsa di ba á:, i ||kã: k''auki siŋ |ne ≠kaka há: ã:, a se-g |ne ||na hĩ ha? a se ||a: !kan au ||kha-ka tí ko:, a se-g |ne !kan si ||ke:n||ke:n ha. He e:, a-g |ne ˍmaĩ, akən |xi: ||kóë ||ko a ||ki he e:, ha |ne ˍ|kati |xi: ||kóë ||ko ha ||ki; ta: ha |k''uã: ʃo-|õä e: |ki: !ke. Hiŋ |ku e:, ha ||a: ||ke:n hĩ, au haŋ k''auki |kweitən ||ke:n ʃo-|õä.'

Another man agreed. This other said to him, 'Why did our brother not speak to thee about it, that thou mightest have been with him? thou wouldst have held the other side of the stick and helped him dig. Then thou wouldst first have spit in thy saliva, and then he would afterwards spit in his saliva; for he was gathering *ʃo-|õä*, which kills people. That was what he went to dig up, though he was not accustomed to dig up *ʃo-|õä.*'

!ketən ˍtai. Hiŋ !gauökən ha !nwa. Hiŋ !gauökən ki !kei ||a: ha !nwa au ha eŋeŋ. Hiŋ |nĩ: ha, hiŋ ≠kakən, 'I ||kã: ˍ||kwaŋ a:, ||k'i: ʃo:, hé: ti, he ĩ siŋ ≠kaki, ti e: ha |ku |kwẽ:ï |kã:.'

The (two) men set out. They follow his spoor. They follow it up to his body. They catch sight of him, they say, 'Our brother it is, sitting fast, just as we said that he would be.'

The man who misused ʃo-|õä

!ku ko:kən ≠kaka !ku ko:, 'I ||kã: kaŋ |kɯ a: k''auki ≠kaka ka:; ŋ siŋ ||na hĩ hã, ŋ siŋ sa: ||ke:n |ki !kei !ho ha.

One says to the other, 'Our brother is the one who did not tell me about it, that I might be with him, that I might come to teach him digging!

!ku ko:kən ≠kaka ha, 'Arróko |kweja dəro, a se arróko ku: |e |i; ta a |kɯ a ||k'oen ||khwitən||khwitən é: a, he i ||kã: ||k'i: ||kóë ʃo hĩ, au haŋ k''auki ||khõã taŋ !hammi. A se ||ka tẽ ʘhokən -||ka:ŋ, a se ||ko sa: ke |i, ŋ siŋ |ki |hiŋ ŋ-ka ʘhokən -||ka:ŋ.'

The other says to him, 'Quickly strike flint and steel, thou shalt quickly light a fire; for thou seest the snakes among which our brother sits fast, though he does not seem to feel fear. Thou shalt burn a fresh twig (of *ʃo-|õä*), thou shalt put fire by me, that I may take out my fresh twig.'

Haŋ tutú: !ku ko:, 'Tsa di ba: á, a k''auki ≠kaka ka: ã:?' !ku ko:kən k''auki ≠kakən, au han tatti e:, na ||khei||khei ||k e:ja, nɪŋ |kɯ koä -!kattu siŋ. !ku ko:ken ≠kaka !ku ko:, 'A kaŋ kwõŋ |kɯ tutú:i ||kã:, ta:, ha k''auki se ≠kakən, au akkən |kɯ se ≠kam ʘpua |nẽ: ha.'

He asks the others, 'Why didst thou not tell me about it?' The other does not speak, because his teeth are closed, they are clenched together. The first man says to him, 'Thou must not question our brother, for he can not speak, until thou hast first helped him.'

Haŋ kúï ≠kup au ʃo-|õä e: !ku:, he e ʃo-|õä -||ka:ŋ. !ku ko:kən kúï ≠ku≠kubbu !ho ʃo-|õä e: !nwanna. !ku ko a:, haŋ !ku: |kam ʃo-|õä e: kúï ≠kup, haŋ !ku: kóïtən |e: !ku ko: |nu|nutu:, haŋ |xi: !ahí ||ko au !ku ko: tsaxáitən. !ku ko:kən !kabbakən úï.

He sets fire to two twigs of *ʃo-|õä* which are new. The second man sets fire to the three pieces of *ʃo-|õä*. The first man takes two pieces of *ʃo-|õä* which burn, he lets the two pieces smoke into the other man's nostrils, he spits into the other's eyes (which are open, but fixed). The other man starts.

The man who misused ʃo-/õä

!ku ko:kən ||xamki !kan |kam ha-ha-ka ʃo-|õä, haŋ kó:ïtən |e: !ku ko: |nu|nutu, !ku ko:kən ||xã:, haŋ !kabbakən uï. !ku ko:kən tuppəm |kam !gwarra ʘpua, ha:ŋ ||ka tẽ ||a: ʘhokən, haŋ ʃo ko |ĩ: !ku ko: !kaxu, haŋ ≠kaka !ku ko:, '!kanna ki au i ||kã: !kaxu-ka tũ-ka tí ko:, ŋ siŋ arróko |ã |hiŋ i ||kã: !gau; ta: ʃo:|õä |kɯ |ka: ha; ta: a ||k'oen, i ||kãŋ -|ka:ti !khoukən.' Haŋ

The second man also takes his own *ʃo-|õä*, he lets it smoke into the other man's nostrils, the other starts again. The first man takes off an arrow point, he burns a twig, he sits cutting the other's chest. He says to the second man, 'Hold for me the skin of our brother's chest on the other side, that I may quickly cut, letting out our brother's blood, for the

arróko |a si ||kakən||kakən !ku ko:. Haŋ arróko xuruxuru ||kóë tẽ ||a: |hóä au |ku kɔ:-ka ||xaukən.

ʃo-|õä is killing him; for thou seest, our brother is trembling now.' He quickly cuts the other in haste. He quickly rubs the burnt wood into the other's blood (the cuts).

Haŋ ≠kaka !ku ko:, 'Å kóä |ĩ: i ||kã: tẽtẽ, he e:, a ˍsaŋ |ne xanna-xanna !ho au i ||kã: !kwa!kwagən, ha !kwa!kwagən-ka ||xaukən se ||xam |hiŋ; á siŋ xuruxuru |ã|ã-ka ku:, i ˍsaŋ |ne ||gwe:tən ha.' Haŋ !k''o-kən !ku ko |k'a. ||khwitən||khwi-takən ˍtaiˍtai úï, au hiŋ |ne ˍkwaŋ ki ˍtai ʃo-|õä ˍ|k'wai.

He says to the second man, 'Thou must cut our brother's thighs, and make long cuts down our brother's legs, that his legs' blood may also come out; thou must rub (burnt wood) into all the cuts, that we may lead him.' He cracks (the second and third fingers of) the other's (left) hand. Snakes come out (of the hole), and glide away taking the *ʃo-|õä* scent.

(People do not kill these *ʃo-|õä* snakes, but let them alone, merely showing them to one another when they see them. These snakes do not go to a man who knows *ʃo-|õä*, he digs in peace because he is a *ʃo-|õä* man. A man who digs *ʃo-|õä* cuts on the outside of both arms above the wrists, and rubs the burnt powder of the plant into the cuts. *||khabbo* was told by a man whom he knew, not to dig *ʃo-|õä* himself, his arms being free from the accustomed marks of a *ʃo-|õä's* man,—*|nu:-ka |ã|ã*, i.e. the cutting of the Bushmen from the other side of the Orange River.—The *|k'ĩ:-||eŋ* are people who live by the Orange River on the Colonial side, who talk both Bushman and Koranna and dig up *ʃo-|õä* on this side of the river. These people cut the backs of wrists as the *|nu-ka !ke* or Bushmen of the other side of the Orange River do. These cuts are called *|nu:-ka |ã|ã*.)

Hiŋ tutú !ku ko:, 'A xa: k''auki taŋ á se ≠kakən, a- se-g |ne ˍtai, tãtã: a, ta: a ˍ||kwaŋ |ne ˍdabba-ĩ; a tsaxáitən-ta ˍdabbaˍdabbajakən ˍ||kwaŋ |ne k''wa tˀain. Hiŋ ˍ||kwaŋ |ne k''wẽŋ a se-g |ne ≠ka-kən, a se-g |ne ˍkóaŋ tãtã a.'

They ask the other man, 'Dost thou not feel as if thou couldst talk, and walk, trying thyself, for thou dost open and shut the eyes; thine eyes opening seems to have become soft (his eyes were no longer fixed, but their lids could move easily). They seem as if thou wouldst speak, as if thou wouldst arise, trying thyself.'

The man
who misused
ʃo-|õä

!ku ko:kən ≠kaka hĩ, 'ŋ tu kaŋ ˍ||kwaŋ taŋ ŋ se ≠kakən; ukən ˍ||kwaŋ se ˍ!ham !kən!kən |kwi: tẽ

The other says to them, 'My mouth feels as if I might talk; ye shall first stretch out my legs (which

ŋ !kwa/kwa:gən, hĩ se ku /nũ:, he e:, ŋ -//kwaŋ /ne tãtã ŋ ; he e:, u /kɯ-g /ne //gwe:tən ŋ, ŋ siŋ /kɯ-g /ne _tai tau tã:ã ŋ !kwa!kwa:gən. He e: ŋ /ne _tai kúï /nũ/nũ: ĩ: ; he e:, u _saŋ /ne !hau u //a: !kɒn _kwan au ŋ, au ka: /ne _tai txe:tən. He e:, ŋ saŋ /ne k''wã:ï:, au ka tatti e:, //neiŋ siŋ !hi:ŋ, au úkən !kɒn _kwan au ŋ. Tá ŋ -//kwaŋ siŋ duru ú //e ; u se //gwe:tən ki /kɔ: //e ŋ, ta: /xuarre //xɒmki /e:ja ŋ eŋeŋ, au hiŋ tatti e:, ŋ k''auki _dóä //gu ʃɔ:, ta: ŋ /kɯ _dóä !kwã: ʃɔ:, au kakən tatti e:, !nwiŋ /kɯ _dóä ʃɔ: //neiŋ; ŋ /kɯ siŋ !ɒhái //kóä //hɔ: au ŋ eŋeŋ, há ŋ sa: //ke:n /e tẽ ʃo-/õä ã:.'

had been drawn up as he sat), that they may loose their stiffness, then I will try myself. Ye shall lead me, that I may walk trying my legs. Then I shall walk loosening the stiffness from them; then ye can loosen your grasp of me, when I walk easily. Then I will drink, when I feel that home is near, when ye loosen your grasp of me. For I must slowly arise and go; ye shall lead me thither, for the cold also has entered my body, because I did not sit wrapped up, but I sat in the cold, for I felt that my kaross had been left at home; I had only slung on my bag to my body, when I came to dig putting *ʃo-/õä* into it.'

!ke kuitakən //gwe:tən hó ha ; haŋ ≠kaka !ke kuitən, 'U _koá: se !kɒn //ʔwi: au ŋ //kũŋ//kũŋ, u se /kɒn _!kwai!ho ŋ ; he é: ŋ /ne _!kwai!khe, ĩ:. He e:, u-g /ne !kɒn !ho ŋ, ŋ se ≠kɒm ʘpua !khe: ku /nũ: au ŋ //k'óë; he ŋ /ne !hau, ŋ _tai !kũï, au ú: /ne //gwe:tən /kɒm ŋ, he e:, i-g /ne tɒm ʘpua _tai //a, au u: tɒm ʘpua _taïja ke. Ta: ŋ !naunko //k'i:ja, he ti hiŋ e:, ŋ !kwa!kwagən _kau_kam, ĩ:, au hiŋ tatti e:, ŋ siŋ //k'i: ʃɔ:, hiŋ taŋ ŋ se _tai tau _!kaitən_!kaitən tin.'

The others (the two man) help him up; he says to them, 'Ye must hold firmly at my arms, that ye may holding raise me up; then I shall stand upright. Then ye shall keep hold of me, that I may first stand stretching my back, and afterwards I shall walk forward, while ye gently make me walk, while ye lead me on, and then we go on gently. For I am still stiff, therefore my legs are trembling, because they feel that I sat fast, they feel as if I should fall down as I walk'

Han ≠kwi≠kwi:ja !kũï. !ke kuitakən ≠kaka ha, 'A _kwaŋ se !kõä !kõä //kau tẽ au !kʔãũ ; a se k''auki !xĩ!xĩ ã.' !ku ko:kən ≠kakən, 'ŋ !kwa!kwa:gən kaŋ e: !naunko _kau _kam, au hiŋ tatti e:, ŋ siŋ //k'i: ʃɔ. ŋ -//kwaŋ se _tai ku ta /i hĩ, he ŋ /ne tã-ĩ hĩ ; ta: hĩ !naunko ta sirritən, au hiŋ tatti, /xuarre /e: ta: ŋ

He staggers forward. The others say to him, 'Thou must tread firmly upon the ground, thou must not drag thyself along.' The other replies, 'My legs are still trembling, because they feel that I sat fast. I must walk, making them warm, then I shall feel them, for they still feel chilled, because the

|nũ|nũäde. ||kẽïŋ se _!ham ≠kɒm ⊙pua ||ka _kau hĩ, he e: ŋ |ne tã:-ĩ hĩ, ĩ. He e:, ŋ |ne _|ka:ti |nuobba !kũ ||a, au hĩ |né ta _|kɒm|kɒm, au ka tatti e:, ŋ |ne _|ka:ti xerre.'

!ke kuitakən !hom ha, 'ŋ kaŋ _||kwaŋ |kwẽ: da.' Haŋ ≠kwi-≠kwi:ja !kũ ||a:.

!ku ko:kən ≠kaka !ku ko:, 'I ||kã:ŋ tuko siŋ ka, i se tɒm ⊙pua _taija hã, ha se _!kɒm ≠kɒm ⊙pua ku |nũ|nũ:, au ||kãïŋja |karaka, au ha _tai ||a: au kammaŋ; ta: !kau ⊙pua _||kwaŋ !xo:wa, ha i siŋ !gauö-kən ki sa: ha !nwa, ã:. He ti hiŋ e:, i _saŋ |ne di ti é: ha |ke:, tá, i _||kwaŋ sin _tai tau !kõäse ha au kammaŋ.'

!ke !kuitakən tɒm ⊙pua _taija hã, hiŋ tutú hã, 'Á siŋ ≠kaka si?' !ku kokən ≠kaka hĩ, 'ŋ kaŋ !naunko ||k'i:ja.' !ke kuitakən tutú: ha, 'A |i:ŋ té: ta?' Haŋ ≠kaka !ke kuitən, 'U kaŋ _||kwaŋ _taba akka ŋ |ĩ:, ŋ |ĩ:ŋ _||kwaŋ |ne twai-ĩ; _k''aogən |ku e:, ŋ |ne ta ||hiŋ||hiŋ ja, ĩ:, au ŋ tatti e:, ŋ eŋeŋ k''auki _kaowa, hĩ siŋ |né ta |i; he ŋ k''auki !naunko _tai kóä ta |i hĩ; he e: ŋ !kwa!kwa-gən-ka !kwa:gən |ne |kɒm, au ka:-g |ne _tai ||a:, hiŋ e:, ŋ eŋeŋ _sa-g |ne |kɒmma, ĩ:, au ka tatti e:, ŋ !kwa!kwagən-ka !kwa:gən |ne ta |i. Ta: ŋ !naunko ≠kwi ≠kwi:-ĩ.'

!ke kuitakən !hom ha, 'A kaŋ _||kwaŋ |kwe: da, akən ≠kaka si.' Hiŋ _tai |kɔ: ||a: au ||neiŋ-ta _|kao. !ke kuitakən tutú: ha, 'Ákən |ne te: tã?' Haŋ ≠kaka !ke kuiten, 'ŋ kaŋ _||kwaŋ |ne |kwe: ta, ŋ k''auki |ne ≠kwi≠kwi:-ĩ, tá, ŋ _||kwaŋ tan ú se |ne !kɒn _kwan au ŋ, ŋ sin

cold is in my knees. The sun must first warm them a little, then I shall feel them in consequence. Then I shall soon walk briskly, when they (my legs) are fresh, when I feel that I shall soon walk easily.'

The others assent, 'I will do so,' He goes staggering forward.

One says to the other, 'Our brother has asked us to take him gently along, until he has lost his stiffness, while the sun shines as he goes along on the way; for the little path is long by which we came following his spoor. Therefore we will do as he tells us, for we will walk along taking care of him on the way.'

The others gently lead him, they ask him, 'Canst thou speak to us?' The other says to them, 'I am still stiff.' The others ask him, 'How is thy heart?' He answers, 'Ye treated my heart well, my heart is comfortable; coldness is what makes me feel lame, because I feel that my flesh is not warm so I do not feel warm, as I have not yet walked making it warm; when my legs' bones become warm as I go along, then my flesh will be warm, when I feel that my legs' bones are warm. For I still stagger.'

The others concur, 'That is so, just as thou didst tell us.' They draw near to the home hill. The others ask him, 'How dost thou feel?' He says to them, 'I feel like this, I do not stagger, but I feel as if ye might loosen your hold of me, so that I might walk by

|ne ||ĩ:, ŋ ˍtai; tá, ŋ ˍ||kwaŋ |ne ˍtai txe:tən; ŋ ˍ||kwaŋ taŋ ŋ se-g |ne !kúïtən, ta: ŋ-ka ˍtai ˍ||kwaŋ |ne ka ||xi||xi.'

myself; for I can walk briskly; I feel as if I can return, for my going is strong.'

!ke kuitakən !hom ha, 'ŋ kaŋ ˍ||kwaŋ |kwẽ: da.' Hiŋ !kən ˍkwan ã:. Hiŋ !khãã |kəm ||a: hã. Hiŋ !kai ||a: !khwa:. !ke kuitakən ≠kaka ha, 'A ˍkwa: se ˍ||guobbo a tu, a se ˍ||kuarri tẽ u ʃo-|õä ˍ|k'wai; he e:, a-g |ne təm ⊙pua k''wẽ:ï, ta: a ||kaŋ-a; a se ˍ!həm ||e ||neiŋ, he e:, a-g |ne ˍ||khwai |xóä|xóä a ||khẽĩ-||khẽĩ, au ã:; he e:, a ˍsaŋ |ne ˍ|kati k''wã ||wẽ:ï:, ĩ:, au a ˍ!həm hã: ã:, a:ta |i, ha |ki |xabba:. He ti hiŋ e:, a-g |ne ˍ|ka:ti k''wã ||wẽ:ï. A ˍkwa: ˍsan |ne k''auki !kaunsiŋja |ha !khwe, ta:, a ˍsaŋ |ku ʃo: !əhuobbakən; ta:, a |ki |ã|ã ˍ||ka:ŋ. He e: a siŋ ˍ!həm |ku |ki á-ka ||neiŋ, |ha ka: ˍ!həm |ku !kwai; |ã|ã se ≠kəm ⊙pua ||kɔ:; he e:, a-g |ne |ĩ: ha; hiŋ e:, a-g |ne |ã:ŋ |ha-ka ||neiŋ, au ⊙hokən e:, si |ã: a ĩ:; hiŋ e:, a se ˍtaba |ha ĩ:.'

The other men agree, 'I think so.' They loosen their hold of him. They walk just in front of him. They go down to the water. The others say to him, 'Thou must rinse thy mouth in order to spit out the *ʃo-|õä* scent, then thou must drink a little, for thou art hungry; thou shalt first go home, then thou shalt bite, strengthening thy teeth with meat; then thou shalt drink plentifully later, when thou hast first eaten hot meat that has soup. After that thou canst drink plentifully. Thou must not sit to windward of thy wife, but thou must sit to leeward; for thou hast new cuts. Therefore thou must first have a hut of thy own, thy wife must first be alone, until the cuts become dry; then thou must cut her. Then thou must sleep in thy wife's hut with the twig with which we cut thee; with that thou shalt treat thy wife.'

!ku ko:kən ˍ||guobbo ha tu; haŋ k''wẽ:ï. Hiŋ ˍtai |hiŋ ||a: au !khwa: tu ||kai, hiŋ !kúïtən !kei ||a: ||neiŋ. Hiŋ sue:ŋ. |aitikən á ha ã:. !ke kuitakən ≠kaka ha |ha, 'Si kaŋ |ku ||a:, |haŋ ||k'i: ʃo:, au haŋ ||kóë ʃo: ||khwitən||khwitən, au ||ka tu; au ha a: k''auki ≠kaka, si-ta !ku ko: se ||na hĩ hã. Haŋ k''ó:ä |ku ú:ï, haŋ ˍtai, au sitən k''auki ≠enna.'

The other man rinses his mouth; he drinks. They go away from the water pit, they return and reach home. They sit. The woman gives him meat. The others say to his wife, 'We went, husband sat fast, while he sat among snakes at the hole's mouth; because he was the one who did not tell, so that one of us might be with him. He arose, he went off, without our knowing anything about it.'

The man who misused *ʃo-|õä*

|aitikən !hom, 'I ˍ||kwaŋ ki e: si ŋ |kwẽ: da, ti e:, ha ˍdóä ||aŋ ||k'i:

The woman assents, 'We thought so, that he had gone and stuck fast.

ʃo:. ŋ -//kwäŋ ka, u /kɯ /kwẽ:ï /kĩ. ŋ -!hɒm /nĩ /ke:, ta: ha á: ka /ki //ka //kóä ke /i, he e: ŋ ã /ne -kóäŋ /hiŋ, ŋ ã: /ne kuŋ.'	I thought that ye would do just so. I now see your friend, for he is the one who makes fire for me, and then I arise, I warm myself.'

❑

Notes

2 … *he saw a snake come …* : '[and get into the hole where the *ʃo-/õä* is]' (3286 rev., note omitted).

29-30 *Ye must follow your friend's spoor …* : '[I think it means friend here, but J.T. says nephew]' (3290 rev., note omitted).

63 … *for he was* **gathering** ʃo-/õä: '/k"ũa: – a word which I *think* is chiefly used [if not wholly] for women's hunting, *!kŭnn* being used for men's hunting. Women hunt for their prey [dig out things]: they hunt their prey; because they feel that they dig out rice, that they may kill it; because they feel that the rice runs about. That is why they kill the rice, when the rice is in the rice hill. [The killing is here a figure of speech, meaning that this is *their* game; for the killing is done later by means of the fire at the women's houses]' (3296 rev. –3297 rev., note omitted).

Interestingly, neither */k"ua* or *!kŭnn* are listed in the *Dictionary*. Here, although it is a man who went out to collect *ʃo-/õä*, the 'women's word' */k"ũa:* is used because it is dug out like *veldkos*.

65-66 … *though he was not accustomed to dig up* ʃo-/õä: 'That is why the *ʃo-/õä* does not know his scent. Because the man knew that he was not accustomed to dig up *ʃo-/õä* which is angry. Because the man knew that he now dug *ʃo-/õä* which was angry, but he did not know *ʃo-/õä*'s digging. He should have understood, but people had not taught him about *ʃo-/õä* digging. And he should have known that people would have taught him, that he might know, the things which the *ʃo-/õä* people did thus on account of it' (3297-3299, text omitted).

87 *He asks the others …* : The original translation says: 'He questions the other man [the patient]' (3302).

155 *The other says to them …* : '[the patient]' (3311).

165-166 *Then I will drink …* : '[He drinks at the water which is near the house]' (3311 rev., note omitted).

206-207 … *when I feel that I shall soon walk easily*: '[his legs being able to move quickly]' (3319 rev., note omitted).

221-222 *Canst thou speak to us?*: '[J.T. says the Bushman question in an interrogative tone, here, altho' he seems to explain to me that it is *not* a question in its meaning.]' (3321 rev., note omitted)

223 *I am still stiff*: '[in my legs]' (3321 rev., note omitted).

237-238 *They draw near to the home hill*: '[a little hill]' (3324 rev., note omitted).

247-248 *The other men agree, 'I think so'*: '[J.T. says "I say so" here but I don't think it can be quite this.] He now says it is their thoughts which agree with him.' (3326 rev., note omitted)

Cursing

Narrator: |Haŋ‡kass'o
Source: '|Haŋ‡kass'o from personal observation'
Dictation date: 16 August 1879
Notebook reference: L.VIII.31: 8741-8743
***Bantu Studies* reference:** Vol. 10 (1936), Part VIII: 161

These are some of the ways that people curse each other.

❑

|xam-ka !kʔe-ta ||k'ao||k'ao ˍ||kwaŋ |k'waija. ˉHĩ ta, 'ˍ!kʔo: ˍäkən !kwi,' au ˉhĩ ||k'ao !ku ko:. ˉHĩ sá ka, 'ˉ|nu !kwi.'

The Busnmen's (modes of) cursing are many. They say, 'Grave Man,' when they curse another man. They also say, 'Departed one.'

ˉHĩ ||xamki ka, 'ˉ|a:,' au ˉhĩ ||k'ao !ku ko:, 'ˉ|a:, a kaŋ ||nau, a k''au ka a ˉ|kukən, a á xau k''wã ≠hannuwa?'

They also say, 'Be killed,' when they curse another man, 'Be killed, dost thou think thou shalt not die, thou who dost not act nicely?'

!ku ko: ˉku, 'ˉ|nu !kwi we, á ka ŋ ||nau, a k''au ka a ˉ|a:?'

That other exclaims, 'O Departed one, dost thou think that thou wilt not be killed?'

!ku ko: ˉku, 'ˉ!kẽjã ˉ!khan |kam ||e á.'

The former exclaims, '* * * * be upon thee.'

!ku ko: á, ha ˉku, 'ˉa ki |kam ||e: á, ta: a k''au ˍdóä k''wã ≠hannuwa.'

That other exclaims, 'Death be upon thee, for thou dost not act nicely.'

!ku ko: ˉku, 'ˉ!ku: |hiŋ we, a kaŋ ||nau, a k''au ka a ˉ|a:?'

The former exclaims, 'O hatch out, dost thou think, thou wilt not be killed?'

❑

Notes

6 *They also say, 'Be killed' ...*: 'They also say [?wish] the other shall/may [?] die, when they say "/a!"' (8740 rev., note omitted).

13 *The former exclaims*: '[who said /a, above]' (8740 rev., note omitted).

13-14 *'**** be upon thee'*: Neither Lucy Lloyd nor Dorothea Bleek translated the word *!kẽjã*. Perhaps it is a variant spelling of *!ke:a*, translated as 'rage' (Bleek 1956).

15-16 **Death** *be upon* **thee** ... : In the notebook the word for 'death', */a*, is translated as 'a fight'. Ju|'hoan people call a concentration of supernatural potency a 'fight' (see Marshall 1961: 351).

thee: 'The other one [shall?] also die.' (8743 rev., note omitted)

16-17 ... *for thou dost not act* **nicely**': The word *ǂhannũwa* is translated here as 'nicely', but it also means 'to be comfortable, happy, good or fortunate' (Bleek 1956). The word describes the behaviour of humans and other animals, and the effect that this has on the social and natural environment (see Part III, 'Hunting after the death of a friend' and Part VIII, 'The sorceror !Nuiŋ-|kúïtən' for examples). When people *ǂhannũwa* each other, then things go well. When people do not *ǂhannũwa*, then conflict is bound to follow, as in this case. The narratives in Part VII describe the ability of game sorcerors (*!gitən)*, both the living and the dead, to make game animals *ǂhannũwa* or not.

18-19 *O hatch out'*: In the notebook translation, this passage is translated as follows: 'Oh! Mayest thou be hatched!' (8743). See 'Things which hatch out'.

Things which hatch out

Narrator: |Haŋ‡kass'o
Notebook reference: L.VIII.31: 8742 rev.
***Bantu Studies* reference:** Vol. 10 (1936), Part VIII: 161

This extract is a note to the previous narrative 'Cursing'. Dorothea Bleek left out an important part of the note however (see 'Note' below).

❑

i|k'ao||k'ao á a, haŋ |kɯ ||ke-||kéja tʃweŋ e: ¯!ku:, !ku ko:kən |kɯ ||k'ao !ku ko: ki |kukən.

This cursing resembles things which hatch out, the one curses the other that he may die.

❑

Note

The first part of the reverso note says: 'It is cursing while/as they curse each other. We say: "This ostrich, it is the one which hatched out here" [i.e. of this eggshell].' (8742 rev.). The basis for the metaphor is clearer now: |Haŋ‡kass'o seems to be comparing the hatching out of curses to the hatching out of ostrich eggs.

Bewitchment

Narrator: |Haŋ‡kass'o
Translation dates: Sometime between 21 May and 15 June 1878
Notebook reference: L.VIII.11: 7009 rev. and 7010 rev.
***Bantu Studies* reference:** Vol. 10 (1936), Part VIII: 161-162

|Haŋ‡kass'o mentions two cases where non-humans (in one instance), and a human (in another), use supernatural potency or 'magic' to get what they want.

❑

¯|kittən¯|kittən,

The name of a little black bird.

Haŋ !hau ||xe:, au haŋ tatti e:, ||kuanna ¯ã |ne é, he ||xe: |ne se ¯||khou ĩ:. He hi |ne ¯hĩ ||xe:-ta ¯|kɔro, au ||xe:-ta !khoa: a kããwa.

It bewitches the ants' chrysalides, when it feels summer is there, and they fly out. Then they eat the flying ants, when the ants' rain has fallen.

!kwi !hau, !ku ko: se _taŋ-a. Haŋ _!gabbetən-ĩ au wai-ta !kwagən, au haŋ !hau !ku ko:. He tikən e:, han _!gabbetən-ĩ au wai-ta !kwagən, !ku ko: se _taŋ-ã á ha, au haŋ tatti e:, ha _taŋ-ĩ. !ku kokən a |khi:.

A man makes a charm, that another may miss (his aim). He throws springbok bones to bewitch the other. That is why he throws springbok bones, that the other may miss like he does, because he misses. The other kills.

❑

Notes

1 *The name of a little black bird:* '*/kittən-/kittən* [the name of a small bird, found in Bushman land, black [or blackish?]. They eat "Bushman Rice" [it] is (*/koro //xĕ*, "flying ants" – ed.), "Bushman Rice" heads (*//xĕ /naŋ*, not in *Dictionary* – ed.), that and Bushman Rice's … (*//xĕ ta !khwoŋ!khwoŋ*, not in *Dictionary* – ed.). The call of the */kittən-/kittən* is '*/korŏkã tchuarri, /korŏkã tchuarri*" ' (7009 rev., note partially omitted).

The bird is probably the Anteating Chat (*Myrmecocichla formicivora*). It is a small bird (about 180 mm long) and sooty blackish brown in colour. It occurs in the shrubby desert environment of !Xam-ka !aũ, where it eats insects, in particular ants and termites. It hunts by dropping onto its prey from an elevated perch, such as a termite mound or bush, especially in summer. In winter it forages mainly by hopping and running on the ground (Anonymous 1999).

2 *It bewitches the ant's chrysalides*: The same word, *!hau*, is used to describe the behaviour of the lizard that lies in a thorn tree and turns the rain clouds back (Part V, 'Lizards and rain').

4-6 *Then they eat the flying ants, when the ant's rain has fallen*: 'J.T. says that *!hau-!hau waken* (not in *Dictionary* – ed.) afterwards, it will go (i.e. fly away?)' (7009 rev. text omitted).

7 *A man makes a charm*: Dorothea Bleek left out the title and a short explanation: 'Explanation of *!hau-!hau*. Missing [one's] aim [it] is; that the other one might not kill' (7010 rev.).

13 *The other kills*: The other man is successful in hunting, so the jealous man who misses his aim wants to curse him out of spite.

SPECIAL SPEECH OF ANIMALS AND MOON USED BY THE |XAM BUSHMEN

From material collected by
Dr. W.H.I. BLEEK and Miss L.C. LLOYD between 1870 and 1880,
edited by D.F. Bleek

A curious feature of Bushman Folklore is the peculiar speech attributes to certain animals and to the Moon. It is an attempt at imitating the shape or position of the mouth of the animal in question. As a rule all clicks are changed either into other special clicks, or into other consonants. In the following pages examples of these peculiar speeches are given, interlined with the same words translated into ordinary Bushman speech.

Photo: Jeremy Hollmann

‘|ʊhére does really seem to have taken pity on me to-day. For ostriches are coming passing.’
Engravings of a row of ostriches and a rhinoceros made on dolerite rock. Britstown District, Northern Cape Province.

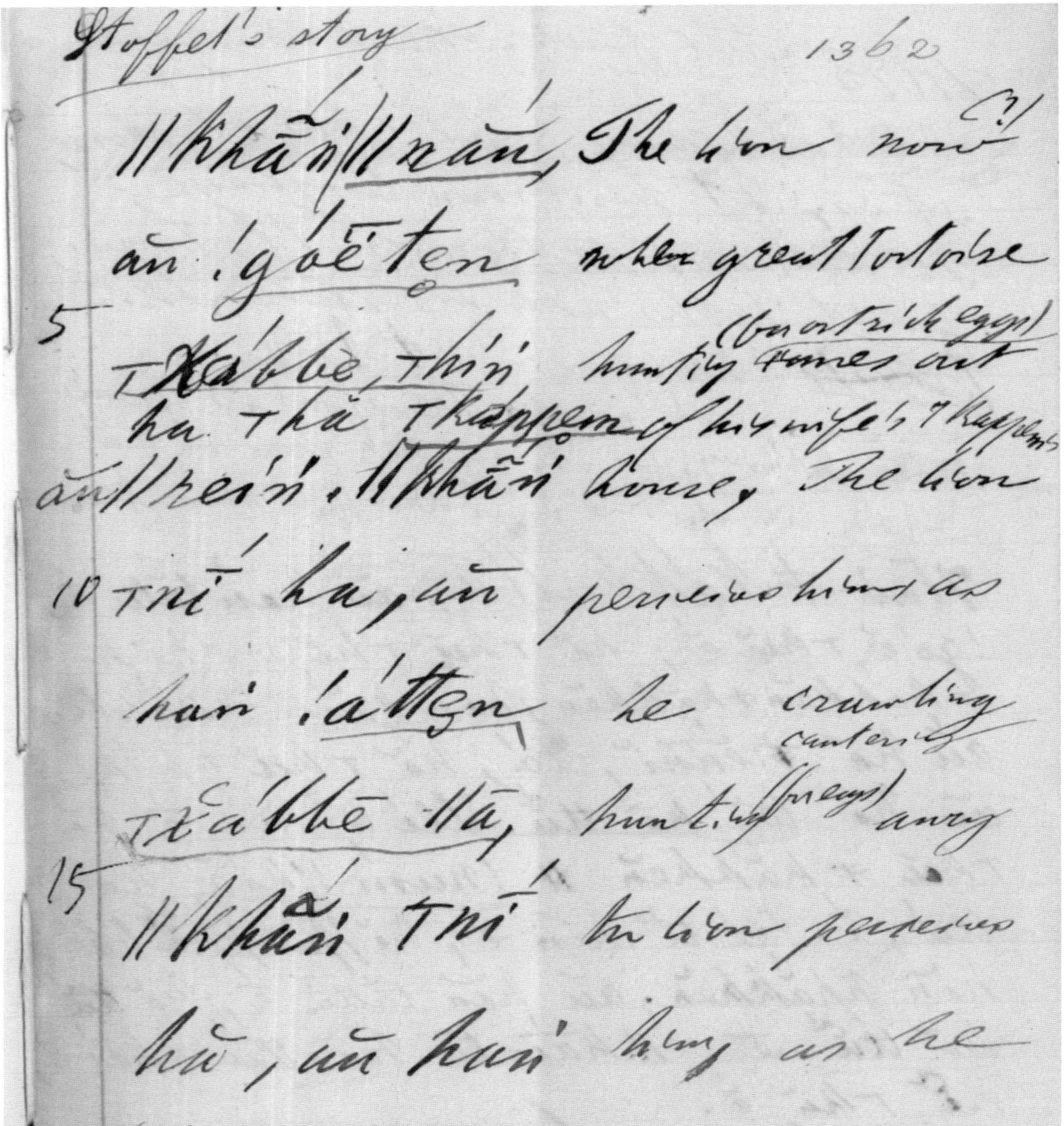
Stoffel's story 1362

||khāï||xau, The lion now

aū !goë ten when great Tortoise

ǂxábbe, ǂhiñ hunting (for ostrich eggs) comes out

ha ǂhã ǂkappem of his wife's ǂkappems

aū||keiñ. ||khãï house, The lion

ǂhí ha, aū perceives him as

hau !áttẹn he crawling

ǂxábbē ||ã, hunting (preys) (cantering) away

||khãï ǂhí the lion perceives

hā, aū hau him as he

!kuttu ||ā stooping goes,

Manuscript page B.XIV: 1362 from |A!kunta's narrative 'The Lions and the Tortoise'

Special speech of animals and moon used by the |Xam Bushmen

All things were once people
– |Haŋ‡kass'o: 'Why the Ostrich does not click' –

Unlike Parts I to VIII, in which Dorothea Bleek selected and arranged narratives around |Xam customs and beliefs, the focus of 'Special speech' is language itself, the language of animals. This was a feature of |Xam that intrigued Wilhelm Bleek (1875:6):

> A most curious feature in Bushman folklore is formed by the speeches of various animals, recited in modes of pronouncing Bushman, said to be peculiar to the animals in whose mouths they are placed. It is a remarkable attempt to imitate the shape or position of the mouth of the kind of animal to be represented. Among the Bushman sounds which are hereby affected, and often entirely commuted, are principally the clicks.

Having observed that |Xam speakers imagined how the clicks would sound when produced by the mouth of an animal, Bleek (1875:6) described how he and Lucy Lloyd put this speech down in writing:

> It need not be said that, if it be by no means easy to write Bushman itself, the difficulty of taking down these animal speeches is by far greater, and before any attempt could be made to translate them into English or Dutch, they had first to be rendered into ordinary Bushman by our informants.

When dictating to Bleek or Lloyd, therefore, the |Xam teachers first spoke in the particular animal's peculiar speech before going back and translating it into 'human' language. Bleek (1875:6) believed that animal clicks were evidence of the probable existence of many more click sounds in Bushman languages:

> The presence of these abnormal clicks in the different kinds of speech, points to the possibility, nay, even to the probability, of the former presence of many more clicks in the Bushman language than the five which are now to be found there.

The 'probability' that the number of click sounds was decreasing fitted in with Bleek's ideas about the evolution of language. One of the reasons Bleek, a comparative linguist, studied |Xam was because he thought that it belonged to the most ancient class of languages. He argued that, as languages changed over thousands of years, they tended 'to throw off the sounds which are difficult in pronunciation, and to render the phonetical mechanism of the language smoother' (Bleek in Deacon & Dowson 1996: 45). In other words, languages became easier to speak because people stopped using sounds that they found difficult to make. Bleek thus reasoned that 'languages [like |Xam] which abound in uncouth and unpronounceable sounds must be presumed to have best retained the ancient phonetic features' (Bleek in Deacon & Dowson 1996: 45). The various click sounds in |Xam were included in the category of 'difficult' sounds.

Linguists today find no support for the idea that languages are evolving from an earlier phonetically complex stage to a simpler one; neither is there any objective way to determine what speech sounds are 'difficult' and 'unpronounceable' (Anthony Traill, email communication, 29 July 2002). In addition to these problems, some of the Early Race sounds are in fact simplifications of |Xam speech rather than, as Bleek believed, evidence of prior complexity. Thus, Wilhelm Bleek's ideas, intriguing as they may have seemed at the time, have not been pursued any further.

The Early Race

Nonetheless, Bleek's hypothesis that the animals' speech incorporated archaic sounds is consistent with the status of these animals in |Xam belief – they are from an earlier time that predated not only the existence of the |Xam people, but even the boundaries between human and other animal species, as well as the stars, sun and planets (Hewitt 1986). Virtually all of 'Special speech' and, indeed, most of the Bleek and Lloyd Collection of narratives, concerns these primeval people (Hewitt 1986: 105). They had a special name, *!Xwe:-/na-se- !kˀe* – the 'first-there-sitting-people' or, as Lloyd called them, the 'Early Race'. Roger Hewitt (1986: 105) estimates that the Early Race was made up of nearly 50 species of animals, including insects and people, as well as non-animal entities such as the stars, sun and moon. The Early Race people looked human and lived much as |Xam hunter-gatherers did; importantly, however, they also had animal characteristics, which not only dictated how they spoke (e.g. 'Why the Ostrich does not click'), but also some of their circumstances, such as where they lived (e.g. 'The Anteater, the young Springbok and the Lynx').

The combination of human and animal characteristics made Early Race society inherently unstable; misunderstandings and disasters were common and occurred because of continual tensions between human rules of behaviour on the one hand, and animal instincts on the other (Hewitt 1986). For example, in the narrative 'The young Dog', the wild dog (*Lycaon pictus*) marries a quagga (*Equus quagga quagga*). The union is disastrous because the wild dog's family (which includes the jackal and hyena, all carnivores) learns that the wild dog has married a quagga person, one of the animals upon which they prey. They act according to their animal natures, killing and eating the quagga, behaviour that renders the institution of marriage untenable.

The tales show that the time of the *!Xwe:-/na-se- !k'e* was formative: it was through the foolish and dreadful exploits of the Early Race that the natural and human, social order of the world as we know it came to be (Hewitt 1986). The extract published in 'Special speech' as 'The Anteater, the young Springbok and the Lynx' is part of a longer narrative that describes an important moment when the differences between animals and people became apparent. This signalled the end of the *!Xwe:-/na-se- !k'e* – from this time onwards, each animal species became separate and their behaviour was fixed (Lloyd 1889: L.IV.42; Hewitt 1986).

Storytelling

Besides their linguistic and mythological interest, the 'Special speech' narratives incorporate characteristics of an oral culture of which people from an alphabetic culture are largely unaware, and which they find hard to understand (Biesele 1993; Sanders 1994). Perhaps the most glaring (and sometimes irritating) feature for readers of transcribed performances of stories is the frequent repetition of phrases and ideas (Hewitt 1986; Biesele 1993; Sanders 1994). In preparing 'The rescue of the Mantis and |Kwammaŋ-a' for publication, for example, Dorothea Bleek omitted many notebook pages – presumably because they were, in her words, 'wearisome repetition' (Bleek 1924: v).

Had |Haŋ‡kass'o been telling the story to an audience in |Xam-ka !au̅, however, the repetition would have had a quite different effect – a listener in an oral culture experiences repeated words and phrases a great deal differently from a reader. In a live performance, each time a phrase is repeated, it is delivered in a particular tone of voice accompanied by certain gestures; repetition is thus a means of emphasis, a form of oral punctuation, creating rhythm and contributing to the mood of the performance (Sanders 1994). Spoken words evaporate into the air as they are uttered. Once written down, however, repetition becomes a bore.

There are many instances of repetition in the 'Special speech' narratives. The |Xam – and |Haŋ‡kass'o in particular (Hewitt 1986) – used short songs or chants to punctuate and underscore specific moments in a narrative ('The Black Crow calling the Jackal', 'The Young Dog', and 'The Anteater, the young Springbok and the Lynx'). In addition, all the |Xam teachers used stock phrases: the two most common are *he ti hiŋ e:* and *he tiken e:* (Hewitt 1986: 237). The first phrase literally means 'these things they are', but may be variously translated in English as 'therefore', 'that is why', as well as 'and so'. The second phrase, *he tiken e:*, literally means 'these things are', and is used in the same way.

The use of vivid and strange, even shocking, imagery is another characteristic of storytelling in an oral culture. Biesele (1993: 43) argues that storytelling is not merely 'cultural froth'; the stories communicate ideas that are important to survival, but the ideas are 'embedded in entertainment' to make them vivid and memorable. For instance, by incorporating information about the behaviour of lions into a story about two man-eaters taking a sleeping man out of his hut at night (see 'The Lions and the Tortoise'), the |Xam teacher |A!kuŋta remembers and imparts a wealth of information about lions.

The 'Special speech' narratives are therefore special in more than one sense of the word – they are examples of how the |Xam language was changed and manipulated by its users. They reveal some of the concerns most central to their hunter-gatherer lifestyle, and provide insights into the performance of folklore and its adaptive significance.

The Blue Crane's speech

Narrator: ||Kabbo
Dictation dates: Sometime between 21 August and 14 September 1873
Translation date: 30 September 1873
Notebook reference: B.XXIV: 2266-2271
***Bantu Studies* reference:** Vol. 10 (1936), Special speech: 163-164

Wilhelm Bleek's description of the 'fable' of the Blue Crane (Bleek 1875: 14):

We have only the beginning of a fable, in which a Blue Crane and some Bushman girls play parts, and in which the Blue Crane talks Bushman in the manner said to be peculiar to him [i.e., by the addition of a *tt* to the end of the first syllable of almost every word].

(2266-2271, translated as far as 2270)

The Blue Crane (Anthropoides paradisea) *is one of six African crane species. Unlike most other kinds of crane, Blue Cranes forage and nest in dryland areas. They eat plants and insects. Adult Blue Cranes form pair bonds and rarely move out of sight of each other. The relationship endures until one of the partners dies. Blue Cranes regularly perform spectacular dances – mated pairs dance together, as well as unmated birds that are looking for a partner (Allan 2001).*

❑

!kwi-/ka:gən ≠kaka hi /ka:gən, '/hau hĩ, i //a: //gauä siŋ !ki: -/ke:
Girls said to each other, 'Let us go and sit in the shade of that
kaŋ !khe, ha-ka -!kann, ta: ha a: tt?ammuwa, ha a:-ka -!kann so ta
camelthorn, its shadow, for it is in full leaf, its shadow seems to be
serritən. I se //a twãĩ i /ka:gən /naŋ, i se hã, i /ka:gən ⊙muiŋ.'
cool. We will inspect each other's heads, we will eat each other's lice.'
-!k?o:gən ≠kakən, 'ŋ kattən katt, ŋ sett //natt hĩ ut, ut sett //att
'ŋ kaŋ ka, ŋ se //na hĩ u, u se //a
The Blue Crane said, 'I do wish, (that) I may be with ye, (that) ye may
twatatt kett, ta:t ⊙moattən doatt ts?itt /kətt ŋ /natt. Ut sett
twãja ke, ta: ⊙muiŋ dóä ts?i: /ki: ŋ /na:. U se
louse me, for the lice do biting hurt my head. Ye shall
!kwarakən att kett ŋ /natt.'
!kwarakən a: ke ŋ /na:.'
eat (the lice) for me of my head.'

Haŋ !khou !kann //k'e: //hittən, haŋ ≠kaka !kaukən, '/nott hi:, itt
'/nau hi:, i
She gathered together the girls, she said to the children, 'Let us go, we

/nett //ott hatt !keitt, i-g /natt sett //att //gauä settən hatt.'
/ne //e ha !ki:, i /ne se //a //gauä siŋ ha.'
go to that camelthorn, that we may go to sit in the shade of it.'

Hiŋ ˍtá:ï !kei //a: ˉ!ki:, hiŋ //gauä siŋ. !kˀo:gən
They went to the camelthorn, they sat in the shade. The Blue Crane

≠kaka !kwã, 'm ʘattʘattde wett, sóëttən /kott satt, att sett
'm ʘaʘaide we, ssˀóëŋ /ko: ssˀa, a se
said to a child, 'O my granddaughter, sit nearby, that thou mayst

karatat tett ŋ /natt, tatt ŋ /natt /kuɯtt ˍdóätt tatt !naut!nauttən
karaka ke ŋ /na:, ta: ŋ /na: /kuɯ ˍdóä ta !nau!nauügən
examen for me my head, for my head feels swarming

aut ʘmottən arr arr, hatt ˍdóätt !kott //kott !khett ŋ /natt. Att
au ʘmuiŋ a: a, ha ˍdóä !ko: //kau !khe ŋ /na:. A
with these lice, which are all over my head. Thou

sett ˍdóätt tsˀitt !xitt tatt kett ʘmuittən.'
se ˍdóä tsˀi: !xi: ta ke ʘmuiŋ.'
shalt biting destroy for me the lice.'

Notes

Dorothea Bleek's introduction reads:

The simplest kind of animal speech is that attributed to the Blue Crane. This bird is the Mantis's sister, and plays a part in several stories. In one very short tale her peculiar speech is given, in which *tt* is added to the first syllable of almost every word.

9 *The* **Blue Crane** *said* …: Wilhelm Bleek first translated the word *!kˀo:gən* as 'heron' (2267 and 2269).

18 **She** *gathered together the girls* …: The notebook translation is 'he' (2268).

Why the Ostrich does not click

Narrator: |Haŋ⌿kass'o
Dictation date: Probably between 11 July and 8 August 1879
Notebook reference: L.VIII.30: 8628 rev.-8629 rev.
***Bantu Studies* reference:** Vol. 10 (1936), Special speech: 164-165

Dorothea Bleek gives the following introduction to this tale:

The use of *t* is also attributed to the Ostrich, only this bird is supposed to have changed the clicks into *t*'s. An explanation of the reason why the Ostrich does not click was given as a note to the following story, which gives examples of this peculiarity of speech.

❑

Tői |ɛnni ||kwaŋ k''auki ⁻!xowa, ta:, hĩ |kɯ taurotauro; hiŋ |kɯ e
The Ostrich's tongue is not long, for it is round; it is

!kwa; hiŋ k''auki ||ke||kéja tʃueŋ kuiten |ɛ|ɛnn he !xo!xoka,
bone; it does not resemble the tongues of other things which are long,

ta:, tői |ɛnni |kɯ kuerrekuerre. He tikən e:, tői k''auki ta '≠,' ĩ.
for the Ostrich's tongue is round. Therefore the Ostrich does not click.

He tikən e:, tői há óä 'ttuẽï da, haŋ tt?e:,' au ha e !kui, haŋ ne
'kwẽï da, haŋ |k'e:,'
Therefore the Ostrich formerly 'dus it poke,' when it was human, it

'ttuẽï da, haŋ tt?e:.' Haŋ |kɯ-g |ne _!gumm, au há |ne e tői.
'|kwẽï da, haŋ |k'e:.'
'dus it poke.' It calls (roars), when it is an Ostrich.

Tői-ta |ka:kakən e: ⁻!khauru.
The hen Ostriches are those which trill.

Tʃueŋ-ta⁻ku _ha óä e !k?e, ||khetən||khetən ||xamki.
All things (that is living creatures) were once people, the beasts of prey also.

❑

Note

12-14 *It calls (roars), when it is an Ostrich. The hen Ostriches are those which trill:* Male ostriches utter characteristic 'booming' calls when proclaiming their territory or displaying to females. The calls sound similar to a lion's roar and consist of a deep 'boo boo booooh hooo', which they repeat several times at short intervals (Folch 1992: 79).

The Ostrich and *ǂkainjatara*

Narrator: |Haŋǂkass'o
Source: '|Haŋǂkass'o, from his maternal grandmother, ǂKammi, and from his mother |Xabbi-aŋ, when asked for it, after the death of her mother'
Dictation date: 13 July 1879
Notebook reference: L.VIII.30: 8628-8636
***Bantu Studies* reference:** Vol. 10 (1936), Special speech: 165-167

One day at a waterhole, in the time of the Early Race, the Ostrich tricked the ǂkainjatara *(a small yellow bird).*

❑

(The *≠kainjatara* is a small yellow bird, numerous in Bushmanland and also seen at the Cape. The *≠kainjatara* was once a man.)

≠kainjatara -//kwaŋ -há óä //khó:ë ssʔo ha |kagən, tőïtən
The *≠kainjatara* once sat among his companions, the Ostrich

|ne |kweŋ !kʔai ssa: !khwa:. Tőï |ne |kweŋ, au hiŋ |há !houwa.
descended to the water to dip up. The Ostrich dipped up, while they sat.

Tőï |ne ⁻|kú !kwitən, tőï |ne -|kammaiŋ. Tőïtən -há |ne kúï,
The Ostrich put away the eggs, the Ostrich loaded herself. The Ostrich said,

'ne tʔe: u ti te: ssʔo:, ha ne ssa tənn tuatuaija nho ttʔe ŋ.'
'|ne |k'e ju !kwi |ke: ssʔo:, ha |ne ssa !kənn !kwa!kwaija !ho //e ŋ.'
'Say to the man sitting yonder, that he shall come to help me up.'

!kʔetən -há |ne kúï, 'Au !kwi á: a?' 'K''auki, k''auki, k''auki,
The people said, 'To this man?' 'No, no, no,

twi te: ssʔo:, haŋ tu á ŋ ttʔe: ha, ha se ssa: tənn tuatuaija
!kwi |ke: ssʔo:, haŋ |ku á ŋ |k'e: ha, ha se ssa: !kənn -!kwa!kwaija
the man sitting yonder, he is the one of whom I speak, he shall come to

nho ttʔe ŋ.' !kʔetən -há |ne ⁻//xã, hiŋ kúï, 'Au !kwi á: a?' 'K''auki,
!ho //e ŋ.'
help me up.' The people again said, 'To this man?' No,

twi te:, ha k''auki é:, ta: twi té ttau ssʔo ha é.'
!kwi |ke:, ha k''auki é:, ta: !kwi |ke !kaun ssʔo, ha é.'
that man he is not; for the man yonder sitting in the middle he is.'

!kʔetən _há |ne kúï, 'Au !kwi á: a?' *'Í, í, í:, kwi tte: ɑ, ha se*
'Í, í, í:, !kwi |ke: ɑ, ha se
The people said, 'To this man?' Yes, yes, yes, that man, he shall
tənn ttuai nho ttʔe ŋ.'
!kənn !kwaija !ho ||e ŋ.'
help me up.'

He ti hiŋ e:, ≠kainjatara _há |ne _táï u ssa:, haŋ |ne _táï
Therefore *≠kainjatara* rose up and came, he went
!khe ssa ha. He ≠kainjatara _há |ne ⁻|keï ha ⁻||kũ haŋ _há |ne kúï,
up to her. And *≠kainjatara* took hold of her arm, she said,
'ne ⁻takki, ŋ ssiŋ tu a: ttette:n au a ⁻ttũ.' He ha _hä |ne ⁻|kẽï
'|ne |ka ki, ŋ siŋ |ku a: !ka!kənn au a ⁻||kũ.'
'Leave hold of me, that I may hold by thy arm.' And she took hold of
≠kainjatara ⁻||kũ, haŋ |ne |ku kúï ≠nuau |kəm ||a ≠kainjatara. Haŋ
≠kainjatara's arm, she snatched up *≠kainjatara*. She
_há |ku-g |ne ⁻!kuxe |hiŋ ≠kainjatara, au haŋ ⁻!khəi ||kho ha
ran away with *≠kainjatara*, while she carried him on her bosom.

Haŋ _há |ne ||nau, !kʔe _!gabbeta ki ||a ha, haŋ _há |ne ta,
When the people threw sticks after her, she sang,

'⁻Nou, xau _dabbetən tuá,	*'|nou, u xau _|gabbetən !khwa:,*
U tte:,	*U |ke:,*
Dabbetən tuá.	*_!gabbetən !khwa:.'*
⁻Nou, xau _dabbetən tuá,	'Grant that ye do not throwing break
U tte:,	Your companion,
_Dabbetən tuá.'	Throwing break.'

Au !kʔetən |ku _!gabbetən ti e:, ha siŋ ||a:, ï:, au ha
While the people threw sticks at the place where she had been, she
|ku ⁻ï ||a: au ti é; !kʔe |ku _!gabbetən ti e:,
really went to this place; the people threw sticks at the place where
há siŋ ||a:, ï:, au há |ku ⁻||xã, ha kúï ⁻suãïjãu ⁻!xuənni, ha |ku ⁻ï ||a:
she had been, while she again turned slanting aside, she really went
au ti é.
to this place.

He ti hiŋ e:, há ka,
Therefore she sang,

'⁻Nou, xau _dabbetən ttuá:	*'|nou, u xau _!gabbetən !khwa:,*
U tte:,	*U |ke:,*
_Dabbetən ttuá:.	*_!gabbetən !khwa:*

Special Speech of animals and Moon used by the the /Xam Bushmen

-Nou, xau dabbetən ttuá:	'Grant that ye do not throwing break
U tte:,	Your companion,
_Dabbetən ttuá:.'	'Throwing break.'

He tikən e: ha _há /ne //aŋ kuɛrre, haŋ /ne tdï //a:, tdï !khe //a //neiŋ.
Then she left off running, she walked along, walking reached home.

Haŋ há /ne //aŋ -!ka //kho ≠kainjatara au _≠karitən. Haŋ há /ne kúï,
She went and put down *≠kainjatara* by Yolk. She said,

'A nhaŋ tte: a; ŋ _ttwaŋ tatti, a _ttwaŋ ttueitəŋ totóä u ssiŋ tɯ-g ne
'A /haŋ /ke: a; ŋ _//kwaŋ tatti, a _//kwan /kweitən kokóä u siŋ /kɯ-g /ne
'There is thy husband; because thou art always like as if ye should be

ttuẽï u, u _koa: tɯ-g ne ttóä tí e: tt?uai, au u ne nhauwa.'
|kwẽï u, u _koa: /kɯ-g /ne //khóä tí e: !kwai, au u /ne !hauwa.'
thus, ye are like one thing, when ye are sitting down.'

Haŋ k''auki /e: ta: tũ, ha _//kwaŋ tatti e: -!xwe-//na-sso-!kwi /kɯ.
She (Yolk) was not in the shell, for she felt she was one of the Early Race.

Haŋ /kɯ e !kwi, tői ʘpuaxaitən /ne é. Tői /ne dá tői
She was a person, the Ostrich's daughter she was. The Ostrich made her

ʘpuaxai ã:. He tikən e:, tői /ne /ki ssa: ≠kainjatara. Tői
daughter of her. Therefore the Ostrich brought *≠kainjatara*. The Ostrich

_//kwaŋ e !kwi. ≠kainjatara ka-ïnja, ≠karitakən /ka-ïnja. Tői,
was a person. *≠kainjatara* was yellow, Yolk was yellow. The Ostrich

_//kwaŋ /kɯ -/kẽï ≠kainjatara, ha se //a -a ha ʘpuaxai ã ≠kainjatara;
caught hold of *≠kainjatara*, that she might go and give him to her daughter;

ta: ≠kainjatara //khóä ha ʘpuaxai. He tikən e:, tői -/kẽï
for *≠kainjatara* resembled her daughter. Therefore the Ostrich caught hold

≠kainjatara, ha se //a -a ha ʘpuaxai ã ≠kainjatara, ≠karitən ã
of *≠kainjatara*, to give to her daughter *≠kainjatara*, to Yolk

≠kainjatara. Tői ʘpuaxai /keŋ e _≠karitən.
≠kainjatara. The Ostrich's daughter's name is Yolk.

Notes

4 *The* **ǂkainjatara** *once sat among his companions*: '*ǂkainjatara* was a man. Therefore the Ostrich caught hold of him, in order that the Ostrich might give him to her daughter. The Ostrich caught hold of *ǂkainjatara* in order that she might go and give *ǂkainjatara* to her daughter; to Yolk. The Ostrich's daughter's name is Yolk.' (8627 rev., note omitted)

'[a little bird whose head and front part of the body is yellow]' (8628, text partially omitted).

42 *When the people threw sticks after her, she sang* …: The *Bantu Studies* version of this song differs slightly from the following translation in this omitted note:

'She said that the other people should grant them that they did not throwing [sticks] break their companion's leg. Allow that ye do not [in] throwing [sticks] break your companion's leg' (8631 rev., note omitted).

50-52 …*she really went to this place* …: '[that is turned and went in a different direction]' (8634, text omitted)

'she ran on, from side to side, in a slanting direction.' (8633 rev., note omitted).

68 *She went and put down ǂkainjatara by Yolk:* |Haŋǂkass'o explains that *ǂkaritakən* or *Yolk* is the name of the Ostrich's daughter.

71-74 *'There is thy husband; because thou art always like as if ye should be thus, ye are like one thing, when ye are sitting down.'*: The *Bantu Studies* translation is unclear. My understanding is that the ostrich mother kidnapped *ǂkainjatara* because her daughter Yolk was not making any effort to find herself a husband.

The Lions and the Tortoise

Narrator: |A!kuŋta
Dictation dates: Sometime between February 1873 and 12 March 1873
Notebook reference: B.XIV: 1362-1392
***Bantu Studies* reference:** Vol. 10 (1936), Special speech: 168-172

This gruesome and detailed story has a popular theme – lions eating people! (see Part II, 'The lion'). The two lions concerned are called !Gu: *(Mat) and* !Haue ta ǂhou *(Belt). They are Early Race characters that now form the stars Alpha and Beta Centauri, the two pointers to the Southern Cross, an important constellation visible in the southern hemisphere.*

Dorothea Bleek describes the Tortoise's speech as follows:

The speech of the Tortoise is characterised by changing the clicks; and some other initial consonants into labials. We have an example of it in the following fragment of a story, belonging to the myths of the Lions who are stars.

❑

||khã:ŋ ||nau, au !góë:tən |xabbe: |hiŋ au ||neiŋ, ||khã:ŋ
The Lion does this, when the Tortoise goes seeking eggs from home, the Lion

|ni: ha, au haŋ !attən |xabbe: ||a:, ||khã:ŋ |ni: ha, au haŋ
sees it, as it trots out to hunt eggs, the Lion sees it, as it

!kutta ||a:, au haŋ !attən |xabbe: ||a:, au haŋ !kutta ||a, au
singing goes, as it trots out hunting, as it goes singing, as

!nuattakən !khe ||a. Haŋ ≠kaka ||a:, au haŋ tatti e:, !góë |kɯ e;
the bow arrives. It talks away, for it feels it is a tortoise;

ha |kɯ |ki ha-ha-ka ≠kakən≠kakən, haŋ k''auki ≠kakən au ha |ẽrr̃i,
it has its own language, it does not talk with its tongue,

ta ha |kɯ ≠kakən au ha tu-ka tũ. He ti hiŋ e:, ha |kɯ ≠kakən
but it talks with its mouth's skin. Therefore it talks

!num ||kóä ha tu, ĩ. He ti hiŋ e:, ha ppu ppẽ: bba, haŋ ppakən, ha |kɯ |kwẽ: |ka, haŋ ≠kakən,
inside its mouth. Therefore, it does like this, it talks,

au haŋ tatti e:, ha tu-ka tũ e: ||kau ta: ha tu ||kaië, hĩ |kɯ e.
for its mouth's skin is that which lies upon the inside of its mouth.

Haŋ !kuttən, 'múttappəm ¯pɛ: bbha:, múttappəm ¯pɛ: bbha:.'
'!nuattən ¯!khe //a, !nuattən ¯!khe //a:'
It sings, 'The bow arrives, the bow arrives.'

He ti hiŋ e: //khã: /ne !ahátta, au haŋ !attən /xabbe //gaueja
Therefore the Lion goes round, as it trots out hunting, seeking
//a: /au tőï !noá. //khã: /ne !khe //e, //khã:-ko:kən /ne ≠kaka //khã:-ko,
for the ostrich spoor. The Lion arrives, one Lion says to the other Lion,
ti e: hĩ se tsʔi: /kao !góë:. !góë:tən ≠kaka //khã:,
that they must bite breaking the Tortoise. The Tortoise tells the Lion,
ti e: //khã: se tsʔi: /kao ha, //khã: se a: !kuko:
that the Lion must bite breaking it, the Lion must give the other (Lion)
!góë !khui-/u, ha se //xam hã: hĩ. //khã: /ku !k'óɛ
the Tortoise loin's root, that he may also eat it. The Lion retorts to
!góë:, ti e: !góë:-ʘua /ku a, ha ha /ku se konn !ho ha,
the Tortoise, that it is a little Tortoise, one he will swallow down,
au ha /ku ≠urru. Haŋ !kũ //a:, haŋ /kẽ-ĩ !góë:, haŋ !num !ao ha,
while it is whole. He goes forward, he seizes the Tortoise, puts it in his mouth,
haŋ konn !ho ha, au haŋ !kar̃r̃a ha !ahai ha-ka //khwai Haŋ konn !khe,
he swallows it down, then he again slings on his quiver. It stands swallowed,
haŋ sukkən //kaitən //khã: /na:, haŋ //kåo !khe //khã: !kũ:-ka /kammiŋ.
it jumps up onto the Lion's head, it stands above the Lion's eyebrows' hair.
!góë:jakən ≠kakən≠kaka //kåo !khe //khã: !kũ:, haŋ ≠kaka //khã:,
The Tortoise speaks standing above the Lion's eyebrows, it says to the Lion,
'Pã:-we:, mma: hĩ, i pphu, i mma: k''wã, i se ppheŋ bbauë
'//khã:-we, /na hĩ, i !xu, i //a: k''wã, i se //k'oëŋ //gauë
'O Lion, let us go to the water, go to drink, that we may look seeking
pam-ka me:-ta mimmi, i se ppxerri hĩ.'
/xam-ka !ʔe-ta //nei//neiŋ, i se /xorri hĩ.'
Bushmen's huts, that we may steal up to them.'

!góë:jakən ≠kaka //khã:, 'a se ppenn mha: hi, ha ppi a: ppiŋja,
'a se !kann /na: hi, ha !kwi a: !kwiŋja,
The Tortoise tells the Lion, 'Thou shalt take out for us, that big man,
ha kóä ppu:wa, i se ppuŋŋa; u se k''auki ppxerri k''ank''ein,
ha kóä //ku:wa, i se !khuŋ ha; u se k''auki /xorri k''ank''ein,
he will be fat, we will go behind him; ye will not steal up deceiving, (though)

u se ppamppa ppxerri. Me se k''auki tu ĩ mmummúntu, ta:
u se təm⊙ua |xərri. !ʔe se k''auki tu ĩ !nu!núŋtu, ta:
ye will gently steal up. People will not hear with their ears, but

ppi a: ppai tumma ta ã: mmummúntu, ha pumm-ĩ au bba:; haŋ
!kwi a: !kwai tumma ta ã: !nu!núŋtu, ha tum-ĩ au ⁻||ga:; haŋ
one man lies listening with his ears, he is listening at night; he

k''auki ppe:nja, ta: ha ppenn, haŋ ppéppe: phiŋ ã: tsʔaxeitən, haŋ ppum-ĩ
k''auki ⊙oënja, ta: ha ⊙oëŋ haŋ !kwé!kwe: |hiŋ ã: tsʔaxeitən, haŋ tumm-ĩ
does not sleep, for he sleeps peeping out of his eyes, he is listening

meiŋ pphappha, au haŋ tatti e:, ha ppakka ppherri: e,
||neiŋ ||ka||ka, au haŋ tatti e:, ha ||kwakka !kerri: e,
inside the hut, for he feels that he is a sensible grown-up person,

ha ppenna bba:.
ha ≠enna ||ga:.
he knows the night.

He ti hiŋ e:, ha ppumm ã ppaukən. Paukakən ppu e ppenja,
He ti hiŋ e:, ha tumm ã !kaukən. !kaukakən |ku e: ⊙oënja,
Therefore he listens for the children. The children are asleep,

pperritən a: mmenna bba:, ha a ppakka bba:, au haŋ tatti e:
!kerritən a: ≠enna ||ga:, ha a ||kwakka ||ga: au haŋ tatti e:
the grown-up is the one who knows the night, he understands the night, because

ha a: tãĩ bba:. Haŋ ppumm-ĩ au bba:, haŋ ppumm-ĩ bba:ga kwərrikwərri:,
ha a: tãĩ ||ga:. Haŋ tumm-ĩ au ||ga:, haŋ tumm-ĩ ||ga:-ga kwarrikwarri:,
he walks at night. He is listening at night, to the night's dangers,

au haŋ tatti e:, ha e pperri:, ha mmenna tsʔa a: tãĩ bba:.
au haŋ tatti e:, ha e !kerri:, ha ≠enna tsʔa a: tãĩ ||ga:.
because he is a grown-up person, he knows the thing which walks at night.

Ha ppumma ppa:, ti e: ppéppe: tãĩŋja tiŋ bba:, ha ha
Ha tumma ta:, ti e:, ||ké||ke: tãĩŋja tiŋ ||ga:, ha ha
He lies listening whether a beast of prey is walking about at night, it

ppouwa bbauë tsʔa a: ha ka ppa hã:au bba:-ka tãĩ,
!khouwa ||gauë tsʔa a: ha ka |ka hã: au ||ga:-ka tãĩ,
smelling seeks a thing which it can kill and eat on the night's walk,

ha-ha-ka _ha au bba:. He ti hiŋ e:, ha ka tãĩnja tiŋ bba: ĩ,
ha-ha-ka _ha au ||ga:. He ti hiŋ e:, ha ka tãĩnja tiŋ ||ga: ĩ,
its going at night. Therefore it is wont to walk about at night,

au ha ka ha se ppu: a ã: mmuřu, ha se ppu: mimiŋ ⊙oáĩ; ha se
au ha ka ha se !khou a ã: |nunu, ha se !khou ||nei||neiŋ |k'uai; ha se
for it wants to smell with its nose, to smell the hut's scent; it will

pphorri miŋ, ha se ppĩ a ppí, ha se bbábbitən ti tãĩ ppí,
|xorri ||neiŋ, ha se |ki a !kwi, ha se !gabbe:tən ti tãĩ !kwi,
steal up to the hut, it will get a man, it will throwing make the man go,

ppíja siŋ mma: kaŋ ppú tiŋ, ha pu:xe ppuŋ hóä, ha pöeŋ ppí
!kwija siŋ ||a: kaŋ !ku: tiŋ, ha !kuxe !kuŋ hóä ha ||k'öëŋ !kwi.
the man will go and fall down, it runs behind, it sees the man.

He ti hiŋ e:, ha pparrukən suttən ho ppí, ĩ, ha pu:xe ti phiŋ ppí, ha
He ti hiŋ e:, ha !karrokən suttən ho !kwi, ĩ, ha !ku:xe ti |hiŋ !kwi, ha
Then it snatches up the man, it runs off with the man, it

pu:xe ku ppúppu-siŋ bba:, ha ppu:xe ppóë ho bba: e: mhodka, au mme
!ku:xe ku ≠kubbu-siŋ ||ga:, ha !ku:xe ||kóë ho ||ga: e: |hodka, au !ʔe
runs penetrating the night, it runs into the night's blackness, while other

kwita mme ppi:ja mma ha tsʔẽ:, au ha mme puxe phiŋ mei ppuko.
kwita |ne !kwi:ja ||na ha tsʔẽ:, au ha |ne !kuxe |hiŋ ≠n:: !kuko:.
men call behind its back, while it runs away carrying off the man.

Ha mme pu:xe ti tãĩja, ha mme mma: ppu: ppe, ha mme pe:nja, haŋ tãĩ, au
Ha |ne !ku:xe ti tãĩja, ha |ne ||a: !kou !khe, ha |ne te:nja, haŋ tãĩ, au
It runs along, it goes and stops, it lies down, it walks on, as

haŋ mhei ˉppa:, au haŋ mhei ti mma ppí, mhei ppəm bba: ppuppi:. Haŋ
haŋ !ahéi ||a:, au haŋ !ahéi ti ||a: !kwi, !ahéi |kam ||a: |kubbi:. Haŋ
it goes carrying, as it goes carrying the man into the bushes. It

ppakən, mhei ti ppe: ppí au ppúppi: ppaië, haŋ ppó:ë ti ppí au
≠kakən, !ahéi ti |e: !kwi au !kubbi: ||kaië, haŋ ||kó:ë ti !kwi au
talks, carrying the man into the bushes' middle, it puts the man down in

ppuppi: ppaië, haŋ mme hĩ: ppí eŋ-eŋ, haŋ mme ppuŋ ppí-ta ssoëŋ.
|kubbi: ||kaië, haŋ |ne hĩ: !kwi eŋ-eŋ-, haŋ |ne !kuŋ !kwi-ta ssoëŋ.
the bushes' middle, it eats the man's flesh, it devours the man's fat.

Mmei kwitən mʔhammi tãĩ au ˉppã:, au hiŋ tatti e:, ˉppã: saŋ
!ʔe: kwitən !hammi tãĩ au ||khã:, au hiŋ tatti e:, ||khã: saŋ
Other people walk in fear of the Lion, for they feel that the Lion may

pxã:, ˉppã: se: hĩ, au ˉppã: mme gauwa ppuko:, ˉppã: si se
||xã:, ||khã: se: hĩ, au ||khã: |ne gauwa !kuko:, ||khã: si se
again come to them, when the Lion approaches another (man), the Lion will

ppí a hã, ˉppã: se pxã, ˉppã: pu:xe ti pʔhiŋja, au mmei pita
|ki a hã, ||khã: se ||xã, ||khã: !ku:xe ti |hiŋ ha, au !ʔe: kwita
seize him, the Lion will again run away with him, while other people

mme pxã, hĩ ppi:ja ppum mma hã. Au haŋ mme mhéi ppí ppummu-siŋ
|ne ||xã, hĩ !kwi:ja !kuŋ ||ha hã. Au haŋ |ne !ahéi !kwi ≠kubbu-siŋ
again call behind him. Meanwhile he carries off the man, penetrating the

bba:, bba: se te:ŋ ha tsĩ:, mme: se k''auki mmi hã.
||ga:, ||ga: se te:ŋ ha tsĩ:, !ʔe: se k''auki |ni: hã.
night, that the night may cover his back, that people may not see him.

Au ha ppu ĩ: ppóë: hóä bba:, mme kwitakən ppu mme paŋŋa ppi ha tsĩ:
Au ha |ku ĩ: ||kóë: hóä ||ga:, !ˀe: kuitakən |ku-g |ne |kaŋŋa |ki ha tsi
While he thus goes into the night, other people are throwing at his back
au ppi, au haŋ ppum mme kaŋ mˀhéi ppa:, au ppau tsĩ:, au hiŋ ppatti e:,
au |i, au haŋ |ku-g |ne taŋ !ɑhéi ||a:, au !kau tsĩ:, au hiŋ tatti e:,
with fire, while he tries to carry away to the back of the hill, for they feel

ppuko siŋ pphərri:ja mme: bba:, au ¯ppã:ŋ mmum ¯ta: hã,
!kuko siŋ ||xərri:ja |e: ||ga:, au ||khã:ŋ !num ¯ta: hã,
the other is disappearing into the night, while the Lion holds him in his mouth,

au ha ppã: tu ppaië, ppã:ŋ ppu ppu:xe tau tsẽ:-ĩ ha, ppãŋ ppu ppu:xe:ja
au ha ||khã: tu ||kaië, ||khã:ŋ |ku !ku:xe tau tsẽ:-ĩ ha, ||khã:ŋ |ku !ku:xeja
inside the Lion's mouth. The Lion runs biting him, the Lion runs along

ki tau tsi: ppu:kən hã. Au ppãŋ ppu:xe mma hã haŋ mme ppɑm u:ï ha tu,
ki tau tsi: |ku:kən ha. Au ||khã:ŋ !ku:xe ||a: ha, haŋ |ne |kɑm u:ï ha tu,
biting him to death. As the Lion runs off with him, he opens his mouth,

au ppãŋ tatti e:, ha tauko pphərri:-ĩ, au ppã:kən tatti e: a
au ||khã:ŋ tatti e:, ha tauko ||kərri:-ĩ, au ||khã:ŋ tatti e: a
and the Lion feels that he is going along screaming, and the Lion feels that

ha kwaŋ mme ppe:n-da, haŋ kwaŋ mme tauko ʘparrakən-ĩ.
ha kwaŋ |ne |kwẽ:-da, haŋ kwaŋ |ne tauko !karrakən-ĩ.
he is acting like this, he is going along snatching.

He ti hiŋ e:, ppã:ŋ tsĩ: ppu:ka ĩ, ha se bbou, ta mme: kwitən
He ti hiŋ e:, ||khã:ŋ tsi |ku:ka ĩ, ha se ≠gou, ta: !ˀe: kwitən
Therefore the Lion bites him to death, that he may be quiet, for other people

saŋ pu:xe ppaiti ppã:, au hĩ ppum-i ppuko.'
saŋ !ku:xe !xaiti ||khã:, au hi tum-i !kuko.'
would run after the Lion, if they heard the other.'

Notes

A note glued into the notebook on pages 1364 rev.-1365, in what seems to be Lucy Lloyd's hand and dated 'Feb/73', says:

[Must try to get the story bodily (? – ed.). It is a little tortoise which has been swallowed whole by a lion; it comes out of the lion's stomach and stands on his eyebrows; and the leads him to all sorts of disappointments; in the way of food and water, he talks thus ... (several untranslated lines of |Xam as spoken by the tortoise follow – ed.).]

The Ichneumon's speech

Narrator: ||Kabbo
Dictation date: Not definitely known. Probably a few days before 5 October 1873, the earliest date recorded in Notebook B.XXIV.
Notebook reference: B.XXIV: 2251-2255
***Bantu Studies* reference:** Vol. 10 (1936), Special speech: 172-173

How the Ichneumon (or mongoose, probably the small grey mongoose, Herpestes pulverulenta*) speaks /Xam*

In the speech of the Ichneumon, the clicks are changed into palatals and compound dentals and sibilants. We have an example of this peculiarity in a speech given by the Ichneumon, after his grandfather, the Mantis, had punished the Mierkats for cutting up his pet eland by depriving them of their possessions.

❑

/ni:tən ≠kakən, ' ts?e, ts?e, ŋ tʃũïŋ ts?arruxu, _kwa: kaŋ dje dji ts?a ade,
' !khe, !khe, ŋ !kõïŋ !arruxu, _kwa: ka ;ne di ts?a ade,
The Ichneumon says, ' Look, look, what my grandfather Mantis has done.

hiŋ e:, ts?e e: hĩ k''auki ts?e ts?wei, tʃa: ts?ɑ:-ga eŋ-ka ku: ts?ɯ e:
hiŋ e:, !?e e: hĩ k''auki se _//kwei, ta: sa:ga en-ka ku: /kɯ e:
hence these people shall not chew (flesh), for all the eland's flesh which

tsjauwa hĩ e: a. Ts?a: kaŋ tsj'e: a, ha tsjuwa, ha _ts?au-gu tswaŋ ts?o
//hauwa, hĩ e: a. Sa kaŋ ⁻/ke: a, ha //ku:wa, ha _!kao-gu //kwaŋ ss?o
was hanging up is here. That eland was fat, so the Mierkats seem to be

k''wa: ã-ka ts?oëŋ. Hiŋ ts?ɯ e: ss?o, ts?a: ts?e au ts?xɔrre:, tʃa:
k''wa: ã-ka ssweŋ. Hiŋ /kɯ e: ss?o, /a: !khe au /xɔrre, ta:
crying about its fat. They are likely to be killed with cold for

dsjyïdsjyï-ta ku: ts?ɯ e:, ts? arruxu ts?i ts?a: hĩ. Dya: a haŋ ts?ɯ a:
ts?yïts?yï-ta ku: /kɯ e:, !arruxu /ki ss?a hĩ. //na: a haŋ /kɯ a:
all their things the Mantis has brought here. This krieboom which

ts?urriŋ jəhiŋ ss?i-ta djiŋ, ha ts?weits?wei e: ts?ɯ e: djauwa hã, tja:
!kɔr̃r̃iŋ /?hiŋ si-ta //neiŋ, ha //khwai//khwai e: /kɯ e: /hauwa hã, ta:
grows out at our hut, is that on which these quivers are hanging, for:

dja: dje tsʔɯ-gən dje tsúïtən sse au tsʔa a: ha-ga tsʔãũtsãũ,
//na: /ke /kɯ-g /ne !ku:ïtən !khe au sa a: ha-ka thʔãũthʔãũ,
the krieboom stands white because of this eland's fat lumps (inside ribs)

hé tsɯ tsoá djweidjweitən. Hiŋ tswaŋ tsʔo tsʔaŋ tsxwein, tsa tsɔttən-
he /kɯ //kóä !gwei!gweitən. Hiŋ //kwaŋ ssʔo taŋ !k''wein, ta. !kɔttən-
which resemble boulders. They apparently feel angry, for the white

tsɔttən e: hĩ tsʔɯ e: tsʔauwa, tsʔar̃r̃a hiŋ tsʔauwa.'
!kɔttən e: hĩ /kɯ e: //hauwa, !kar̃r̃a hiŋ //hauwa.'
karosses are those which hang, still they are hanging.'

Notes

3-4 *'Look, look, what my grandfather Mantis has done …'*: The word *!arruxu* is translated as Mantis. A note to this extract explains that '*!arruxu* is a second name for the Mantis, also sometimes applied to his wife, the Dassie'.

10-13 *… the Mierkats seem to be crying …*: 'A note states that, 'the Mierkats don't cry with tears, they cry with their thoughts they think so much about it' (2251 rev.).

The Mierkat, (more commonly spelt 'Meerkat'), *Suricata suricatta,* is a type of mongoose that lives in large underground warrens (Kingdon 1997).

16 *… all their things the Mantis has brought here*: The original note reads: 'The Mantis has dreamt about the Mierkat's things, and as he has dreamt they have risen up and transported themselves to the neighbourhood of his hut. The family on waking find them there.'

|Kaggen had the power to actively dream things to happen (see Part VI, 'More about |Kannu') – he was the |Xam's first *!gi:xa* (Lewis-Williams 1996). He could also talk to his own possessions and order them about (Alan James 2001: 42-43 and 159-160, 'The things of |Kaggen speak').

The rescue of the Mantis and |Kwammaŋ-a

Narrator: |Haŋ‡kass'o
Dictation dates: February 4-6, 8-10, 1878
Notebook reference: L.VIII.2: 6196-6231 and 3: 6232-6236
***Bantu Studies* reference:** Vol. 10 (1936), Special speech: 174-73

Dorothea Bleek's introduction to this narrative:

A further example of the Ichneumon's speech, together with some peculiar speech by the Dasse, the Mantis's wife is found in one version of the rescue of *-/kwammaŋ-a* and the Mantis after they have been buried under falling stones and discovered by the Crow messengers.

A note by Dorothea Bleek at the conclusion of the narrative.

(The Ichneumon's speech was not translated by Miss Lloyd either into ordinary Bushman or into English. I have been able to translate it, because it is very similar to the speeches in another version of the same story, but there are a few words of which I cannot be sure.

The difficulties of translation are increased by the many different spellings given to the same words. I have reproduced them all as in the original.—D. F. BLEEK.)

Dorothea published a version of this narrative in Mantis and his friends*: the story is entitled 'The Dasse's Story and the Crow's Story' (Bleek 1924: 47-50).*

≠xóä, hiŋ kóä !nuí:, hiŋ kóä //xuagən, hiŋ e: -há óĩ //a:
The Elephant and the Giraffe and the Rhinoceros were those who went

/ki /hiŋ -/kwammaŋ-a-gu, o !kauruwəkən //xamki //a:,
to take out */kwammaŋ-a's* party, while *!kauru*, (the Mantis's wife) went too,

!kó:äkən //a:. He //a //k'oen, ti e:, tukən /e: ta: he, ti e:, ti-g /nu //khóä
the Porcupine went. They went to see where the men were, whether it seemed

!k?e se /ki /ha hi ã tukən. He tikən e:, hi
as if the people would take out the men for them. That was what they

//a //k'oeŋ hi.
went to see.

(Omitted text: 6198-6200)

Whether it seemed as if the people would take out the men for them. That is what they went to see, that they might see if it seemed as if the people would take out the men for them. That is what they went to see. Then the Elephant and the Giraffe and the Rhinoceros and ǂKum!kwe and the Giraffe, these people and !Kauru's people (!Kauru is the Dasse, | Kaggen's wife) with them and the Porcupine [the porcupine's other name is !koä (6199 rev., note omitted)], they were going to see whether the men were, whether it seemed as if the people would take out the men for them. !Kauru and the Porcupine they were going to see, whether it seemed as if the people would take out the men for them. That is what they went to see.

Hiŋ |ne ||k'oen, ||ka ||ka ti e:, !kauögən -||kwaŋ |ne !kũ!kũï, !kauõgən
They saw that stones had fallen, big

e: !kui!kuíta, he -||kwaŋ |ne !kũ!kũï. He tikən e:, hi |ne ≠ĩ:, ti e:, tukən
stones had fallen. Then they thought that the men

-||kwaŋ -k''óa se |hiŋ, ta: !kauögən e !kui!kuíta hi -||kwaŋ |ne !kũ!kũï.
could be got out, for the stones which had fallen were big.

-|!kwammaŋ-a xukən -||kwaŋ |ne ||khou ≠ka:-siŋ, o !kóäkən ||k'oen !khe.
|kwammaŋ-a's face became visible, while the Porcupine stood looking.

He tikən e:, !kó:ä ≠ĩ:, ti e:, |kwammaŋ-a -||kwaŋ -k''óa se |hiŋ, ta:, ha
Then the Porcupine thought, that *|kwammaŋ-a* could be got out, for his

xu -||kwaŋ |ne ||khou ≠ka:-siŋ, o !kʔetən |ne |kɛ|kɛm úï !kauögən e !khe
face became visible, when the people took off the stones which stood

!ahíta ha xu. He tikən e:, !kó:ä -||kwaŋ ||k'oen !khe, ti e: -|kwammaŋ-a
upon his face. Then the Porcupine stood watching for *|kwammaŋ-a's*

!kaugən -||kwaŋ |ne ||khou ≠ka:-tiŋ. He ti hiŋ e:, !kóä -||kwaŋ ||k'oen !khe
body to become visible. Then the Porcupine saw as she stood,

(Omitted text: 6206-6209)

… looking that it seemed as if the people would take out |Kwammaŋ-a for his body became visible. Then the Porcupine saw as she stood that |Kwammaŋ-a was taken out. The people took out |Kwammaŋ-a. Then the Porcupine stood and saw that the people took out |Kwammaŋ-a. |Kwammaŋ-a was taken out, while the Porcupine stood looking. Then the Porcupine gave thanks/jumped for joy that the people had taken out |Kwammaŋ-a for her,

The rescue of the Mantis and /Kwammaŋ-a

ĩ:, o ti e: -|kwammaŋ-a -||kwaŋ |hiŋ. He ti hiŋ e:, !kóä -||kwaŋ |ne
that *|kwammaŋ-a* was taken out. Then the Porcupine gave

||hĩ-ĩ, ti e:, !kʔe -||kwaŋ |ne |ki |ha ha ã -|kwammaŋ-a.
thanks, that the people had taken out *-|kwammaŋ-a* for her.

!kaurukən a: |ku ||k'oen !khe:, o haŋ tatti, haŋ k''auki ˍdóa |ni:
!Kauru was the one who stood looking, because she could not see

|kaggən, ta: !kauögən |ku ˍdóa |ki !haŋ-a |kaggən. He ti hiŋ e:,
the Mantis, for the stones had shut in the Mantis. Therefore

!kauruwo |ku ||k'oen !khe:, o haŋ tatti e:, ha k''auki |ni |kaggən.
!Kauru stood looking, because she did not see the Mantis.

(Omitted text: 6210-6211)

That is why she stood looking because she did not see the Mantis. Therefore she stood looking.

He ti hiŋ e:, ha ||nau, ha |ne ||k'oen, ti e:, !kˀe |ku-g |ne ta hi !ku
Then when she saw that the people meant

se ¯|ka: |kaggən, haŋ |ne ≠kaka !kˀe, ti e:, hi ˍ||kwaŋ se |ki |ha ka ã
to leave the Mantis, she told the people to take out for her

|kaggən.
the Mantis.

He ti hiŋ e:, !kˀe ˍ||kwaŋ |ne !kann!kann ||kud: !ho !kauögən, he
Then the people took hold and uncovered the stones, and

!kˀetən |ku-g |ne !kann !k''erri |hiŋ |kaggən. He ti hiŋ e:, |kaggən
the people pulled out the Mantis roughly, hurting him. Then the Mantis

|ne |i|iŋ o |kaggən tũ:, ĩ:, o !kauögən e !k''erri ha eŋeŋ. He e:,
complained about his skin, for the stones were hurting his body. Then

!kauruwo |ne kúï, '!kammam, m kamm kam, m |kam, a !hamm dimm amkam kam|kam.'

'!kau-we:, ŋ kaŋ ka, ŋ |ke:, a ˍ!nam dí akka ke |kaggən.'

!kauru said, 'O person, I wanted, I told you to treat well for me the Mantis.'

He !kˀe-g |ne |ku !kann!kann ||kud:tẽ !kauögən, he !kˀe-g |he |ku !kann
Then the people took hold and laid aside the stones, and dragged

!k''erri |hiŋ !kaggən. He ti hiŋ e:, |kaggən |ne |i|iŋ, ĩ: o |kaggən tũ:.
out the Mantis roughly. Then the Mantis moaned about his skin.

He ti hiŋ e:, |kaggən |ne |i|iŋ, |kakkakən |ne ¯||kerri, ĩ:, o han tatti e:
Then the Mantis moaned, the Mantis screamed, because

ha tũ: ˍ||kwaŋ taŋ kwokwoŋ-a. He ti hiŋ e:, ha |ne ¯||kerri, ĩ:, o ha tũ:,
his skin was aching properly. Therefore he screamed about his skin,

The text from this point on page 6215 until page 6219 was abridged in *Bantu Studies*. Here is the translation from the notebook:

(Omitted text: 6215-6219)

Therefore he screamed because his skin was really hurting properly. Therefore he screamed. He kept on screaming about his skin, because his skin was aching properly. Therefore he screamed about his skin for he felt that the stones had skinned him. Therefore he screamed about his skin, for he felt that the stones had skinned him. Therefore he screamed about his skin, because the stones had skinned him. Therefore he screamed about his skin when he first moaned. Then he screamed; when he had first moaned about his skin. Then he screamed, for he felt that his skin was really hurting properly. Therefore he screamed, because his skin was really hurting properly,

o haŋ tatti e:, !kauögən -//kwaŋ !kwara ha. He e:, ha /ne -//kerri, ĩ:, o
because he felt that the stones had skinned him. So he screamed, after
ha -!hamm /i/iŋ ã: tũ:; ha /ne -//kerri, ĩ:, o haŋ tatti e:, ha tũ: -//kwaŋ
he had first moaned about his skin; he screamed, because his skin was
dóä taŋ kwokwóŋ-a.
really hurting properly.

Haŋ -//kwaŋ /ne duru //a:, hĩ !kˀe, o -/kwammaŋ-aŋ -//kwaŋ //a:,
He limped home with the people, while !*kwammaŋ-a* went along,
-/kwammaŋ-a a: /ku twai-i. /kakkakən a: /xóäkən/xóäkən-ĩ,
!kwammaŋ-a was comfortable. The Mantis was the one who went staggering along,
ha a:, !kˀe -tai tau //ahóbbakən//ahóbbakən //au //kho ha xu,
it was he whose face the people were anointing, as they went, to heal it,
o ha -tai tau /xóäkən/xóäkən-ĩ, o han tatti e:, ha -//kwaŋ -dóä //kaŋ-a.
while he went staggering along, for he felt that he was hungry.
He ti hiŋ e:, ha -tai tau /xóäkən/xóäkən-ĩ, o han tatti e:, ha -//kwaŋ
Therefore he staggered as he walked, for he felt that he was
-dóä //kaŋ-a. He ti hiŋ e:, !kˀe /ne -tai tau //ahóbbakən//ahóbbakən //au
hungry. Meanwhile the people walked on anointing
//kho ha xu, o !kˀetən ta, ha xu se //au siŋ, ha se kwe: -tai //a
his face, for the people wished his face to heal, that he might go quietly
!kˀe, ha se !kúïtən. He ti hiŋ e:, ha -//kwaŋ /ne !kúïtən, ĩ:.
with the people, that he might return home. So he went home.

He e:, ha //kaxai !kˀɔkən /ne //aŋ k''wa: /xumm ha, ĩ, o ti e: ha /ku
Then his sister the Blue Crane cried pitying him, because he was
//khó:ä o twitwi:tən. He ti hiŋ e:, ha //kaxai k''wa: /xumm ha ĩ:, o há-ka
covered with wounds. Therefore his sister cried pitying him for his
-!gó:ë, ti e:, ha /kaggən, ha kukuá: dí -!gó:ë, o !kˀe
misfortune, because he, the Mantis, had suffered misfortune, while the people

The rescue of the Mantis and /Kwammaŋ-a

e: ‗≠kwaija, o há-ka didi:. He tikən e:, !k²e |ne ‗≠kwaija, ĩ:
were scolding him for his doings. Therefore the people scolded him,

o há a: k''auki tu:ï !k²e e: hi ≠kakən ha. Ta:
because he did not listen to what the people said to him. For the

|ni ⊙pua |ke:, a ‗há ka siŋ ≠kaka ha ã:, o ‗|kwammaŋ-a: ≠kaka
young Ichneumon there had often spoken to him, for ‗|kwammaŋ-a had spoken

|ni ⊙pua ã:, he |ni ⊙pua |ne ≠kaka ha !kóïŋ |kaggən.
to the young Ichneumon, and the young Ichneumon had spoken to his Grandfather the Mantis.

He |ni ⊙pua ‗há: |ne kú:ï, 'ŋ tʃóïŋ wé:, ibó kaŋ ka, ŋ
'ŋ !kóïŋ wɛ:, ibo kaŋ ka, ŋ
And the young Ichneumon said, 'O my grandfather. Father wishes me

tts²akka há:, a koá: k''auki sse ttss²a: ttsse:nttsse:n zza zzá tsse:n
≠kaka ha ã:, a koá: k''auki se ss²a: k''e:nk''e:n ||na |‚na, k''e:n
to tell thee that thou must not come to play tricks there, playing

tsséï taŋ. Íbókən tssué: dza, haŋ tssakka ke, ŋ ssiŋ tsswé: kú, ŋ ttssakka
|kwẽ:i a.(?) Ibokən |kwẽ:i da, haŋ ≠kaka ke, ŋ siŋ ‚kwe:i u, ŋ ≠kaka
like this. Father thus spoke to me, I should say this, I should tell

ha, a sse k''auki ss²á ttse:nja zzá, dze:n dzéï taŋ. He ti hiŋ e:, (?)
ha, a se k''auki ss²á k''e:nk''e:nja ||na ||neiŋ |kéï a. He ti hiŋ e:,
thee, thou shouldst not come to play tricks at houses like this. That is what

ibó kaŋ ttssakka ke, ŋ siŋ ttssakka ha; tsá: a k''auki ta ‗tssóa,
ibó kaŋ ≠kaka ke, ŋ siŋ ≠kaka ha; ta: a k''auki ta ‗k''óa,
Father said to me, I should speak to thee: for thou wert not willing,

i ssiŋ ttssakka ha ã:, tsá a ka tssá tse:ntse:nja zzá
i siŋ ≠kaka ha ã:, tá: a ka ss²a k''e:nk''e:nja ||na
that we should talk to thee, but thou didst come playing tricks at

dzen a tsxara. He ti hiŋ e:, ibó ka, ŋ tssakka há:, ŋ ssiŋ kukú,
||neiŋ a |xara. He ti hiŋ e:, ibó ka, ŋ ≠kaka ha ã:, ŋ siŋ kukúï,
a strange house. Therefore Father wishes me to speak to thee, I must thus

ŋ a ttssakka ha, a sse k''auki ttss²a: tsse:ntsse:nja zzá, tse: e: tsxára
ŋ a ≠kaka ha, a se k''auki ss²a: k''e:nk''e:n ||na, !k²e e: |xara
tell thee, that thou shouldst not come playing tricks at other people's

hé‗ta dzeŋ. Tsa:, a k''auki ta tss²õä, á ssiŋ tʃóä, i: ssiŋ ttssakka ha.
hé-ta ||neiŋ. Ta:, a k''auki ta ||khóä, á siŋ ≠gouwa, i siŋ ≠kaka ha.
houses. But thou art not willing to be silent, that we may speak to thee.

Tsa:, a ka dza ttsse:nttse:n zza zzá, tsé e: tsxára, hí-ta dzeŋ. Hẽ, ŋ ta,
Ta:, a ka ||a k''e:nk''e:ŋ ||na ||ná, !k²e e: |xara, hí-ta ||neiŋ. He ŋ ta,
But thou dost go to play tricks there at stranger's houses. And I feel,

ŋ tssóïŋ wɛ:, a k''auki dzóä ttssú:ï; tsa: á ka tss?á ttse:nttse:n
ŋ !kóïŋ wé:, a k''auki //khóä tú:ï; ta: á ka ss?a k''e:nk''e:n
o my Grandfather, thou dost not seem to listen, but thou dost come to play

zza zzá, akən ttssé:ï ¯tsa, a k''auki ˍdzóä ttssú:ï, hiŋ e:, á
//na //ná, akən /kwẽ:ï /kã, a k''auki ˍk''óä tú:ï: hiŋ e:, á
tricks there, thou dost act as if thou hadst not listened, for thou

ka ts?á:, ttsse:nttsse:n zza zzá. Tsá, a ssiŋ ssiŋ zzó a: ttssú:ï,
ka ss?a:, k''e:nk''e:n //na //ná:. Tá, a siŋ siŋ //kho á: tú:ï,
didst come playing tricks there. For if thou hadst seemed to listen,

a kóä k''auki ssin ttsse:nttsse:ŋ, o a ssiŋ ttssú:ï. Tsá:,
a kóä k''auki siŋ k''e:nk''e:n, o a siŋ tú:ï. Tá:
thou wouldst not have played tricks if thou hadst listened. For

a ˍdzóä ssiŋ ssiŋ dzo a: ttssú:ï, a koá k''auki ssiŋ ttsse:nttsse:n.
a ˍk''óä sin siŋ //kho a: tú:ï, a koá k''auki siŋ k''e:nk''e:n.
if thou hadst really seemed to listen, thou wouldst not have played tricks.

Ákən ttssé:ï tssá:, a k''auki ˍdzóä tssú:ï, hiŋ e:, a ˍdzóä ttsse:nttssen,
Akən /kwẽ:ï /kwã, a k''auki ˍk''óä tú:ï, hiŋ e:, a ˍk''óä k''e:nk''e:n,
Thou dost act as if thou hadst not listened, for thou dost play tricks,

ákən tssé:ï tssá:, a k''auki ˍdzóä ttssú:ï.'
akən /kwẽ:ï /kwã, a k''auki ˍk''óä tú:ï.
thou dost act as if thou hadst not listened.'

Notes

2-3 *The Elephant and the Giraffe and the Rhinoceros were those who went ...*: An important character, ǂKum!kwe, has been left out of the list between the Giraffe and the Rhinoceros – 'ǂKum!kwe once was a man; that is why his name was ǂKum!kwe. He lives in our country. He always says '*ǂku ǂku*'. He sounds as if a man were throwing stones there, when he falls upon his buttocks.' (6195 rev.–6196 rev., note omitted)

28 *... for the stones which had fallen were big*: 'The men must come out, for stones had fallen, stones which were big had fallen.' (6203, text omitted)

32-34 *...for his face became visible ...*: 'That is why the Porcupine thought that |Kwammaŋ-a must be got out.' (6204-6205, text omitted)

73 *!kauru said, 'O person ...'*: In the notebook translation, this is 'O people' (6213).

106 … *for he felt that he was hungry*: 'Therefore he walked staggering with hunger, for he felt that he was hungry.' (6222, text omitted)

116-118 … *because he was covered with wounds*: The phrase is repeated: 'Therefore his sister cried pitying him, because he was covered with wounds' (6224, text omitted).

125 … *because he did not listen to what the people said to him*: 'He did not seem as if he had heard the people who spoke to him, for he kept on going to tease there, he did not seem as if he heard what the people had said to him' (6226–6227, text omitted).

146 *Father said to me, I should speak to thee*: 'You should not go teasing about at houses. Then father said to me I should speak to thee' (6229–6230).

Roger Hewitt (1986:147) explains that |Kaggen and the Ichneumon have:

> … a joking relationship with each other… Their relationship is also strengthened by the fact that whereas |Xam males regarded their fathers' parents as their 'lent' grandparents, they regarded their mothers' parents as their 'real' grandparents. Thus the formal relationship between |Kaggen and the Ichneumon was doubly close. In contrast to this |Kawammang-a (sic – ed.) and |Kaggen were in a mutual avoidance relationship and this is emphasised by the necessity for |Kwammaŋ-a to address all of his comments to |Kaggen through his son …

The Black Crow calling the Jackal

Narrator: ||Kabbo
Dictation dates: Some time in July 1872
Notebook reference: B.IX: 921-929
***Bantu Studies* reference:** Vol. 10 (1936), Special speech: 179-180

The Black Crow (the Cape Rook, Corvus capensis*) calls the black-backed Jackal* (Canis mesomelas) *to try and adopt the Dawn's Heart Star's child. The jackal in turn calls the Blue Crane.*

Dorothea Bleek's original introduction:

The Jackal uses 'a strange labial click, which bears to the ordinary labial click ʘ the same relation that the palatal click ≠ bears to the cerebral click!' This is Dr. Bleek's explanation of the sound, given on p. 6 of A brief Account of Bushman Folklore. In one of Miss Lloyd's notes she writes 'the jackal has a pat lip click.' She writes it ♀. Dr. Bleek writes it ⌽. According to my recollection of the manner in which Miss Lloyd pronounced the click, I should say it had something of a strongly plosive p in it.

There is an example of this speech in an episode in the myth of the Dawn's-Heart. This star hides its child under leaves for its mother, the Lynx, to find it. Other animals and birds come first and try to claim it, but the child mocks at them. They speak to each other about it.

||hóë:tən a: !kwi:ja kɔro, he e: kɔrokən |ne ssˀa ĩ:. !gauë-|ĩ-ʘuakən
The Black Crow calls the Jackal, then the jackal comes. Dawn's-Heart's child

|ne kurri:tən kɔro, kɔrokən |ne !k'wein, au ||hóë:tən !k'weinja.
mocks the Jackal, the Jackal gets angry, as the Black Crow got angry.

Kɔrokən |ne !kuï: !kˀo, '¯⌽ba:-au-¯wa:, ⌽o-wɛ:, ⌽me u ssa:, a ⌽me !kˀo-wɛ:, |ne u ssa:, a-g |ne
The Jackal calls the Blue Crane 'Bow wow, o Blue Crane, come that thou mayst

⌽poëŋ ⌽pã: a: a, aurugu-⌽ua a: a.' !kˀo:kən a:-g |ne ≠kakən, ti e:ha se ||k'oëŋ !kwã: a: a, auruku-ʘua a: a.'
see this child, this fine child.' The Blue Crane says that she will

||a: ||k'oëŋ !kwã:, ã: kɔro !kwi: ha ã:. Rrurrurrurru, |nakki ŋ ||a:
go to see the child, to which the Jackal called her.' *Rrurrurrurru,* let me go

||k'oëŋ !kwã, a: kɔro !kwi: ŋ ã, ŋ siŋ ||óä:kən di m ʘpa:xai ã:,'
to see the child, to which the Jackal called me, that I may make my daughter of her.'

Kɔrokən ≠kakən !kˀo, 'ɸattən ɸu ssa, a se ɸoëŋ.'
'!attən !u ssa, a se ||k'oëŋ.'
The Jackal says to the Blue Crane, 'Run forward, that thou must see. 'The

!kˀokən ≠kakən, '|nakki ŋ |ne !attən !kũ ||e.' !kˀokən ||nau ha !nauŋkɔ !á:ẽ
Blue Crane says, 'Let me run forward.' While the Blue Crane still walks

||a:, haŋ dauko !kuttən ha ||kũ |na, ti e: |garra ssoëŋ e ha
on, she sings in going of her shoulder, that Krieboom berries sit on her

||kũ |na. Haŋ tá:ẽtá:ẽja ti !kuttən,
shoulder. She walks along singing,

> *'|garra kaŋ ssóë:ŋja ŋ ||kũ |na,*
> 'The Krieboom berries sit on my shoulder,
>
> *|garra kaŋ ssóë:ŋja ŋ ||kũ |na.'*
> The Krieboom berries sit on my shoulder.'

Haŋ |ne tá:ẽ !kei ||a: !gauë-|ĩ:-ʘuakən ʃo. Haŋ ≠kakən ti e:,
She arrives at the seat of the Dawn's-Heart's child. She says that,

!kwã a: a ha xa: k''óä dóä |kwẽ:-u kɔro !kwi: ŋ ã:, haŋ k''auki tan-ʘua
this child seems to be just as the Jackal told me, it is not a little

!kú:ïta. !kuko: kɔrokən ≠kaka ha, 'Ha i ɸeŋ ɸhcẽ: ɸi:ja
'Ha i ||keŋ ||hcẽ: !kwi:ja
white. The other, the Jackal says to her,' Our friend the Black Crow told

ŋ ã:, ŋ siŋ ɸkaŋ ka, ŋ di m ɸpuaxai ã:. ɸpa:ŋ ɸu-g ɸme ɸuerritən ŋ.
ŋ ã:, ŋ siŋ ||kuaŋ ka, ŋ di m ʘpuaxai ã:. !kwãŋ |ku-g |ne kurritən ŋ.
me of her, I wanted to make my daughter of her. The child mocked me.

He ti hiŋ e:, ŋ ɸme ɸpi: a ĩ:, a se ɸxam ssˀe ɸpenn ɸpã: a: a,
He ti hiŋ e:, ŋ |ne !kwi: a ĩ:, a se ||xam ssˀa ≠enn !kwã a: a,
Then I told thee about it, that thou shouldst also come to know this child.

ha ɸpu ɸme ɸperritən ŋ.'
ha |ku |ne kurritən ŋ.'
which mocked me.'

!kuko: !kˀo:kən ≠kaka ha, 'ŋ kattən ||kwattən se datt m ʘaxatt ã:.'
'ŋ kaŋ ||kwaŋ se di m ʘuaxai ã:.'
The other, the Blue Crane says, 'I wanted to make my daughter of her.'

Special Speech of animals and Moon used by the the /Xam Bushmen

The Black Crow calling the Jackal

!kuko: kərokən ≠kaka ha, ' a kaŋ ʘkwaŋ ʘkɯ se ĩ:, ta m ʘpɯ ʘme ʘenn.'
' a kaŋ ||kwaŋ !kũ se ĩ, ta ŋ |kɯ |ne ≠enn.'
The other, the Jackal say's, 'thou didst come forward for I know.'

Note

37-40 *... this child seems to be just as the Jackal told me, it is not a little white*. An omitted note on 925 rev. explains that 'she (i.e. the Blue Crane) is praising the child'.

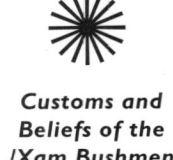

The young Dog

Narrator: |Haŋ‡kass'o
Source: '|Haŋ‡kass'o from his maternal grandmother ‡Kammi'
Dictation date: 10 July 1879
Notebook reference: L.VIII.29: 8603-8614 and 30: 8615-8627
***Bantu Studies* reference:** Vol. 10 (1936), Special speech: 180-186

The title of this narrative in Lucy Lloyd's 'A short account of further Bushman material collected' (1889: L.IV.40) is 'The Quagga, who was poisoned by her husband, !Kuinssi/kauoken'.

Dorothea Bleek's introduction:

In the following story there is another longer example of the speech of the Jackal together with the speech of the Hyena, who uses the click ≠ indiscriminately.

The 'Dog' (!kuiŋ-si) referred to here is probably the Wild Dog. In /Xam folklore the Dog's relatives are the Jackals, the Hyenas and the Blue Cranes. The Dog marries the Quagga, but the relationship is doomed once the Dog's relatives learn that his wife is a Quagga.

!kuiŋ-si-_/káuökakən /ne /haŋ /e //k'hwi. !kuiŋ-si_/kauökakən /ku-g /ne e
The young Dog married into the Quaggas. The young Dog was

!kwi, ¯!xwe-//na-ss?o !kwitən /ku e. Ha-ka !k?e _//kwaŋ /ku e koro-gu
a man, one of the 'Early Race' he was. His people were the Jackals,

!gwãĩ-gu, !k?o-gu. Ha _//kwaŋ tatti e:, !k?e e //na ha, hĩ _//kwan e.
the Hyenas, the Blue Cranes. He felt that the people who lived with him they were.

_!goë taŋ _há oä /kẽã: //k'hwi //nuaŋ-ka tı ⊙pua, haŋ /ne ¯!numm !ko
The Tortoise once took a little piece of the Quagga's liver, she put

hĩ, haŋ /ne /ku səm, ¯//kou tẽ ĩ. He //k'hwi ⊙pua
it into her mouth, she closed her mouth upon it. And the little Quagga

/ne /ku ¯!kaunu ha tu, haŋ /ne /ku //ka ĩ hĩ au /i. He ha /ne /ku ¯/ka
tried to open her mouth, she burnt it with fire. Then she left

-!góë. Haŋ |ne |ku u:ï, haŋ |ne |ku ⁻!kúïtən, haŋ |ne ||aŋ ≠kakka ha xóä.
the Tortoise. She arose, she returned home, she went to tell her mother.

(*||k'hwi ||uara -||kwaŋ ⁻|kuwa !kaukən ã ha ||nuaŋ, haŋ |ne |kou|kou ⁻|kəmma*
(The mother Quagga put away for the children her liver, she cut off

!kaukən ï:. Haŋ |ne a ⁻a kaukən; haŋ |ne |kou ⁻|kəmma !khwã a:,
for the children from it. She gave to the children; she cut off for this child

ha ã ||nuaŋ-ka ti ⊙pua, ha |ne |kou ⁻|kəmma !khwã a ha ã ||nuaŋ-ka ti ⊙pua.
a little piece of liver, she cut off for that child a little piece of liver.

Ha -há |ne kúï, 'U -koá k''auki se a ⁻a |kagən au ŋ ||nuaŋ, ta: |kagən
She said, 'You must not give to your companions of my liver, for they

se ≠kaka hĩ-ta !k?e.')
would tell their people).'

Ha xóäkən -há |ne kúï, '⁻ŋ hŋ, !khwã we, tsara xa a:, a ka ||kan-di
Her mother exclaimed, 'Alas, o child, why is it that thy foolishness

|kwëï tã ã:? A xa k''au -saŋ |ne ⁻tã !góë, au á |ku ⁻a
is like this? Wilt thou not feel bereavement, when thou hast given

-!góë ŋ ||nuaŋ?' (-!góëtən ≠ni |hiŋ ||nuaŋ au
to the Tortoise of my liver? '(The tortoise took away the liver from

||k'hwi ⊙pua; ha xóäkən ⁻≠i, ti e:, ha ⊙puaxai a: ⁻a
the little Quagga; her mother thought that her daughter had given

-!góë ã ha ||nuaŋ.)
to the Tortoise of her liver).

Au -!góëtən -há |ne úï, haŋ |ne ⁻!kuïtən. -!góë |ne ||aŋ
Meanwhile the Tortoise arose, she returned home. The Tortoise went

xattən |hiŋ ||k'hwi ||nuaŋ. Haŋ |ne |ke⁻|kəmma kɔro-gu ||nuaŋ-ka tikən-
to spit out the Quagga's liver. She cut off for the Jackals pieces of

tikən, kɔro-gukən |ne tsəmm ⁻ĩ hĩ. Hiŋ há |né ta,
liver, the Jackals tasted them. They said,

'φpíä, φpíä, tsa φpiŋ-si -φpuaökən -k''öä -döä φpaŋ ss?o φpi ã?'
'⁻||kã ⁻||kã, tsa !kuiŋ-si |kaúökən -k''öä -döä |naŋ ss?o ||k'hwi ã?'
'Excellent, Excellent, How is it that the Young Dog has married a Quagga?'

Hiŋ |ne ⁻a !kuko:, !gwãĩ, ||nuaŋ-ka ti ko:, !kuko:,
They gave to the other one, the Hyena, another piece of liver, the other,

!gwãĩ |ne tsəmm hi. !kuko: !gwãĩŋ -há |ne kúï, ⁻≠kəã, ⁻≠kəã,
the Hyena, tasted it. The other, the Hyena, said, 'Excellent, excellent,

≠kuiŋ-si ˍ≠kauökən ˍk''óa ss²o ≠ke ¯≠kou, haŋ ≠haŋ ss²o ≠k''ui. ≠ne ¯a
!kuiŋ-si- |kauökən k''óä ss²o !kẽï ¯||ou, haŋ |haŋ ss²o ||k'hwi. |ne ¯a
the Young Dog must truly have married a Quagga. Give to

≠kőïte ≠k²o ã ≠nuaŋ-ka ti ≠kua, ha ≠ne ≠kamm ki.'
!kőïte !k²o ã ||nuaŋ-ka ti ⊙pua, ha |ne tsamm hĩ.'
Grandmother Blue Crane a little piece of liver, that she may taste it.'

Hiŋ ˍhá |ne ¯a !k²o ¯ã ||nuaŋ-ka ti ⊙pua, !k²okən
They gave to the Blue Crane a little piece of liver, the Blue Crane

|ne tsamm hĩ. !k²okən ˍha |ne tsamm ||nuaŋ, !k²okən ˍha |ne kũ,
tasted it. The Blue Crane tasted the liver, the Blue Crane exclaimed,

'¯||kã, ¯||kã, m ⊙pua⊙puaïdi !kuiŋ-si- ˍ|kauökən ˍk''óa sso !kẽï ¯||ou,
Excellent, excellent, my grandson the Young Dog must truly

haŋ |haŋ ss²o ||k'hwi. ¯|ka, ha se ssé, ŋ siŋ ≠kaka ha ã,
have married a Quagga. Wait, let him come, that I may tell him about it,

ta: ||k'hwi ˍdőä |ku a:, ha |haŋ ss²o ha.'
for it must be a Quagga whom he had married.'

He !kuiŋ:si ˍ|kauökən ha |ne ssa:, hiŋ |ne saŋ ≠kaka ha, ti e:,
And the Young Dog came, they came to tell him that

||k'hwi ˍdőä |ku a:, ha |haŋ ss²o ha; haŋ ˍdőä se |kha ||k'hwi.
a Quagga must be the one whom he had married; he should kill the Quagga.

He tikən e:, !kuiŋ-si ˍ|kauökən ˍha |ne ¯||keŋ ||kukən ¯!kwagən, au
Therefore that Young Dog stuck in (poisoned pointed) bones, while (his)

|aitikən kaŋ ˍ!hau sso: ha xóäkən-gu. Haŋ |ne ˍ||keŋ |'kukən !kwa:kn.
wife was visiting her parents. He stuck in the bones.

He |aiti ˍha |ne ¯!kúïtən ssa:. |aitikən ˍha |ne kúï, '|ne ¯koä ki,
And the wife returned home. The wife said, 'Make room for me,

ŋ |ne !khwi.' Ha ˍ||kwaŋ ka, gwai |ha: ha au ||neiŋ,
that I may make the bed.' She wanted her husband to go out of the hut,

ha se !khwi akən. Gwaitən ˍhá |ne kúï, '|ku teŋ ¯ssa:, te ŋ
that she might make the bed nicely. The husband said, 'Lie down, for I

|ku |kedda !khwija.' He ha |ne |ku |e ||a ||neiŋ, haŋ |ne |ku ¯||kou siŋ
have just made the bed.' And she went into the hut, she sat down upon

!kwa, he !kwa |ku-g |ne kúï ¯≠kãũ siŋ ha ||khwãĩ, haŋ |ne |ku sueŋ !khwa:
a bone, and the bone pierced her buttock (?), she sat down breaking

!kwa. He ha |ku | nau, haŋ kúï, haŋ sueŋ, haŋ |ku ¯||kou sin !kwa ko:,
the bone. And when she turning about sat down, she sat upon another bone,

haŋ /kɯ sueŋ !khwa: ha. He ha ˍhá /kɯ ˉu /hiŋ //a, au tʃueŋ-ta !kaukakən
she sat breaking it. And she rose up, she went out, while the little ones

/kɯ /ne //kóäkən //na hĩ ha xóä.
altogether accompanied their mother.

He tikən e:, hĩ ˍha /ne ˍtáï tau ˉ!kuttən. Hiŋ ˍhá /né ta,
Then they walked along singing. They said,

'*ˍ!gáökən ˉwe:,*	'O poison,
ˍ!gáökən ˉwe:,	O poison,
ˍ!gáökən ˉwe:,	O poison,
ˍ!gáökən ˉwe:,	O poison,
ˍ!gáökən ˉwe:,	O poison,
ˍ!gáökən se !kənn !ho	Let the poison hold up
Itau /ĩ:,	Our mother's heart,
Itau se //a k''wã	That our mother may go to drink
Au !khou-/kui:.'	At Neck-vulture.' (a water pool).

!kaukakən ˉ!kuttən; hiŋ ta, ˍ!gáökən ˍkoá se ˉa ha xóä
The children sang; they said that the poison should allow their mother's

/ĩja siŋ !naunko !khe, ha xóä se //a k''wã, ha se ˉ!hou,
heart to stand a while, that their mother might go to drink and afterwards

ha ˉ/kukən, au ha k''wã.
die, when she had drunk.

Haa xóäkən ˍhá: //a:. Hiŋ ˍhá ka,
Their mother went along. They sang,

'*ˍ!gáökən ˉwe:,*	'O poison,
ˍ!gáökən ˉwe:,	O poison,
ˍ!gáökən ˉwe:,	O poison,
ˍ!gáökən ˉwe:,	O poison,
ˍ!gáökən ˉwe:,	O poison,
ˍ!gáökən se !kənn !ho	Let the poison hold up
Itau /ĩ:,	Our mother's heart,
Itau se //a k''wã	That our mother may go to drink
Au !khou-/kui:.'	At Neck-vulture.'

He hĩ ˍhá /ne ˉ!k?ai //a !khou-/kui:. Ha xóäkən /ne k''wẽ:ï. Haŋ /ne
And they went down to Neck-vulture. Their mother drank. She was

/kɯ k''wẽ:ï, k''wẽ:ï, k''wẽ:ï, k''wẽ:ï, haŋ /ne /kɯ kuakkən, haŋ /ne /kɯ ˉ/kukəŋ;
drinking, drinking, drinking, drinking, she vomited she died;

he ha /kɯ-g /ne //khóë ta: !khoa:, !kou ta !khoa tu !khou.
and she lay by the water, on the water's bank.

Kɔro-gukən |ne |ku ⁻||khuĩ ha, hiŋ |ne ⁻|kẽĩ ha !noa, !gauökən ki !k?ai
The Jackals traced her, they found her footprints, followed down

||a ha !noa au !khoa:. Hiŋ |ne |ouwi ha, au haŋ ta:, hiŋ
her footprints to the water. They caught sight of her as she lay, they

|ne !khe ||a: ha, hiŋ |ne ||aŋ |ĩ: ha, |ĩ: ha, |ĩ, |ĩ,, |ĩ, hiŋ |ne ||kɛ:äkən |ku ||ɛnn
went to her, they went and skinned her, cut her up, they altogether dwelt

!khoa:. Hiŋ |ku-g |ne ⁻hã |ki ha.
at the water. They were eating her.

||k'hwi-ta !kaukakən ˍhá ˈku k''wa: ||na. !kukokən ˍhá |ne ⁻||kaiten
The Quagga's children were crying there. One of them climbed up on

kɔro-ka ⁻!nu, haŋ ⁻||khou sso hĩ. He ha ˍhá |ne ||nau, kɔro-gu⁻wa !xãũã,
the Jackals' branch nut, she sat upon it. And when the Jackals were boiling,

ha ˍhá |ne ||nau, ha ||k'oen ti e:, sueŋja |ku-g |ne |ki !haŋ-a !koã xu,
when she saw that the fat covered the top of the pot,

ha ˍhá |ne ⁻tsunn ha tsaxáitən-ta !khwetən, he ha tsaxáu-ka !khwe-ta
she winked pressing out her tears and her tears

ˍhá |ne tattən ⁻||kou siŋ !koã, !koã |ne ⁻|ki. Kɔro ˍhá |ne kúĩ,
fell upon the pot, the pot clove asunder. The Jackal exclaimed,

'ŋ-ka ǂpua, ŋ-ka ǂpua, tsara ˍkoá: ǂpiá ke ǂpua?'
'ŋ-ka !koã, ŋ-ka !koã, tsara ˍkoá: !khwa: ke !koã?'
'My pot, my pot, what can have broken for me the pot?

He !gwãĩ ˍhá |ne ||xamki !xãũä. He ||k'hwi ʘpua ˍha ||nau ha ||k'oen,
And the Hyena also boiled. And when the little Quagga saw

ti e:, !koã |ne ⁻kũ, he sueŋja |ne !ahítiŋ !koã xu, ha
that the pot was boiling and the fat was upon the top of the pot, she

|ne ⁻tsunn ha tsaxáu-ka !khwetən, he !khwe⁻ta |ne tattən ˍ||kou siŋ !koã,
winked pressing out her tears, and her tears fell upon the pot,

!koã |ne ⁻|ki. !gwãĩ ˍhá |ne kúĩ, '⁻ĩ, ⁻ĩ, ⁻ĩ, ŋ-ka sueŋ, n-ka sueŋ,
the pot clove asunder. The Hyena exclaimed, 'Alas, alas, alas, my fat, my fat,

ǂkã, tsara ˍkoa: á ǂka ke ǂkoã?' !kuko: kɔro ˍhá |ne kúĩ,
ˍ||kã, tsara ˍkoa: á !khwa: ke !koã?'
oh dear, what can have broken for me the pot?' The other, the Jackal, said,

'ǂpu we:, a kaŋ ǂpu a: ǂpuen ǂpuã a:, haŋ ⁻ǂpi ǂpia ǂpe ǂi.'
'!ku we:, a kaŋ |ku a: ||k'oen !koã a:, haŋ ⁻|ki ||ka !khe |i.'

Special Speech of animals and Moon used by the the /Xam Bushmen

The young Dog

'O person, thou art the one who seest this pot, it clove asunder on the fire.'
!kuko:kən ˍhá |ne kúï, ' ¯≠kaŋ, ŋ kaŋ k''auki ≠enna, tsa a ≠koã ¯≠ki ã?'
' ¯|keŋ, ŋ kaŋ k''auki ≠enna, tsa a !koã ¯|ki ã?'
The other said, My 'friend, I do not know why the pot clove asunder?'
He ||khwi-ta eŋ ˍhá |ne ||gwi:.
And the Quagga's meat was finished.

!kuiŋ-si ˍ|kanökakən ˍha |ne ¯||xã, haŋ |haŋ ha !kouki ʘpua. He e:,
The Young Dog again married his younger sister-in-law. And then
ha ʘpuai-|houkən |ne |k'abbe ha, há ka ha se ¯||xã, ha !kha ha
his parents-in-law spoke together about him, that he would again kill his
!kouki ʘpua, hiŋ e:, ha |haŋ ha !kouki ʘpua,
younger sister-in law, since he had married his younger sister-in-law,
au haŋ |kha |aiti; haŋ ¯||xã, haŋ |haŋ ha !kouki ʘpua.
when he had killed his wife; he again married his younger sister in-law.
Ha ʘpuai-|houkakən |ne |k'abbe ha, hiŋ |ne !ho ¯!ku. He hi
His parents-in-law talked together about him, they held a dance. And they
|ne ||gwitən. He e:, há |ne ||gwitən hĩ ha ʘpuai-houkən. ||k'hwi e: |k'waija
played. And then he played with his parents-in-law. Many Quaggas
|ne |ku !khe ||k'e: ã:. Hiŋ |ne |ku !k?õä !xwumm ha, hiŋ |ne |ku !k?õä
surrounded him. They trampled him to pieces, they trampled
kúï |nuaŋ|nuaŋ ã, |khi: ha.
breaking his bones, killed him.

Notes

Khoi-San folklorist Sigrid Schmidt uses this tale to discuss general characteristics of 'Khoisan Magic Tales' (Schmidt 1996: 111-113).

20-22 *The mother Quagga put away for the children her liver, she cut off for the children from it*: Other Early Race people also cut off body parts to feed themselves and their children: the Zorilla, weasel or muishond (*!ko:a*) cuts itself up and eats itself (L.VIII.13: 7158-7205); the *!kha§-u* (a lizard of the genus *Agama*) brings home his own flesh as food (L.VIII 12: 7114-7118; 13: 7119-7156).

86 *And she went into the hut …*: 'She was a person [a woman]. The quaggas were formerly people.' (8612 rev., note omitted)

106-107 *That our mother may go to drink at Neck-vulture*: 'The meaning of this name (*!khou-/kui:* – ed.) appears to be literally "Neck-vulture" or "Neck-vultures". It is the name of a place; the locality of which unknown to "Jantje". He heard its name from his maternal grandmother, ‡Kammi. I think the water pool must have been fine.' (This last sentence is translated from the |Xam and must therefore have been dictated by |Haŋ‡kass'o – ed.)

109 *The children sang ...*: 'The children were two' (8613 rev., note omitted).

140 *They were eating her*: 'The Quagga's children were crying there: "The quagga's do not a little cry if another one is wounded; for, they cry, [they] make a noise together" [The Bushmen are wont to say to things which are numerous, they say that they [the things] make a noise [together]], if they smell the scent of blood.' (8618 rev., notes omitted)

144 *... the Jackal's branch hut*: 'I think that it seems to have been high, like the houses [referring to kilns] which are here; for, the people say that they were high.' (8619 rev., note omitted)

149 *... she winked pressing out her tears ...*: Lewis-Williams (1996) points out that 'winking' (|Haŋ‡kass'o used the word *tsunn*, elsewhere ||Kabbo and Diä!kwain use *dabba*) is associated with dying, dreaming rain and bewitchment, and therefore with shamanism or sorcery. In the current story, on two occasions, the tears of one of the Quagga's children fall upon a cooking pot containing her mother's remains, causing the pot to split in two. This is clearly another case in which winking has a magical effect. See Part IV, Introduction, for more about winking.

163 *Alas, alas, alas ...*: 'She cried about the fat' (8622 rev., note omitted).

174 *The other said ...*: 'She said 'Oh! Companion!' (8623 rev., note omitted).

The Jackal's song

Narrator: ||Kabbo
Dictation dates: Sometime between 21 August and 14 September 1873
Translation date: 1 October 1873
Notebook reference: B.XXIII: 2159
***Bantu Studies* reference:** Vol. 10 (1936), Special speech: 186

Wilhelm Bleek's description from his 1875 report (1875: 15):

The Jackal's song, in the peculiar Jackal dialect of Bushman, with its extraordinary click.

Dorothea's introduction:

A further example of the Jackal's click is given in the following song.

❑

ϕáta ki ϕgau _kɔro, ϕgau _kɔro-we:, ϕgau _kɔro,
!atta ki _/go kɔro, _/go kɔro-we, _/go kɔro,
Canter for me little Jackal, o little Jackal, little Jackal,

ϕáta ki ϕgau _kɔro, ϕgau _kɔro-we:, ϕgau _kɔro,
!atta ki _/go kɔro, _/go kɔro-we, _/go kɔro,
Canter for me, little Jackal, o little Jackal, little Jackal,

ϕata ki ϕgau _kɔro, ϕgau _kɔro-we:, ϕgau _gɔro,
!atta ki _/go kɔro, _/go kɔro-we, _/go kɔro,
Canter for me, little Jackal, o little Jackal, little Jackal.

❑

Note

Dorothea Bleek added the following:

(Two notes by Miss Lloyd state,

1. The click is a *pat* click made by the lips.
2. This *_/go koro* is the name for quite a young Jackal who can neither see nor walk).

The Moon's speech

Narrator: |A!kuŋta
Dictation dates: Sometime between 13 and 21 March 1873
Notebook reference: B.XV: 1469-1482
***Bantu Studies* reference:** Vol. 10 (1936), Special speech: 187-189

Why the Moon speaks like a shoe.

Dorothea Bleek's introduction:

The most difficult click of all is one used by the Moon, the Hare and the Anteater; Dr. Bleek wrote it ??. He describes it as follows: '? ? is a click made by the Moon instead of the other clicks (v.z. ! / //≠) except the lip click. It is made by curling up the tongue backwards in a sort of roll and then withdrawing the turned up part of the tongue from the upper palate.'

In Miss Lloyd's notes on the special clicks she writes: 'The Moon has a kind of side click in the middle of the mouth, the point of the tongue being turned up and back to the roof of the mouth. This click has a kind of palatal crook to it.'

An example of this click is found in one very long version of the Moon and Hare story. The moon tells the Hare, that his mother will come to life again, and that, therefore, he need not cry. The little Hare does not believe him and continues to cry, saying that the Moon is deceiving him. The Moon becomes angry, threatens to beat his mouth and curses him. In cursing him he begins to use this peculiar speech.

❑

!ka! karrokən |kwẽ: da haŋ ≠kaka !nãũ ⊙ua, ti e: ??nãũ ⊙ua tatti e:
The Moon thus says to the little Hare, that the little Hare is

ha ??kuɯ e ??gebbi ⊙ua. He ti hiŋ e:ha-g ??no??nunntu ??ki:ja ĩ:, au
ha |kuɯ e |gebbi ⊙ua. He ti hiŋ e: ha-g !no!nunntu !ki:ja ĩ:, au
a little fool. Therefore his ears are red, because of

??gebbitən di i. Haŋ k''auki ??kwakka.
|gebbitən di i. Haŋ k''auki ||kwakka.
the foolish doings. He is not clever.

!ka!karrokən ≠kakən ã: |eřři: ||kã:xu, au haŋ tatti e:, ha |eřři:
The Moon speaks with the side of his tongue, because his tongue

!ahi!ahi: ʃiŋ ha !ga!garrakən xu. He ti hiŋ e:, ha ≠kakən ã: /ẽrri /emm
is upon his palate (?). Therefore he speaks with his tongue's tip
au haŋ tatti e !ka!karro /ku e, ha /ku ≠kakəŋ hã-hã-ka kumm, hɛ ha:
because he feels he is the moon who tells his story, and he
??kwe:ŋ ??kwa ĩ:, au han tatti e: !ka!karro /ku e, !kuitən k''auki e, /kwẽ:ĩ /kwã: ĩ:,
does so, because he feels that he is the Moon he is not a person,
ha se ≠kakən akkən, ta: !ka!karro /ku e. He ti hiŋ e: ha /ku ≠kakən
who will speak nicely, for he is the Moon. Therefore he tells
!ka!karro-ka kumm ĩ:, haŋ k''auki ≠kakən !kui-ta kumm, ta ha /ku ĩ:
the Moon's story, he does not tell a person's story, for he thus
≠kakən, ha /ku ĩ: ≠kakən !ka!karro-ka kukummi.
speaks, he thus tells the Moon's stories.

He ti hiŋ e: ha /ku ≠kakən !ahi //ko:ä /ẽrri-ta ti ko:, au han
Therefore he speaks turning up the other part of his tongue, for he
tatti e: !kukən /ku e. He ti hiŋ e:, ha /ku ≠kakən !kukən-ka kukummi,
feels that he is a shoe. Therefore he tells the shoe's stories,
au han tatti e: !kui k''auki e, ta: !ka!karro /ku e. Haŋ e /kaggən
for he feels that he is not a man, but is the Moon. He is the Mantis's
!noá-ka !kukən, au han tatti e:, /kakkən /ku a: !kwi:ja ha /kẽ,
foot's shoe, and he feels that it was the Mantis who called his name.
ha se di !kukən.
he will act like a shoe.

He ti hiŋ e: ha ??kwẽ: da ĩ: haŋ ??kakən, au haŋ tatti e: ha ≠kakən ha !kwẽ: da ĩ: haŋ ≠kakən
Therefore he speaks like this, for he feels that he speaks
//kei//keija !nãũ, haŋ /kwẽ: da haŋ ≠kakən, au haŋ tatti e: ha /ku ĩ:
like the Hare, he speaks in this manner, for he feels that he merely
??kaken a: ??ẽrri:, haŋ /ku ĩ: ≠kakən //kei//keija /õã. /õä ha ≠kakən ≠kakən a: /ẽrri:
speaks with his tongue, he merely speaks like the Hare. The Hare speaks
/õä-ga ≠kakən≠kakən, haŋ /ku /kwẽ: da ??kakən. ??õäŋ ??kwẽ: da ≠kakən. /õäŋ /kwẽ : da
the Hare's language, he speaks like this. The Hare does like this
??õäŋ ??kakən. /õäŋ ≠kakən kúï !kwãŋ ha xoá, haŋ ≠kakən ha xoá-ka /õäŋ ≠kakən.
the Hare talks. The Hare talks like his mother, he tells his mother's
kukummi, ha xoá-ka kukummi e: ha xoá ≠kaken hĩ. Hɛ: !nãũ ʘua
stories, his mother's stories as she tells them. And the little Hare
thumm-ĩ hĩ au ha xoá ≠kakən; haŋ /ne ≠kakən kúï: !kwãŋ ha xoá, au han

listen's to his mother's speech; he talks just like his mother, because he

tatti e:, ha ó:ä ≠kakən kúï: !kwaŋ ha xoá, ha ó:äkən ??kwẽ: da, haŋ ??kakən,

feels that his father talks like his mother, his father talks like this,

au han tatti e: ha ??kakən //kei//keija ha /ha, haŋ ??kwẽ: ??kwe, haŋ ≠kakən !kwẽ: da

for he feels that he speaks like his wife, he does like this, he

??kakən; hiŋ ??kuı hĩ-ka ku: ??kakən kumm a: ??kwai, au hiŋ tatti e:,

≠kakən; hiŋ /kuı hĩ-ka ku: ≠kaken kumm a: !kwai, au hiŋ tatti e:,

speaks; they all tell one story, for they feel that

hĩ ??kuı ??kakən hĩ-hĩ-ta ??kakən, hiŋ k''auki ??kakən ??ei-ta ??kakən,

hĩ /kuı ≠kakən hĩ-hĩ-ta ≠kakən, hiŋ k''auki ≠kakən !?ei-ta ≠kakən,

they talk their own language, they do not talk the people's language,

ta hĩ ??kuı ??kakən hĩ-hĩ-ta kukummi, au hiŋ tatti e:, kum ko: k''auki

ta hĩ /kuı ≠kakən hĩ-hĩ-ta kukummi, au hiŋ tatti e:, kum ko: k''auki

for they tell their own stories, as they feel that another story is not

??na, ha hĩ se ??kakən hã. Ta: hĩ ??kuı ??kakən kumm a: ??kwaï, hiŋ k''auki

//na, ha hĩ se ≠kakən hã. Ta: hĩ /kuı ≠kakən kumm a: !kwaï, hiŋ k''auki

there, that they may tell. For they tell one story, they do not

??kakən ??ei-:ta ku:-ka kukummi; ta: hĩ ??kuı ??kakən??kakən kúï: ??kwãŋ

≠kaken !?ei-ta ku:-ka kukummi ; ta: hĩ /kuı ≠kakən≠kakən kúï !kwãŋ

tell the people's stories; for they speak like

??hu??hu:, au hiŋ tatti e:, ??hu??hu: ??kwẽ: da ??hu??hu: ??kakən.

/hu/hu:, au hiŋ tatti e:, /hu/hu: /kwẽ: da /hu/hu: ≠kakən.

baboons, for they feel that baboons talk in this manner.

Notes

12 … *he speaks with his tongue's tip* …: 'Anteater, hare and moon all three talk in this ugly manner' (1470 rev., note omitted).

25-27 … *he feels that he is a shoe*: |Kaggen created the moon by throwing his leather shoe up into the sky (Bleek 1875: 10; Bleek 1924: 4-5).

The Anteater, the young Springbok and the Lynx

Narrator: |Haŋ‡kass'o
Source: '|Haŋ‡kass'o from |Xabbi-aŋ his mother, his maternal grandmother ‡Kammi, and his step grandmother Tuai-aŋ'
Dictation dates: 26, 27 June 1879
Notebook reference: L.VIII.29: 8561-8602
***Bantu Studies* reference:** Vol. 10 (1936), Special speech: 189-197

Dorothea Bleek's original introduction:

The use of the same click by the Anteater is given in the following story:

Wilhelm Bleek's description in the 1875 Report *gives a useful summary of this story (Bleek 1875: 13):*

The Anteater inquires from a flock of springbok ewes, one after another, whether her child is a female. Each mother answers that hers is a male, until, at last, a foolish springbok confesses that her child is a daughter. The anteater offers to hold the child, so that the springbok should eat some of the anteater's food. The latter then springs into a hole with the kid, and tells the mother, who is crying for her child, to go. The male springbok scolds his wife for having lost their child. ... On account of her husband's anger, the springbok mother sends the lynx to recover her child for her. The lynx slips into the anteater's hole underneath the young springbok, and, pushing her out, runs off with her. The anteater, trying to follow, is caught in the bowstring of the lynx, as in a sling. Disengaging herself, she again proceeds to deliver to the lynx her important messages concerning the nature and habits of the different animals.

❑

|kukəntĕ ̠||kwáŋ ho óä ¯!kauŋ ssˀo |huru. Haŋ e !kwi, !xwe-||na-ssˀo
The Anteater sat in the mouth of her hole. She was a person, one of
!kwi. Haŋ ||na ||neiŋ, au haŋ ka ||xe: se ¯||ko.
the Early Race. She stayed at home, as she wanted the ants' eggs to dry.
Waïtən |kɯ-g |ne !koã ¯||xĩ ||a: wai ã:, au haŋ ssˀo: ||k''oen. Wai

The Springbok travelled passing by her, as she sat looking. The Springbok

//ua//uarrakən há ka,
mothers sang,

‘ ˍã ˍã ˉhŋ, ‘ ˍã ˍã ˉhŋ,
wai-⊙pua we, O Springbok child,
ˉ⊙puoinja ki. Sleep for me.
ã ã ˉhŋ, ˍã ˍã ˉhŋ,
wai-⊙pua we, O Springbok child,
ˉ⊙puoinja ki.’ Sleep for me.’

Wai //uara a: /ki !khwã, haŋ ˍhá /ne kúï, ‘??khwã ka ˉtsara ka ??he a?’
(To) a Springbok mother who had a child she said, ‘What kind of child is it?’

Wai //uarakən ˍhá /ne kúï, ‘!khwã !aháin !kwa ˍ!kwanraŋ ˍ//kwaŋ /ku e: ha
The Springbok mother said, ‘The child’s navel’s (?) * * * is that which he

/k’’wa: ĩ:, !khwã gwaiïtən é.’ He /kukəntẽ ˍhá /ne kúï ‘??k?ũ ??a:, ??k?ũ ??a:
cries about, it is a male child.’ And the Anteater said, ‘Begone, begone,

au a k’’auki ??kẽja ??khe. A kaŋ ??k?ũ ??khe.’ Wai e: xau /ki
au a k’’auki !kẽja !khe. A kaŋ !k?ũ !khe.’
do not stand talking. Go away.’ Springbok which had not

!kaukən, hiŋ ˍhá !khe kau ˉ!koã, au ha /ni: wai //uara a /ki
children travelled along, then she saw a Springbok mother which had

!khwã, wai-⊙pua a ˉ≠enni. Haŋ ˍha /ne ˉ//xã, haŋ kúï ‘??khwã ka tsara
a child, a very little Springbok. She again exclaimed, ‘What kind of child

ka ??khe?’ Wai //uarakən ˍhá /ne kúï,’ !khwã gwai ⊙pua ke:.’
is here?’ The Springbok mother said, ‘It is a little male child.’

/kukəntẽŋ ˍhá /ne kúï, ‘??k?ũ ??e, ??ku ??k?ũ ??e.’ Wai //uarakən ˍhá
The Anteater exclaimed, ‘Go away, do go away.’ The Springbok mother

/ne !k?ũ //a:. Wai //ua//uarrakən ˍha ˉ//xĩ //e toukən hã, au haŋ ˍhá ˉ//k?oen ss?o.
went away. Springbok mothers passed along, while she sat watching,

au haŋ //k’oen ˍ//gauë ss?o au wai //uara a: ka /ki !khwã. Ha /ni:
while she sat looking for a Springbok mother who had a child. She saw

//uara a: /ki !khwã. Haŋ ˍhá /ne kúï, ‘??khwã ka tsara ka ??he a?’
a Springbok mother who had a child. She exclaimed, ‘What kind of child is it?’

Wai //uarakən ˍhá /ne kúï, '!khwã gwai ⊙pua kaŋ e,' au wai
The Springbok mother said, 'A little male child it is,' while a Springbok
//uara a: /gebbi, haŋ ˍhá kaŋ ˍ/ká:gən ssa:. Haŋ
mother who was foolish was following in the distance. She (the Anteater)
ˍhá ka, '??khwã ka tsara ka ??ke a?' Wai //uarakən ˍha /ne kúï, '!khwã
said, 'What kind of child is that?' The Springbok mother said, 'A little
gwai ⊙pua ke:.' Haŋ ˍhá ka, '??k?ũ ??e, ??ku ??k?ũ ??e.' Haŋ ˍhá //k'oen ss?o.
male child it is.' She said, 'Go forward, do go forward.' She sat looking.
He wai //uara a: /gebbi haŋ /ne /kwẽï /kĩ, haŋ //a:, !gwe ho //a: ha.
And the foolish Springbok mother thus went along, went along in front of her.
Haŋ ˍhá /ne kúï, '??khwã ka tsara ka ??ke?' Wai //uarakən ˍhá /ne kúï,
She said, 'What kind of child is that?' The Springbok mother said,
'!khwã /atti ⊙pua kaŋ e.' Han ˍhá /ne kúï, '??ki sse ha, ??ki ssa ké ha,
'A little female child it is,' She said, 'Bring her, bring her to me,
ŋ ??k'oen ha.'
that I may look at her.'

He wai //uarra haŋ /kwẽï /kĩ, haŋ ssa:; wai //uarakən
And the Springbok mother in this manner came; the Springbok mother
/ne !khe ssa ha: wai //uarakən /ne /kwẽï /kĩ, haŋ !haŋ !khe: ssa. He ha ˍhá /ne kúï,
came up to her; the Springbok mother in this manner came up. And she said,
'??ki ??há ha, ??ki ??há ke ha, ŋ //k'oen ha.' He wai
'Take her out, take her out for me, that I may see her.' And the Springbok
//uara ˍha /ne /ki /hiŋ wai ⊙pua; wai //uarakən /ne á ha ã
mother took out the little Springbok; the Springbok mother gave her the
wai ⊙pua. Haŋ há /ne kúï, 'A sse ??khe ??e ¯??xe ??ke ta:,
little Springbok. She said, 'Thou shalt go to the ants' eggs lying there,
a sse ho hĩ, a sse hã hĩ, ta:, a e //uara.' He
thou shalt pick it up, thou shalt eat it, for thou art a mother.' And
wai //uara ˍhá /ne !khe //a: //xe:, haŋ ˍhá /ne ˍ/gomm ¯!k?auŋ ¯//ho,
the Springbok mother went to the ants' eggs, she scooped it into the bag,
au !kukəntẽ ˍhá /ne u ¯/e /huru, /ki /e: wai ⊙pua. Haŋ
while Anteater went into her hole, taking the little Springbok. She
/ne /ku !k?auŋ ss?o:. Haŋ /ku ¯!kauŋ ss?o /huru //xã:xu,
sat near the mouth (of the hole). She sat by the side of the hole's mouth,

haŋ k''auki /e: ta:.
she was not in it.

He wai //uara ˍhá /ne ssa:, haŋ ˍhá /ne kúï, ' A xa de? a xa de?
And the Springbok mother came, she said, 'Where art thou? where art thou?

A-g /ne /auwa ke !khwã. A-g /ne akke !khwã, ŋ /ne sse ˍtä̃ï. He
Let me see my child. Give me my child, that I may go.' And

/kukəntẽ ˍhá /ne kúï, '¯??ki: ta ??huru ˍ??nomm dʒwaïïtən-tu.' Haŋ /ki
'ˍ/e: ta /huru ˍ!nomm dʒwaïïtən-tu.'
the Anteater said, 'in the inside of the hole.' She made

≠enniŋja ha ˍdomm, au haŋ ka, wai //uarra siŋ ka, he kaŋ
her throat small, because she wanted the Springbok mother to think she was

¯/e ta. Wai //uarakən ˍhá ka, 'Óẽja, /hiŋ ssa:, a akke ã !khwã.
far inside. The Springbok mother said, 'Hallo there, come out, give me my child

¯/nu !kwi we, /hiŋ ssa:, a akke ã !khwã. A kaŋ kwoŋ /ku /ki /eja ke !khwã?'
O accursed one, come out, give me my child. Why hast thou taken in the child?'

'¯??ki ta ??huru ??nomm dʒwaïïtən-tu.'
'In the inside of the hole.' (said in a very tiny voice).

He wai //uara ˍhá /ne /kwẽï /kĩ, haŋ k''wá:ä //a:, au haŋ ˍhá /ne /hiŋ ssa
And the Springbok mother thus went crying away, while she came out

/huru, haŋ /ne ¯!kauŋ siŋ ¯ssa:, haŋ /ne //k'oen ssʔo, au wai
of the hole, she came to sit in front of it, she sat looking at the Springbok

//uara. Haŋ ˍhá /ne ta, 'N ˍ??kwaŋ ??ke:ja ¯ha, ti e:, a ˍk''óã ssʔo ka,
mother. She said, 'I told thee, that thou didst seem to think,

a ??ha: ka ŋ,' au wai //uarakən ˍhá /ne !khe //a: !kʔe kuitər.
thou wert as clever as I,' while the Springbok mother went to the others.

He wai gwai ˍhá /ne //aŋ kúï, '/auwa ke !khwã, !khwã xa de?'
And the Springbok husband said, 'Show me the child, where is the child?'

He wai //uara ˍhá /ne kúï, '/kukəntẽ ˍ//kwaŋ a: /ki /e:ja ¯ke
And the Springbok mother said, 'The Anteater is the one who took from me

!khwã au /huru.' He gwai /ne //ken ¯/ki ha /noá //kha-tu,
the child into the hole.' And the husband piercing clove her feet (between

au /kukəntẽ /ne //kaiŋ /ki wai ⊙pua.
the first and second toes), while the Anteater was fondling the little Springbok.

/kukəntẽ ˍhá /né ta,
The Anteater sang,

'ŋ ka ??na,	*'ŋ kaŋ /ne,*	'I am,
ŋ ka ??na,	*ŋ kaŋ /ne,*	I am,
taŋ kaŋ ??e:.	*taŋ kaŋ ˉ/e:.*	going in.
ŋ ka ??na,	*ŋ kaŋ /ne,*	I am,
ŋ ka ??na,	*ŋ kaŋ /ne,*	I am,
taŋ kaŋ ??e:.'	*taŋ kaŋ ˉ/e.'*	going in.'

Haŋ ˍhá /ne k''aise wai ⊙pua; wai ⊙puakən /ne ˉki
She brought the little Springbok up; the little Springbok grew up,

au haŋ k''aise /ki wai ⊙pua. Han /ne kúï '!khoukau' au wai ⊙pua
while she let her grow up. She said, '*!khoukau*' for the little Springbok's

/kẽ. Wai ⊙puakən /ne dí ˉ!kwi-/a, au haŋ k''aise /ki wai ⊙pua.
name. The little Springbok became a maiden, while she brought her up.

He tikən e:, /ku-g-!nuiŋ-gu /ne /k'abbe ha, ĩ. /ku-g-!uiŋjaŋ ˍhá /ne kúï,
Then the Lynx and his people plotted against her. The Lynx said,'

'ˍ//guattən a: se /haŋ !khoukau, há se k''auki ˉa /kukəntẽ se /nĩ ha.'
'The Cat shall marry *!khoukau*, he shall not let the Anteater see him.

//kauëtən ˍhá /ne kúï, '/ku-g-!nuiŋ á se /haŋ !khoukau, ha
The Leopard said, 'The Lynx shall be the one to marry *!khoukau*, he

ˉtt?ainja, há a /kukəntẽ k''auki se /nĩ ha, ta: /kukəntẽ ˍsaŋ /ku /nĩ
walks softly, him the Anteater will not see, but the Anteater might see

ˍ//guattən, ta: ˍ//guattən k''auki ˉtt?ain kwɔˉkwaŋ-a, ta: /ku-g-!nuiŋ a:
the Cat, for the Cat does not walk really softly, but the Lynx is one who

ˉtt?ainja.'
walks softly.'

He tikən e:, /ku-g-!nuiŋ ˍhá /ku-g /ne ssa, ssa, ssa, haŋ /ku-g /ne /kwẽï
Then the Lynx came, came, came, he acted in this manner,

/ki, haŋ !gwe tiŋ //neiŋ. He ha ˍhá /ku-g /ne //nau, /kukəntẽŋ /ne /k'wã,
he lay opposite the home. And he watied till the Anteater was fetching water,

haŋ /ku-g /ne ˉu, !kou tiŋ ssa /kukəntẽ. Haŋ /ku-g/ne ≠kakən //na ha /aiti
he got up and slipped past the Anteater. He talked with his wife

ã:, haŋ ˍhá /ku /nė ta, '/kukəntẽ kaŋ ˍdóä ku á, a xóäken k''auki ˍdóä é,
about it, he said, 'This is really an Anteater, it is not really thy mother,

ta: /kukəntẽ ˍdóä /kш á, a xóäkən ˍdóä /kш e wai, ˍkwi a: /tara haŋ
for it is an Anteater, thy mother is a Springbok, a different person she
ˍdóä /kш á, a xóäkən k''auki /kwẽ.' Haŋ /ne /kш ˍttonnu /hiŋ ˍ/a: au //neiŋ,
is, thy mother is not like this.' He crept out of the home,
haŋ /ne /kш /kwẽï /kĩ, haŋ te:ŋ //a:.
he went to lie down.

/kukəntẽŋ ha /ne /kш ssa: //neiŋ, haŋ /ne /kш ˍssaŋ //ka /ki ¯//xe:.
The Anteater came home, she came to put the ants' eggs to dry.

//kõïŋ /ne ¯/e:, hiŋ /ne ¯⊙puoin. /ku-g-nuiŋjaŋ /ne /kш ˍtonnu /e ssa:.
The sun set, they slept. The Lynx came creeping in.

/kukəntẽŋ ˍhá ka, '??koukau we, ??ne teŋ ??ko: ??a: ki, ˍtsara a ¯??kou tiŋ
The Anteater said, 'O *! khoukau*, lie close to me, what has brushed past
ŋ ã?' Ha ⊙puaxaitən ˍhá ka, 'Tsara itau //nau //neiŋjaŋ k''auki kuerrija
me?' Her daughter said, 'Why does mother forget, the home is not rounded
ã:, au ti e: ha ˍ!ham a: k''auki /xerri kuerrija //neiŋ.'
off at the place where she lately did not scratch rounding off the home.'

'Xau ŋ ??kwaŋ ??khõã tsa a ¯??kou tiŋ ŋ ã.' Ha ⊙puaxaitən ˍhá ka, 'Tsara
'Xau ŋ ˍ//kwaŋ ≠xõã ts?a a ¯//kou tiŋ ŋ ã.'
'But I felt something brush past me.' Her daughter said, 'Why art
a //ka, a k''au ˍ//kwan a: k''auki /xerri kuerrija //neiŋ?'
thou obstinate, art thou not the one who did not scratch rounding the home?'

He !gauë ˍhá /ne !khwai: he !ku-g-!nuiŋ ˍhá /ne /kш ˍre¯u /hiŋ ˍ/a:, haŋ
And day broke, the Lynx crawled out, he
/ne /kш /kwẽï /kĩ, haŋ kúï tt?abbu tiŋ //a:.
acted in this manner, he stole aside.

/kukəntẽŋ ˍhá /kш-g /ne kúï, 'M ⊙puaxai ??khoukau, akən tsko se ??ne hi
The Anteater said, 'My daughter *! khoukau*, thou shalt now be with
ŋ, i se ??kwã. Ha ⊙puaxaitən ˍhá /ne kúï, 'ŋ kaŋ ˍdóä /kш //na //neiŋ; ta:
me, we will fetch water.' 'Her daughter said, 'I want to stay at home; for
ŋ k''auki taŋ ŋ ka: ˍtáï.' 'A ??ke ˍdóä á ¯hi, ta: a siŋ ??na
I do not feel like going.' 'Thou shouldst give to us, for thou didst stay

??neiŋ au ??kú:ï, akən ˍdóä á ˉhi:.' Ha ⊙puaxaitən ˍhá /ne kúï, 'ŋ kaŋ
at home yesterday, thou shouldst give to us.' Her daughter said, 'I ought

ˍdóä /ku //na //neiŋ, ta: ŋ k''auki taŋ ŋ ka: ˍtáï, ta: ŋ ˍsaŋ /ku //na hĩ
really to stay at home, for I do not feel like going, but I will be with

á au !gauë.' He ha ˍhá /ne kúï, 'A ˍ??kwaŋ se ĩ:, a se ??kwe:nja
thee tomorrow.' She said, 'Thou shouldst do this, thou shouldst fetch water

ˉhi, a ˍsaŋ ??k?o:kən ˉhi, ta: ŋ ??ku ??khouwa tiŋ, hŋ ti é ;
for us, thou shouldst gather wood for us, for I must seek about at this place ;

ŋ siŋ ??ku ˉ??kuïtən.' He ha ˍhá /k'wa //a:, ĩ:.
I will then return home.' And she went to fetch water.

/ku-g-!nuiŋjaŋ /ne /ku ˉu, !kou tiŋ ssa: ha:. /ku-g-!nuiŋjaŋ ˍhá /ne kúï,
The Lynx arose, slipped past her. The Lynx said,

'A ˍkoá: se /ku doˍddottən.' Haŋ a ts?erre /kukəntẽ, /kukəntẽ ˍkoá:
'Thou shalt be blinded,' He bewitched the Anteater, the Anteater should

k''auki se antau /hĩ //xe:. Hiŋ /ku ˉ/ku //xe:.
not quickly see the ants' eggs. They (Lynx and Springbok) packed up ants' eggs.

Hiŋ ˍhá /ku //nau, /kukəntẽŋ /ne ˉ!kai //a /k'a, hiŋ /ku-g /ne ˍtáï.
They did this, when the Anteater was going along the river-bed, they went away.

/kukənteŋ ˍhá /ku-g /ne //khuetən //na. He ˍkɔttən ˍhá /ku-g /ne
The Anteater was making a hole there. Then the Patridge did

/kwẽï /kĩ, ˍkottakən //khou ssa:. ˍKɔttakən ˍhá /ku-g /ne kúï, 'Kɔttau-we:,
this, the Patridge came flying. The Patridge said, 'O mate,

!khoukau ˉsiŋ kau ˍ!k?onn //a:.' /kukəntẽŋ ˍhá /ne kúï, 'ˉ??nwe:' He
!khoukau has run away.' (?) The Anteater said, 'Coming.' And

ˍkottən ˍhá /ne kúï, 'ˍKɔttau ˉwe:, !khoukau ˉsiŋ kau ˍ!k?onn //a.' /kukən-
the Partridge said, 'O Mate, *! khoukau* has run away.' The Ant-

-tẽŋ ˍhá !ne /ku ˉ!hu: /hiŋ au !k?o, haŋ /ku-g /ne /kwẽï /kĩ, haŋ ˉ!kuxeja
eater got angrily out of the hole, she did this, she ran

//neiŋ. Haŋ ˍhá /ne /ku !khe //a //neiŋ, haŋ /ne /ku ˉ!ko: //neiŋ. Haŋ ˍhá
home. She arrived at home, she found the home empty. She

/ne /ku kúï, 'M ⊙puaxai, m ⊙puaxai, m ⊙puaxai, ˉ??nu ??kwi di ˍkoá a:
said, 'My daughter, my daughter, my daughter, what bad man can have

??ki ˍtáïja ke ??khwã?' He ha ˍhá /ku kúï, //gubugu, //gubugu, //gubugu,
carried off the child from me ?' And she went bumpety, bumpety, bumpety,

⊙phãĩ, //gubugu, //gubugu, ⊙phãĩ. Ha-ka ⁻!kuxe /kɯ e: ka,
bump, bumpety, bumpety, bumpety, bump. Her running it was which went

//gubugu, //gubugu, //gubugu, ⊙phãĩ, //gubugu, //gubugu, //gubugu ⊙phãĩ.
bumpety, bumpety, bumpety, bump, bumpety, bumpety, bumpety, bump.

Haŋ k''auki ⁻//kou hóä !kˀãũ, ta: ha /kɯ //khó:ë hóä !kˀãũ. Haŋ /ne ka
She was not above the ground, for she was underground. She went

//gubugu, //gubugu, //gubugu, ⊙phãĩ, //gubugu, //gubugu, //gubugu, ⊙phãĩ.
bumpety, bumpety, bumpety, bump, bumpety, bumpety bumpety, bump.

He !khoukau ˍhá /ne //aŋ kú:ï, ' K''au-dəro we, akən ssˀo ka, ŋ k''au /kɯ
And !khoukau, said, 'O young man, thou dost seem to think, I shall not

se !kənn tau !kˀũ; a koá siŋ tã-ĩ !kˀãũ, e: i ˍtáï ⁻//khou !khe hĩ.
be pulled down; thou shouldst feel the ground on which we are walking.'

He /ku-g-!nuiŋ ˍhá /ne kúï, 'A ˍ//kwan siŋ tã-ĩ, he e:, a ˍsan /ne /k'eja
And the Lynx said, 'Thou must feel it, then thou canst tell

ke, au a ⁻tã, ti e:, !kˀãũ e:, a ˍtáï ⁻//khou !khe hi, hĩ de kúï tã
me, if thou dost feel that the ground on which thou art walking is

ˍhõˍhõä.' Hiŋ ˍhá //a:.
trembling.' They went on.

/kukəntẽ /ne //nau, /kukəntẽŋ hiŋ ssa:, /kukəntẽŋ /ne /uwi hĩ,
The Anteater did this, when she came out, she caught sight of them,

au hiŋ //khóë ⁻//a. He ha ˍhá /kɯ-g /ne !xaiti //a hĩ. Haŋ /kɯ-g /ne kúï ⊙puãĩ,
as they went by. And she followed after them. She popped up to look,

haŋ /kɯ-g /ne kúï ⁻!kˀũ ĩ:, haŋ /kɯ-g /ne ⁻/e. He tikən e: !khoukau
she dropped back, she went underground. Then !khoukau

ˍhá /kɯ-g /ne kúï, 'K''ao-dəro we, !kˀãũ e:, ŋ ˍtáï ⁻//khou !khe hĩ,
said, 'O young man, this ground on which I am walking

hiŋ tuko di kúï tã ˍhõˍhõä.'
really feels to be trembling.'

He tikən e:, /ku-g-!nuiŋ ˍhá /kɯ-g /ne ˍtáïˍáija ti ha !kənn
Then the Lynx walked along while he held

kúï ˍtxuomm au !nũï. Haŋ /kɯ-g /ne hauru !kuŋ //kho //a: !nũï au /aiti,
the bowstring in a loop. He cast the bowstring round the woman,

he ha /kɯ-g /ne !kənn /hiŋ ssa: /kukəntẽ, au !nuiŋ koä ⁻sebəu siŋ ha
and he pulled out the Anteater, while the bowstring was round her

ˍdom. /kukənteŋ ˍhá /kɯ-g /ne kúï, '⁻ʔʔa, a ʔʔnaʔʔna, a di ʔʔkʔʔruiŋ,
throat. The Anteater said, 'Destruction, thou there, do thou become a Lynx,

a _táï_táïja ??khóë tiŋ ¯??ga:.' *|ku-g-!nuiŋjaŋ _há |ne ||xamki kúï, '¯|a,*
which walks about at night.' The Lynx also said. 'Destruction,

a ||na||na, a dí |kukəntẽ, a _táï_táïjà ||khóë tiŋ ¯||ga:.' *Haŋ _há ka,*
thou there, do thou become an Anteater, which goes about at night.' She said,

'¯??a, a ??na??na, a dí ??ku-g-??nuiŋ, a _táï_táïja ??khóë tiŋ ¯||ga:.'
'Destruction, thou there, do thou become a Lynx, which walks about at night.'

|ku-g-!nuiŋjaŋ _há ka, ' ¯|a, a ||na||na, a dí |kukəntẽ, a
The Lynx said, 'Destruction, thou there, do thou become an Anteater, which

_táï_táïja ||khóë tiŋ ||ga:.'
walks about at night.'

He ha _há |kɯ-g |ne ¯!küïtən, au !ku-g-!nuiŋjaŋ |kɯ_g |ne ||a:
Then she went home, while the Lynx went on

hi kau wai ⊙pua, au wai ⊙puakən tatti, ha |kɯ-g |ne ¯!küïta:
with the little Springbok, for the little Springbok felt, she was returning

ha-ka !kˀe.
to her people.

Notes

Title *The Anteater, the young Springbok and the Lynx*: Although Bleek and Lloyd always referred to the 'Anteater', it is not clear whether they mean the Scaly Anteater (the pangolin, *Manis temminckii*) or the Antbear (the Aardvark, *Orycteropus afer*). Both eat ants, both have underground burrows and both are nocturnal. On the basis of their distribution, it is more likely to be the Aardvark. The springbok (*Antidorcas marsupialis*) is a gazelle-like antelope found in arid parts of southern Africa, like those parts of the Northern Cape Province where the |Xam lived. The Lynx or, more properly, the Caracal (*Caracal caracal*), is a small carnivore with a preference for drier parts of the country.

4 *…she wanted the ant's eggs to dry*: *||xe:* are ant chrysalides or Bushman rice, an important and nutritious *veldkos* in |Xam-ka !aũ.

20 *The Springbok mother said …*: 'They [the springbok] were formerly people' (8560 rev., note omitted).

20 *The child's navel's [?] …*: The missing phrase is *!khwa !uhain !kwa!kwannaŋ*. The word *!kwa!kwannaŋ* is not in the *Dictionary*.

73 *Take her out* ...: 'From the kaross, the kaross in which she carried the little Springbok. [It] was a *!k'issi*; she [the mother springbok] had made a kaross [*//henni*, "a little *!k'aussi* in which they carry a little child that is the one which they call *//henni*"] of it' (8568 rev., note omitted). Neither *!k'issi* nor *!k'aussi* are in the *Bushman Dictionary*.

78-80 *Thou shalt go to the ants' eggs lying there, thou shalt pick it up, thou shalt eat it* ...: 'She was deceiving the Springbok mother, in order that she might take the little Springbok inside.' (8569 rev., note omitted)

96 ... *in the inside of the hole* ...: 'This is said in the smallest and most squeaking of voices' (8571 rev., note omitted).

110-112 ... *while she came out of the hole, she came to sit in front of it*...: The 'she' here is the Anteater.

124 *And the husband piercing clove her feet*: 'She was a Springbok, she was a person' (8574 rev., note omitted).

144 *Then the Lynx and his people plotted against her*: 'They were talking, the Bushmen call it */'kabbe*; the Boers call it '*konkelen*' 'to plot' 'to intrigue'. (8576 rev., note omitted)

169 ... *thy mother is not like this*: 'He taught the girl' (8581 rev., note)

'And the Anteater returned' (8582, sentence omitted).

180-183 ... *the home is not rounded off* ...: The Anteater's 'daughter' – the kidnapped Springbok child – tells her that she brushed against a bulge in the wall of the tunnel and has imagined that it was an intruder.

238 ... *she found the home empty*: 'She missed the child at the house' (8592 rev., note omitted).

How Bushman women show admiration for the Horse

Narrator: |Haŋ‡kass'o
Dictation dates: 14 August 1879
Notebook reference: L.VIII.31: 8737-8740
***Bantu Studies* reference:** Vol. 10 (1936), Special speech: 197-198

This extract does not include the special speech of any animal; Dorothea Bleek included it for reasons she mentions in the original introduction to this narrative:

Here may also be added a piece showing the reaction of the |xam Bushmen to the horse, a new animal introduced by the White man.

❑

Hĩ ˍ//kwaŋ ka ˍ//naiŋja bara, he bara /ne k''ɛnn. Au bara tatti,
They (the women) click at a horse, and the horse feels proud. When the horse feels
hĩ //naiŋ, bara /ne k''ɛnn, au bara tatti, ha ˉtumm-ĩ hĩ, au hĩ !kuttən
that they click, the horse feels that he listens to them, while they sing
//na bara tsˀĩ:. He tikən e:, !kˀe tá ka, bara ˍ≠ná:ˉä,
there behind the horse's back. Then people say, the horse dances,
au ha ˉ//kuara //a:.
as he canters along.

(*/han≠kassˀo* tells me that he does not know the song which the women sing on these occasions, as it is a woman's song. Note by L.)

Hiŋ //xamki !kuppəm, hiŋ k''auki !kuppəm twaitən ˉ//ka: hĩ.
They (the women) also play at *! kuppəm*, they play it beautifully.
//gwitən ˍ//kwaŋ é, !kˀe-ta /ka:gen-ka //gwitən. Hiŋ ˍ!guá:ï ˉ!nuiŋ au
A play it is, a women's play. They strike (slap) the kaross with
hĩ /k'a/k'a. Hiŋ ˉ//kau ssˀo ˉ!nuiŋ; ˉ!nuiŋjaŋ /ne ˉ!khou ssˀo hĩ
their hands. They sit upon the kaross; the kaross is between their
tẽtẽ-ta kammaŋ. Hiŋ /ne ˍ!guá:ˉï ˉ!nuiŋ, an hĩ ˉ//kau ssˀo ˉ!nuiŋ.
thighs. They strike the kaross, as they sit upon the kaross.
Hiŋ /ku tuɔrreja !nuiŋ, hiŋ /ne ˉ//kau ssˀo ˉ!nuiŋ, au ˉhĩ tuɔrreja
They roll up the kaross, they sit upon the kaross, when they have rolled

!nuiŋ; ⁻hĩ |ne ⁻||kau ssˀo ⁻!nuiŋ, ⁻hĩ |ne !kuppəm. ⁻!nuiŋ
the kaross; they sit upon the kaross, they play *!kuppəm*. The kaross's

||ˀuóbbe ₋||kwaŋ ⁻!xwaŋ bara e: hĩ |k'waija, au hĩ ⁻||kuara ||a:, ti e:
noise sounds like many horses when they canter along, when

⁻!nuiŋ ka, 'bbúbbu(p), bbúbbu(p), bubbu(p), búbbu(p).'
the kaross says, 'bubbu (p), bubbu (p), bubbu (p), bubbu (p).'

Special Speech of animals and Moon used by the the /Xam Bushmen

---

Notes

(Notes. They sit upon the lower part of their legs, holding the upper part of their legs somewhat apart, and the rolled (or folded) up kaross tightly between the knees.

⁻||naiŋ is to make a sharp lateral click, used as an admiratory ejaculation by Bushman women. L.)

How Bushman women show admiration for the Horse

In another place the verbs used to distinguish four of the clicks are given. (p. 8727r.)

⁻||naiŋ to make a lateral click,
! kwara to make a cerebral click,
⁻!khwaitəŋ to make a palatal click,
|i|iŋ to make a dental click.

Remark about a parrot

Narrator: |Haŋ‡kass'o
Dictation date: Sometime in July 1879
Notebook reference: L.VIII.29: 8556 rev.
***Bantu Studies* reference:** Vol. 10 (1936), Special speech: 199

Dorothea Bleek's introduction is as follows:

The following remark on a parrot seen at Mobray is given.

❑

ˉKwarritən a !xwaŋ !kui, ta: haŋ |kui '||' u !kwi.
A bird which sounds like man, for it says '||' like a man.

The difference between the Bushman and European way of using the tongue

Narrator: |Haŋ‡kass'o
Notebook reference: L.VIII.29: 8528 rev.
***Bantu Studies* reference:** Vol. 10 (1936), Special speech: 199

Dorothea Bleek introduced this short but perceptive comment as follows:

A Bushman defines the difference between Bushman and European methods of articulation.

❑

|xam-ka !kˀetən |kui ≠kakən au hi |enni !kauükən, au |hũˉ|hũŋaŋ
Bushmen talk with the body of their tongue, while Europeans
|ne é: ≠kakən au hĩ |enni |ɛmm.
are those who talk with the tip of their tongue.

BUSHMAN GRAMMAR

Introduction

Dorothea F. Bleek's *Bushman Grammar*

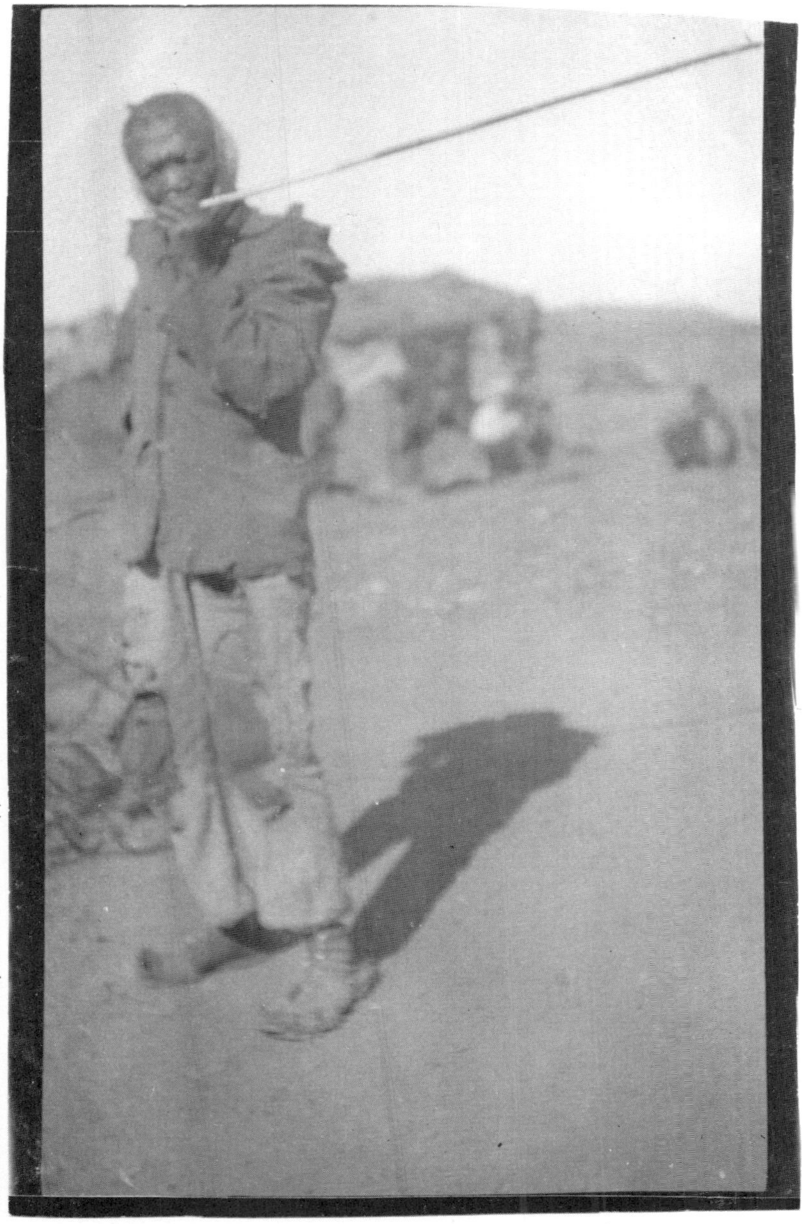

Photo: Dorothea Bleek, courtesy of UCT, BZE 97/20 (4)

'|Kãũnũ used to strike the bowstring, and then clouds came up while we were asleep'. |Xam Bushman playing bow, Prieska.

Introduction

The academic and general fascination for the material on the |Xam language, anthropology, and literature recorded in the late nineteenth century by Wilhelm H.I. Bleek and Lucy C. Lloyd is still extensive today. Surprisingly, the language itself received relatively little attention after the death of the Bleek family members involved in this research. It is all the more fortunate, therefore, that Dorothea F. Bleek's grammar sketch (1928-30), one of the few linguistic documents on the |Xam language, is republished here.

The classification of |Xam

Contrary to the popular assumption that the San (alias Bushman) peoples of southern Africa are a homogeneous population, they comprise many different groups that are distinguished, among other things, by their language. Three language families and one isolated language can be identified, which have not been shown to be related genealogically to each other. The establishment of the three major families namely Khoe (Central Khoisan), Ju (Northern Khoisan), and Tuu (Southern Khoisan) – derives from Dorothea Bleek's pioneering research.

|Xam belongs to the Tuu family, more specifically to a major branch – the !Ui, which was distributed over most of South Africa and adjacent parts of southern Namibia. The other major Tuu branch is Taa, found in central-eastern Namibia and south-western Botswana. Only one !Ui language, which Dorothea Bleek called 'N||ng', has survived to this day. 'N||ng' is spoken by a few old people living in the Northern Cape, north of the Orange River.

The |Xam language was spoken by people who lived in the Cape interior, west and south of the Orange River. It remains unclear how far |Xam extended into the areas closer to the coastline where Khoekhoe languages were also spoken. (It cannot even be stated with any confidence that the San languages of these areas belonged to the Tuu family.)

Given such a vast geographical distribution, it is not surprising that |Xam – like other San languages – was not a homogeneous language. In fact, it is more appropriate to speak of a dialect cluster or 'language complex' in which there exists a close dialectal proximity between neighbouring speech varieties, but a far greater linguistic divergence – even mutual unintelligibility – between varieties that are remote from each other.

The main informants for the research carried out by Wilhelm Bleek and Lucy Lloyd in the 1870s spoke Flat and Grass |Xam, two neighbouring varieties found in the Northern Cape along the Hartbees and Sak Rivers, between Kenhardt in the north and the Kareeberg in the south.

Other sources on the |Xam language

The extensive documentation by Bleek and Lloyd of Flat and Grass |Xam is not the only source on the |Xam language. Apart from the short word lists that Bleek and Lloyd collected from other |Xam language varieties, there are four more substantial bodies of data that were assembled in other research contexts.

The first and earliest relevant data goes back to Hinrich Lichtenstein, who published material on several indigenous languages encountered by him on his travels through the wider Cape region in the early 1800s (Lichtenstein, 1808:1811-12). Although his data on the San language (simply referred to as 'Buschmannisch') is difficult to evaluate in terms of the San's exact origin and linguistic structure, it is reasonably clear that it represents various forms of |Xam.

The second body of data was Wilhelm Bleek's recording of the |Xam dialect spoken in the Achterveld, east of Calvinia, in 1866. While this data was the basis of the material published by Bleek (1869) and Müller (1877), it awaits a more extensive linguistic treatment. The original field notes are part of the Bleek and Lloyd Collection held in the Manuscripts and Archives Department of the University of Cape Town Libraries.

Theophilus Hahn, responsible for the third body of data, carried out a study of the |Xam language shortly after the research done by Bleek and Lloyd. There are several indications that his informant was also a speaker of the Flat |Xam variety. Unfortunately, he did not publish his material in any complete form, and only parts of it are accessible through its presentation by Müller (1888).

The fourth and final body of data stems from Dorothea Bleek herself, who besides being extensively involved in the analysis and editing of the material collected by her father and aunt, carried out a short field trip in 1910-11 to the Kenhardt and Prieska districts. The locations of her study and the origins of her informants also indicate a Flat |Xam dialect background. The data she recorded is incorporated in the Bleek and Lloyd Collection at the University of Cape Town.

From her trip, Dorothea Bleek reported that the |Xam language was no longer spoken by all members of the group, suggesting that it was in the final stage of language death (see Traill 1996). Thus, her work marks the endpoint of a then one hundred-year-old tradition of firsthand research on |Xam.

Linguistic analyses of |Xam and Dorothea Bleek's grammar sketch

Owing to various circumstances, including the untimely death of Wilhelm Bleek in 1875, the two main researchers were unfortunately not able to subject |Xam to a thorough linguistic analysis. In published form, they left only a few – but important – commentary notes in Bleek & Lloyd (1911).

To date, only two published linguistic descriptions of |Xam exist. One is in English, namely that by Dorothea Bleek contained originally in two subsequent issues (1928/29 and 1929/30) of the *Zeitschrift für Eingeborenen-Sprachen* and republished here, and one is in German by Meriggi (1928/29), which appeared simultaneously in the same journal. A modern linguistic analysis of Flat |Xam can be found in Güldemann (Güldemann, T. Forthcoming a, b, c), to which the reader is referred for a more current approach to the language in the context of the enormous increase in knowledge on these languages and the more advanced methods of the general discipline.

Dorothea Bleek's |Xam sketch is of particular importance for the linguistic research on the language because she and Lucy Lloyd worked together for a long time on the material collected in the 1870s. Therefore, it is likely that her study reflects to a large extent the deep insights that her aunt, as one of the two firsthand researchers, had reached in the course of many years of intensive work with the language and its speakers.

At the same time, Dorothea Bleek noted in her Introduction that parts of her analysis 'are based as much on my own experience [from her field trip in 1910-11] as on their notes [her father and aunt]'. The integration of Dorothea Bleek's own knowledge on |Xam and other San languages is the reason why her presentation of the data may deviate considerably from that of Wilhelm Bleek and Lucy Lloyd, in particular her simplified transliteration. The reader should be aware of this fact and is advised to revisit the notebooks for the purpose of studying the sound structure of the language since a modern analysis could make use of the fine-grained and thus variable transcriptions in the original field notes.

A comparison between the two sketches by Dorothea Bleek and Meriggi also reveals several differences in presentation and analysis. Although Meriggi had received comments by Dorothea Bleek on parts of his study, he contributed his own perspectives on the language, apparently based on a different linguistic background.

|Xam has been an extinct language for almost a century now. However, the extensive number of sources on |Xam and their diverse range, together with a more sophisticated approach to this highly complex language group in general, justify the belief that further research will allow scholars to reach a good understanding of its linguistic structure. The academic dedication of the early scholars, among them Dorothea Bleek, is a legacy that will enable future researchers to bring this still little known language to the attention of the linguistic public.

Tom Güldemann
Max Planck Institute for Evolutionary Anthropology/Linguistics, Leipzig, Germany
gueldema@rz.uni-leipzig.de

BUSHMAN GRAMMAR.

A grammatical sketch of the language of the */xam-ka-!k'e*

by Dorothea F. Bleek.

Introduction.

A number of different Bushman languages are still spoken in parts of South Africa, und we have records of others that have died out. This sketch deals only with the speech of the Bushmen who lived south of the Orange River, who all from east to west spoke one language with slight dialectical variations. They called themselves */xam-ka-!k'e* or */xam* people, the word having no other meaning than nationality. It is spelt */kham* by some writers. The tribe is almost extinct, but the language was fully written down fifty to sixty years ago by my father, Dr. W. H. I. Bleek, and my aunt, Miss Lucy Lloyd. This grammar is based on the folklore collected by them.[1] I have myself visited old Bushmen in Prieska and Kenhard districts some years ago, and my remarks on pronunciation are based as much on my own experience as on their notes.

The tribe living north of the Orange River in Gordonia and Griqualand West call themselves *//ŋ-!ke* or 'home people'. Their language is related to the */xam* speech. So is the language of the tribe found in the eastern Transvaal at Lake Chrissie, who call themselves Batwa, the Swazi word for Bushman. Other allied tongues are those of the extinct Bushmen of the Orange Free State and Basutoland, of the */auni* on the lower Nossop, of the Bushmen of Kakia in southern Bechuanaland, who call themselves Masarwa, a Sechuana name for Bushmen, and of the */nu-//en* who inhabit the country round the upper Nossop and the Auhoup. These form one division of Bushman languages which I call the Southern Group.

Very different languages are spoken beyond the Tropic of Capricorn. On the land stretching from the north-west side of the Oas-Ngami road to about the 19⁰ east longitude we find the *≠au-//en* or *//k'au-//en,* generally called Auen by Europeans; north of these live the *!kuŋ,* whose boundaries extend from Ngami to about the 18⁰ south latitude and from about the 22⁰ to the 19⁰ east longitude in the south, and to about the 16⁰ in the north; to the west of the *!kuŋ* scattered

[1]) cf. Specimens of Bushman Folklore collected by W. H. I. Bleek and L. C. Lloyd edited by the latter, with an introduction by G. Mc Theal, translation into English, illustrations and appendix; London (G. Allen) 1911. SS. XL—468.

over the South West Protectorate the *hei-//kum.* The latter have to a great extent adopted Nama as their speech, but their own language, still found in some isolated villages, is closely allied to the former two. All three are distantly related to the Southern Group. I call this the Northern Group.

In the wedge-shaped space between the Tropic of Capricorn and the Oas-Ngami road are tribes speaking languages which have a good deal of resemblance to Hottentot. Among them are the Tati Masarwa, who appear to call themselves *hie-tʃware,* the *tanna-kwe,* the *tsau-kwe,* the *tsoro-kwe,* the *!giŋ-kwe* and the *naron* or *//ai-kwe;* the latter are the most westerly of the group and their speech has the greatest likeness to Nama. I call this the Central Group.

In this sketch I am dealing with the */xam* language only, so for convenience sake I use the word Bushman to apply to this tribe only, to the Bushman of the old Cape Colony to whom the name was first given.

Orthography.

Bushmen do not open their mouths much in speaking, it is therefore not easy to distinguish the vowels clearly. Slurred indefinite vowel sounds are in the majority and often vary slightly with individual speakers.

We find: *i, i:, e, e:, a, a:, ɑ, ɑ:, ɔ, ɔ:, u, u:, ʌ, ə:, y, y:, ɯ, ɯ:.*

There are the diphthongs: *ei, ai, au, ao, aɔ, oi, ɔi, ua* and *ɔa* often turning into *wa,* and *ia* turning into *ja.*

All vowels and diphthongs may be nasalized, which is indicated by ~ above the vowel or vowels. If two vowels occurring together are to be pronounced separately, I have placed the trema ¨ over the second.

The following consonants occur:

p only after the labial click or in foreign words, exclamations, and imitations of sound, in the latter it may be at the end of a word.

b occasionally at the beginning, more often in a dissyllabic word.

t very frequently used both at the beginning, and in dissyllabic words.

d chiefly at the beginning of words.

tʼ and *dʼ* probably occur occasionally. Some of the double letters at the beginning of words in 'Specimens of Bushman folklore' may represent them, but do not always do so; they generally indicate the more noisy manner of sounding consonants common to Bushmen.

k occurs very frequently at the beginning of words either alone or following a click, occasionally in words of two syllables.

g is used in the same manner as *k*, but less frequently.

k' and *k''* occur either alone or after a click. The latter sound is a very loud plosive croak. In Specimens of Bushman Folklore *k'* is written ⌣ and *k''* *y*.

m is rarely used at the beginning of a word, more frequently at the end of a syllable.

n only occurs after clicks at the beginning of words, except in some forms of the first personal pronoun sing. and in words connected with animals' cries, but it is very frequent at the end of a word or syllable.

ŋ occurs alone as the first personal pronoun sing., and in "no", it is very frequent at the end of words.

r is only used at the beginning of a word in exclamations; then it is rolled properly. In the middle of a two syllabled word it occurs frequently, but the rolling is very slight, the sound is often nasal, sometimes almost *l*. There is no real *l* in the language.

f v only occur in imitations of sound, as of the wind. They are bilabial.

w j are frequent, but not at the beginning of words; they seem to have developed from vowels.

s ʃ are only used at the beginning of words sometimes after *t*. They often change in different local dialects.

z ʒ are likewise only used at the beginning of words sometimes after *d*, but are far less frequent.

h is used at the beginning of a word either alone or after a click or *k*.

x is used at the beginning of a word alone or after a click or *k*. The position of the tongue varies according to the following vowel, being further forward before front vowels than before back ones.

So far I have followed the orthography of the International Phonetic Association. For the clicks I use the old signs well known to all students of Bushman and Hottentot languages.

6*

The clicks are implosive sounds with a double closure, formed either by pressing the tongue against the teeth or palate, or the lips together, while the back of the tongue touches the velum, or the glottis is closed, more often the former. By lowering the tongue the air space is increased, then the front closure is withdrawn, the air is sucked into the half-filled space and makes the click. After the front release comes the back release, which may be silent or not. If it is not silent, a velar sound follows the click, unless it is the lip click; if it is silent, a vowel or *h* follows. Only the nasal sound can be made at the same time as the click, in which case it would be more correct to put ˜ above the click, rather than *n* after it. But in Bushman the click always seems to come first, and has always been written first, so I have kept to this orthography.

The Bushman vocabulary proper has five clicks:

/ the dental or alveolar fricative click is formed by pressing the front of the tongue against the teeth or alveolus and releasing it gently with a sucking sound.

! the retroflex plosive click is made by pressing the tip of the tongue against the palate and snapping it off smartly as if imitating the drawing of a cork.

// the retroflex fricative click is made by spreading the tip of the tongue across the palate and releasing it gently, perhaps letting the air in at the sides. This click somewhat resembles the Bantu lateral click.

ǂ the alveolar plosive click is made by pressing the front of tongue far forward on the alveolus, almost on the teeth, and snapping it off smartly.

⊙ the lip click is made by pressing the lips together and releasing them as in a kiss.

Clicks always stand at the beginning of a word, or of a syllable in a compound word. The following examples will show in what manner they are used:

/a	to fight	*!a:*	along	*//a*	to go	*ǂabakən*	to burn
/ha	husband	*!ham*	first	*//hagən*	to equal	*ǂhau*	to jump
/ka	to leave	*!kã*	to await	*//ka*	wet	*ǂka:*	bare
/kha	stick	*!khau*	bee	_*//khã*	lion	—*ǂkhara*	feather
/xã	to shoot	_*!xagən*	crow	*//xã*	again	*ǂxama*	to fetch
/k'a:	riverbed	*!k'ao*	to skin	*//k'ao*	cursed	*ǂk'ana*	to call
/ga	hippo	*!gã*	frog	*//ga:*	night	*ǂgabətən*	to throw
/na	head	*!na*	winter	*//na*	there	*ǂna*	to forget

/ is sometimes used with a glottal release before vowels as
/ʔãũ bone,

⊙ may be followed by *p, b, m* or *h*.
⊙pwa little, *⊙bu:-ta* to rain gently, *⊙mwaiŋja* to kiss, *⊙ho* wood, tree.

Some writers subdivide the retroflex clicks further according to the position of the tongue on the palate. As this movement of the tongue is automatic, the click being made a little further forward before a front vowel than before a back one, I do not think it necessary to express it in writing.

No other clicks are used in the ordinary vocabulary, but in Bushman folklore the speech of certain animals and of the Moon is distinguished by the recurrence of some particular sound at the beginning of each noun and verb instead of the ordinary click or consonant. Some of these sounds are clicks. Thus the Jackal has a lip click described as bearing the same relation to the ⊙ click, as the alveolar plosive click bears to the alveolar fricative click. I have never heard these special clicks from a Bushman; from hearing my aunt pronounce the Jackal's click, I should say it is a strongly plosive *p*'. The Moon, the Hare and the Anteater have a most unpronounceable click made "by curling up the tip of the tongue backwards in a sort of roll and then withdrawing the turned up part of the tongue from the palate". This click has a sort of palatal croak with it. The Ichneumon's speech is distinguished by replacing all initial clicks and consonants by *ts*' or *tʃ* or *tj* or *dy*. The tortoise changes initial sounds into labials, the Blue Crane adds *t* to most words.

The four clicks /, !, //, ≠ are common to all Bushman and Hottentot languages, the lip click ⊙ is found in all languages of the Southern group, but nowhere else.

Tones.

Bushman words may vary in meaning according to the tone in which they are spoken. There are three tones to be distinguished, high, middle and low. The middle tone I leave unmarked. The high tone is indicated by placing ‾ before a syllable, the low tone by placing _ before it. There are very few examples of rising or falling tones on one syllable, but often the low tone is followed by the middle tone or the middle tone by the high tone, rarely the other way round. The variation in tone among the Southern Bushmen is not so great as among the Northern Group.

The following examples show the use of the tones: *ha* he, *_ha* auxiliary of past tense; */kẽ⁻ĩ* to seize, */kẽ ĩ* follow *_!gauö* to poison, *_dɔä* could, *ŋ* I, *_ŋ⁻ŋ* no, *⁻ĩ_ja* yes; this last word is not pronounced staccato, as the negative is, but falls from the high to the low tone without arrest of breath.

Tones are also used descriptively to denote quantity or distance. The larger or farther a thing is, the higher is the tone of the adjective or adverb describing it.

The accent in Bushman is generally on the first syllable, always if the syllable has a click. The few cases of accentuated second syllables I mark with an accent ′. This occurs most frequently in reduplications.

Before leaving the subject of pronunciation I will give a Bushman's comparison of his method of speaking with a European's: */xam-ka-!k'etən /ku ≠kakən au hi /eni !kauükən, au /hũ⁻/hũŋaŋ /ne e: ≠kakən au hi /eni /ɛm.* 'The Bushmen talk with the body of their tongue, while the Europeans are those who talk with the tip of their tongue'.

The Vocabulary.

In my MS Bushman dictionary there are three and a half boxes of words without clicks, seven and a half of words with clicks. Of these, two boxes hold words with /, three hold words with !, two hold words with //, while the words with ≠ and ⊙ share half a box between them. Yet if we count up the words with and without clicks on half a dozen pages of "Specimens of Bushman Folklore" taken at random, we find that less than two fifths are words with clicks, more than three fifths are words without clicks. This shows that the words in most frequent use are without clicks.

Among the words beginning with a vowel or *h* we find nearly all the pronouns and demonstrative adjectives, most of the prepositions and conjunctions, a few adjectives and adverbs, some verbal particles and a few much used verbs, but hardly any nouns.

Among words beginning with consonants but without clicks we find a moderate number of nouns, about twice as many verbs, some adjectives and adverbs, many grammatical particles, a few pronouns, prepositions and conjunctions.

Among words beginning with clicks we find countless nouns and verbs, some adverbs, mostly with the form of verbs, and very little else.

Words of one syllable are in the majority. Some words of two syllables are reduplications or compound words, but not all; a number are formed of root and endings.

The Noun.

Gender.

Bushman has no genders referring to sex; in fact it has only slight signs of any classification of nouns at all. The pronouns referring to nouns have two forms, one used only in the singular, — *ha* he, she, it, *a:* who,which, that —, and one mainly used in the plural, — *hi* they, *e:* who, which, that —. The latter forms are however used with certain nouns where the singular number is clearly indicated. This looks as if there had been two classes of nouns in the singular, and that the plurals of both had been the same, and now outwardly agree with the second classes singular, that is to say as far as the pronouns are concerned. There is no distinguishing feature in the nouns themselves. Some of these are: *_//gai* shoulderblade, *tũ* skin, *//na:* kareeboom, *//neiŋ* hut, *hɔro* eggshell. They are all things, not persons, but the majority of things belong to the first class.

The terms of relationship show traces of endings referring to sex. In masculine terms we frequently find a nasal vowel or *ŋ* at the end of the word, in feminine terms we find the endings *xai*, *ti* or *te;* or *x* at the beginning of the word. According to Krönlein *xai* is 'to cohabit' in Nama, and *xais* is often used for 'wife'. *Te* and *ti* are feminine plural endings in Nama. In Bushman we find:

//kã brother, *//kaxai* sister; *⊙pwoŋ* son, *⊙pwaxai* daughter; *ɔã* father, *xoä* mother; *!kõïŋ* grandfather, *!kõïte* grandmother, *//k'ʼen* child's father-in-law; *//k"aiti* child's mother-in-law. The last named word seems to contain the adjective */aiti* female; male is *gwai.* These adjectives follow the nouns they qualify. Occasionally they are used alone as man and woman. Their irregular plurals *tukən* males, men, and *!kagən* females, women, are joined to the nouns they qualify by the possessive particle, or they may be used alone. This looks as if they were really nouns, though sometimes used as adjectives, especially as they correspond to roots of words for men and women in other Bushman languages.

Case.

Nouns have a simple form always used in the objective case and sometimes in the nominative, and an emphatic nominative formed by adding *-kən* to the simple form. After a long vowel this may be modified to *-gən,* after *i* and *e* to *-tən,* and after a diphthong or nasal vowel it can be shortened to *ŋ*. If the noun already ends in *kən, gən* or *tən* in the simple form, these endings are changed to *kakən* or *takən* in the emphatic form, sometimes shortened to *ka:* or *ta:*. If the simple form ends in *ŋ*, the emphatic form adds *-aŋ* or *-jaŋ*.

The possessive case is formed by adding *-ka* to the simple form. This particle may be changed to *-ga* or *-ta* according to the rule shown above. The thing possessed follows the possessor.

The vocative case is made by adding *-wε* to the simple form.

The dative has no special form; it is expressed by position or by a preposition. The dative precedes the accusative.

Number.

There is no particular form for the dual, the plural is formed in different ways, mostly by reduplication, occasionally by an ending, or by both. The following tables show the different forms:

I. Reduplication of the simple form.

	Singular.	Emphatic.	Plural.
foot	*!nɔa*	*!nɔaŋ*	*!nɔa!nɔa*
hand	*/k'a*	*/k'akən*	*/k'a/k'a*
mouth	*tu*	*tukən*	*tutu*
eggshell	*hɔro*	*hɔrokən*	*hɔrohɔro*
lung	*ʃo*	*ʃokən*	*ʃoʃo*
stone	*/kou*	*/kougən*	*/kou/kou*
perforated stone	*!kwe*	*!kwetən*	*!kwe!kwe*
night	*//ga:*	*//ga:gən*	*//ga//ga:*
ravine	*!kwiri*	*!kwiritən*	*!kwiri!kwiri*
dog	*!kuiŋ*	*!kuiŋjaŋ*	*!kuiŋ!kuiŋ*

II. Reduplication of the emphatic form.

thing	*ti*	*tikən*	*tikəntikən*
bed-skin	*!ki:*	*!ki:tən*	*!kitən!ki:tən*
bow	*/hou*	*/houkən*	*/houkən/houkən*
hill	*_/kao*	*_/kaokən*	*_/kaokən_/kaoken*
net	*/ũĩ*	*/ũĩŋ*	*/ũĩŋ/ũĩŋ*

III. If the singular is already a reduplication, the plural is a reduplication of the forms with -kən.

	Singular.	Emphatic.	Plural.
whirlwind	//go//go	//go//gokən	//gokən//gokən
bush, a certain	/kwe/kwəri	/kwe/kwəritən	/kwəritən/kwəritən
beast of prey	//kei//kei	//kei//keitən	//keitən//keitən

IV. Joining the simple and emphatic forms.

face	xu:	xu:kən	xuxu:kən
fight, death	/a:	/a:kən	/a/a:kən
fieldmouse	//khou	//khoukən	//khou//khoukən
tortoiseshell	_!gəë	_!gweitən	_!gwei_!gweitən
spot	ǂu:	ǂu:kən	ǂuǂu:kən
gland	–ǂk'wã	–ǂk'wãŋ	ǂk'wã–ǂk'wãŋ
head	/na	/naŋ	/na/naŋ
leg	!kwa:	!kwa:gən	!kwa!kwa:gən

The tendency to shorten the first half of the reduplication shown by these examples, is more marked in the following:

shoulder-blade	–//gai	_//gaitən	_//ga_//gaitən
dark stripe on buck	ǂhãĩ	ǂhãĩŋ	ǂhaǂhãĩŋ
thigh bone	!kuï	!kuïtən	!ku!kuïtən

V. Nouns ending in -kən, -gən, -tən, -ŋ form the plural

a. by reduplication of the root only:

black crow	_!ka:gən	_!ka:_kakən	_!ka:_!ka:
silver jackal	!gwitən	!gwitakən	!gwi!gwi
hut	//neiŋ	//neiŋjaŋ	//nei//nei and //nei//neiŋ
kaross	!nwiŋ	!nwiŋjaŋ	!nwi!nwi

b. by joining the root and the whole word:

star	/kwatən	/kwatakən	/kwa/kwatən
korhaan, vaal	_!kaukən	_!kaukakən	_!kau_!kaukən
tick	!ke:n	!ke:naŋ	!ke!ke:n
barblet	//kukən	//kukakən	//ku//kukən
feather brush	_!koäkən	_!koäkakən	_!ko_!koäkən

VI. Nouns ending in -*m* or -*n* take *a* or *i* after the reduplication.

	Singular.	Emphatic.	Plural.
story	*kum*		*kukumi*
tip	*/ɛm*		*/ɛ/ɛmi*
collarbone	*!khʌm*	*!khʌmaŋ*	*!kha!khʌmi*
stone pipe	*_!kan*	*_!kanaŋ*	*_!kan_!kana*

VII. Nouns of two or more syllables form the plural by reduplication of the first syllable only.

wrist	*//khɔrɛ*	*//khɔrɛtən*	*//khɔ//khɔrɛ*
mother animal	*//kwara*	*//kwarakən*	*//kwa//kwara*
little bird	*k'eni*		*k'ek'en*

This is particularly marked in compound nouns formed with *xu* face, surface, or *tu* mouth, hole.

hunting ground	*!kauxu*	*!kauxukən*	*!kau!kauxu*
back	*tsəŋxu*	*tsəŋxukən*	*tsētsəŋxu*
chest	*!ka:xu*	*!ka:xukən*	*!ka!katənxu*
stomach	*/kouxu*	*/kouxukən*	*/ku/kutənxu*
ear	*!nuntu*	*!nuntukən*	*!nu!nuntu*
belly	*!kautu*	*!kautukən*	*!kau!kautəntu*
arm hole	*//khatu*	*//khatukən*	*//kha//khatu*

VIII. *R* and *t* in the second syllable often change in the plural.

blister	*gouru*	*gourukən*	*gougoutən*
edge	*!ara*		*!at!atən*
stone knife	*//kuru*	*//kurukən*	*//kutən//kutən*
pipe	*!xɔro*	*!xɔrokən*	*!xɔtən!xɔtən*
larynx	*¯!həre*	*¯!həretən*	*!hatən!hatən*
Koranna	*!kwara*	*!kwarakən*	*!kwatən!kwatən*
breastbone	*//gɔro*	*//gɔrokən*	*//gɔtən//gɔtən*
jackal	*_kɔro*	*_kɔrokən*	*_kɔtən_kɔtən*
cat	*_//gwatən*	*_//gwatakən*	*_//gwa_//gwara*
old woman	*/nutara*	*/nutarakən*	*/nu/nutatən*

IX. Other irregular reduplications.

old man	*/nuk'au*	*/nuk'aukən*	*/nukən/nukənk'au*
youth	*k'audɔro*	*k'audɔrokən*	*k'auk'aurukən*

	Singular.	Emphatic.	Plural.
middle	*//kaie*		*//ka//katənĩ*
mouse	*!henixa*	*!henixakən*	*!he!heniŋxa*
white man	*/hũ*	*/hũŋ*	*/hũ/hũnaŋ*
body	*!kauükən*		*!kau!kauwaŋ*
place	*!kwei*	*!kweitən*	*!kwei!kwɔreaŋ*
eye	*tsa‾xau*	*tsa‾xaitakən*	*tsa‾xaitən* and *tsatsa-xukən*
fool	*/gebi*	*/gebiwakən*	*/gi/gitən* and */gebitən-/gebitən*

X. Some plurals are formed without reduplication by adding one of the endings *-kən, -gən, -tən, -ŋ.*

bone	*!kwa*	*!kwakən*	*!kwa:gən*
tree	*⊙ho*	*⊙hokən*	*⊙ho:gən*
branch	*/khwe*	*/khwetən*	*/khwetən*
stick	*//kha*	*//khakən*	*//khaitən*
young girl	*//hi:*		*//hi:tən*
sister	*//kaxai*	*//kaxaiten*	*//kaxukən*
sieve	*‾!k"wi*		*‾!k"witən*
metal knife	*!gwara*	*!gwarakən*	*!gwatən*

XI. Some plurals are formed by adding *-de* or *-di* with or without reduplication.

son	*⊙pwɔŋ*		*⊙pwɔnde*
brother	*//kã*	*//kaŋ*	*//kʌnde*
brother-in-law	*!xa:*		*!xa!xa:de*

In these three examples *de* seems identical with a plural for 'man' found in the *//ŋ* Bushman language, in the following it seems to stand for *di* things, doings, corresponding to a singular *ti* thing deed.

lath	*!kwainti*	*!kwaintiken*	*!kwa:rde*
little birds	*//gəritənti*	*//gəritəntikən*	*//gəritənde*
screen of bushes	*//kuï*	*//kuïtən*	*//kuï//kuïde*
eyeball	*!gəritən*		*!gwiri!gwiride*
fingernail	*//kũru*	*//kũrukən*	*//ku//kudi* and *//ku//kuti*

XII. Some nouns denoting persons form the plural by adding *-gu:*, usually to the emphatic form. This ending, which in Nama denotes the masculine plural, may be added to a proper name or the name of a personified animal to express 'family', 'friends'.

	Singular.	Emphatic.	Plural.
father	*oä*	*oäkən*	*o:kəngu:* parents
„	*bobo*		*bo:kəngu:*
mother	*xoä*	*xoäkən*	*xoäkəngu:*
„	*mama*	*mamaŋ*	*mamagu:*
husband or wife	*/ha*	*/hakən*	*/haukəngu:* husband and wife
brother-in-law	*!khwĩ*	*!khwĩ:ŋ*	*!khwĩ!khwi:ŋgu:*
jackal, the	*kəro*		*kərogu:* the jackal and party
Jantje	*//kabo*		*//kabogu:* Jantje and his people

XIII. Irregular plurals.

thing	*tsa*	*tsakən*	*tʃueŋ* and *tʃwitʃwi*
egg	*!kauï*	*!kauïtən*	*!kwitən*
child	*!khwã:*	*!khwã:ŋ*	*!kaukən*
little sister in law	*!kouki*		*!koukukən*
person, man	*!kui, !kyi*	*!kuitən*	*!k'e:*
man, male	*gwai*	*gwaijakən*	*tukən*
woman, female	*/aiti*	*/aitikən*	*/ka:gen* women, mates

XIV. A number of nouns have no separate form for the plural. Many names of animals are among these, for instance: springbok *wai*; ostrich *toï*; hartebeest *!'wa:*; lion *_//khã:*; black korhaan *_kwa_kwara*; eland *s'a*; ox *xəro*; beetle *ʒu:*; butterfly *dadabasi*; moth *gəro*; ichneumon */ni:*; owl *!hũ!hũ*; baboon */hu/hu*; elephant *≠xəë*;

also names of plants, as

thornbush *!naba*; kareeboom *//na:*; grass */khe:*; berry */gara*;

also parts of the body, as

thumb *//əhái*; liver *//khã:*; skin *tũ:*; neck *!kou*; nose */nũnu*; throat *_dəm*;

and some other nouns, as

bead */k'i:*; sorcerer *!gi:*; hole, den *!kwe!kwe*; winter *!na:*.

Examples of the declension of nouns:

Singular.

	bag	leg	hut	fieldmouse
Simple	*//ho*	*!kwa:*	*//neiŋ*	*//khou*
Emphatic	*//hokən*	*!kwa:gən*	*//neiŋjaŋ*	*//khoukən*
Possessive	*//ho-ka*	*!kwa:-ga*	*//neiŋ-ka*	*//khou-ka*
Vocative				*//khou-wε*

Plural.

Simple	*//ho//ho*	*!kwa!kwa:*	*//nei//nei*	*//khou//khoukən*
Emphatic	*//ho//hokən*	*!kwa!kwa:gən*	*//nei//neiŋ*	*//khou//khoukakən*
Possessive	*//ho//ho-ka*	*!kwa!kwa:-ka*	*//nei//nei-ta*	*//khou//khoukən-ka*
Vocative				*//khou//khoukən-wε*

Singular.

	ostrich	white man	hyena	son
Simple	*toï*	*/hũ*	*!gwãĩ*	*⊙pwɔŋ*
Emphatic	*toïtən*	*/hũŋ*	*!gwãĩn*	*⊙pwɔŋ*
Possessive	*toï-ta*	*/hũ-ka*	*!gwãĩ-ta*	*⊙pwɔŋ-ka*
Vocative	*toï-wε*	*/hũ-wε*	*!gwãĩ-wε*	*⊙pwɔŋ-wε*

Plural.

Simple	*toï*	*/hũ/hũ*	*!gwãĩgu:*	*⊙pwɔnde*
Emphatic	*toïtən*	*/hũ/hũnaŋ*	*!gwãĩgu:kən*	*⊙pwɔndekən*
Possessive	*toï-ta*	*/hũ/hũ-ka*	*!gwãĩgu:-ka*	*⊙pwɔnde-ka*
Vocative	*toï-wε*	*/hũ/hũ-wε*	*!gwãĩgu:-wε*	*⊙pwɔnde-wε*

Pronouns.

Personal.

The personal pronoun has no gender referring to sex. We find the following forms:

Singular.

	1st person	2nd person	3rd person	
Simple	*ŋ, ka*	*a*	*ha, hã*	*ki*
Emphatic	*ŋ-ŋ, kakən, ka-ŋ*	*a-a, akən*	*ha-ha, hã-hã, haŋ*	*ki-hi*
Possessive	*ŋ-ka, ŋ-ŋ-ka*	*a-ka, a-a-ka*	*ha-ka, ha-ha-ka*	*ki-ta*

Plural.

Simple	*i*	*si*	*u*	*hi, hĩ*
Emphatic	*i-i, itən,*	*si-si, sitən*	*u-u, ukən*	*hi-hi, hĩ-hĩ, hiŋ*
Possessive	*i-ta*	*si-ta*	*u-ka*	*hi-ta, hi-hi-ta*

No exact rule can be given for the use of the two forms of the 1st person; *ŋ* is far more often used than *ka,* which often but not invariably appears in subordinate clauses. Nor does there seem to be any fixed rule for the use of the nasal in the third person; it seems to depend on individual choice. The use of *hi* for *ha* in the 3rd person singular has been explained above under 'gender of nouns'.

In the 1st person plural the form *i* includes the person or persons addressed with the speaker, the form *si* excludes those addressed. In Nama *si* is also used in the exclusive forms of the 1st person plural.

Before nouns denoting relationship or parts of the body the possessive particle *-ka* is generally dropped.

my wife *ŋ /ha*; my hut *ŋ-ka //neiŋ*; thy grandfather *a !kõïŋ*; thy bag *a-ka //ho*; his mouth *ha tu*; his bow *ha-ka /hou*; the lion's head *_//khã: /na*; the lion's home *_//kha:_ga //neiŋ*.

Relative.

The relative pronoun has two forms only: *a:* refering to all pronouns in the singular, and to the singular of all nouns which take the personal pronoun *ha;* and *e:* to all pronouns and nouns in the plural and to the singular of those nouns which take the personal pronoun *hi.*

A: and *e:* are apparently nominatives, they stand at the beginning of the subordinate clause. To express the objective case, *a:* and *e:* precede the verb, which is followed by *ha, hi,* or *ĩ:*; the latter is contracted from *au ha* or *au hi,* to him, to them. For example:

!kui a: /kha wai *!kwa:gən e: ha _kworetən hĩ*
man who kills springbok. bones which he gnawed them.
//gəro e: !kwa:gən !ʌhí so hi
breastbone which bones upon sit it, (the breastbone on which the bones are) *haŋ //kei//kei !ˀwa: a: /ku:ka*
he resembled hartebeest who died.

Demonstrative.

The demonstrative adjectives *ha* and *hi* 'this, these,' are similar in form to the personal pronouns 'he, they,' but are spoken with more emphasis. They precede the nouns they qualify. *A:‾a* that, *e:‾a* those follow the nouns they qualify. They probably represent the relative pronouns and the verb 'to be'. *!kwi a:‾a* man who is, that man. *!keˀe: ‾a* people who are, those people.

!ke: yonder is also used after the noun it qualifies with or without the following *¯a*. *a χu /ke: ¯a* thy face yonder, *¯!kẽĩ /ke:* the boy yonder.

Reflexive.

The reflexive pronouns myself, thyself etc, when used emphatically, are translated by *//ẽ* or *//ẽĩ*, which often has the form of a verb. *i /ku //ẽĩ, i !χaiti ha* we did ourselves, we follow him = we followed him ourselves. *hi se //ẽĩ, hi //k'ɔen* they may themselves, they see = that they may see for themselves. *//ẽĩ* is similar to the root of the 3rd personal pronoun in Nama.

If not emphasized, the reflexive pronoun is rarely used and is identical with the personal pronoun.

Interrogative.

The interrogative pronouns who? what? are expressed by the words for person and thing with an interrogative ending *-de*, followed by one of the interrogative verbal particles *xa, ba, /nu*; *!kui* is shortened to *!ku*.

!ku-de xa a:¯a? what person is that? who is that?
tsa-de ba ¯a? what thing is it? what is it?

The Adjective.

Bushmen do not use many adjectives, they are less interested in the quality of anything than in its actions. Adjectives follow the nouns the qualify and are often preceded by the relatives *a:* and *e:*.

⊙ho a: t'ain bush which soft, a soft bush; *//go//go !keri* whirlwind great, the great whirlwind; *!kaukən e: ǂen* children who small, small children; *hã: e: akən* food which good, good food.

Most adjectives are the same in singular and plural. As exception, we find the indefinite adjective *ko* other, plural *kw:tən*, and the following adjectives of size:

	Singular	Plural		Singular	Plural
tall	*!xo:wa*	*!xo!xo:ka*	short	*/yri*	*/ytən*
large	*!kuïja*	*!kuï!kuïta*	small	*ts'ɔre:*	*ts'etən*
round	*kɔrekɔre:*	*kɔritənkɔritən*	little	*⊙pwa*	*-ka !kaukən*

These last two are almost nouns, *kɔrekɔre:* being also 'a ball' and *⊙pwa* turning into 'children' with the possessive particle in the plural, as *//ho ⊙pwa* little bag, *//ho//ho-ka !kaukən* bags children, little bags. In several other Bushman languages ⨀*pwa* means 'child' and probably did so once in the */xam* language.

As mentioned under 'gender of nouns' the words *gwai* male and */aiti* female can be used either as adjectives or nouns. Their irregular plurals are certainly nouns, for when used to qualify a noun they are joined to it by the possessive particle. */ka:gən* has the double meaning of 'mates, companions,' and 'women'. *gwai* can be used as 'big, strong' as well as 'male'.

!kui gwai man, strong person	*toï gwai* male ostrich, strong ostrich
!k'e-ta tukən men	*toï-ta tukən* male ostriches
!kui /aiti woman	*toï /aiti* female ostrich
!k'e-ta /ka:gən women, men's mates	*toï-ta /ka:gən* female ostriches

Ku 'all' is also joined to the noun it qualifies by the possessive particle. *!'ãũ-ka ku:* all the earth; *ti-ta ku:* the whole place; *i-ta ku:* we all.

Numerals.

There are three numeral adjectives in Bushman:

!kwai one */ku:* two *!nwəna* three

They may follow the nouns they qualify directly or after the relatives *a:* and *e:*. Thus we find

!kui a: !kwai and *!kui !kwai* one man

!kaukən e: !ku: and *!kaukən !ku:* two children

/ka:gən e: !nwəna and */ka:gən !nwəna* three women

!kwai is sometimes used for 'alone'. There are no other numerals.

The Adverb.

Adverbs are difficult to distinguish from verbs in Bushman. They are often used in both capacities. Thus we find:

oä, u:i away and to leave	*//kaitən* up and to ascend
//a thither „ to go	*//kau* upon „ to mount
sa hither „ to come	*//koe* down „ to descend
/e: in „ to enter	*/hiŋ* out „ to come out
!ʌhí in front of and to head	

Besides these there are a number of words which we translate as adverbs but which are clearly used as verbs, for the subject is always repeated after them by a pronoun; yet they are never used without another verb following. Among them are:

_mai first; */hau* afterwards; *!hʌm* later; *//xã:* again; *!kana* repeatedly; */kwẽĩ* thus; *//nau* then or as follows.

!kui⁻/a a: _mai, ha /e: xwara; xoäkəngu: /ku /ne !heu, hiŋ sa. The girl did first, she enters the spring; the mothers did afterwards, they come.

Other adverbs show that they have once been verbs by taking as ending one of the particles *ki, ko, kau* which are used to join verbs.

kau, kauki not; *!ka:gən !ka:gənkau* early; */kai:ti* later; *//xʌm, //xʌmki* also; *!naunko* still, yet.

These adverbs precede the verbs they modify; so do *≠xʌn-⊙pwa* subsequently and *tʌm-⊙pwa* gently, a little, which seem from the ending to be derived from nouns. Adjectives are often used as adverbs without any change; these generally follow the verb. We find:

akən good, well; *!hanũwa* comfortable, comfortably; *!nu:* angry, angrily; *kwe:* quiet, quietly; *twaiï* sweet, sweetly.

Other adverbs do not show their derivation clearly They sometimes precede and sometimes follow the verb, but are always close to it. *//kwẽ:i* 'very' generally follows the adverb it modifies.

The Preposition.

There is really only one preposition in Bushman *au* or *ɛ*, which can mean 'to, for, at, in, with, on account of'. It directly precedes the noun it governs. The other words we translate with prepositions are really adverbs or verbs, and retain their place before the principal verb.

!kaukən se /a: ha au //kuru the children will cut it with a knife

ha !ʌhí tiŋ !kaukən he in front lay the children, he lay in front of the children

hiŋ /e: s'o //neiŋ they in sat house, they sat in the house.

Many verbs need no preposition where we employ one: *ta, tiŋ* to lie in or at; *≠χi:* to shine upon; *tum* to listen to.

The Conjunction.

All conjunctions stand at the beginning of the clauses or sentences they introduce. We find the following:

au or *o*	when, as because, while
ta:	for, because, but
he or *hɛ*	and (joining sentences)

he ti hiŋ e:	then, therefore (lit 'these things they are')
he tikən e, he e:	(the above shortened)
ti e:	that (lit. 'things which') introduces the subordinate clause, if a conjunction is used at all.
koä	and (joining words) is always preceded by a plural pronoun, for example:

/kagən hiŋ koä /kwamaŋa mantis they and */kwamaŋa*, the mantis and */kwamaŋa*

Sometimes *koä* is dropped and the pronoun alone remains:

!gwãĩgu: //kwaŋ e:, hiŋ kərogu:. hiŋ //hoëgu:

the hyenas were (there), and the jackals, and the crows.

(To be continued.)

BUSHMAN GRAMMAR.

A grammatical sketch of the language of the /xam-ka-!'e

by Dorothea F. Bleek.

(Continuation.)[1]

The Verb.

In conjugating a verb the different persons are not distinguished save by the subject; one says: *ŋ ǂkakən* I speak; *a ǂkakən* thou speakest; *oä ǂkakən* father speaks; *sitən ǂkakən* we speak; *ukən ǂkakən* you speak; *hi ǂkakən* they speak; */ka:gən ǂkakən* the women speak.

Two or three verbs can be strung together in a sentence, sometimes joined by one of the particles *ki, ko, kau, ti, to, tau, si,* or by */ki* 'to take', sometimes without any connection. It is possible that the adverbs and prepositions which have also a verbal meaning are really verbs used in this manner.

/ha /ki sa wai the husband takes comes springbok, brings the springbok.
!khwã:ŋ /ne //kara so child did bask sit, the child sat basking.
ŋ ˍkoä ˍtã:i kau !nu:i I must walk and bark, I must bark as I walk.
oäkən siŋ ˍ/kame:n ki //a !kwitən father did carry and go eggs, took the eggs.
ha se !khe tau !nau he will stand and bury (it).
ha se //a di /ki siŋ ha he will go make take sit it, he will go to sit preparing it.

Moods and tenses are formed by placing one or more verbal particles or auxiliaries before the verb in chief. A few of these can be used as independent verbs, others are not found alone though they may once have been so used. These particles do not correspond exactly with one mood or tense in English, it is therefore difficult to give exact rules for their use, particularly when several are employed together, but the following examples will show the most usual meaning. Occasionally also the verb takes an ending, generally when it can be translated as a participle. Sometimes however the ending seems to include the object. There are evidently so many more ways of expressing nuances of action in Bushman then in English, that we shall see many different Bushman forms translated by one and the same English expression.

[1]) cf. Vol. XIX, p. 81—98.

se indicates the future or subjunctive. It is generally used in clauses expressing the effect of the preceding clause. Sometimes it can be translated by 'must'. It may be derived from *sa, si* 'to come'. *!kwiŋ fo ǂĩ, ti e:, !kwiŋ se /ka ha, au !kwiŋjaŋ k''auki se /ka ha* the dog seems to think that the dog will kill it, but the dog will not kill it.

/kao –!kwa: !kʔwa: !khou, //xa ʘpwa se _/kamme:ŋ !kʔwa:
cut break hartebeest's neck, (that) sister little may carry hartebeest's

/na:.
head.

haŋ !kurukən!kurukən //kau ta: !kwa: /na: ts'ĩ-ta !ʔãũ, ha se
he dries (his feathers) upon lie water's head's back's earth, he will

!hau ha _ta:ẽ u.
afterwards he walk away, i. e. he dries his feathers lying upon the water's bank, that he may afterwards walk away.

he e:, to:ï se aro:ko /ku:kən ĩ: then ostrich will quickly die from it; *he ti hiŋ e:, i se _tai au //kõĩŋya /e:ta* therefore we will go when the sun has set.

!kwi gwai se ǂkʌm-ʘpwa _taba /ki /e: ʃo-/õä _/kwai au ha /ha
the man must first work put in herb scent on his wife,

he e: ha se-g /ne _tai //koë !khe ha /ka:gən.
then she may walk among stand her mates, i. e. the man must first work scenting his wife with herbs, so that she may walk about among her companions.

siŋ indicates the past tense, also the perfect, pluperfect and subjunctive perfect. It may be derived from one form of the verb 'to sit'.

!kʔwa:gən siŋ ka, ŋ /kvm u !hãũ au ha ts'axau.
hartebeest did want, I take away thong from his eye, i. e. the hartebeest wanted me to take the thong away from his eye.

ts'wa:-ga !kʔe:-ta kukumi hɛ: //kabogu: siŋ ǂkaka hu hĩ,
Flat's Bushmen's stories which the Jantjes have told you them,

hɛ e: i se xóäxóä hĩ, ta: //kabo k'auki !naunko !ki kum
they are we will write them, for Jantje not still gets story

a: ha se ǂkaka.
which he may tell, i. e. the Flat-Bushmen's stories, which Jantje and his people have told you are what we will write, for Jantje no longer hears a story that he may tell.

/kagən kukui:tən /k'e:, ha siŋ /kai:tji //k'oen ha:-ʘpwakən !/gwitən
Mantis answering said, he had just seen springbok little play

//koë !khe: ǂxoä-ka !kauken.
among stand elephant's children, i. e. the Mantis answered that he had just seen the little springbok playing among the little elephants.

ŋ ǂĩ:, ti e: ŋ !ku siŋ !ke!ke _k'agn, _!k'aku siŋ //na
I thought that I would await the crow, the crow might be with

ŋ, ha siŋ //k'oen !kwi:tən.
me, it might see the eggs.

s?aŋ, _saŋ appears to be one form of the verb *si, sa* 'to come'. Sometimes it can be translated as 'come', at others it expresses future or conditional action. It is often used with other particles.

hiŋ _s?aŋ !gua:n !?auŋ !khe hiŋ !kɔtən.
it came to join upon stand its top of neck, i. e. it came to join onto the top of its neck.

hɛ e: kɔ:ro _saŋ _hami ha /na: then the jackal will fear his head.
!kwi /akən ǂĩ ti e: ha _saŋ //kau ki //kaiten !huiŋ eŋeŋ the girl thougt that she would throw up the *!huiŋ* roots.

oä perfect or pluperfect.
!kwi a: ‾a _oä tuko _a: ‾a man this has really been here, i. e. this man has really been here.
hiŋ e ha //kaxai /ne ǂenna, ti ė: ha _oä !xwəni, ti e: ha !k'ɔ/k'a _oä sɔe:nja !khwã then his sister would know, that he had turned back, that his hands had been upon the child.

ha indicates the past. It is generally used with other particles. The word is identical with the verb 'to come' in Naron and Hottentot, and similar to the Bushman *‾hã* 'to go'.
!kwi /akən _ha //k'oen ha the girl looked at him.
he ti hiŋ e:, /aiti _ha /ne /kau/kau ho u:i ha !nu:!nuŋtu: therefore his wife cut away his ears.

/ne expresses either the indicative or imperative. In the indicative it may denote a state, when it may be translated by the verb 'to be', or a habitual action, or a simple continuation of the narrative.
!khou /ne _kɔ:iŋ. !kwaitəntu:wa //ko:wa, hĩ /ne xube !kuŋ !/e. !kauka-g /ne /ni: ha the honey is lean. The flowers having dried, they break off. The children saw him.
ts'uïts'uïtən /ne /ke:tən hi /ka:gən, /ne ‾hã: the things call to their mates, go.

/ne ǂkaka ke a-a-ka kum tell me thy story.

//kəi//kei-wɛ, /ne //kaotən s'a: o beast of prey, rise up.

/ku a narrative particle, either past or present, often used similarly to the verb 'to be'.

/kaggən /ku a: /kərruwa !kauken the Mantis was one who cheated the children.

ha /na: ka /ku _mai, hi /hiŋ //e, au ha eŋeŋja: /ku //nũ: /na:; ha /na: /ku !ŋõä ã his head is wont first to go out, while his body is behind the head; his head looks round.

!kaukən /ku !kei //a: //neiŋ the children reached home.

he /ku !ki:ja they are red.

ha /na: /ku /hoä:ka his head is black.

/ku /ne, /ku-g /ne is often used in narratives; it seems to express either continuous action, or a repetition of the preceding tense.

ha /ku-g /ne /kan/kan au !ku!ku, au haŋ /ku-g /ne butən xa au ha _//ŋai he was stepping along with his shoes, while he jogged along with his shoulderblade.

hi /ku /ne dabba-ĩ it opens and shuts its eyes, i. e. it is opening and shutting its eyes.

he tikən e:, ha xóa /ku-g /ne _taba_taba, ha xóakən /ku-g /ne /ki //a ha ã hã therefore, his mother worked and worked, his mother brought him food.

/ne /ku likewise used in narratives to carry on any tense.

!khwa: kaŋ _ha ¯oa //haita !kwi /a, au !kwi /akən //na //neiŋ; !kwa:-gən /ne /ku !khau ha, he !khwa: /ne /ku /hiŋ ĩ: the rain formerly courted a girl, while the girl was at home; the rain scented her, and the rain went forth on account of it.

_dəa 'must, can', or a past tense. It is generally used with other particles.

/hũ: _oä _dəä e: /ka _!hoä !kʔe Boers must have been those who killed off the people.

ŋ !nəa kan k'auki _dəä ĩ:ja my foot can not do so.

ŋ /ke /ku _dəa /kurrija //na//na: kə:ro-ka //neiŋ, au ŋ k'auki //e ŋ-ga //neiŋ, ŋ /ku _dəo !ʌhaitən uĩ: I there have been writhing at the jackal's hut, and I did not go to my home, I had to limp away.

ŋ a: _ha: k'au _dəa !ku:xe I am the one who was not able to run.

_kóä 'must' or 'should' is usually followed by another verbal particle or a verb of motion.

u _kóä se //ka: hi: !kuttau you must burn for us to Sirius.

a _kóä /ne se /e: //ko:ä ke _!kə:a au //ho-ʘpwa thou must pack up for me stamped meat in the little bag.

ŋ ‗kóä ‗tãẽ /ha !xwe; u ‗kóä ‗tãẽ /kuŋ ʃo ŋ I must walk to the wife first; you must walk behind me.

k''ɔa, k''oa, ‗k''oä 'should, seems to', may also be translated 'must'.

haŋ /ne ta ti e: ha /eni ‗k''oä k'auki si /'xã: ŋi //k'i: tiŋ he wished that his tongue should not again stick fast.

au ka ‗k'oä /ku se /ne di /a: while I was obliged to fight.

to:i a: /xara ha k'oä e a different ostrich she seems to be.

kwa: and *kwaŋ* also *‗kwa* and *‗kwaŋ*, are generally used in one of a series of clauses to express sequence or effect. They may be translated 'shall', 'should' or 'must', or by an adverb 'then', 'henceforth' etc.

ŋ /kõiŋja /ne /k'e: ŋ, ŋ kwaŋ k'auki ‗!kaitən-ĩ //kərri my grandfather told me, I must not throw stones at the bird.

hĩ ≠en‾a ti e: ʃo /õä ‗/kwai ‗saŋ ‗!kwa:ŋ, ʃo /õä ‗/kwai ‗kwaŋ //kʔuere hĩ /ĩ they know that the herb scent would be angry, the herb scent would hurt their hearts.

!khwetən ts'u //koe ta: ŋ-ka //neiŋ //kaië, au akən kwaŋ /ku //keri //na au !khwa: the wind blows into my hut's middle, while thou art just screaming there about the rain.

ŋ ka !aruxu kwaŋ k'auki ≠ĩ: I wish the Dassie should not think.

ha //nɔeintuwa: si-g /ne /kwẽ: da, ha kwa: /ne //kʌm//kʌm his chest will be thus, that he may bellow.

au ha ≠gou /ki ʃo, ŋ kwa: /ku ĩ:ja while it sat silent, I consequently did so.

au //kõiŋ a: //hiŋ s'a, ha kwa: /ne !khe while the sun comes out, he still stands.

//kuaŋ seems to emphasize the following verb; it is sometimes merely narrative, sometimes adverbial in meaning.

!kwiŋ //kuaŋ e a dog it is.

//koxaitən ‗kuaŋ //khõä a Kafir it seems (to be).

tʃweŋ e: ‗darakən hĩ ‗//kuaŋ /ne e things which move they are.

ibogu ‗//kuaŋ /ke: ‗/kamɛn s'a: our fathers yonder come carrying.

haŋ /ne aroko ho: //kha, au haŋ tatti e:, ha ‗//kuaŋ /ne ≠hau≠hau ĩ: he quickly picks up the stick, because he is just springing away.

ŋ ‗//kuaŋ /ne ho akkən ŋ-ka tʃwitʃwi, au kakən /ne ≠gouwa, ŋ ‗//kuaŋ siŋ /ne ‗/kamɛŋ akkən hĩ I picked up nicely my things, while I was at peace, I carried them nicely.

ka 'to wish', 'to mean', 'to intend' is also used to express habitual action or a state.

au haŋ ka, ha si /ki /e: /k''i: a: !nuntu for he wishes, he shall stick in beads to his ears.

ŋ ǂī, ti e:, ŋ ka ŋ !nɔa se_!hʌm kwəre I think that I want my foot first to cool.

ha ka-g /ne //a !kwi!kwisitən ‾/ni: he meant to go to tell lies to the ichneumon.

/ha !gwāīŋ a: ka aroko _/kamɛŋ ti sa to:i-ta !kwitən the male hyena is one who quickly carries off the ostrich eggs.

he e: !nwa: ka !khe wai then the arrow stands in the springbok.

ha a: ka //ku: wa; /ku:i /ku a: ka _kɔ:iŋ he is one who is fat; the broody ostrich is one who is lean.

kaŋ expresses continuous action or a state.

/ga: ra kaŋ swe: nja ŋ //ku: /na: the berries are sitting on my shoulder.

/auā !khwā, !khwā kaŋ k'ʼwa: listen to the child, the child is crying.

au /a a:, ha kaŋ da: ha au !kauxu about the fight which he had been making on the hunting ground.

ha-g /ne !ʌhái ho //khwai, au /ni: ja kaŋ //k'oen !khe: //neiŋ he slung on the quiver, while the ichneumon stood looking at the hut.

ŋ kaŋ ‾//kaŋ_a I am hungry.

si kaŋ e: /k'abbe:ja we are those who conspired.

ta, tā 'to feel' is used in the same sense as *ka*.

si ta si di si ⨀pwaxai au hā-hā we thought we should make our daughter of her.

to:i k'auki ta ǂkaka !kʔe an ostrich does not talk to people.

he e:, !gwāī ta !khwai!khwai hī they are those whom the hyena frightens.

tan 'to feel', 'to seem', is also used to emphasize the following verb.

ha k'auki taŋ //ku: he does not feel tired.

ti taŋ, to:i se /ka ha it seems, the ostrich will kill him.

ŋ taŋ ts'auwa I do milk.

!kwi taŋ /ke sa:, !kɔīŋ taŋ /ke sa: a man yonder comes, Grandfather yonder comes.

kië 'would' used after conditional clauses.

ta ha //nau, ha xa /kwēī /kwē/kwā:, ha di, hiŋkië se_tai hī ha for she knew, if she did not act in this manner, they would go out with her.

In many cases a number of particles are used together. The following are some combinations frequently found.

_ha oä, _//kuaŋ _ha oä, kaŋ or *taŋ _ha oä* are often used at the beginning of a story, where we should say 'once' or 'once upon a time'. They have generally been translated 'formerly'.

!xwe-//na-s'o !kui _//kuaŋ _ha oä /haŋ-a ǂneru a man of the early race once married a *ǂneru* bird.

_!kha¯ü _//kuaŋ _ha oä ka the lizard once sang.

/kui: _ha oä da hi //kaxai au ¯!kui the vultures formerly made their sister of a person.

!khwa kaŋ _ha oä //haita !kui/a the rain once courted a girl.

!khwe taŋ _ha oä /ku ǂgouwa the wind was formerly still.

kaŋ s'aŋ 'will'

ŋ kaŋ s'aŋ _/ka:ti _!gwa: /ki a tu I will soon beat thy mouth.

ŋ kaŋ s'aŋ i: I will come.

_k''oä _dəä 'must have'

ŋ _k''oä _dəä //khwaitən//khwaitən I must have been mistaken.

au ha ¯/k''oä _dəä mai, ha !ʌhi ho ŋ while he must have first passed in front of me.

au hĩ _k''oä _dəä !khwetən /ki /xoë for they must have disturbed the place.

/ne and */ku* or both are often used with particles expressing tense without apparently affecting the meaning.

/hu/hu _ha /ne //aŋ _//gauë hĩ the baboons went to seek it.

he !gauë_/ĩ _ha /ku /ne /k'e: ha !kouki-⊙pwa and the Dawn's-Heart scolded his younger sister-in-law.

se /ku-g /ne or */ku se-g /ne* are equivalent to 'will be doing'.

!khwa /ku se-g /ne kãũ, /ki se wai the rain will be falling, bringing the springbok.

i se /ku-g /ne /xã-a wai we shall be shooting springbok.

Interrogative particles.

/nũ, /nu expresses a question, doubt or possibility.

aken /nũ k''au ʃo _doä¯g /ne _//kwakka? dost thou not seem able to understand?

ŋ k'' auki ǂenna, ti e: !kui /nũ e I do not know whether it be a man.

/ka:gen tutu: ha ĩ, ti e:, ha /nu k''au /na: /k'e ĩ the women asked, whether it had not seen the men.

hiŋ _//kuaŋ //khoä hĩ /nũ !kõã they seem as if they may be travelling.

ba is used in direct questions.

a ba /ku /uru: wa ha !khwã? hast thou forgotten this child?

u ba siŋ se /ku //a: /ã !kõiŋ? have you been and cut up the old man?

ha ǂkaka /ni:, ts'a ba a:, !kõiŋ _//kuaŋ ʃo da: /a:? she said to the ichneumon, what is it that the old man seems to have?

de, di is used in direct and indirect questions, but with a second interrogative particle. *ti de* 'what place,' stands for 'where,' *tsa de* 'what thing' for 'what' or 'why', *!ku de* or *!ku di* 'what person' for 'who'; there is even an example of *dekən* used as 'who'. We might almost look upon the particle as adjective, adverb, or pronoun.

ra is another particle used in questions with a second interrogative. It generally follows *tsa* 'thing' and may be translated by 'what' or 'why'.

xa when used with one of the above mentioned interrogatives certainly expresses a question, occasionally it is used without them as a negative, expressing 'lest' or 'unless'.

//neinjaŋ /nu //na ti de? where is the house?

tsa de ba a:, u—//kuaŋ //kōā /kī:—ā //kaxai? what is it, you have really got sister?

a xa de? where art thou?

/ōā xa de? where is the hare?

ŋ xa si //kaitən ti de? where shall I ascend?

a—a: !kain ⊙pwa, a xa /ke: swe:ŋswe:ŋ ti k''wa? thou little orphan, art thou sitting there crying?

tsa de xa e, he !khwā k''auki ≠kakən ke? what is the matter that the child does not speak to me?

!khwā—wɛ, tsa ra xa a:, a—ka //kandi //kwēi tā ā? o child, why is it that thy foolishness is like this?

!ku di xa a: /na: !kuttau? who was it saw Sirius?

haŋ !xe:ī ha !k'a!k'a, !kuko xa se !nī: he he hid his hands, lest the other should see them.

See also the example to *kiē*.

Verbal endings.

-ī The termination *-ī* to a verb expresses duration of action, corresponding to the forms with the present participle.

au hiŋ tatti ⊙ho //kɛn-ī hī as it felt the bush was pricking it.

he eŋ-eŋ _dɔā-g /ne _darakən, hɛ —k'oā e:, hi ≠ko:-ī, ī: its flesh is able to move, that must be why it is shrinking away from it (the second *ī:* is the pronoun).

he tikən e:, /kaggən /ne //kabo-ī !khwa therefore the Mantis was dreaming about the child.

-ā, -a after a verb expresses duration or repetition of action, it can sometimes be used as a participle.

/hu /hu a: kaŋ hā-a //xī hoā a baboon who feeding went by.

ha oā se //karro-ā !k'e e: !kau!kau !ʌhi!ʌhi !khe !kukən !kukən that his father might take aim at the people who sit upon their heels.

a In the cases quoted above the ending *a* or *ã* remains distinct from the verb in pronunciation, but there is another ending *a* which connects itself more closely with the verbal root in one of the following ways:

(1) In short verbs the final *e* or *i* turns into *a*. Such verbs are *se, si* 'to come', *//e* 'to go', *di* 'to do', *hĩ* 'to eat', *//ke* 'to burn', */ki* 'to kill', */i* 'to cut', */ni* 'to see', */xi* 'to shoot'.

(2) In longer verbs, especially in those ending in a diphthong or *n* the *a* is joined to the root by *w*, or *j*, forming *-wa* or *-ja*, as *//kei//keija, /korruwa, !kammenja.*

(3) Verbs ending in *kən* or *tən* change these syllables into *ka* and *ta*, *ǂkaka, tatta.*

(1) The rules governing the change of *i* and *e* to *a* are not clear; sometimes the latter form expresses the perfect, sometimes it is used after *se* as the subjunctive, sometimes it seems to be used as an applied form, but then again there are cases where no reason can be found for its use.

haŋ hĩ: kerru-ka !kaukən he eats young bushes

sitən k''auki !naunko hã: to:i eŋ-eŋ we have not yet eaten ostrich flesh.

ha ka, ha /ka tsa, ha se hã: to:i eŋ-eŋ he thought he would kill something, that he might eat ostrich flesh.

ŋ k''auki taŋ, ŋ se tãẽ ha:ŋ I do not want to walk feeding myself.

!na: ko:wa se /kɯ-g /ne se another winter will come.

//go//go ⊙pwa:kən /ne sa hĩhĩ a little whirlwind came to them.

sa:gən sa:, sa:gən /ke sa the eland comes, the eland yonder comes.

sitən k''auki se //k'oen !ka!kauru,o si /xã: ⊙pwai we may not look at the moon, when we have shot game.

(2 and 3) The endings *wa, ja, ka, ta* seem to indicate the imperative, an applied form, a participle, or the passive.

\/kaggən kɯ a: /korruwa !kaukən the Mantis is one who cheated the children.

haŋ //kei//keija ha /ku:ka he seemed as if he were dead.

!kˀwa: /na: //k'oen//k'oenja //nũŋ ta ŋ ts'əŋxu the hartebeest's head lay looking behind my back.

au haŋ /xoroka sa as he rustling came.

hiŋ /xerrija //kuĭtən-ka !k'ãũ they scratch up the screen's earth, or they scratch up earth for the screen.

haŋ /ne tor̃ritor̃rija //koë: he having whirled round fell.

mamaŋ ǂkakka kė mother told me.

//koĭŋ se !karaka hĩ !k'ãũ the sun should warm for them the earth.

//khweitən//khweita /ku sa: lying come forward.
haŋ ǂkakkən kweitənkweita !kwā: it speaks whispering to the child.
/ne ǂkakka ke speak to me.
//k'oenja ti e: look at this place.

These endings may be forms of a verbal particle *a* or *a:* sometimes still found before the verb, probably denoting past action. A similar particle in the Auen language denotes the repetition of any tense. As this particle is almost identical with the singular of the relative pronoun, it is difficult to say which is meant after nouns in the singular. *ŋ xoä a: ǂkakka ke* may be 'my mother was the one who told me' or 'my mother told me'. But in the following instance the *a* follows a noun in the plural, so it is clearly not a relative. *!kʔe a !hʌn!hʌn _tai* the people had gone hunting.

That the *a* may be a verbal particle sometimes preceding the verb is indicated by the fact, that the endings *wa* and *ja* are occasionally found attached to the noun, yet affecting the verb, not merely emphasizing the noun.

i se _tai, au //kõinja /e: ta we will go, when the sun has set.
/kaggən tũwaŋ !karokən!karokən suttən /hiŋ hĩ au !kaukən /k'a/k'a the Mantis's skin snatched itself out of the children's hands.

The ordinary emphatic form of *tũ* is *tũn.*

//khetən//khetən saŋ hĩ ⊙pwai, au ⊙pwaija /ku:kən ta the beasts of prey would eat the game, while the game lay dying.

In the following example the particle seems attached to both noun and verb.

!kwaitəntu:wa //ko:wa, hĩ /ne /xubu the flowers having dried, they break off.

The participle in *a, wa, ja, ka, ta* is occasionally used as the passive.

!k'ãũ /ne ǂkaǂkaka the ground is made light (lit up).
!kwã gwai ⊙pwakən a !kauwa ha /k'a a little boy is cut in this hand.
!ka!karro //kuaŋ /a: the moon has been cut.

Many adjectives seem to be simple participles of verbs.

!k'ãũ-ka ku: ǂxi: ja all the earth is bright (shining).
!k'ãũ /ne !ki: ja the earth is red.
ha siŋ _doã khwija, ka ku-gmuiŋ ku a khwija it had to be cunning, for the lynx was one who is cunning.

Reduplication of the verb.

Reduplication expresses either repeated, continuous action such as might be translated 'kept on doing', or else transitive and causative action.

!kwaŋ !ku: tĩ !k'wa: /na: the child let fall the hartebeest's head.

ha //kaxukakən !ku!ku: tĩ /kaggən-ka eŋ-eŋ her sisters let fall (one after another) the Mantis's flesh.

/kaggən-ka eŋjaŋ ǂhauǂhau //k''e: the Mantis's flesh sprang together, kept springing together.

ha /ne !kattən!kattən //koä !khe //a: he running went before the wind.

haŋ kiki ha he makes himself grow, from *ki* 'to grow'.

ha se tã:ẽ !kwain!kwain ha !nəa!nəa he will walk strengthening his feet, from *!kwain* 'to grow strong'.

a a: saŋ /ki/ki !khwãŋ thou art the one who shall take care of the child, from *!ki* 'to get, have, bring'.

kuï

A very frequent form of expressing action is the use of the verb *kuï* before the chief verb, which is often an imitation of sound; such a phrase as 'it went pop', 'er machte plumps'.

kuï alone generally means 'to speak, say'. It is often used with another verb of speech.

he ha kuï: ta ti e:, ŋ siŋ //xʌm ta he and he said: feel that which I have also felt.

he mama kukuïtən /k'eja ke and mother speaking said to me.

When used with other verbs *kuï* corresponds more to 'to make' or 'to do' in so far as it need be translated at all.

he //go:gən kuï tʃətto //ko ha /na: o ha //kua/;kua and the tortoise made slide in her head to her neck, i. e. and the tortoise drew her head into her neck.

ha /ku-g /ne kuï //nip(p) au /khwã ⊙pwa he makes nip to the little child, i. e. he catches hold of the little child.

haŋ /ne kuï //khabbe(t) ã: /khwĩ he fended off his brother-in-law.

he ti /ku di kuï taŋtaŋ !khwa: !kʌn !haŋ si tsaxaitən these things made to feel water holding shut our eyes, i. e. it seemed as if the rain were closing our eyes.

Syntax.

The sequence of the sentence or clause is the direct one: subject, verb, object; or amplified: connective, subject, verbal particle, verb, indirect object, direct object, extension.

Only in the Imperative does the subject occasionally follow the verb, for example:
_amm //k'oen ju //xabbitən//xabbitən /na: gwai first look ye at *//xabbitən//xabbitən*'s big head.

Where there are several subjects they are first enumerated, then repeated by a pronoun. Several verbal particles may precede the chief verb or verbs, for as stated above, several verbs can be strung together to express one action. One of these verbs, where there are two or more, has generally an adverbial effect indicating place or manner. An extension of the verb expressed by a noun with a preposition follows the verb, and has more the nature of an indirect object with a preposition.

The whole speech is broken up into small clauses, joined either by connectives which precede the subject, by relatives, or by the meaning. Many of these clauses are adjectival phrases, others are adverbial phrases with the form of verbs, after which the subject is repeated (see Adverbs, Part 1).

he ti hiŋ e:, *haŋ /ne ku: /e _//khã: tu au /xabba:,* *haŋ /ne*
these things they are, he did fill in lion's mouth with soup, he did

/kei /e: _//khã:ŋ /na: au !kɔõ, *au haŋ tatti (ta ti) e:*
put in lion's head to pot for he felt thing which (or this)

ha //ko:äkən /ki /e: _//khã: /na: au !koã; ha si //ko:äkən /ka_//khã:
he altogether put in lion's head to pot; he will altogether kill lion

au /xabba-ka /i; au han (ta ti) tatti e:, ha e /gwãĩ a dattən
with soup's heat; for he feels thing this, he is hyena who deceives

!kʔe kuitən, haŋ ǂkakkən, he ti hiŋ e:, ha ǂkakka _//khã:, ĩ:.
people other, he speaks, these things they are, he spoke to lion, of them.
i. e. therefore, he poured soup into the lion's mouth, he put the lion's head into the pot, while he felt that he altogether put the lion's head into the pot, that he might altogether kill the lion with the soup's heat; while he feels that he is a hyena who deceives other people, he speaks, therefore he talked to the lion about it.

The *ĩ:* that finishes so many sentences is sometimes clearly a part of the relative, referring back to a preceding pronoun or demonstrative, but occasionally it seems only a final 'in this manner', 'like this', 'on account of it'.
he _//khã: tuĩ, o ha k'ʾwa: //na, he_//khã: /kʌm sa ha ĩ: and lion heard, as she cried there, and lion came to her on account of it.

The use of the adverbial phrase *//nau* is shown in these examples:

he /xʌm-ka /nuk''o //nau, haŋ //k'e:gən !/a: /aitji à:,
and Bushman old man did this, he gathering wood went for wife of it,

/aitji se //ke: //kau //khɔ o !kuï-se, ha /auaxi _//khã:, e _//khã:ŋ
wife should make fire upon place on *!kuï-se,* he espied lion, as the lion

!khai /hiŋ sa:, ti e:, k''audɔro siŋ !khai /hiŋ sa: he,
crossing over came, place this, youth had crossing over come it, i. e.

and an old Bushman, as he went along getting wood for his wife, in order that his wife might make a fire above the *!kuï-se,* espied the lion, as the lion came over the hill at the place which the young man had come over.

Di-xɛrretən _//kuaŋ _ha oä //nau, _//khã //kuarakən !/na !khwa: /kuenja,
Di-xɛrretən once did this, lioness mother at water was dipping up,

haŋ /ne //aŋ /kuen //na, Di-xɛrretən ta ti e: (tatti e:), _//khã
she had gone to dip up there, *Di-xɛrretən* felt this thing, lioness

a: !kan!kan //k'e:ja !k?e-ta !kaukən, au _//khãŋ tatti,
was one who gathered together people's children, for lioness felt thing,

_//khã e ‾//o:sa, //nwaintu; he tikən e:, ha /ne !kan!kan
lioness was weak in chest; these things are, she did gather

//k'e: !k?e-ta !kaukən, !kauka: siŋ //na ha, !kauka siŋ
together people's children, children might be with her, children might

da: ha ã; ta ha e ‾//o:sa, he ha k''auki di /gi: tfueŋ.
do for her of it; for she was weak, and she not does hard things.

The following examples show adjectival phrases:

he tikən e:, !kaukən e: !ku:, hi _ha /ne ui, hiŋ /ne /kʌm
these things are, children are two, they did arise, they did reach

//a hĩ-ta !k?e.
go their people, i. e. therefore two children arose, they went away to their own people.

!kui a: a, haŋ /ki !xui!xui.
man who here }
man is here } he has feather brushes. This man has feather brushes.

Repetition seems the most striking feature of Bushman speech. Every part of a story is generally told over and over again with slight alterations in the forms of speech, for instance:

he tikən e:, !khwã _ha /ku-g /ne ‾ki, ĩ:; haŋ /ku-g /ne di
these things were, child was growing, during them; it was becoming

kui //kho ti e: ha siŋ /kuẽ ĩ:. he tikən e:
making to resemble thing which it had been like it. these things were
/kaggən _ha /ne sa:, ĩ:; au haŋ sa: //k'oen; he ha _ha /ne
Mantis did come, during them; while he came to look; and he did
/kuẽĩ ⁻/ki, haŋ _tai sa:. haŋ _ha //nau, au haŋ _tai tau //k'oenja
like this, he walking came. he did as follows, as he walking and looking
⁻sa:, haŋ /ne /ouwi !khwã, au !khwãŋ /ne /kara s'o:.
came, he espied child, as child did basking sit, i. e. then the child grew; it became like that which it had been. Then the Mantis came, while he came to look; and he in this manner walking came. While he came walking and looking, he espied the child, as the child was sitting in the sun.

Poetry.

The repetition found in the stories is even more evident in the poetry, which consists in short sentences or phrases recurring again and again with very small changes, and an occasional chorus of sounds, not words. A good example is the Blue Crane's song:

/ga:ra /ku swe:nja ŋ //ku/na:,
berries are sitting on my shoulder (arm's head),
/ga:ra kaŋ swe:nja ŋ //ku/na:,
berries do sit on my shoulder,
/ga:ra haŋ swe:nja ŋ //ku/na:,
berry it sits on my shoulder,
!ga:ra kaŋ swe:nja ŋ //ku/na:,
berries do sit on my shoulder,
/ga:ra kaŋ kaŋ ⁻/ke: ho,
berries are up here, (yonder placed),
rrru kaŋ ⁻/ke: ho,
rrru are up here,
/ga:ra kaŋ kaŋ ⁻/ke: ho,
berries are up here,
rrru kaŋ ⁻/ke: ho,
rrru are up here,
kaŋ kaŋ ⁻/ke: ho,
are are up here,
/ga:ra rru kaŋ ⁻/ku: ha.
berries rru are put on it.

REFERENCES

Allan, D. 2001. The Blue Crane. Imperilled national icon. *Africa Birds and Birding* 6(4): 30-39.

[Anonymous]. 1999. *Roberts' Multimedia Birds of Southern Africa*. Westville: Southern African Birding.

Apps, P. 1992. *Wild Ways: A Field Guide to the Behaviour of Southern African Mammals.* Halfway House, South Africa: Southern Book Publishers.

Archer, F. M. 1990. Planning with People – Ethnobotany and African Uses of Plants in Namaqualand (South Africa). *Proceedings of the 12th Plenary Meeting of AETFAT. Mitteilungen aus dem Institut für Allgemeine Botanik, Hamburg*: 959-972.

Archer, F. M. 1994. *Ethnobotany of Namaqualand. The Richtersveld.* MA Thesis, University of Cape Town, South Africa.

Biesele, M. 1975. *Folklore and Ritual of !Kung Hunter-gatherers*. PhD Thesis, Harvard University Cambridge, Massachusetts.

Biesele, M. 1993. *Women Like Meat: The Folklore and Foraging Ideology of the Kalahari Ju/'hoan.* Johannesburg: Witwatersrand University Press.

Biesele, M. 1996. 'He stealthily lightened at his brother-in-law' (and thunder echoes in Bushman oral tradition a century later). In: Deacon, J. & Dowson, T. A. (Eds) *Voices from the Past. /Xam Bushmen and the Bleek and Lloyd Collection.* Johannesburg, South Africa: Witwatersrand University Press, 142-160.

Bleek, D. F. (ed.) 1924. The Mantis and his Friends. Bushman Folklore. Cape Town: Maskew Miller.

——— 1928-30. Bushman grammar: A grammatical sketch of the language of the |Xam-ka-!k'e. *Zeitschrift für Eingeborenen-Sprachen*, 19:81-98, 20:161-174.

——— 1931. Customs and Beliefs of the |Xam Bushmen. Part I. Baboons. *Bantu Studies* 5: 167-179.

——— 1932a. Customs and Beliefs of the |Xam Bushmen. Part II. The Lion. *Bantu Studies* 6: 47-63.

——— 1932b. Customs and Beliefs of the |Xam Bushmen. Part III: Game Animals. *Bantu Studies* 6: 233-249.

——— 1932c. Customs and Beliefs of the |Xam Bushmen. Part IV: Omens, Wind-making, Clouds. *Bantu Studies* 6: 323-342.

——— 1933a. Beliefs and Customs of the |Xam Bushmen Part V. The Rain. *Bantu Studies* 7: 297-312.

——— 1933b. Beliefs and Customs of the |Xam Bushmen. Part VI Rain-Making. *Bantu Studies* 11(4): 375-392.

——— 1935. Beliefs and Customs of the |Xam Bushmen: Part VII. Sorcerors. *Bantu Studies 9*: 1-47.

——— 1936a. Beliefs and Customs of the |Xam Bushmen. Part VIII. More about sorcerors and charms. *Bantu Studies 10*: 131-162.

——— 1936b. Special Speech of Animals and Moon used by the |Xam Bushmen. *Bantu Studies* 10: 163-199.

——— (Ed.) 1956. *Bushman Dictionary*. American Oriental Series 41. New Haven, Connecticut: American Oriental Society.

Bleek, E. & Bleek, D. 1909. Notes on the Bushmen [Introduction]. In: Tongue, M. H. *Bushman Paintings*. London: Clarendon Press, 36-44.

Bleek, W. H. I. 1873. *Report of Dr Bleek concerning his researches into the Bushman language and customs, presented to the Honourable the House of Assembly by command of His Excellency the Governor*. Cape Town: Cape Parliamentary Paper.

Bleek, W. H. I. 1875. Second report concerning Bushman researches, presented to both Houses of the Parliament of the Cape of Good Hope, by command of His Excellency the Governor. Cape Town: Government Printer.

Bleek, W. H. I. 1869. The Bushman language. In Noble, Roderick (Ed.), *The Cape and its People and Other Essays by South African Writers*. Cape Town: Trübner, 269-284.

Bleek, W. H. I. and Lucy C. Lloyd. 1911. *Specimens of Bushman Folklore*. London: George Allen.

Boonzaier, E., Malherbe, C., Smith, A. & Berens, P. 1996. *The Cape Herders: A History of the Khoikhoi of Southern Africa*. Cape Town & Johannesburg: David Philip & Athens: Ohio University Press.

Boycott, R. C. & Bourquin, O. 2000. *The Southern African Tortoise Book*. Revised and expanded edition. Hilton, KwaZulu-Natal, South Africa: O. Bourquin.

Branch, B. 1998. *Field Guide to Snakes and Other Reptiles of Southern Africa*. 3rd Edition. Cape Town: Struik Publishers.

Butler, F. G. 1997. Nose-bleed in shamans and eland. *Southern African Field Archaeology* (6): 82-87.

Deacon, H. J. & Deacon, J. 1999. *Human Beginnings in South Africa: Uncovering the Secrets of the Stone Age*. Cape Town: David Philip.

Deacon, J. 1986. 'My place is the Bitterpits': the home territory of Bleek and Lloyd's |Xam San informants. *African Studies* 45(2): 135-155.

Deacon, J. 1988. The power of a place in understanding southern San rock engravings. *World Archaeology* 20(1): 129-140.

Deacon, J. 1996a. Archaeology of the Flat and Grass Bushmen. In Deacon, J. & Dowson, T. A. (Eds) *Voices from the past. |Xam Bushmen and the Bleek and Lloyd Collection*. Johannesburg: Witwatersrand University Press, 245-270.

Deacon, J. 1996b. A tale of two families: Wilhelm Bleek, Lucy Lloyd and the |Xam San of the Northern Cape. In: Skotnes, P. (Ed.) *Miscast: Negotiating the Presence of the Bushmen*. Cape Town: University of Cape Town Press, 93-113.

Deacon, J. 1997. 'My heart stands in the hill': rock engravings in the northern Cape. *Kronos. Journal of Cape History* (24): 18-29.

Deacon, J. & Dowson, T. A. (Eds) 1996. *Voices from the Past. /Xam Bushmen and the Bleek and Lloyd Collection.* Johannesburg: Witwatersrand University Press.

Dean, R. & Milton, S. 1991. *Galium tomentosum*, a yarn for the birds. *Veld & Flora* 77(3): 82-83.

Doke, C. M. 1927. The importance of Bantu Studies in South Africa. *The Umpa* 12(1).

England, N. M. 1968. Music among the Zu/Wasi of South West Africa and Botswana. Unpublished Ph.D Thesis. Cambridge, Harvard University.

Folch, A. 1992. Family Struthionidae (Ostrich). In Del Hoyo, J., Elliot, A. & Sargatal, J. *Handbook of the Birds of the World.* Volume 1, Ostrich to Ducks. Barcelona: Lynx Edicions, 76-82.

Guenther, M. G. 1996. Attempting to contextualise |Xam oral tradition. In: Deacon, J. & Dowson, T. A. (Eds) *Voices from the Past. /Xam Bushmen and the Bleek and Lloyd Collection*. Johannesburg: Witwatersrand University Press, 77-99.

Guenther, M. G. 1999. *Tricksters and Trancers.* Bloomington: Indiana University Press.

Güldemann, T. Forthcoming a. Phonology: Other Tuu languages. In Voßen (Ed.).

Güldemann, T. Forthcoming b. Morphology: |Xam of Strandberg. In Voßen (Ed.).

Güldemann, T. Forthcoming c. Syntax: |Xam of Strandberg. In Voßen (Ed.).

Hewitt, R. L. 1986. *Structure, Meaning and Ritual in the Narratives of the Southern San.* Hamburg: Helmut Buske Verlag.

Hollmann, J. C. 2002. Natural models, ethology and San rock-paintings: piloerection and depictions of bristles in south-eastern South Africa. *South African Journal of Science 98* (November/December): 563-567.

How, M. W. 1962. *The Mountain Bushmen of Basutoland.* Pretoria: J. L. Van Schaik Ltd.

James, A. 2001. *The First Bushman's Path. Stories, Songs and Testimonies of the /Xam of the Northern Cape.* Pietermaritzburg, South Africa: University of Natal Press.

Katz, R. 1982. *Boiling Energy. Community Healing among the Kalahari Kung.* Cambridge, Massachusetts: Harvard University Press.

Katz, R., Biesele, M. & St. Denis, V. 1997. *Healing Makes our Hearts Happy: Spirituality and Cultural Transformation among the Kalahari Ju/'hoansi.* Rochester, Vermont: Inner Traditions.

Keeney, B. 1994. *Shaking out the Spirits.* Barrytown, New York: Station Hill Press.

Keeney, B. 1999. *Kalahari Bushmen Healers.* Philadelphia: Ringing Rocks Press, in association with Leete's Island Books.

Keeney, B. 2003. *Ropes to God: Experiencing the Bushman Spiritual Universe.* Philadelphia: Ringing Rocks Press.

Kruger, J. C., Skinner, J. D. & Robinson, T. J. 1979. On the taxonomic status of the Black and White Springbok. *South African Journal of Science 75* (September): 411-412.

Lee, R. B. 1967. Trance cure of the !Kung Bushmen. *Natural History* 76(9): 31-37.

——— 1968. The sociology of !Kung Bushman trance performances. In Prince, R. (Ed.) *Trance and Possession States*. Montreal: R.M. Bucke Memorial Society, 35-54.

Le Roux, P. M., Kotze, C. D., Nel, G. P. & Glen, H. F. 1994. *Bossieveld. Grazing Plants of the Karoo and Karoo-like Areas.* Photographs by C. D. Kotze. Bulletin 428. Pretoria: Department of Agriculture.

Lewis-Williams, J. D. 1981. *Believing and Seeing: Symbolic Meanings in Southern San Rock Paintings.* London: Academic Press.

—— 1982. The economic and social context of southern San rock art. *Current Anthropology* 23(4): 429-449.

—— 1987. A dream of eland: an unexplored component of San shamanism and rock art. *World Archaeology* 19(2): 165-177.

—— 1988. 'People of the eland': an archaeo-linguistic crux. In Ingold, T., Riches, D. & Woodburn, J. (Eds) *Property, Power and Ideology.* Oxford: Berg, 203-211.

—— 1992. Ethnographic evidence relating to 'trance' and 'shamans' among Northern and Southern Bushmen. *South African Archaeological Bulletin 47*: 56-60.

—— 1996. A visit to the Lion's House. In: Deacon, J. & Dowson. T. A. (Eds) *Voices from the Past.* Johannesburg: Witwatersrand University Press, 122-141.

—— 1998. Quanto? The issue of 'many meanings' in southern African San rock art research. *South African Archaeological Bulletin 53*: 86-97.

—— 2000. *Stories that Float from Afar: Ancestral Folklore of the San of Southern Africa.* Cape Town: David Philip.

Lewis-Williams, J. D. & Biesele, M. 1978. Eland hunting rituals among northern and southern San groups: striking similarities. *Africa* 48(2): 117-134.

Lewis-Williams, J. D., Blundell, G., Challis, W. & Hampson, J. 2000. Threads of light: re-examining a motif in southern African San rock art. *South African Archaeological Bulletin 55*: 123-136.

Lewis-Williams, J. D. & Dowson, T. A. 2000. *Images of Power: Understanding San Rock Art.* 2nd Edition. Johannesburg: Southern Book Publishers.

Lichtenstein, H 1808. Bemerkungen über die Sprachen der südafricanischen wilden Völkerstämme, nebst einem kleinen Wörterverzeichnisse aus den gebräuchlichsten Dialecten der Hottentotten und Kaffern. *Allgemeines Archiv für Ethnographie und Linguistik*, 1: 259-331.

—— 1811-12. *Reisen im südlichen Afrika in den Jahren 1803, 1804, 1805 und 1806,* 2 volumes. Berlin: Salfeld.

Lloyd, L. C. 1889. *A Short Account of Further Bushman Material Collected.* London: David Nutt.

Marshall, L. 1957. N!ow. *Africa* 27(3): 232-240.

—— 1961. Sharing, talking, and giving: relief of social tensions among !Kung Bushmen. *Africa* 31(3): 231-249.

—— 1962. !Kung Bushman religious beliefs. *Africa* 32(3): 221-251.

—— 1969. The medicine dance of the !Kung Bushmen. *Africa* 39: 347-381.

—— 1999. *Nyae Nyae !Kung beliefs and rites.* Cambridge, Massachusetts: Peabody Museum of Archaeology and Ethnology, Harvard University.

McCall, D. F. 1970. Wolf courts girl: the equivalence of hunting and mating in Bushman thought. *Papers in International Studies: Africa Series* No. 7: v, 1-19. Ohio University Center for International Studies.

Meriggi, P. 1928-29. Versuch einer Grammatik des |Xam-Buschmännischen. *Zeitschrift für Eingeborenen-Sprachen*, 19: 117-153, 188-205.

Mills, G. 2001. *African Predators*. Photographs by M. Harvey. Cape Town: Struik Publishers.

Mossop, E. E. (Ed.) 1935. *The Journal of Hendrik Jacob Wikar (1779) and the Journals of Jacobus Coetse Jansz (1760) and Willem van Reenen (1791)*. Cape Town: Van Riebeeck Society.

Müller, F. 1877. *Grundriß der Sprachwissenschaft 1, 2: Die Sprachen der wollhaarigen Rassen, II. Die Sprachen der Buschmänner*. Wien: A. Hölder, 25-29.

——— 1888. *Grundriß der Sprachwissenschaft 4, 1: Nachträge zum Grundriß aus den Jahren 1877-1887, Die Sprache der /Kham-Buschmänner (/kham-ga 'e#) im Norden der Cap-Colonie*. Wien: A. Hölder, 1-18.

Newman, K. 1990. *Newman's Birds of Southern Africa*. Cape Town: Southern Book Publishers.

Orpen, J. M. 1874. A glimpse into the mythology of the Maluti Bushmen. *The Cape Monthly Magazine* IX: 1-10.

Pager, H. 1975. *Stone Age Myth and Magic as Documented in the Rock Paintings of South Africa*. Graz: Akademische Druck.

Puff, C. 1978. The genus Galium L. (Rubiaceae) in southern Africa. *The Journal of South African Botany* 44(3): 203-279.

——— 1986. Part 1 Rubiaceae, Fascicle 2 Rubioideae (Second part): Paederiaeae, Anthospermeae, Rubieae. In: Leistner, O. A. (Ed.) *Flora of southern Africa* 31: 1-79. Pretoria: Botanical Research Institute.

Sanders, B. 1994. *A is for Ox: The Collapse of Literacy and the Rise of Violence in an Electronic Age*. New York: Vintage Books.

Schaller, G. B. 1972. *The Serengeti Lion. A Study of Predator-Prey Relations*. Chicago: University of Chicago Press.

Schmidt, S. 1996. The relevance of the Bleek/Lloyd folktales to the general Khoisan traditions. In: Deacon, J. & Dowson, T. A. (Eds) *Voices from the Past. /Xam Bushmen and the Bleek and Lloyd Collection*. Johannesburg: Witwatersrand University Press, 100-121.

Shearing, D. 1997. *Karoo*. Illustrations by K. Van Heerden. South Africa Wild Flower Guide 6. Cape Town: Botanical Society of South Africa.

Skaife, S. H. 1987. *African Insect Life*. Revised by J. Ledger. Cape Town: C. Struik Publishers.

Skinner, J. D. & Louw, G. N. 1996. *The Springbok,* Antidorcas marsupialis *(Zimmermann, 1780)*. Transvaal Museum Monograph No. 10. Pretoria: Transvaal Museum.

Skotnes, P. (Ed.) 1996. *Miscast: Negotiating the Presence of the Bushmen*. Cape Town: University of Cape Town Press.

——— 1999. *Heaven's Things: A Story of the /Xam*. LLAREC Series in Visual History. Cape Town: University of Cape Town Press.

Stow, G. W. 1930. *Rock-Paintings in South Africa from Parts of the Eastern Province and the Orange Free State*. Introduction and descriptive notes by D. F. Bleek. London: Methuen & Co Ltd.

Thomas, E. M. 1995. *The Tribe of Tiger. Cats and their Culture.* Paperback edition. London: Orion Books, Ltd.

Traill, A. 1996. !Khwa-ka hhouiten hhouiten, 'The rush of the storm': the linguistic death of |Xam. In: Skotnes, P. (Ed.) *Miscast. Negotiating the Presence of the Bushmen.* Cape Town: University of Cape Town Press, 161-183.

Van Wyk, B.E. & Gericke, N. 2000. *People's Plants. A Guide to Useful Plants of Southern Africa*. Pretoria, South Africa: Briza Publications.

Vinnicombe, P. 1975. The ritual significance of eland *(Taurotragus oryx)* in the rock art of southern Africa. In Anati, E. (Ed.) *Les Religions de la Prehistoire.* Capo di Ponte: Centro Preistorici, 379-400.

Vinnicombe, P. 1976. *People of the Eland: Rock Paintings of the Drakensberg Bushmen as a Reflection of their Life and Thought.* Pietermaritzburg: University of Natal Press.

Voßen, R. (Ed.). Forthcoming. *The Khoisan Languages.* London: Routledge.

Yates, R. & Manhire, A. 1991. Shamanism and rock paintings: aspects of the use of rock art in the south-western Cape, South Africa. *South African Archaeological Bulletin* 46(153): 3-11.

INDEX